The Countess of Longford is a CBE, a Fellow of the Royal Society of Literature and an Hon. D.Litt. of Sussex University. Her previous publications include *Victoria R.I.* (which won the James Tait Black Memorial Prize and is also published by Abacus), *Jameson's Raid*, *The Royal House of Windsor*, *A Pilgrimage of Passion: The Life of Wilfrid Scawen Blunt*, *Eminent Victorian Women*, *Elizabeth R*, *The Oxford Book of Royal Anecdotes*, *Darling Loosy: Letters to Princess Louise* and her memoirs, *The Pebbled Shore*.

Also by Elizabeth Longford in Abacus

Victoria R.I.

WELLINGTON

Elizabeth Longford

An *Abacus* Book

First published in Great Britain as *Wellington: The Years of the Sword* and *Wellington: Pillar of State* by George Weidenfeld and Nicolson Limited in 1969 and 1972. First published in this abridged one-volume edition by George Weidenfeld and Nicolson Limited in 1992. This edition published by Abacus in 2001 Reprinted 2002

A CIP catalogue for this book is available from the British Library.

ISBN 0 349 11291 6

Printed and bound in Great Britain by Bookmarque Ltd, Croydon, Surrey

Abacus An imprint of Time Warner Books UK Brettenham House Lancaster Place London WC2E 7EN

www.TimeWarnerBooks.co.uk

To the descendants of
the First Duke of Wellington
and the Second Earl of Longford,
Gerry Wellington and Frank, and
in memory of my daughter
Catherine Pakenham

Contents

Illustrations

Acknowledgements for Illustrations

The author and publishers wish to thank His Grace the Duke of Wellington for his kind permission to reproduce pictures 1, 2, 4, 5, 15, 17, 18, 19, 27, 38, 47 and 54. Numbers 3, 6, 9, 10, 13, 14, 26, 30, 32, 33, 44 and 55 are reproduced by the kind permission of the board of Trustees of the Wellington Museum. The author and publishers would also like to thank the Mansell Collection for permission to reproduce numbers 7, 8, 12, 16, 20, 21, and 31; the British Museum for numbers 23, 36, 41, 45, 46, 50; the Bibliothèque Nationale for numbers 24 and 25; the Royal Military Academy Sandhurst for number 28; Mr M. C. Farrar-Bell for number 11; the Hon. Mrs Bonham for number 42; Wellington College for number 40; Macmillan & Co for number 39; the RAMC Historical Museum for number 35; the Walker Art Gallery, Liverpool, for number 49; and Miss Barbara Murray for number 52. Number 51 is reproduced by permission of *Punch* magazine and numbers 37, 43 and 48 are in the possession of the author.

The author would also like to thank Miss Sophie Baker for her photography; Miss Jane Flower for the gift of number 48; and Miss V. Lloyd and Mr W. Clarke for their kind help.

Maps

A Calendar of Events in Wellington's Career
1769–1852

1769	*1 May*	Birth of Hon. Arthur Wesley, Dublin.
	15 August	Birth of Napoleon Bonaparte, Corsica.
1781		Death of father, 1st Lord Mornington. Enters Eton.
1784	*Summer*	Leaves Eton. At Brighton with tutor.
1785		Brussels, with mother.
1786	*16 January*	School of Equitation, Angers, France. Returns England end of year.
1787	*7 March*	Ensign.
	25 December	Lieutenant.
1788	*February*	Arrives Ireland as ADC to Lord-Lieutenant.
1789		French Revolution.
1790	*April*	MP for Trim, Ireland.
1791	*30 June*	Captain.
1792	*September*	Courting Kitty Pakenham.
1793	*1 February*	France declares war on Britain.
	30 April	Major.
		Proposes to Kitty Pakenham; rejected.
	30 September	Lieutenant-Colonel.
1794		Commands brigade Flanders; withdrawn 1795.
		Napoleon commands French artillery, Toulon.
1796	*3 May*	Colonel in the army.
	June	Sails for India in command of 33rd.
1797	*February*	Arrives Calcutta; next eight years in India.

1798		Richard, 2nd Lord Mornington, arrives as Governor-General, having changed family name back to Wellesley. Irish Rebellion.
1799	*Spring*	Invasion of Mysore.
	4 May	Storming of Seringapatam, death of Tipoo Sultan.
		Governor of Mysore. Richard created Marquess Wellesley.
1800		Union of Great Britain and Ireland. Defeat of Dhoondiah Waugh.
1801		Resignation of Pitt, Addington Prime Minister. Arthur Wellesley superseded.
1802	*March*	Peace of Amiens ratified.
	29 April	Major-General.
1803	*May*	Renewal of war against France.
	6 August	Outbreak of Second Mahratta War.
	12 August	Capture of Ahmednuggur.
	23 September	Battle of Assaye.
	29 November	Battle of Argaum.
	15 December	Surrender of Gawilghur.
1804	*1 September*	Order of the Bath.
		Napoleon crowned Emperor; Pitt Prime Minister again.
1805	*10 March*	Embarks for home; calls at St Helena.
	10 September	Reaches England.
	20 October	Napoleon defeats Austrians at Ulm.
	21 October	Nelson's victory at Trafalgar.
	2 December	Austerlitz; Austrians and Russians crushed.
	December	Arthur Wellesley takes a brigade to the Elbe.
1806	*23 January*	Pitt dies; succeeded by coalition Ministry of 'All the Talents'.
	30 January	Succeeds Cornwallis as Colonel of the 33rd.
	February	Returns home; posted to Hastings.
	1 April	MP for Rye, Sussex; later for Mitchell, Cornwall; Newport, Isle of Wight.
	10 April	Marries Kitty Pakenham in Dublin.
		Napoleon decrees blockade of Britain (Continental System).

1807 *3 February*   Birth of Arthur Richard Wellesley, son and heir.

March   Tory Ministry of Duke of Portland.

3 April   Arthur Wellesley joins Government as Chief Secretary of Ireland.

9 July   Treaty of Tilsit between Napoleon and Tsar Alexander of Russia.

31 July– 30 September   Copenhagen expedition.

1808 *16 January*   Birth of second son, Charles.

Spring   Risings in Iberian Peninsula against Napoleon.

25 April   Lieutenant-General.

12 July   Arthur Wellesley in temporary command of expeditionary force to Portugal.

1 August   Troops begin landings in Mondego Bay.

17 August   Battle of Roliça.

21 August   Battle of Vimeiro; Arthur Wellesley superseded.

31 August   Convention of Cintra; later recalled to England for Court of Inquiry.

1809 *16 January*   Death of Sir John Moore at Corunna, Spain.

April   Arthur Wellesley resigns Chief Secretaryship, sent in command of force to defend Portugal.

12 May   Crossing of the Douro and capture of Oporto.

27 June–4 July   Enters Spain.

6 July   Marshal-General of Portuguese Army.

27–28 July   Battle of Talavera.

4 September   Viscount Wellington of Talavera.

Autumn   Retreat to Portugal; orders secret construction of Lines of Torres Vedras (September).

Withdrawal of Walcheren expedition; Portland resigns; Perceval Prime Minister.

1810   Wellington perfects his 'defensive system'.

	April	Napoleon foresees trouble with Russia; marries Marie-Louise of Austria; cancels plan to command in Peninsula himself.
	10 July	Ciudad Rodrigo, Spain, surrenders to French.
	28 August	Almeida, Portugal, surrenders to French.
	27 September	Battle of Bussaco, Portugal.
	8 October	Wellington enters Lines of Torres Vedras.
	14 October	French discover Lines and refuse to attack.
1811	*5 March–8 April*	French retreat to Spain.
	11 March	Surrender of Badajoz to French.
	3–5 May	Battle of Fuentes de Oñoro.
	5–12 May	First siege of Badajoz.
	11 May	Surrender of Almeida to Wellington; garrison escapes.
	16 May	Battle of Albuera.
	19 May–10 June	Second siege of Badajoz.
	31 July	General (local rank).
	Summer–autumn	Retreat to Portugal.
1812	*8–19 January*	Siege and storming of Ciudad Rodrigo.
	February	Earl of Wellington; Grandee of Spain with title of Duque de Ciudad Rodrigo.
	16 March– 6 April	Third siege and storming of Badajoz.
	11 May	Assassination of Perceval; Lord Liverpool Prime Minister.
	May	Napoleon begins invasion of Russia.
	17 June	America declares war on Britain.
	22 July	Battle of Salamanca.
	12 August	Entry into Madrid.
	18 August	Marquess of Wellington; Generalissimo of Spanish armies (22 September).
	19 September– 21 October	Siege of Burgos.
	22 October– 19 November	Retreat to Portugal; French retreat from *Moscow (October–December)*.
	December	Wellington visits Cádiz and Lisbon; Portuguese title of Duque da Victoria.
1813	*1 January*	Colonel of Royal Regiment of Horse Guards.

4 March	Knight of the Garter.
21 June	Battle of Vitoria. Field-Marshal.
25 July	First assault on San Sebastián abandoned and city besieged by Wellington; same day French invade passes of Pyrenees.
28–30 July	Battle of the Pyrenees (Sorauren).
31 August	Second assault and fall of San Sebastián; same day Battle of San Marcial.
7 October	Crossing of Bidassoa into France.
16–19 October	Napoleon defeated at Battle of Leipzig.
31 October	Surrender of Pamplona.
10 November	Battle of the Nivelle.
December	Battles of the Nive and St Pierre.
1814 *February*	Crossing of the Adour and investment of Bayonne.
27 February	Battle of Orthez.
	Bourbon Prince at Wellington's HQ.
4 February– *19 March*	Abortive peace negotiations with Napoleon at Châtillon.
1 March	Treaty of Chaumont against Napoleon (Quadruple Alliance).
31 March	Entry of Allies into Paris.
6 April	Abdication of Napoleon.
10 April	Battle of Toulouse; end of Peninsular War.
16 April	Treaty of Fontainebleau with Napoleon.
24 April	Louis XVIII returns to France.
28 April	Napoleon sent to Elba.
3 May	Wellington created Duke.
4 May	In Paris for Review of troops by King.
24 May–8 June	Mission in Madrid.
30 May	First Peace of Paris signed with France.
14 June	Farewell to troops at Bordeaux.
23 June	Returns to England for celebrations.
5 July	Ambassador to the French Court.
August	Leaves for Paris, surveying defences of Low Countries on the way.
22 August	Arrives Paris Embassy.
15 September	Congress of Vienna opens informally.
24 December	Treaty of Ghent; end of American War.

1815	3 January	Secret Treaty between Britain, France and Austria.
	8 January	Battle of New Orleans.
	3 February	Wellington arrives Vienna as British Plenipotentiary.
	1 March	Napoleon lands in France.
	7 March	Congress hears of Napoleon's escape from Elba.
	13 March	Congress outlaws Napoleon.
	19 March	Louis XVIII flees from Paris.
	20 March	Napoleon enters the Tuileries. The Hundred Days.
	25 March	Treaty of Chaumont against Napoleon renewed.
	28 March	Wellington leaves Congress of Vienna.
	4 April	Enters HQ in Brussels.
	April–June	Assembly of Allied army under Wellington.
	9 June	Final Act of Congress of Vienna.
	15 June	Napoleon crosses Belgian frontier; captures Charleroi.
		Duchess of Richmond's ball.
	16 June	Battles of Ligny and Quatre Bras.
	17 June	Prussians retreat to Wavre; Wellington follows to Mont-Saint-Jean.
	18 June	Battle of Waterloo.
	21 June	Wellington crosses frontier into France.
	21–22 June	Official news of Waterloo reaches England.
	3 July	Surrender of Paris. Treaty of Saint-Cloud.
	8 July	Second Restoration of Louis XVIII. The White Terror.
	7 August	Napoleon exiled to St Helena.
	22 October	Wellington Commander-in-Chief, Army of Occupation.
	20 November	Second Peace of Paris.
1816	February	Wedderburn-Webster libel action.
	25 June	Incendiary attempt on Wellington's house.
	July	Visit to England.
	Autumn	Discussions with Madame de Staël.
	26 December	Flying visit to London.
1817	9 January	Troop reduction announced.

	July	Visit to England.
	October	Appointed Allied referee on French reparations.
1818	*10 February*	Assassination attempt by Cantillon.
	October–November	Congress of Aix-la-Chapelle.
	21 November	End of Occupation.
	26 December	Appointed Master-General of Ordnance in Liverpool's Cabinet.
1819	*16 August*	Peterloo.
	Autumn	Six 'Gag' Acts.
1820	*29 January*	Death of George III. Accession of George IV.
	23 February	Cato Street Conspiracy.
	Summer–Autumn	Trial of Queen Caroline.
	19 December	Appointed Lord-Lieutenant of Hampshire.
1821	*5 May*	Death of Napoleon.
	5 August	Accident to ear; deafness.
	12 August	Suicide of Castlereagh.
	October–November	British representative at Congress of Verona.
1823–1827		Political duel with Canning.
	10 May	Daniel O'Connell founds Catholic Association.
1824	*16 September*	Death of Louis XVIII. Accession of Charles X.
	December	Wellington defeated by Canning on recognition of South American Republics.
1825	*March*	'Cottage Plot' against Canning.
	April	Wellington propounds plan for Catholic Emancipation.
	1 December	Death of Tsar Alexander I. Accession of Tsar Nicholas I.
	December	Monetary crisis.
1826	*February–April*	Mission to Russia.
	29 December	Constable of Tower of London.
1827	*5 January*	Death of Duke of York. Wellington Commander-in-Chief.
	17 February	Lord Liverpool suffers stroke.
	9 April	Canning Prime Minister.
		Resignation of Tories. Wellington also resigns command of Army.

	8 August	Death of Canning. Goderich Prime Minister.
		Wellington resumes command of Army.
1828	*8 January*	Goderich resigns.
	9 January	Wellington Prime Minister.
		Forced to resign command of Army.
	March–May	Repeal of old Test and Corporation Acts.
		Cabinet friction over Corn Laws and parliamentary reform.
	20 May	Huskisson and Canningites resign.
	July	Clare election. Irish crisis.
	1 August	Wellington broaches Catholic question with King.
	August–December	Wellington works behind scenes for Emancipation.
1829	*20 January*	Lord Warden of Cinque Ports.
	10 February	Suppression of Catholic Association, but Tory split on Emancipation issue. Wellington orders 'rightabout face'.
	21 March	Wellington v. Winchilsea duel at Battersea.
	13 April	Catholic Emancipation.
	9 May	Elder Brother of Trinity House.
	1829 Winter– 1830 Spring	Severe economic distress.
1830	*26 June*	Death of George IV. Accession of William IV.
	26–29 July	French Revolution of 'July Days'.
		Flight of Charles X to England; usurpation of Louis Philippe.
	August	Wave of Continental revolutions.
		Irish agitation for repeal of Union.
	August– November	Rising of agricultural workers under 'Captain Swing'.
	2 November	Wellington refuses parliamentary reform.
	15–16 November	Defeat and resignation.
		Grey Prime Minister.
1831	*22 April*	1st Reform Bill thwarted; King prorogues Parliament.
	24 April	Death of Kitty Wellington.

	27 April	Apsley House stoned.
	8 October	Lords defeat 2nd Reform Bill.
	12 October	Apsley House stoned again.
1832	*7 May*	Lords defeat 3rd Reform Bill; 'May Days' of near-revolution.
	15 May	Wellington fails to form Government; Grey recalled; Wellington abstains.
	7 June	Great Reform Bill becomes law.
1833		Critical period as Leader of Lords.
1834		Chancellor of Oxford.
	8 July	Grey resigns; Melbourne Prime Minister.
	14–15 November	William IV dismisses Whigs, summons Wellington.
	15 November– *9 December*	Refuses premiership; caretaker for Peel.
	9 December	Foreign Secretary. Peel Prime Minister.
1835	*7 April*	Fall of Conservatives. Leader of Opposition in Lords for next six years. Bi-partizan policy.
1837	*20 June*	Death of William IV. Accession of Queen Victoria.
	Summer	Agitation for Six-Point Charter and repeal of Corn Laws.
1838	*Spring–Summer*	Wellington clashes with ultra-Tories. Anti-Corn Law League founded.
1839	*May*	Bedchamber Plot.
	19 November	Acute seizure.
1840	*February*	Two more attacks.
	Summer–Autumn	The Hungry Forties. Riots in industrial areas.
1841	*Summer*	General Election. Peel Prime Minister. Wellington enters Cabinet without office.
1842	*February*	Peel announces tariff reforms and income tax.
	August	Wellington resumes command of Army, holding it for rest of life. Irrational anxieties over defence. Chartist and Irish agitation.
1843	*14 October*	Arrest of O'Connell.
1845	*October*	News of Irish potato famine.

	November	Peel proposes repeal of Corn Laws.
	6 December	Cabinet split. Wellington supports Peel (though against his policy); Stanley opposes.
		Peel resigns.
	20 December	Russell fails to form Whig Government. Peel recalled by Queen.
1846	*Spring*	Wellington urges peers to 'right about face' on Corn Laws.
	26 June	Corn Bill passes in Lords; Peel defeated on Coercion in Commons same day; resigns.
1846–1852		Wellington retires entirely from party politics.
1847		The Statue affair.
1848	*January*	Affair of the Burgoyne letter on defence.
	February	French Revolution, flight of Louis Philippe to England. Wave of European revolutions.
	10 April	Wellington as Commander-in-Chief defuses great Chartist demonstration.
1850		Ranger of Parks.
1851	*1 May*	Great Exhibition.
1852	*February*	Fall of Russell; Derby Prime Minister.
	14 September	Death at Walmer Castle, aged 83 years 4 months.
	18 November	Burial in St Paul's.

Introduction

At the beginning of the year 1769 two phenomenal characters in world history, Wellington and Napoleon, were awaiting birth. They were born within three and a half months of each other, Wellington in May, Napoleon in August. Some two hundred years later I was researching a new two-volume biography of Wellington to mark the bicentenary: *Wellington: The Years of the Sword*, published in 1969, and *Wellington: Pillar of State*, in 1972. The present single volume is an abridgement of the two.

As with all abridgements it has been necessary to cut out many favourite 'frills', such as a fair number of footnotes; also some fringe stories of Wellington's family life; and a good deal of his later preoccupations after he had retired from both military and political activities – for instance, his position as Chancellor of Oxford University and as Warden of the Cinque Ports. This has resulted in my keeping twice as much from the original *Years of the Sword* as from the *Pillar of State*. I hope that despite (or because of?) sometimes ruthless cutting, a sharp, accurate portrait of this remarkable character will emerge.

It has always been easier to present an arrogant egotist redeemed by genius, such as Napoleon, than a hero such as Wellington with unfashionable qualities like reserve and a curious humility to set against his forceful personality and memorable wit. The Duke of Wellington, to quote his own words, has been 'much exposed to authors', besides being much 'exposed' in the sense of criticized and even debunked. Nevertheless, his recorded life has achieved what Sir John Plumb once demanded of history: 'May history help to sustain man's confidence in his destiny.' A study of the Great Duke's life does precisely that. And that example is no less effective when the hero dives headlong into blunder and odium than when he enjoys spectacular triumphs.

Since I began my researches over twenty years ago, there has been much welcome growth in the study of Wellington but not, I think, change in fundamental attitudes. There is major growth in study and preservation of the battlefields. The foundation of the Waterloo Committee both in London and Brussels came in the nick of time. In about 1972 the Belgian government put forward a plan to drive a motorway across the middle of the battlefield. Alerted by John Beith the British ambassador in Brussels and by Emmanuel Meeus, the Eighth Duke of Wellington and Gerald Templar mounted a vigorous campaign that defeated this proposal. The motorway was diverted round the edge and in 1973 the Waterloo committee was set up to prevent the reemergence of any such scheme. Through its agency, together with the Association of Friends of the Waterloo Committee and their excellent Journal, it has expanded our interest in that eternally challenging subject. The small but dynamic museum in the village of Waterloo itself does justice to both sides in the campaign, the courageous French as well as British, Dutch-Belgians and Prussians; while the shops and mementos scattered over the battlefield no longer suggest, as once they did, that Napoleon won the Battle of Waterloo. Most important, that great landmark, the Château of Hougoumont, has been restored so far as is humanly possible to the state it was in at 9 am on 18 June 1815. New points of interest have emerged in the course of the work. Was the poet Victor Hugo right, for example, in describing the famous well at Hougoumont as choked with the bodies of dead French soldiers? When it was drained for preservation purposes the only relics found were a few horses' bones.

Perhaps most interesting of all to the general public is the moderate but very impressive proliferation of monuments. Apart from the Gordon monument, Waterloo's memorials twenty years ago were virtually shared between the French and the Dutch, the latter of whom had scored a double victory over their British allies: the outstanding Dutch *Butte de Lion* (Lion Mound) both celebrated the part played by the Prince of Orange and his forces in the battle, and also deceived British tourists into saluting what they thought was the *British* lion at last! Today one can visit many recently erected, simple but moving memorials to the British who fought and fell on 18 June, among them General Picton. Besides the Waterloo Committee and its ramifications, I must also pay tribute to the expansion and development of the National Army Museum in Royal Hospital Road, Chelsea, along with its supporting association of Friends; to the Guards Museum in Birdcage Walk; and above all to the Wellington Museum at Hyde Park Corner, housed in the Duke's home, Apsley House. Thanks to the energies of the 8th Duke of Wellington, Elizabeth Esteve-Coll, Director of the Victoria and Albert Museum (which is in overall charge of Apsley House), and Jonathan Voak, Curator of the Wellington Museum, interest is spread by entertainments, such as appropriate concerts, a one-man play on Wellington acted by Roger Wimbush and various lectures. In a south-coast town near where I live, there has sprung up the thriving Bexhill Hanoverian Study Group, an example of local enterprise publicizing the fact that the King's German Legion, which served in Wellington's campaigns, had their barracks in Bexhill.

The news from Portugal and Spain, dealing with the Peninsular War rather than Waterloo, is equally heartening. On the three separate occasions that I researched there in the 1960s, only the Portuguese authorities had restored or memorialized some of their celebrated sites. Heroic efforts had made the Lines of Torres Vedras live again, while Wellington's great British–Portuguese victory of Bussaco was rendered easy to map out and follow. But in Spain the famous battlefields – Talavera, Vitoria, the Pyrenees – were in danger of being overgrown or overbuilt. It was only thanks to information given by local tradesmen and farmers that I was able to identify some parts of them. When the flourishing Anglo-Spanish Society in London kindly invited me to address them after my *Years of the Sword* was published, they shared my concern with preservation of the Peninsular battlefields.

Today Sir Julian Paget, Bt, editor of the *Guards Magazine* and foremost among modern interpreters of Wellington, has a splendid story to tell of Talavera in 1990. He describes how the Spanish Government had driven a motorway straight across the battlefield of Talavera. 'Early in 1988 the bulldozers turned up thousands of human bones, and it was realized that they had disturbed a mass grave from 1809', containing, it was thought, the remains from both sides. 'It was too late to change the motorway, but, as the result of strong protests by the British Ambassador in Madrid, the Duke of Wellington and the Wellington Society, the Spanish Government undertook to erect a monument nearby to all those who died at the Battle of Talavera.' This they did, and in October 1990 wreaths were laid on the huge Monument at a simple but moving ceremony in the presence of the Talavera Regiments and their Colonels. 'Britain was appropriately represented by Brigadier the Duke of Wellington, formerly Royal Horse Guards (The Blues), while Spain had the Duque de Albuquerque, and the French had their military attaché and the senior Colonel of their Talavera Regiments.' On the Sunday before, Sir Julian and David Chandler, the distinguished military historian, had taken a guided tour round the battlefield. Its events can still be identified, despite the motorway – perhaps an encouragement to other would-be preservers of historic sites. I am grateful to Sir Julian for allowing me to quote here from his article in the *Guards Magazine*.

Several other anecdotes concerning the Great Duke have been related to me since my book was first published and I would like to quote them here. A Peninsular story recounts Wellington as saying (in 1811) that he was once caught 'like a rat in a bottle' – the analogy being based on a conjuring trick he had witnessed in India, where muskrats were sucked into bottles by means of a vacuum inside. When one of the General's guests protested that they must have been either very small rats or very big bottles, Wellington replied characteristically, 'Very small bottles and very large rats.' The story has often been retold at Wellington's expense, for instance by B. R. Haydon and Professor Gilbert Murray. In Murray's account he is represented as a senile old soldier. However, in *A King's Story*, the memoirs of the Duke of Windsor, a new light is thrown on the 'bottle' stories that authenticates Wellington's. HRH recalls how Mr Gunner, the college porter at Magdalen, Oxford, where he was an undergraduate, used to perform his famous trick – inserting a banana in the neck of a bottle filled with burning paper and watching the vacuum suck it down with a thud. He adds, 'The only time my father King George V came to Oxford to see me I had Gunner perform this feat for his special benefit. "By God," said the King appreciatively, "that is one of the darnedest tricks I ever saw." ' It may be doubted whether the King used an Americanism to describe his experience, but otherwise he was almost certainly watching the same Indian trick as Wellington had witnessed nearly two hundred years before.

An anecdote dated 1812 touches on the storming and capture of Badajoz by a 'Red-coat', Lt Macpherson of the 45th Foot (later Sherwood Foresters) who was wounded in the side as he led his men up the scaling ladders. He was passed by Wellington's brother-in-law General Hercules Pakenham, also severely wounded, who cried out, 'We shall meet again.' (Did he mean in heaven? But both survived.) Macpherson returned to the attack, fought his way to the Castle tower, tore down the French tricolour flying on top and replaced it, in the absence of a Union Jack, with his own red jacket. Lieutenant-Colonel A. A. Dean relates that his old regiment still celebrates Badajoz Day by hoisting a red coat on the flagpole.

A third anecdote gives a typical glimpse of Wellington near the end of his life. Sir John Stephenson recalls a story handed down in his family and originating with Sarah Lady Lyttelton, royal governess to Queen Victoria's children. 'When the Duke wrote to accept the Queen's invitation to be godfather to her son [1850] he mentioned that if she should be thinking of giving the boy [later Duke of Connaught] his godfather's name, it was Arthur.' Sir John goes on to ask me, 'Was that true modesty on the part of your hero, as I have been brought up to believe?' I'm sure it was.

By gracious permission of Her Majesty the Queen I have been given access to the Royal Archives, Windsor, and by gracious permission of Her Majesty the Queen of the Netherlands, to the Archives in the Royal House, The Hague. I warmly thank the Royal Librarians, Mr Robert Mackworth-Young and Mr Pelinck, for all their help. Through Mr Pelinck I would also like to thank the Dutch military experts for their valuable suggestions. Likewise I do not forget my great debt to His Excellency the Netherlands Ambassador.

In the sad loss of the 7th Duke of Wellington early in 1972, it was some consolation to me that he was able to read the whole of my book in manuscript, and to give me the incalculable benefit of his advice and criticism up to the last. The depth and detail of his knowledge of the 1st Duke was unique. He expressed it in racy conversation, in his wonderful collection of memorabilia and in the fascinating books on his great ancestor that he edited or compiled. His loss to scholarship is indeed heavy. I can never thank him and his family enough, particularly for the complete freedom they allowed me in pursuing the path of biography wherever it might lead. Fortunately for the cause of continuity and development his son Valerian, the 8th Duke, is the generous guardian of family history and has opened Stratfield Saye House to the public, setting up the impressive new museum together with the Great Duke's historic funeral car. I must also thank Mr Francis Needham and Mr Antony Grant, secretaries respectively to the 7th and 8th Dukes, for their constructive criticism of my manuscript, proof- reading and patient help of all kinds.

I would like to express my very warm thanks to others who have allowed me to use unpublished papers: Lord Raglan, Lady Albemarle, Sir Anthony Weldon, Mrs Freda Loch, Comte Sebastien Foy; l'Abbé Chapeau, Angers University; Mr Edmund de Rothschild; the Rector of

Maynooth College, Dublin; the Curator of the Archives, Household Cavalry Museum, Windsor; and the former and present curators of Apsley House, Victor Percival and Jonathan Voak. I am most grateful to the latter and to Elizabeth Esteve-Coll, Director of the Victoria and Albert Museum, for inviting me to lecture on Waterloo in the Waterloo Chamber of Apsley House with slides from the V & A collection.

For my visits to the Portuguese battlefields I am immensely indebted to the Gulbenkian Foundation, and to Mr J. C. Thornton, Miss M. H. Knott, Miss M. O'Donovan, and Mr F. P. Almeida Langhane. I must thank Colonel Francisco Eduardo Baptista for his untiring energy and thoughtfulness; though expecting to be conducting a male researcher through the Lines of Torres Vedras, he bore the truth with fortitude. Without the initial enthusiasm of His Excellency the Portuguese Ambassador none of this could have taken place, and I thank him most warmly. Sir George and Lady Labouchère were the kindest of hosts in Madrid; Sir Nicholas and Lady Henderson (authors themselves) and Mme Piru Urquijo were perfect leaders of the expedition; my sister-in-law Lady Mary Clive located half-obliterated sites with the flair of yet another fellow author and biographer; His Excellency the Spanish Ambassador was extremely kind in answering questions, as were Professor Clavería and Miss Thain of the Spanish Institute, and Professor Pabón in Madrid. A very special word of thanks is due to His Excellency the Chilean Ambassador for his translations. I am indeed grateful to Sir Roderick and Lady Barclay for their hospitality during the 150th Anniversary of the Battle of Waterloo, and to the Aberdeen family for inviting me to be present at the ceremony at the Gordon Monument.

For giving me the benefit of their expert knowledge I wish to thank especially Mr and Mrs Jac Weller, Field-Marshal Lord Templer, Colonel Sir Thomas Butler, my brother-in-law Mr Anthony Powell, Sir Arthur Bryant, Mr Tom Goff, Reverend J. C. Bowmer (Librarian at Epworth House), my brother-in-law Mr Donald McLachlan, Major C. J. D. Haswell, Lt Col J. G. O. Whitehead, David Chandler, Mr A. S. Bennell, Sir Roy Strong and Dr John Hayes (former and present Directors of the National Portrait Gallery); the staffs of the National Army Museum, the Household Cavalry Museum, the Imperial War Museum, the Indian Section of the Victoria and Albert Museum, the India Office Library, India House, the French Embassy, the National Library of Ireland, the Irish State Papers Office, the Public Record Office of Northern Ireland and Mr A. P. W. Malcolmson, the Public

Record Office, Somerset House, the London Library, the British Library, Chelsea Public Library, Kent County Archives, the Jockey Club, the British Medical Association, Madame Tussaud's, the West Sussex and Surrey Records Offices and County Archives, Mr D. W. King and the Ministry of Defence Library, Mr D. S. Porter and the Bodleian Library, Mr J. T. Eubank, Jr and Rice University (for Miss Jenkins's letters); Brig. D. A. Pringle, Duke of York's Royal Military School; Mr J. R. Dineen, Royal United Services Institute Library; Mr William Reid, National Army Museum; Commander C. H. Tyers, Naval and Military Club; Atalanta Clifford, Guards Museum; Mr C. Dobson, House of Lords Library; Mr A. E. Barker and the SPCK; the late Lord Cromer K. G.; Mr T. L. Ingram and Barings Bank; Mr P. Montague-Smith, Editor of Debrett; the Town Clerks of Rye and Winchelsea.

I would like to thank all those who have kindly put me in touch with material for this book: Lord Charteris, Lord Adeane, my aunt Mrs Jean Braddell, Professor Edmund Ford, Mr Martin Gilbert, Reverend C. C. Ellison (Meath Historical Society), Reverend R. J. Kent (St George's Church, Dublin), Reverend Edwin Starke, Mr Frederic Raphael, Mr Richard Buckle, Miss Margery Weiner, Mrs E. de Winton, Sir John Betjeman, Major-General John Sheffield, Mr John Kerslake, Dr John Roebuck, Mr David Colville, Mr G. Handley-Taylor, Mr M. C. Farrar-Bell, Mr Joseph Bryan III, Captain Gerrard, Miss Joan Cooley, Mr A. P. Ryan, Dr Patrick Kelly, Lord Head, Mr Michael Glover, Mr Francis Boyd, Commander Burrows, Mr Alan Tillotson, Mr R. W. Houssman, Mr W. G. Constable, Mrs Fortescue-Hitchins, Mr R. Bucknall.

In dealing with Wellington's later life I have been greatly helped by those who have lent me new material. I thank the 5th Marquess of Salisbury and his librarian Miss Clare Talbot, Miss Carola Oman, Mr J. Bennett, Mr Francis Bamford, Mr John Sparrow, Mrs Georgina Battiscombe, Lord Kenyon, Admiral Sir F. Dalrymple-Hamilton, Mrs Hardy-Roberts, Major John Maxse, Mrs Lettice Miller, The Hon. Mrs Anne Fremantle, Mme Christianne Besse, Lord Dunsany, Mr Kenneth Rose, Mrs N. Tweddell, Mr Tom Cullen, Mrs Margaret Dodger, Mr George Huxley, Mr W. T. Oliver, Brig. K. Thompson, Mrs Ruth Adam, Lady Moran, Mr J. Ford, Mr R. Speaight, Mr Gervase Huxley, Captain P. B. Backhouse, Mr Esmond Warner, Mrs F. B. Maggs, Mr P. Skottowe, Miss Mary Lutyens, Brig. P. H. C. Hayward, Mr Brian Inglis, Professor G. Best, Mr H. Bolitho, Dr S.

Pasmore, Mr R. de Stacpoole, Col. R. J. Longfield, Miss J. Harrild, Lady Limerick, the Hon. Mrs Arthur Pollen, Mrs Tonge, Mr J. Mannering, Mr R. H. Irrmann, Mr B. J. Buxton, Dr Alec Vidler, Mr Derek Hudson, Mr J. F. Vernon, Group Captain G. Knocker, Mrs M. R. Cowie, Mr R. Boulind, Mr E. Franklin, Mr L. Drucker, Mr G. Lewin, Mr J. Showers.

I would also like to thank those who have answered my queries relative to the Duke's later years or suggested corrections in my account of his earlier ones: Lord Anglesey, Mr John Ehrman, Mr M. G. Brock, the Hon. Gerard Noel, Mr P. J. V. Rolo, Miss Susan Ertz, Mrs J. H. Fisher, Col A. C. T. White, VC, Brig. R. G. S. Bidwell, Miss Grizel Grey, Mr C. Seed, Dr Dorothy George, Mr Richard Ormonde, Professor M. R. D. Foot, Mr John Terraine, Mr A. Brett-James, Mr C. Clive-Ponsonby-Fane, Mrs R. Craddock, Lt Col I. H. Stockwood, Brig. P. Kivy, Brig. S. C. Dumbreck, Mr D. Young, Mr G. Spencer, Mr B. Sweet-Escott, Mrs S. J. Morton, Mr D. Parsons, Mrs A. Moffat, Brig. H. Bozner, Mr Hugh Farmar, Mr John Robbins, Mr R. A. Chatter, Mr Harford Montgomery Hyde, Mr Denys Forrest, Mr L. Smith, Mr Michael De-la-Noy, Mr Peter King, Mr Jerit-Jan Colenbrander and Brig. Sir Mark Henniker, Bt.

Sir Mark's letter of October 1973 especially delighted me. While challenging the Raglan MSS in which Wellington was said by Fitzroy Somerset to have left the final choice of the Waterloo position to a trusted staff officer, he has a paean of praise for the performance of Sir Harry Smith's wife Juanita on the battlefield. Sir Mark's father possessed a charger in 1914 named Juanita and Sir Mark himself 'was told about the lady at a very tender age. She was a great "one" [the town of Ladysmith was to be called after her] and rode a phenomenal distance on the day of the battle of Waterloo. I once won a trophy,' he adds, 'for riding fifty miles in a day, but it was nothing compared with what Juanita did in 1815. Today we are a puny race.'

Since the new writing on Wellington and his family in the last twenty years, I would say that the hero's true character is better understood than it was fifty years ago. Among the new studies are: *Waterloo – Battle of Three Armies*, edited by Lord Chalfont; *The Great Duke* by Sir Arthur Bryant; *The Eldest Brother*, a definitive life of the Marquess Wellesley by Iris Butler; and most recently *The Iron Duke* by Lawrence James. I have been privileged to write the introductions to other recent books on Wellington: *The Duke* by Philip Guedalla (reprinted 1974); *Your Most Obedient Servant – James Thornton – Cook to the Duke of Wellington*; *A Soldier's*

8

Wife – Wellington's Marriage by Joan Wilson. The Wellington Lectures now delivered annually at Southampton University (of which Field- Marshal Lord Carver gave the first on 'Wellington and his Brothers' and I the third on 'Wellington and Mrs Arbuthnot') should keep the fires burning near the Duke's Hampshire home.

I conclude by thanking all those friends and family who have read all or part of the book at whatever stage: Sir Basil Liddell Hart, my sister-in-law Lady Violet Powell, Mrs Angela Lambert, Mr Paul Johnson, Mr Harold Kurtz, Mr Ian Robertson, and Miss Anna Collins who generously volunteered research on newspapers and pictures. Professor Lord Briggs, Dr G. Kitson Clark and Professor Kevin Nowlan did me the honour of reading the page proofs of the chapters on British and Irish political history. I am most grateful to my publisher Lord Weidenfeld for having given me the original idea of the book and to Mr Anthony Cheetham for his enthusiasm for this new edition; to Tony Godwin and Mrs Gila Falkus; to Allegra Huston, Natalina Bertoli and Elizabeth Blumer; and to Mrs Agnes Fenner for her very intelligent typing. I thank yet again my first agent and friend Graham Watson, and now the incomparable Mike Shaw. My daughter Antonia made many suggestions and devised the title *Years of the Sword*, my son Thomas shared valuable Irish nuggets, Paddy, Michael and Kevin read various chapters, while Judith, Rachel and Valerie helped me greatly with cutting and shaping. To Frank I owe the inspiration of his life-long devotion to the subject and his preliminary shortening of the whole of *Pillar of State*; not forgetting the fact that he was born great-great- nephew of Kitty Pakenham, first Duchess of Wellington.

1

Retained for Life

Wellington is a national hero. His countrymen today, whether they feel exalted or irritated by the breed, cannot deny that he belongs to it. His name still issues a challenge. The challenge may change with time and the password need renewing. But there is still an encounter – or a collision.

Where did he get his magic? It is possible to examine the Duke item by item. He had brilliant military talents, an antagonist of genius and Europe for an arena. But an itemized hero explains nothing. Somehow he must be caught in action, in flight like a great meteorite wrenched off from the mass of humanity: blinding, molten, irresistible. No doubt he will cool in time, like the meteorite, and then rough edges will begin to appear; cracks, excrescences and other eccentricities. The Duke had his share. There is nothing unheroic about that. The British even find it endearing. 'England expects every man to do his duty' – and every great man to do much else besides, some of it, as the Duke would have said, 'rather curious'.

At first sight, one of the Duke's more curious traits was a studied indifference to his own history. 'The Duke of Wellington has nothing to say to the forty or fifty Lives of Himself which at present in the course of being written', were the words with which at the age of seventy-one he dismissed one of these hapless authors. No doubt the present biography, like so many of its predecessors, would have received the same unfailing discouragement. As for the Duke's pedigree, he liked to represent it as something unknown and unknowable. When he was seventy-four and had long been the most famous member of a leading family, a certain Samuel Gordon wrote from Aungier Street, Dublin, to ask for the name of a book dealing with Wellington's ancestors, the Wellesleys, in the days of Cromwell. Wellington replied as if the Wellesleys of County Meath were no more or less traceable than the Sam Gordons of Aungier Street: 'He has no knowledge of any person from whom or place at which Mr Gordon could procure Information on the matter referred to. . . .'[1] A fuller knowledge of the great man's character would have warned his correspondent what to expect. His taboo was no aberration but an expression of principle. It can only become intelligible, therefore, as his life story unfolds. Meanwhile, his picture of a family tree shrouded in the mists of history, with which he loved to baffle enquirers, must yield to more recent research.

The Wellesleys came from Somerset. When did the family go to Ireland? No documentary evidence has survived, but a respectable authority, William Lynch, implies that it was with Henry II in the 1170s. Writing in 1830, Lynch stated that the Wellesleys had held the hereditary office of Standard Bearer to the King 'since time immemorial' – meaning, apparently, since the reign of Henry II. He described how Henry's former Standard Bearer had thrown down the royal banner during a battle against the Welsh and run away. He was superseded by a Wellesley whose conduct on the battlefield was more reliable. The new Standard Bearer would, of course, accompany King Henry when he invaded Ireland.

By the reign of Henry III there is documentary evidence of a Wellesley in Ireland. He went over in 1226 on 'King's business' and bought property in Dublin. From the latter half of the fourteenth century onwards these Wellesleys lived entirely in Ireland, steadily amassing land by marriage or services rendered. There was Sir William, Member of Parliament in 1372, Keeper of the Castles of Kildare and Carbery, Justice of the Peace for Kildare and Kilkenny, Sheriff of Kildare. A Patent Roll of 1400 recorded that he was 'retained by the King for life with a salary of £20 a year'. Gerald Wellesley, or 'Garret [the Irish form of Gerald] Wesley' as he called himself, served on the Grand Jury at Trim in Meath. His wife was Elizabeth Colley. Their son, Garret Wesley II, lacked one advantage – an heir. On whom should he bestow the Wesley name and fortune?

The Colleys in fact had Wellesley blood, and the childless Garret II could not do better than choose his first cousin Richard Colley, younger son of his maternal uncle Henry Colley of Castle Carbery, only fifteen miles away. Richard Cowly, Cooley or Colley never had to decide which way to spell his name, for in 1728 he was to change it to Wesley by adoption, and in 1746 to Mornington by ennoblement. Here in Richard Wesley, an Irish Georgian gentleman born about 1690, civilized and eccentric, was the Duke of Wellington's grandfather.

What did these six centuries of a strikingly homogeneous past mean for Wellington? Behind him stretched an embattled English race who had occupied an alien land, marrying strictly with their own kind and becoming not only a ruling caste but a ruling garrison. It would be hard for Wellington to escape from such a heredity. Especially from that William de Wellesley, Knight, who had been 'retained by the King for life' at a salary of £20 a year. The phrase was to be echoed almost word for word centuries later by Arthur Wellesley, Knight, Viscount, Earl, Marquess, Duke. Though the retaining fee was to change amazingly, the spirit would remain the same.

Garret Wesley III was born on 9 July 1735, the musical prodigy who was to be Wellington's father. While still in his nurse's arms the baby listened attentively to his father's playing – for Richard 'played well (for a gentleman) on the violin';[2] and though 'indolence' prevented the child from composing until the advanced age of nine, the next four years saw amazing progress.

Young Garret's godmother, Mrs Delany, reported enthusiastically on this 'most extraordinary' thirteen-year-old. He was already composing and excelled at the violin and the classics. While indulging his son's tastes Richard Mornington had not curbed his own, so that when he died in 1758 the Wesley fortune was somewhat impaired, though his heir still had the substantial income of £8,000 a year. Garret, the new Lord Mornington, was twenty-three. He married Anne Hill, eldest daughter of Arthur Hill (afterwards Lord Dungannon), a strong-minded girl of sixteen with no fortune. Mrs Delany later decided that the young Morningtons 'seemed' very happy, though their future was doubtful. Anne lacked 'judgement', as her son Arthur was also to discover.

Lord Mornington prospered in the arts and paternity if not in the six per cents. He was created an Earl in 1760, Doctor and then Professor of Music at Trinity in 1764 for his sacred compositions, madrigals, catches and such enchanting glees as '*Here in cool grot*'. In 1760 his son and heir, Richard Colley Wesley, was born, followed by William in 1763, Anne in 1768, and in 1769 his third surviving son, Arthur. Then came two younger boys, Gerald Valerian born in 1770 and Henry in 1773. All the boys were destined to have distinguished careers, some brilliant, Arthur the most dazzling of all.

The 1760s were not a prosperous time for Ireland. The poor in their squalid cabins, existing on a diet of potatoes and milk, were increasing as fast as the Wesleys and there were far more of them, so that the population, which had been under 2 million in 1706, would be 4½ million by the end of the century. The whole hinterland depended on a subsistence economy where gangs of peasant desperadoes gave the misery a voice. Ireland's first Coercion Act was passed just four years before Arthur Wesley's birth.

The lucky stars looked down on the hero's birthday – though on precisely which day has never been agreed. Wellington himself always kept it on 1 May. The place of his birth is also disputed. There is evidence based on local tradition, but only on tradition, for Dangan Castle, the Wellesley home. There is ingenious support for a premature birth on the road between Dangan and Dublin. And there is no valid argument whatever for a variety of suggestions including Trim, Mornington, 114 Grafton Street, a house opposite 6 Merrion Square and the Dublin packet-boat at sea.

Dublin newspapers, however, which were published at the beginning of May, announced the birth of a son to the Countess of Mornington 'a few days ago' in Merrion Street, where, at No. 6, stood Mornington House. Despite Wellington's own inveterate distrust of newspapers, in this case they must be assumed to know best. At 6 Merrion Street (now 24 Upper Merrion Street) on 1 May 1769 the future Duke of Wellington was born.

On 15 August of the same year was born Napoleon Bonaparte.

2

Odd Man Out

The childhood which has almost no annals is not necessarily happy.
Wellington's grim reticence about his youth fits into the impression of a frustrated fourth child, conscious of latent powers but
inhibited by two clever elder brothers and two promising younger ones.

No one bothered to leave behind a description of the child's
appearance, though one surviving contemporary portrait, a silhouette,
gives the impression of a delicate, even poetic face. The nose already
has a faint downward curve, unusual in childhood. The lips form a line
that is almost sedate. His eyes were always of a brilliant light blue; his
hair was brown.

As a small child, Arthur attended the Diocesan School, Trim. This
was his first and last experience of Irish education. By moving to
London his father prevented him and his brothers from acquiring what
Arthur's future brother-in-law, Edward Pakenham, called 'a singularity of pronunciation that hereafter might be a disadvantage . . . in
society'.[1]

The London preparatory school was Brown's establishment in
Chelsea. He did not speak well of it. The shilling tip he once received
while a pupil there from his eldest brother Richard, was well-matched
by the school's modest educational provisions. They ensured that
Arthur would enter Eton singularly ill-equipped. He admitted to his
future biographer, the Rev. G. R. Gleig, that he was 'a dreamy, idle and
shy lad'.[2] Indifferent health, explained one of his schoolfellows, gave
Arthur a careless and lethargic manner. He would never take part in
playground games but 'lounged' against a large walnut tree watching
the players and picking out those who cheated.

The Mornington parents were 'frivolous and careless personages',
according to Arthur's brother Richard. It is unlikely that Arthur heard
much about current affairs during these early school years. Yet there
was much to discuss both abroad and at home.

American colonists were not losing their War of Independence as expected; by 1778, in fact, they had gained allies in Spain and France. Irish Protestants sprang to arms, spreading wild rumours of a French invasion and pouring their money into costly volunteer corps in return for which they fiercely demanded commercial equality with England. Irish Catholics in 1778 were placated with another partial Relief Act, to lure them into the Army.

By the end of 1781 General Cornwallis had surrendered to General Washington, and Arthur Wesley's father was dead.

So far, Arthur's outstanding gift was intense love of music and skill in playing the violin. It was not a gift to be prized by his widowed mother. The late Lord Mornington's orchestra had filled no mouths at Dangan. Under a cloud of family indebtedness that compelled refulgent Richard, now Lord Mornington, to leave Oxford without a degree, Arthur entered Eton in autumn 1781, carrying his shyness with him.

There were no compulsory, organized games at Eton and even the most casual cricket or boating did not attract Arthur. Lonely and withdrawn, he preferred the grounds of the Manor House where he boarded, playing at the bottom of the garden and jumping over a broad black ditch. He had no aptitude for the classics and his younger brother Gerald was soon his scholastic superior. Richard felt no compunction about settling with their mother to remove Arthur from Eton, in order that all the available funds might be concentrated on Gerald and Henry. This she did at the end of the summer half, 1784.

Wellington did not choose to set eyes on Eton again until 22 January 1818, thirty-four years after his own schooldays. By then he was visiting his two sons who were boarding in his old house. He inspected the garden – but what had become of the broad black ditch over which he had jumped so often? 'I really believe I owe my spirit of enterprise,' he said with his laugh like a war-whoop, 'to the tricks I used to play in the garden.'[3] The stream, with its banks of black mud, had been filled in, but a subsidence in the lawn must have indicated – as it still does – where Arthur Wesley had played his tricks.

It seems odd that an alumnus so lukewarm when young, so indifferent when old, should have paid to his *alma mater* the highest tribute in his power: 'The Battle of Waterloo was won on the playing-fields of Eton.' Of all Wellington's alleged *obiter dicta*, this is perhaps the best known. Yet probably he never said or thought anything of the kind.

This 'laconic' (as Wellington's epigrams used to be called) did not make its first appearance until three years after his death. In 1855 an eminent French writer and parliamentarian, Count de Montalembert, visited Eton in search of material for his projected book on the political future of England. The writer picked up something that the orator in him turned to good account: '. . . one understands the Duke of Wellington's *mot* when, revisiting during his declining years the beauteous scenes where he had been educated, remembering the games of his youth, and finding the same precocious vigour in the descendants of his comrades, he said aloud: *"C'est ici qu'a été gagnée la bataille de Waterloo."* '

There is no mention here of 'playing-fields'; therefore no justification for later attempts, based on this passage, to praise (or deride) Wellington for advocating organized games. His remark, in 1818, that jumping over the broad black ditch had produced his own 'spirit of enterprise', could be used only, if at all, to prove that the battle of Waterloo had been won by a small, odd-man-out in the Manor House garden.

Arthur was now an awkward fifteen; he visited the famous 'Ladies of Llangollen' that summer of 1784, and made a poor showing. These two ladies, Lady Eleanor Butler and Miss Sarah Ponsonby, described as 'the most celebrated virgins in Europe', had rejected the vanities of eighteenth-century Ireland and fled together to the mountains of north Wales, there to cultivate a romantic friendship. (Arthur was to remember them fifty years later looking like two little old men as they stood side by side outside their cottage with hair cut short, mannish jackets, top hats, and a cat and a dog.) When their rather odd neighbour, Lady Dungannon, brought over her grandchildren, Miss Sarah regaled her cousin, Mrs Tighe, with an account of Arthur's backwardness.[4]

A few weeks later the London home broke up. Lady Mornington, like many another financially embarrassed Briton, decided to live in Brussels until the tide turned. Arthur was packed off to Brighton for some much-needed tutoring with the Rev. Henry Michell. At the beginning of 1785 he went with his mother to the home of a Brussels advocate, M. Louis Goubert. But a year with Arthur in Brussels, which meant a year with Arthur's violin, was enough for Lady Mornington. She returned home herself and sent him to France, to prepare for that last refuge of square pegs – the Army.

Prejudice against the Army was almost universal. At home there was no police force, so that the strong arm of the law was represented by companies of red-coats whose discipline, behaviour, pay and billets even by eighteenth-century standards were deplorable. Even Tories, even Wellington himself would never cease to feel a deeply historical, thoroughly British reserve towards the standing army. What a career to choose for a son growing up in an abysmal decade. But what else could be expected, with Arthur's sorry record? 'I vow to God I don't know what I shall do with my awkward son Arthur,' complained Lady Mornington to her daughter-in-law, William's wife. He was 'food for powder and nothing more'.[5]

To prepare himself for this uninviting future Arthur was dispatched to the historic Royal Academy of Equitation at Angers in Anjou. Here the sons of the nobility and gentry from all over Europe had been trained for two centuries in the manly arts. Angers was no mere riding-school. Among past pupils had been George Villiers, 1st Duke of Buckingham. Gauche, sixteen-year-old Arthur Wesley was hardly a reincarnation of George Villiers, who had descended on Angers aged nineteen, 'loving everybody and avid of amusement'; but Angers was just the place to give Arthur the civilized *politesse* if not *panache* he needed.

Arthur's name headed the list of entries for 1786: '*Mr Wesley, gentilhomme Irlandais, fils de Mylaidi Mornington, pensionnaire, entre le 16 Janvier.*' With two sons of Irish peers for boon companions, Mr Walsh son of Lord Walsh, and Mr Wingfield, son of Lord '*Portscowz*' (Powerscourt), this '*groupe des lords*' as they were called, would make for the eating-houses of the town centre in the evening, where their college uniforms of scarlet coat, yellow buttons and sky-blue facings mingled with the blue or silver-grey of the French garrison.

Angers must have been largely responsible for the change which was soon noticed in Arthur. Admittedly the English boys (108 out of 334 Academicians during his year) tended to keep aloof, and he and his friends had a tiresome habit of dropping small change out of their windows on to the heads of passers-by. He spent some of his happiest hours playing on a sofa with his white terrier Vick.[6] This is perhaps the reason why his later feats as a rider were to excel in valour rather than grace, despite the Academy's motto of 'Grace and Valour' – in that order. Nevertheless, the impression given by many of his biographers that he left Angers with nothing much more than a good French accent, because nothing much more was available at a place like Angers, cannot be accepted.

Wellington would certainly have preferred a university education, as he was himself to make clear. But short of that, Angers did him proud. It was to make him one of the most cosmopolitan of great Englishmen. M. de Pignerolle, the director and a Frenchman, was the first to detect the signs of brilliance which had been invisible to Arthur's countrymen. Towards the end of Arthur's residence a young Irish peer and his governor were entered as boarders. The letter enquired of Pignerolle if he had any English boys of promise. Pignerolle replied that he had 'one Irish lad of great promise, of the name of Wesley . . .'[7]

If Angers had a weakness it was one that Arthur himself would have been the last to admit. In Marcel de Pignerolle the Academy had a director dedicated to the *ancien régime*. Lord Stanhope tells how one evening at dinner in 1840 in the dining-room at Apsley House, the Duke fixed his eyes on a pair of portraits of Louis XVIII and Charles X in their royal robes. 'How much better after all,' he reflected smiling, 'these two look with their *fleurs-de-lis* and *Saint-Esprits*, than the two corporals behind, or the fancy dress in between!'[8] The corporals were Europe's royal war-lords, Alexander of Russia and the King of Prussia in uniform, while the fancy dress was George IV painted by Wilkie in Highland kilt and bonnet.

The new Arthur made an instantaneous impression. His mother is said to have caught sight of him for the first time at the Haymarket Theatre, after he returned to London towards the end of 1786. 'I do believe there is my ugly boy Arthur,' she exclaimed incredulously, for he had shot up, his hair was well powdered and his cheeks were bright.[9] Not that the military prospect could now be allowed to recede. Richard dashed off a letter to the Duke of Rutland, Lord Lieutenant of Ireland, the moment Arthur arrived:

Let me remind you of a younger brother of mine, whom you were so kind as to take into your consideration for a commission in the army. He is here at this moment, and perfectly idle. It is a matter of indifference to me what commission he gets, provided he gets it soon.[10]

If Arthur saw this brotherly message he would not have felt unduly resentful. No doubt he would have preferred civilian life, but it was never his way to carry opposition beyond a certain point.

On 17 March he was gazetted Ensign in the 73rd Highland Regiment. Years later, his Irish-born friend, John Wilson Croker, remembered, or thought he remembered, the Duke telling him about a unique incident and decided to put it in his own *Memoirs*.*

Can you spare me five minutes [he therefore wrote to the old Duke on 15 November 1850], to tell me whether my recollection of one of the most remarkable passages of your life (as I think) is correct? Did you once tell me that the very day (or week) that you *first joined the Army* you had a private soldier & all his accoutrements & traps separately weighed, to give you some insight into what the *man* had to do & his power of doing it?[11]

Wellington's reply was certainly no less characteristic than the story he was asked to vet:

I have frequently calculated the weight of each of the articles which the Soldier carried. . . . But I don't think that I made this calculation on the day I joined a regiment or ever said that I had made it at that period! In the orders respecting the examination of Officers for Promotion I have required that this knowledge should be attained.†

Some such order may well have given rise to a legend like Croker's; on the other hand, Wellington's answer to Croker may be a vivid example of his passion for what today would be called 'debunking'.

On 24 October 1787 the Duke of Rutland died and the Morningtons promptly closed in on his successor, Lord Buckingham, the Viceroy designate, whose fat red face expressed kindly greed and who had already got Richard a seat on the English Board of Treasury. He at once yielded to this new clamour: by 4 November Lord Mornington was already thanking him for having appointed Arthur one of his aides-de-camp at 10s. a day. His private income was £125 a year. Auspiciously on Christmas Day 1787 Arthur was gazetted Lieutenant in the 76th Regiment of Foot. On 23 January 1788 Arthur was transferred into the 41st and a day or two afterwards Lady Mornington 'consigned' him to his new lord and master, from their London home in Henrietta Street, Cavendish Square. She sent the Ladies of Llangollen two lyrical letters to prepare them for the new Arthur who would call on his way to Holyhead: 'he really is a very charming young man, never did I see such a change for the better in any body . . .' Before this letter arrived, Arthur and his grandmother, Lady Dungannon, had already visited the Ladies. Eleanor Butler noted in her journal that they had

* John Wilson Croker (1780–1857). MP for Downpatrick, 1807, founded the *Quarterly Review*, 1809, secretary to the Admiralty.

† Order signed by Wellington on 14 May 1850: '[Officers] should know the weight of the knapsack, the weight of the soldier's firelock, of his pouch with or without the ammunition . . . of his accoutrements with or without the bayonet, of the bayonet with or without the scabbard.'

dropped in shortly after breakfast on 28 January, adding: 'A charming young man. Handsome, fashioned tall [five feet nine inches] and elegant.' His charm had worked even upon his problem grandmother, for the journal continued, 'She was in the best Temper'.[12]

On 1 February 1788 he sailed into Dublin Bay. All seemed set fair for the legendary return of the younger son to his native country, from whose shores he had departed in a sombre disguise of reserve and silence. Or was Ireland, alike in her frustration and her poetry, her despair and her rapturous hopes, to remain forever inimical to his kind of genius? 'The Irish politicks are vastly too intricate for a *volume* to describe,' wrote Lady Sarah Napier a year before he arrived. 'There is no *system* or regularity here.'

As it happened, regularity was to be Wellington's guiding star.

3

Food for Powder

The Ireland to which Arthur Wesley returned was quiet – the quiet before the storm.

This happy state dated from 1782 when the Irish orator, Henry Grattan, had risen to his feet under the magnificent chandeliers of Parliament House and saluted Dublin's first independent Parliament: 'Ireland is now a nation.' Since then a wave of national confidence had swept over Dublin inspiring Protestants and Catholics, Whigs and Tories alike to build, to drain, to trade, to make their city the most beautiful in Europe. Even in the unkempt countryside a few valiant landlords were intensifying their campaigns for improvement. Richard Edgeworth was spreading lime far and wide, as was another ardent landlord nearby, his cousin, Lord Longford.

Dublin Castle alone, the seat of all power, was in no state to lead an Irish renaissance. Arthur Wesley found an arrogant junta installed whose one aim was to bind the upper classes to themselves and to the British connection by four golden chains: titles, pensions, sinecure posts and highly paid jobs.

The Vicereine unkindly called Arthur and his colleagues her 'awkward squad'. But despite their inexpertise supper would be duly served in the Round Room where the rompers, dashers and rattlers of the *bon ton* flocked to eat the Castle roasts and ragouts, washed down with Tokay, burgundy, champagne and iced sherbet, to the sentimental measures of a German band. When the Lord Lieutenant, his Privy Council and aides at length rejoined the ladies, having endlessly toasted everything from the glorious and immortal victory of William III to the no less glorious and immortal victory of the favourite race-horse of the day, 'the Keeper of the Seals could not keep his legs – the Speaker could not articulate a syllable – the King's Solicitor suffered judgement to go by default'[1] – and the aides were in no state to help anyone.

Wesley's most pressing danger was not to become food for powder

but food for sharks. Gambling was an obsession and soon he was
borrowing money wherever he safely could, for instance from his
landlord, a bootmaker on Ormonde Quay. Nor did certain financial
misfortunes of his grandmother and elder brother warn him to live
quietly. News came in November 1788 that Lady Dungannon, having
quit Wales for a jollier life at Hampton Court, had been arrested for
debt, conducted by two bailiffs and six 'Marshall Men' to a sponging
house, where she met and entered into lively conversation with a Mr
Cavendish's mistress, until the horrified Morningtons arrived and bore
her away, Lady Mornington 'shocked and provoked by her mother's
want of feeling or shame'.[2] She was forthwith shipped abroad to a
French convent with her great-grand-daughter Mary, William's eldest
child, as chaperone.

This débâcle did not encourage Richard to keep Dangan afloat. His
whole estate was mortgaged in any case, and there were debts of
£16,000. A generous spendthrift himself, he was living with a French
courtesan, Mademoiselle Gabrielle Hyacinthe Rolland, by whom he
constantly had children. He paid all Lady Dungannon's debts,
nonetheless, and brought her home again within six months, just
beating the French Revolution.

On both sides of Arthur's family there was thus a spendthrift strain,
balanced by a flair for harsh rectitude in his mother and 'a little pepper'
in his mother's father. Which was to be his master, the frivolous or the
serious? The anecdotes that survive of his Irish life when he was
between nineteen and twenty-one show the two elements evenly
matched.

There were stories of picnics outside Dublin to which ladies refused
to go if 'that mischievous boy' Arthur Wesley was also invited. A young
Mrs St George, however, who had been lent Dangan for her honeymoon, noticed him favourably. He was 'extremely good humoured and
the object of much attention from the female part of what was called "a
very gay society" '. There was the story of an unruly Arthur fined for
beating a Frenchman and seizing his stick in a Dublin bawdy-house.
The narrator of this incident was inclined to forgive the young offender,
since he later made a habit of beating Frenchmen and taking their
batons. Arthur's appearance before the magistrates was scarcely worth
noting, considering the plague of duelling and fighting in Dublin all
through this period.

In another episode the Castle aide-de-camp was found reading
Locke's *Essay Concerning Human Understanding*. If Arthur was engaged

upon improving his own understanding, who or what had inspired him? Marcel de Pignerolle may have started it. Very likely the Ladies of Llangollen had introduced him to the little room leading out of the salon that was their library. Lastly, it is possible that the Castle aide-de-camp had already met a bookish and extremely charming girl, three years younger than himself, who was destined to play a bitter-sweet role in his life.

Kitty Pakenham, Lord Longford's second daughter, lived about thirty miles from Dangan Castle at Pakenham Hall, Castlepollard, in County Westmeath. She and the future authoress, Maria Edgeworth, were friends and distant cousins, Maria being five years older than Kitty and as uncompromisingly plain as Kitty was pretty. Indeed, according to the Edgeworths Kitty had 'an indefinable beauty'. Wellington's biographers usually put his first meeting with Kitty sometime in 1792 when he was twenty-three and she twenty. It may have been earlier. Kitty at seventeen or eighteen, that is in 1789 or 1790, would certainly have been presented at the Viceregal Court where Arthur, from his place of vantage behind the throne, would have seen her. Her gaiety and glowing complexion, her bobbing curls and exquisite figure made her a great favourite up at the Castle.

Even if Arthur's excursions into the *Essay Concerning Human Understanding* were not the result of a budding literary friendship, they would surely have promoted one. For how could Kitty, always retiring with a book to the window-seat of the library at Pakenham Hall, fail to be interested in a most unusual young cavalry officer who in public clanked his spurs and in private read Locke?*

The struggle within Arthur Wesley was to take place over the next five or six years against the background of a viceregal court which had brought dissipation to a fine art. From 1789 onwards it had to face the growing tremors caused by the French Revolution.

To the supporters of Pitt, among whom Arthur's family numbered themselves, it seemed that France in 1789 had gone mad. When Bastille Day came round again on 14 July 1790 the Ladies of Llangollen gazed apprehensively at a crimson sunset and Eleanor wrote in her journal:

The sky like a sea of Blood. I tremble for France.[3]

---

* Wesley transferred to the cavalry (12th Light Dragoons) without promotion in June 1789.

The Wesley interests steadily moved away from an Ireland again becoming disaffected. Anne Wesley, now a regular beauty, was seen by Fanny Burney in a stage-box in London with her mother. In January 1790 Anne married a safe Englishman, Henry Fitzroy, son of Lord Southampton.

A Wesley must of course still sit for the family seat of Trim, but the up-and-coming William, who had succeeded Richard as MP, wanted to move on. Arthur cut his political teeth on Trim, by standing as its candidate.[4] He cut some remarkably sharp ones in the March of 1790, blackballing an attempt by Trim to present the Freedom of the Corporation to the nationalist leader, Grattan. Arthur won hands down – forty-seven votes to twenty-nine, as he reported to Richard with a sigh of relief:

I hope you'll approve of all I have done, really I was in the most difficult situation I ever experienced & only got out of it by sticking up manfully to what I first said.

Just as manfully he turned down the usual requests for land and loans (not to mention the repayment of £70 owing by Richard), on the ground that these transactions would 'vitiate his return' at the coming General Election. But it was not his kind of life, and he knew it. He ended his letter pointedly with an enquiry after Richard's health and a suggestion: 'I am still of the same opinion with regard to your going abroad & hope you will accept my offer to accompany you.' All this gives more than a hint of the future man and politician: of the life-long determination to act rightly if possible, 'manfully' in any case, and of dislike for jobbery.

Election day duly arrived on 30 April 1790. Arthur, having been successfully declared MP for Trim, reported to his brother that it had gone off much better than he expected.[5] Slim and pink-cheeked, he sat for two years under the splendid cupola of Dublin's Parliament House without opening his mouth. Today he and his friends would be called lobby-fodder; in 1791 Wolfe Tone had another name for them – 'the common prostitutes of the Treasury Bench'.

Wolfe Tone was the intense, white-faced young nationalist leader whose 'United Irishmen', founded in this year, demanded Catholic emancipation and parliamentary reform. Richard Mornington, meanwhile, was content to leave Tone and all other Irishmen to the growing bigotry of the Castle, for he himself was pulling still further out of Ireland. In 1791 he sold Mornington House.

Arthur wrestled with his problems in the country like a glorified estate manager. He acted as umpire throughout 1792 between the family agent, John Page, and a tenant named Locker who occupied some cabins on the Dangan estate and was in arrears of rent. Through Page, Wesley was in touch with the most hated class in Ireland. As absenteeism grew among landlords, pretensions grew among agents. The stubborn John Page wished to evict Locker. Eviction was a problem which was to concern Arthur deeply in the years to come.

A major problem enterprise was to sell the Kildare estates profitably and to hold crumbling Dangan together until it too could be sold – for Mornington had decided to sever even the tenuous links with Ireland of an absentee landlord. Arthur himself was always drawing on the agent for loans: there were debts to Page totalling 79 guineas, but considering that Arthur had only recently achieved a captain's pay (in the 58th Foot in 1791 with an exchange into the 18th Light Dragoons in 1792), it was almost to his credit that his debts were not larger. Debts were perhaps inevitable. They were not a good springboard for matrimony.

By 1792 Arthur Wesley and Kitty Pakenham were openly courting. Even John Page knew about it, for Captain Wesley's letter to him dealing manfully with Locker's case was mailed from Castlepollard, 16 September 1792, and headed 'Coolure' the day before.

Castlepollard was the Pakenhams' nearest village. Its market square always smelt of cow-dung and turf-smoke and its cabin-lined road led to 'the Castle', as everyone called Pakenham Hall. Coolure was the home of Kitty's uncle, Captain Thomas Pakenham, RN, half-an-hour's walk from 'the Castle' and standing, three-storied and alone, on the wild shores of Lough Derravaragh.

No more delightful setting could have been found for young love. Thomas Pakenham had all the geniality of a naval captain and the lake was enchanting, especially in the evening, with its islands dotted here and there, its flotillas of wild-fowl and its echoing hills, echoing perhaps to the sound of Arthur's violin. The park had been duly landscaped in its time, and now Arthur could escort Kitty home by the short cut round the lake and up through her father's 'black red bog', whose draining and cultivation the traveller Arthur Young had admired. Lord Longford was not brilliant like the Professor of Music, but Young had found it exhilarating to meet 'so spirited an improver'. In any case, Captain Wesley did not have to deal with him, for he died that very year and was succeeded by Kitty's brother Tom. Tom saw no reason to throw away his popular sister on a penniless suitor and would do nothing to encourage the Castle aide who, now that Mornington House was sold, found his way more and more often to the Longford town house in Rutland Square.

Arthur did his best, none the less, to raise himself in the eyes of Tom and his sister during the first months of 1793. Suddenly he became articulate and began to speak in Parliament. In January he seconded the Address from the Throne, deploring the imprisonment of Louis xvi and the invasion of the Netherlands by the French, and congratulating his own Government on what he hoped would be a reasonably liberal attitude towards the Roman Catholics. By February Louis xvi was dead; England and France were at war; and Ireland, in the manner of high politics, was again placated with a substantial measure of Catholic Relief.

In the spring days of 1793 the thoughts of Arthur Wesley turned to Pakenham Hall. Mildly burdened by debt and as mildly flushed by debate, he decided to try his luck with Kitty Pakenham. He failed. His offer was rejected because he could not keep her on a captain's pay in the 18th Light Dragoons, nor on the pay of a major in the 33rd Foot, nor even of a lieutenant-colonel in that same regiment: for thanks to loans from Richard he managed to buy two promotions in the crisis year of 1793. No doubt she said good-bye to her lover softly and civilly. For him it was the parting of the ways.

This year was also to be the parting of the ways for France and for Europe. Nothing would be the same again. Fanny Burney heard that 4,000 refugees had arrived in England after the 'September Massacres' of the year before, among them Mme de Staël and Fanny's future husband, the Chevalier d'Arblay. M. de Pignerolle had clung on at Angers, but the magnificent establishment was reduced by 1792 to five horses. Now, in 1793, the Terror swept France. The *ci-devant* Director of Angers Academy was only one among many hundreds to lose his life.

Arthur faced the truth about himself. His problem was not just being a younger son. Part of him was still standing aloof, a dilettante, under the walnut tree in the school playground, but with a violin bow, not a shadowy baton in his hand. With Kitty, he had made one serious attempt to become committed. That had been positive. Now he must take negative action, destroy everything that stood in the way of his military vocation. First, the card-playing in the Dublin clubs. Next, the violin.

He burnt it in the summer of 1793 with his own hands: burnt the hours strolling beside the little waves at Coolure, the bouquet of wine at Angers, the dozing in Brussels, the mooning by the Thames at Eton and the lingering on the ancient bridge over the Boyne at Trim; burnt all the dreams and poetry going back to his childhood when he had listened enraptured to his father's playing.

What was to take their place? Regimental accounts. From now on they took up much of his time, though not unpleasantly, for he was a master of detail. As a lieutenant-colonel with war at hand he had to make all rough financial paths smooth, as he had done (and was still doing) for Richard's affairs in Meath. Figures had no terror for him; indeed, as Duke of Wellington he often told his friend, Robert Gleig, about his special talent for 'rapid and correct calculation'.

Only a few of his friends touched in their memoirs on the loss of a musician and his violin. One added sombrely that Wellington always disliked any mention of this 'circumstance'.

He had made the break. Now, as so often after a climax, there lay before him not the immediate vision of the promised land, but the frustration of asking and asking for the means to get there.

He found himself compelled for the next two or three years to do the very thing which in later life he could not endure in others. To beg for favours. To write polite letters requesting patronage. The trend was always towards the Army. Would Richard request Mr Pitt to desire Lord Westmorland to put him in one of the flank corps being formed that summer of 1793 to support the Dutch? 'If they are to go abroad, they will be obliged to take officers from the line, and they may as well take me as anybody else. . . .'[6] But somewhere between London and Dublin the cup slipped and he was still a Castle aide-de-camp.

Another autumn came and another expedition was planned, this time to the Normandy coast. The 33rd were to join it under the command of Lord Moira. Arthur resigned his Trim seat. Dangan Castle had also been disposed of. Neither had the old pull, since he was no longer allowed to ride over to Pakenham Hall on a September day and pay his court to Kitty.

1793 passed gloomily into 1794. Nothing had come of Lord Moira's expedition. Anti-Jacobin madness engulfed England. *Habeas corpus* was suspended in May 1794. Wolfe Tone was trapped and exiled to America, while his United Irish Society followed the Volunteers into liquidation. There were no spurs to be won in Ireland.

At last Lord Moira's army was ready to sail again. He was to reinforce the Duke of York in Flanders with 10,000 new men including Arthur Wesley and his 33rd.

Some time before he sailed, a brief but far from unimportant letter was sent to Kitty Pakenham, dated bleakly 'Barracks *Tuesday*'. Arthur had just received Lord Longford's final determination against their marriage. This was punishment enough, he said, for any offence he might have caused by having written to her recently and by writing again now. Nevertheless he could not accept that all was over. As Lord Longford's decision was founded upon 'prudential motives', an improvement in Arthur's situation could alter everything. There followed a sentence of which the last phrase was decisively to alter Arthur's life. If something did occur to make Kitty and her brother change their minds – 'my mind will still remain the same'.[7]

To an honourable man, those seven words would be binding.

In June 1794 he left Cork for Ostend, privileged to see active service for the first time – and under the worst possible conditions.

Nothing could have turned out more fortunately. He saw the effects of a divided command, of no properly organized food supply or winter clothing. In short, as he told Stanhope forty-five years later when his friend was suggesting that the Dutch campaign must have been very useful to him: 'Why – I learnt what one ought not to do, and that is always something.'[8]

Lieutenant-Colonel Wesley's initiation began at Ostend, where he was put in command of a brigade which he brought round, as a rearguard, by sea to Antwerp. Then came a chaotic and hopeless attempt to hold Belgium, followed by an autumnal retreat into Holland and an arduous stand upon the River Waal from October 1794 until January in the new year.

General Winter arrived in November 1794 with ferocious frosts and fought on the side of the French. When Colonel Wesley thought the enemy were about to go into winter quarters until the spring – 'I think it impossible for any troops (even the French) to keep the field in this severe weather'[9] – they came speeding down the frozen canals, rolled up the Dutch, seized all their ports and sent the exhausted red-coats staggering towards Hanover into a new intensity of cold and wretchedness. In order if possible to silence the rumbles in Parliament against Pitt and his bungled campaign, the chief command was withdrawn in December from the Duke of York. 'To say that I shall not feel this as a severe blow,' protested the Duke vehemently to his royal father, 'would be contrary to my own character. . . .'[10] The public, however, viewed His Royal Highness's character rather differently:

> The noble Duke of York.
> He had ten thousand men,
> He marched them up to the top of the hill,
> And he marched them down again.

As one of the unhappy ten thousand who had done the marching, Arthur hoped for home in December. But he was kept an extra six weeks on the banks of the Waal by the French, sleeping in his clothes and turning out once or twice every night. It was no compensation that they were 'perpetually chattering' to his men across the river and offering to dance the *carmagnole* for their amusement.[11]

Nor was there any encouragement for the high command. 'I was left there to myself with my regiment . . . thirty miles from headquarters,' he later told his friend, Lord Ellesmere, 'which latter was a scene of jollifications, and I do not think that I was once visited by the Commander in Chief.'

'The infantry regiments,' continued Wellington to Ellesmere, 'were as good in proper hands as they are now [1837], but the system was wretched.'[12] The system, in fact, was a scandalous traffic in commissions developed over the past ten years by which army brokers ('rascally crimps') created a flood of new field officers out of anyone who could pay, from schoolboys to keepers of gambling dens and worse.*

At headquarters no one knew anything at all. Those fighting in the field had to depend for information on letters from England. 'The real reason why I succeeded in my own campaigns,' concluded Wellington to Stanhope, 'is because I was always on the spot – I saw everything; and did everything for myself.'[13]

Miserable and hungry, Arthur's brigade marched doggedly towards the River Ems and so to Bremen and the Weser, more and more often breaking rank to loot, or to add their frozen bodies to the snowy heaps of dead men and horses that lined the roads. A certain old Colonel Watson of the Guards had warned Wesley back in Belgium what to expect:

You little know what you are going to meet with. You will often have no dinner at all. I mean literally no dinners, and not merely roughing it on a beefsteak or a bottle of port wine.[14]

---

* Sir Walter Scott stated that baby boys and even young ladies might have commissions bought for them: 'We know ourselves one fair dame who drew the pay of captain in the —— dragoons, and was probably not much less fit for service than some who actually did duty.' (*Memoir of the Duke of York*, 1827.)

Emphatically there had been no spurs to win; though Lieutenant-Colonel Wesley was at least congratulated by headquarters on an action he had fought at Boxtel in Holland, on 15 September 1794. This was the first military engagement of his life. There had been a charge by a French column. With commendable steadiness his infantry obeyed Wesley's orders to hold back their fire until the last moment. Then, at his command, they drove off the enemy with rolling volleys of musketry. Thoughts about these tactics, about a proper supply-service, and about officers who looked after their men, accompanied Wesley on his voyage home at the beginning of March 1795, and remained with him for the rest of his life.

When he arrived back in Ireland a palace revolution with nation-wide consequences was about to sweep the Castle.

The old junta had successfully opposed a fresh attempt by Pitt to introduce Catholic Relief. Fitzwilliam, a reforming Lord Lieutenant, was recalled to England on 25 March. Dublin went into mourning and his carriage was drawn through streets draped in black. So ended the 'Fitzwilliam episode', as it was called. But it was an episode which started a gale.

'Here is a whirlwind in our Country,' wrote Maria Edgeworth in April 1795. Within six months the whirlwind had become uncontrollable. The prohibited United Irishmen burst up again like dragon's teeth, sworn now to bring off a French invasion of Ireland followed by an armed rebellion.

Amid this excitement, home for Arthur merely meant yet another round of begging and rebuff. Everything seemed to be repeating itself – Arthur back at the Castle as a frustrated aide-de-camp, Arthur MP for Trim again, a desperate urgency in Arthur's pleas for something to do. Probably inspired and certainly backed by Richard, he decided to open with a bumper request: to become Secretary at War – no less. It was a forlorn hope but worth trying, for as Secretary at War he would leap from scarcely £500 a year to £1,800. He had still not decided whether he was a soldier or a politician. Lord Camden was unimpressed, and in June Arthur had lowered his sights to a civil department – something either at the Revenue or Treasury Boards.

. . . I hope I shall not be supposed to place myself too high in desiring to be taken into consideration . . . [but if these Boards] are considered too high for me, of course you will

31

say so. . . . You will perhaps be surprised at my desiring a civil instead of a military office. It is certainly a departure from the line which I prefer.[15]

Nothing came of it. The last wild throw, made by Richard possibly without Arthur's knowledge, was to offer his brother as Surveyor-General of the Ordnance – a position already occupied by Kitty's uncle, Captain Thomas Pakenham of Coolure. Lord Camden agreed, but Arthur himself turned it down for obvious reasons. An indignant Tom Pakenham attributed the attempt to oust him to 'a deep laid scheme of Mornington's'.

This embarrassing affair seems thoroughly to have shaken Arthur's confidence and health. At any rate, he is next heard of at Southampton in September 1795, resolved to sail to the West Indies with the 33rd, but laid up with a bout of fever. His physician, Dr Hunter, prescribed four kinds of pills besides 'the Strasberg liniment'. If the Strasberg liniment should fail to effect a cure ('Can be used with the best success for dogs and horses') he must strengthen it with two tablespoonfuls of the fat of a freshly killed fowl.[16]

While Richard and Dr Hunter thus worked hard on Arthur's behalf, Lord Camden wrote that he would be 'very glad' to make some arrangement satisfactory to Colonel Wesley 'against you come back from the West Indies'.[17] There was a genial touch of humbug in the Viceregal phrase, 'against you come back'. If Arthur was not killed either by the French or by a tropical fever it would probably be because he was drowned before either of the other enemies had a chance to attack; and in fact it was from this last fate that he was saved by a miracle. Of his convoy, seven transports were wrecked by a storm on Chesil Beach soon after they had left Portsmouth. After waiting a few more weeks until December, the fleet again put out to sea, this time in the teeth of a winter gale which not surprisingly dispersed them for good. Wesley's ship was among the lucky ones which after seven wild weeks on the ocean were blown back to England. The 33rd wintered at Poole. In April 1796 they were turned round again and sent in advance of Wesley to India.

India! In contemporary jargon, a switch from the West to the East Indies meant stepping out of the white man's graveyard into the treasure-house of the Orient. Richard felt that after so many setbacks he could not advise Arthur to decline such an 'advantageous station'. As soon as his constituents, his debts and his health – the last two still troublesome – made it possible for him to sail, he must catch up with his regiment.

Once the decision to leave England had been taken it was mainly a question of how the colonel should deal with his debts – for Arthur, through rapid transfers, was a full colonel at twenty-seven. As he waited at Portsmouth for the fair wind his debts were still outstanding but under control. There were substantial loans from Richard, and £955 14s. 8½d. owing to the agent, John Page, who thought this 'serious sum' ought to be mentioned to Lord Mornington in case Colonel Wesley never returned. But if the colonel felt the slightest 'delicacy' about speaking of the debt, let him just leave a written paper with my Lord; 'may all happiness & success attend you wherever you go'.[18]

How, then, did Arthur Wesley stand with himself and the world at this crucial point in his life?

Arthur was twenty-seven years old, chronically frustrated and in constant ill-health. No doubt the two were connected. His income was paltry, and his debts, though 'of a size that would not much disturb a person of less scrupulous honour', had necessitated odious begging letters which made an indelible impression.

Indigence and indebtedness had killed young love. If Lord Longford, Kitty's brother, had adopted Arthur Young's advice on how to assess a prospective husband – "'Tis true I hear many excellent things of him; but does he farm hugely? Are his turnips clean? . . . these are points much more to the purpose than the common rubbish of character ye common mortals attend to' – the answer must have been that there was not a turnip, clean or unclean, to offer Kitty. Nothing but the 'rubbish of character'.[19]

Among the 'rubbish' lay a secret resolve to read. The passage to India gave it a fine excuse. From Dublin Arthur brought his small library, to which he added in England over fifty pounds' worth of books. Among the Oriental dictionaries and maps, the military manuals and histories of India, were Voltaire, Rousseau, Frederick the Great, Maréchal de Saxe, Plutarch's *Lives* and the *Caesaris Commentaria* – in Latin; for philosophy, Locke and *Human Understanding* reappear; for theology, five volumes of Paley, gilt; and for the good of his Anglo-Irish soul, twenty-four volumes of Swift at 2s. 10d.

Arthur and his trunkload of books followed the 33rd at the end of June. Ireland was already a month away. It had been high time to break out from the Castle, where his spirit had been a prisoner for more than nine years. Perhaps, indeed, he had never yet known what it was to feel truly free.

4

Ascendancy in the East

The voyage to the Cape he found tolerable, as he raced to overtake his regiment in a cruiser. Cape Town itself was enlivened by the presence of two sisters, Jemima and Henrietta Smith, also on their way out to India. Jemima was 'a satirical and incorrigible flirt'. He paid court to Henrietta who had a 'pretty little figure and a lovely neck'. ('Neck' was the polite term for bosom.) No doubt she was glad to receive it, for young Captain George Elers who noticed the lovely neck also remembered that her admirer was 'all life and spirits . . . with a remarkably large aquiline nose, a clear blue eye . . . remarkably clean in his person . . . spoke at this time remarkably quickly' – in fact, a remarkable person.

The second half of the passage, confined to a slow troop-ship and lasting from September 1796 to mid-February 1797, was in Wesley's own words 'most tedious'.[1] Neither his travelling library nor the impact of strange continents and oceans could take the edge off his impatience. 'Most tedious' remained his first and last comment on a passage to India which must be regarded as one of the most significant in British history.

With the beginning of the hot season only a month away, Calcutta immediately whirled the 33rd and its colonel into hectic festivities. There were gentlemen's 'seats' all round the city, and where there were seats there were feasts. On St Patrick's day Colonel Wesley, as a newly arrived Irishman, was asked to preside at the usual dinner, which he did, notes William Hickey, the diarist, 'with peculiar credit to himself'.[2]* Three days later another Irish soldier arrived, Major-General John St Leger. Hickey gave a house-party for him at his 'little château' at Chinsurah, an imposing brick and stucco mansion with verandahs and Doric pillars, to which Colonel Wesley was invited.

---

* Hickey puts these and subsequent events in 1799, but all or most of them must have occurred in 1797. He wrote his memoirs at Beaconsfield in 1813.

Hickey fell into a state of continuous excess. The most 'dangerous' parties, he found, were those held by the 33rd. Hearing that Colonel Wesley 'with a few other equally strong heads' was to be present at one hard-drinking session to which he had been invited, he at first declared himself too ill to join their 'jovial crew'. Unwisely he later yielded to the 33rd's persuasion and found himself round a table with 'eight as strong-headed fellows as could be found in Hindostan'. Hickey's excruciating headache lasted for two days and nights. 'Indeed, a more severe debauch I never was engaged in in any part of the world.'[3] He had not been trained at Dublin Castle.

Despite this haze of jollity the 33rd were supposed to be preparing for an autumn campaign.

Once again, Arthur had plunged into a land crying out for change. India was full of troubles, among them multiple corruption. Rapacity was not the prerogative of any one man, institution or colour. Warren Hastings was picked out for special notice; but in fact every grade of the East India Company, from its Court of Directors at Leadenhall Street in the City of London to its network of military and civil servants out East; every rank in His Majesty's Army; the numerous independent merchants living in the three British Presidencies of Bengal, Madras and Bombay; and the whole array of native Indian rulers – all alike expected to make their fortunes quickly and easily out of India.

The affair of the Nabob of Oudh illustrated the complexities of the Indian game. Incomparably larger than all the European territories, the Indian princely states, including Oudh, covered most of the huge sub-continent. There had been a time when the Mogul Empire, centred in Delhi, imposed some kind of unity on these states. But by 1797 the 250-year-old Empire had fallen into decay, and the Europeans, having inserted themselves into the interstices, were pushing their way through the ruined fabric like banyan or peepul trees in a crumbling fort, until nothing remained but heaps of loosened stones and spreading trees. Britain had her powerful root-system. French influence, despite Clive's victories, remained strong in its trading centres; and there was a largish piece of Portugal at Goa.

The problem was, how could the two main European rivals strengthen themselves against each other in India, now that war had broken out between them in Europe?

One way was by getting control of an Indian princely state. The French had done so in Oudh. Another was by attacking the Dutch colonists in Java or the Spanish in the Philippines, if the shifting alliances and hostilities in Europe changed them from harmless planters into springboards for French invasion.

Almost on arrival Colonel Wesley found himself in the thick of it. He wrote with suppressed excitement to Mornington on 17 April 1797 that there was to be a large expedition against the Spanish colony of Manila in the Philippines. The 33rd was to sail with the contingent from Bengal; his own name had been mentioned as the Deputy Governor's choice for chief command. His contempt for his rivals was matched by a consummate though reasoned confidence in himself, founded on the large force which would be at his disposal, and the equally large dose of 'pusillanimity' at the disposal of the enemy. His own 'exertions' would compensate for his want of experience.

Here was a great commander in embryo.

At the back of his mind there were also his debts. 'Of course the Chief Command of this expedition would make my fortune,' he burst out at the end of this candid letter. 'Going upon it at all will enable me to free myself from debt, therefore you may easily conceive that I am not very anxious for the conclusion of a peace at this moment.'[4]

His half-serious fears of peace were premature. But by 20 May he knew that his misgivings about the chief command were justified. He was not to lead the Bengal force after all. Lord Hobart, the Governor, had selected General Braithwaite on grounds of seniority. With a good adjutant-general, a good quartermaster-general and a good army, Lord Hobart argued, the Commander-in-Chief did not matter. 'But he is mistaken,' wrote Arthur severely, 'if he supposes that a good high-spirited army can be kept in order by other means than by the abilities & firmness of the Commander in Chief.' A snub delivered to General St Leger by Colonel Wesley about the same time confirms the impression of a new, sharp intellect at work in India; one crackling with pent-up energy, bold enough to say no to anybody, but less ready than formerly to take no for an answer.

Whether or not because of Irish horsy enthusiasm, St Leger supported a memorandum to establish Indian Horse Artillery. 'Without being regularly bred to Artillery,' commented Colonel Wesley, 'it is not difficult to perceive the advantages which would attend such an establishment. . . .'[5] It was not difficult to see the disadvantages. There was no supply of horses. The most Colonel Wesley would consider was an emergency unit of eight horse-drawn guns and four howitzers; for the rest, bullocks were best.

There was probably more to it than St Leger's horses versus Wesley's bullocks. Wesley's letter gives a feeling that he was not going to have anyone, even the man destined to assume supreme command of the whole Manila expedition, careering about the East, smoking 'sagars', roaring out patriotic songs and transforming his battlefields into Irish races. Indeed, small things were happening under Wesley's nose to cause him reservations about the rip-roaring society of which he was now an ornament. After three months 'entirely free from ague', he had contracted a slight fever in June.[6] And there was the gambling of the 33rd.

At last in July 1797 came news from Arthur's family. Mornington was to be Governor of Madras at once and afterwards Governor-General of India. Congratulations poured from Arthur's pen – so glad Mornington was coming – sure he would manage to preserve his health – would do everything possible to help.[7]

Having indirectly heard of the possibility of Mornington's appointment a fortnight earlier, he had already sent home some blunt views on the Indian scene. Taking the 'natives' and the climate together, India was 'a miserable country to live in, and I now begin to think that a man well deserves some of the wealth which is sometimes brought home, for having spent his life here.' One could not punish offenders with imprisonment or whipping, as at home, for this would cause loss of caste; in any case their learned men (if Arthur's Indian histories were to be believed) taught that God punished crime, which was in their eyes quite sufficient. 'Notwithstanding all this,' he assured Mornington, 'being here for a few years would place you in so high a situation for the remainder of your life, that I should like to see you Governor-General.' Not that he himself expected to derive more advantages from his brother's appointment than he would from any other Governor-General, owing to 'rules on patronage in India'. (If the brothers intended to obey these rules, they were the only people in India who did.) It was sad that Mornington had to leave his wife and children behind. This was perhaps mitigated by the news that their mother had at length visited her daughter-in-law, Richard's former mistress and since 1794 his wife. Arthur believed that 'nothing but absurdity prevented it being done sooner'.[8]

Compared with the heavily burdened Mornington – five children for ever illegitimate, despite their mother having been made an honest woman – Arthur seemed bleakly free from family cares. He complained more than once during this summer of 1797 of not having received a single letter from home since he had left in the previous June.

Meanwhile preparations for the Manila expedition kept him sweating at his desk. He was aware that 'the higher classes of Europeans' kept healthy by taking more care of themselves and using more 'conveniences' and 'luxuries' than the lower orders.[9] Before embarkation he therefore issued thirty-six paragraphs of hygiene drill, to be observed by the men on board ship.

In the event, it was a member of the 'higher classes' who failed lamentably to add his three parts of water to wine. Hickey had persuaded Arthur to take on as chaplain to the 33rd the nephew of his friend Mr Scawen, a young man named Blunt. They sailed in August. After only three days at sea the unfortunate clergyman got 'abominably' drunk and rushed out of his cabin stark naked among the soldiers and sailors, 'talking all sorts of bawdy and ribaldry and singing scraps of the most blackguard and indecent songs'. Such was his shame on afterwards hearing of these 'irregularities' that he shut himself up and refused to eat or speak. Colonel Wesley was informed. He instantly rowed across to Blunt's vessel and sent for him. The wretched man declined to appear. Wesley then descended to Blunt's cabin and talked to him like a father:

. . . what had passed was not of the least consequence as no one would think the worse of him for the little irregularities committed in a moment of forgetfulness . . .[10]

Colonel Wesley's broad-minded and kindly attempts to 'reconcile Mr Blunt to himself' were not successful. In ten days he forced himself to die of contrition.*

Arthur had got as far as the Malay Archipelago and was writing an encouraging letter to the patient John Page in Ireland when disastrous news reached Bengal. On top of the momentous mutinies at Spithead and the Nore which, until settled, were a threat to England's lifeline, came the news that yet another of her allies, Austria, had followed Prussia and Spain into a peace treaty with the enemy. Vast French armies had been released from Europe for aggression round the world, while the defenders of the British Empire in India were standing off Manila, a thousand miles away. The Bengal and Madras armies were abruptly ordered to return at once to their respective headquarters at Fort William and Fort St George.

An Irish emergency had already in 1797 had its repercussions in India. General Lord Cornwallis, who had been intended for Calcutta while Mornington went to Madras, could not now be spared from

---

* See William Golding's *Rites of Passage*, founded on this anecdote

38

home. At the end of this chain of reaction Lord Mornington emerged as Governor-General of India, appointed on 4 October 1797. To the unconcealed mortification of his rival Lord Hobart, he had soared past the Madras Presidency straight to the top.[11]

The Ascendancy had failed in Ireland. In India, on the contrary, might not creative minds like those of the three Wellesley brothers – Richard, Arthur and Henry, Richard's secretary – be welcomed? Those were the days before racial prejudice had poisoned the British Raj and the celebrated Indian, Rajah Rammohun Roy, was predicting with enthusiasm that 'forty years of contact with the British would revivify Indian civilization'. The three brothers were about to embark on their first period of brilliant cooperative effort. But for a start, Arthur had to adjust himself to a small change in his style.

Plain 'A. Wesley', as he had been accustomed to sign himself tersely from birth, had to go. Richard had persuaded his ever-obliging cousin Sir Chichester Fortescue, Ulster King of Arms, to allow him to impale the de Lacy Lion Rampant in his escutcheon. This armorial *coup* had been projected with a view to a step in the peerage. Pitt loyally advanced 'the strong claims of the closest personal friendship' to press a marquessate for Mornington upon George III.[12] The King resisted; but meanwhile Richard had put a finishing touch to his reconstructed lineage.

The family name had been 'Wellesley', not 'Wesley', for many hundreds of years; 'Wellesley' it should be again. Three extra letters were not to be sneezed at, in the acquisitive fairyland of heraldry. Henry was already 'Henry Wellesley'. There was nothing for it but that 'A. Wesley' should change too.

5

Tigers of Mysore

T he interval between the Manila fiasco and Lord Mornington's
comet-like descent on Calcutta (with a long, glittering tail of
baggage which provoked some unfavourable comment) had not been
wasted by Arthur. He nosed around the southern Carnatic, staying in
'humdrum' Madras, whose gardens Hickey had found inferior to 'the
most barren part of Hounslow Heath'.[1] Wellesley's attention, however,
was directed to a character who lived beyond Madras, in Mysore,
bearing no small resemblance to the brigands of the Heath itself.

All reports, including Arthur's to Richard, made it clear that the
formidable Moslem ruler, Tipoo Sultan, the Tiger of Mysore, was in
alliance with the French.

Lord Mornington reacted more violently to this news than even the
alert Colonel of the 33rd expected. He decided that the Tiger of Mysore
should learn once for all who was king of the jungle. He would gather an
army forthwith and settle Tipoo early in 1799. Arthur, with his
cautious diplomatic instincts, and fortified by the frantic pleas of
Madras officials not to stir up tigers unnecessarily, strongly counselled
Mornington to have patience and negotiate. But the Governor-General
determined to use his brother as a go-between in selling his forward
policy to Madras. By July Arthur was doing his best in singularly
distasteful circumstances.

The new Governor of Madras, Lord Clive, proved to be of a 'heavy
understanding'. Richard nicknamed him Puzzlestick. It took Arthur
five hours to convince Lord Clive that Richard did not intend to
'precipitate the country into war'.[2] (If Clive's understanding had been
brighter Arthur might have taken even longer.)

Arthur was ordered in August to bring the 33rd from Calcutta to
Madras, ready for the fray. A note of restiveness invaded Arthur's
letters to his younger brother Henry during that autumn, due to the
endless diplomatic intrigue needed to keep the peace with Clive and
prepare for war with Tipoo. His policy involved isolating Clive from his

officials, particularly his secretary, Josiah Webbe. Most of Arthur's letters to Henry on this delicate subject were written partly or wholly in what passed for code. On 19 October he advised that the 'S.G.' (Supreme Government) should avoid disputes with Clive even on petty subjects, as disputes would erect 'the little men such as 10 [10=W=Webbe] who have to handle them, into great ones'.[3] Arthur's furtive job was not made more palatable by the fact that he still half agreed with 'the little men'. When Richard wrote to him on 21 October for his opinion on the crucial question of war or no war, he had to reply that there were strong reasons for simply making Tipoo accept a British ambassador and expel the French; he would willingly go as envoy himself.

His ambivalent attitude to the war did not prevent him from working overtime to organize supplies of bullocks, grain and money. On the last day of October he was too busy to put a letter to Henry into code, though one sentence was an obvious case for the treatment:

I have likewise prevailed upon Lord Clive to appoint a commissary of stores . . . instead of trusting to the vague calculations of a parcel of blockheads, who know nothing, and have no data.

Within two months of Arthur's last groan the tension was relaxing. Lord Clive responded to his blandishments and supported the war policy. Most of Arthur's own doubts were repressed. He summoned Richard to Madras for personal supervision of the final rupture with Tipoo. Up till the end of November 1798 there had been a risk that fresh troops sent to reinforce the Madras army might snatch the 33rd's place on the battlefield from under Arthur's nose. But on the 29th he received a reassuring note from the Commander-in-Chief. The Colonel of the 33rd was in fact destined to hold an extensive command.

'The plot thickens so quickly,' wrote Arthur to Henry from the camp of their ally the Nizam of Hyderabad on 28 December 1798, that he would not have time to meet the Governor-General in Madras before marching. If information were needed Henry must come to him, where incidentally he would get his first sight of an Indian camp – 'a curiosity of its kind'.[4] In this cool phrase Arthur described the vast, ungainly caravanserai he was preparing to shepherd southwards: 150,000 camp followers advancing inside a hollow square around which circled a guard of 6,000 cavalry.

Lord Mornington gave the order to invade Mysore on 3 February 1799. Tipoo was still sending civil messages which ended with the wish, 'Continue to rejoice me with happy letters'.[5] But though the letters continued they became progressively less happy. British preparations were far advanced. So was the season. And the news of Nelson's victory on the Nile, still comparatively fresh, made them suddenly feel a match for the French in Mysore or anywhere else in India. So let Arthur stop his 'croaking', especially his 'fears & fancies about money' (Richard had just raised a loan to finance the expedition) and take heart from the universal praise which had been lavished on his own late command of the Nizam's contingent.

I wish to God the whole were under your direction; but even as it is, I think our success is certain. . . .[6]

His 'croaking' brother was not so sure. But he had at least achieved one success already – against Richard himself. The over-excited Governor-General cherished a design to take the field in person. Fortunately he asked Arthur's advice first who replied bluntly:

All I can say upon the subject is, that if I were in General Harris's [the Commander-in-Chief] situation, and you joined the army, I should quit it.

Arthur himself did not get on with Harris nor did he admire his talents. But to upset Harris at this juncture would damage the 'public interest'.

Arthur managed to get the whole hungry camp supplied with grain 'through bullying day and night', without costing the public a single shilling. 'I bustled through the difficulty,' he explained to Henry in a graphic sentence. Yet General Harris had not 'sufficiency of spirit' to give credit where credit was due; and as 'there is nothing to be got in the army but credit', Harris's neglect was hard indeed to bear. 'I was much hurt about it at the time', he wrote a month later. Now, however, 'I don't care . . . and shall certainly continue to do every thing to serve General Harris, and to support his name and authority'.[7]

Virtue had its reward. The Nizam's Prime Minister decided that as a European officer had to command his army in the field, it had better be the Governor-General's brother. So after supplying it, bringing it south and at last being praised for his efficiency in a General Order from Harris, he was delighted to find himself at the head of this large force, with his own 33rd added to it as a European stiffener.

One officer was not pleased. David Baird, twelve years older than Wellesley and a major-general, had been captured by Tipoo's father,

Hyder Ali, and kept in irons for over three and a half years at Seringapatam. He had hoped to forget his past sufferings in some glorious new action, such as Manila. Arthur Wellesley had been picked for it. Now Wellesley was to command the Nizam's contingent. Baird sent General Harris 'a strong remonstrance'.[8] It did him no good.

As was to be expected, Wellesley's few letters *en route* for Seringapatam were totally devoid of scenic comment. Not a word of the luxuriant rice-fields and sugar plantations round Bangalore, nor of the hilly, dense country as they turned south for the capital.

Things had not gone altogether well. Early on the march it was apparent that Major Shee of the 33rd was neglecting his duties. Some of his men were marching without arms or equipment. When Wellesley remonstrated, Shee replied rudely that he was 'extremely sorry', not for any misconduct but for Colonel Wellesley having been 'so much misinformed' as to censure him.[9] And a lot more in the same strain. Wellesley's reply was coldly furious.

This is not the first time I have had occasion to observe that, under forms of private correspondence, you have written me letters upon public duty, couched in terms to which I have not been accustomed.[10]

Next time he received such a letter he would send it straight to the Commander-in-Chief.

Apart from these disturbances in the 33rd, general progress was retarded by mismanagement and misfortune. The Nizam's army had started out over-loaded. Its 120,000 bullocks died in droves. Arthur reported to Henry that his friend Captain Malcolm, in charge of the Nizam's sepoys, 'leads the life of a cannister at a dog's tail'. He himself was 'not a little fagged'.

It was Tipoo who made them pull themselves together. As they struggled out of thick jungles in Mallavelly on 26 March, they were suddenly confronted with a ridge crowned by elephants. This was the first sign of Tipoo's brave bid to defeat the invaders before they reached his capital. Two thousand of his French-trained troops advanced in column on the 33rd who held their fire 'with the utmost steadiness' until the enemy were sixty yards away; then came the deadly British volleys tearing holes in the close-packed columns; confusion spread and Wellesley's cavalry easily scattered them.

By 5 April the Allies had completed a sweeping arc around Seringapatam and were encamped two miles beyond it to the west. Arthur finished a letter to Mornington on a buoyant note: there was no more squabbling, 'and we shall be masters of this place before much time passes over our Heads.'[11] He was right; but first he had to go through one of the most unpleasant experiences of his life.

Though the Allies outnumbered Tipoo their position was in one respect hazardous. Numerous enemy outposts were concealed between the Allied camp and the city, mainly in five great 'topes' (thickets) of cocoa, bamboo and betel. Enemy rockets were already dropping among the Allied tents. No siege-works could safely begin until this dangerous ground had been cleared. Wellesley, partly as a diversion, was ordered to 'scour' one of the thickets known as the Sultanpettah Tope.

The ground inside this tope was scored with irrigation canals from four to six feet deep. Even after a thorough reconnaissance it would have been difficult terrain to negotiate in stifling darkness. But there had been no chance to reconnoitre. It was impossible for Wellesley to locate the quarter from which a counter-attack was coming or even to rally his own troops for a disciplined withdrawal. He had certainly achieved a diversion, but that was all. Lost, separated from the unfortunate 33rd and dismally aware that he had failed, he stumbled into headquarters several hours later to make his report to General Harris.

'Near twelve,' wrote Harris in his journal, 'Colonel Wellesley came to my tent in a good deal of agitation, to say he had not carried the tope. It must be particularly unpleasant to him.'[12] Wellesley's second-in-command made sure that it was even more unpleasant than necessary by circulating a story that he had eventually been found fast asleep with his head on the mess-room table. Some said that but for his relationship to the Governor-General, 'he never would have had a chance of getting over this affair.'

Twelve soldiers who had been taken prisoner in the tope were carried into Seringapatam and killed by having nails driven into their skulls or their necks wrung by Jetties (Hindu 'strong men'). Those who were killed outright during the fighting, like young Lieutenant Fitzgerald, turned out to have been the lucky ones.[13]

The whole horrible episode made an indelible impression on Wellesley. He wrote to Mornington on 18 April from camp:

I have come to a determination; when in my power, never to suffer an attack to be made by night upon an enemy who is . . . strongly posted, and whose posts have not been reconnoitred by daylight.[14]

The fact that Lieutenant Fitzgerald's brother, the Knight of Kerry, was one of his closest Irish friends, would have helped to keep the memory alive. As in 1794, events had taught him 'what not to do'. This time he was learning from that rare phenomenon, a failure of his own.

On the following morning, 6 April, all the enemy outposts were cleared. Wellesley again led the attack against the ill-fated Sultan-pettah Tope, this time with complete success.

Now at last the siege-works could begin, following each other with rhythmical precision according to the hallowed ritual of the master, Vauban – batteries, parallels (trenches), zigzags (connecting lines) to more advanced parallels and batteries, the enemy guns silenced, and then – the breach.

On several occasions Tipoo put out peace-feelers:

I have adhered firmly to the treaty; what then is the meaning of the advance of the English armies. . . ? Inform me. What need I say more?[15]

He 'needed' to say that within twenty-four hours he would surrender the fort and large areas of Mysore, send four sons as hostages and a huge indemnity. Instead he waited six days and then offered to dispatch vakeels (envoys) and hold a conference. On Mornington's instructions Harris refused the vakeels and pressed on with the siege.

There was a shattering roar on 2 May. A shell had fallen on a rocket magazine inside Tipoo's fort. Black smoke belched up in a huge plume laced with fiery stars, plunging into ominous shade the fort's long, low white walls, the shining roofs of Tipoo's palace, the sugar-white minaret of his elegant mosque, the flat boulders of the River Cauvery which encircled the island of Seringapatam, and the shell-shattered trees, banks and aloe hedges that concealed the British siege-works.

By noon next day the breach was 'practicable' and bamboo scaling-ladders were silently carried into the trenches at dusk.

On the morning of 4 May 1799 the order went out for the assault. David Baird volunteered to take command of the 4,000 storming troops. At 1.10 pm the towering Baird leapt from his trench and bellowed, 'Now, my brave fellows, follow ME and prove yourselves worthy of the name of British soldiers!'[16] The defenders smashed into them with muskets and rockets; but the leaders of the storming party or 'forlorn hope' (from the Dutch *verloren troop*, 'lost troop') were already across the almost dry river-bed. They reached the summit of the breach within six minutes, where they planted a British flag. Thousands of defenders fled, some of them tearing off their turbans to use for sliding down into the inner ditch. All Tipoo's elaborate outer defences, built under French supervision, were abandoned. Ten French officers surrendered. All was over bar the looting.

A search meanwhile was made for Tipoo in the palace, which it was thought would be his last refuge. The Tiger of Mysore was not there.

The day had opened gloomily for Tipoo with an ominous report from his astrologers. Ascetic, cruel, brave and profoundly religious, his habit had been to study the sacred books and make notes on them. Seated on a throne shaped and striped like a tiger, with a pearly canopy crowned by the gold and jewelled Uma bird, he would say it was better to live like a tiger for two days than for two hundred years like a sheep. He died like a tiger.

Fighting and killing to the last in a bloody mêlée at the North Gate, he fell wounded, was lifted by his attendants into the soft palanquin that he had always scorned, and was then shot dead by a British soldier who fancied the jewel in his turban. In the macabre torchlight his body was recognized by an amulet on his right arm and dragged out from a huge pile of corpses. It was so warm that Wellesley felt the heart and pulse. The dark eyes were open, the expression stern but dignified as in life. He was buried next day beside his father, Hyder Ali, in the Loll Baug garden of cypresses, with the river rising in a tigerish storm which, if it had come sooner, might have saved him. In his pocket-book was found a prayer: 'I am full of sin; thou art a sea of mercy. Where thy mercy is, what became of my sin?' With all his sins he was a remarkable man.

Utterly exhausted by the tension, heat and violence of the assault, Baird asked General Harris for his troops and himself to be temporarily relieved. Arthur Wellesley was therefore appointed acting Governor of Seringapatam. Next day, 6 May, he was confirmed in his onerous but lucrative post.

The first intimation of this change came to Baird in an unfortunate way. While leisurely breakfasting in Tipoo's palace with his staff, he was presented by Colonel Wellesley with a sheet of official paper and the awful *fait accompli*:

'General Baird, I am appointed to the command of Seringapatam.'

The huge Scot rose to the occasion. Ignoring Wellesley, he turned to his dumbfounded subordinates and roared out the word of command. 'Come, gentlemen, we have no longer any business here.'

Breakfast, however, was business of a kind and Governor Wellesley intervened graciously: 'Oh pray finish your breakfast.'[17]

Once outside the palace, Baird hit back with a rasping letter to Harris: 'Before the sweat was drying on my brow, I was superseded by an inferior officer.'

This was his third grievance and the first ill-fated reference to supersession. It was to haunt Baird and Wellesley by turns for months.

To restore order among the inhabitants and to keep order among the victors was Arthur's most urgent task. The congested island (only $3\frac{1}{2}$ by $1\frac{1}{2}$ miles) was an appalling scene of chaos – loot, murder and Tipoo's live tigers, which were habitually chained up outside his palace, 'getting violent'. He soon had four looters swinging from gibbets in key streets. Not that he particularly blamed them; for what could you expect, as he wrote to Richard, from troops who had been through so much? These drastic measures ended the crisis, brought the peasants back to the city and got the bazaars open again to feed the army. The head of the Hindu royal family, a child whose throne had been usurped by Hyder Ali, was restored.

Distribution of prize-money was always a sordid and rapacious aftermath of victory. In the end the total treasure was estimated at £1,143,216. General Harris got £150,000, the sepoys and Indian surgeons about £5 each and Colonel Wellesley £4,000.

Arthur at last was solvent. Unless he paid back all he owed to Richard. For his prize-money by no means covered his expenses. These had quadrupled since the campaign began and the Government had not yet made any allowances.

The consequence is that I am ruined . . . I should be ashamed of doing any of the dirty things that I am told are done in some of the commands. . . .[18]

Knowing the 'quite scandalous dilatoriness' of the Government, Richard handsomely insisted on postponing his own repayment.

To thwart the 'sharks' Arthur sent Tipoo's robes and turbans, which they planned to auction, to Fort William, and as a gift for Richard, Tipoo's musical tiger. Who knows how many happy hours Tipoo spent feeding his hatred of the British on the sight and sound of this horrible toy? Pinned beneath the carved claws of the royal beast lay a man, presumably a servant of the Company, whose left hand waved helplessly while a shrill, intermittent scream came out of his mouth, to the accompaniment of the tiger's savage growls. A pipe organ inside the tiger and his victim was responsible for this hideous concert, which could be varied by playing eighteen ear-splitting notes on a keyboard in the tiger's belly. Richard presented 'Tipoo's Tiger' to the Court of

Directors and the famous Uma bird to George III.* He added the same bird, looking appropriately like a peacock, to his own coat-of-arms.

Another honour with an all too distinctively Hibernian flavour was bestowed on Richard on 2 December 1799. Having been from the age of twenty-one an Earl in the Irish peerage he was raised, with the same limitation, to a Marquessate. The Directors added an annuity of £5,000 a year for twenty years, to keep it up. But to the friend of the English Prime Minister an *Irish* Marquessate was just 'a double gilt potato'.[19]

When Harris's army departed in July 1799 Colonel Wellesley took command of the remaining troops in Mysore. Two things stand out in Wellesley's Mysore command: the military experience derived from pacifying brigand-infested new territories, and the resolve, carried out over three years, to give its peoples a firm and just rule. The Governor-General also suggested that he might begin by collecting anecdotes for a history of the siege; Colonel Kirkpatrick, his own military secretary, would make a good compiler, 'but he has an Iron pen'. The future Iron Duke never had any love for such histories, with their certainty of provoking controversy. Fortunately he was soon engaged upon more congenial business.

A Mahratta freebooter, one of the smaller tigers of Mysore named Dhoondiah Waugh, had been lying in Tipoo's dungeon awaiting a horrid end. The assault on Seringapatam enabled him to escape. Gathering round him Tipoo's wild men he lived off the defenceless villages of the Deccan, at first eluding capture by Wellesley's troops through swift movement and local intelligence. Pushed inexorably northwards, Dhoondiah at last vanished out of the Deccan into Mahratta country. Suddenly, early in 1800, Dhoondiah's name cropped up again. A skirmish took place with Dhoondiah's bandits in which, as Arthur remarked, 'the gentlemen succeeded against the blackguards.'[20] By April 1800 there could be no doubt: 'our old adversary Dhoondiah Waugh is in force'. Indeed he was now calling himself the King of Two Worlds.

The king of earth and heaven was chased through Mahratta territories and back into the Deccan. In July his camp was captured, and on 10 September 1800 he was caught unawares, his 5,000 cavalry routed and he himself slain. His four-year-old son was found afterwards cowering among the baggage. The soldiers picked him up and galloped

---

* The Uma bird is at Windsor Castle while the tiger is a favourite exhibit at the Victoria and Albert Museum, though today its growl is somewhat asthmatic.

after the colonel, who at once made himself responsible for little Salabut Khan's future.

Another personal note struck on 10 September was the 'great swift charge' of four regiments headed by the Colonel of the 33rd himself. This was the first and last time that Arthur Wellesley led a cavalry charge.

Wellesley's hunting down of Dhoondiah sharpened the Governor-General's awareness of his brother's military distinction. The admirable settlement of Mysore had led him to believe that dear Arthur was after all destined to shine in the civil rather than the military sphere.[21] Possibly he was also reflecting the still strong prejudice against soldiers, and paying Arthur the compliment of considering him too good for the Army.

Now all this was over. A new approach was to be made to Arthur. It would demonstrate that the Governor-General considered his brother the best man in India for a military assignment of the most urgent and special nature.

Two papers marked 'Private & Secret' were addressed to Arthur by his brother, the Governor-General, on 5 November 1800. They were to prove gunpowder to Arthur's equanimity.

The great man informed him that owing to the French threat to India he proposed to attack the Isle de France (Mauritius), the only French naval base in East Indian waters. Arthur would take command of the invasion force, set off secretly, and having arrived, capture the Isle de France in one night. On no account must Arthur mention the plan to anyone, not even Lord Clive.

Great Jealousy will arise among the General Officers, in consequence of my employing you; but I employ you, because I rely on your good sense, discretion, activity and spirit; and I cannot find all these qualities united in any other officer in India who could take such a command.[22]

This looked to Arthur like his chance at last. He promptly got himself recalled from Mysore and wrote enthusiastically to Richard that he expected to reach Trincomalee on 22 December 1800. In case of victory he would leave Mornington (as he still called his brother) to decide whether he should remain in Mauritius or return to Mysore.

It is absolutely indifferent to me which I do, and I shall be glad to be in that place in which I can be of most service.[23]

Within three weeks Arthur had become far from indifferent. If after all, warned Richard, he decided that the armament assembled by Arthur at Trincomalee must be used against Egypt instead of Mauritius, the force would have to be commanded by a general, not a colonel. Arthur reacted hotly. The general would almost certainly be Baird. He felt sure that when Richard had given the first orders he intended him to command the army *at all events*.[24] His embarrassed brother could not deny it. Since his decision to appoint Arthur he had been personally confronted by a furious Baird resolved not to be passed over a fourth time in favour of the Governor-General's brother.

When Arthur heard of Baird's protest he sympathized. But that was no reason, as he was to repeat obstinately over and over again, why the wrong done to Baird should be righted at his expense. His reputation had been irreparably damaged: for it would be said that if the Governor-General, who was known to favour his brother, superseded him, there must be something very wrong with him. The expedition had been switched back to Batavia – but with Baird in command. Why Baird, not Arthur, for Batavia?

At the end of January 1801 an overland despatch arrived from home which seemed to answer Arthur's last question. Writing on 6 October 1800 from Downing Street, Mr Secretary Dundas announced that the forthcoming expedition from India was after all to be part of a grand joint affair against the French in Egypt. Batavia was off. Command of the Indian contingent 'should be given to some active and intelligent officer. . . .'[25] So it was all Dundas's fault that Colonel Wellesley could not command.

Arthur was not appeased. As he pointed out later, the Dundas despatch mentioned neither Baird's name nor that of any other general. In fact its phrase, *some active and intelligent officer*, might have been made to fit Arthur himself.

Everything now seemed to conspire against him. His brother Henry did not return from leave in England until too late. 'Had I been here in time,' he wrote to Arthur, 'I think I could have prevented [Baird's] appointment.'[26] Worse still, the confirmation of his 'supersession' did not reach Arthur at Trincomalee in time to save him from plunging yet further into the mire.

The date was 10 February 1801. Unwisely assuming that he was still in command of the Trincomalee troops but aware from a copy of Dundas's despatch that they were to go to the Red Sea instead of Batavia, he decided without any instructions to provision them forthwith in Bombay. His good friend Frederick North, Governor of Ceylon, was horrified. If Dundas's despatch meant that he should go anywhere, it meant that he should go to Suez. If the worst came to the worst, North wrote, and the Bombay bullocks failed, Colonel Wellesley could always pick up some horses and camels from Arabia instead.

This was not the way Arthur was accustomed to talk about his precious bullocks. *Horses* instead? He was aboard the *Suffolk* ready for the Bombay passage by 15 March, informing North firmly from his cabin that 'Articles of provision are not to be trifled with, or left to chance'.[27] Colonel Wellesley was to receive a very sour welcome in Bombay.

Arthur still considered Lord Wellesley's conduct indefensible. His supersession still rankled. From Bombay he wrote to Henry: 'I was at the top of the tree in this country. . . . But this supersession has ruined all my prospects. . . . However, I have lost neither my health, spirits, nor temper in consequence thereof.'[28]

This was brave but untrue. As he continued feverishly to probe the wound the next thing he knew was that he had been attacked by a genuine fever, the Malabar Itch, caught by sleeping in a strange bed on the way from Ceylon. Arthur was ordered to plunge himself into baths of nitric acid so strong that the towels on which he dried were burnt. As for his letters, large sulphurous yellow stains on the flimsy rice paper seem to this day an all too appropriate background to the caustic accounts of his wrongs.

Paradoxically it was Baird himself who, on reaching Bombay on 31 March in the *Wasp*, turned out to be a much needed dove of peace. Such had been Arthur's spleen that he had made up his mind to quit the Army and India for ever. But Baird showed himself so sympathetic to his stricken junior – 'the General behaved to me as well as a man could' – that Arthur decided to go to Egypt after all as Baird's second-in-command. He was able to write to a friend:

My sense of the original injustice is somewhat blunted. . . . I must ever look back upon the last five months as the most interesting in my life.[29]

This sudden swing from despair to cheerfulness – part disposition, part will-power – was characteristic of him. He was never a man of iron, in the sense of lacking temperament. The Iron Duke had even a certain volatility all his own.

Despite this upward swing, he had not really 'got the better of' (a favourite phrase) the Malabar Itch nor of the grievance. By writing a long recapitulation of his supersession on 18 April to Lord Wellesley, he seems to have caused the fever to strike again. He confessed this time to being 'very ill'.[30] Because of the renewed eruption on his skin he had finally to cancel his '*laudable*' intention of catching up Baird in Egypt. (The sarcastic italic was Arthur's and underlined his bitterness.) Fate decided that he should remain aloof in Bombay. It was just as well, for the ship in which he had intended to sail went down with all hands.

He himself put down the recurrence of his illness to the spring tides at Bombay. Henry, who was the estranged brothers' go-between, knew better. It was the Supersession Itch.

There was one redeeming factor, Mysore. When more or less recovered from the physical itch, Arthur had taken up his old command again in May 1801 at Lord Clive's urgent request. In Mysore things were prosperous though the army, officers and men alike, had deteriorated during his absence. Nevertheless the picture was gratifying. India needed him. He took Henry's advice, given with some reserve since Henry himself was ill, not to leave 'this hateful country' just yet.[31] Arthur felt qualified, out of his own bitter experience, to give some advice in return.

I know but one receipt for good health in this country and this is to live moderately, to drink little or no wine, to use exercize, to keep the mind employed, and, if possible, to keep in good humour with the world. The last is the most difficult, for as you have often observed, there is scarcely a good humoured man in India.[32]

The uses of moderation, including therapeutic good temper, were of course not the discovery of Arthur Wellesley, but he was well in advance of most Anglo-Indian thinking, including that of William Hickey who boasted in 1802 of having saved the life of a fevered friend by pouring four bottles of claret down his throat every twenty-four hours.[33]

Arthur's admirable recipe for health – good temper – he could not yet follow, despite valiant efforts. Indeed, ill-humour drove him to a step (the passage to Bombay) which even Fortescue describes in a hushed voice as 'a very bold one for a mere colonel to take', and which he himself in later years would have regarded as rank insubordination.

He and the Governor-General were still corresponding after mid-1801 through intermediaries. Great events were needed – peace in Britain and war in India – to bring these two remarkable brothers together again in a new alliance.

This time it would have to be a true alliance between equals. Arthur Wellesley was emerging as one who did not suffer superiors gladly. 'We want no Major-Generals in Mysore,' he remarked on hearing that an officer of this superior rank had landed in India. Team-work with 'such people' as seemed likely to come his way gave him the itch. As he wrote to Henry during the wretched aftermath of his supersession:

'I like to walk alone. . . .'[34]

6

That is all India

Strange things were happening in England and Ireland, though the news trickled through in the usual haphazard way, through merchant captains in Madras. Arthur nevertheless learnt the fact of Pitt's resignation on 5 February 1801, as early as June that year. Things looked 'very bad indeed':[1] for a new administration would be too weak to carry on the French war.

Pitt's successor, Henry Addington, a portentous mediocrity, was already beginning to 'treat' when Arthur first heard about the change of government. By 1 October a preliminary treaty with France was agreed amid public rejoicing. Up went the fireworks, down went the price of bread. In March 1802 the Peace of Amiens was ratified.

The East India Company pounced with joy on the opportunities given by peace and the removal of Dundas, Lord Wellesley's friend, from the India Board. They set about putting Wellesley's policies into reverse. Officials, some of them with dubious even criminal records, who had only recently been swept out of their grimy corners by the Governor-General's stiff broom and sent packing to England, were suddenly returned to sender, without compliments, by the Company. One of Lord Wellesley's most creative projects, a college for civil servants in Calcutta, was summarily wound up and the chance to re-educate the ignorant young men who came out to govern India abandoned. Arthur predicted a wave of 'greediness' and 'dishonesty' among the Company's new placemen:

I have determined that as soon as . . . I find that it is intended to introduce the new system of dubashery* and rapacity into this country, I shall withdraw, and I believe every honest man . . . will do the same.[2]

He himself knew a good deal about 'dubashery and rapacity' in Seringapatam and how, if unchecked, they could spread like a plague.

---

* A *dubash* was an Indian secretary, agent or middleman, and *dubashery* meant corrupt dealings by European officials through these agents

The trouble had begun while Arthur was away campaigning. Soon after he returned to Seringapatam in 1801 he forwarded to the Commander-in-Chief 'an interesting account of the sale of the Company's salt petre by Lieutenant-Colonel Mandeville & his lady, etc., etc.,' in their private house. The 'etceteras' stood for the fact that Colonel Wellesley had assembled a Commission of officers to inquire into the embezzlements, and that there would be a determined effort by the Europeans to make Nellahtomby Dubash, the Lascar storeman, the scapegoat.

Almost at once, however, it emerged that 'Nelly' (as the men called Nellahtomby) and his mates had committed all their enormities under orders, and when he made a statement implicating the commissary, Captain Macintire, the Commission refused to enter it on their minutes. Next morning they were forced to record something far worse – that Nellahtomby's desk had been broken open during the night by Captain Macintire and all the incriminating evidence stolen or destroyed. In the end all the officers were convicted, Colonel Mandeville and his lady being the worst offenders. While others were merely stealing cannon and brass pigs from the arsenal and mint, the Mandevilles had stripped the copper bands from the pillars of the Mysore palace. Reorganization of the whole arsenal was undertaken by Wellesley, Macintire being replaced by a Captain Freese, of whom more will be heard.

Stealing from a Company itself highly rapacious was by no means the gravest offence which Colonel Wellesley had to deal with. The very lives of the civilian inhabitants were endangered by types like Lieutenant Dodd. This officer had forcibly obtained money from Indians by torture – making them stand in the sun with boxes of stores on their heads. Wellesley felt certain that Dodd had flogged Basur, a goldsmith, to death and then made the villagers swear that Basur had poisoned himself. And Dodd's sentence? Six months' suspension of rank and pay and – a reprimand. In the New Year of 1802 the shamefaced authorities had to inform Wellesley of Dodd's desertion. His description had been circulated – straight and well made (alas, in limbs only), last seen on a Bombay boat at midnight, 3 February, 'carrying with him a tall stout Bay horse'. It was thought that William Dodd and his stout horse intended to offer their services to the Mahrattas.

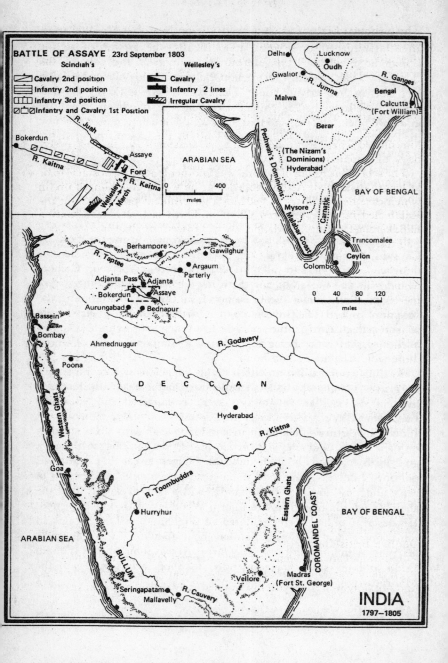

BATTLE OF ASSAYE 23rd September 1803

Scindiah's

- Cavalry 2nd position
- Infantry 2nd position
- Infantry 3rd position
- Infantry and Cavalry 1st Position

Wellesley's

- Cavalry
- Infantry 2 lines
- Irregular Cavalry

Bokerdun

R. Juah

R. Kaitna

Assaye

Ford

R. Kaitna

Wellesley's March

0   400

miles

ARABIAN SEA

Delhi

Lucknow

Oudh

Gwalior

R. Jumna

R. Ganges

Malwa

Bengal

Calcutta
(Fort William)

Berar

Peshwah's Dominions

(The Nizam's
Dominions)
Hyderabad

BAY OF BENGAL

Mysore

Malabar Coast

Carnatic

Trincomalee

Ceylon

Colombo

0   40   80   120

miles

Berhampore

Gawilghur

R. Taptee

Argaum

Parterly

Adjanta Pass

Adjanta

Bokerdun

Assaye

Aurungabad

Bednapur

Bassein

Bombay

Ahmednuggur

R. Godavery

Poona

D E C C A N

Hyderabad

R. Kistna

Western Ghats

Goa

R. Toombuddra

Eastern Ghats

BAY OF BENGAL

Hurryhur

COROMANDEL COAST

ARABIAN SEA

BULLUM

Vellore

Madras
(Fort St. George)

Seringapatam

R. Cauvery

Mallavelly

INDIA

1797–1805

The turbulent Mahrattas were being vigilantly watched by Wellesley. On 29 April 1802 his command was strengthened by his promotion to the rank of major-general (though only on the India list). And that spring, as if to clear the decks, Major-General Wellesley was freed from two encumbrances.

One of these was Colonel Shee, under whose erratic surveillance during Arthur's absence his precious 33rd had become a nightmare of drunkenness and brawling. Wellesley had been quietly trying to get him moved when death, heralded by a 'spasmodic fit' lasting several days, anticipated his wish.[3]

The rebellious Rajah of Bullum was another long-term obstacle to be at length dislodged. Arthur hoped that he would give himself up, in which case he would try to get him a government provision. But the Rajah fled into the Western Ghats and was last seen with 'only a handkerchief on his head and short drawers on his *breach*';[4] on 9 February a reward of 1,000 pagodas offered by Major Munro accomplished his betrayal and capture.

In November 1802 General Wellesley heard privately of an act of violence in Central India – 'the terrible defeats'[5] of two Mahratta chiefs, the Peshwah of Poona and Scindiah of Gwalior, by a third, Holkar of Indore. The Governor-General felt he could not ignore such heaven-sent discord in the formidable Mahratta Empire. He determined to use it as an excuse for humbling all its marauding horsemen, dispersing its infantry and finally safeguarding its neighbours, especially the threatened Nizam of Hyderabad. It was also an opportunity to defy the 'cent per cent rascals' of Leadenhall Street on a scale which would make the Mysore campaign look like an economy drive. From the opposite angle, it seemed a conclusive reason why the two Wellesley brothers, despite the Company's 'enormities' and their own repeated threats to resign, should remain at their posts.

As a start to the new campaign, the Governor-General concluded a 'subsidiary alliance' in December 1802 – with the Peshwah. This treaty, called after the Peshwah's refuge at Bassein, shifted the whole balance of power in Central India. Until the Treaty of Bassein, the Peshwah had been titular head of the Mahratta Confederacy. Now he was a 'protected prince' or, like the rulers of Hyderabad, Mysore and Oudh, a British puppet.

Arthur had always been alert to the dangers of 'subsidiary alliances', but if there was to be a second Mahratta war he intended to be in it. And not only in it, but with his scope greatly increased because of it.*

* First Mahratta War, 1761; second, 1803–5; third, 1817

'You are dying of the cramp,' Addington had once told Richard before he went to India. All these talented Wellesleys tended to die of the cramp and Arthur in particular constantly needed fresh chances to develop the strength that he felt was in him. The Mahratta command seemed made for him.

The first thing was to get the Peshwah back into Poona. At once, the piecemeal lessons which Arthur had learnt from sporadic Mahratta outbreaks on his borders were brilliantly integrated. He brought his army safely across the fords of two rivers, the Toombuddra and Kistna, in March and April 1803, and in order to be ready for the rise of these and the other great rivers which criss-cross India, he ordered Major Doolan to start immediately making basket-boats. He had both studied his Caesar and acted 'much as Alexander the Great seems to have done'.[6]

A smooth advance brought him within sight of his goal by 8 April. News reached him on the 19th that the Mahratta Governor of Poona intended to burn it down before evacuating. To restore the Peshwah to a smoking ruin would have been a fatal blow to prestige. So Wellesley, with 400 cavalry, covered forty miles that night – in all, sixty miles in thirty-four hours – expecting every moment to see a black pall above the city. When he dashed into Poona on the 20th it was in turmoil but untouched.

By the middle of May the Peshwah was back on his *musnud* (throne). The question was now whether the other Mahratta powers could be induced to leave him there. In General Wellesley's urgent opinion, a relentless 'harrying' of the Mahrattas by troops who could move with 'celerity' was the best tactics.[7] But the Governor-General was so much harried himself by Company criticism that the chance to rush the Mahrattas into speedy peace was lost.

On 4 June 1803 General Wellesley marched out from Poona. During the next two days the Mahratta armies gathered menacingly on the Nizam's frontier. On 26 June General Wellesley was given plenary political and military powers. Whether by negotiations or war, his orders were to 'restore the tranquillity of the Deccan'.[8]

Once again the Governor-General had over-ridden 'jealousy' (this time 'among the Residents'[9]) in favour of his brother.

The breakdown of negotiations and declaration of war took place on 6 August 1803.

The first necessity was to seize Scindiah's great hill-fortress of Ahmednuggur, among the strongest in India and plumb on the Nizam's frontier. After a 'brisk and gallant contest' on 8 August 1803 the outer fortifications of the town were captured. Two days later a battery of four guns, skilfully placed, opened fire on the fort and continued pounding away until on the 12th the garrison surrendered. Inside were found ample provisions and 'trifling articles' belonging to Scindiah – swords, dirks and pistols, looking-glasses and bawdy pictures.[10] The episode that made most impression on Wellesley was that of a young soldier knocked from the highest rung of a scaling-ladder who picked himself up and immediately raced to the top of the town wall again, to be first over. Who was he? asked the General. A volunteer from the 78th, he was told, named Colin Campbell.* Wellesley promoted him to brigade-major and before he left India made him his private secretary. It was to be a favourite joke that he had first seen Sir Colin Campbell, Governor of Ceylon, 'in the air'.[11]

The success of Ahmednuggur may have led Wellington later to underrate the infinitely more formidable problems of reducing Peninsular fortresses when defended by outstanding and resolute Frenchmen. Napoleon's attack on him as merely a 'Sepoy General' was false from the start and finally proved the most deadly boomerang. Wellington's Indian sieges were a different matter. The quality of resistance put up was not very relevant to Badajoz or Burgos in Spain. If Napoleon had called him a 'Sepoy siege-master' it would have been crude propaganda but less ludicrously wide of the mark.

While the Governor-General was as usual commending his brother's 'alacrity', Arthur had already marched from Ahmednuggur, resolved on bringing Scindiah and the Bhoonslah of Berar to a battle. By crossing another great river, the Godavery, he managed to manoeuvre Scindiah northward away from Hyderabad. But on the 23rd Wellesley received intelligence that Scindiah's cavalry had already escaped him, though there was still time to catch his infantry in their camp, which was only six miles away. Wellesley at once made a swift reconnaissance on a good horse, entailing a circuit of four miles. He was astonished by what he saw. Instead of infantry alone opposing him, Scindiah's whole army was still there, spread over seven miles of shimmering plain, where the green parrots, vultures and kites flashed, circled or hovered

---

* Sir Colin Campbell (1776–1847). Not to be confused (as has happened in the editing of Ellesmere's *Reminiscences*) with Sir Colin Campbell, Lord Clyde (1792–1863), hero of the Indian Mutiny.

in the incandescent light. Thousands of cavalry stretched from Bokerdun on the left to merge into infantry and artillery in the centre and round the village of Assaye on the right. A river, the Kaitna, protected their front. This was a position of considerable strength. The two brilliant commanders, de Boigne and Perron,* who had been responsible for transforming the Mahratta hordes into relatively modern armies with European equipment and officers, had done their work well.

The general had to think quickly. Stevenson, his second-in-command, had lost his way; it was a case of Wellesley's 7,000 of all ranks against six times that number. If he attacked it must be with troops who had already marched twenty-four miles that day. He turned to an Indian *vakeel* (envoy) and asked what he thought would be the result of a battle. The man replied with Oriental politeness that 'the battle was not always to the strong'.[12] The gamble was in fact prodigious, such as only a fool or a genius would dare. General Wellesley ordered the advance.

The first crisis came when they heard how steep and rocky were the Kaitna's banks and the guides declared there were no fords. At once Wellesley's genius took over. Still pressing on, he saw through his glass, below Assaye, to the right, two other villages facing each other on opposite banks of the Kaitna.

I immediately said to myself that men could not have built two villages so close to one another . . . without some habitual means of communication . . .[13]

There must be a ford, whatever the guides said. He sent a staff officer on ahead who duly found the ford. How did Wellesley come to make his inspired guess?

When one is strongly intent on an object, common sense will usually direct one to the right means.[14]

Strongly intent though he was, his inevitable delays over the ford problem had given the Mahrattas time to strike camp and form into a dense line behind the Kaitna. Fortunately for him they failed to occupy the ford. But as his men marched diagonally towards it they fell under a hot cannon-fire. The head of Wellesley's orderly was blown off while he was actually crossing. The headless trunk, spouting blood, remained in

* Perron was French, and at the time of Assaye was in Hindustan. De Boigne was a Savoyard with British nationality, and had trained Scindiah's martial races on British lines, with many young British officers, all of whom left when war was imminent

the saddle for a few moments while the terrified horse plunged and reared among the general's staff, scattering them far and wide, until at last its ghastly burden slid into the water.

Once across, Wellesley calculated that the ground would favour him, or rather that he could force the enemy to conform to his idea of its most advantageous use. A tributary stream, the Juah, flowing parallel to the Kaitna but behind Assaye until it joined the main river well below the village, presented him with a tongue of land under a mile wide, which he could just fill with his small army. This would deny 'the overwhelming deluge of native cavalry', as he called them, any space for manoeuvre. There was no slackening in the Mahrattas' cannonade, but Wellesley intended to attack their left immediately, where it lay along the Kaitna, roughly at right angles to his position.

All at once it became clear to the staring British that something strange was happening. The Mahrattas were changing front, not scientifically perhaps, but such a manoeuvre was totally unexpected. The Mahratta infantry and guns were soon face to face with the British, between the two streams, with their left on Assaye. Wellesley could not avoid a corresponding adjustment in his own front line on the extreme right, nearest Assaye; for the Mahratta manoeuvre had dangerously lengthened his front. He still intended to open his attack against the infantry on the Kaitna (now the Mahrattas' right), correctly reckoning that once their right and centre had been pushed back to the Juah their left and Assaye would fall. Now, however, he must first order his pickets on the right wing to move outwards and make room for detachments coming up on their left to fill in the gaps. Meanwhile the murderous cannonade had redoubled. Wellesley could wait no longer.

We attacked them immediately, and the troops advanced under a very hot fire from cannon, the execution of which was terrible.[15]

Terrible it was; but not enough to save Scindiah's artillery from the fury of Wellesley's centre and left. There was no resisting them. They captured or cut down the first line of brave Mahratta gunners at their posts and went on to destroy the second line, despite an audacious ruse of some of the first-line gunners. These feigned dead until the victorious British had swept over them, when they sprang to life again, turned about and fired into their captors' backs, only to be shot down in their turn. Deprived of their guns the Mahratta infantry showed no mind to stand and fight. This was what Wellesley had foreseen. This should have turned directly into his irresistible push from the left towards the

Juah. And so it would have, but for the sudden intervention of dire calamity on his right.

Colonel Orrock, whether dazed by the fire or unable to halt his rightward movement, or simply misunderstanding an order, had led his pickets, followed by the 74th Highlanders, straight at the guns under Assaye. Theirs not to reason why. It was one of those 'unlucky accidents' for which Wellesley could never blame Orrock, though it accounted for half his total losses.[16] The issue trembled in the balance.

With no thought but to save the remnants of their comrades, the 19th Dragoons under Colonel Maxwell and the 4th Native Cavalry dashed in together, the latter brought forward from the reserve by Wellesley himself in the nick of time. The rescue was made. The tide turned. Wellesley went on to drive in the Mahrattas along the Juah, while Maxwell and his 19th charged down upon the remaining infantry under their German commander, Pohlmann.* Last to leave the field were the Mahratta horse who, in Fortescue's words, 'rode sullenly away'. Victory was complete.

Assaye had been a close-run thing. The day was all but lost in a stupendous massacre under its walls. It was won in rivers of blood – 'the bloodiest for the numbers', as Wellington was to recall grimly, 'that I ever saw. . . .'[17] To the enemy's 1,200 killed and 4,800 wounded he lost 1,584 killed, wounded and missing, 650 of them Europeans. In one company the officer and forty-four men out of fifty were killed. Every mounted field and staff officer lost a horse, Colin Campbell three. Wellesley's bay was shot under him and his grey Arab was piked.

On the darkening battlefield the victors dropped exhausted and slept among the ungathered dead. Arthur, at first sleepless and mourning, sat for a time with his head on his knees. Visions of his heroic Sepoys, of his vital European regiments, of the officer who had lost one arm against the Bullum Rajah and broken the other hunting but who had charged with his bridle in his teeth waving his sword in his single, mutilated hand – all the courage and the carnage floated before him. When he at last slept it was only to be awakened by a recurring nightmare – 'a confused notion that they were *all* killed. . . .'[18] Had it been worth it? Less than a month later he was writing:

I acknowledge that I should not like to see again such loss as I sustained on the 23rd September, even if attended by such a gain.[19]

* Pohlmann's First Brigade was the only one of de Boigne's famous five brigades (really divisions) present at Assaye and it was Pohlmann who gave Wellesley his hard fight.

This was to be by no means the last time that melancholy would follow a great victory. But years later, when his battles were distant memories, his friend, little Mr Chad of the diplomatic service, asked him what was 'the best thing' he ever did in the way of fighting.

'Assaye,' replied the Duke of Wellington sombrely. He did not add a word.[20]

It was *his* victory. Without his nerve and willpower it could not have happened. Colin Campbell of the 78th was the first to pick out the quality which made Wellesley such an incomparable leader on the field:

The General was in the thick of the action the whole time . . . I never saw a man so cool and collected as he was . . . though I can assure you, till our troops got the orders to advance the fate of the day seemed doubtful. . . .[21]

The echoes of Assaye were to roll on triumphantly into Wellington's middle and old age, and after. A visitor to the battlefield in 1829 sent him an account. The mango under which Arthur Wellesley directed the battle had died of its wounds and been carried off for firewood. But would his Grace accept the gift of a box made from wood hewn from its roots by his Lordship's humble servant, Lieutenant J. E. Alexander? The Duke, as was his custom, would not.

A century later an Indian writer, J. R. Jeejeebhoy, eloquently declared that the victor of Assaye 'rose in his tent . . . on the 23rd of September, 1803, and before sunset found himself universally famous'.[22] This was suitably Byronic. 'His path thereafter,' he added, 'was ever strewn with the sweet flowers of a nation's gratitude.' Looking no further than Arthur's last full year in India, 1804, the flowers in some places would have seemed to the hero of Assaye thinly strewn.

By the end of 1803 the various British armies had between them won a whole series of victories.

Wellesley's army entered Berar on 25 November. At 3 pm on the 29th he and Stevenson, after marching in burning heat since 6 am, joined forces at Parterly, six miles north of the River Purna, a tributary of the great Taptee. Wellesley had detected Stevenson's approaching troops before anyone else.

'How can you tell Colonel Stevenson's dust from any other dust?'[23] asked an admiring Indian on his staff. Immediately after Stevenson's arrival Wellesley climbed a tower to look for the enemy. Only five miles to the north, on an absolutely flat plain in front of the village of Argaum, he saw a seething mass of enemy horse and foot. He had ten or eleven thousand to put against them. Nevertheless he marched straight for the plain and the battle.

A great sea of high corn made the enemy invisible to his vanguard until the very moment when they emerged into the plain, a moment made terrible by the sudden concentrated fire of fifty Mahratta guns. Even Wellesley was at first somewhat alarmed by this development and rode forward to investigate. He was quickly reassured.

'We shall have time to take these guns before night,' he remarked confidently. His advance-guard, however, plunged backwards into two Sepoy battalions behind them, both composed of the heroes of Assaye who notwithstanding their fine record panicked and fled. Once more this was a moment of crisis on which the fate of an army hung.

Wellesley first tried showing himself to the fleeing Sepoys in a vain attempt to rally them. At last he calmly sent them to the rear to be re-formed and then brought them forward again himself, under cover of his own far fewer guns, into their original positions. After it was all over he said frankly, 'If I had not been there to . . . restore the battle, we should have lost the day.'[24]

By 4.30 pm all his troops were in line and he gave the word to advance. After a fierce collision between Sepoys and a wild horde of screaming Arabs, Wellesley's cavalry leapt after the Mahrattas, killing, capturing and rounding up men, horses, camels, elephants and thirty-eight cannon under the hectic light of the moon.[25] His total losses were 562, hardly one-twentieth of his force.

Gawilghur, a vast, impregnable fortress if ever there was one, high up between the headwaters of the Taptee and the Purna, gave the Bhoonslah's defeated infantry an incomparable chance to make a last stand. They were perhaps 30,000 strong. For some reason they failed to seize it.

The siege necessitated the most violent exertions on Wellesley's part. In order to direct his now ailing second-in-command, he had to ride over to Stevenson's camp every day by a circuitous mountain road, a matter of fifty miles there and back in the blazing heat.

According to the history books the place was taken by assault in a few hours on 15 December 1803. Stevenson certainly stormed the northern wall of the outer fortification in fine style. Did he really have to assault the main fortified area to the south-east, the base of whose rampart would have defeated a mountain goat? And how did Wellesley's column in the south-east corner manage to get in, *if opposed*, despite incredible obstacles? The problem has mystified one of the very few military historians (if not the only one) to explore this fantastic fastness. 'Three reasonably effective troops of Boy Scouts armed with rocks could have kept out several times their number of professional soldiers.'* The only possible answer is that resistance collapsed before a general assault became necessary. The affair cost Wellesley only fourteen killed and 112 wounded, a small price indeed compared with Assaye. He was reaping the benefit of the moral ascendancy he had established at Assaye and Ahmednuggur.

Treaties negotiated by Arthur with Scindiah and the Bhoonslah vastly extended the 'subsidiary alliance' system and convinced the sanguine Governor-General, against Arthur's initial doubts, that 1804 would see the last Mahratta fish, Holkar, in the net. But the system was already showing its weakness. The pivotal alliance with Scindiah proved a delusion and Holkar, certain of no danger from that quarter, inflicted a defeat on General Lake's army under Colonel Monson in Malwa of such appalling dimensions that 'the national military character'[26] seemed to have been plunged back into the bad old days.

Besides Monson's 'retreat, defeat, disgraces and disasters',[27] Arthur saw many things in the India of 1804 to make him wince. His recent treaty with Scindiah he felt had been dishonoured by his brother's refusal to let Scindiah keep his capital of Gwalior:

I would sacrifice Gwalior, or every frontier of India, ten times over, in order to preserve our credit, for scrupulous good faith. . . .[28]

His position as major-general on the Madras (i.e. the Company's) staff he considered to be 'of an ambiguous nature', since it had never been confirmed in England by the Duke of York.

Finally there was the question of his health. William Hickey had once commented with a mixture of relish and commiseration on a Dutchman's tombstone to be found on the Coromandel coast:

> Mynheer Gludenstack lies interred here,
> Who intended to have gone home last year.[29]

---

* Mr Jac Weller made a unique examination of the sites of Wellington's Indian battlefields and sieges in 1968, and most kindly informed the present writer of the results of his topographical discoveries, including the deductions to be drawn from them. As well as suggesting that the all-out assault was unlikely, Mr Weller argues that the alleged slaughter of the whole garrison of many thousands was probably an exaggeration also, since Gawilghur was a hill-fort of such immense size that most of the able-bodied garrison could have escaped.

Was this to be Arthur's fate? He suffered more and more often now from spasms of rheumatism, lumbago and ague; and when not physically feverish was consumed with a burning desire to go home: 'I am anxious to a degree which I can't express to see my friends again'.[30] At last, after many doubts and disappointments, he made up his mind on the night of 16 February.

Parliament had sent thanks for 'memorable services' in the Deccan; an old friend 'Beau' Cradock, now Sir John, brought out the Order of the Bath for him to Madras, and quite in the spirit of bygone Dublin pranks, pinned it on his coat, like Santa Claus, while he slept.[31] His fortune amounted to over £42,000; enough, as he told Cradock, to make him independent but not a Nabob. That was what he wanted: for as Henry had once written to him, 'you care less about money than any man I ever yet knew.'[32]

A golden vase worth 2,000 guineas, a sword worth £1,000, besides countless addresses from gallant officers and illustrious civilians, expressed praise and thanks. His most heartening address had come from Mysore on 16 July 1804.

We, the native inhabitants of Seringapatam, have reposed for five auspicious years under the shadow of your protection . . . when greater affairs shall call you from us, may the God of all castes and all nations deign to hear with favour our humble and constant prayers for your health, your glory, and your happiness.[33]

Here was one timeless memorial left behind in India to the 'Sepoy General' – the impress of his work and character. Another was of that whimsical kind which is sometimes bequeathed by the great to a countryside. A huge jutting peak above the village of Khandalla in the Western Ghats, known locally as the Cobra's Head, was to become The Duke's Nose.

On 10 March 1805 Sir Arthur Wellesley sailed thankfully in HMS *Trident*. Her captain, Benjamin Page, in time to come presented the Corporation of Ipswich with a bust of Wellington, surprisingly designated 'The Napoleon of India'. Apart from sea-sickness, the voyage was refreshing, especially the month's stay in St Helena. Its climate seemed to him, as it did not to Napoleon, 'the most healthy I have ever lived in', restoring his physical health. 'I am now convinced that if I had not left India,' he wrote to Malcolm from the island, 'I should have had a serious fit of illness.'[34] Oddly enough Napoleon was to occupy the very house where Arthur had stayed, The Briars, while Longwood was being prepared for him.

On 10 September 1805 the *Trident* dropped anchor in the Downs, off Dover. It was the fifth anniversary of Wellesley's victory over Dhoondiah.

Some time after 1815 Arthur's old governor at Angers, General Mackenzie, who had known his youthful lack of stamina, asked him to explain his extraordinary endurance on the field of Waterloo. What had caused this change? The Duke replied promptly:

'Ah, that is all India.'[35]

It was indeed all India – the ability to live for three years on end in tents, to remain for hours in the saddle, to train troops not naturally good at marching to set up record after record. 'Marches such as I have made in this war, were never known or thought of before.'

From physical toughness sprang prodigies of industry with the pen. His *Indian Despatches*, stiff with memoranda and enlivened with letters on all subjects from war and peace to women and potatoes, were to entrance the whole world, including their author, when they came to be published. 'They are as good as I could write now' – 'the same attention to details' – 'fresh' – 'amusing'. *The Times* was awed and delighted by the incessant tramp of transport bullocks through the thick volumes.

How did he manage to write so many letters in the midst of active operations? asked Stanhope. The Duke gave one of his great replies: 'My rule always was to do the business of the day in the day.'[36]

Industry was backed by 'alacrity' which made him always seek out 'forward' officers with 'dash'. It was inexorable necessity which afterwards introduced caution into a naturally bold temperament.

From regimental experience in India he learnt how to handle large bodies of men, his command having risen to 50,000 in 1804. 'I have often said that if there were eight or ten thousand men in Hyde Park, it is not every general that would know how to get them out again. . . .'[37] From the combination of experience and study came his famous 'attention to detail', which gave to the sick their cots and quilts, to the healthy an exact mixture of arrack and water, and to the bullocks a precise speed and load.

Many of these concerns were material. What had India taught him about human beings?

The 'native inhabitants of Seringapatam' were not alone among Indians in regarding his justice and fairness with 'wonder'. Native customs were always to be respected, whether it was a question of who owned dancing girls 'as long as their persons are worth having', or of insisting that the search of Tipoo's zenana for arms should be 'as decent and as little injurious to the feelings of the ladies as possible'.

Notwithstanding this and many other signs of sympathy, he felt no particular sentiment in favour of black skins, such as Thomas Clarkson, William Wilberforce and the Anti-Slave Trade Society were expressing in England. He would not have two half-caste officers, said to be 'as black as my hat', in the 33rd. They might be 'intrinsically as good as others', but the 33rd was not a Sepoy regiment.[38] A place for everything and everything in its place. That was regularity. That was the ideal.

Government and Company officials often infuriated him, but he in turn was not above recognizing his own faults. The Mahratta war had caused many violent disagreements with Bombay, and on 7 January 1804 he wrote disarmingly to the Governor: 'I really believe that I may sometimes have complained without much cause.'[39]

His officers he exhorted to remember that they were 'gentlemen and soldiers' – in that order.[40] Gentlemen did not accept bribes. Major Doolan once naively reported that the Rajah of Kittoor had offered him 4,000 pagodas and Wellesley 10,000 to take Kittoor under the Company's protection. Arthur soundly berated him:

. . . I am surprised that any man, in the character of a British officer, should not have given the rajah to understand that the offer would be considered an insult. . . .[41]

The crestfallen Doolan replied that he had merely thought a cash payment would test the Rajah's sincerity. He would in future invariably comply with all his colonel's instructions, 'as my only Wish, is to Merit your approbation'. He was forgiven.

Colonel Wellesley practised what he preached.

'Can you keep a secret?' he said to a Rajah who had offered him £50,000 for information about his negotiations with Scindiah.

'Yes!' replied the Rajah eagerly.

'So can I.'[42]*

To the rank and file he gave two watchwords, 'discipline and regularity',[43] which would protect them against their besetting sin – intoxication.

---

* A similar story is told of Moltke in the 1870 war:
'Can you keep your mouth shut?'
'Yes.'
'So can I.'

68

His own besetting sin, according to Captain Elers, was certainly neither 'party' nor intoxication nor anything else of that kind.

Colonel Wellesley had at that time a very susceptible heart, particularly towards, I am sorry to say, married ladies. . . .[44]

Elers' sly verdict was coloured by disappointments over patronage in later years; nevertheless there seems no doubt that Arthur's interest in women and theirs in him had grown while in India. With his quick speech, ready laughter and muscular, well-built figure, rather over middle height, he was an attractive man who lost nothing from his 'strongly patrician countenance' and the glitter of 'something strange and penetrating' in his clear blue eyes. In the emotionally charged atmosphere of Anglo-Indian society, full of 'great hospitality and conviviality, seasoned with some female jealousies of attention & etiquette, & squabbles for precedence', not to mention a shared passion for amateur theatricals, the handsome major-general might well have been tempted to act as a Don Juan. Perhaps in imagination he did sometimes play that role. For an exhilarating collection of romantic fiction was listed for his voyage home, including *Love at First Sight, Illicit Love, The Rival Mothers, The Supposed Daughter* and *Lessons for Lovers*.[45] But for the most part Arthur Wellesley stood out as a chivalrous though somewhat detached figure, more likely to make aphorisms than to make love.

One relationship with a married woman may have been of a more serious nature.

Captain John William Freese of the Madras Artillery, whom General Stuart had appointed Commissary of Stores at Seringapatam in July 1802, had a young and very pretty wife, General Stuart's daughter. She had given birth to a son, Arthur, on the seventh of that month, to whom Arthur Wellesley stood godfather. Poor little Mrs Freese lost her eldest son in the following October, which may have drawn her and Arthur together, for he loved children. At any rate, he lost his heart to the captain's wife and shocked his censorious aide-de-camp, Captain West. But Mrs Freese's husband, according to Captain Elers, did not object.[46]

Arthur rode it out, and Arthur's friend John Malcolm continued to send him brief news of 'little Mrs Freese' until, in 1807, his small godson was brought home from India by General Cunningham to live with an aunt. But when Arthur Freese arrived his aunt was dead. General Cunningham at once thought of the boy's godfather. Would

Wellesley have him? Little Arthur was four; the same age as Salabut Khan when Colonel Wellesley rescued him from the Deccan battle-field. (One of Wellesley's last acts in India had been to leave money for Salabut's education.) Of course he took in Arthur Freese, and on 20 June 1807 Malcolm wrote to him from India of Mrs Freese's intense relief.

I never saw Mrs Freese better, and your accounts of Arthur which she read to-day have made her mad with joy. Why do you shave the poor boy's eye-brows – & endeavour to alter God's works – In Scotland red hair is a *Beauty* at least it was *five centuries* ago.[47]

Her son was to grow up and flourish in the Duke's home and incidentally to throw some interesting new light on its inmates. For many years the portrait of a dark-haired beauty with shining eyes hung in Apsley House, whether to remind Arthur Freese or Arthur Wellesley of a lost gleam may never be known.*

It remains to round off the Indian story with a better documented affair of Arthur's 'susceptible heart'.

Two well-meaning intermediaries had combined in 1801 to re-awaken the memory of Kitty Pakenham. The first was Colonel Beresford, lieutenant-general of the Ordnance at Dublin Castle under Thomas Pakenham of Coolure, the master-general, who wrote:

I know not if Miss Pakenham is an object to you or not – she looks as well as ever – no person whatsoever has paid her any attention – so much I say having heard her name and yours mentioned together – I hear her most highly spoken of by Mrs Sparrow. She lives so retired that nobody ever sees her . . .[48]

Beresford enclosed a letter for Arthur from the charming Mrs Sparrow – 'she talks so handsomely of you, you ought to be flattered' – whose message, though now lost, is not hard to guess. For Arthur replied fully to Olivia Sparrow, who was the wife of General Sparrow, daughter of Lord Gosford and Kitty's best friend:

August [1801]

You may recollect a disappointment that I met with about 8 years ago, in an object in which I was most interested. Notwithstanding my good fortune, and the perpetual activity of the life which I have led, the disappointment, the object of it, and all the

---

* The portrait of dark-haired Mrs Freese is now at Stratfield Saye. Both Arthur Freese and his father had sandy hair.

circumstances are as fresh upon my mind, as if they had passed only yesterday. How much more would they bear upon me if I was to return to the inactivity of a home life?

Upon the whole I think that for many reasons referable as well to another person as to me, I am better away; but I acknowledge that I am very anxious to go home. . . .

I have answered your questions candidly, and have stated facts which tend rather to my own humiliation . . . because I wish to shew you that the merit of your friend is still felt, and because I know that you will not mention them (to more than six full assemblies).

Fortune has favoured me upon every occasion and if I could forget that which has borne so heavily upon me for the last 8 years, I should have as little care as you appear to have.

When you see your friend do me the favour to remember me to her in the kindest manner.[49]

Which was it that bore so heavily upon him? Love or humiliation?

Whether or not Mrs Sparrow broadcast Arthur's 'facts' to six full assemblies, she certainly forwarded his letter post-haste to Kitty. Poor Kitty's often unmanageable emotions broke loose in her reply to Olivia:

Dublin, *May 7th* [1802]

God Almighty forbid he should either remain an exile from his country or be unhappy in it. Olivia you know my heart . . . as well as I know it myself you know how sincerely I am interested in his happiness, and you can imagine what gratitude I feel . . . for his kind remembrance. My dearest Olivia you know *I* can send no message, a kind word from me he might think binding to him and make him think himself *obliged* to renew a pursuit, which perhaps he might not then wish or my family (or at least some of them) take kindly. . . .[50]

As Kitty wrote on, three steady facts emerged: that she still loved him, that her family were still lukewarm about him (except for Aunt and Uncle at Coolure under whose cheerful roof the courtship had begun), and that despite Olivia's assurances she desperately feared Arthur was becoming lukewarm about her.

He now desires to be kindly remembered, but do not you think *he* seems to think the business *over*, in a former letter to you his words were I believe 'You cannot say more to her than I feel'. Do you recollect? Olivia I am afraid of saying a word ever since your letter arrived for fear it should be his name. So then the sooner I hear from you the better pray write soon.

Like all intermediaries, Kitty's dearest friend both acted as a safety-valve and kept up a good head of steam.

Letters continued to pass between Olivia Sparrow and Arthur Wellesley until at last in 1805 the time came to put it all to the test. One thing at any rate was clear. His longing to get home was not only due to ill-health or bad relations with Leadenhall Street. Nor was there any doubt of whom he was thinking when he told Lord Wellesley, 'I am anxious to a degree which I can't express to see my friends again.' Nor to what he referred when he wrote to Cradock, 'I am not rich in comparison with other people, but very much so in comparison with my former situation. . . .' Even the Mrs Freeses now fell into place. They were the way in which he chose to learn his *Lessons for Lovers*. They sharpened the soldier's nostalgia and desire for family life. And being married ladies, they preserved him in that interesting state which Kitty had described as 'Free'.

7

My Dearest Kitty

———

Arthur Wellesley was home after nine years, if home was the word. His mother was still living in a house off Cavendish Square; but there was no intimacy here. A Dublin acquaintance, Sir Jonah Barrington, meeting Arthur again in the Strand, did not recognize the 'sallow' stranger, and Arthur had to stop him with the words, 'Have you forgotten your old friend?'[1] He had been fêted all over India; in England he was hardly known, and the 'rattles' of the *bon ton* were ill-equipped to discuss Assaye. Yet he must still bend his mind to the East, to the defence of the whole 'Wellesley system' in India to a sceptical Whitehall and hostile Leadenhall Street. Richard was no longer Governor-General. On the voyage home Arthur had learnt of his abrupt and ignominious dismissal.

From September 1805 onwards the hope of serving in a European war absorbed Arthur. He had arrived home to find a Third Coalition just concluded by Pitt – Britain, Russia and Austria against the newly crowned Emperor Napoleon – and there was the prospect of a British expeditionary force to support it. Less than half his mind can now have been on the empire of the Mahrattas. Meanwhile, by a historic coincidence, his first encounter with the civilians of Whitehall brought him face to face with the very heart and genius of the war.

At the Colonial Office in Downing Street on 12 September 1805 Arthur Wellesley was waiting to see Lord Castlereagh. Also waiting in the little ante-room for an interview was a naval gentleman with only one arm, whom Arthur immediately recognized. The gentleman could not be expected to know the crop-haired, sunburnt major-general from India, nine years younger than himself. But neither did the major-general expect to be treated to quite such a display of Nelson's notorious egotism:

He entered at once into conversation with me, if I can call it conversation, for it was almost all on his side, and all about himself, and, really, in a style so vain and silly as to

73

surprise and almost disgust me. . . . I suppose something that I happened to say may have made him guess that I was *some-body*. . . .[2]

At any rate, Nelson left the room for a moment, found out who the general was and returned to dazzle him with a very different version of the Nelson touch.

All that I thought a charlatan style had vanished, and he talked . . . with a good sense, and a knowledge of subjects both at home and abroad, that surprised me equally and more agreeably than the first part of our interview had done; in fact, he talked like an officer and a statesman. . . . I don't know that I ever had a conversation that interested me more.

What did they discuss? Wellington recalled to Croker that Nelson had dwelt on 'the state of this country' and 'affairs on the Continent'. He expressed the hope that Wellesley might be appointed to attack the French in Sardinia – strategic 'good sense' compared with the expedition to Hanover that Pitt was actually planning.

By the narrowest of margins providence had succeeded in bringing together the heroes of Trafalgar and Waterloo for the best part of an hour. On the following day, 13 September 1805, Nelson left London to join HMS *Victory* at Portsmouth. Wellesley had only just arrived in London after a quarter of his life spent abroad. During the years of battle ahead he became fond of invoking 'the finger of Providence' to explain extraordinary pieces of good fortune. On this earlier occasion he felt that Lord Castlereagh's keeping his two visitors waiting long enough to discover one another's worth, had been a matter of luck.

Meanwhile, Castlereagh obstinately insisted that the Governor-General should have found some 'middle way' of saving India without a Mahratta war. 'From this supposed project,' wrote Arthur sadly to his brother, 'I could never drive him.'[3] Yet, while Castlereagh resisted Arthur's pleas he came to believe in the advocate's personality and skill. At a crucial moment in Arthur's career this was to make all the difference.

Pitt was visiting George III at Weymouth when Arthur arrived in England, but within a few days of returning home he invited General Wellesley to ride with him from Wimbledon Common to London. Arthur continued to his brother:

We rode very slowly [Pitt's health was crumbling] and I had a full opportunity of discussing with him and explaining all the points in our late system in India [of alliances] to which objections had been made, which were likely to make any impression upon him. . . . Upon all these his mind appeared to be satisfied.

It was fortunate that Pitt seemed satisfied, for Arthur had arranged to leave London next day to take the cure in Cheltenham. It was a cure which he hoped would lead to his recovery from rheumatism and possibly also from loneliness, disappointment and humiliation.

A week or more before his journey Arthur had received a letter from Olivia Sparrow; he sent her an interesting reply.

... I see evidently that you imagine that I am unworthy of your friend & I have not vanity enough to assert that I am otherwise. All that I can say is that if I could consider myself capable of neglecting such a woman I would endeavour to think of her no more. I hope that you will find that I am not quite so bad as you imagine I am.

So Arthur was going to have a chance to prove himself. But where and when? Clearly in Cheltenham, whither Mrs Sparrow must have summoned him.* It was after the meeting in Cheltenham that he hoped Mrs Sparrow would find him 'not so bad'. Mrs Sparrow herself had been neglectful in one respect, for he continued:

You have not told me what is to become of your friend in the Winter. Does she remain in Ireland? Shall I go over to see her?

Arthur then went on to break to the eager go-between some unpleasant news. Through no fault of his own, all might yet come to nothing.

The Government were about to dispatch a force to the Elbe, hoping to rescue the King's ancestral Hanover from the French. He therefore ended his letter to Mrs Sparrow on a subdued note:

I am very apprehensive that after having come from India for one purpose only I shall not accomplish it: & I think it not impossible that if the troops under orders for embarkation should be sent to the Continent, I shall be ordered to go with them, & possibly never see you or her again. ...

If Arthur really believed that he had left India 'for one purpose only' – to see Kitty Pakenham again – his mood was more romantic than he afterwards admitted. More important than his mood, however, was the letter which he had written to the young Kitty about 1794 before leaving Ireland, containing a phrase which he was not likely to forget: 'my mind will still remain the same.' If Kitty still wanted him, his old pledge stood and he was hers. Only the lady herself, or death somewhere on the foggy Elbe, could release him.

Fortunately for the success of his chivalrous enterprise, the first

* See Mrs Arbuthnot's Journal, 27 June 1822, where she noted that the Duke of Wellington had told her Lady Olivia Sparrow (as she then was) 'sent for him' on his return to England.

detachment of troops for Hanover (which did not include Arthur) was not after all destined to embark until the end of October. But there was still one country visit to be fitted in before he could take the road to Cheltenham.

On the way there, he had to call in at Stowe, the seat of Lord Buckingham, where he 'underwent a bore for two days' discussing Lord Wellesley's future with his fat old friend; he recommended his brother 'to remain neutral for some time, and observe the course of events'.

When Arthur at last reached the agreeable spa of Cheltenham it would have been as well if he had remembered his own sage advice to Richard – 'remain neutral for some time'. His love for Kitty was far from compelling. Indeed it is fairly certain that, with other young men about town, he had been drawn to the company of London's most bewitching courtesan, Harriette Wilson. Nevertheless he met General and Mrs Sparrow at Cheltenham by arrangement. Olivia was 'very charming'. Her task was not difficult. She must have already written to Kitty giving her a glowing account of Arthur's faithful love, together with his letter of the 24th. An answer from Kitty would arrive soon. All she had to do meanwhile was to go on being charming, while Arthur went on proving that he was 'not quite so bad' as she pretended to imagine.

Kitty's answer was sent to Olivia on 8 October. It is clear from the long, distraught sentences that *she* was Olivia's problem, not Arthur.

Your letter arrived just as I was leaving Langford Lodge. Olivia it does agitate me. . . . What can I say, I can know nothing of his mind but what you have told me you assure me he still regards me he has authorized you to *renew the proposition* he made some years ago but my Olivia I have in vain sought in his letter for one word expressive of a wish that the proposition should be accepted of. . . . I think he wishes to be ordered abroad and perhaps he is right for I am very much changed and you know it within these last three years, so much that I doubt whether it would now be in my power to contribute [to] the comfort or happiness of any body who has not been in the habit of loving me for years like my Brother or you or my Mother.[4]

Kitty's predicament was intelligible enough. To read her letter right through is to receive the impression of some sense, much sensibility, but above all of emotional unease. What had happened three years ago to make her write that she was 'very much changed' and – almost accusingly to Olivia – 'you know it'? Her friends declared she had lost her round pink cheeks pining for Arthur. 'She is now very thin and withered (I believe pining in his absence helped to make her more so)',

wrote the Hon. Mrs Calvert in the following May.[5] Others asserted
that she had been scarred by smallpox. This was not true and was
contradicted in writing after the death of Wellington by her beloved
niece Catherine Foster, *née* Hamilton, only daughter of Kitty's sister
Helen.

Often had the Duchess [Kitty] been heard to laugh at the impudent and ill-natured
untruth, which soon became a current report, that she had been disfigured by the
smallpox, an invention which was the more daringly absurd from the impossibility of
its falsehood not being evident to all who personally knew her. The unblemished
texture of her skin and the extreme beauty of her teeth, together with the
extraordinarily youthful appearance of her delicate little figure were always too
remarkable ... to leave any possibility of any *mistake* representing her personal
appearance excusing the *misstatements* which were very generally made.[6]

The beginning of the 'change' in Kitty had another cause, and a clue
is found in the brief love-story of Kitty Pakenham and Galbraith Lowry
Cole. This young man, who was to become one of Wellington's
Peninsular officers, proposed to Kitty 'two or three years before'
Arthur's return from India. According to Cole's family, Kitty 'played
fast and loose with his affections'. In proof, his grand-daughter quotes a
letter of 20 October 1802 from Lowry's brother William, Dean of
Waterford, to another brother, Arthur:

... Lowry since that love affair with Kitty Pakenham seems like a burnt child to fear
the fire. ...

Suppose the fire had burnt Kitty also? The affair was certainly no
flash-in-the-pan, for Kitty's brother Ned returned on sick leave from
the West Indies early in 1806, just in time for her wedding, but
expecting to find her engaged to – Lowry Cole.

The pieces of the jigsaw begin to fall into place. *1801*: Colonel
Beresford reported to Wellesley that Kitty looked 'as well as ever – no
person whatsoever has paid her any particular attention'. *May 1802*:
Kitty wrote to Olivia that 'he' (Colonel Wellesley) seemed to think 'the
business *over*', and anyway a renewal might cause 'vexation' to her
family. *Mid-1802*: Kitty herself considered the business was over and
therefore allowed Cole to court her. He proposed and was accepted.
Later 1802: Mrs Sparrow intervened. Citing Arthur's letter from India
as proof of his continued attachment, she begged Kitty to remain
faithful to him. Olivia won, as she always did, and the Cole engagement
was broken off. But the unfortunate Kitty, torn between the conflicting
pressures, fell into a decline. (Three years later Mrs Calvert was

remarking that 'she looks in a consumption'[7] and her doctor, Sir Walter Farquhar, advised her to take great care of herself.) Today we should probably say that she had a nervous breakdown.

Gradually and painfully she struggled back to health. By the time Olivia told her that Arthur was on the way home at last, she seemed almost her old self again. But ever since 1802–3 her temperament had been different, as Mrs Foster made clear towards the end of the passage already quoted:

An air of dejection and melancholy paleness was all that could have been wished otherwise in the amiable Duchess. . . .

Kitty's agitated letter of 8 October gave Mrs Sparrow the chance to draw back. But she showed the letter to Arthur. Without having set eyes on Kitty for at least eleven years, he sent her a formal proposal of marriage. It was a strange reflection on his fatalistic state of mind, in which the study of personal happiness found so little place.

Within three weeks or so Arthur received from Kitty a joyful if still somewhat nervous acceptance:

I should be the most undeserving of beings were I capable of feeling less than gratitude in return for the steadiness of your attachment. . . . To express what I feel at this moment would be quite impossible. I will therefore only say that I am conscious of a degree of happiness of which till now I had no idea.[8]

But ought they not to meet first? asked Kitty.

It is indeed my earnest wish to see you, besides the pleasure it must give me to meet again an early and truly valued friend, I do not think it fair to engage you before you are quite positively certain that I am indeed the very woman you would chuse for a companion a *friend* for life. In so many years I may be much more changed than I am myself conscious of. If when we have met you can tell me . . . that you do not repent having written the letter I am now answering I shall be most happy.

Kitty had thus conscientiously repeated the offer to release him. More than ever now he was bound to ignore it.

A copy of this letter was dispatched by him to Mrs Sparrow – he could not 'bear to part with' the original – together with two other letters which he had received on the same day, presumably from Kitty's brother and mother giving their consent. 'Now my dearest friend,' he wrote to Mrs Sparrow, 'you may wish me joy for I am the happiest man in the world.'

The war in Europe was still on Arthur's mind. He had received his answer from Kitty on 4 November. It was a date of private satisfaction neatly sandwiched between national tidings, first of disaster, then of a tragic triumph. On 20 October Napoleon had eliminated the Austrian army at Ulm. The day after Ulm came Nelson's victory on 21 October at Trafalgar, and on 6 November its announcement in England, together with the heavy news of the hero's death. Despite the almost unbearable loss, the nation recognized that it was Pitt's energy which had made Nelson's triumph possible. On 9 November, Lord Mayor's Day, the Prime Minister was thanked at the Guildhall Banquet for saving Europe. It was Pitt's day. Arthur Wellesley was present to hear the Prime Minister's reply, unforgettable in its brevity and grandeur.

I return you my thanks for the honour you have done me; but Europe is not to be saved by any single man. England saved herself by her exertions and will, as I trust, save Europe by her example.[9]

The Duke of Wellington described it with enthusiasm but equal brevity to his friend Stanhope thirty-three years later: 'That was all; he was scarcely up two minutes; yet nothing could be more perfect.'

One more memorable encounter took place between Pitt and Arthur Wellesley before each set out on his travels – Arthur to the Continent, Pitt to eternity. Taking the young soldier into his confidence, the Prime Minister predicted that Napoleon would be checked as soon as he met with 'a national resistance'; that 'Spain was the place for it, and that then England would intervene.' Ten years later, at a dinner in Paris after Waterloo, Arthur Duke of Wellington recalled this remarkable prophecy.

Was the whole story apocryphal? An unpublished letter from Wellington seems to support it. 'I happen to know', wrote the Duke in 1847, 'that Mr Pitt before he died was in communication with the Spanish government.' The extraordinary thing was that Pitt's young confidant was to become the instrument through which his prophecy was fulfilled.

Arthur was now at Deal, on the point of taking a brigade of infantry to reinforce the thousands of British troops already in north Germany, wasting their time in supporting a Prussian offensive that never came off. He only hoped this expedition would be more fortunate than its predecessor in November – 'but it does not look like it'.[10]

He was right. Napoleon had finally crushed the Austrian and Russian armies at the battle of Austerlitz. The news, when it came, broke the Third Coalition and Pitt's heart. For the few weeks that remained to him, his face was stamped with what his friend William Wilberforce called 'the Austerlitz look'.

That February Arthur Wellesley, without having fired a shot but with a greatly augmented salary, was brought home again.

The outlook seemed grey. Pitt had died on 23 January 1806, just over a week after receiving his friend Lord Wellesley, the newly arrived ex-Governor-General of India, at his bedside. Arthur was put in command of 'a few troops' at Hastings – 'the old landing place of William the Conqueror', as he explained to the historically-minded Malcolm in India.[11] But there was no prospect of it becoming the landing-place of Bonaparte. How could Sir Arthur Wellesley, KB, submit to such paltry employment? asked one of his friends. His answer became famous.

I am *nimmukwallah*, as we say in the East; that is, I have eaten of the King's salt, and, therefore, I conceive it to be my duty to serve with unhesitating zeal and cheerfulness, when and wherever the King or his Government may think proper to employ me.[12]

This was the first time that Arthur Wellesley had expressed an idea so familiar to his ancestors of the Irish Pale – 'retained for life'. That it came to him first from India was significant, for India was his most formative period. Wellington was a man in whom an idea, once it had taken root, struck wide and deep. He became possessed by it. The idea of the retained servant, the *nimmukwallah*, was to send up marvellous shoots.

Hardly had Arthur accepted the fact that he was to be retained at peaceful Hastings, than he was faced by high excitement elsewhere. The trouble that he had predicted in Parliament over the 'Wellesley system' blew up in the person of a retired Anglo-Indian merchant named James Paull. This strange character had made a large fortune in Oudh, partly through 'ingenuity', and partly through the benevolence of Lord Wellesley. In the course of two years Paull's initial gratitude to the Wellesleys had turned into profound vindictiveness. While in Oudh he had researched into the details of Henry's unpopular treaty with the Nabob. He was now busy exposing it in Parliament. His indictment was that the Wellesley administration had squandered public money, including a grant of 30,000 rupees to Arthur in the Deccan. His aim was to have Richard Wellesley impeached.

When Lord Castlereagh advised Arthur to enter the House of Commons and defend his brother from the back-benches, he agreed.

He was offered the seat of Rye and on 1 April declared elected. The Army had granted him leave. A supper, tea and cold collation for the burgesses cost him £269 16s. 0d., with an added £50 for the poor instead of bunting.[13] He used the remainder of his leave to make the journey, so familiar in youth, to Ireland, there to marry Kitty Pakenham.

He had been warned. But the sight of his faded, thirty-four-year-old bride, chaperoned by her maiden aunt, Lady Elizabeth Pakenham, was a shock all the same. 'She has grown ugly, by Jove!' he whispered into the ear of his clergyman brother, Gerald, who was to marry them. Arthur decided afterwards that he had not been 'in the least' in love with her. As he was to tell his friend Mrs Arbuthnot in 1822:

I married her because they asked me to do it & I did not know myself. I thought I should never care for anybody again, & that I shd. be with my army &, in short, I was a fool.[14]

The ceremony took place on 10 April 1806, in the Longfords' same drawing-room that had been the scene of his early, unsuccessful courtship. It was in the parish of St George's, Dublin, where to this day the church register can be seen, containing their two names:

The Honble. Sir Arthur Wellesley, K.B., to the Honble. Catherine Dorothea Sarah Pakenham of this parish by the Rev. G. Wellesley.

The honeymoon was short (Arthur's leave expired after six days) but not too short for Maria Edgworth's curiosity about his appearance to be satisfied. She wrote that he had been seen at Dublin Castle.

Sir Arthur is handsome, very brown, quite bald and a hooked nose.[15]

The baldness must have been an illusion caused by Arthur's close-cropped hair. At a time when powdered hair and *queues* tied with ribbon were the fashion (and obligatory in the services), the eccentric Wellesley kept his hair unpowdered and cut short. He was always remarkable for his plain common sense.

At the end of a week – for Arthur took an extra day's leave – he returned alone to his duties in England. His bride was presented at Court to Queen Charlotte, who made the most of a romantic opportunity.

'I'm happy to see you at my court, so bright an example of constancy. If anybody in this world deserves to be happy, you do. But did you really never write one letter to Sir Arthur Wellesley during his long absence?'

'No, never, Madame.'

'And did you never think of him?'

'Yes, Madame, very often.'[16]

They came to live at 11 Harley Street. There had been a moment when the Wellesleys might have removed into the more spacious house opposite. For Kitty was expecting a baby. But Arthur's careful instincts forbade him to take a more expensive place than necessary. So the agent received a polite note of refusal:

> Hastings, *September 14th, 1806*
>
> Sir,
>
> . . . It appears to me that the house you mention in Harley Street opposite No. 11 is very dear. I shall therefore be satisfied with No. 11 unless you should hear of one that will suit me better at a reasonable expense.[17]

On 19 September he wrote to Richard that his regiment had marched to Portsmouth to embark; 'Yet I have heard nothing of being employed.' So he had asked Lord Grenville to chivvy the Duke of York. 'It is such an object to me to serve with some of the European armies. . . .' Even if it meant leaving Kitty. The earliest surviving letter written to Kitty by Arthur after their marriage shows already the tip of the iceberg floating towards this ill-assorted couple. 'Domestic annoyances' was the name.

> Deal, *December 6th, 1806*
>
> My Dearest Kitty
>
> I send underneath, an order for 50 Pounds; but I wish you would not send it till you want the Money as the Bankers will not have it in their hands, till they have disposed of some stock of mine. George [an unspecified manservant] is to have 14 Shillings a week Board Wages, & if he should want more, or not be satisfied give him Warning; for it is high time to draw a line.
>
> Ever Your's most affectionately
> A.W.[18]

Time to draw a line. . . . Wellington was a great man for drawing lines.

8

The Gilt Potato

The year 1807 began with Arthur still playing his 'most difficult and unpleasant game'[1] on the back-benches. Difficult, because the Ministry he supported – the coalition now called with increasing sarcasm, 'All the Talents' – contained Whigs who were attacking his brother. Unpleasant, because this was precisely the kind of ambivalent situation against which his straightforward nature revolted. Rescue came from an unexpected quarter.

Unhappy Ireland was once more poised to fulfil her ironic role in British politics – the destruction of British governments. There was a violent reawakening of Catholic passions. The Talents Ministry proposed to soothe them by throwing open the Services to all 'Dissenters'. King George III intervened with a resounding no, demanding from his Cabinet a pledge never again to raise the Catholic spectre. The Cabinet replied by resigning on 25 March 1807, the very day on which one of their only really 'talented' measures passed into law – abolition of the slave trade.

The King sent for the infirm 3rd Duke of Portland: he controlled the agonies of the stone with quantities of laudanum, slept prodigiously and hardly ever spoke. He formed a Tory government with Castlereagh back at the War Office and Canning as Foreign Secretary.

Who was to rid the ailing Prime Minister of a turbulent Ireland? At last the Duke of Richmond, as Lord Lieutenant, made the sacrifice. As his Chief Secretary he selected Arthur Wellesley.

This was the end of Wellesley 'neutrality'. From now on he was a Tory, though still with a soldier's aversion to 'party'. The situation in Ireland would prove demanding. But at least the potato this time was suitably gilt. No less than £6,566 a year was earmarked for the Chief Secretary's salary.

Arthur had changed his constituency from Rye to Mitchell in Cornwall after the dissolution of 1806, and was to change it again in 1807 to Newport, Isle of Wight. But these electoral shufflings affected his life a good deal less than an event which took place at 11 Harley Street on 3 February 1807.

Kitty gave birth to a son and heir, Arthur Richard. Sir Arthur was hanging about when Lady Salisbury looked in and invited a by no means reluctant Arthur to hunt at Hatfield. The only surviving letter that refers to his son's birth was written three days afterwards from Hatfield to his mother-in-law, Lady Longford. Arthur expressed his thanks for her attention to Kitty's health 'in the late disturbing & critical moments'.

His frail wife was now in her thirty-sixth year. It was something of a miracle that she had produced a child safely, especially in the prevalent conditions of lying-in chambers. Her mother would have seen to it that all the well-fitting Georgian casements at No. 11 were tightly closed and the room kept stiflingly hot by a roaring fire in the efficient grate. But Kitty survived. She was pregnant again in May, a month after they moved to the Chief Secretary's lodge in Phoenix Park.

Arthur's robust method of allaying Kitty's various fears was kindly meant but more suitable to a subaltern with a slight scratch than a properly anxious mother. When baby Arthur caught measles at only five months old, his father wrote cheerfully from London where he had returned to his Parliamentary duties.

I have no apprehensions for the Meazles being convinced that it is a mild disorder, & one that has no bad consequences, if the Patient is well taken care of as it is going off.[2]

To Wellington, illness was always something to be 'got the better of' with as little fuss as possible.

A week later an outcrop of 'domestic annoyances' caused a few mild protests from Arthur to his 'dearest Kitty'.

London, *July 25th, 1807*

. . . I am much concerned that you should have thought of concealing from me any want of money which you might have experienced. . . . I acknowledge that the conclusion I draw from your conduct upon the occasion is that you must be mad, or you must consider me to be a Brute, & most particularly fond & avaricious of money. Once for all you require no permission to talk to me upon any subject you please; all that I request is that a piece of work may not be made about trifles . . . & that you may not go into tears because I don't think them deserving of an uncommon degree of attention.[3]

Once for all – trifles – tears – mad – Brute. The approach seemed somewhat formidable. Kitty was not mad nor Arthur a brute. But his forthright attempts to set her on the right road 'once for all' merely scared her into further incompetence.

The Ireland to which Arthur had returned as Chief Secretary was not the country he had left. There was now no reason why he should ever want to set eyes on Dangan again. It had been rented by a nationalist in order to have a mansion for entertaining Napoleon, when the latter came to liberate Ireland. (The nationalist's loyalist brother had prepared a cage for Bonaparte in Cork.) By 1807 Dangan was no longer kept up like a gentleman's residence. Its fine trees were hacked down, their stumps left standing like gravestones, its walks overgrown – not quite the idea of a Chief Secretary's early home.

If Wellington was ever chaffed for being an Irishman and replied with a notorious quip, it was just possibly during this period:

Because a man is born in a stable that does not make him a horse.

Mornington House had fared better than Dangan, but like all great places after the Union, its value had dropped catastrophically, by 1802 to £2,500. There was no lack of people to tell Arthur how Dublin had been ruined by the Union. He agreed with Kitty's friends, the Edgeworths, in deploring the landlords who had removed themselves to England after the Union and thus increased the evils of absenteeism.

Only the wretched cabins remained eternally unaltered, with the same ragged families inside, the same sprouting weeds on the roof, and the same holy pictures on the walls, mingled with the prints of the exquisite singer, Mrs Billington, who had taken Ireland by storm in 1783 and was reputed mistress of the Duke of Portland in his heyday.

In this familiar yet changed scene, it was Arthur Wellesley's overriding task to distribute the Irish patronage. It had to be done so as to produce the maximum number of bought-up Government supporters in Parliament. For patronage in both parties was still the great adhesive, as Wellesley recognized:

We must keep our majority in Parliament, and . . . that can be done only by a good use of the patronage of the government.[4]

Dubashery no doubt, but of the most hallowed kind. And when a job-hunter went too far (like a certain Mr Meeke, whose name belied his nature) Arthur could always show a touch of the old iron:

You are rather high in your demand of an office . . . but I hope to place your friend if he be more moderate than you are.[5]

The new Chief Secretary had arrived at the Castle just in time for the 1807 elections. Wexford, after great exertions, produced an unexpected

Tory success. The first Tory candidate, it is true, got rid of his Whig opponent by killing him in a duel; but as this was 'reckoned fair in Ireland', wrote Arthur, 'it created no sensation' and another Tory candidate was elected.[6] A hard-pressed colonel in Clare, however, could see no hope of being elected unless Sir Arthur took a hand in the removal of the hostile local sheriff. But again the Chief Secretary had to draw a line. 'I am sorry to tell you,' he wrote, 'that there is no precedent whatever for the dismissal of a sheriff ... excepting for gross misconduct.'[7]

In agreeable contrast to these and many other difficulties was the contest for Downpatrick in Ulster of the young lawyer, John Wilson Croker, a great find on Arthur's part. On 21 May the Tories of Down were in the lead and Croker wrote: 'The popery war-whoop was sung against us but we out-sang them.'[8] By the 23rd they were home and dry – with a majority of twenty-five out of 141.

And so entered into Parliament, into history, literature and above all into Wellington's life-story, John Wilson Croker. Posterity must do him a kind of homage for the incomparable memory which enabled him to record so much of Wellington's conversation in his master's authentic voice.

The joy of Croker's victory was somewhat impaired by the threat of a petition against corrupt practices and an avalanche of solicitations.[9] Lady Elizabeth Pakenham, Kitty's spinster aunt, requested a job for a friend. Arthur explained his 'delicate situation' and suggested she should apply instead to her nephew, Lord Longford; to which she answered that Longford, alas, had a rule never to solicit except for his own brothers. Lord Wellesley desired a post in the Revenue 'at an early date' for Tim Hickey, his boatman in India; Arthur's mother sent four pages of demands. It was almost a pleasure to receive his brother William's more relaxed appeal:

I hope the other applications I have made will be attended to in time. . . . Sydenham* was discovered viewing Blenheim the other day with a whore – they went by the names of Mr. and Mrs. Thompson – O the Profligacy of the Age!!![10]

How did Arthur Wellesley defend the profligacy of political practices? He was never very convincing and indeed admitted that they could not be defended 'in the abstract' but – in Ireland, however, 'in my day at least, almost every man of mark in the state had his price'.

---

* Thomas Sydenham, Lord Wellesley's aide-de-camp in India and a family friend.

Fortunately for Arthur, patronage was not his sole concern. The Government's road was also paved with good intentions towards the Catholics.

In an interview with a Catholic nobleman, Lord Fingall, Wellesley promised that the Catholic laws, though not at present open to reform, would be administered by him 'with mildness and good temper'.[11] Nevertheless, despite all the mildness and good temper, an aggressive young Catholic lawyer named Daniel O'Connell began to organize the disaffected. There was plenty of material to hand. At country fairs maypoles were being set up as 'trees of liberty', and even among those too old to fight, the Castle found 'a deep rooted antipathy to Great Britain'.[12]

A resounding new triumph for Bonaparte abroad had as usual fanned Irish hopes. On 29 June 1807 Wellesley heard of 'a great action' having taken place on the 14th.[13] It was the rout of Russia at Friedland. In July the two Emperors, Napoleon and Alexander, met on their celebrated raft in the River Nieman at Tilsit.

'I hate the English as much as you do yourself,' said the Tsar as he stepped aboard.

'If that is the case, then peace is already made,' said Napoleon. They proceeded to divide the Continent between them.

The defence of Ireland had always been one of the Chief Secretary's duties and the 'summit conference' at Tilsit turned Wellesley's thoughts, nothing loth, towards his true profession. He had toured from Dublin to Cork with his brother William in July and August of the year before, visiting martello towers, barracks and rivers. Now he used his experience to rule out more martello towers and simply recommend a larger naval station at Bantry Bay.

I lay it down as decided that Ireland, in a view to military operations, must be considered as an enemy's country. . . .[14]

This was precisely how he had written about Malabar in India. Throughout his adult life he had moved between two British ascendancies, in the East and the West, each, as he was honest enough to admit, maintained by force. Of the army in the East he had written:

They feel they are a distinct and superior class to the rest of the world that surrounds them; . . . and they show in what manner nations consisting of many millions are governed by 30,000 strangers.[15]

Irish Protestants had the same 'high notions', being possessors of the soil, as he often said, 'by right of conquest'. While he had been away in India, many liberalizing ideas had percolated from France to Britain, even to the ruling classes. They had not reached India. Arthur Wellesley was untouched by French heresies. This was his misfortune. But he was compensated by remaining, throughout the gloomiest years of England's struggle against France, completely free from any uncertainties or fears. At all times he was prepared to fight.

Some time before the end of May 1807 Arthur Wellesley heard that the Government were yet again planning an expedition to the Continent, though its object was secret. Immediately he determined to leave Ireland. Otherwise people would say that he had avoided active service 'in order to hold a high civil office'. The Chief Secretaryship was a highly gilt potato.

Within ten days it was settled that Arthur should leave Ireland at once but carry on his Irish business in London until the expedition actually sailed. Several letters went to Admiral Tom Pakenham, one asking him to settle with Kitty about her going to Coolure. There were to be no 'tears over trifles' in this quarter. He told the Lord Lieutenant:

I have not written to Lady Wellesley upon [the expedition]; and it is as well not to say anything to her about it till it will be positively settled that we are to go.[16]

Keeping his excitable wife in the dark until the last moment was to become his rule.

Another letter to Tom informed him that the troops from Ireland for the expedition must be in England by the 22nd, so would he help 'hurry the fellows away'? If any of the 'fellows' were Marines, Arthur was responsible for a proposed reform in their sleeping quarters. He had written the year before that if their numbers were to be kept up, some arrangement would be needed 'for stowing them in the Barracks'. Hammocks would be the best mode, since 'the beastly practice of two great hulking fellows stark naked sleeping together would be done away with'.[17] He was to go on the expedition, and Kitty had to be told at last. Just before embarkation he sent her a loving note from Sheerness to say that Lord Longford was at Deal to see off his young brother, Hercules Pakenham, who would come under Arthur's command. Edward Pakenham also was going. 'God Bless you,' he ended, 'my dearest Kitty.'

Thankful to be off, he embarked on 31 July 1807 in the *Prometheus*. His destination was to all but the Government and Service chiefs, unknown.

Through channels kept strictly to himself George Canning, the exceptionally active Foreign Secretary, had discovered certain 'secret articles' in the Treaty of Tilsit. The Emperor had already decreed in 1806 the closure of all Continental ports to British trade. After Tilsit, the noose was to be fatally tightened by the surrender to him, if necessary, of Europe's remaining neutral fleets, those of Portugal and Denmark. Napoleon might even use the fleet at Copenhagen to invade England. With brilliant foresight – or unethical effrontery, depending on how the total situation is regarded – Canning ordered neutral Denmark to place her excellent fleet in Britain's safe custody until the end of the war. Otherwise he would get it on the same terms by force. The indignant Danes refused and the British Navy set sail.

At the time, Canning's 'courage and initiative', as Professor Asa Briggs calls it, struck many Whigs and Radicals as being utterly reprehensible. Charles Napier, a serving soldier of twenty-five, wrote, 'now every one says – *Poor Danes!* A soldier cannot fight an enemy he pities with proper spirit.'[18] But to Wellesley and the majority then, and to the majority of historians now, Britain's desperate necessity was rightly Canning's law.

The actual operation was quick and fairly clean, for British regulars were fighting the Danish militia. Lord Cathcart led the expedition with 'a steady old guardsman' named Sir Harry Burrard as his second-in-command.[19] Sir David Baird commanded a division and Sir Arthur Wellesley a brigade. The latter was to play a crucial part.

On 16 August he was ordered to land with an advance guard not far from Copenhagen; the army followed and the city was duly invested. Ten days later a sudden danger loomed in the shape of a relieving force of Danish regulars. Wellesley was given the task of cutting it off. This he proceeded to do, clearing the enemy out of their entrenched positions at Köge, a town south-west of Copenhagen. There were no further attempts to relieve the city.

Wellesley's whole action cost him only 172 casualties, though the Danes fared a good deal worse. Now it was a question of whether to bombard and storm the beautiful city, if, as seemed certain, it would not surrender. Wellesley felt they ought to find some less barbarous way of reducing it. Fortunately, after three days of a sporadic cannonade, the garrison surrendered on 5 September. To Bonaparte's rage, the British had thus narrowly forestalled his own army of 30,000 men waiting at Hamburg to take over Denmark themselves.

Major-General Sir Arthur Wellesley, KB, as a reward for gallantry, was appointed one of the three British Commissioners to arrange the terms of capitulation. During the Danish campaign, however, he heard that the Lord Lieutenant insisted on having him back. He was still Chief Secretary.

Three consequences of this brief martial interlude were important to him: further experience in handling the population of an invaded country, assertion of his own authority, and the association of his name at last with service in Europe.

His kindness towards the luckless Danes brought him a rewarding letter from one of his Danish opposite numbers who was 'penetrated with gratitude for your human and generous conduct'.[20]

One other event connected with the Copenhagen campaign was to prove of some importance to Wellesley. Lord Grosvenor had taken with him on the expedition a favourite mare named Lady Catherine, got by John Bull out of a mare by the Rutland Arabian. She was found to be in foal and sent home. When her offspring, a strong chestnut, was born later in England, he was called Copenhagen.

Arthur had reached England on 30 September. For the next eighteen months it was back to the old Irish treadmill, with intervals for performing his duties in London or cosseting Kitty. 'Lady Wellesley,' he informed the Irish Chancellor on 7 December, 'is in a situation which will not permit her to go from the neighbourhood of Town at present.'[21] On 16 January 1808 she presented him with a second son, Charles.

The threat of invasion had once more receded, making Ireland a little less of 'an enemy's country'. During that autumn of 1808, with the Danish fleet safely in English harbours, the Portuguese navy had also been rescued at the eleventh hour from Napoleon's clutches. He had declared war on Portugal on 20 October. As the French conquerors – General Junot and his tatterdemalion troops – staggered into Lisbon from Spain, they heard that the coveted ships, with the Portuguese royal family on board, had vanished over the horizon to Brazil two days before.

So Wellesley was able to devote himself again to 'mild government'. He considered how reforms in schooling might draw Catholic and Protestant children together; he wondered whether the tithe and rent problems might not be solved by eradicating absentee clergy and landlords; he prepared an embargo on corn exports in case of a potato famine.

But his heart was not in it. Or rather, the task of reforming Ireland was too heart-breaking. He wanted to leave. 'I shall be happy to aid the government in any manner they please,' he had written to Canning somewhat desperately on 17 October 1807, 'and am ready to set out for any part of the world at a moment's notice.'[22]

Successive British governments had not been backward in devising wildcat assaults all over the world. Now Canning had a scheme for bringing in the New World to defeat the tyrant of the Old. Luckily, Wellesley also was brought in. He was required to cooperate with the emissary of Venezuelan revolutionaries, General Miranda, in planning an insurrection in his native Spanish America against Napoleon's ally, Spain. Wellesley at once pointed out some of the project's more disastrous flaws. Yet as the youngest lieutenant-general in the Army, promoted in April 1808, Arthur Wellesley wished as ardently as any Minister to take advantage of a crack in Napoleon's colossal empire. In June 1808 he gladly accepted the command of 9,000 men assembled at Cork to invade Spanish America.

Meanwhile the chasm into which Napoleon was ultimately to fall had opened in old Spain the month before. Early in May 1808 the popular Spanish king, Ferdinand VII, was summoned by Napoleon to Bayonne, forced to abdicate and replaced by the King of Naples, Joseph Bonaparte. Patriotic Spain spontaneously burst into flame. This was high-toned insurrection. This Wellesley could applaud – 'there was advantage to be derived from the temper of the people of Spain'. This was Napoleon's crack of doom.

All of which would be 'much facilitated', as Wellesley wrote dryly but with true vision, not by sailing away to South America, but by 'alarming' Bonaparte at home.

The arrival of a Spanish deputation in England the very next month, June 1808, and a Portuguese one in July urging joint attacks on the common enemy, made sure that the opportunity should indeed not be missed. The destination of Arthur's whole force at Cork was switched to the Iberian peninsula. In a state as near to euphoria as Arthur ever reached, he made his last preparations in London. They included a stormy interview with General Miranda.

An extraordinary interview was held by Arthur with Father James Robertson, OSB, the monk who became a British secret agent. A distinguished Spanish general, the Marquess de la Romana, and his impressive army were being used by Napoleon as part of his occupation forces in Denmark. If someone could only get a message to Romana describing the new situation in Spain and the need for him there (four spies had already tried and died), the British Navy would do the rest. Arthur invited the monk to Harley Street on 31 May and broached the subject with characteristic force.

'Tell me, Mr Robertson, are you a man of courage?'

'Try me, Sir Arthur.'

'That is what we mean to do.'[23]

'Romana' Robertson, as he came to be called, carried out his mission brilliantly after many thrilling adventures. As a result, the fleet was able to conjure 9,000 excellent soldiers out of Denmark and into Spain and to present Arthur Wellesley with his most valued Spanish general.

John Wilson Croker attended a farewell dinner at 11 Harley Street alone with Sir Arthur and Lady Wellesley. After Kitty had withdrawn, Croker found that his host had fallen into a brown study. What was Sir Arthur thinking about?

Why, to say the truth, I am thinking of the French that I am going to fight: I have not seen them since the campaign in Flanders, when they were capital soldiers, and a dozen years of victory under Buonaparte must have made them better still. They have besides, it seems, a new system of strategy which has out-manoeuvred and over-whelmed all the armies of Europe. 'Tis enough to make one thoughtful; but no matter.

Sir Arthur had been thinking aloud. Now he made a memorable prediction.

My die is cast, they may overwhelm me, but I don't think they will out-manoeuvre me. First, because I am not afraid of them, as everybody else seems to be; and secondly, because if what I hear of their system of manoeuvre, is true, I think it a false one as against steady troops. I suspect all the continental armies were more than half beaten before the battle was begun – I, at least, will not be frightened beforehand.*

Arthur had faithfully served his apprenticeship in India and Ireland. Through all he had been *nimmukwallah*. Now, in his fortieth year, he was ready to leap on to the world stage. His aims were limited to what was termed 'a particular service' – the 'absolute evacuation of the Peninsula by the troops of France' – his army was small but good, his energies only waited to be released. Napoleon, about to enter his fortieth year, was master of that stage and had been for years; his armies were enormous, his ambition megalomaniac. In the year 1808 each took a decisive turning: Napoleon towards his downfall, Wellesley towards fulfilment.

* Croker, vol. I, pp. 12–13 and Greville, 14 Dec. 1839, a shortened version of the above.

9

My Die is Cast

A problem faced Wellesley at Cork. The impression made by his armament was a mixed one.

His 9,000 men were to be reinforced on landing in the Peninsula by 5,000 troops now afloat off Spain, under his future second-in-command, General Sir Brent Spencer. But Wellesley was desperately short of horses for cavalry, artillery and supplies. His small wagon-train had to be deflected from its original duty of putting down 'Thrashers' and 'Liberty Rangers' in Ireland, and he could count on fewer than 350 cavalry sabres. At least there were 229 drummers and trumpeters. It was to be hoped that the cities of the Peninsula would resemble Jericho.

Wellesley's infantry, on the other hand – the 'steady troops' of his last talk with Croker – were the best England had assembled in memory. Britain had young champions in John Moore and Arthur Wellesley. The Government had also increased the militia to 200,000 men, some of whom would volunteer for the regular army serving abroad and make the best of soldiers, and had added 45,000 new recruits to the regular army in 1807–8. In that army there was henceforth to be short hair. Pigtails were cut off, sponges issued and powdered heads washed. Arthur Wellesley's cropped head would no longer be mistaken for baldness.

At the famous Shorncliffe camp, Sir John Moore had trained his unique Light Division of highly disciplined men in whom individual initiative was at the same time encouraged. At Woolwich, Colonel Shrapnell had invented a secret new weapon officially known as spherical case shot, though it was later called by his name, generally minus the last letter ('shrapnel'). When exploded in the air by several consecutive fuses, it had a long range and wide spray of bullets which the enemy were to find 'very dreadful' and Wellesley 'of great benefit'.

By no means all the great Peninsular names were as yet with his army, but there was Rowland Hill, the beloved 'Daddy' Hill who looked like a benevolent coachman and with whom Wellesley expressed himself extremely rejoiced to be serving again:

... and I hope that we shall have more to do than we had on the last occasion [Copenhagen] on which we were together.[1]

On his staff was Lord Westmorland's son and heir, Lord Burghersh, a dashing aristocrat of twenty-four with a mop of wavy hair. For aide-de-camp, a handsome, apple-cheeked young man of nineteen had been recommended by the Duke of Richmond, a young man who was to make smooth, as far as possible, the path of Wellesley's whole life. It was not only Fitzroy Somerset's intelligence, but his phenomenal truthfulness and exactitude in describing a situation and carrying out an order, that Arthur prized. Dr Hume, another man destined to play no small part in his life, public and private, was in charge of the wounded.

Up to the very end Wellesley was still wrestling with Irish patronage – who should be Deputy Warehouse Keeper of Stamped Goods? The Warehouse Keeper of Unstamped Goods, to be sure – but at last the time came for his waiting troops to be brought back to their transports from excursions, exercise and billets ashore, thoughtfully organized by Wellesley and Hill.[2] On 12 July, one day ahead of his army, Wellesley put to sea in the *Donegal*. He intended to employ part of the passage in learning Spanish from Lady Eleanor Butler's prayer book, a sensible parting gift from the Ladies of Llangollen.

Having transferred on the 13th into the fast cruiser, *Crocodile*, General Wellesley was soon in contact with the Spanish Junta at Corunna, where he found a strong patriotic disinclination for British officers or men. Wellesley could not yet be expected to recognize this as a danger signal. He wrote home enthusiastically: 'It is impossible to describe the sentiment which prevails throughout the country.'[3] On the 24th he reached Oporto, where there was an ardent British 'factory' based on the historic port wine trade, and a no less ardent bishop, head of the Supreme Junta of Portugal. To him Wellesley allotted the pastoral task of collecting hundreds of oxen and pack-mules for his transport, while the Portuguese general, Bernadin Freire, was persuaded to march south to Leiria on the Lisbon road, and there meet Wellesley's army with stores of food and 6,000 troops.

Meanwhile Wellesley had sailed southwards to confer with Admiral Cotton, near Lisbon, on the proposed landing of his army in Mondego Bay. Anchorages were strictly limited on 'this iron coast', as Wellesley called it, while Lisbon was defended by a string of seventeenth-century but still 'respectable' forts in the Tagus estuary.[4] At Figueira da Foz, on the other hand, where the River Mondego poured into the Atlantic, there was an ancient fort of golden stone which the valiant students of nearby Coimbra University had seized from the French. Admiral Cotton put in some of his marines, and Wellesley decided to land there. He reached Mondego Bay on 30 July. Here the old demon of supersession caught up with him once more.

A letter from Lord Castlereagh awaited him marked 'Secret'. It informed him that the French army in Portugal under General Junot was much stronger than at first suspected; that the British expeditionary force was therefore to be increased by 15,000 men; that, finally, the command of such a large armament would have to pass from Wellesley to Sir Hew Dalrymple, with Sir Harry Burrard as second-in-command. Wellesley should continue his preparations against Lisbon without waiting for the arrival of Sir Hew and Sir Harry; but the list of new commanders finished with Sir Arthur Wellesley at the bottom.

Sir Hew Dalrymple, nearing sixty, had only once seen active service – in the disastrous Flanders campaign of 1793–4. He sent Wellesley a report of affairs in Spain no less damping than his own presence was soon to be in Portugal: the Spanish would not admit their British Allies to any of their fortresses, and General Spencer had failed signally to conciliate them.

Wellesley's reaction to Sir Hew's and Castlereagh's letters was characteristic. 'I hope that I shall have beat Junot,' he wrote to his confidant, the Duke of Richmond, 'before any of them arrive, then they will do as they please with me.' On 31 July, in anticipation of an immediate landing, he issued his first General Order of the Peninsular War:

The troops are to understand that Portugal is a country friendly to his Majesty. . . .

This uncompromising assertion was to stand between the soldiers and a multitude of favourite sins, beginning with robbery and ending with rape. It was to be repeated endlessly and disobeyed as often; it was to cost many soldiers a brutal flogging and not a few their lives. But without Portuguese cooperation the war would have been lost.

There were to be six women to every hundred men (drawn by lot before embarkation amid screams and swooning), the men to have one pound of biscuits and one pound of meat every day, with wine added if the meat was salt; the women to be on half-rations and no wine, however salt the meat.

The landings began on 1 August. As was feared, several boats capsized in the roaring surf and a number of unfortunates were drowned. The survivors scrambled over the red granite rocks, burning and bare except for tufts of samphire. Next day Wellesley issued a stirring proclamation to the inhabitants:

> PEOPLE OF PORTUGAL
> The time is arrived to
> rescue your country

The landings were all completed by 8 August. On the 10th Wellesley struck camp and entered Leiria next day after a twelve-mile march made intolerable to his unhardened troops by deep sand, blistering sun and the celebrated nerve-racking shriek from the wheels of wooden ox-carts.* Under the lofty magnificence of Leiria Castle, Wellesley and Freire met in fierce dispute. Freire insisted that the march to Lisbon should be through the protecting mountains to the eastward, Wellesley by the exposed westward road which alone would keep him in touch with his store ships. Nor could Wellesley supply Freire's 6,000 men as well as his own. In the end it was agreed, though still with many growls, that Wellesley should arm, feed and take with him just seventeen hundred of Freire's light troops.

Junot meanwhile had sent a French veteran, General Henri François Comte de Laborde, to hold up Wellesley's advance on Lisbon at the first suitable battleground. So Wellesley reached Alcobaça and hurried on towards Obidos, a village of one long street. Just before he arrived the first engagement of the Peninsular War took place.

It was what Wellesley called 'a little affair of advance posts', when a detachment of the 95th Rifles successfully drove off French pickets at the windmill of Brilos, but then 'foolishly' entering into a pursuit, ran into the French rearguard. General Spencer went to their rescue, but not before some loss. 'The troops behaved remarkably well,' wrote Wellesley indulgently, 'but not with great prudence.'[5]

Laborde had drawn up his 4,000 men in front of the whitewashed hamlet of Roliça, about eight miles away in the centre of a wide valley

---

* Virgil spoke of '*stridentia plaustra*'; the Portuguese had an onomatopoeic word for it, '*chiar*'.

surrounded by a horse-shoe of rugged mountains. Over the eastward range his colleague General Loison might appear at any moment with 5,000 reinforcements. It was Wellesley's aim to strike before the second army arrived.

At dawn next morning, 17 August 1808, he marched his men into the plain and deployed the centre of his three scarlet columns before the admiring French with great pomp and noise, in order to distract their gaze from two other columns which were to steal right and left around the horseshoe and take them in the rear. Laborde, however, was too capable a veteran to be caught. He dexterously withdrew to a second position of immense strength behind the village. Suddenly Colonel Lake of the 29th, without waiting for the rest of the British centre, dashed up a narrow gully and miraculously reached the top, only to find himself cut off behind Laborde's lines. He himself was killed and almost all his men were casualties before help could reach him. His action changed the battle of Roliça from an inconsiderable occasion to a perilous drama.

On realizing the disaster, Wellesley at once ordered a general advance. A swarm of British skirmishers doggedly fought their way up the mountain clefts. The infantry followed close behind and took over the whole westward half of the ridge, while the British left also began to close in. There was no option for Laborde but to retreat. For a time he withdrew in good order; then the dams of discipline burst and his army poured away, abandoning three of their five guns.

Wellesley described the battle with awe rather than triumph. It was 'a most desperate' action; 'I never saw such fighting as in the pass', and the French showed 'their best style'.[6] Clearly it would need something more than Roliça to drive the French out of Portugal.

Wellesley awoke from a night in the open near Roliça to hear that 4,000 reinforcements from England were off the coast. He at once marched to cover their disembarkation at the mouth of the River Maceira from the hills round Vimeiro, a peaceful village with a stone bridge over the Maceira. The landings took place in the pink-bouldered estuary on the 18th, 19th and 20th, not without the usual drownings. On the evening of the last day, the sloop *Brazen* brought in the first of the lieutenant-generals destined to supersede Wellesley, Sir Harry Burrard.

Wellesley immediately rowed out through the surf to propound to Sir Harry his plan for next day – a swift march south to Mafra, the important royal town north of Lisbon. From Mafra he would outflank

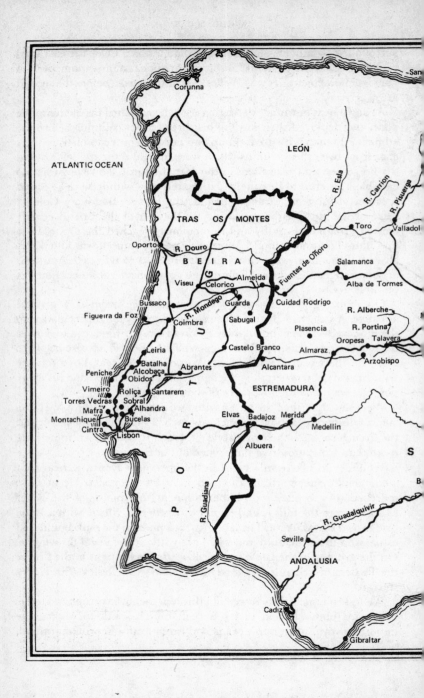

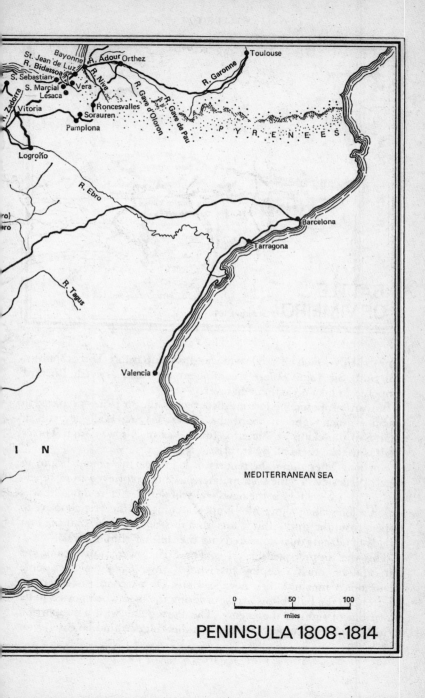

PENINSULA 1808-1814

MEDITERRANEAN SEA

Toulouse
Bayonne
St. Jean de Luz
R. Adour
Orthez
R. Bidassoa
R. Niva
S. Sebastian
Vera
R. Gave d'Oloron
S. Marcial
R. Gave de Pau
Lesaca
R. Garonne
R. Zadorra
Roncesvalles
Vitoria
Sorauren
Pamplona
P Y R E N E E S
Logroño
R. Ebro
Barcelona
(ro)
ero
Tarragona
R. Tagus
Valencia
I   N

0   50   100
miles

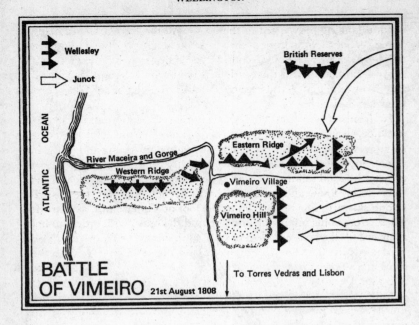

Wellesley

Junot

British Reserves

OCEAN

ATLANTIC

River Maceira and Gorge

Western Ridge

Eastern Ridge

Vimeiro Village

Vimeiro Hill

BATTLE
OF VIMEIRO 21st August 1808

To Torres Vedras and Lisbon

Junot's army which he had learnt was drawn up before Torres Vedras. But until Sir John Moore's contingent had also arrived, Burrard proposed to take no action whatever.

Burrard proposed but fortune disposed. While Sir Harry prepared to spend a quiet night on board the *Brazen*, leaving Wellesley still in charge of the camp at Vimeiro, Junot was on his way from Torres Vedras to take them all by surprise.

Not long after midnight reports of a French movement began to reach Wellesley. To the Commander-in-Chief, reprieved from super-session for twelve hours, the news was wonderful. Before dawn he was up on a long ridge above his camp, watching for the French army to appear from the south. But it was from the east, at 9 am, that the first clouds of tell-tale dust appeared and the shifting glint of arms.

This was an unlooked-for crisis. The French were now turning his left; and he must redeploy his whole army. Coolly he led some thousands of men into their new positions. On a second, easterly ridge he drew up the bulk of his army, ordering the men when posted to lie down out of sight of the enemy. The Portuguese with a supporting British brigade occupied a smaller parallel ridge behind, in case Junot tried a flanking movement to the north. All these troops were behind Vimeiro. South, or in front of the village, rose a round green hump with a flat top, known as Vimeiro hill. Here Wellesley posted the rest of his army. And here began the battle of Vimeiro on 21 August 1808, with the advance of four dense French columns, their right led by Laborde, their left by Loison.

In front of the Grenadiers, according to hallowed Napoleonic practice, swarmed a darting mass of *tirailleurs* (skirmishers), supported by guns, whose ritual act consisted in stinging, flustering and confusing the enemy lines until they were sufficiently distraught to fall an easy prey to the solid infantry behind. This time none of the magic worked.

Wellesley knew all about the peril of French *tirailleurs*. He posted a strong skirmish line of his own at the foot of Vimeiro hill, armed with rifles. Most of his infantry waited behind the crest, with orders to hold their fire till the last moment. In front of them twelve guns were drawn up against the first French group of seven. As the French went in they were met in rapid succession by obstinate rifle-fire, a brief cannonade and then, suddenly, a thin red line of British infantry – 'thin' because only two deep, so that every weapon could fire – delivering its 'rolling' musket-fire company by company down the whole line and gradually wrapping itself round the head of the leading French column, until its deadly hail poured into the French flanks as well as front. The French general tried in vain to form his huge rectangular column (thirty men broad by forty-two deep) into line, and thus bring the rear ranks of his muskets into play. The British fire was too hot for this manoeuvre. His column began to •disintegrate. All at once the French bundled themselves headlong to the bottom of Vimeiro hill. After the battle a pair of victims of this savage fight, one French and one British, were found in deathly embrace skewered together by the same bayonet.

Three more French columns advanced against the hill, only to meet the same lapping, murderous fire from the thin red lines. They lost eleven guns and had a first taste of the new 'shrapnel' fired from British howitzers. The next stages, however, gave Wellesley some bad moments. After a bout of unpleasant street-fighting in Vimeiro village, he decided to try a cavalry charge on the disordered French columns. The 20th Light Dragoons accordingly dashed forward at a breakneck gallop that ended in fiasco, the horses bolting, most of their riders casualties, the colonel dead and little damage inflicted on the enemy. This was the first but far from the last time that Wellesley was to see British cavalry go out of control.

On the ridge behind Vimeiro fighting had broken out at 10.30 am, half an hour before the assaults on the hill collapsed. Here the British repeated their earlier tactical triumphs. Springing up unexpectedly from behind a precipitous crest, 3,000 British muskets drove three French brigades down into the valley and away to the north of the ridge. Here there was a temporary setback, when the French were reinforced, but by bringing the 29th round himself to attack the French right flank, Wellesley again managed to establish a column *v.* line duel, which ended for the fifth time that day in a mob of broken French infantry fleeing down a blood-stained slope. This was the moment to turn a defeat into a rout.

Wellesley galloped impetuously up to Burrard, who had by now arrived and raised his hat. The soldiers watched him intently. Then in a loud voice clearly audible to his staff Wellesley exclaimed:

'Sir Harry, now is your time to advance. The enemy are completely beaten, we shall be in Lisbon in three days.'

Sir Harry hesitated and Wellesley pressed him again.

'We have a large body of troops which have not been in action; let us move them from the right to Torres Vedras, and I will follow the French with the left.'[7]

The French had in fact fled eastwards, leaving Torres Vedras and the road to Lisbon open. It was Sir Harry's chance.

But Sir Harry had said no once and he said it again. 'Wait for Moore.' It was not a pun but a fatuity. Wellesley turned away in disgust, remarking to his officers that they all might as well go and shoot red-legged partridges.

The glow of Vimeiro nevertheless hung over Wellesley for another few hours. In jubilant letters to his brother William and the Duke of Richmond he described himself as 'the Child of Fortune'.[8] Thanks to Junot he had been able to prove, what he had long suspected, that the fabled French shock tactics would melt before steady troops, well led. Richmond responded in due course with equal zest. There was 'something whimsically providential', he reflected, in Junot forcing a glorious victory upon Arthur at the very moment the command was passing. 'You must have bribed him to attack you when he did.'

By the end of next day the glow had vanished. The vultures and the effluvia from the dead made the whole army yearn to march. From having been 'the most fortunate of men', Wellesley suddenly found himself in a 'very delicate' position. On 22 August the army's third Commander-in-Chief in twenty-four hours, Sir Hew Dalrymple, took over; he totally ignored his young subordinate's plans for an advance, though the army still came to Wellesley on every detail, refusing to take orders from anyone but 'their old General'. In fact, the two men were from the start at loggerheads.[9]

Junot now deftly intervened. Choosing his subtlest negotiator, the remarkably ugly General Kellermann, he sent him under a flag of truce to propose a treaty for the total evacuation of Portugal by the French. As the Frenchmen galloped into Sir Hew's camp there was a sudden alarm at what was thought to be a surprise attack. From Wellesley's point of view an attack would have been better than the intrigue into which he now slithered.

To cut a long and dismal episode short – the kind of episode that Wellesley always detested – terms for a forty-eight-hour armistice were agreed to on 22 August, that greatly benefited the victorious British army, moderately assisted the defeated French and desperately shocked the uncomprehending peoples of Portugal and Britain. All the French-occupied fortresses were given up and the royal flag of Portugal waved once more on St George's Castle, Lisbon. Since Burrard had thrown away the chance of annihilating Junot, every responsible man, and more especially Wellesley, welcomed this as the only other way of freeing Portugal at once and absolutely.

Scarcely anyone, however, and certainly not Wellesley, accepted Kellermann's detailed interpretation of the main agreement. While it was inevitable that the French army should be repatriated, together with their property, and in British ships, it was a peculiarly disagreeable shock that French 'property' was found to include church plate melted down, two state carriages belonging to the Duke of Sussex and the Portuguese royal family's cambric sheets from Mafra run up into shirts for Loison.

The proposed armistice terms of the 22nd were read over to Wellesley at Sir Hew's request and criticized by him; they were then drafted by Sir Hew and Kellermann alone, Wellesley having left the room. Kellermann signed. Sir Hew was about to sign also when Kellermann astutely suggested that Wellesley should sign instead, since he and Kellermann were of corresponding rank. Kellermann's more devious reason was to get the actual victor of Vimeiro thoroughly involved in a treaty which he knew would be unpopular and might be rejected.

Against his better judgement, without even reading the final draft, Wellesley signed. He was afterwards to regret his action deeply. Why did he do it?

His first motive was one of principle: he agreed with the armistice in principle (though not in detail). Second, 'good nature', as he himself wryly called it: a wish to do what 'they' asked. It was a weakness of character, perhaps, and one that seems strange and inconsistent in a so-called Iron Duke. Until it is remembered that only machines, like the steam-boat called *Iron Duke*, are made of the same metal throughout.

The armistice was duly transformed into a convention. It was ratified on 31 August by Sir Hew and by Junot. Next day the British headquarters were moved nearer Lisbon to Cintra. Wellesley neither negotiated nor read a word of the final document (though of course he knew the gist) until it was published in the *London Gazette Extraordinary* on 16 September 1808, as the Convention of Cintra. It created a furore.

A very popular radical journal, the *Political Register*, launched a bitter attack on all three generals, asking whether they could even be described as curs who allowed a mastiff (Junot) to carry off their bone? 'No, not so; for they complacently carry the bone for him.'[10] Three stanzas of Byron's best invective in *Childe Harold* were devoted to it:

> Britannia sickens, Cintra! at thy name;
> And folks in office at the mention fret,
> And fain would blush, if blush they could for shame.
> How will Posterity the deed proclaim!

Posterity has in fact proclaimed the deed extremely sensible, though in September 1808 everyone was feeling 'sickened', and none more so than Arthur himself. 'I am sick of the state of public Affairs,'[11] he wrote to William on 6 September, and to Richmond on the 27th, 'since the arrival of the great generals, we appear to have been palsied, and every thing has gone wrong.' But there was one audacious thing he could still do for his devoted army before he went home to face the music. He could make sure they had a commander worthy of them. Sir John Moore was now in Portugal and clearly the man. First the political breach between Moore and the Government, who sensed in him a taint of Opposition, must be healed. Wellesley, believing himself to be the ideal go-between, wrote to Moore offering his services.

... the Commander in Chief must be changed, and the country and the army naturally turn their eyes to you. . . . Although I hold a high office under Government [Chief Secretary of Ireland], I am no party man; but . . . I think I have sufficient influence over them, that they may listen to me upon a point of this description. . . . In times like these, my dear General, a man like you should not preclude himself from rendering the services of which he is capable by an idle point of form.[12]

The *nimmukwallah* was at work again. But now a new ingredient had appeared in the developing concept: the need for some measure of neutrality within the party system.

Moore, touched by Wellesley's unexpected overture, agreed to meet him at Queluz, the charming little rose-pink palace outside Lisbon. Wellesley told Moore that the army had confidence in only two leaders, the two whose unorthodox conference was now taking place at Queluz. One or other of them must stay to liberate Spain.

And you are the man – and I shall with great willingness act under you.[13]

But for the Convention of Cintra and its humiliating and protracted effects, he would no doubt have done so – and perhaps lost his life, like Moore, or his arm, like Baird.

Next day Wellesley embarked for England, to defend himself. He and his officers landed at Plymouth on 4 October. He was looking, according to a stray observer, 'low and nervous',[14] and expecting, as he said cheerfully, 'to be hanged drawn & quartered; or roasted alive', or at any rate 'shot like Byng'.[15]

However, I shall not allow the Mob of London to deprive me . . . of the satisfaction which I feel in the consciousness that I acted right.

Arthur was putting a bold face on it, as had been his fashion ever since he sailed from Trincomalee without orders, seven years before.

Nevertheless there was a chill feeling of having been sent back to start. Confidently as the Child of Fortune had told Croker three months earlier, 'my die is cast', where was he now? The die was back again, rattling disconsolately in the box.

10

Cintra and Charybdis

Politically conscious London vented its wrath on Sir Arthur, and for good measure included his whole family in the attack. For he was the only politician among the three culprits of the Convention. Cobbett* wrote to Lord Folkestone, who had acted for James Paull against Lord Wellesley over India:

How the devil will they [Wellesley and friends] get over this? . . . It is evident that *he* [Arthur] was the prime cause – the only cause – of all the mischief, and that from the motive of thwarting everything *after he was superseded*. Thus do we pay for the arrogance of that damned infernal family.[1]

Though the Duke of Richmond begged Arthur not to mind 'the whispers of those who dislike the name of Wellesley',[2] his three brothers minded very much. William managed to relieve his feelings in 'cursing and swearing' but Henry had been taken ill with vexation. The persistent attacks on Richard's Indian government had received their quietus in April that year, when James Paull, having lost £300 at a gambling club, blew out his brains. But Richard had lost a hundred times as much in the huge costs of his defence. While waiting to be cleared, Richard could not hold office; frustration produced indolence and indolence carried him unresisting into a life of indiscretion. 'In spite of his Idleness,' Arthur had written to William two days after Roliça, 'he would have been in Office before now if he had not taken to whoring.'[3]

The Government had been forced to recall Sir Arthur's two successors and announce a military inquiry into the Convention to open on 14 November, when all three generals would be examined. Arthur took Richmond's advice to remove himself temporarily to

---

* William Cobbett (1763–1835), the famous Radical author and politician with a huge following, published the *Political Register* every week from 1802 until his death. Imprisoned 1810–12 by the Government for denouncing the flogging of mutineers. Beneath his radicalism were many conservative emotions, as expressed in his *Advice to Young Men* (1829) and *Rural Rides* (1830).

Ireland – 'All in this country but the rebels,' wrote Richmond, 'are anxious for your return' – and he was back at the Castle by 20 October. His departure did not escape Cobbett's malicious notice. The *Political Register* took the opportunity to remind its readers of how ignominious had been the recent arrival in London of the victor of Vimeiro:

he had the discretion not to make any noise upon his landing. He snugged it in, in the Plover sloop. . . . It was not thus that he used to enter Calcutta. . . .

Having sarcastically mentioned Indian 'triumphal arches' and 'thousands of gilded barges', Cobbett went on to ask why Arthur Wellesley, this 'Chevalier de Bain', this conqueror of 'Monseigneur le Duc d'Abrantes [Junot] en personne' had come home. Could it be that 'he is come home for the purpose of avoiding another meeting with the Tartar Duke, or any of his like'? This imputation of cowardice stung Arthur into thoughts of a libel action. William dissuaded him, 'But be sure your cause will go to Leeward if you do not come here to watch and guide it.'

This gloomy prediction crossed a letter from Dublin full of Arthur's usual cheerful cynicism and self-confidence. He felt 'quite at ease' about the inquiry, for his case was stronger than William seemed to think.

At last the Court of Inquiry assembled, in the Great Hall of Chelsea College (now Hospital). Sir David Dundas presided. When the result came it was a fumbling anticlimax. Since the Court were determined not to blame either Sir Hew or Sir Harry and could not in justice blame Sir Arthur, everybody was right, though in violent mutual contradiction.

By six votes to one on 22 December 1808 the Court approved the Convention. By four to three they reluctantly accepted its details. But neither Dalrymple nor Burrard ever held command again; a blessing for which the much maligned Convention has since been given credit.

Arthur Wellesley was back yet again in Ireland. His mood fitted the glum spirit of the times. Kitty cannot have found this thwarted hero easy to please. Throughout the Cintra episode he had frequently stressed his need for 'patience and [good] temper', a sure sign of strain. The marriage had jogged along fairly happily for the first two years but in 1808, with another year of Arthur's constant travels between Phoenix Park and Harley Street, Kitty began running to her various

Irish cousins with tales of his coldness and neglect. Sorry as they all felt for her at first, she eventually alienated some of even this faithful band by her complaints.

It was during these difficult days that London's most aspiring courtesan, Harriette Wilson, claimed in her *Memoirs* to have consoled 'the Duke of Wellington'.

Harriette was the darling of the dandies. Among her lovers were the Marquess of Lorne, the Marquess of Worcester, son and heir of the 6th Duke of Beaufort, and many other glittering Regency names. She was queen of the 'demi-reps', mistress of the Game of Hearts and altogether an extremely vivacious if not beautiful London-bred *gamine*.

'The Duke', as she consistently called Wellesley, was said one day to have approached a certain Mrs Porter's notorious establishment in Berkeley Street on foot, 'rapped hastily' on her door, and as 'one of her oldest customers' demanded a meeting with Harriette Wilson. When Mrs Porter made some practical difficulties, enlarging upon Harriette's 'wildness' and 'independent' life, he interrupted impatiently: 'Nonsense! it is very well known that the Marquess of Lorne is her lover.' Mrs Porter surrendered to superior generalship and agreed to approach Harriette. Picking up his hat, he gave a final brief command. 'And make haste about it. I shall call for your answer in two days.'[4]

Harriette, burdened by debt (for Lorne was stingy and anyway going to Scotland), arranged to receive 'the Duke' a few days later. She described how he arrived punctually at 3 pm, bowed, said 'How do you do?' and then in silence tried to take her hand. She withdrew it.

'Really, for such a renowned hero, you have very little to say for yourself.'

'Beautiful creature! where is Lorne?'

'Good gracious, – what come you here for, Duke?'

'Beautiful eyes, yours!'

'Aye, man! they are greater conquerors than ever Wellington shall be; but, to be serious, I understood you came here to try to make yourself agreeable?'

'What child! do you think that I have nothing better to do than to make speeches to please ladies? . . . You should see me where I shine.'

'Where's that, in God's name?'

'In a field of battle.'

According to the *Memoirs* he now became her constant visitor, but 'a most unentertaining one' who seemed to her in the evenings, when he wore his broad red ribbon of the Bath, to look 'very like a ratcatcher'. On one of these occasions she claimed to have teased him about Cintra.

'Do you know . . . the world talks about hanging you?'

'Eh?'

'They say you will be hanged, in spite of all your brother Wellesley can say in your defence.'

'Ha! what paper do you read?'

'It is the common talk of the day.'

'They must not work me in such another campaign,' the hero of Vimeiro is said to have replied smiling, 'or my weight will never hang me.'[5]

What is to be made of all this? In the passage just quoted she certainly has caught Arthur Wellesley's quick, peremptory speech, noted by all his friends, as well as the paternal touches and wry humour. Even the taciturnity broken by rather naïve gestures of homage sound perfectly authentic. However, in contrast to the genuinely 'Wellingtonian' touches, her account is full of equally remarkable improbabilities: his wearing the Order of the Bath to visit a *cocotte*, his boasting of battle honours.

Harriette Wilson was writing her *Memoirs* in 1824. She was living in Paris with a disreputable Colonel Rochfort, harbouring a grudge against the Beaufort family who she felt owed her a pension in return for not having married Lord Worcester. She decided to try her hand at authorship as a solution for her troubles. Her impresario in the enterprise was a rascally publisher named Joseph Stockdale, who published works of scandal and pornography, as well as excellent maps of the south of France which Wellington's army found very useful. Each of Harriette's former beaux was to be given the chance to buy himself out of the *Memoirs* by the payment of £200.

On 16 December 1824 Stockdale dispatched one of these charitable offers to the Duke of Wellington:

24 Opera Colonnade.

My Lord Duke,

In Harriette Wilson's Memoirs, which I am about to publish, are various anecdotes of your Grace which it would be most desirable to withhold, at least such is my opinion. I have stopped the Press for the moment; but as the publication will take place next week, little delay can necessarily take place.

The Duke of Wellington's reply to this unpleasant document has disappeared, but not without leaving a resounding echo behind which is now a part of the English language:

Publish and be damned.

According to legend, Wellington wrote these words in flaming red ink right across Stockdale's letter and posted it back to him. How much truth is there in this cherished tradition?

Stockdale's actual letter is at Apsley House and has nothing on it except the blackmailer's own slime.* A second letter from Opera Colonnade, however, shows that the Duke had indeed told Stockdale to go to hell and take Harriette with him. Stockdale's reply to the Duke's defiance was dated 28 December 1824.

Mr. Stockdale was certainly not aware that the Duke of Wellington had been written to, much less threatened by Harriette Wilson now Rochfort. . . .

Mr. Stockdale has purchased one half of the property of Harriette Wilson's Memoirs; his chief motive in which was to protect, as well as he could, any friend, who might be disagreeably implicated in them. Instead of exulting, he was grieved & pained, far, very far beyond what he shall attempt to describe, in the discovery of the prominent figure which the Duke of Wellington & the Marquess Wellesley cut, in those pages, from which S. [*sic*] was anxious to obliterate them, though it would diminish the interest of the work, & its consequent produce, perhaps, not less than £5,000. Indeed as a friend of that illustrious house, S. does not hesitate to say that twice that sum would be a cheap purchase of the destruction of those details, which, a few hours will place beyond the possibility of redemption. . . .

When published early in 1825 Harriette Wilson's *Memoirs* took by storm a shocked world. The Duke of Wellington figures prominently eight or nine times. Mrs Arbuthnot, his greatest woman friend of this period, asked whether he had really known 'this woman'. He replied frankly:

he had known her a great number of years ago, so long tho' that he did not think he should remember her again, that he had never seen her since he married tho' he had frequently given her money when she wrote to beg for it. . . .[6]

Thanks to Mrs Arbuthnot, it is now possible to see the outlines of what really happened through the mists of Harriette Wilson's fund-raising fiction.

The 'great number of years ago' (dating back from 1825) when Wellington knew Harriette Wilson represented the months between September 1805 and March 1806 – a matter of twenty years earlier. He had just returned from India and was somewhat at a loose end (until firmly whipped in by Olivia Sparrow). Since Harriette did not appear

---

* Wellington frequently drafted his answers on the blank spaces left by his correspondents; occasionally he crossed the original writing; sometimes he used pencil instead of dark ink, but never red ink.

on the scene until about 1803, he cannot have met her before he went to India. But he almost certainly paid earlier visits to Mrs Porter's house in Berkeley Street, from which Harriette later conducted her affairs. These would have taken place between 1795 and 1796, while he was gloomily hanging about London, rejected by Kitty Pakenham and waiting to set sail. Captain Elers, a friend of Indian days, told the story of a beautiful Mrs Sturt who, when stranded in Madras on the way to join her husband, had appealed to 'her old friend Colonel Wellesley'. Generously and characteristically he at once made out an order on his banker for £400. Captain Elers added that Mrs Sturt had originally emanated from 'the establishment of a notorious woman living in Berkeley Street'.[7] Surely none other than the procuress, Mrs Porter.

What more natural than that Major-General Wellesley should have returned to his old haunts in 1805? Or that he should have ordered Mrs Porter, as 'one of her oldest customers', to produce for him this new talk-of-the-town called Harriette Wilson? Or that the actual hero of Assaye should have been conveniently transformed into the future hero of Portugal, Spain and Waterloo?

So the Stockdale–Wilson combine published, hoping that the Duke would be damned.

Or should we question Wellington's own veracity? Did he conceal from Mrs Arbuthnot some of the truth in February 1825? His confidence in Mrs Arbuthnot was complete. Why should he lie to the keeper of his conscience?

The winter of 1808 and spring of 1809, when Harriette Wilson says she saw so much of 'the Duke', were not seasons favourable to courtesans. This was the time when the celebrated Mary Anne Clarke scandal broke over the head of the Duke of York.

The very day after the Royal Commander-in-Chief had signed the report on the Convention of Cintra and sent a copy to Dalrymple (20 January 1809), Colonel Wardle, MP, stood up in the House of Commons and moved for an inquiry into the Duke of York's conduct as Commander-in-Chief.

For weeks to come Cintra and all Wellesley's troubles were driven out of the public mind. Colonel Wardle's inquiry was instituted. As if in an earthquake, a mass of underground corruption at the Horse Guards suddenly became exposed to the country's horrified gaze. It was shown that another clever, witty and conscienceless London *gamine*, Mary Anne Clarke, had used her position as the Duke of York's mistress to augment the irregular allowance he made her by selling under the counter and at cut prices, commissions, promotions and exchanges. The burning question was whether the Duke of York had known that this criminal traffic was going on.

Though Mary Anne entranced the Members of Parliament who questioned her, the ravishing gown of blue silk barely concealed an implacable little fury. She had been dismissed by her royal lover in 1806 and had found a quick and sure way to revenge. How amusing to be able to tell goggling Members that she sometimes had had to remind the Commander-in-Chief of his nefarious promises by pinning a note on their bed-curtains. When Mrs Clarke later had the bright idea of dragging Arthur's name into the scandal, he wrote:

The House was in a roar when she mentioned my name; but I was happy to find that not a single man, not even Folkestone, imagined that I knew anything about the matter.[8]

But he was no longer so 'positively certain' of York's ignorance. He was still optimistic enough to believe, however, that these revelations would actually enhance Britain's reputation abroad,

as it will be manifest to the whole world ... that these transactions, which have deservedly created so much indignation, have been carried on by the scum of the earth.

During March Wellesley came to believe with the vast majority – which today no one can doubt – that York 'must have suspected Mrs Clarke's practices'.[9] He endorsed the general view that certain moral standards were necessary in public men. On 17 March the Duke of York resigned from the Horse Guards and next day was replaced as Commander-in-Chief by old Sir David Dundas.

None of this boded well for General Wellesley. Though the Duke of York had never favoured him since India, Dundas was to prove no less unhelpful than York to his future command. For an atmosphere of timidity, especially as regards promotions, now pervaded the Horse Guards.* It was understandable; but intensely annoying to a general who wanted nothing more than to collect the best possible staff.

Finally, the relevance of Mary Anne Clarke to Harriette Wilson should now be clear. Arthur Wellesley, it must not be forgotten, had arrived back in England under heavy fire. Scarcely had the Cintra guns been silenced before the great Clarke cannonade opened. So powerful was it that one stray ball at least came bounding towards Arthur. Was

* George Napier gives an account of his asking, or trying to ask Dundas for promotion. Having enquired after George's health, Dundas replied to every question on promotion, 'Wear flannel, Major, wear flannel.' (*Early Life of Sir George Napier*, p. 81.)

it likely that he would choose these months of crisis to renew relations with another member of Mrs Clarke's dangerous sisterhood?

It happened that at this very time Arthur Wellesley himself was once more expecting a responsible command.

During November 1808 Spanish resistance had collapsed under a tremendous French onslaught directed by Napoleon in person. Madrid was again in French hands. Wellesley's new friend, Sir John Moore, was driven from Spain in December, and though he heroically evacuated all but a few thousand stragglers from his suffering army and saved both Cádiz and Lisbon, he himself fell at Corunna on 16 January 1809.

Sir David Baird lost an arm, young Harry Burrard, Sir Harry's son and Moore's aide-de-camp was killed. Whig support for the war died too. Beginning with the Grenvilles and going right through to Cobbett, the Opposition was totally disillusioned. Napoleon had not even bothered to stay in Spain but handed over to Marshall Soult. By the end of March 1809 Soult was in Oporto and the Portuguese of Lisbon were clamouring once more for aid; this time, it would seem, in vain.

Arthur Wellesley had followed with horror the story of the retreat to Corunna. 'Beau' Cradock had now assumed chief command but was clearly unfit for it. General Beresford, at the invitation of the spirited Portuguese whose language he spoke, was reorganizing the Portuguese army. But Beresford had a long way to go before Portugal could defend herself. Worst of all the hero Moore, before he died, had said that if Spain fell Portugal could not be held. Who now dared draw the sword?

Arthur Wellesley, rehabilitated but only just, used the month of March to cut through all obstructions with his pen.

'I have always been of opinion that Portugal might be defended whatever might be the result of the contest in Spain. . . .' These were Wellesley's challenging words in a memorandum of 7 March to Lord Castlereagh. They challenged Moore's pessimism, though Wellesley entirely dissociated himself from Tory attacks on Moore's conduct. The conditions of success, he continued, were 20,000 British troops including 4,000 cavalry; a reconstituted Portuguese army; and the Spaniards to keep at least some of the huge French armies pinned down in their country. On the basis of these brave words Castlereagh battered down the Cabinet's resistance.

Wellesley's orders from the Government, nevertheless, reflected a certain stringency in the situation:

The defence of Portugal you will consider as the first and most immediate object of your attention.[10]

Any combination with Spain should on no account be undertaken without the express authority of the British Government.

On the day before Wellesley's memorandum of 7 March, a sensational event had scandalized London society. Arthur's sister-in-law, Lady Charlotte Wellesley, wife of his brother Henry and mother of four young children, eloped. She went off in a hackney coach with Henry, Lord Paget, probably the best cavalry officer in the Army. With the names of Wellesley and Paget linked in such a way, it was inevitable that the Peninsular expedition should be deprived of Paget's skill in the arm where Arthur would need it most – the cavalry.

Yet another family convulsion, this time still nearer home, was to agitate Arthur's last weeks in England. Kitty's youngest brother, Henry, had run into debt through gambling and persuaded her to lend him the housekeeping money. Arthur's imminent departure for Portugal brought in all the unpaid bills, Kitty could not settle her accounts and one of the tradesmen dunned Sir Arthur. His anger was unforgiving. She had misappropriated his funds.

This painful episode spoilt the last days together of husband and wife. Its echoes were to haunt Arthur's memory for the rest of their married life.

By the beginning of April his preparations were almost complete. Sir David Baird, one-armed since Corunna, regretfully handed over his own favourite aide-de-camp, Captain Alexander Gordon, on 2 April to General Wellesley, wishing Arthur success in his command 'wherever it may be'.[11] (The public did not yet know.) His Irish business still had to be concluded. Either the recollection of a recent attack by Samuel Whitbread on his dual office in 1808, or his own second-sight, warned Wellesley to resign his seat in Parliament and office in Ireland. Croker wa left to handle the routine business until a successor was appointed. In due course Croker became his successor.

The spring of 1809, as it turned out, was to be the last time Wellesley held office in Ireland or indeed set foot in that country. His work there ended on characteristic notes of personal affection and social construct-tiveness. On 2 April he asked Richmond to allow the Irish-born Ladies of Llangollen pensions of £50 each. And the last letter from him now lying in the Irish State Papers Office is a plea to start draining 'the Bogs & Morasses of Ireland'.[12] One bog at least stood no chance of being drained until Wellesley himself became Prime Minister – the anti-Catholic laws. Meanwhile, the 'enemy country' showed that he had not gone altogether unappreciated. One of the Dublin guilds gave him a new-year present – a silver box containing its Freedom, for his 'private worth' and high military talents, 'highest amongst the heroes that this your native land has given birth to'.

Harriette Wilson claims that 'the Duke of Wellington' paid her two farewell visits before he left.

Early one morning before she had finished breakfast he called, but proved to be 'impenetrably taciturn'. At length he broke the silence.

'I wonder you do not get married, Harriette!'

'Why so?' He did not answer.

'I was thinking of you last night, after I got into bed,' he began again.

'How very polite to the Duchess. Apropos to marriage, Duke, how do you like it?'

'I was thinking – I was thinking that you will get into some scrape, when I go to Spain. . . . I must come again tomorrow, to give you a little advice.'

'Oh, let us have it all out now, and have done with it.' But he took a hasty leave. Harriette affirmed that she was not sorry, for she had found him 'very uphill work'.[13]

His last alleged visit took place a few hours before he 'betook himself again to the wars', and was more to her liking. She burst into tears at the thought that she might never see this man again, who had relieved her from 'many duns'. He kissed her cheek, told her to look after herself, to leave her address for him at Thomas's Hotel as soon as he returned, and if she wanted anything in the meantime to 'write to Spain'.

'Do you hear?' wiping her eyes and kissing them; 'God bless you!' He hurried away.[14]

Harriette had no doubt been through many a parting scene with soldiers going to the wars and knew how to describe one.

He never once returned on leave during the five years of his Peninsular campaign, beginning in 1809. Therefore Harriette's next circumstantial account of his turning up 'unexpectedly' and provi-dentially on short leave from the Continent was another of her inventions. But she was certainly ill and penniless. In her distress she doubtless wrote to Wellington in Spain and he replied with the usual banker's order and letter. Perhaps that letter even contained something like the remark which was attributed to him by Harriette during the invented visit he paid her while on an imaginary leave.

'I have thought of you, very often, in Spain; particularly one night, I remember, I dreamed you came out on my staff.'[15]

11

The Hideous Leopard

Napoleon's orders were that Wellesley's army, like Moore's, was to be driven into the sea. He had hit upon a peculiarly offensive name for his opponent. Not a British lion, king of beasts, but an emaciated leopard, hideous and heraldic. The innovation was effective (though somewhat overworked by Napoleon), ridiculing as it did the creatures on the Royal Standard and the English character. 'The hideous leopard contaminates by its very presence the peninsula of Spain and Portugal,' declared Napoleon to his soldiers in 1808. 'Let us carry our victorious eagles to the Pillars of Hercules. . . .'

Wellesley's task, in reverse, was to drive those eagles, broken-winged, back if possible to the Pyrenees. For a moment, however, it looked as if the leopard would be driven into the sea without any help from the French.

One of those storms which Arthur believed always accompanied his travels almost wrecked his ship, the *Surveillante*, during his first night at sea, 14 April 1809. His aide-de-camp, Colin Campbell, was sent by the captain to request Arthur to put on his boots and come up on deck, for the end was near. Wellesley replied that he could swim better without his boots and would stay where he was. Neptune subsided, and another touch was added to the legend of imperturbable calm.

He arrived on 22 April in the Tagus to find Lisbon *en fête* in his honour. Its magnificent Black Horse Square was crowded with merrymakers who had banished Cintra from their thoughts. There were groups dancing to castanets and drums, plump ladies in painted litters or sedan chairs with white head scarves and fichus, short handsome gentlemen in tricorne hats decorated with bunches of ribbon and a motto across the front – 'Conquer or Die'; peasants in long straw cloaks, white shirts, blue drawers and black shovel hats, pilchard dressers, lemonade sellers, chestnut roasters blowing grains of salt with a palm leaf on to their nuts to give them a bloom; beggars carrying round written accounts of their sad stories for the charitable Portuguese to read, and mendicant friars with Saint Anthony's image to kiss; ballad singers thumping out future triumphs for Arthur Wellesley on guitars, and special tableaux at the theatre where Victory placed a wreath of laurels on the head of a noble figure with a splendid nose.[1]

Only two days after his arrival Wellesley made one of his quick decisions. He would march north immediately and rescue 'the favourite town of Oporto' from Marshal Soult. Having succeeded, he proposed to return south leaving Marshal Ney 'to the war of the peasantry which has been so successful. . . .'[2]

This was Wellesley's earliest tribute to the gallant Spanish guerrillas who first made their spontaneous appearance on the scene that year.*

Half-way down the rugged Portuguese border he would cross into Spain, bringing his army of 26,000 to cooperate with the septua-genarian Spanish captain-general, Don Gregorio García de la Cuesta, against Marshal Victor in a drive on Madrid.

His plan was by no means lacking in dash and optimism. His Peninsular allies, though intensely patriotic, had recently shown their ardour in somewhat alarming ways. His old enemy, the Portuguese General Freire, had been murdered in March by his compatriots for cowardice; and in the same month the Spanish General Cuesta was routed at the battle of Medellin, having been ridden over by his own cavalry who in turn were shot for desertion by the Junta at Seville.

Despite this hyperactivity, Wellesley was careful to detach General Mackenzie with 12,000 men from his small army to guard Lisbon against Victor while he himself was in the north, instead of relying on Cuesta. He joined his troops at Coimbra on 2 May and spent the inside of a week revolutionizing the Anglo-Portuguese army. For the first time he introduced into the British Army autonomous divisions. He toughened his Portuguese infantry by putting one battalion into each of five British brigades. He strengthened his skirmish line by giving every brigade a permanent company of riflemen. All this was the practical result of Vimeiro. He had digested its failures and successes – the raw Portuguese troops who had not been able to stand alone; the British infantry who had held back their fire so steadily when protected by the riflemen's screen.

Thanks partly to an informer, Wellesley now knew that Soult's army was 23,000 strong (rather more than he had reckoned, and all

---

* In Spanish a 'guerrilla' means a little war and those who wage it are 'guerrilleros' The word 'guerrillas' is used here and throughout in the accepted English sense.

veterans), against his own 17,000 supported by Beresford's 6,000 Portuguese. On 12 May he reached the suburbs of Oporto. His troops were on the threshold of the greatest adventure of the Peninsular War.

At 2 am on that morning of 12 May 1809 Wellesley's men had heard a thunderous roar over the River Douro, which flowed majestically through steep hills between them and the city. It was Soult blowing up the bridge. He knew that the British were advancing in force. He did not guess how quickly. The marshal sat up all through the night of the 11th putting the last touches to a methodical plan for evacuation. At 9 am next morning, exhausted but well satisfied, the tall French marshal went to bed.

Wellesley, meanwhile, stood on the terrace of the Serra Convent opposite the city, training his glass intently upon the deep, forbidding river at his feet. Above its precipitous banks to the left he could see the twin-towered Cathedral and his friend the Bishop's palace. On the right the cliffs were steeper still; but a narrow path zigzagged up towards an isolated square stone building behind a high wall.

Wellesley looked unostentatious enough in his plain blue coat, short cape and plumeless cocked hat; but the quiet dress concealed a man thirsting for action, however spectacular, to surprise the enemy.

At this crucial moment one of his scouts made his way into the silent group on the Serra hill. The scout was Colonel Waters, a famous daredevil of the future. His present proposal suited his temperament.

The River Douro, which according to Soult should have been bridgeless, boatless and totally impassable, could in fact be crossed. A Portuguese barber had noticed four large wine-barges lying unguarded on the French side, but concealed from their view by overhanging cliffs. He had also managed to find a solitary skiff, paddled it over to the south bank, and having hidden it in the rushes under the Serra slopes, reported to Waters. Should he paddle back for the barges?

Waters was promptly ordered to collect volunteers. He organized a splendidly mixed party of six brave Portuguese – a barber, a Prior and four peasants – to help him bring these sitting targets across the three hundred yards of sunlit, open water.

Not a sentry noticed, not a gun fired. Soon the makeshift transports, shaped like clumsy gondolas, lay hidden with the skiff under the south bank, ready to take the first soldiers over. The time was 10.30 am. Now it was up to Wellesley.

'Well, let the men cross.' No histrionics. No hat-waving. Yet the command was in fact a cry of 'Death or Glory!'

The perilous ferrying began. Thirty by thirty, the soldiers filed into their barges. At the end of an hour only 600 had got across. But led by a company of the Buffs (3rd Foot) they had made good use of their time and numbers.

The square building to the right in which Wellesley had shown such interest turned out to be the Bishop's Seminary, now standing empty. Into it ran the first small boat-load. They banged the iron gates shut and proceeded to fortify their heaven-sent, ecclesiastical bridgehead. It was covered by British howitzers which Wellesley had brought into place on his hill opposite.

At noon he put down his glass for a moment to scribble a note to Beresford. 'My advance Guards are crossing in Boats; & the French Picquets are evacuating the Town.' He would follow them as soon as possible but the bridge would not be repaired till tomorrow, '& the passage by Boat goes on but slowly'.[3]* When, after a full hour, French artillery and infantry at last launched fierce attacks on the Seminary from the hill behind, they were all scattered – by the same rolling volleys and shrapnel that had caused havoc at Vimeiro.

Soult meanwhile was sleeping. An orderly rushed four steps at a time up the stairs to the room where his staff were still at breakfast, shouting that the English were coming over the water . . . were in the town. Soult, roughly awakened, refused to believe it.

But already the northern banks of the Douro were spotted with British red-coats clambering up into the steep, narrow streets, and a stream of French fugitives was pouring helter-skelter out of the town into the rugged country beyond. A throng of Portuguese citizens swarmed down and ferried over the British in mounting numbers. Soult's personal attempts to rally his men failed. He was forced to follow the stampede, abandoning a thousand sick and wounded in his hospitals and a very fine meal on his table. General Wellesley had the pleasure of sitting down to it at four in the afternoon.

Oporto was liberated. Next day, when all the troops and guns were across the Douro, the pursuit began.

So did torrential rain. Up into a wilderness of crags, mud, tossing pines and hissing torrents the exhausted Allies dragged their mules and guns. In vain. Soult's fleeing army, always just ahead, jettisoned more

---

* This note is now among the Raglan Papers with nine others like it Its peculiar interest lies in the fact that a carbon copy was sent to Beresford, this being Wellesley's original pencilled note. The pencil is so faint that the present writer found it easier to read from the copying ink on the back of the paper, with the help of a mirror.

1 *Arthur Wesley, future Duke of Wellington, aged about 11, by an unknown artist.*

2 *Arthur Wesley as Lieutenant-Colonel of the 33rd, aged about 26, by John Hoppner. Given by Arthur to his brother Richard in 1841, who said of it: 'It is admirable; much of the best which exists of you; the likeness is perfect and conveys the true expression of your countenance.'*

3 *Battle of Assaye, 23 September 1803.*

4 *Major-General the Hon. Sir Arthur Wellesley, K.B., by John Hoppner, 1806. The portrait represents Wellesley in India.*

5 Above *Sir Arthur Wellesley, by Robert Home, 1804. The star and ribbon of the Bath were added later, as the news of Wellesley's appointment to the order did not reach India until 1805. 'It belonged to the poor Duchess,' wrote the Duke about this portrait, and it still hangs at Stratfield Saye.*

6 Above right *Harriette Wilson.*

7 *Catherine Dorothea Sarah ('Kitty') Pakenham, Viscountess Wellington, by Slater, 1811. Maria Edgeworth commented: 'Lady Wellington is not like: it is absurd to attempt to draw Lady Wellington's face; she has no* face; *it is all countenance.'*

8 *'A procession of Hampshire Hogs', inspired by Cobbett and his* Weekly Political Register, *marches to London with a Loyal Petition 'humbly shewing that the Convention with Junot was a cursed humbug upon Old England! and that the Three damned Convention Signers ought to be Hanged Drawn and Quartered ...' The three generals are seen swinging in effigy.*

9 *Capture of Oporto, 12 May 1809. On the right is the Serra Convent with Wellesley holding up his telescope; in the centre, across the River Douro, is the Bishop's Seminary.*

10 *Torres Vedras, the town with its fortress on the right, 1810.*

11 *Self portrait of Kitty at Tunbridge Wells, c.1810, sketched in watercolours to 'amuse' her brother-in-law, Harry Stewart, in Ireland. Home-made slippers were her speciality. She was later laughed at for never being without an old basket. The saddle is placed well back on the animal's crupper to give the rider's liver a good shaking.*

12 *Storming of Badajoz, 6 April 1812. Notice the spikes and sword-blades in the breach and the flooding in the foreground.*

13 *'The Beau', 1812, by Juan Bauzit, watercolour. Wellington is shown in civilian clothes – dark blue great-coat and grey breeches.*

14 *Battle of Salamanca, 22 July 1812.*

15 *Wellington's triumphal entry into Madrid, 12 August 1812, a bronze relief at Stratfield Saye by Robert Jefferson, with the caption 'The Events of War are in the Hands of Providence alone' – said to be the Duke's reply to congratulations from the Cortez.*

16 *Wellington, drawn in chalk by Francisco Goya, Madrid, 1812. Wellington started up in a rage during one of the sittings, when Dr McGrigor confessed that he had disobeyed orders on the march.*

17 Below *Battle of Vitoria, 21 June 1813, by Captain Marston, who took part in the action. ''Tis but a bad picture,' wrote Croker in 1834, but it hung in the billiard room at Stratfield Saye and was so accurate that Wellington used it to demonstrate to Croker how he won the battle. Wellington is in the centre riding Copenhagen, behind him is the hill of Arinez, and to the left and right are the bridges of Mendoza and Nanclares.*

18 Below *Crossing the Bidassoa into France, 1813. Wellington is watching the troops accomplishing their surprise march through the water.*

and more of their baggage, cannon, arms and even wounded whenever their pursuers showed signs of gaining on them. French reprisals against the Portuguese peasants encountered on their flight stirred Wellesley to his coldest fury.

. . . I have seen many persons hanging in the trees by the sides of the road, executed for no reason that I could learn, excepting that they had not been friendly to the French invasion . . .[4]

In retaliation, no savagery seemed too terrible to their Portuguese victims. They tortured French stragglers, burnt the abandoned wounded alive and were known to have sawn an officer in half.

Soult and his desperate ragamuffins managed to stagger over the Spanish border on the fifth day of the pursuit. Slightly earlier Marshal Victor, away to the south, had at last bestirred himself and raided over the same border in the opposite direction. Wellesley turned to face this new, not unexpected threat, and to open the second phase of his planned offensive – the drive into Spain.

On 22 May 1809 he was back in Oporto and taking a breather to write to William among others. Would the whole country this time share his satisfaction?

Once more Portugal was clear of the French. (Victor had quickly retired again.) The whole incredible affair of Oporto had cost Wellesley only twenty-three killed, ninety-eight wounded and two missing. Something like another 400 were added to his casualty list by the pursuit, 200 of them sick. Soult lost altogether 4,000 veterans.

Nevertheless Soult's retreat made nothing like the stir of Moore's. When England's small and precious army lost 5,000 men it was rightly a matter for public lamentation. To Napoleon, whose stupendous victories were only achieved by even vaster sacrifices, the loss of Soult's 4,000 was quite endurable.

More than that, the same sour feelings which had spoilt the aftermath of Vimeiro developed in England after the crossing of the Douro: disappointment that the results of such gallantry were not more brilliant. Wellesley's failure to catch Soult was indeed to cost him dear in two or three months' time.

Wellesley's real concern, however, was not with the Government's latent disloyalty but with the Opposition's scathing abuse. They had never wholeheartedly backed this second Peninsular expedition, nor the choice of commander. They expected him to fail as their hero Moore had failed, and when Samuel Whitbread read Wellesley's victory despatch, he declared in Parliament that Sir Arthur's account was 'an exaggeration'.* Winding up an acid correspondence in September 1809, Wellesley wrote to Whitbread:

I will not enter into any statement of our affairs in this part of the world; I daresay that you will hear and read enough, and speak more upon them than some of us will like. . . .[5]

Now that the dust of contemporary faction has settled, the crossing of the Douro stands out for the triumph it was. Wellesley had acted with audacity but without rashness. His infallible eye for ground told him that a passage could be attempted and the Seminary – a natural fortress – defended long enough for his purposes. The advice he gave to Beresford on this, Beresford's first independent command, put one side of his military faith in a nutshell:

Remember that you are a commander-in-chief and must not be beaten; therefore do not undertake anything with your troops unless you have some strong hope of success.[6]

When that strong hope existed, as at Oporto, his philosophy was always to 'make a dash at the enemy'. Oporto proved once for all that 'he was a safe general and not a cautious one'.[7]

For the time being Marshal Victor relapsed into dilatoriness. Wellesley used the pause to deal with defects in his army. There were plenty of them. Less than three weeks after Oporto he was writing:

The army behave terribly ill. They are a rabble who cannot bear success any more than Sir John Moore's army could bear failure. I am endeavouring to tame them. . . .[8]

His army's besetting sin was plunder. He intended to 'tame' them by sending the worst corps home and punishing individual offenders on the triangle. Three or four hundred lashes were calculated to tame even the most spotted leopards, except perhaps the ironically named 'Belem Rangers', who were convalescents in Belem hospital and presumably too weak to be lashed but not too weak to rob.

Wellesley also developed one of his curious but revealing theories about military grievances.

---

* Soult had in fact a force of 10,000 men supported by many cannon, every one of which the French lost.

We are not naturally a military people; the whole business of an army upon service is foreign to our habits, and is a constraint upon them. . . .[9]

Before all dissatisfactions could be removed, the 'impecunious' state of his army, as he called it, had become a major scandal. He wrote bitterly to Villiers, the British Minister, from Coimbra:

We are terribly distressed for money. . . . I suspect the Ministers in England are very indifferent to our operations in this country.[10]

Ironically, the 'indifferent' Ministers sent him permission to enter Spain just about this time, together with reinforcements – but still no money. He wrote again to Villiers on 11 June:

the ball is at my foot, and I hope I shall have strength enough to give it a good kick: I should begin immediately but I cannot venture to stir without money.[11]

Bonaparte of course would have kicked forthwith. His armies lived off the country, by forcible requisitioning amounting to robbery. Wellesley would not kick off until he could pay cash.

The problems of paying for the war had in fact only just begun. They were not to be solved until a financier with prominent blue eyes, light reddish curls and an astute humorous expression, took a hand. This was Nathan Mayer Rothschild, founder of the London House of Rothschild in 1803–4. In one year alone he was to transmit £11 million in Continental subsidies and remittances to the Peninsula, his brother James in Paris being rumoured to possess suits of female clothing in which he personally smuggled bullion to Wellington through the French lines.

The Treasury's failure in 1809 did not help the General in settling on a joint plan of campaign with his difficult Spanish colleague, General Cuesta. Two days after his letter about the football he was writing gloomily to John Hookham Frere, Minister at Seville, that but for 'the obstinacy of this old gentleman', the British and Spanish armies could between them have intercepted Victor after Soult's defeat – 'the finest game that any armies ever had. . . .'[12]

Part of the delay, at least, was due to the 'torpid' Cradock. He had been sent by Wellesley to Cádiz at the end of April to change £100,000-worth of Spanish gold into Portuguese dollars and was expected back in mid-May. 'Beau' Cradock stopped nearly a month and 'amused himself' (as Arthur informed William sarcastically), not returning until 15 June.[13]

Wellesley's final money arrived at last on 25 June. He marched on the 27th. His infantry began crossing the border into Spain on 4 July.

A detailed plan of campaign had still to be agreed. On 10 July there took place at the Fort of Miravete, Almaraz, the famous first meeting between the Allied generals. It was not a success. Thanks to a chronic dearth of good maps and an incompetent guide, Wellesley kept Cuesta waiting five hours. Though Cuesta showed all the courtesy of a Spanish nobleman, it was not very convenient to have his troops reviewed by torchlight. The flickering gloom, however, was all too symbolic of the Spanish evolutions. Wellesley could see no sign of professionalism among the officers, no manoeuvrability among the men. Courage was their one shining feature, shared to the full by Cuesta himself. Despite the injuries he had received from his cavalry riding over him at Medellin he had the tenacity to fight on, though leading his armies from inside a huge coach drawn by nine mules until he reached the actual battlefield, when he submitted to being hoisted into the saddle and held in place by four Sancho Panzas.

A four-hour discussion between Cuesta and Wellesley followed the torchlight review. An agreement was reached to join forces on 21 July at Oropesa and from there to advance on Victor together, while the Spanish General Venegas intercepted the French from the south-east. As soon as Victor heard of the Allies' arrival at Oropesa, he realized that with only 20,000 men against their combined 55,000, he must hastily retreat behind the River Alberche a few miles to the north-east of Talavera. The Allies decided to attack him simultaneously at dawn on the 23rd.

Wellesley was up at 2 am. When no Cuesta appeared he rolled himself in his cloak and took one of his celebrated pre-battle naps. At 6 am there was still no Cuesta. Wellesley rode over to his camp and found the old man reclining disconsolately on his loose carriage cushions by the Alberche bridge. His army was too tired, he said; he had not reconnoitred sufficiently; the bridge might not bear his artillery. They would attack next day.

Next day there was no Victor to attack. He had flitted eastwards during the night. Wellesley's scouts warned him that other French armies in Victor's direction were concentrating. Nor had the movement of Venegas materialized.

It was now Wellesley's turn to refuse to join Cuesta in a foolhardy chase after Victor on the 24th, especially as the Spanish commissariat had let him down as badly in July as the British Treasury had in June.

Was Wellesley being unfair? A modern Spanish historian, Pablo de Azcarate, points out that Wellesley himself seemed far from sorry at Cuesta's failure to attack on the 23rd.* His letter to Frere of 24 July concluded with the words:

that omission I consider fortunate, as we have dislodged the enemy without a battle, in which the chances were not much in our favor.[14]

It would be unfair to Wellesley to take these words as his considered opinion. In military matters (though not in politics) he tended to look on the bright side until he knew the worst. In this case he knew the worst all too soon, and the word 'fortunate' was not repeated. His final opinion was expressed to Lord Stanhope in 1833. After rather handsomely giving Cuesta credit for being 'sensible' as well as brave, he admitted that his obstinacy of 23 July had proved fatal.

If he had fought when I wanted him to at Talavera, I have no hesitation in saying that it would have cleared Spain of the French for that time.[15]

There can be no doubt that the Allies missed a unique chance, nor that the people of Britain, when they heard the full story, were right to look upon 23 July as the blackest day of the campaign. But they were wrong in attributing Cuesta's recalcitrance to the fact that it was a Sunday. As Wellington remarked of this *canard* to Stanhope: 'he made many other foolish excuses, but that was not one of them. . . .'

Kitty Wellesley, however, evidently swallowed the story, for she noted in her journal with asperity:

Sir Arthur intended to attack Victor on the 23rd but was prevented by Genl. Cuesta. His reason is said to have been that it was Sunday. . . .[16]

Kitty had made a romantic resolution when her husband said good-bye on 8 April 1809. She would keep a journal in which their respective activities, recorded on opposite pages, would afterwards tell her exactly what her hero had been doing at every moment of her daily round. It was mid-July before she could summon up energy to begin.

London. July 16th. Sunday. Very late this morning. Heard Arthur a lesson. Arthur Freese his catechism.

July 17th. Rose very late from fatigue. Wrote to Sir Arthur. . . . I heard to-day that Sir Arthur was proceeding to Madrid, Heaven prosper them! Longford and I dined early and went tête-à-tête to the play, 'Killing no Murder.'†

July 18th. The British Army on its March.

---

* Pablo de Azcarate, *Wellington y Espana* (1960).

† By Theodore Hook, a popular writer of light comedy; later author of a life of Baird.

Cuesta had plunged after Victor on the 24th in the deluded conviction that the French were fleeing before him. In fact Victor had retired *pour mieux sauter* – having joined forces with General Sebastiani and King Joseph. Cuesta was in a 'scrape', as Wellesley had predicted. He made a precipitate retreat to the Alberche. Before Victor's attack had fully developed, Wellesley himself was in a 'scrape', due to the negligence of a British brigade.

Wellesley had gone out with two divisions to cover Cuesta's return to Talavera. On 27 July, while on the way back, Donkin's brigade took an unorthodox siesta and were surprised by stealthy French skirmishers. Wellesley happened to be at the top of the Casa de Salinas, an isolated stone building, from one of whose twin towers he was making his customary investigation of what lay on the other side of the surrounding olive and cork groves. Suddenly he caught sight of French light troops under the Casa's walls. With a wild clatter he and his staff dashed down the steep stairs, leapt on to their horses and spurred out of the courtyard peppered by the desultory bullets of French soldiers who fortunately did not know at whom they were firing. This was Wellesley's narrowest escape of the Peninsular War.

Wellesley rallied Donkin's brigade himself and then retreated to Talavera 'in face of both armies'. Two British battalions had been broken, losing 440 men to the French 100. It was not an auspicious beginning.*

The battle of Talavera has always caught men's imagination since Byron wrote his ominous lines:

> Three hosts combine to offer sacrifice,
> To feed the crow on Talavera's plain.

Two of the hosts, Spanish and British, were already being posted while Wellesley was emerging from the Salinas affray. Talavera's plain, the site he had chosen, was a mile wide, divided in half by a shallow stream, the Portina, which flowed from the northern mountains through a lower ridge which it cut into two hills, behind a redoubt, and eventually into the town. The battle was to be fought on either side of the Portina line, almost as in a game of French and English, mainly between the two ridges and the redoubt. Wellesley posted all his forces

---

* The Casa de Salinas or Serranillas can still be found by the traveller, though the present inhabitants of Talavera do not easily recognize either name. After many enquiries by the writer in 1966 it was at last identified by an ice-cream vendor as the block of agricultural flats which he supplied

to the west of the stream, so that the road to Portugal was behind them. Of the two key ridges, the higher was called the Medellin. This he occupied, leaving its opposite number, the Cascajal, to the French. In the exposed sector between the Medellin hill and the redoubt he placed mainly British troops; the bulk of Cuesta's army was given a cultivated area extending from the redoubt to the town, defended by breastworks. The battle began – accidentally – on the evening of 27 July 1809.

It happened by stages. First, some distant French dragoons indulged in casual shooting at Spanish pickets in Cuesta's section. Cuesta's whole front line suddenly responded with an enormous reverberating salvo. Next moment two thousand raw Spanish soldiers, terrified by their own thunder and shouting 'Treason!', were shocked into head-long flight to the rear, where they sacked Wellesley's baggage wagons in company with some British paymasters, commissaries and stragglers. The extraordinary rout then poured down the road to Portugal, spreading alarm and despondency, including the news that the French had won.

The episode made a lasting breach in Wellesley's trust. It was not that he ever minded troops running away – 'They all do at some time or other,' he explained to Croker – as long as they came back.[17] The Spanish levies had not come back and they had robbed his baggage.

Cuesta had his own reaction. He ordered a decimation: two hundred of the captured deserters to be executed after the battle in cold blood. On Wellesley interceding for them, Cuesta reduced it to forty.

At sunset on that day, Wellesley's army could see huge masses of French rolling in from the east like banks of indigo cloud. Some of the British rank and file began to look pale even in that rosy light, but their officers had no doubt they were as steady as ever.[18] The test came before it was quite dark.

Marshal Victor, aware that the lines opposite were still disturbed by the Spanish exodus, like the sea after a storm, determined to chance his arm on a night attack. It was a bold, if not reckless bid, but nearly succeeded.

General Hill's reliable division, which should have been in the front line on the Medellin, had inadvertently been assigned to the rear. There was a sudden uproar and shouts of 'The hill! the hill!' 'Daddy' Hill heard the turmoil in front but thought it was 'the old Buffs, as usual making some blunder'. In fact it was the 9th Léger swarming up the shadowy slopes with drums beating and cries of '*Vive l'Empereur*', to overwhelm a force of Hanoverians who, believing themselves to be in

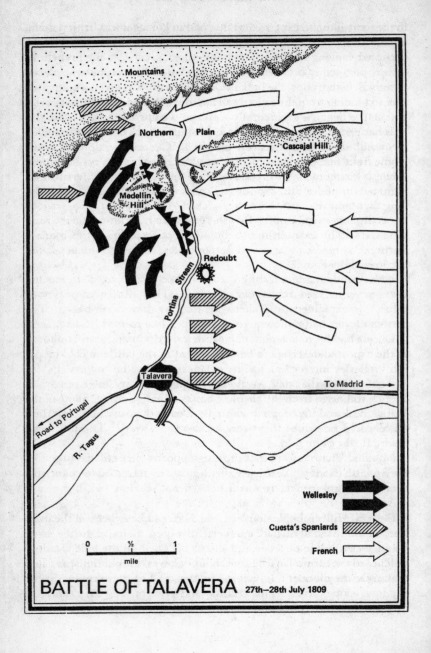

Mountains

Northern   Plain

Cascajal Hill

Medellin
Hill

Redoubt

Portina Stream

Talavera

To Madrid →

Road to Portugal

R. Tagus

Wellesley

Cuesta's Spaniards

French

0   ½   1
mile

BATTLE OF TALAVERA 27th–28th July 1809

the second line, had eaten their few wheat grains and settled into an uneasy sleep without posting pickets. Both Wellesley and Hill rode up in the darkness to investigate the firing. Before Hill knew where he was, he had plunged into the thick of the fighting and almost been dragged from his horse by a French skirmisher. He galloped himself free, ordered forward his division including the 29th, and had the satisfaction of hearing, if not seeing, this gallant regiment, heroes of Roliça and Vimeiro, topple the enemy off the Medellin crest into the Portina gulley below. Both sides lost over 300 men; and but for the 29th the British might have lost this crucial ridge and so the battle. With difficulty Wellesley restored his positions. He then lay down on the ground, wrapped in his cloak, for a few hours of sound sleep before the murderous dawn.

As the red sunrise of 28 July 1809 spread behind the huge black silhouette of the French army, 40,000 men could be counted with ease by the watchers on the Medellin, facing their own force of 20,000. All at once a signal gun on the Cascajal opposite opened up the French barrage. Fifty-four cannon, aided by swirling smoke and mist which an easterly breeze blew across the Medellin, prepared the way for three dense French columns to advance. British skirmishers retired in textbook style, but so slowly as to mask Hill's field of fire. 'Damn their filing!' he swore; 'let them come in anyhow.'[19]* Then it was column against line, as at Vimeiro. Wellesley had made his infantry lie down or wait behind the crest until the French were in position to take the full blast of close-range, rolling volleys. In less than two hours of bloody fury all three attacks had failed.

A truce was called during the fierce glare of the early July morning while soldiers from both sides drank from the fouled stream. On the Cascajal the French held a council of war, Marshal Victor angrily demanding one more assault on the Medellin. Joseph and Jourdan were for withdrawal, leaving Soult to take the Allies in the rear, but Victor's bad temper triumphed.

At 11 am the French drums beat a recall to the eagles. Blue and scarlet uniforms, mingling down at the Portina, drew apart; there were nods and smiles, a final hand-shake here and there, and they were ready once more to be foes.

This strange scene at Talavera was the rehearsal for a regular procedure throughout the Peninsular War, and was encouraged by at

---

* This is said to have been one of the only two occasions when 'Daddy' Hill swore.

least some of their leaders. Wellington described to Croker in 1828 how the advance-posts would always give each other notice of an imminent attack, the French calling out, '*Courrez vite, courrez vite, on va vous attaquer.*' Wellington added:

I always encouraged this; the killing of a poor fellow of a vedette [scout] or carrying off a post could not influence the battle and I always . . . sent to tell them to get out of the way.[20]

Around noon Wellesley could see a formidable dust-cloud raised by fresh French troops. He sent over to Cuesta for reinforcements, who responded promptly.

There followed in fierce succession two immensely powerful French assaults upon the British centre – the third and fourth attacks of the battle. The first of them, an advance in column of 4,500 infantry and eighty cannon, was received, absorbed and broken by British and Spanish artillery-fire combined with what can now be called Wellesley's usual infantry method. After Wellesley's death-volleys had done their work not a single piece of artillery was still in French hands; nor had they fired a shot.

Now came the half-hour which was to decide the battle. The fourth French attack, though heavier than the rest, looked certain at first to meet the fate of all its predecessors. From his post on the Medellin, Wellesley could see his long, raging lines battering the heads of the French columns, which gradually disintegrated. The end seemed near; until he realized that one brigade of Guards and two of the King's German Legion, mad with excitement, had hurled themselves right over the Portina and far into the second, unbroken mass of French columns beyond. Six hundred out of the Guards' 2,000 fell, and the 'ugly hole' which they had left in their own front was about to be filled with a roaring tide of French cavalry and guns, ready to break up the whole shallow British battle-line from the rear. The fate of the day depended on how Wellesley handled this crisis.

Though weak in reserves and threatened everywhere, he somehow contrived to lay his hands on 3,000 heroic men, enough to do the trick. Hill was ordered down from the Medellin with the 48th, and Mackenzie up from the redoubt with the 24th, 31st and 45th. Into the gaping centre marched the resolute 48th, opening their ranks for a moment to allow the remnants of the Guards to pass through to the rear and then, in Napier's words, 'resuming their proud and beautiful line'. To the exhilaration of all, the Guards and the King's German Legion reformed behind them with a loud hurrah. The French, on the verge of superlative victory, were held. Their commander, Lapisse, was killed; their spirits flagged; thousands of horribly dripping bayonets thrust ever more feebly until it was clear that the ghastly combat in the centre had petered out. Victory at Talavera had been plucked from their grasp.

No regular pursuit of the beaten French could be undertaken. Only Cuesta's troops were fresh enough and Wellesley would not move them. The tactful reason he gave in his official despatch (29 July) was that the ground they already held was too 'important'.[21] In a private memorandum of 28 July he revealed the true reason: 'the Spanish troops are not in a state of discipline to attempt a manoeuvre. . . .'*

Next morning, 29 July, when Wellesley might have reformed his armies, the French had all gone. They knew, though he did not, that Soult would be there in command of another French army within a week. There was nothing for Cuesta to do but to march out his forty thieves, dressed in white, and shoot them.

In the late afternoon after the battle a running flame had caught the grass on the Medellin, making a horrible roast of dead horses and scorching the wounded, as if to offer a final 'sacrifice', in Byron's words, to the god of war. 'Never was there such a Murderous Battle!!' said Wellesley.[22] He had been outnumbered two to one in the fighting and had lost over 5,000 men, a quarter of his force engaged; the French over 7,000. He himself had been bruised by a spent bullet, Mackenzie killed and all his staff wounded or their horses shot. It sounded like Assaye. Wellesley decided it was worse.

The battle of Talavera was the hardest fought of modern times. The fire at Assaye was heavier while it lasted; but the battle of Talavera lasted for two days and a night.[23]

Kitty received the news of her husband's victory on 14 August. Her reactions were entirely characteristic.

Thank God his exertions have been crowned with the success they deserve and, tho our loss has been dreadful, yet the events of the 27th & 28th July will ever be thought of with pride by this country, and ought to fill the Spanish nation with gratitude.

If Arthur had seen that last line he would have laughed sardonically.

Kitty was able to finish her diary for 14 August on an ecstatic if somewhat distracted note:

* The date of this memorandum, 28 July, occurs on the copy in the Raglan Papers. The date is important, since Professor Azcarate argues that Wellesley criticized the Spanish for indiscipline only *after* he had broken with them towards the end of August.

I was myself incapable of anything. Walked up & down the room till, quite exhausted, I went to bed with feelings most different from those which afflicted me yesterday. . . .

The King and Prime Minister, though each racked with personal gloom – George III over Princess Amelia's illness and Portland over his own – decided to rejoice the hero of Talavera with a peerage which, but for Cintra, would have been his after Vimeiro. Arthur's brother William discussed the news in a long letter of 22 August, complaining mildly about his difficulties in finding a suitable title. Why had not Arthur left instructions before he went abroad? William of course was joking. He knew his brother too well to suppose that he, unlike Richard, would ever ponder a title before it was conferred. The College of Heralds could not allow time for Arthur to be consulted, so William had to plump. He plumped for 'Wellington'. How he reached his decision was explained in the same letter:

after ransacking the Peerage and examining the map, I at last determined upon Viscount Wellington of Talavera and of Wellington, and Baron Douro of Welleslie in the county of Somerset – Wellington is a town not far from Welleslie . . . I trust that you will not think that there is anything unpleasant or trifling in the name of Wellington. . . .[24]

Arthur found it neither trifling nor unpleasant. Instead he expressed the highest approval. Kitty, on the other hand, was not enthusiastic.

Broadstairs. August 26th – Lord Henniker called in the evening to congratulate me on Sir Arthur's Peerage. I regret his former stile [*sic*] and title – that of Wellington I do not like for it recalls nothing. However, it is done & I suppose it could not be avoided.

Arthur signed his new name for the first time on 16 September 1809, his elevation to the peerage having been gazetted on 4 September. At the end of a dry letter about finance to John Villiers he wrote:

> Believe me, etc.
> Wellington.

This is the first time I have signed my new name. Would the [Portuguese] Regency give me leave to have a *Chasse* at Villa Viçosa?[25]

It would be an honour to have Viscount Wellington hunting anywhere.

Croker composed a poem on Talavera for which Arthur sent somewhat ironical thanks – 'I did not think a battle could be turned into anything so entertaining' – and he was painted by a Portuguese. Beneath his name on the engraving they wrote the single glorious word,

Invicto. Premature shouts of triumph were anathema to Arthur. He hastily scribbled under the offending epithet: 'Don't halloo till you are out of the wood.'[26]

12

Retreat to Portugal

For the space of just one day after the Talavera victory all seemed well and the road open to Madrid. Next day, 30 July 1808, came an alarming report. Marshal Soult had evacuated Galicia, and once more with properly equipped soldiers instead of tatterdemalions was at the Pass of Baños ready to advance. On 8 August Wellesley (as he still was), wrote that he now had 'the whole host of Marshals'[1] against him in Estremadura – Soult, Ney, Mortier, Kellermann, Victor, – as well as the King, Sebastiani and 5,000 men from Suchet's corps. Unless Soult, in particular, was stopped, he would cut Wellesley's life-line with Portugal. It was this which was to change Wellesley's victory into retreat.

An Anglo-Spanish conference was called, nerves taut on both sides. Wellesley chose to deal with Soult. Cuesta promised to look after the British wounded in Talavera until they could be moved. Harrowing scenes took place as Wellesley's army marched out, some of the sick crying to their comrades not to desert them, others limping or even crawling along the road until the last British baggage-wagon and camp-follower had vanished.

Wellesley duly reached Oropesa on 3 August, only to be met by two pieces of bad news. Austria was rumoured to have made peace with Napoleon and Cuesta, threatened by Joseph, had packed up his baggage as soon as Wellesley left Talavera and was marching to join him. Fifteen hundred British wounded were left to the French. It was not that Wellesley feared for their safety. The French would (and did) care for them well. It was what he called 'the disgrace'. Part of his triumph over Soult at Oporto had lain in compelling him to abandon a thousand wounded in the town. Cuesta had now caused Wellesley to lose half as many more. There needed only the Junta's utter failure to supply his army with food and transport, for him to wash his hands of Spain and fulfil his threat to return to Portugal.

To do Wellesley justice, he did not pretend that his own army was blameless. The women were an especial problem. George Napier wrote that it was far more difficult to control the camp-followers after Talavera than soldiers of ten times the number. The only way, he added,

is to have plenty of provosts, to hang and flog them without mercy, the devils incarnate.[2]

The flogging of women was later to land Wellington in trouble. But as he explained to Lady Salisbury:

It is well known that in all armies the Women are at least as bad, if not worse, than the men, as Plunderers! and the exemption of the Ladies would have encouraged Plunder![3]

'The Ladies', their husbands and babes-in-arms would dive into the cellars of plundered houses and paddle up to their middles in seas of wine, until the 'Bloody Provost' arrived. Then there would be a drunken dash for safety and the women, who could not run as fast as the men, would be caught, in the words of a Highland soldier, with 'sax and thirty lashes a piece on the bare doup'.[4] Among the soldiers, robbery of beehives was a favourite crime, the 4th Division being known for their prowess as 'honeysuckers'. What could you expect from a starving army in a land flowing with wine and honey, if nothing else?

Enormous bitterness was generated on both sides by the supply question; indeed, the echoes can still be heard today. In Spain it is argued that Wellesley's army was well-fed until he announced his withdrawal, when the Spaniards naturally ceased to feed soldiers who were abandoning them. But in face of Wellesley's complaints of hunger and half-rations *before* Talavera, this argument has only limited force. On the other hand, Wellesley was mistaken in believing as he did that his Allies deliberately starved him, while living off the fat of the land themselves. There was no fat left in the plains of Extremadura after the French had scoured them. Nor would the ordinary diet of Spanish peasants have seemed anything but starvation to British beef addicts. (Wellington once observed that the Irish were happiest in a wine country, the Scotch on pay-day and the English when there was plenty of beef.)

On 4 August Wellesley crossed the Tagus at Arzobispo and began his circuitous, painful and long-drawn-out exodus from Spain; an exodus sometimes brought to a halt but never reversed.

One of the brighter interludes occurred on 8 August when the Junta rewarded him for Talavera with the captain-generalship of their forces – too late – and six beautiful Andalusian horses. Two contrasted events quickly followed, both on 12 August; General Cuesta left and Lord Wellesley arrived. A paralytic stroke deprived Cuesta of the use of his left leg. In place of John Hookham Frere, the retiring British Minister, arrived the man who should have been a tower of strength to Arthur's cause: his brilliant eldest brother. Kitty's great friend, Mrs Calvert, heard that Lord Wellesley's reception was delirious. The cheering people took out the horses from his carriage and drew it into Seville, one large lady eventually seizing 'his little lordship' in her arms, covering him with kisses.

Arthur did not welcome Richard's arrival, being thoroughly disgusted with his brother's personal record. Richard was trying to separate from his wife who, however, refused to vacate the Wellesley mansion, Apsley House at Hyde Park Corner. Unfortunately the incorrigible Richard was involved with a whore called Sally Douglas. His arrangements for bringing this friend to the Peninsula caused a long delay in his departure and therefore more scandal. Added to the vexations of Richard's presence was the burden of Henry's future. Henry had already gone through the preliminaries of his divorce, but was once again living with Charlotte. 'I understand that she is already *under his protection*,' lamented Arthur to William.[5] He could not understand how Charlotte's brother, Lord Cadogan, could allow his sister to live '*& perform*' with a man from whom she had been divorced by the Church;

& I conclude that Poor Henry will again be dragged through the Mire, & will marry this blooming Virgin again as soon as she will have been delivered of the consequences of her little amusements.*

The situation, however, was not quite as Arthur imagined. Re-marriage was not contemplated. The handsome Lord Paget had gone to fight at Walcheren, leaving Charlotte in need of 'protection'. As for Gerald Valerian, born in 1809, Henry refused to admit that he was his son. It was left for Kitty, with Arthur's blessing, to adopt this 'miserable little Being', as Kitty called him, out of the motherliness of her heart. 'The wretched infant is rejected by every body.'[6]†

* A daughter, born to Charlotte in 1810, of whom Henry Paget was the father (Marquess of Anglesey, *One-Leg*, p. 109).

† Gerald Valerian Wellesley (1809–82). He became Queen Victoria's much loved Dean of Windsor.

The sight of Henry's woebegone elder children had a salutary effect on Kitty. She invited them all to dinner on 23 August and wrote that night in her journal:

they are strong instances of the dreadful evils which the loss of a Mother inflicts upon Children. . . . Let no degree of Suffering, O my God, tempt me to forsake my Children!

In mid-September thousands of the sick, dying and dead from Walcheren were being landed at south-east coast ports. Kitty dared not go near her favourite Ramsgate pier for fear of catching the awful 'Walcheren fever' – dysentery. 'The sight of the Fleet is as dreadful as it was magnificent some weeks ago,' she mourned. The Whig Opposition were in a fury over the Walcheren débâcle and their mounting wrath spilled over on to Wellesley and the Talavera campaign. 'I am convinced that in six weeks' time,' said Lord Grey, 'there will not remain a single British soldier in the Peninsula except as a prisoner.'[7] He denied that Wellesley had won a victory; the captured guns did not prove anything; the French might have found it 'convenient' to leave them behind.

Nevertheless, the faith of the Peninsular army in their leader remained unshaken. It was reflected in the objective remarks of a young Swiss officer who had served under and loved Sir John Moore. Lord Wellington, he decided, seemed rather more than his age, despite his tall, neat figure, expressive features and piercing glance. He was said to be very energetic, prompt in decision, and 'always on his own at that. . . .'

He has the liking and confidence of the Army, who agree in thinking him resourceful, enterprising, and ambitious. I have heard him – wrongly, I think – accused of hauteur, though he is far from having the attentive affability we so admired in poor Sir John Moore. . . .[8]

But there was one matter where Wellington had the distinct advantage. Moore had minded desperately the attacks made on him, whereas 'Lord Wellington laughs at all the calumnies the papers publish.'

Castlereagh himself was in dire trouble that September. He discovered that after a long intrigue Canning had persuaded Portland to oust him from the Cabinet by laying on him all the blame for Walcheren and the Talavera retreat. Portland's dilatoriness in not moving Castlereagh at once caused the fall of the Government. Canning, Castlereagh and Portland all resigned, and Castlereagh and Canning fought a duel on Putney Heath on 21 September, Castlereagh wounding Canning in the thigh and Canning shooting a button off the lapel of Castlereagh's coat.

The old King turned his back on the horrid event. 'I know two Cabinet Ministers have fought a duel,' he said, 'but I don't want to hear any more about them.'[9] He was not so mad as they thought.

When the news of the duel reached Wellington on 6 October he was shocked.

It will confirm in the minds of all men despicable opinions which they have had of the publick servants of the state.[10]

Nevertheless he told William in a most significant letter of 22 October that he would continue to support the Tories, with one important proviso.

. . . I don't conceive that I ought to embark in politics to such an extent as to preclude my serving the Country under any administration that may employ me.

Wellington in fact did not expect the Tories to last and was prepared to serve under the Whigs. The war came first. He must not be asked as a party politician to surrender the command he held as a soldier. This line of thought, briefly unfolded to Sir John Moore in the *tête-à-tête* at Queluz, now inspired him to a full-scale attack on the party mentality.

. . . I never felt any inclination to dive deeply in party Politics; I may be wrong but the conviction in my mind is that all the misfortunes of the present reign, the loss of America, the success of the French revolution etc. etc., are to be attributed in a great degree to the Spirit of Party in England; & the feeling I have for a decided party politician is rather that of contempt than any other. I am very certain that his wishes & efforts for his party very frequently prevent him from doing that which is best for the Country. . . .[11]

The new Tory Government, described by Mrs Calvert as 'a set of dolts',[12] was headed by a lawyer, Spencer Perceval. He was an evangelical, fanatically opposed to Catholic Emancipation. The best his admirers could say of him was that he was clever and an 'honest little fellow'.[13] History has been less than kind to him, for he was to prove courageous also. The two most distinguished members of the former Government – Canning and Castlereagh – were both out, Lord Liverpool was War Minister, William Wellesley-Pole was Irish Chief Secretary and the Marquess Wellesley was haled back from Spain to cast his lustre over a dull crew by becoming Foreign Secretary. Henry was another to benefit. He was appointed in place of Richard at Seville, to work as closely with Arthur as in India.

For Arthur himself there was a new and serious challenge. He must convince a shaky Government not to throw in its hand at Lisbon as well as in Walcheren.

Wellington was operating on a knife-edge. It was his delicate task to convince the Government that retreat from Spain had been inevitable while evacuation of Portugal would be disastrous. As regards the first proposition, his troops were with him to a man. 'There is not a man in the army,' he had written in August, 'who does not wish to return to Portugal'.[14] Hunger and fever since then, in the unhealthy Guadiana valley around Badajoz, had not changed their mood. Only the sunny-tempered Ned Pakenham, newly arrived as assistant adjutant-general, thought the Spanish people unfortunate rather than disloyal. 'I am one of the few,' he wrote home on 20 December, 'who exceedingly regret leaving Spain.'[15]

Wellington had taken two steps in the interest of his second proposition – the defence of Portugal – one secret, the other open (since it involved the Spanish army).

On 10 September, as unobtrusively as possible, he visited Lisbon. The next few weeks he spent in riding all over the hilly quadrilateral between Lisbon, Torres Vedras, the coast and the Tagus. With him rode his chief engineer, Colonel Richard Fletcher, who on 20 October received a twenty-one-point memorandum full of references to 'damming', 'redoubts', 'barriers' and 'signal posts', and introduced by a thousand-word essay on how these mysteries would enable the position they had surveyed to be held against any sweep by Napoleon's eagles, winter or summer.[16] It was a classic case of Wellington seeing for himself. When any problem was reported or question put to him he would always reply:

'I will get upon my Horse and take a look; and then tell you!'[17]

The result of these particular rural rides would be seen in due course, when thirteen months of closely guarded secrets came to an end and Wellington was ready to astonish the world with his Lines of Torres Vedras. Meanwhile he used his evenings in Lisbon to pull up some of his officers, issuing a General Order requesting these officers to cease their misconduct towards the Portuguese inhabitants. It was generally believed that he had limited all Lisbon leave to twenty-four hours, since no reasonable man needed longer than that in bed with a woman.

While thousands of palisades and fascines were being secretly

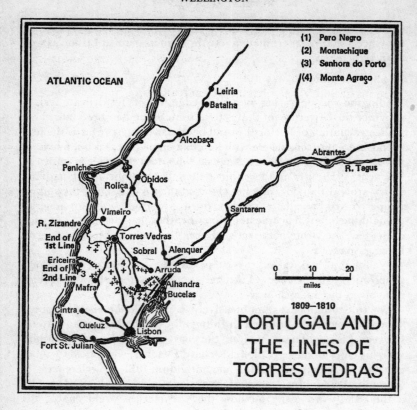

ATLANTIC OCEAN

(1) Pero Negro
(2) Montachique
(3) Senhora do Porto
(4) Monte Agraço

Leiria
Batalha

Alcobaça

Abrantes

R. Tagus

Peniche

Roliça
Obidos

Vimeiro

Santarem

R. Zizandre

End of 1st Line

Torres Vedras

Sobral
Alenquer

Ericeira
End of 2nd Line

3

Mafra

1 4
+ +
2

Arruda

Alhandra
Bucelas

0   10   20
miles

Cintra

Queluz

Lisbon

Fort St. Julian

1809–1810

PORTUGAL AND THE LINES OF TORRES VEDRAS

indented for at Torres Vedras, Sobral and Lisbon, Wellington set off again at the beginning of November to Cádiz. In the interests of Portuguese defence, it seemed important to save the Spanish armies from annihilation. This might prove impossible. There had been a 'September Plot' against the inept Junta. They fled to Cádiz where Wellington found them planning a string of autumn victories to rehabilitate themselves. Aghast at such suicidal folly, he tried to dissuade them, but in vain. In November, this Spanish army was utterly broken to pieces at the battles of Tamamès and Ocaña. The Central Junta abdicated on 29 January 1810, preparatory to handing over to an elected Cortes. On 1 February King Joseph Bonaparte, bent on acquiring the easy wealth of Andalusia, entered Seville. Except in Cádiz, open Spanish resistance had collapsed. So, it appeared, had

Wellington's hope that Spain might yet do something to stem the new French flood now being released against the Peninsula by Napoleon.

This was where the paradox of Peninsular warfare came in. Wellington himself was the first to appreciate it. From his new headquarters at Viseu, high up on its breathtaking plateau among the mountains of Portugal, he wrote to Lord Liverpool at the end of January 1810 about Spain's last hope.

It is probable that, although the armies may be lost and the principal Juntas and authorities of the provinces may be dispersed, the war of partizans may continue.[18]

Spain was to be saved, in fact, not by grape-shot, greybeards and grandees, but by hardy guerrillas and the sudden flash of the knife. These peasants spontaneously organized themselves into small, do-or-die bands: Juan-Martin Diaz called 'El Empecinado', the dweller-by-the-stream in the Guadalajara mountains; Julian Sanchez, the farmer in Old Castile whose family had been murdered by the abhorred French dragoons. When Moreno presented some captured silver plate to his native town, he enriched it with a handful of French ears, some with earrings.

By a special kind of nemesis, the ease with which Napoleon's armies flowed right over the country gave the partisans their chance. The enemy were spread far but spread thin. Even the basic force of 200,000 veterans which Napoleon was compelled to keep, year after year, in Spain, would never be safe from the noon-day ambush and the things that went bump in the night.

The partisans represented the one form of 'irregularity' which Wellington not only prized but paid for, whenever an intercepted French despatch, often gruesomely bloodstained, was brought into his camp. The partisans were gradually trained for the regular army by Wellington's British scouts.

Most of these picturesque British scouts were either killed or captured in the end, including the greatest of them, Major Colquhoun Grant: 'he was worth a brigade to me', said Wellington when he heard that Grant was a prisoner; 'I wish he had not given his parole. . . . I should have offered a high reward to the guerrilla chiefs for his rescue.'[19] The guerrillas were devoted to him and nicknamed him 'Granto el Bueno' – the Good – to distinguish him from the unpopular John Grant known as 'Granto el Malo'. Wellington preserved among his papers some of Grant's original intelligence reports. Neatly marked No. 1, No. 2 and so on in Grant's precise, spiky hand, they looked more as if they had been penned in some commodious office than by candlelight behind the enemy lines. Every one of them came direct to Wellington.

Grant was in fact not given the proper treatment of a prisoner on parole and made a fabulous escape in 1814, to handle Wellington's intelligence before Waterloo.

The main weakness of Wellington's intelligence seems to have been in cracking the French codes. He told Sir William Napier after the war that he would have given £20,000 to anyone in the Peninsula who could decipher King Joseph's letters as Lady Napier had done for her historian husband.[20] By 1813 there was some specialization at headquarters – and also many bright ideas from home. Lord Bathurst sent Wellington a box of shoes with false soles 'for conveying written intelligence in an unsuspected manner'.[21]

One more group which deserved (and received) well of the Commander-in-Chief were his religious 'irregulars'. James Warren Doyle, an Irish student for the priesthood at Coimbra University, volunteered to collect information. The Irish College at Salamanca, under its remarkable rector, Dr Patrick Curtis, ran an even better known intelligence service. During the war the College practically shut down. In 1809, for example, there were only four names on its books – Burke, Shea, O'Grady, O'Kelly – and these four, having gone off as guides and interpreters in Sir John Moore's army, remained with Wellington's. Relays of young Irish novices, previously known as somewhat 'turbulent students', became spirited intelligence officers.

It was not surprising that Napoleon, feeling all these sinister drains on his resources, should have later come to speak with loathing of 'the Spanish ulcer'.

1810. London. January 1st. Began this year by wishing every happiness to my Husband, comfort to those who need it, and a continuation of happiness to the happy.

Kitty's husband was one of the happy. He had laid his plans and was ready to take on all comers. When the French reinforcements arrived, he told William on 4 January,

I hope we shall do tolerably well even if *Boney* should come to drive the Leopards into the Sea.[22]

His army under his eagle eye – and nose – was at last 'improved'. Though its plundering could be 'infamous' at times, he would do anything to get his army their legitimate supplies. There was one occasion when a staff officer visited a large estate to procure forage. He returned empty-handed. Wellington asked why.

'I was told I would have to bow to the noble owner, and of course I couldn't do that.'

'Well, I suppose I must get some myself.'

A few days later the forage began pouring in. How did he do it?

'Oh, I just bobbed down.'[23]

In February 1810, when Wellington was voted a pension of £2,000, Creevey organized a petition from the Common Council of London against it. Wellington believed that the petitioners were hoping to have him once more, as after Cintra, '*en spectacle* at Chelsea'; but again he did not care:

they may do what they please, I shall not give up the game as long as it can be played.[24]

The petitioners failed. William reported that they had not made 'the smallest impression'. There was no Court of Inquiry into Talavera at Chelsea. The war went on. It remained to strengthen the morale of the British Government before the French armies arrived.

Blunt accounts by William of Richard's love affairs had convinced Arthur that no help was to be expected from the Foreign Secretary. In March William understood from Lord Wellesley's Cabinet colleagues that he hardly ever visited his office or spoke in the House of Lords, that nobody could get access to him.

By May, it was true, William heard that Richard had 'entirely got rid of the expense of Moll' – but now he was flirting with the outcast Canning, a liaison not much better in William's eyes than the one with Moll.

At the War Office, Liverpool was more industrious but scarcely less irritating. Napoleon had made another leopard speech on 4 December 1809:

When I shall show myself beyond the Pyrenees the frightened leopard will fly to the ocean, to avoid shame, defeat and death.

Liverpool therefore pointed out that in view of Napoleon's forthcoming arrival in the Peninsula, the possibility of Portugal's fall and the consequent need for an army to defend His Majesty's own dominions, 'the safety of the British Army in Portugal is the first object which his Majesty has in view'.[25] This, as Wellington remarked hotly to William, was 'ludicrous enough'. The British Army had gone to Portugal – in order to be safe! Inconsistently Wellington was also instructed by Liverpool not to evacuate Portugal until it was 'absolutely necessary'. There was also a queasy suggestion that it might be better to embark furtively from Peniche rather than openly from Lisbon. Of Wellington's many robust replies the most effective was sent on 2 April.

First, he was not going to be driven out of the Peninsula by the ghost of Sir John Moore. Second, he was not so keen on 'desperate battles' as the Government seemed to imagine: he had stood in two positions for six months, despite his Allies' impatience to strike and his officers' – or some of them – to quit. Third, if he did have to evacuate it would be from Lisbon not Peniche.

. . . I feel a little anxiety to go, like gentlemen out of the hall door . . . and not out of the back door, or by the area.[26]

A month after this manifesto, Napoleon handed over his 'Army of Portugal' to the fifty-two-year-old Marshal André Massena, the 'old fox' who had been winning spectacular victories for France ever since he led the attack on Arcole in 1796. 'Massena, the Spoilt Child of Victory, is in our front',[27] wrote Wellington grimly to Lord Wellesley on 4 June.

A major shift in the French Empire's foreign policy during late 1809 and early 1810 had precluded Napoleon from taking on the Spanish command himself. The Austrians offered the Corsican usurper their Emperor's daughter, Marie-Louise, in marriage. The barren Josephine was accordingly divorced and Napoleon married Marie-Louise, 1–2 April 1810. At the same period the Emperor of the French saw war with Russia loom ahead and left the Peninsula problems to Marshal Massena.

There were 350,000 French soldiers in Spain, 100,000 of them fresh troops. And Massena's reputation alone would suffice to win the war, as Napoleon assured his redoubtable lieutenant in a flattering effort to dispel a touch of war-weariness. Massena modestly relayed this heartening compliment to his staff at Salamanca, where they waited to burst through the twin northern gateways into Portugal: Ciudad Rodrigo on the Spanish side of the frontier, Almeida on the Portuguese.

Marshal Ney, Massena's brilliant second-in-command, appeared with 30,000 veterans before Ciudad Rodrigo on 2 July 1810 and invested it. Immediately there was a universal outcry. Wellington must march to the relief of this key fortress and its valiant old Governor,

General Herrasti. Wellington did not move. The white-haired Governor was compelled to surrender on 10 July. Ney gallantly gave him back his sword, congratulated him and shook hands. At that moment there was no doubt which leader commanded the Spaniard's greater respect, Ney or Wellington.

It had been the hardest of decisions for Wellington. But the Walcheren fever had made havoc of Lord Liverpool's efforts to reinforce him, and he could not trust his 33,000 troops, many of them raw recruits, against Ney's soldiers. He stood at Celorico in Portugal. Edward Pakenham understood and admired his strategy and 'steadiness'. On the day after Herrasti's surrender Ned wrote to his mother predicting that the French, by dividing their huge forces, had not

reserved that commanding power to make the Leopard jump into the Sea – for my part I think it will take the Emperor (after His family Efforts) to move us at all.[28]

They were all beginning to enjoy the leopard business.

General Robert Craufurd of the Light Division made up for Wellington's 'steadiness' at Celorico by a month of extreme audacity on the line of the River Coa. Contrary to Wellington's instructions he held up the French advance into Portugal by daredevil skirmishing, only just giving himself time to dart back to safety, after losing over 300 men. Wellington, who desperately needed brilliance in his generals and had found it in Craufurd, could not bring himself to have Craufurd court-martialled.

There were other staff problems to be faced as well. Few of the new officers sent out to him by the Horse Guards possessed the solid ability and agreeable temperament of an Edward Pakenham or a Lowry Cole. Though Kitty had jilted Cole in Arthur's favour, Cole served his brilliant rival with devotion and skill, writing to his sister in February 1810:

I never served under any Chief I liked so much, Sir J. Moore always excepted, as Lord W. He has treated me with much more confidence than I had a right to or could be expected from anyone.[29]

There was General Sir William Erskine, drunken, 'blind as a beetle', according to a fellow officer,[30] and probably mad, whom he had sent home 'indisposed' the year before. Back he came in 1810, along with other known disasters such as Generals Lumley and Lightburne and Colonel Landers. Wellington gave Colonel Torrens, Military Secretary at the Horse Guards, the full blast of his indignation:

Really when I reflect upon the characters and attainments of some of the General officers of this army . . . on whom I am to rely . . . against the French Generals . . . I tremble: and, as Lord Chesterfield said of the Generals of his day, 'I only hope that when the enemy reads the list of their names he trembles as I do.'[31]

He was eventually delivered from Erskine when the unfortunate general committed suicide at Lisbon in 1813. Meanwhile there was the further problem of his second-in-command. Poor Lord Liverpool racked his brains. He had four good candidates all of whom declined (Lord William Bentinck because he was 'so despondent about the cause in the Peninsula') and it had to be Sir Brent Spencer again.[32] The news brought no joy to Wellington. Sir Brent was a great courtier, supposed to have made a secret royal marriage to George III's daughter, Princess Augusta, known as 'Puss', and Wellington did not trust him to support the cause when on leave:

On the contrary the Royal Family at their dinners or their Card parties would make him say what they please, & he would swear to it afterwards.[33]

To Lord Liverpool, an unrelenting Tory, he sent a special request.

I only beg you not to send me any violent party men. We must keep the spirit of party out of the army, or we shall be in a bad way indeed.[34]

Another dangerous weakness was 'croaking' – the contemporary word for grumbling and defeatism. In spreading doubts about Wellington's strategy the croakers incidentally gave away intelligence to the enemy about the numbers and positions of his army, through letters home which got into the newspapers. Wellington often suggested censorship, but the nineteenth century knew nothing of Official Secrets Acts until 1879. Secrecy depended on individual discretion, as when Colonel John Colborne of the 52nd, Wellington's best officer in the Light Brigade, wrote to his sister in 1810, 'Remember, my letters are sacred and must not be repeated'.*

One arch-croaker, in Wellington's view, was Charles Stewart, adjutant-general and half-brother of Castlereagh. He had to be got rid of after much friction, including at least one scene when the Commander-in-Chief reduced the adjutant-general to tears. But with a remarkable talent for management, Wellington never allowed their

---

* (Moore-Smith, p. 147, 9 November 1810.) Field-Marshal Sir John Colborne, 1st Baron Seaton (1778–1863) A brilliant product of the Shorncliffe training under Sir John Moore. Governor-General and Commander-in-Chief, Canada, 1838. He was over six feet tall, had an aquiline nose second only to Wellington's, and a winning nature.

relations to be completely severed. Nor did he let himself brood too much over croaking and criticism.

As a result of 'never-minding' and remaining friendly, Wellington was able to buy from Stewart before he went home his young charger, Copenhagen.

It would not have been the British Army without some complaints of the Naval arm also, and Wellington told William he was 'teazed to death' by the interference and ingenuity of Admiral Berkeley in all matters from the commissariat to the artillery, but especially in planning for an emergency embarkation.

I tremble when I think I shall have to embark the Leopards in front of Bonaparte aided by such a man, who has already twenty new invented modes of putting Leopards into Boats. . . .[35]

As usual, Wellington learnt in the end how to handle an awkward human phenomenon. The culmination came on 2 December 1811 when he actually wrote to Liverpool asking *not* to be relieved of the Admiral: 'it is impossible for two officers to be on better terms than we are.'

There were some who would have turned the tables on Wellington, declaring that he did not give enough encouragement to his subordinates. Even the tactful William had found something amiss with the Talavera despatch.

. . . I never read so clear or so modest a statement. I have but one fault to find with it – you are not warm enough in Praise of your officers. . . .[36]

Another fault was said to be a certain haughtiness at his own table. Only young Lord March, Lord Fitzroy Somerset and Captain Burgh, later Lord Downes, were thought to be completely happy members of his military 'family'.

It was quite true that Wellington, in looking for able young men for his personal staff, preferred ability with a title to ability without. All commanders were accustomed to select their military family from their actual families or close friends, most of whom in Wellington's case were members of the nobility. Lord March, whom Wellington called 'the best fellow I ever saw', was the eldest son of his great friend the Duke of Richmond. The Beaufort family, from whom Fitzroy Somerset sprang, was to be allied three times over with Wellington's, Fitzroy himself marrying one of Wellington's nieces, while his eldest brother, Lord Worcester, having been rescued from the arms of Harriette Wilson and sent out to Wellington in the Peninsula, married another of his nieces, and after she died, yet another.

Wellington always liked the *jeunesse dorée*. No doubt the obvious delight he took in their dashing style and uninhibited spirits created jealousies. But when ability was missing no youth, however golden, was permitted to remain.

Failure to take his senior staff officers into his confidence was one more fault. Two historians have studied this trait in action but reached conflicting conclusions. Sir Charles Oman discovered that of all his generals, Craufurd, Beresford and Hill were the only ones with whom he 'condescended' to talk freely, so that Picton and Cole complained; while Sir John Fortescue found he wrote freely only to Hill, Cotton and Cole, so that Craufurd and Picton complained.[37] The fact is that for a public man he had astonishingly little of that desire to be loved by the many, to win wide affection by giving it widely, such as Nelson possessed. Wellington's innate reticence developed into something that ill-will could mistake for pride. But whatever Wellington's officers may have lost through his contracted human sympathies, they gained immeasurably from his super-human composure and reserves of strength at a crisis.

After the fall of Ciudad Rodrigo it was known that Massena would besiege Almeida. The two fortresses stood facing one another like the castles across a chess board, with Elvas and Badajoz as the corresponding pair in the south. Once Massena had captured the two northern castles his road to Portugal would be open. He would be a long step nearer to saying checkmate. On 26 August 1810 he began shelling Almeida. With reasonable luck, however, Wellington could expect the town to hold out until possibly the end of September. But the 'child of fortune', as Wellington liked to call himself, was not to be in luck this time. Indeed, what Oman calls 'the greatest accident of the War' was about to befall him.[38]

Barrels of gunpowder were being carried from the main powder magazine inside Almeida Cathedral on Sunday 27 August to the cannon on the walls. One keg happened to be leaky and left a long trail of gunpowder behind it. A French shell accidentally ignited this trail; the flame ran all the way back to the great Cathedral doors, open for lading, where more ammunition caught fire and in turn set off the main magazine inside. Suddenly, in a tempest of fire and smoke and crashing masonry, like a nineteenth-century print of Judgement Day, the whole Cathedral, castle and town centre vanished. Hundreds of the garrison died. The survivors forced Governor Cox to surrender, which he did at noon on 28 August 1810.

The moment had almost come to put Wellington's secret plan for the defence of Portugal into action. It was to centre on a compact, deliberate retreat into a gigantic fortress. And if possible – if that 'old fox' Massena could be lured into committing such a *bêtise* – there would be one great battle on the way there in a position of his own choosing. Fought partly to hearten the croakers, it would be a battle of prestige.

By the middle of the first week in September he had moved his headquarters back from Celorico to Gouveia. There he stood until the third week, receiving accurate information from his intelligence service about Massena's advance, and bargaining with Massena for the lives of each other's prisoners caught sniping or straggling in the Beira mountains.

The snipers were Wellington's. Known as the *Ordenanza*, these Portuguese peasants operated in their traditional woollen caps, short brown cloaks and breeches 'negligently drawn over their bare legs',[39] carrying old blunderbusses, pikes and pruning knives. In vain Wellington insisted to Massena that the *Ordenanza* called up under ancient Portuguese law were as much serving soldiers as those in the militia. Massena had them all executed at the price of his own stragglers' lives.

There was an incipient feeling of confidence in Wellington's camp, even though the fall of Almeida had caused the Whig Opposition and the Portuguese Regency Council to redouble their croaking in the expectation of instant evacuation. A defensive strategy of which the core at Torres Vedras was still invisible could not be expected to win applause.

Which road would the 'old fox' Massena take to Coimbra, and so onwards to Lisbon? Wellington heard to his amazement on 17 September that Massena was advancing by the road through Viseu. 'There are certainly many bad roads in Portugal,' he wrote to Stuart with grim satisfaction, 'but the enemy has decidedly taken the worst in the whole kingdom.'[40] 'Not a soul anywhere; all is abandoned,' wrote Massena glumly; 'our soldiers find potatoes . . . and only live to meet the enemy.'[41] Massena had touched the fringe of a 'scorched earth' policy. Even with the 350,000 pounds of bread found in Almeida, it was not a well-fed army which invaded Portugal.

Massena's extraordinary choice of route (due to misleading maps and ignorant guides), though more than welcome to Wellington, meant a sudden and swift change of plan. The divisions of Hill and Leith were ordered back at once from the fortified heights above the River Alva to an equally strong position to the north. This was the famous ridge of Bussaco. All along Bussaco's towering hog's back, running north and south for almost ten miles, Wellington stationed his sixty cannon and army of 51,000 men, half British and half Portuguese – a somewhat thin barrier of men perched upon a mighty barrier of mountain. A staff officer, on being asked by an artillery officer for a map of Bussaco to send to England, replied: 'You only have to draw a damned long hill, and that will be sufficiently explanatory.'

Past Bussaco's southern end wound the River Mondego, under a strange, perpendicular cliff of grey granite. Deep heather covered its sides and summit, broken by boulders of black basalt and pink and grey limestone. Solid stone windmills stood here and there on high plateaux. At the loftiest point of all, two miles from its northern end, Wellington established his headquarters in the wooded and walled Convent of Bussaco. Every room was occupied by his staff, except for the Prior's and that of one monk who managed to fill his up with lumber. From a narrow, cork-lined cell with white-washed walls and brick floor, Wellington issued his final orders of 26 September 1810. His soldiers, most of them concealed behind the *massif*'s crest, were to eat a cold evening meal and lie down without fires in total darkness and eerie silence. He knew that Massena would force a head-on collision next day. No flanking movement to north or south. Head-on, against the mountain. It had been almost too much to hope for, but it was going to happen.

Massena had unaccountably delayed at the village of Mortagoa, eight miles from Bussaco, between the 19th and 25th. He explained to Napoleon that he was waiting for supplies; others believed that he was resting his mistress 'Madame X'.[42] She rode everywhere with him dressed in an aide-de-camp's uniform. Ney had to shout the results of a very inadequate reconnaissance through Massena's bedroom door. No doubt she had found the Viseu road rough going. By the 26th, however, Wellington could see Massena's army of over 65,000 men assembled on the eastern hills opposite.

As black night fell in tense stillness over Bussaco, innumerable French bivouac fires across the valley sprang into cheerful life.

13

They Shall Not Pass

<hr>

At daybreak on 27 September 1810 Wellington reconnoitred his outposts. One commanding officer was found to be drunk through nerves and was quietly removed. 'A man gets nervous,' Wellington explained years afterwards, 'thinking of his own responsibility; and then he takes to brandy – want of confidence in himself, there's the evil.'[1] It was an evil from which Wellington never suffered, to the inestimable advantage of his army.

He also found that fog had moved in even more decisively than Massena. From his high command-post outside the Convent walls he could see nothing of the three French corps below, whose bivouac fires had made them so distinct the night before: the IInd Corps under General Reynier occupying the hamlet of San Antonio de Cantaro opposite Wellington's centre; then the VIth under Marshal Ney in the village of Moura to Reynier's right; lastly the VIIIth Corps under Junot in reserve. Wellington could not see even his own riflemen on the lower slopes, though ever since dawn ominous sounds had been coming up from below. Skirmishers of both armies were in contact. All at once, about 6 am, the heads of four French battalions under General Heudelet burst upwards through the mist.

This was the start of Massena's dawn attack. It had been assigned to Reynier, whose 14,000 troops were to assault the central section of the ridge, using a cart-track from San Antonio which crossed it from east to west.* During a long, hectic hour it looked as if Reynier might succeed, though Heudelet's attack had failed. Eleven battalions under General Merle made towards Lightburne's brigade on Picton's left, where Wellington himself stood, plain and workmanlike in his usual plumeless cocked hat and a grey greatcoat. He soon had two six-pounders

<hr>

* Today this old track can be seen clearly from Bussaco as it leaves the hamlet of San Antonio and begins to climb the ridge; but about half-way up it becomes a mere jumble of loose rocks, until it finally hits a new forestry road, running laterally along the ridge, and disappears.

trained on them, though at long range. Distracted by fog, the guns and Allied skirmishers away to their left, they swerved diagonally in that direction and accidentally hit on a weak spot in Wellington's line. It was a lucky accident for Merle. The Allies' light troops were easily driven in. Some of Merle's *voltigeurs* (special companies of skirmishers) dashed ahead and reached the rocks on the summit. If they could be supported, the whole tide of Reynier's powerful 1st Division would soon be rolling over the crest.

Wellington ordered down two more six-pounders to blast the French flanks with grape and canister. Picton, splendidly eccentric in his night-cap, personally rallied the disordered light companies and brought them back to support the brave men who, from right and left, were fighting the battle of the gap. These were the 8th Portuguese, Major Gwynne's half of the 45th and above all that great fighting regiment of Irishmen, some of whom knew only enough English to get by on parade, the 88th Connaught Rangers. Into the enemy's front the Portuguese musketeers poured their steady volleys, while Alexander Wallace, the Connaught Rangers' fiery colonel, shouted, 'Now, Connaught Rangers . . . when I bring you face to face with those French rascals, drive them down the hill!'

Though there were eleven French battalions against only four Anglo-Portuguese, Merle's men were exhausted by their steep, fast climb with packs on their backs through the boulder-strewn scrub. Under Wallace's onslaught their foremost ranks toppled backwards on to those behind, until suddenly the whole mass broke and rushed headlong down the mountain-side, Allies and enemy, bayonets and bodies, drummers and drums, bouncing from rock to rock pell-mell to the bottom.

'Upon my honour, Wallace,' cried Wellington riding up, 'I never witnessed a more gallant charge than that just now made by your regiment.'

It was nearly 7 am. In the pearly air above the mountain, shafts of sunlight were dissolving the mists; on the slopes the carnage was still partly hidden. Now, between the two bloody avalanches of debris left by Heudelet and Merle, the third French attack began. Seven more battalions of Reynier's 2nd Division, marched superbly upwards, led by their highly distinguished young general, Maximilien Foy. It was Foy's duty to force his way over. He came within an ace of success. Indeed, but for one of those strokes which demonstrated Wellington's genius on the battlefield, Foy would have been there. His leading

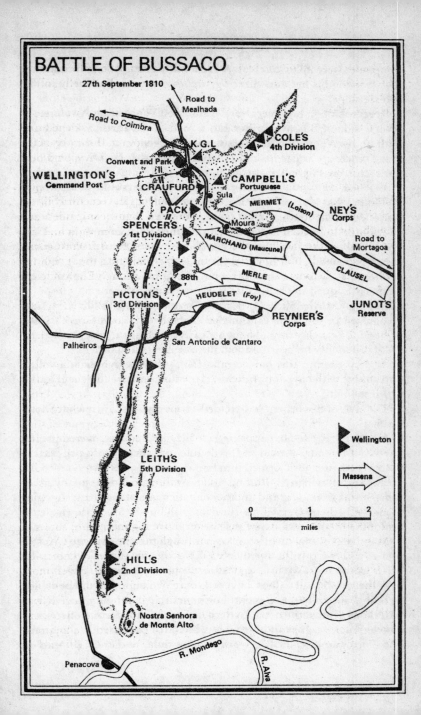

BATTLE OF BUSSACO

27th September 1810

Road to Mealhada

Road to Coimbra

K.G.L

COLE'S
4th Division

Convent and Park

WELLINGTON'S
Command Post

CRAUFURD

CAMPBELL'S
Portuguese

Sula

PACK

MERMET (Loison)

NEY'S
Corps

SPENCER'S
1st Division

Moura

MARCHAND (Maucune)

Road to
Mortagoa

88th

MERLE

CLAUSEL

PICTON'S
3rd Division

HEUDELET (Foy)

JUNOT'S
Reserve

REYNIER'S
Corps

Palheiros

San Antonio de Cantaro

0   1   2
miles

Wellington

LEITH'S
5th Division

Massena

HILL'S
2nd Division

Nostra Senhora
de Monte Alto

Penacova

R. Mondego

R. Alva

companies were up to the crest. A French officer leapt on to the topmost rock, waving his hat and cheering; *tirailleurs* swarmed to the lip of the reverse slope.

Reverse slopes, however, were Wellington's speciality. All along the reverse side of Bussaco's ridge ran a road of red earth, widened and built up by Wellington for just such an emergency. In the midst of the first French upthrusts he had ordered Leith's 5th Division, who held the sector on Picton's right, to move to their left, if not themselves threatened, along the hidden lateral road. They could then support Picton in what looked like being the crucial struggle. General Hill was stationed on the southernmost point of the ridge known as the Senhora da Monte Alto, which he had reached at the last moment by a brilliant march unknown to Massena. He was now to move at his discretion into the gap opened by Leith. Hill's vacant space was left to the care of the Senhora. It was a bold decision. And announced with sufficient boldness to quell the fears of at least one young officer.

Captain Moyle Sherer, who was serving in Hill's division, had recognized in the three columns of 'black enormous masses' his first sight of a French army. Thoughts of Austerlitz, of Jena flooded his mind. Suddenly he heard a loud, deep voice issuing orders:

'If they attempt this point again, Hill, you will give them a volley, and charge with bayonets; but don't let your people follow them too far down the hill.'

The style of this order – 'so decided, so manly' – was just what Sherer needed.

Just as the French hat appeared aloft, Leith, having covered the last stretch of the lateral road at the double, advanced on to the plateau with his 9th and 38th formed into line and waving his own plumed hat in answering defiance. Rolling volleys tore into Foy's column, Foy himself was wounded, and another chaotic mass of fugitives, sweeping along with them Heudelet's survivors, again streamed down to the bottom of the mountain and the shelter of their guns.

Marshal Ney meanwhile had seen through the thinning mist Merle's first *voltigeurs* crowning the heights. This was his signal to launch his VIth Corps from Moura, and after capturing Sula opposite him, to rush the paved road to the Convent so that Wellington would be caught in both front and rear. General Loison marched out with twelve fresh battalions against the north-eastern face of the mountain, between two wooded ravines. Inexorably they pushed a tough force of 1,400 British and Portuguese Rifles (*Caçadores*) out of Sula, and then climbed on towards two targets high above them, Ross's battery of six guns and the round, white, Allied command-post, Sula Mill.

Twenty yards from the top the French prepared to run in upon the guns. But Ross's artillery, having duly expended their last shot, galloped off to the rear. In their place, drawn up by Wellington on the Sula road behind Craufurd's solitary figure and totally invisible even to the front ranks of climbers below, nearly 1,800 infantry of the 52nd and 43rd (Light Division) waited, motionless and silent. Suddenly General Craufurd swept off his hat and sent his great voice clanging among the rocks. 'Now, Fifty-Second! Avenge the death of Sir John Moore!'[2] The echoes rolled back to him. 'Charge! charge!' he shouted, 'Huzza!' In a moment, 'eighteen hundred British bayonets went sparkling over the brow of the hill.' William Napier's thrilling words must find a place in any story of Bussaco, even though they managed to associate an unutterably horrible charge with the haunting beauty of a waterfall. The Napier brothers were there to see the awful tornado of bullets, discharged at ten paces, slice off the heads of the leading French columns, while broad tongues of fire curled round their flanks. Down, down into the valley, sprawling and slithering over boulders streaming with blood, went thousands of Napoleon's soldiers the fourth time that day. Yet for this cruelly exposed army, four times was not enough.

Three-quarters of an hour after his 1st Division had started, Ney sent in eleven more battalions under General Marchand on the left of the two ravines. Victory seemed assured, for only four battalions, and these all Portuguese, faced them on the summit. They knew nothing of what a small nation in arms, inspired by Wellington, could do. Its young soldiers delivered a fire as deadly as its veteran British allies. For all his resolution Marchand had to retreat from an impossible enterprise.

Massena's first trial of the despised Portuguese army and its leopard partners had resulted in 4,600 French losses to 626 British and 626 Portuguese – an exact Allied sharing of casualties as of valour. Wellington had resoundingly beaten Massena, the man he was afterwards to consider Napoleon's ablest general.

What happened next day was scarcely surprising, since part of the 'old fox's' army was still untouched. Wellington heard on 28 September that his left flank had been turned in the defiles north of Bussaco. Though in private he hotly blamed the Portuguese commander, the blow was to prestige rather than strategy. He had envisaged an ultimate withdrawal into the heart of the fortress that was Portugal – now ready and waiting to receive him. There he would stand and defy the French invaders until, in good time, he was strong enough to push them out. That evening Wellington resumed his retreat. With Bussaco as brightly lit by deceptive camp fires as it had been dark the night before, his first troops slipped away past Penacova and its ruined Moorish castle at the southernmost tip of the ridge, and marched out on to the Coimbra road. Behind him on the mountain he had left an olive tree in the Convent garden planted with his own hands and a legend of Anglo-Portuguese glory that has not yet disappeared. His lookout point, now shut in by plantations, is marked by a flat, inscribed stone. Two sail-less windmills, one by Moura and the other on Sula hill, carry plaques stating that they were the command-posts of Massena and Craufurd respectively. At the Sula gate outside the Convent park a tall obelisk has been raised topped by a glass star (switched on for the anniversary) and surrounded by a railing of cannon barrels standing on their muzzles. Nearby is a museum where models of the valiant Allied soldiers can be seen, all the Portuguese brown-eyed, all the British blue. For the Peninsula, such a wealth of historic memorials is inspiring. In the splendidly fantastic palace (now a hotel) built beside the old Convent by King Ferdinand II, huge battle scenes in blue and green tiles keep fresh the legend of 'Lord W'. Inside his cell is a plaque to 'The Glorious General'.

The Allies streamed through Coimbra with the French at their heels. Massena wrongly expected to have them beaten and flying for their ships in a week. Wellington rightly believed he was making for safety, but he kept his secret still.

The citizens of wealthy Coimbra had failed to take the 'scorched earth' measures that the frontier towns had so heroically achieved. A torrent of wretched families loaded with baggage which should long ago have been removed or destroyed, struggled over the Mondego bridge with Wellington's army, while their abandoned houses flamed behind them. Terrified inmates of prisons and asylums, smelling the fires, screamed from barred windows to be let out. The British soldiers freed them, so that among the desperate horde that poured down the Lisbon road was a quota of murderers and madmen. Some of the victors of Bussaco made their own crazy contributions to the scene. Despite Wellington's incessant orders against plunder, one soldier staggered out of Coimbra laden with a huge gilt mirror. He and the mirror were hung up together on the roadside by the 'bloody Provost' –a ghastly confrontation.

Massena's army rampaged through the deserted city looting everything they could lay hands on, from rings on the fingers of corpses in graveyards to the priceless scientific instruments in the University. Though Ney tried to stop the sacking, Junot did not hesitate to help himself. Massena lost his communications with France. As he raced south the militia and *Ordenanza* closed in behind him, sealing all the exits. The besieger was besieged; though he did not yet know it. Nor did he yet know that when Wellington's army made their usual day's march on 8 October 1810, they were in fact entering the Lines of Torres Vedras. The leopard had been driven into the hills instead of the sea. There was a great difference.

People at home reacted to recent events much as Wellington expected. William assured him on 27 October, 'Your Battle of Bussaco is universally admired.' But in a letter to William of 4 October Wellington had shown himself prepared for Talavera-type criticism:

The Croakers about useless battles will attack me again about that of Bussaco; notwithstanding that our loss was really trifling.[3]

Among the many captured documents brought to Wellington's camp after Bussaco were Massena's despatches taken off a French officer making his way to Paris disguised as a Spanish peasant. One paper consisted of a question and answer prepared by Massena to assist the officer through an awkward interview with Napoleon's chief-of-staff.

Q. Do you think you will get to Lisbon?
A. Everything makes us hope so; the English being in full retreat, and the French full of confidence in their General-in-Chief.[4]

Massena did indeed expect to reach Lisbon within a week. Nevertheless, if Wellington had been asked, 'Do you think you will halt Massena short of Lisbon?' he would have answered with better reason, 'Everything makes us hope so.'

The entry into the Lines of Torres Vedras on that first day went as smoothly as a machine.

Not that these so-called 'lines' greatly resembled the continuous lengths of stone wall or earthworks which might at first spring to mind. The Lines of Torres Vedras were essentially groups of hill-forts commanding all highways and passes to Lisbon. Yet though this is broadly true, it misses their full subtlety; for where the scarping* of long

---

* Scooping away earth to make a more or less perpendicular rampart.

mountain ranges provided continuous barriers, the Lines were indeed lines.

Each contingent was met and led to its appointed defence post. By evening many progress reports had reached Wellington. Picton, for instance, wrote that he had entered Torres Vedras itself,[5] the town which was to give its name to the whole defence system.

Torres Vedras – the old towers – was one of the most ancient towns of Portugal. It had its river, the Zizandre, its aqueduct, its Moorish castle high on a hill. Its inhabitants were employed on the military works. All trees which might give cover to the French invader were felled and the wood used for revetting (facing) gun embrasures and ditches, while the tops of the trees formed *abattis* – twig entanglements on forward slopes. The Moorish castle had become Redoubt No. 27 in Wellington's total of 152 forts. But for all its elaboration and fame, the first line of fortifications of which Torres Vedras formed a part was not Wellington's strongest. Running for twenty-nine miles from the sea coast to the Tagus at Alhandra, it was originally intended only to hold up Massena until the army could fall back into the impregnable defences of the second line behind.

This second chain of fortifications, extending for twenty-two miles from the coast to the Tagus, was roughly parallel to the first but began six miles to the south. Even on a still day the surf below the westernmost fort of all, No. 97, came boiling into narrow ravines between inaccessible cliffs. No enemy could land here, but there was an estuary not far off. Therefore here, high up among stunted gorse and juniper, thistles and rock roses, Fletcher's peasants had hacked out a ditch, scarp, counter-scarp and traverse, with gun embrasures for many batteries covering the estuary. Every few moments came a defiant boom from the sea; the redoubt's own guns could boom in cross-fire with Forts 96 and 95, the latter being another Torres Vedras on a small scale. The gigantic pile of Mafra had become an entrenched camp. Twenty redoubts bristled with guns round the *tapada* (royal park). After nature's prodigious masterpiece, the Pass of Montachique, the second line wound on eastwards, with a thick knot of forts at the next pass, Bucelas, until it reached the green Tagus valley where there were rice-fields, salt-pans and breeding grounds for bulls and tiny red dragonflies. At the end of this line a strong group of redoubts had established a potent cross-fire with Admiral Berkeley's gunboats on the river.

And so southwards again to the third line. An embarkation point in case of dire necessity was the real purpose here, and the third line centred on two miles of shore around Fort St Julian, in the Tagus estuary between Lisbon and the sea. This was also the main landing-place for the army's and population's food. Everyone, including Wellington, preferred to emphasize the latter aspect of the third line.

Back in the first of Wellington's lines the entry of troops continued throughout 8, 9 and 10 October, according to plan. Queries flowed in from all over the Lines about reinforcements, cavalry support, when to destroy bridges. Across one of General Sontag's moans about the Portuguese militia Wellington wrote in his habitual thick, rather illegible pencil for the attention of the military secretary, James Bathurst:

Tell him that I will attend to the enemy's movements & take care to have troops sufficient in any quarter likely to be attacked; & that I am responsible that the troops I lead in any situation are of a sufficiently good description and sufficiently numerous to defend their fort; & to do what I require of them.[6]

They had Wellington and that was sufficient.

By 10 October 1810 the Allied army was all inside the Lines, apart from cavalry patrols. It was from one of these patrols, captured near Alenquer, that the French cavalry commander, Montbrun, received a puzzling piece of news. They had been on their way back, said the British prisoners, to 'the Lines'. The Lines? It was the first Montbrun, or any other Frenchman, had heard of them.

On the 12th Massena's vanguard drove in Wellington's outposts at Sobral. Wellington at once withdrew his forces from the village to the place appointed for them three miles to the south – the immensely strong, fortified camp on the heights of Monte Agraço, a fastness towering above all other mountains in the Torres Vedras peninsula. From the top could be seen the white houses of Sobral where the French, in turn, sat looking at Monte Agraço. This was where Wellington decided to make his stand. This was where he hoped Massena would launch his second Bussaco.

This also happened to be where Massena discovered what the captured cavalry patrol had meant by 'the Lines'. On 14 October Junot overran some light defences at the foot of Monte Agraço – and suddenly laid bare the hidden strength behind. He retired to Sobral and informed Massena. That old fox gave a rocket to the stupid officers who had not told him about the Lines. They explained lamely, 'Wellington has made them.' 'The devil,' shouted Massena, 'Wellington didn't make the mountains!'

So Massena had to do what Wellington did always: get upon his horse and see for himself. On that same 14 October he made an extensive reconnaissance. Then he re-entered Sobral merely to sit down for a month and await reinforcements. Wellington and his officers were much disappointed. So he gave a 'grand Ball, previous dinner, and concluding supper' at Mafra on the occasion of Beresford being created Knight of the Bath. Edward Pakenham agreed that such 'an amusement' with 50,000 of the enemy a few miles off might seem like 'madness'; on the contrary, the Mafra ball gave confidence to the capital and pride to the Portuguese army – '*Viva*!!!'[7]

Ned's '*Viva*' was not misplaced. For when the French turned back from Monte Agraço on 14 October 1810 the tide of French conquest in Europe turned also. The skirmish at the foot of the mountain had caused only sixty-seven Allied and 120 French casualties. Such a limited action; such prodigious results.

Sickness among Massena's troops, besides acute shortage of all supplies, soon made a further retreat necessary. Taking advantage of a blanketing fog during the night of 14 November, Massena's army silently decamped without having to fire a shot. Who was the Child of Fortune now? For a few days Wellington attempted a pursuit. On 24 November he called it off, leaving Marshal Massena to be dealt with by General Starvation.

No less than for Massena, reinforcements were a major problem for Wellington. An angry conviction grew in his mind that the Government's failure to reinforce him, or to settle arrears of army pay, was due to lack of confidence in his Peninsular campaign. When England herself was invaded, 'we shall heartily repent all the little dirty feelings which have prevented us from continuing the contest elsewhere.' Yet, concluded Wellington gloomily, as soon as the Prince of Wales became Regent, he would 'change everything'.[8] In other words, he would bring in his friends the Whigs, who would promptly withdraw the army and leave the Peninsula to Napoleon.

Instead, the Prince Regent turned against the Whigs. William gleefully reported 'chop fallen faces' among the Opposition, 'who were all cock-a-hoop before'.[9] Portugal would not be abandoned.

Troubles of a different kind still haunted the Portuguese Regency Council. The Sousas, a great city family, were not able to persuade every peasant to carry out the scorched earth policy. From the other angle, scorched earth meant scarred people: fifty thousand died of hunger behind the Lines, munching the yellow thistles that grew among the redoubts. It was a large number out of a population of two and a half million. And what were they suffering for? Wellington's 'cautious system' or 'defensive system',[10] as he himself called it, did not at first seem worth such sacrifices.

The Sousas naturally abhorred all anti-clericals from Liberals to Freemasons, especially the latter who had been instituted in Portugal by the French invaders. Wellington found this out almost too late. Enormous scandal was caused by his officers staging their customary Masonic activities while in Lisbon. One procession in particular, of January 1810, narrowly escaped being shot at and stoned.[11] Wellington at once issued a General Order requiring his officers to refrain from

an amusement which, however innocent in itself, and allowed by the law of Great Britain, is a violation of the law of this country, and very disagreeable to the people.[12]

Unfortunately the Portuguese were under the impression (and still are) that Wellington himself was a Freemason in more than a purely technical sense. This was a mistake. True, he had been initiated at Trim Lodge as a very young man. He never went near that or any other Lodge again. Later on he developed a powerful antipathy to anything and everything that might conceivably be regarded as a secret or subversive society.

Wellington's own dislike for the Sousas, whom he referred to predictably as 'these gentry'[13] never got much beyond colourful language. In this case everyone was deeply aware at bottom of fighting for the same cause.

Christmas Day 1810 in the Lines. Fog as usual. A message from Craufurd's advance post, the same one that had come almost every day for weeks, said that it was too thick to see anything but the sentries, though 'the Drums were heard as usual'.[14] As usual, desertions. Two men from the Brunswick Corps went over to the French, while two boys, one a scullion of Pierre Soult's, deserted to the Allies. Then there were invitations from the French in Santarém to watch amateur theatricals, invitations from the English to watch football and horse-racing. The French were hungry, as usual; but not yet hungry enough.

New Year's Day 1811 in London. Kitty's journal seemed to echo the muted atmosphere of an advanced post in the Lines: all listening and waiting. Yet the journal was not quite as usual. There was a new note of asperity. At least it showed that she had some spirit. Unfortunately there was no guarantee that she would not use it against Arthur's friends when he came home.

January 1st . . . Lady Liverpool kindly asked me to spend the day with her. I did so: the company a set of stupid Lords who were anything but pleasant. I behaved very ill and expressed what I thought of them.

April 13th. Letters from Portugal: all well to the 27th. Spent the day at home alone. I will at last observe the advance of my Children, I will at last rise in tolerable time, I will at last keep resolutions so often repeated, so often broken.

Needless to say, Kitty's 'at last' was still a dream. Her journal broke off abruptly a week later and did not begin again for seventeen months. Something else, however, had actually happened – at last. On 5 March, in yet another dense fog, Massena had struck camp and was off.

The French had a start of thirty miles over Wellington, whose staff had given up all hope of Massena ever going. In the great race north, each commander had his difficulties. Massena's wretched army had been reduced to under 46,000 and even little luxuries for Madame X had to be smuggled through the English lines.[15] Wellington's soldiers were still plundering, and in January 1811 he had had to make a reasoned plea for a reform in the recruiting system, to get a better type of regular soldier.

It is expected that people will become soldiers in the line, and leave their families to starve, when if they become soldiers in the militia, their families are provided for.[16]

What was the result of this inconsistency?

That none but the worst description of men enter the regular service.

Granted that Wellington's army was not perfect, it was improving as fast as Massena's deteriorated. 'We are becoming a more efficient and better army every day', he wrote to Liverpool just before the pursuit began.[17]

A series of exciting rear-guard actions lasted until the middle of March. Up till then Massena had intended merely to break through into an unscorched district, and to renew the march on Lisbon. Thanks to Trant's militia, however, and Wellington's tactical skill, Massena was manoeuvred away from the Mondego and forced to make a dash for the Spanish frontier.

On 15 March he gave the crucial order. All impedimenta including ammunition were flung away and pack animals hamstrung. The pursuing Allies were reminded of Soult's ghastly retreat from Oporto, only this time it was far worse. Ravines, pits, ditches, huts and chapels revealed their sickening collections of skeletons and decomposing or fresh bodies, some of them half burnt or mangled by torture, to extract information about hidden food and wine. Ned Pakenham described to his brother Tom 'the acts of horror actually committed by these fiends of hell'.[18] It seemed hardly possible that these were the same civilized Frenchmen who had once warned them, while still in the Lines, not to worry if they heard 101 cannon-shots: it would only be a *feu de joie* in honour of the birth of Napoleon's son, the King of Rome.[19]

Despite Ney's defensive brilliance, Wellington felt so sure of victory by 20 March that he sent his troop-transports home. The front and back doors out of Portugal were thus voluntarily closed. Two days later Marshal Ney was sent involuntarily back to France. Massena had ordered a ludicrous swerve to the south against Plasencia. Ney rightly called it madness and wrongly defied his superior.

A week's agonizing tramp through barren mountains soon forced Massena to turn east again. On 3 April Reynier's IInd Corps narrowly escaped extinction at Sabugal. But for the fog on the battlefield and the denser fog in General Sir William Erskine's mind, the Light Division and cavalry would have taken the French in flanks and rear. Even as it was they caused 760 French casualties to 179 of their own, having fought 'one of the most glorious actions British troops were ever engaged in'.[20]

That night Massena ordered a general retreat on Ciudad Rodrigo, across the River Agueda. Five days later he and Madame X entered Salamanca, his base. Napoleon had given him an impossible task. Portugal could not be subdued by less than 100,000, as Wellington had always said. But since Napoleon insisted that there were never more than 30,000 leopards – Portuguese being a species of animal that he simply did not count – 65,000 French soldiers seemed plenty. Considering these handicaps and the assistance of Madame X, Massena's extrication of his army from Portugal was a triumph of skill.

On 10 April 1811 Wellington issued a proclamation:

The Portuguese are informed that the cruel enemy ... have been obliged to evacuate, after suffering great losses, and have retired across the Agueda. The inhabitants of the country are therefore at liberty to return to their homes.

Massena's 'great losses' amounted to 25,000; Wellington's to less than a sixth of that number.

Everyone, even the Opposition, rejoiced. Three weeks later when a vote of thanks was passed by both Houses for Wellington's campaign, William felt Parliament had never been 'more unanimous'. Lord Grey was 'highly flattering', Ponsonby (another Whig leader) 'very handsome', Canning 'very complimentary'. And miracle of miracles, costive old Sir David Dundas at the Horse Guards actually gave Wellington leave to *promote* six majors and twelve captains!

The Portuguese war represented the solid virtues of caution and economy of force by avoidance of big battles. Beside a battery at Alhandra was to stand a monument to the Lines of Torres Vedras: a pillar surmounted by the figure of Hercules, with the inscription, NON ULTRA – *They Shall Not Pass*.

They did not pass. But there was more to it than that. After the retreat, the stand. After the stand, the advance. In the final advance against Massena, Wellington's army had shown a new talent of immense significance, manoeuvrability. And he had predicted exactly a month earlier: 'the war is now likely to take on a new shape. . . .'

14

The Keys of Spain

The new shape of war demanded radical changes in Spain. Without a secure hold on its two border fortresses of Ciudad Rodrigo and Badajoz, Wellington's war could never become properly offensive.

Up till the beginning of March 1811 the Spaniards at least held Badajoz, though under siege by Soult. Well aware of the fortress's increasing peril, Wellington despatched Beresford on 8 March to its relief. When Beresford arrived, it was to besiege Badajoz, not to succour it. But the treacherous Governor, José Imaz, surrendered it to Soult on the 11th. In Wellington's bitter words, Badajoz had been 'sold'.

The answer to most Spanish problems, thought Henry Wellesley at Cádiz, was to 'make Arthur Generalissimo'. Arthur agreed; but Henry was foiled by three awkward facts. General Blake, a Spaniard of Irish descent whom Henry described as very popular because he had won one battle and lost only seventeen, was desperately jealous. The slogan 'Arthur for Generalissimo' received no powerful backing at home. Wellington let the matter of his Spanish command drop. The problem of Badajoz could not be dropped so easily.

As soon as Massena had been driven back into northern Spain, Wellington decided to see for himself how Beresford was proceeding in the south. Having minutely instructed Beresford regarding the immediate investment of Badajoz, Wellington started back again at a gallop on 25 April and 'returned to us', in Ned's jubilant words, 'exactly in time'.

Young Johnny Kincaid of the Rifles had been eaten up with curiosity when he joined the Peninsular army in 1810 to see the famous general. Since Wellington frequently visited the Torres Vedras outposts, Kincaid was soon satisfied. 'He was just such a man as I had figured in my mind's eye,' he wrote. A man who could be picked out from hundreds of others dressed in the same uniform. Now, on Wellington's whirlwind return to the northern army in April 1811, Kincaid spoke for all:

we would rather see his long nose in a fight than a reinforcement of ten thousand men any day.[1]

On 2 May 1811 Massena ordered an advance upon Almeida of 48,000 men and thirty-eight guns.* Wellington, curiously symmetrical with forty-eight guns and 38,000 men, stood waiting on the border. Part of his army was at Badajoz; many of his troops were sick again; and one of his divisions, the 7th, was fresh from England, though it perhaps made up for lack of military experience by possessing one of the best diarists of the Peninsular war, Private W. Wheeler of the 51st. Wheeler had landed at Lisbon in March, making the Englishman's usual remarks about the excess of filth and priests. (His solution was to draft all able-bodied clergy into the forces, using the rest to clean up the streets.)

The Man of Energy, as Ned called Arthur, posted his centre in a position after his own heart. A rugged hill crowned the village of Fuentes and shaded off southward into a long plateau; behind its crest his main force could be concealed. Dared he hope that Massena would at last oblige with a frontal assault?

Early in the morning of 3 May Wellington was out with his glass sweeping the straight white road from Ciudad Rodrigo. He saw five of Massena's divisions emerge from the woods of cork and ilex. By 2 pm it had begun. Ten French battalions launched themselves across the River Dos Casas, made a brief lodgement behind rock or wall and were hurled back over the blood-stained water. As at Bussaco, Massena's head-on collision failed. Next day, 4 May, there was a grim lull. That evening, providentially, General Robert Craufurd returned to his Light Division from leave. He was just in time. For throughout the next day, 5 May, Wellington's army was to be under constant pressure with the possibility of defeat never far off.

Massena's flanking movement to the south began all too well; there seemed nothing to stop him. A few French prisoners brought in to the Allied camp and questioned as to how many of Massena's men were in the attack, replied, 'The whole French army'. The awful news was rushed to Wellington.

'Oh! they are all there, are they? Well, we must mind a little what we are about.'

His famous imperturbability had never been more needed. Two

---

* Oman gives this figure of 48,000. General Sir James Marshall-Cornwall (*Massena*, p. 240) says Massena had only 45,000, while Massena himself would not admit to more than 35,000.

hours after dawn the crisis was desperate: Wellington's right overrun, the 7th isolated, Fuentes exposed in flank and rear, the relief of Almeida in sight. Wellington took the bold course. He ordered Craufurd and the Light Division to go in and bring back the broken battalions into the lines. Let the road to Portugal be lost; he trusted his troops not to need it. Nothing would induce him to uncover Almeida.

Now followed under the eyes of the admiring Commander-in-Chief one of the most polished displays in military history. Surrounded by swirling eddies of French dragoons, Craufurd covered the retreat of the 7th with a series of rhythmical evolutions which suddenly transformed the deadly orthodoxy of Hyde Park reviews into a dance of life. Defying the enemy cavalry to approach his invincible infantry squares; holding off their artillery with short cavalry charges until his horses, in Wellington's words, 'had not a gallop in them';[2] and, as his squares formed by turns into column, protecting their retirement with the six guns of Bull's Horse Artillery, he brought his own Light Division and the crippled 7th to safety.

Wellington meanwhile had realigned his army to meet the new situation. His front now lay at right angles along the plateau, one leg running back westwards, with its hinge on Fuentes church – a position not without danger. Massena did his best to exploit it. Attack after attack carried the French up to the church; wave after wave of defenders, each new contingent sent in by Wellington in the nick of time, drove them down again to the river.

The decisive moment came at noon, when the Allies had lost the village and the huge plumes of Bonaparte's Grenadiers seemed to be everywhere, almost up to Wellington's command-post on the plateau above. All now depended on the Connaught Rangers. Pakenham had been sent to ask if they might clear the village. Wellington gave the order and Pakenham galloped back.

'He says you may go – come on!'[3] With ferocious yells the Irishmen charged, sweeping all before them. The once picturesque Spanish village was in utter ruin but victory was won. (Wellington later asked the British Government in the detached manner that concealed his feelings for a contribution to the restoration of Fuentes: it had recently become a battlefield and had not been 'much improved by this circumstance'.)[4] Massena had fought his last battle and lost. On 10 May at dawn a staff officer, Lord Aylmer, rushed into Wellington's room while he was shaving, with the news that the French had decamped.

'Ay, I thought they meant to be off; very well,' said Wellington,[5] and he went on scraping at his determined chin.

Having retreated to Ciudad Rodrigo, Massena later announced to the astonished world – a victory. Nevertheless, something had happened on the night of 10 May 1811 to give Massena a shred of excuse for his claim.

Three volunteers were paid 6,000 francs each to get a message into beleaguered Almeida, ordering Governor Brennier to break out. He should fire three salvoes at intervals of five minutes starting at 10 pm to indicate 'message received'. Two of the volunteers were caught and shot; the third got through, mostly on all fours. Next night Massena heard the signal guns. Well satisfied, he made off for Ciudad Rodrigo.

Wellington of course had taken steps to prevent a sortie. By audacity on Governor Brennier's part, however, and dismal apathy or errors on the part of five British officers, the garrison blew up Almeida and got away. Wellington was angrier than he had ever been: 'the most disgraceful military event,' he stormed, 'that has yet occurred to us.'[6] As usual the preposterous General Sir William Erskine was involved. But it was a mere colonel who was blamed; he shot himself.

The army was deeply shocked by this disaster and some blamed Wellington for hierarchical prejudice, causing him to make a colonel the scapegoat for a general's sins. Over a century later a librarian at the War Office was still accusing Wellington of 'heartlessness' in this affair.* Was he guilty?

Wellington's passions had undoubtedly been aroused. Incompetence, including foolhardiness, seemed to meet him at every turn. The problem remains as to why Wellington did not seize this golden opportunity of eliminating the ludicrous Erskine at last. The answer again emphasizes the vein of fatalism or stoicism in his character. He had already tried desperately to get rid of this man and failed, for Erskine had more influence at the Horse Guards than the 'Sepoy General'. Therefore Wellington, according to his creed, must make the best of a bad job – which would hardly be achieved by telling the world that one of his generals had lapses through taking a drop too much.

William Wellesley-Pole, however, was permitted to know Arthur's true feelings. He received a caustic note from Spain on 15 May:

. . . I begin to be of opinion with you that there is nothing so stupid as a gallant officer. . . . I am obliged to be everywhere and if absent from any operation something goes wrong.[7]

* F. J. Hudleston, *Warriors in Undress*, p. 18.

The truth was that the humiliation of Almeida had gone far to wipe out the glory of Fuentes, and when the Government decided not to move a vote of thanks for that battle, Wellington could not but agree. On 16 May he set off southwards once more, sensing perhaps that Beresford's siege of Badajoz might be another of those operations where, in his absence, 'something goes wrong'.

Beresford had opened the siege at the beginning of May. His artillery was a collection of brass museum pieces from the lately re-fortified walls of Elvas, stamped with the names of long-dead kings. This pack of sick bloodhounds, for ever 'drooping at the muzzle', were expected to batter down the giant among all the many bastions and towers of Badajoz – Fort San Cristobal. Naturally no progress was made and when, after a week, Beresford heard that Soult was coming up behind him, he abandoned the abortive siege and turned to meet Soult at the battle of Albuera. Wellington was on his way south, but had not arrived.

> Oh, Albuera! glorious field of grief!

The awful paradox of this British victory gained by Beresford at Albuera near Badajoz on 16 May 1811 was not likely to be overlooked by Byron. The carnage on both sides was appalling. Beresford had actually ordered a retreat when the twenty-six-year-old Henry Hardinge took it on himself to urge upon a willing Lowry Cole the absolute necessity of throwing in the 4th Division, orders or no orders. And so the bloody tide turned. On the victorious side not enough men were left alive to collect their dead – those terrible dead of the Peninsular battlefields, who, stripped by human kites, lay buried stark naked until the wolf came down from the mountains.

> For with his nails he'll dig them up again.*

Beresford sent in a report of the battle dwelling less on the glory than the grief. Wellington, however, foresaw the disastrous effect of the despatch's 'whining' tone. 'This won't do,' he said shortly, 'write me

---

* (John Webster, *The White Devil*, Act V scene IV). Dr Adam Neale first saw Webster's line acted out by the wolves at Vimeiro. Goya immortalized, if that is the right word, the stripping of the war dead in his drawings, now in the Prado, Madrid. When Lieutenant William Bragge saw Albuera a year after the battle the ground was white with bones

down a victory.' After all, it was a victory. Soult had been forced to retire.

Having changed the tone of the despatch, Wellington's next thought was to encourage his subordinates and friends. The shattered Beresford, whose trouble Ned Pakenham had diagnosed weeks ago as 'Anxiety', received a steadying message:

You could not be successful in such an action without a large loss, and we must make up our minds to affairs of this kind sometimes, or give up the game.[8]

Wellington visited the awful scene of battle on 21 May, and came upon one famous regiment 'literally lying dead in their ranks as they had stood'[9] – a thing he had never seen before. The effect on his army was to make his long nose among them more prized than ever.

'Men of the 29th,' he said when visiting some of the wounded, 'I am sorry to see so many of you here.' A veteran replied,

'If you had commanded us, my Lord, there wouldn't be so many of us here.'[10]

The second siege of Badajoz, opened by Wellington immediately on arrival, was to show how right the men of the 29th had been.

'Badajoz may fall,' he wrote to Charles Stuart in Lisbon on 8 June, 'but the business will be very near run on both sides. . . . I have never seen walls bear so much battering.'[11] The first assault, on 6 June, had in fact already failed; three days later came the second, also a failure. When he heard that 60,000 French were closing in on him he ordered the siege to be raised. On 17 June he retreated with the whole army across the River Guadiana.

Everyone was pleased in his own way, even the more malicious Whigs. Soult and Governor Philippon of Badajoz congratulated one another, for the town had been on the verge of surrender through starvation. Wellington's soldiers were equally thankful to depart. Work in the trenches beforehand was suffocating. They had had to storm the breach before it was completely practicable, the ladders were too short and the main assault-party lost its way. The French had finally lost their appetite for Bussaco-like engagements against Wellington, while Wellington's knowledge of their numerical superiority prevented him from attacking them. 'The devil is in the French for numbers!!!' he wrote on 12 July. The result was that he defied them from strong positions above the River Caia, a tributary of the Guadiana, for a month and then marched north towards Ciudad Rodrigo. Pakenham as usual spoke for the whole army:

Lord W's judgment in withdrawing his troops on the very day he did, – His countenance afterwards in front of very superior numbers, – His wonderful transfer under the influences of the most disappointing circumstances . . . arising out of the want of skill of another [Beresford], – have if possible raised him higher in the Estimation of his Soldiers.[12]

Soult at last returned gladly to luxurious Seville with his regal ambitions undimmed, while Massena's successor, Marshal Marmont, was left to handle Wellington.

It was good to be rid of Massena at any rate, even though General Foy believed that he had long ceased to be great. The unlucky general had received his dismissal a few hours after his great *coup* at Almeida. To Wellington he would always remain the one marshal who had kept him awake at night.

His successor, August Marmont, Duke of Ragusa, was altogether different. Youngest of the marshals (only thirty-six against Massena's fifty-two), he was well educated, a new type of opponent for a new shape of war.

When Wellington moved north, sickness was his worst enemy. At one time 17,000 men were on the sick list. Young William Bragge of the 'Galloping Third' (Heavy Dragoons) staved off the dysentery for a time by wearing flannel and avoiding fruit; in the end he succumbed to 'King Agrippa'.[13] Wellington himself was off colour for a fortnight and had to modify his spartan regime of riding and writing, as described by Tomkinson: up at 6; 6 to 9 writing, breakfast; visit of heads of all departments until 2 or 3; riding till 6; dinner; 9 till 12 writing. He was in fact reorganizing his whole army. Enough cavalry had been accumulated at last and, by heroic planning, he brought his first siege-train including iron guns up from Lisbon to Almeida.

On 18 December 1811 he wrote to his brother-in-law, Culling Charles Smith, second husband of his widowed sister Anne, for a travelling barouche. 'It must be a Barouche in which I can sleep':[14] breadth of axle-trees not to exceed five feet eight inches; low on the ground or it would overturn; lined with common Russia leather. Wellington received his barouche in April 1812, sent out in the transport *Freelove*.

Next to illness, the difficulty of finding first-class generals still provoked him most. The man he needed was General Lord Paget. But it might make a bad impression at Cádiz to invite so soon the seducer of

Henry's wife. In any case William doubted whether Paget would accept: 'If I know anything of Ld. Paget's character he will not stoop to waive his Rank to serve under you. . . .'[15] For the rest, he had still to solve the eternal problem of leave. Apart from fevers, many generals had 'business', one put his shoulder out, another reported his spleen 'out of order'[16] – a complaint which poor Arthur sometimes seemed to share. His invaluable commissary-general, Robert Kennedy ('who is as well as I am'), was lured home by his wife. One agreeable change could be recorded in Wellington's staff. General Graham, victor of Barrosa, replaced Sir Brent Spencer as second-in-command, 'which I am led to hope,' wrote Pakenham, 'may induce our friend [Wellington] to indulge himself a little more, although he has proved Himself near an Iron man.'[17]

There could be little indulgence for the Iron Man at this moment. In August he blockaded Ciudad Rodrigo and on the 27th cautiously repeated to Lord Liverpool his conviction that the war was entering a new phase:

We have certainly altered the nature of the war in Spain; it has become, to a certain degree, offensive on our part.[18]

Less than a month later Marmont relieved Ciudad Rodrigo and caught Wellington, through a rare failure to concentrate, with his army dangerously strung out. There were some critical moments between 25 and 28 September. At El Bodon, in particular, Picton's 3rd Division was isolated but saved itself by a brilliant movement across an open plain swarming with French cavalry. Forty times the Connaught Rangers heard the French bugles sound the charge; forty times the horsemen drew off, thwarted. Picton's assistant adjutant-general, Hercules Pakenham, described 'this imposing force Pounding us and ready to Charge in case of confusion. However, they never dared it, after we got together.'[19]

Wellington himself had narrowly escaped capture on the 25th by mistaking a party of French Chasseurs for his own Hussars, whom the Horse Guards had recently had the bright idea of putting into French-type caps. A year later he was laughing at this and similar incidents in his life as a soldier:

Although I had the family eye of a hawk, I have frequently been within an ace of being taken, and have more than once been obliged to take to my 'scrapers'. . . .[20]

After Marmont's revictualling of Ciudad Rodrigo, the Allies went into cantonments for three months from 1 October, to recover their health.

While the colder weather in the Peninsula did its healing work and the agues vanished in a round of gaiety – hunting, dinners and balls for the superior officers, dancing the fandango with village belles followed by hot chestnut suppers for the rest – there were signs that the war was again losing support at home. It was true that when someone at Carlton House had begun to praise Wellington's victories in the north, the Prince Regent burst out –

'Damn the north! and damn the south! and damn Wellington!'[21]

Suddenly the help which Wellington failed to find in the English Court was furnished by none other than the Emperor of the French.

Napoleon, who would neither return to Spain after the autumn of 1808 (possibly the most fatal failure of his career) nor leave well alone in Peninsular affairs, ordered Marshal Suchet to be reinforced at Valencia with 15,000 of Marmont's best men. Wellington promptly decided to open the siege of Ciudad Rodrigo in the new year.

On the night of 8 January 1812, 450 volunteers under Colonel Colborne seized the main outwork, situated on a dominating hill named the Great Teson, from which they had a clear view of the town's defences. Ciudad Rodrigo, with its system of ancient ramparts strengthened by modern works, and its square Moorish castle facing the Roman bridge over the Agueda, looked (and still looks) a remarkably compact, defiant fortress. Digging the trenches for the siege was an odious business; the ground was snow-covered and the cutting tools sent out from England abominable. The contractors' profits always seemed to take precedence over the army's parallels. Wellington considered the whole 'cutlery' situation 'shameful'. Listening to the growing bombardment, Private Wheeler and his shivering comrades longed for the assault to begin.

It began on 19 January. Two breaches were by now pronounced practicable. Wellington wrote out the order to attack sitting calmly on the Great Teson with guns booming all around him: 'the attack on Ciudad Rodrigo must be made this evening at 7 o'clock.' He dared not wait, for Marmont was at Salamanca.

Picton's 3rd Division was to storm the main breach to the right, near the Salamanca gate, Craufurd's Light Division the smaller breach to the left, supported by minor incursions. Every attack succeeded. Picton launched the 88th led by Colonel Mackinnon with the words, 'Rangers of Connaught! It is not my intention to spend any *powder* this evening.

We'll do this business with the *could iron*,' and he rode off, pounding the sides of his hog-maned cob. The Irishmen obeyed orders. One young volunteer addressed his bayonet after its first success: 'Holy Moses! how easy you went through him!'[22] Suddenly a huge mine exploded beneath them, blowing Mackinnon sky high, but incidentally laying bare the defences to the survivors. In they poured; while events no less dramatic were passing on the left.

Captain George Napier had asked and received a 'favour' of Craufurd: to lead the storming party of 300 volunteers from the 52nd, headed by the 'forlorn hope' of twenty-five under Lieutenant Gurwood, future editor of Wellington's *Despatches*. Here in the lesser breach reigned a fiery inferno of leaping and falling figures, part of a human tide which moved inexorably forward, dependent on the resolution of each individual soldier to make up for the technical deficiencies of the engineers. Craufurd was hit in the spine, Colborne in the shoulder, Napier in the arm, Gurwood in the head; but after lying stunned in the ditch Gurwood came to and 'cut off in search of the Governor' (in Harry Smith's slightly envious words) who duly rendered him his sword.[23]

Meanwhile the town had been captured by columns of heroic troops who promptly turned into a horde of drunken maniacs. Trigger-happy in the Cathedral square, they suddenly began shooting at doors, windows, roofs and stars until, as Kincaid wrote, some heads were 'blown from shoulders in the general hurricane'. At last the voice of Sir Thomas Picton with the power of twenty trumpets recalled them to reason. But even twenty trumpets blaring hell, besides many brave officers bashing crazy heads together with broken muskets, could not save Ciudad Rodrigo from being sacked.

Next morning Wellington, from his austere headquarters in the little Montarco palace, watched the victorious 52nd march out. 'Who the devil are those fellows?' he asked, as a series of bizarre apparitions passed in front of him festooned in silk gowns and carrying hams, tongues and loaves on the points of their *could iron*.[24]

Then came the turn of the wounded, the dying and lastly those for whom death was too good an end – deserters to the enemy found hiding in the town after its capture. 'Eleven knelt on one grave,' under orders 'to be shot to death three times', recalled Harry Smith with a shudder.[25] Kincaid, in the same regiment, said that Wellington pardoned all with good characters up to the time of their desertion, which apparently amounted to five out of the eleven.

Craufurd's wound was mortal and he died in slow agony, begging Wellington to forgive him for his intrigues. 'Craufurd talked to me as they do in a novel,' said Wellington afterwards.[26] In telling Lady Sarah Napier that George's arm had been amputated, Wellington showed himself once again a master of the right approach:

... Having such sons, I am aware that you expect to hear of those misfortunes which I have more than once had to communicate to you.[27]

He had divined Sarah Napier's feelings perfectly, for she replied with deep emotion a month after the storming:

I can with truth assert that *nothing* has had so much the power of consolation to me as your letter ...[28]

Wellington was no less concerned about the humbler wounded. Soon after the siege, on hearing at dinner that some sick soldiers had been dumped out of doors, he rode thirty miles that night to their bivouac, ordered them to be carried into the officers' quarters, rode back next night to see if he had been obeyed and finding the sick men thrown out again, had them finally brought in and the officers cashiered.

After the burials and the executions, the stock-taking. Wellington congratulated his army on 'the brilliant results of their labours and gallantry'. As in the far-off days of Ahmednuggur, the siege had gone through without a hitch – the only one of Wellington's Peninsular sieges to do so.

The Government elevated him from Viscount to Earl, with a pension to suit of £4,000. William characteristically feared that Viscount Douro would be an 'awkward' title for his son, and hoped to discover a better name. Wellington stopped him at once. Whether he liked 'Douro' or not it happened to be the name his faithful Portuguese soldiers called him by.

The Spanish Cortes meanwhile created him Duke of Ciudad Rodrigo and a Grandee of Spain. The man who carried his victory despatch to the Cortes was Don Miguel de Alava, the devoted Spanish liaison officer destined to concoct the best of all epigrams on the Iron Man:

General Alava told me [wrote Stanhope in 1831] that when he travelled with the Duke and asked him what o'clock he would start, he usually said 'at daylight'; and to the question of what they should find for dinner, the usual answer was '*cold meat*'. '*J'en ai pris en horreur*,' added Alava, '*les deux mots* daylight *et* cold meat!'[29]

At daylight on 6 March 1812 Wellington suddenly slipped off quietly to Badajoz hoping, no doubt, that it would be third time lucky.

This time the army was not to hurl itself disastrously against the impregnable strength of Fort San Cristobal across the river, but to breach the city walls in the south-east by Fort Picurina and the lunette (small detached work) of San Roche, while Picton and Leith escaladed the Castle and the north-western ramparts. Wellington's guns were now iron, not brass. Nevertheless there were weaknesses still.

The required corps of sappers and miners had not been provided by the Government, and Wellington's line regiments were no better as amateur engineers than they had been before. The fortress itself had been given more teeth by its remarkably ingenious Governor, Armand Philippon. The huge ochre walls and angular bastions thirty feet high 'frowned' down on the besiegers, reminding them that Badajoz had earned a reputation for strength through blood ever since it was wrenched from the Moors in 1229.*

Badajoz was invested on 16 March. The first parallel was dug on 17 March in a tempest. Starting on St Patrick's day seemed to the numerous Irish a good omen. Fort Picurina was successfully stormed in streams of fire discharged by the defenders amid a tumult of rockets and alarm bells, and the yells of the combatants. There was bad news for Wellington on 29 March. Marmont was marching westward towards Ciudad Rodrigo. At Badajoz the breaches would scarcely have been passed by the great siege-master, Vauban, as 'practicable'. Wellington was nevertheless forced to declare them so. He dared not wait.

The climactic night came on 6 April 1812. William Grattan of the Connaught Rangers noticed that a desperate calm had descended on the ranks of tattered, tanned soldiers waiting in their open-necked shirts and trousers rolled up. Grattan had observed the same thing before the storming of Ciudad Rodrigo: 'a determined severity' – 'an indescribable *something* about them' that caused admiration and awe. Here it was again at Badajoz, and Grattan repeated the telling phrase: 'a certain *something* in their bearing'[30] that marked them both as the priests and victims of Moloch.

It happened to be Easter Sunday. After the issue of twenty-seven paragraphs of instructions by Wellington, the Light and 4th Divisions were to be launched into hell at precisely 10 pm. As the minutes ticked away and the two armies lay enshrouded in a humid mist, silent except for the intermittent '*Sentinel! Gardez-vous*' exchanged between French

---

* Even today there is an eerie and intimidating waste land among the old fortifications, unpaved and dimly lit, where at night hordes of what the Victorians used to call 'street Arabs' delight in springing out to storm passing cars.

sentries, some of Kincaid's comrades remembered pleasantly the orgy after Ciudad Rodrigo's fall while others, grown 'incredibly savage', resolved to avenge the blood of their comrades shed twice already under those sinister walls. At last, still in quivering darkness, the silent advance into the breaches began. Suddenly a single fireball scattered a dazzling radiance, catching the two sides in the split second before they clashed: black figures clustering thickly on the ramparts behind glinting *chevaux de frise* and enormous shells; below them the scarlet columns of the British advancing like streams of burning lava. Inky blackness again. Next moment the whole thing blew up. In the lurid glare of innumerable separate explosions, all the 'forlorn hopes' were dashed to pieces by hundreds of powder-barrels rolling and roaring from the ramparts. The storming-parties found the slope over which they had to climb bristling with iron 'crows-feet', while the ditch, instead of being filled up with rubble, had been cleared by Philippon's orders and either spread with *fougasses* (small mines) or left pitted by huge holes. Nevertheless, as if driven on by a whirlwind, the multitude behind bounded over the dead and dying and forced their way across planks studded with spikes a foot long; only to be faced on the summit by a long array of captured sword-blades set in immense beams fastened down with chains. Baffled and murderous, some of the men forced their comrades in front on to the swords, thinking to make a bridge over their bodies. Not one got across. Forty times and more the bugles rang out and the doomed columns answered their officers' frenzied cries to advance with a loud hurrah. There was never an answering British shout from above; nothing but taunting enemy voices crying out, as the live shells, grenades and fireballs were tossed over the walls, 'Come up and take Badajoz!'

Wellington stood with his staff on a hillock only slightly screened from the fire, calmly, it seemed, reading the dreadful reports by candlelight. But his chief medical officer, Dr McGrigor, saw his jaw drop and his face turn deadly pale as the last appalling news came in of utter collapse in the breaches. Dully he asked someone to take an order.

'Go over immediately to Picton and tell him he must try if he can succeed in the Castle.'[31] Why should any of the subsidiary attacks by escalade succeed, when the stupendous massed assaults had failed? Picton was wounded and so was Hercules Pakenham; but an indomitable will to get over and a thinning opposition at last brought victory.

'Huzza, there is one man up!' On this frail beginning the 45th built a secure lodgment. Hundreds flew over and the Castle was in Allied hands. There was no need for the 3rd Division to batter their way into the town through the Castle gates, for the bugles of the 5th were already sounding in the streets. Taken in the rear, the great French defence at the breaches dissolved away, and the spent survivors of the Light and 4th Divisions marched into Badajoz unmolested. It had fallen in just twenty days.

The town was deathly still though the street lights were shining. Every shutter was closed, for the inhabitants knew better than to come out and welcome soldiers they had hoped would be beaten. According to the barbarously logical rules of war, a town that refused to surrender deserved to be sacked – unless of course the inhabitants, as distinct from the garrison, were friendly. The British had never found Badajoz friendly. And so, in the small hours of 7 April 1812, pandemonium broke loose. The troops had been through hell – the inundations transformed into fiery lakes of 'smoking blood', the spikes, the shredded bodies, the corpses piled so tight and high they were still warm in the morning. Release from one hell only plunged them into another. Every door was battered in, old men were shot, women raped, children bayonetted. A nun dragged into the street by two soldiers prevailed on one of them to spare her; the other promptly stepped back a pace, took aim and shot his friend dead.

The awful night passed but next morning the army was still mad with drink. Wellington issued (7 April) a General Order – stern, though ambiguously worded: 'It is full time that the plunder of Badajoz should cease.' This did not necessarily mean that he approved of first-degree plunder, so to speak, though Oman thought so, and so no doubt did most of his soldiers.

W. Bragge of the 'Galloping Third' (King's Own Dragoons): *the Survivors richly deserved the liberty of plundering the Town.*
J. Donaldson of the 94th: . . . *we were allowed to enter the town for the purpose of plundering it.*
W. Tomkinson of the 16th Light Dragoons: *The dead and dying in the breach were the most shocking thing ever seen, and perhaps a little plunder was necessary to drown the horror.*

And John T. Jones, the siege historian, admitted that he had passed lightly over the pillaging, because the French were always so much worse.

It is highly unlikely that Wellington thought his troops 'deserved' to plunder. The testimony of one of his aides-de-camp, James Stanhope, is flatly against it. 'He fulminates orders,' James Stanhope wrote in his journal, 'and will hardly thank the troops, so angry is he.' Wellington never forgot the scenes of debauch. 'I remember,' he recalled to his friends years later, 'entering a cellar and seeing some soldiers lying on the floor so dead drunk that the wine was actually flowing from their mouths!'[32] Did Wellington, nonetheless, regard a moderate sacking as a deterrent? Oman adduces a letter he wrote to Canning in 1820 as proof that he did. If he had put the garrison of Ciudad Rodrigo to the sword, argued Wellington, in this letter, he would have saved 5,000 Allied lives at Badajoz: 'the practice which refuses quarter to a garrison that stands an assault is not a *useless* effusion of blood'.

Too much weight should not be attached to these words. Wellington was discussing the advantages of annihilating a stubborn garrison, not of massacring the civilian inhabitants. More important, he had mounted a favourite hobby-horse – the thesis that progress was not always forward – when he tried in 1820 to debunk for Canning's benefit 'the humanity of modern warfare'. No one could suppose that he would actually have favoured the slaughter of General Philippon (who incidentally surrendered at San Cristobal on the 7th) in addition to the sacking of Badajoz. What he could not resist was a superficially logical argument, however perverse in reality, that gave him an opportunity to lambast the 'modern' world.

On the morning after the siege another Wellington showed himself to his deeply astonished staff. He visited the dead on the *glacis*, and seeing so many of his finest men destroyed – his total losses were nearly 5,000 – he broke down and wept. They had never seen it happen before. Then, still sunk in grief, he went back and wrote to the War Minister:

The capture of Badajoz affords as strong an instance of the gallantry of our troops as has ever been displayed. But I greatly hope that I shall never again be the instrument of putting them to such a test. . . .[33]

He had not felt like that since Assaye.

To realize how unusual for those times was Wellington's emotion, it is only necessary to compare the reactions of others on the field and at home. Picton, for one, was completely nonplussed by Wellington's tears.

'Good God, what is the matter?' he exclaimed.[34] Wellington began cursing and swearing at the Government for not giving him enough sappers and miners. It was the best he could do to explain the inexplicable.

At home, Mrs Piozzi wrote an account of a conversation about Badajoz on 26 April.*

* Mrs Piozzi, formerly Mrs Thrale, friend of Dr Johnson, writing to Mr Alexander Leak, 26 April 1812.

Genl. Donkin says it was a glorious sight – the storming of Badajoz; and that old John Duke of Marlbro' would have rejoiced to see the Courage of our officers & men. . . . 51 of the First Rank were knocked down from the Scaling Ladders & died cheering their soldiers.

Fifty-one leaders down at a blow. That was glory.

Yet the terrible fall of Badajoz was not without its barrack-room humour, nor even its moment of romance. That 'impudent fellow' Harry Smith, as Kincaid called him, had carried off a lovely Spanish girl of fourteen from under Kincaid's nose. She and her elder sister fled from the stricken city to the British camp, their ears bleeding where the earrings had been brutally ripped off. Everyone wanted to marry her but Harry Smith succeeded.* As for the traditional jokes, 'You know Ben Battle,' they used to say, 'who left his legs in Badajoz breaches?' And what about Colonel Fletcher, a canny Scot, being hit where it hurt most – in the purse? A bullet from Fort Picurina had forced one of his own dollars into the groin.

Napoleon's latest orders to Marmont, written on 9 May 1812 just before he himself set out for Moscow, were also something of a joke, though a bad one. Quite unaware of the changed position in the Peninsula, he informed Marmont portentously: 'it is necessary to maintain an offensive posture. . . .' The posture was not for him to dictate, now that both the keys to Spain were in Wellington's hands.

---

* Sir Harry Smith (1787–1860), has been mentioned already as a Peninsular diarist. Assistant adjutant-general to Sir Edward Pakenham, New Orleans, 1815; assistant quarter-master-general, 6th Division, Waterloo; Governor of Cape of Good Hope. Married 1812 Juana Maria de los Dolores de Leon (1798–1872), after whom Ladysmith in South Africa was named

15

Grandeur and Misery

Napoleon's remote control of his marshals reached its nadir of effectiveness with the luckless Marmont, Duke of Ragusa. He had forbidden Marmont to support Soult in the south. Instead, his 'offensive posture' was to consist in a renewed attack on Portugal. Wellington's only fear was lest the Spaniards should yield up Ciudad Rodrigo and Almeida to Marmont as they had surrendered Badajoz to Soult a year earlier. He hurried north to revictual them, not without some grumbling to William:

I never saw anything like the Spaniards yet!! I am now tied by the legs till I can get these d—d places well provisioned.[1]

Fortunately Hill's legs were able to work for Wellington in the south. He destroyed the French pontoon bridge at Almaraz on the Tagus, thereby cutting all communication between Marmont and Soult west of Toledo.

There was only one blot on Hill's brilliant campaign. A cavalry action conducted by General Slade resulted in a fiasco that stung Wellington beyond endurance. He wrote to Hill in a fine passion:

I entirely concur with you in the necessity of inquiring into it [Slade's disaster]. It is occasioned entirely by a trick our officers of cavalry have acquired of galloping at every thing, and then galloping back as fast as they gallop on the enemy. They never . . . think of manoeuvring before an enemy – so little that one would think they cannot manoeuvre, excepting on Wimbledon Common. . . .[2]

The cavalry never forgave Wellington for his 'Wimbledon Common' letter.

With extensive command of the Tagus, Wellington at last had the pleasure of choosing between two almost equally inviting prospects: the freeing of southern Spain from Soult or an attack on Marmont, now returned to Salamanca. A victory in central Spain could carry the leopards to the Pyrenees. Throughout May and early June, therefore, Wellington made his multitudinous preparations for the great central thrust, including plans for diversionary attacks. It seemed enough for one man, even an Iron Man, to do. But from the end of May onwards he had to face the possibility of a dramatic challenge from home.

One element of drama was already a fact. On 11 May 1812, in the lobby of the House of Commons, a merchant named Bellingham, whose business had been ruined by the war, shot dead Spencer Perceval. From Wellington's angle the consequences could be very good, because Richard might become Prime Minister, and among the 'Oriental dreams' of which his enemies accused him was the drive for an all-out war effort. Arthur, however, could not quite see Richard back in the Cabinet. In expressing sympathy with Richard over his recent resignation he had written:

In truth the republic of a Cabinet is but little suited to any man of taste or of large views.[3]

Nevertheless the Prince Regent sent for his old crony and asked him to try to form a new government. Not, curiously enough, to become Prime Minister. Simply to find out who would serve.

Enquiry revealed that not a single leading figure in either party, excluding Canning, would serve if Lord Wellesley were Prime Minister.

By 9 June Wellington knew the truth: that there was to be a continuation of the old Tory Ministry but under Lord Liverpool, with Castlereagh still at the Foreign Office and Lord Bathurst in Liverpool's place as War Minister. Wellington was not the man to simulate more confidence than he felt, and Liverpool received a letter from the Peninsula which may or may not have encouraged him to soldier on:

You have undertaken a gigantick task and I don't know how you will get through it.

Wellington did not believe Liverpool would succeed, unless he had both Canning and Castlereagh in his Cabinet – which seemed impossible. 'However there is nothing like trying. . . .'

At the end of June more bad news drove him from scepticism to anger. Not only had Richard been excluded from the Government altogether but William, out of misplaced loyalty, had voluntarily stayed outside. Lord Liverpool was informed that though the Commander-in-Chief in the Peninsula was 'perfectly satisfied' with Bathurst as War Minister, his satisfaction ended there.

I am much annoyed at the breach which prevails between your Govt. and Lord Wellesley, and particularly that Pole is no longer in office. . . .[4]

William received an even sharper rebuke, since Arthur's chances of getting the desperately needed money for his soldiers' and muleteers' pay would be more remote than ever.

It was to take another year to convince him that Liverpool's 'steady and continued exertion on a moderate scale', as Professor Asa Briggs calls it, was in fact a war-winning policy. Meanwhile Wellington was to continue feeling uneasy, lest by losses or lack of victories he himself should shake Liverpool's supposedly precarious power. In the midst of battles and sieges he never ceased writing letters home to try to get his brothers back into the Government. Without these political anxieties it is unlikely that he would have been found at Burgos, for instance, risking both too little and too much.

As usual Wellington kept his own counsel about his next moves. 'As you have left us,' he wrote on 28 May 1812 to George Murray, his valued quartermaster-general, 'I will not *tantalize* you by entering on our plans for the remainder of the campaign. . . .'[5] If Wellington's real object was to avoid leakages rather than tantalization, it was in line with a steady policy.

Ned Pakenham hazarded that 'the Peer', as Wellington was now increasingly called, 'possibly may look southward again'.[6] Contrary to all their expectations the Peer was looking eastward, and on 13 June 1812 he and his army crossed the River Agueda at Ciudad Rodrigo, *en route* for Salamanca. Forty-three thousand British and Portuguese supported by 3,000 Spaniards covered the parched plateau in four days. It was good to be advancing again under a commander they trusted, even if they did not quite understand him. Arty or Nosey to the rank and file, Douro to the Portuguese, the Eagle to the Spaniards,* the Peer or the Beau to his officers, he had become an object of keen interest to the whole army. Lieutenant Arthur Shakespear, a contemporary of Bragge in the same regiment, afterwards recalled one awe-inspiring moment during the advance on Salamanca: 'I saw the Duke of Wellington quietly pull his boot off & scratch his foot!'[7]

They reached the famous university city on 17 June 1812, where the splendid Roman bridge over the river Tormes, with its green mats of sinuous water-weed, drowsy sandbanks and ancient water-mills gave a false impression of peace. Three forts, built out of the ruins of twenty colleges and thirteen convents, had been left garrisoned by Marmont

---

* 'The Spanish Officers and Troops used to call me the Eagle.' (*Wellington MSS*. Duke of Wellington to Angela Burdett-Coutts, 4 October 1848).

when he retired from Salamanca at Wellington's approach. They would have to be reduced before the Allies could advance farther. (Bragge heard that the French would have pulled down the Cathedral as well, but for a heavy contribution paid by the agonized clergy.)

Meanwhile, Wellington deliberately let pass an opportunity on 21 June to attack Marmont near the village of San Cristobal, just north of Salamanca. Why did he do so? Henry Tomkinson and many other officers could not understand it, since the French were outnumbered and the whole object of the campaign was to destroy Marmont's army: 'we all agreed,' wrote Tomkinson, 'Lord Wellington had some unknown reasons. . . .'[8] To the old soldier, Private Wheeler, however, the reason was obvious. Wellington was too well posted on the reverse slopes behind San Cristobal to risk coming down after Marmont. 'Damned tempting!' he exclaimed to his aide-de-camp, James Stanhope, 'I have a great mind to attack 'em!'[9] But he resisted the temptation; while Marmont for his part suppressed any curiosity he may have felt to explore the ridge. Deadlock followed. At the end of four days Marmont retired behind the River Duero (as the Douro is called in Spain), incidentally picking up some much needed reinforcements on the way. This was a pity. But with a government as supposedly weak as Liverpool's to back him, Wellington did not feel justified in sustaining the 'great loss' which even a victory at San Cristobal must have entailed.

And so the first part of the campaign ended for Wellington in little better than a draw, though, the Salamanca forts having surrendered on 27 June, he was able to drive out any regrets over San Cristobal by a triumphal entry into the city. Illuminations in Philip v's imposing Plaza Mayor were followed by a *Te Deum* in the Cathedral, and everywhere he went the Spanish ladies kissed him.

The situation at the beginning of July 1812 was realistically if baldly summarized by Wellington for the sick General Graham:

Marmont will not risk an action unless he should have an advantage; and I shall certainly not risk one unless I should have an advantage; and matters therefore do not appear likely to be brought to that criterion very soon.[10]

To the disappointment of both armies there followed three tedious weeks of marching and counter-marching, the two armies sometimes parallel and within cannon-shot, each commander waiting for the other to make the first mistake. The sun was 'scalding hot', the nights bitter. 'I never suffered more from cold,' recollected Wellington, 'than during the manoeuvres of the days preceding the battle of Salamanca.' He also suffered a narrow escape from French cavalry, when a spectator in the Light Division saw him and Beresford galloping out of a mêlée with drawn swords, the former not looking 'more than half pleased'.[11] Wellington indeed was recovering from utter exhaustion after taking the Salamanca forts, though only his confidant William was informed.

I was never so fagged. My gallant officers will kill me.[12]

If Wellington's importunate officers would not let him sleep in bed there was always the remedy of a nap snatched on a hot hilltop, aromatic with thyme and lavender. His staff well remembered one day of pitiless windings by the two armies locked together like angry serpents, when their Commander-in-Chief suddenly flung himself down with a newspaper over his head and strict instructions about calling: 'Watch the French through your glass, Fitzroy. . . . When they reach that copse near the gap in the hill, wake me.'[13]

At last this vile phase came to an end, as Wheeler knew it would: 'for two such armys cannot long remain near each other without doing something'.[14] On 20 July there was a final grand spurt for the river Tormes near Salamanca. Marmont, whose lightly equipped troops depressed the British by always marching just a little faster than they could, was determined to outstrip Wellington and cut him off from his base at Ciudad Rodrigo. Wellington, inexorably resolved to prevent him, sketched his strategy to his staff: he would cross the Tormes if Marmont did, cover Salamanca as long as possible and fight no action 'unless under very advantageous circumstances'. This in effect meant an almost certain retreat.[15] As he stood map in hand a round shot fell unpleasantly close; he moved a little, still talking.

No eve-of-battle has ever been more exciting than that of Salamanca. Just as Wellington's rearguard, the Light Division, were stepping out of the river in beautiful order on to its left bank, a colossal thunderstorm broke. Major and Mrs Dalbiac of the 4th Dragoons were smothered in the folds of their tent when stampeding horses caught in the ropes, and the major saved his wife only by rushing with her in his arms and depositing her under the nearest gun-carriage.

On 22 July 1812, at daybreak, the strange race started again. Now parallel to one another but with the French as ever slightly in front, the two armies swept south-westward towards the Ciudad Rodrigo road on which Wellington's departing baggage-train was already stirring up a cloud of dust. For the first stage of the retreat to Portugal had begun. Suddenly, right ahead of them, there came into view two remarkable features dominating the long valley – the Greater and Lesser Arapiles. These odd, steep, flat-topped little hills, one just 400 feet high, the other somewhat higher and separated by only a thousand yards of deep, dusty red earth, formed the northern and southern gateposts of a wide, grassy amphitheatre through which at a distance ran the road to Ciudad Rodrigo. Once sighted, the Arapiles naturally became the object of a fiercely stepped-up race for possession. The French, with their greater swiftness, seized the Greater Arapile. Wellington occupied the Lesser, as well as the village of Los Arapiles, standing on the northern edge of the amphitheatre and sheltered by a long ridge behind. The capture of their respective Arapiles, however, though it focused the opposing armies, was not the most decisive move in the game on that morning of 22 July. The crucial event was Wellington's order to his 3rd Division, hitherto left behind on the far side of the Tormes, to march out of Salamanca and take up a screened position near the village of Aldea Tejada, well to the Allied right. Pakenham was now its divisional commander for Picton, still incapacitated, had asked Wellington to put Ned in his place.

When Marmont saw Pakenham's dust-cloud behind the hills it never crossed his mind that this was not just another Allied contingent in retreat. Without this mistake the marshal would not have made the next fatal move. He rapidly extended his left wing under Generals Thomières and Maucune. His aim was to cut off the Allied retreat by outflanking their right – a laudable aim considering that Marmont looked upon the British much as Wellington regarded the Spanish: brave men who stood 'like stocks' but could not manoeuvre.

Wellington had half expected Marmont to offer him a '*pont d'or*' back to Portugal. Instead his telescope showed him through the pearly Spanish light what looked like a movement against his right wing. Could this be the chance 'for which I had long been anxious'?[16] His 5th and 4th Divisions were promptly ordered up to Los Arapiles, with the 6th and 7th in reserve. Another searching look through his glass told him there was still time – for a late breakfast. He galloped into the farmyard where his officers were picnicking, to the braying of donkeys and popping of *tirailleurs* behind outlying stone walls. Wellington told them to hurry up. He refused to dismount but bit at a chicken leg in his fingers. While he was still 'thumping about, munching', an aide-de-

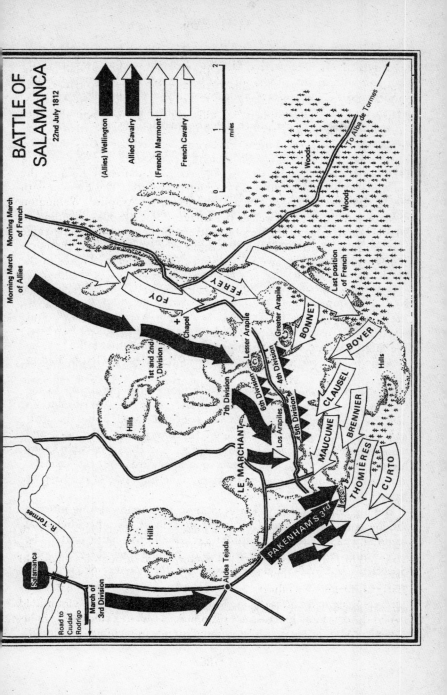

BATTLE OF SALAMANCA
22nd July 1812

(Allies) Wellington

Allied Cavalry

(French) Marmont

French Cavalry

miles

Morning March of Allies

Morning March of French

Road to Ciudad Rodrigo

Salamanca

R. Tormes

March of 3rd Division

Aldea Tejada

Hills

Hills

Hills

PAKENHAM'S 3rd

LE MARCHANT

CURTO

THOMIÈRES

BRENNIER

MAUCUNE

CLAUSEL

BOYER

BONNET

7th Division

6th Division

5th Division

4th Division

Los Arapiles

Lesser Arapile

Greater Arapile

Chapel

1st and 2nd Division

FOY

FEREY

Last position of French

Woods

Woods

To Alba de Tormes

camp brought more news of the French left. Wellington chucked the bone over his shoulder, seized his glass, looked over the low farmyard wall and with a curt, 'By God! that'll do', spurred his horse up the slippery shale of the Lesser Arapile. Suddenly he shut his telescope with a snap.

'*Mon cher Alava*,' he exclaimed to his Spanish liaison officer, '*Marmont est perdu!*'

The French were over-extended and a fatal gap had opened between their left and centre.

Next moment Wellington was off like the wind to Aldea Tejada where Pakenham and the 3rd Division had just arrived. No scribbled notes by aides-de-camp at this critical moment. He tapped his brother-in-law on the shoulder.

'Ned, d'ye see those fellows on the hill?' pointing to the French left. 'Throw your division into column; at them! and drive them to the devil.'

'I will, my lord, if you will give me your hand,' replied the emotional Ned. A group of staff officers standing round noticed how pale Wellington was, but he gave his brother-in-law his hand without relaxing 'his usual rigidity'. As soon as Ned had gone, however, Wellington turned with a triumphant expression to his staff:

'Did you ever see a man who understood so clearly what he had to do?'[17]

At the same moment a cannon-shot flying from the Lesser to the Greater Arapile tore into Marmont's side, destroying two ribs and an arm. Napoleon's youngest marshal was out of the battle almost before it had begun. For Pakenham it was the chance of a lifetime – and Salamanca was to give him his hour of glory. 'Pakenham may not be the highest genius,' wrote Wellington soon afterwards, but his 'celerity' and 'accuracy' in carrying out orders made him 'one of the best we have'.[18]

Having set the 3rd Division in motion, Wellington sprang into the saddle again and personally carried to each of his other divisional commanders an equally abrupt but no less effective battle order. The Opposition afterwards tried to stir up trouble over these 'Laconic Speeches'; but William Bragge expressed the younger officers' view when he wrote home:

although not the language of the Marlboroughs . . . it is very much this modern Hero's style of addressing his Generals and is found to answer equally well.[19]

Meanwhile at close on 5 pm Pakenham initiated Wellington's master-stroke. Supported by D'Urban's Portuguese cavalry on his right flank, he led the 3rd Division swiftly through the concealing dips and folds between him and Thomières, covered by some of Wellington's sixty cannon and strong in the muskets of Wallace, Campbell and 2,000 Portuguese – altogether nearly 6,000 veterans who had been fighting and winning together ever since Bussaco. The first strike was made by the Portuguese Dragoons. Through scattered bushes, smoke and swirling red dust, D'Urban all at once caught sight of the head of a French infantry column. He charged; behind him the British infantry closed in, Pakenham's generally 'boiling spirit' cool as it had never been before. Thomières' men, taken completely by surprise, managed to fire no more than one burst into Wallace's brigade before the famous rolling musketry of the 74th, 88th and 45th opened up on them. The French infantry crumpled and Pakenham shouted to Wallace, 'Let them loose!'[20] The habitual, grim silence of the fighting British was rent by ear-splitting cheers as they went in with the bayonet. Thomières himself fell dead, two-thirds of his leading regiments and half his entire division casualties and all his share of Marmont's seventy-eight guns taken. 'The crash was magnificent!' wrote Pakenham. After the crash, the captures: prisoners, colours and an eagle. Most noble, continued Pakenham, was his own continued advance upon Maucune's Vth Corps supported by Wellington's main forces further to the east, especially by the Heavy Dragoons of gallant General Le Marchant who lost his life: 'the Fellow died Sabre in hand,' lamented Pakenham, 'giving the Most Princely Example. . . .'[21] Even the reserved Wellington was carried away by the spectacle of Le Marchant's superb dash balanced by iron control. 'By God, Cotton,' he shouted to the divisional commander, 'I never saw anything so beautiful in my life; the day is *yours*.'[22] He was never to see that particular perfection again.

At the end of the attack begun by Pakenham, two French divisions were irreparably broken and a third (Brennier's) disabled; indeed, over a quarter of Marmont's army was defeated. It was this action which inspired a Frenchman to say that at Salamanca Wellington beat 40,000 men in 40 minutes.

No struggle against Napoleon's veterans could be a walkover, and as Wellington shuttled in division after division diagonally from the left, there were serious setbacks on the 4th Division's front. Pack's Portuguese failed to storm the Greater Arapile. The rest of the division were now faced by a fresh corps under Clausel. In a terrible confrontation General Lowry Cole was severely wounded and his men put to flight. At this critical juncture Wellington was ready, as always, to plug the hole. He brought up the 6th Division, and Clausel's valiant attempt to turn the tide eventually ebbed away in the destruction of two more French corps and a desperate rush by the survivors for the sheltering woods and the bridge of Alba over the Tormes.

With the end of daylight, Wellington's chance to turn the pursuit into a rout also passed away. It was called off by Wellington on the 25th. In any case the victory was overwhelming: 14,000 French casualties at least, to 5,000 Allied. And so Private Wheeler, with the phlegm of countless of his fellow-countrymen, dropped down on the edge of the battlefield, content to build himself a comforting wall of dead Frenchmen against the cutting wind and to fall into a sound sleep.

Salamanca did something for Wellington which none of his previous victories had achieved. Suddenly the world realized that this indomitable stonewaller had become 'almost a Marlborough' – to use the expression of General Foy, the only French commander to survive the battle with his corps intact.

Hitherto we had been aware of his prudence, his eye for choosing a position, and his skill in utilizing it. At Salamanca he has shown himself a great and able master of manoeuvres.[23]

On the Allied army his personal imprint was stronger than ever. He had been ubiquitous – one moment launching the 3rd Division, the next riding forward with the 5th, then giving the order '7th Division, advance!' – and all the time bearing an apparently charmed life. 'Our Chief was everywhere,' wrote Pakenham, 'and Sadly Exposed himself; – in his preservation our little prayers were heard most surely.'[24] The little prayers at any rate seem to have saved him from injury by a spent bullet which went through his holster and cloak.

William Napier of the Light Division discovered a different but no less impressive Wellington behind the endless galloping and staccato commands.

I saw him late in the evening of that great day . . . he was alone, the flush of victory was on his brow and his eyes were eager and watchful, but his voice was calm and even gentle . . . he seemed only to accept this glory as an earnest of greater things to come.[25]

Salamanca was as much a ladder as a landmark. The problem was how to make the most of his victory. It had aroused a fever of hope. The Russian débâcle was still hidden in the future and Salamanca held the world stage. Arthur conveyed something of the effervescence in Spain to William:

The people of Salamanca swear that my Mother is a Saint; & the daughter of a Saint, to which circumstance I owe all my good fortune!!! Pray tell her this.[26]

He added dryly,

The Marhattas [*sic*] formerly discovered that she was a Marhatta!

Some of his officers already saw Paris shimmering at the end of a few days' march. And there was his own desire to keep the Government going with Peninsular successes. Militarily he might have preferred an immediate follow-up against Clausel and the 'Army of Portugal'. But considering his own army's growing lack of food, money and health, the more glittering alternative was a second triumphal entry, this time into Spain's first city, Madrid.

Wellington's victorious army entered the capital on 12 August 1812, driving before them the Intrusive King, as the Spanish nationalists called Joseph Bonaparte. (Those Spaniards who could tolerate an alien monarch admired Joseph for his moderate and reformist rule, calling him 'Tio Pepe', Uncle Joe.) Wellington's soldiers found it almost impossible to describe the ecstasy of welcome. Private Wheeler was not unwilling to progress 'slowly' forward among 'the most bewitching and interesting little devils I have ever seen', into a city hung with gold and silver draperies, lighted with tall wax candles and loud with bells and '*vivas*'. Wheeler found he had only one penalty to pay for so much bliss: 'It was to be kissed by the men.'[27] To William Bragge the city's sole imperfection was its 'paltry' Company of Comedians, whose 'most applauded Actor amused us with using the Pot de Chambre . . . previous to going into Bed, which Scene concluded the Play'. Wellington wrote simply, 'I am among a people mad with joy. God send my good fortune may continue, and that I may be the instrument of securing their independence and happiness.'[28]

There was much serious work to be done even in tumultuous Madrid, if this goal were to be attained: the enormous treasure-trove from the Retirofortress to be distributed, including guns, shoes galore and two more eagles; the usual General Orders to be issued against plunder (Wheeler calmly stole all the English books from the Royal Library); and preparations for the next move. Nevertheless the son of a saint was not to be let off with less than the best in the way of glory. The Cortes gave him the Order of the Golden Fleece, and he received a gracious letter from Maria Teresa de Bourbon accompanying the Collar which had belonged to her father, the Infante Luis. Francisco Goya, supreme artist of the war, painted him incomparably, bare-headed on horseback in his blue Spanish cavalry cloak; and if there is a restiveness in his eye and carriage more Spanish than Wellingtonian, it is not often that the cause of international fraternity is served by genius.*

It was while Goya was painting him that an incident occurred that threw a flood of light on Wellington's character. He had sent for his relatively new inspector-general of hospitals, James McGrigor, and in his friendliest manner asked him about the state of the wounded between Salamanca and Madrid. Now McGrigor had studied his chief. McGrigor, however, still had a lot to learn. He blandly disclosed that on his own initiative he had redirected the main pockets of sick on to a better route than the one fixed by Wellington.

The face Goya was studying changed. Wellington started up in a rage. How dared McGrigor alter his orders? Goya was aghast. McGrigor pleaded the danger to life, the losses at Talavera through delays. All no good.

'I shall be glad to know who is to command the army? I or you? I establish one route . . . you establish another. As long as you live, Sir, never do so again; never do anything without my orders.'

Suddenly the voice dropped and he sat down. Would Dr McGrigor dine with him that evening?[29]

On 22 September the end for which Wellington's brother Henry (now Sir Henry Wellesley, KB) had worked so long was gained at last: the Spanish Cortes created him Generalissimo of all their forces, with an estate near Granada named Soto de Roma.

Not to be entirely outdone, the English Prince Regent created him a Marquess with a grant of £100,000 by Parliament towards a future home.

Kitty's journal had at length restarted in September 1812. Her object as before was 'to compare in what I am engaged while He, the object of my thoughts, is engaged abroad'. And so on 9 September she began:

At one o'clock went to the Poles: found Mr Pole very angry with me for not having gone to the Ball last night: it was given in honour of Lord Wellington's victory and taking possession of Madrid. . . . I could not go.

* This was the only painting of Wellington executed by Goya from life; x-rays have now revealed that it was painted over a portrait of King Joseph, whose dim shadow still lingers behind the Duke's head, where he hangs today in the Waterloo Gallery, Apsley House.

Tunbridge Wells. September 29th. Being determined not to be held up *en spectacle* and finding myself totally unequal to attending the ceremony of putting up the Eagles [captured at Salamanca and Madrid] I thought my best plan was to leave town. I did so, and wrote to Lady Liverpool from Sevenoaks to excuse myself.[30]

Lady Liverpool was a staunch friend of Kitty's but even she must have felt this was not the way for a hero's wife to behave. Eventually the eagles had to be brought to Kitty. 'They are mine!' she cried, kissing them hysterically, and fainted away.[31]

If Kitty felt ashamed, there were no signs of it for once in her journal; indeed it registered a sense of steady improvement. Judging by Ned's letters, Kitty's emergence from her old state of lethargy seems to have been due to her mother giving her a new domestic 'philosophy'. The tragedy was that however fast Kitty moved, Arthur ran faster still. The gap between them was widening.

For the moment, however, it seemed to be Arthur who was faltering in the race. During the next three months – September, October, November 1812 – the painfully frank Dr McGrigor wrote that 'everything went wrong with him'. Yet his hopes had been high.

After Madrid he started north to drive Clausel's 'Army of Portugal' out of Valladolid, capture Burgos and – who knows? – spend the winter of 1812 on the Ebro, the last great river before the Pyrenees. He needed fortune's face, not her back, to bring off such coups. The idea of wintering on the Ebro in 1812 was in its way as improbable as Napoleon's dream of wintering in Moscow.

Even now his detour to the north against Clausel was only doing what had to be done anyway, sooner or later, but at the back of his mind was the glimmer of a greater game.*

The town of Burgos has never forgotten that it was the birthplace of that eleventh-century ruffian, the Cid. The great cathedral, magnificently ornate, is joyless. Its strange Santo Cristo, with human hair and limbs of rhinoceros hide, broods over rather than protects it – in the same way that the ruined castle, on its remote eyrie, broods over the city. William Bragge, who fell in love with Madrid, found Burgos 'one of the worst large Towns I have seen in Spain. . . . The People horridly

---

* Military historians have not been slow to criticize his performance after Salamanca, but they seem to have under-estimated his desire to help the Government at home – a factor brought out again and again in his unpublished letters to William Wellesley-Pole (*Raglan MSS*).

ugly and what is rather remarkable for Spaniards excessively dirty'; he had no wish to go farther north, 'except to embark'.

There are signs that the march from Valladolid to Burgos, and now the sight of its castle, had much the same effect on Wellington. All his attempts to corner the 'Army of Portugal' on the way there had failed and it had escaped eastwards again. Looking at Burgos Castle for the first time through his telescope he was unpleasantly surprised by the strength of its outwork, keep and double walls clinging to a precipitous rockface. He had been told that Burgos was a relatively minor obstacle. Though he captured the outwork on 19 September, thanks to the gallantry of a kilted young major, Edward Somers-Cocks, his report on the operation was symptomatic of a grey mood: 'I doubt however that I have the means to take the castle which is very strong.'[32] All the subsequent attacks confirmed his worst fears. The leader of one storming party failed to understand his instructions, lost the way and was shot down with Wellington's plans in his pocket, which the French understood all too well.

The death of Cocks on 8 October while he was rallying his men seems to have knocked the heart out of Wellington. An outstandingly daring Intelligence officer, he was Wellington's *beau idéal* of a soldier. Nobly born (his father was Earl Somers), dedicated to his profession but even fonder of field experience than of the new military colleges, Wellington probably saw in him the young eagle who would soar above Britain's pitiful generals. At the funeral his look of sheer despair prevented his friends from speaking to him.

The loss of Cocks highlighted the deficiencies of the men left behind. As the siege dragged on, the positive contributions of some officers were as irritating as the failures of others. One Marine officer arrived at headquarters with a new bayonet exercise which would render one Briton equal to twelve Frenchmen. This reminded Wellington's staff sourly of the Marine who had earlier invented an '*artificial hill*' – a tall pole on which the Commander-in-Chief would be hoisted to survey the enemy.[33]

'Damn me, Sir, I may tumble down and break my neck!' objected Wellington.

'Oh! my Lord, *if that is all*, you may send up one of your aides-de-camp.'

A Portuguese 'projector' wanted to burn up the French army with convex glasses. Burgos, however, was remarkable for a sunless month, deteriorating into icy deluges. When all the inventions had been rejected and the last assault delivered and repulsed (18 October) Wellington miserably decided to abandon 'this d—d place'.[34] Pakenham wrote that it was 'some what provoking' to have 100 siege-guns at Madrid with Wellington so short, and military historians have argued that Pakenham or Popham and his Marines could have got siege-guns across to Burgos from Madrid or Santander in time. The three siege-guns he depended on, christened optimistically by his soldiers Thunder, Lightning and – because it had lost one of its trunnions – Nelson, were eventually reduced to Nelson alone. Ironically, the army slipped out of Burgos after dark on Trafalgar Day, 21 October, with wheels muffled in straw. By now it was high time. Wellington was under immediate threat of being cut off by the advancing French armies.

A serious though short-term result of the Burgos fiasco was a drop in Wellington's magic. Even the war-weary Bragge had expected Burgos to be captured somehow: 'as Lord Wellington in all his military Career never missed taking a Fort, I do not imagine he is going to be outdone at Burgos'.[35] When the hero was in fact outdone, temporary disillusionment followed. Dr McGrigor noticed his frequent 'bad humour'. A pleasanter thought on which to leave gloomy Burgos is that Wellington faced history taking all the blame himself. Lest he should damage the very politicians he had aimed to strengthen, he wrote on 23 November to the Prime Minister:

I see that a disposition already exists to blame the Government for the failure of the siege of Burgos. . . . It was entirely my own act.[36]

And to a group of friends many years later:

It was all my fault; I had got, with small means, into the forts near Salamanca. The Castle was not unlike a hill-fort in India and I had got into a good many of those. I could get into this, and I very nearly did it but it was defended by a very clever fellow. . . .[37]

Another very clever fellow, Napoleon Bonaparte, evacuated Moscow just three days before Wellington extricated himself from Burgos, each beginning what was to prove the most agonizing retreat in his career.

Wellington's soldiers had the advantage of plunging straight into the Spanish wine-country between Burgos and Salamanca, though for some of them the vats of newly fermented liquor were as lethal as Russian snows. Twelve thousand soldiers got drunk at Torquemada, and what looked like banks of dead bodies lined the road, only waiting to be picked up by the enemy. Yet despite the gruesome crimes (and punishments) that marked Wellington's hectic retreat to Salamanca – 35,000 Allies pursued by 60,000 French – he and Hill were united by 8 November on the Tormes. The wounded at Salamanca had been moved ahead of Wellington, a great coup for Dr McGrigor of which he took full advantage. He said boldly:

'My lord, you recollect how much you blamed me at Madrid . . . when I could not consult your lordship, and acted for myself. . . . *Now* if I had not, what would the consequences have been?'

Wellington was not going to be drawn into an argument about exceptions to his rule.

'It is all right, as it has turned out,' he retorted; 'but I recommend you still to have my orders for what you do.'[38]

McGrigor, though he became very fond of Wellington, always considered this insistence on orders a 'singular' feature in his character. McGrigor was mistaken. What was truly singular was Wellington's desire and ability to keep the whole elaborate organization of his army in his own hands. Given this system, a fanatical insistence on orders was not singular but essential.

On 15 November rain began to fall and the Allied army marched out to face the rigours of the last lap – to Ciudad Rodrigo.

All might have continued to schedule but for a blunder by Wellington's new quartermaster-general, Colonel James Willoughby Gordon. As officer responsible for routing the army's supply column during the retreat, he misdirected it twenty miles wide of Ciudad Rodrigo, so that the men got no rations whatever during the last days. With the French on their heels, rain on their heads, mud sucking off their shoes and nothing to eat but the acorns that fed wandering herds of pigs, these prodigal sons fell into a 'savage sort of desperation',[39] quarrelling, cursing, plundering, straggling, starving and dying in thousands. Sir Edward Paget, commander of the 1st Division who had lost an arm at Oporto, was seized from his horse by daring French skirmishers; while three other generals formed what Wellington afterwards sarcastically called a 'Council of War' and decided to disobey their marching instructions. In consequence they led their men into an impasse and had to be rescued by a furious Wellington.

'What did he say?' asked the diarist Charles Greville when Fitzroy Somerset told him the story.[40]

'Oh, by God! it was far too serious to say anything,' replied Wellington's *fidus Achates*. Others present, however, remembered that after a terrible pause the Commander-in-Chief had remarked icily:

'You see, gentlemen, I know my own business best.'

It is also said that while riding in search of the truants Wellington met the officer in charge of the baggage.

'What are you doing, sir?'

'I've lost my baggage.'

'Well, I can't be surprised . . . for I cannot find my army.'

Despite the murmurings at Burgos, the vast majority still welcomed his familiar, plainly dressed figure with a mighty shout, 'Here he comes!'[41] But even among these enthusiasts some cooled after an episode that had its beginnings in the bleak, hungry early hours of 17 November.

Wellington was awakened with a start by the loud rattle of musketry. The enemy falling upon his flank patrols? Not this time. The firing came from his prodigal sons, especially those in the 3rd Division, who had been agreeably disturbed by the sudden charge of hundreds of black pigs across their front. Discipline was thrown to the winds and the ravenous men scattered far and wide on an impromptu pig-shoot, incidentally wounding two Dragoons, falling in large numbers into French hands and giving Wellington his fright. Two days later, on 19 November, Ciudad Rodrigo was reached. Wellington's prodigal sons, however, were far from being welcomed home by a forgiving father.

Two of them had already been hanged for 'the shameful and unmilitary practice of shooting pigs in the woods. . . .' Now it was the officers' turn to be indiscriminately pilloried in the most sweeping and explosive circular ever issued by Wellington. Never had he commanded or even read about an army, he thundered, which had so gone to pieces.

Yet this army has met with no disaster; it has suffered no privations which but trifling attention on the part of the officers could not have prevented . . . nor . . . any hardship excepting . . . the inclemencies of the weather when they were most severe.

He did not question the gallantry of officers; what he wanted to see was 'minute and constant attention' to orders.

This tirade, running to well over twelve hundred words, did not end as so often with a disarming, 'I may be wrong', but with an attack on the slowness of British cooking which the proud officers of Moore's old Light Division, in particular, regarded as an unfair comparison with the French. Like today's boy scouts Moore's 'Shorncliffe boys' prided themselves on their nimbleness in kindling a flame with a couple of wet sticks. When they remembered with what labour their men collected firewood while the French simply tore down the nearest door; and how they lugged up monstrous iron kettles from the rear while the French carried light tin kettles along with them, the comparison seemed doubly odious. Here was a new touch added to the image of what Pakenham called the 'Iron man'. Already admirably iron in his own self-discipline and endurance, he now seemed inflexibly iron in his demands upon others. Later, he was to make no bones about the right way of running an army:

There is but one way; – to do as I did – to have A HAND OF IRON. The moment there was the slightest neglect in any department J was down on them.[42]

The notorious circular, though intended only for his commanding officers, soon found its way into regimental files and so into Opposition newspapers. It was probably true, as Tomkinson heard, that Wellington afterwards regretted his outburst. Many vexations had been simmering during the retreat from Burgos and like the French kettles he boiled quickly. If he had waited a few weeks his main anxiety – the bitter disappointment at home – would have been removed. For Bathurst assured him that his decision to retreat was honoured; foreign opinion considered his retreat the acme of fine generalship.

His army recovered quickly. In their winter quarters the men revelled in cheap food and tobacco, the officers – 'sporting-mad' according to Harry Smith – in beagling, fox-hunting and the occasional wolf-hunt, or 'the continual tramp up to Oporto', as Pakenham called it, to buy pipes of port for their families at home. Reinforcements kept arriving: there was even a rumour, circulated by a spy, that the Tsar was sending 15,000 men; this, however, proved false and no Russians were to be seen during the following June marching through Castile with snow on their boots. He had lost 5,000 men on the retreat but sent 20,000 French prisoners home. A less exacting commander would have lost far more. All Spain south of the Tagus was free and the guerrillas elsewhere rampant.

At the end of a tremendous year he rode off to Cádiz to see what he could do for the Spanish army but with wider prospects in mind. After all, he was the Child of Fortune, and on 10 December he wrote resolutely to Beresford, 'I propose to get into fortune's way. . . .'[43]

16

Vitoria

———

Cádiz gave its new Generalissimo a lyrical welcome.

> Ahe Marmont, onde vai, Marmont?

They chanted the anti-French song composed at Cádiz when Marmont retreated from Salamanca. As always when his own praises were sung, Wellington listened coolly. As soon as the head of the landau in which he rode was lowered and the hero's face and figure became visible, a torrent of enthusiasm broke over him. 'The Eagle! The Eagle!' they shouted, seizing and clinging to his hands. A few ardent glances slid off on to the young Fitzroy Somerset riding with him, and there were renewed cries of joy at such a pair of impossibly red, English cheeks – '*Mirar el Rubio!*'[1] On the return ride to headquarters in January 1813 Wellington described his success with the wry elation which his friends had learnt to expect:

> I was very well received at Cádiz and Lisbon and throughout the country and I ought to have somebody behind me to remind me that I am 'but a man'.[2]

The Horse Guards and Prince Regent also wished to spoil instead of damning him. He was made colonel of the Blues, and given the Garter. Arthur had neither studied nor worked for this honour; he had to ask Garter King at Arms whether the ribbon was worn from the right or left shoulder.

Official confirmation of the French disaster in Russia brought further hope that he might 'yet do well'. With his elevation since Salamanca into a European personage, he was deferentially consulted by the Cabinet as to whether in the new circumstances he should be sent to open a second front in Holland or in Hanover. He had not the slightest hesitation in saying No. The fact was that by early February 1813 he had made an audacious plan for driving the French right out of Spain; and from what he knew of his generals it was highly improbable that such a plan would succeed under anybody but himself. At the beginning of March Colonel Torrens reported signs of renewed trouble on the domestic front from Mary Anne Clarke and the Princess of Wales. 'I wish both these *aimable women* were hanging at any of your outposts,' he wrote. 'We must have a victory from you . . . to put these things out of the public mind.'[3]

Wellington was almost ready to oblige with a victory. While he seemed to be entirely absorbed in running Portuguese foxes to earth, he was in reality hunting down the many evils that had tormented his army during previous campaigns. There were to be tents to replace the hated bivouacking in the open, and prefabricated hospitals under the efficient Dr McGrigor. The suggestion had come from the doctor and been received in silence until suddenly, while walking up and down with McGrigor outside his headquarters one morning, Wellington said, 'By the by, your hospitals are ordered out and may soon be expected.'[4] The only good suggestion of McGrigor's that Wellington rejected was the introduction of French-styled *ambulances*.

With the new tents to be carried on army mules, the officers were sternly ordered to find other conveyances for their own baggage; a not inconsiderable problem, since even a young subaltern like George Robert Gleig, who joined Wellington's army in February 1813, brought with him a bulky kit.

1 Regimental jacket; wings & lace; 2 grey trousers; white, coloured & flannel waistcoats; flannel drawers; 12 stockings, 6 shirts, 1 pelisse; 3 prs. boots, 1 shoes.[5]

This, however, was nothing to Lieutenant Ker of the 9th Dragoons who according to William Bragge brought fifty boxes out to the Peninsula that year:

He is a pretty Man, remarkably neat and wears a Blue Velvet Forageing Cap, gold Tassel and Band of the same edged with white Ermine. How nice.[6]

As at home, there was always a little trouble with '*aimable women*' — the Portuguese girl, for example, who ran off with Lieutenant Kelly and whom Wellington ordered to be sent home on condition she was not put in a convent. It now turned out, wrote General Cole, that the lovers had already been married by the Caçadores' chaplain; should she still be 'given back to her mother'?[7]

At last by mid-May everything was ready. Great was the excitement among the troops in recognizing old friends again after the long months in winter quarters, from fellow-soldiers down to the very mules, Portuguese boys and trulls. Most of their grudges against Wellington had melted away in the spring sunshine, and one of his generals, F. Robinson, wrote in April:

The former want of success has made no impression on our people, they place such confidence in their Hero, that no one questions his conduct. He is their idol, for whom they will offer their lives as freely as they will drink his health. . . .[8]

Their idol's greatest triumph during the months of preparation had been to bring his enormously cumbersome bridging-train from the Tagus to the Douro, without the enemy catching the faintest echo of its loud, discordant progress. This pontoon train, however, was by no means Wellington's only secret. His evasiveness about strategy had at once struck a newcomer like Larpent: that day for instance when he had begun talking blandly about spending next winter in Portugal.

'But we have eaten nearly all the oxen in the country', interposed the Commissary-General pointedly.

'Well, then, we must set about eating all the sheep,' said Wellington, 'and when they are gone I suppose we must go.'

Go? What exactly did he mean? Go forward into Spain or back to Britain? No one cross-questioned him. But his favoured quartermaster-general, George Murray, ventured a quip.

'Historians will say that the British army . . . carried on war in Spain & Portugal until they had eaten all the beef and mutton in the country, and were then compelled to withdraw.'[9]

Wellington did not care what historians would say as long as the enemy did not guess.

The success of Wellington's new advance into Spain depended upon two strategic surprises, both typical of his imaginative mind and secretive methods. Instead of leading his whole army out along the obvious Salamanca road, he divided it into two unequal parts, riding personally with the smaller contingent of 30,000 men, in order to deceive the French into thinking this was his main thrust.

Having entered Salamanca on 28 May, he coolly handed over his command to Hill and slipped away next day towards the northern mountains, where General Graham with the real invasion force of 60,000 men was trudging through country considered impassable by the French. No one dreamt that Wellington would deliberately launch his soldiers, far less guns, into the formidable wilderness of Tras os Montes. Nevertheless it was on this secret march of Graham's that Wellington pinned his hopes of outflanking the French line on the Douro. William Bragge, armed with six pounds of tea, an English cheese and a keg of brandy, was one of those who set out buoyantly with Graham's army longing to see the 'new Route into Spain'.

A rough ride of fifty miles brought Wellington on 29 May to Miranda do Douro on the border, where the river boiled and seethed at the bottom of a ravine. Those travellers who wished to cross it clambered into a wicker basket and were wound over by a primitive system of ropes and windlass. Time was short and Joseph must be outflanked before he had time to concentrate. Without the Army of Portugal, Joseph's force was no more than 60,000.

Next day, 30 May, Wellington galloped into Graham's camp. Here all was anxiety. How get the army over the rushing River Esla, a tributary of the Douro? Bragge and his fellow Dragoons had already decided that the secret route, the like of which had never before been attempted by British cavalry, had much better have been left alone. But though there was some croaking, Wellington's personal popularity had been too thoroughly restored to languish now. The Heavy Dragoons had recently received from him 350 guineas for horses and guns captured at Salamanca, besides 1,500 dollars for an earlier success at Llerena: 'he is again a fine Fellow,' wrote Bragge.[10] He would lead them safely into Spain.

'Farewell Portugal! cried Wellington, turning his horse round and waving his hat as he crossed the frontier for the last time, 'I shall never see you again.'*

Once on the Esla, it was speedily decided to send the first troops over by the ford of Almendra. The wild river, full of melted snow, swept a number of unlucky Brunswickers and ten men from Wheeler's 51st to their death; the others were dragged across clinging to a stirrup or horse's tail of Grant's Hussars. These then fixed the famous pontoon-bridge, and the rest of the army marched over it.

Now began the second stage of this incredible May–June campaign. Wellington suddenly turned his army north again into more bleak hills, this time turning the French on the line of the Ebro. Such an astonishing manoeuvre, with the French border at the west end of the Pyrenees as its target, made sense only if Wellington could effect a total revolution in his supply system.

---

* This story was told to General Donkin by Picton who was with Graham's army. Donkin considered it almost too 'theatrical' to be true of Wellington, but could not doubt Picton's veracity. Donkin probably did not know that Wellington had been an enthusiastic amateur actor in India. There seems no reason to doubt the story; indeed it is easy to overdo the picture of Wellington as the stern, silent Englishman

This in fact he had accomplished in the second of his great surprises. Lisbon and Oporto were abandoned as his twin bases in favour of Santander on the Bay of Biscay. He had staked his future on cooperation between the Army and Navy – an issue which rarely if ever made its appearance in British history without causing a furious paper war between the Services.

All 'offensive postures' had meanwhile vanished from Joseph's army, and his very name Intrusive King became more and more of a mockery as he was extruded from town after town, beginning with Valladolid, by the remorseless but invisible pressure of the enemies on his flank. At 7 am on 13 June these unseen enemies were astonished to hear a tremendous explosion to the south of their march. It was King Joseph blowing up Burgos. And now as Joseph still retreated and Wellington's four great parallel columns, all streaming inexorably eastwards like apocalyptic rivers, began to descend from the barren uplands, an attempt was again made by Wellington's officers to stop him going further.

Why not end this brilliant campaign here and winter luxuriously on the Ebro? 'I thought differently,' Wellington recalled to Croker.

I thought that if I could not *hustle* them out of Spain before they were reinforced, I should not be able to hold any position in Spain when they should be. . . .[11]

He had risked saying 'Farewell Portugal' and did not intend to eat his words.

The hustle began on 17 June. Joseph's armies, discovering on that date that the River Ebro, like the Douro, Carrion, Pisuerga and Arlanzon before it, had been turned, immediately poured back still further along the Royal Road into the valley of Vitoria, with the Allies on their tail. Vitoria's ten-mile-long plain, lying aslant like a diamond among the surrounding hills, was cut diagonally from corner to corner by the road and also, more waywardly, by the River Zadorra. This 'merry brawling trout-stream', as Fortescue calls it, was spanned by a dozen stone bridges and curled itself at the valley's western end into the writhing loops and bends of a whip-lash in action. The slim golden spires of Vitoria stood out on an eminence two-thirds of the way across the plain to the east. The town was the centre of a five-pointed star: the Royal Road sweeping in from Madrid in the south-west and out to Bayonne in the north-east; the northern road to Bilbao, the southern road to Logroño on the Ebro, at the edge of a mountainous plateau whose fantastic sandstone rocks looked like houses and the houses like rocks; and lastly the bad road running out due east to the fortress of Pamplona in the Pyrenees.

Joseph drew up his 57,000 men and eighty guns in three defensive lines behind the Zadorra. The King did not forget to have stands erected in the town from which the people might watch him beat the English. He did forget to break down the Zadorra bridges.

On 19 June the spirited Arthur Kennedy found himself bivouacked in the hills only three leagues outside Vitoria, close to 'the *great Lord*, as he is called (and certainly no one deserves the appellation more justly) . . . and thus two great personnages reposed their bones near each other!' Kennedy's hungry troops were lucky to find an abandoned French dinner consisting of seven sheep. Next evening he climbed a hill to take a look at Vitoria. In front of it lay 'an enormous host'. Word flew round the Allied camp that the *great Lord* would be in that glittering city next night or die on the spot.

Dawn broke on 21 June 1813 in a cold, drizzling mist. But after Salamanca, rain before battle could only be a good omen. Wellington's aim was bold and simple: with his 78,000 men divided into four columns supported by seventy guns, to cut King Joseph's Royal Road to France and destroy his army. A flanking swoop on the left by Graham was to do the actual cutting. On the right wing Hill would make a strong feint in and above the village of Puebla, where the fact that six centuries earlier the Black Prince had fought and won would help to convince Joseph that this hallowed ground was Wellington's chief concern. Wellington himself commanded the two central columns. The French, more interested in great frontal attacks, expected Wellington to come at them *en masse* across the Zadorra from the west.

At about 8.30 am the first shots of the battle were fired, when Hill sent a splendid brigade of Spaniards up the precipitous heights of Puebla, supported by Cadogan's 71st Highlanders. Below in the defile the rest of Hill's corps were massed under their divisional commander, William Stewart, whose orders were now to advance against Vitoria by the Royal Road after the Puebla heights had been secured.

Notwithstanding much bloodshed and heroism at Puebla, the battle of Vitoria was not to be won on the right. Wellington had posted himself on a westward slope overlooking the Zadorra. Opposite him, above the poplars that fringed its banks, he could see a feature which

BATTLE OF VITORIA
21st June 1813

Allies
French

LONGA

1ST and 5TH GRAHAM

REILLE

To Bayonne

To Pamplona

Hills

Baggage

Vitoria

REILLE

REILLE

Royal Road

To Bilbao

R. Zadorra

To Logroño

DALHOUSIE 7TH

PICTON 3rd

Mendoza and Bridge

Margarita

D'ERLON

D'ERLON

Arinez Village

The Hill of Arinez

Tres Puentes

Villodas

KEMPT

Hair Pin Bend

WELLINGTON

GAZAN

GAZAN

Heights of Puebla

Nanclares

COLE 4th

MORILLO

CADOGAN

2nd HILL

R. Zadorra

Hills

Puebla Village

miles

was to prove the focal point of the coming struggle. This was the hill of Arinez, a conical mound in front of the village of that name, covered with stunted lavender and harebells and joined by a saddle to a second hillock which ran down towards the river. Wellington could see the French high command clustered together on the summit of Arinez. Behind the hill he devoutly hoped Graham was debouching on the Bilbao road and only waiting to rush forward, according to instructions, until Wellington's own columns were engaged. But there was already a serious hold-up in Wellington's centre columns and his whole carefully synchronized plan was in jeopardy.

Cause of all the trouble was the Earl of Dalhousie, commander of the left-centre which comprised his own 7th Division and Picton's 3rd. The situation was something of a tinderbox. Dalhousie happened to be one of the two 'newcomers' who had gone astray on the retreat from Burgos. And now he had lost his way over the mountains and was keeping them all waiting. It was probably during these fevered moments that Arthur Kennedy saw Wellington riding by on Copenhagen with a 'pensive' look. But precisely as 'the Lord' passed along the road, the mist dissolved and the stagnant military situation suddenly began to move.

An enterprising peasant was brought before Wellington at about midday with the astonishing news that the bridge of Tres Puentes between Picton and the extreme point of the hairpin bend was totally unguarded. Wellington promptly changed the plan he had formed to storm the bridge of Villodas into a surprise dash for Tres Puentes. Kempt's Light Brigade followed the peasant at the double through the scrubby juniper bushes that covered the hillside down to the river's outer bend. On the far bank, a towering perpendicular cliff completely hid them from the French. They passed the bridge unscathed except for their unlucky guide, who was decapitated by a cannonball. Here they again settled down, somewhat puzzled to be on the French side of the river, and waiting for the battle to begin.

If Wellington was impatient, Picton was beside himself. He rode to and fro hitting his horse's mane with his cane and swearing: 'Damn it! Lord Wellington must have forgotten us.' At last an aide-de-camp came galloping up, but with his eyes searching the mountains.

'Have you seen Lord Dalhousie?'

'No, sir! I have not seen his lordship: but have you any orders for me, sir?'

'None.'

'Then pray, sir, what are the orders you do bring?'

'Why, that as soon as Lord Dalhousie, with the Seventh Division, shall commence an attack upon that bridge,' pointing to Mendoza, 'the Fourth and Sixth [Light] are to support him.' Picton's passions boiled over. The idea, the monstrous idea that another division, the 7th, should fight in his front. He drew himself up and bawled at the flabbergasted aide-de-camp:

'You may tell Lord Wellington from me, sir, that the Third Division under my command shall in less than ten minutes attack the bridge and carry it, & the Fourth and Sixth may support it if they choose.' Turning to his men, he ordered them forward in language that would have made the reforming Radicals shiver:[12]

'Come on, ye rascals! – Come on, ye fighting villains!' This grave and grand insubordination was the beginning of victory. For it in fact carried out Wellington's design, though in an unorthodox way. An onlooker watched the 3rd as it 'swept like a meteor' across the 7th's path, then on through grape and round-shot towards the hill of Arinez, Picton cursing and yelling, dressed like a mad bonfire guy in a broad-brimmed top hat (he was suffering from eye trouble) and blue coat.

By now the whole line of the Zadorra was aflame, the 4th and Light Divisions having been launched across their allotted bridges and fords by Wellington himself, while the French retreated from all the river bends in rolling clouds of dust and smoke. The deafening cannonade from both sides was echoed by Graham's guns at last roaring in the northeast and by Hill's quickening assault on Gazan's southern flank. By 3 pm or soon after, Picton had torn a great rent in the French centre; he joined forces with two more infantry brigades under Wellington's personal leadership; together they all drove at full speed for the north side of Arinez hill and the village beyond.

There is more than one personal glimpse of Wellington during the great battle for this hill, the same hill on which three hundred of the Black Prince's knights had fallen. One moment Arthur Kennedy caught sight of the familiar figure in a 'grey frock' issuing orders 'with the sangfroid of an indifferent spectator'.

A fiery barrage, wrote Kennedy, was the enemy's expiring effort. For the Allied infantry led by Picton on the flank and Wellington in the centre succeeded in driving them off the hill and village. The French never managed to establish firm new lines behind Arinez. Inch by inch they gave way on all sides.

Further to the north, Harry Smith managed with gay effrontery to bounce the slow Dalhousie into giving him the privilege of capturing d'Erlon's key village of Margarita.

'What orders, my Lord?' asked Smith twice in peremptory tones, for his brigade, sent up to support Dalhousie, was coming under fire. 'What orders?'

'Better take the village,' muttered Dalhousie uncertainly to his quartermaster-general, whom he was consulting before giving Smith an answer. Smith overheard and did not wait for more.

'Certainly, my Lord,' and he made off at once in order not to hear them calling him back. After the victory Dalhousie paid him a generous compliment.

'Upon my word, sir, you receive and carry out orders quicker than any officer I ever saw.'

Smith replied with a flourish: 'You said, "Take the village." My Lord, there it is! Guns and all.'[13]

There they were, guns, arms, baggage, food, money, women and all. There were so many women in Joseph's army that a French officer described it as '*un bordel ambulant*' – a mobile brothel.[14] And now it was all abandoned. For that was the final and inconceivable end to the battle of Vitoria when, after 5 pm, the news was shouted by the French from column to column that King Joseph had ordered a general retreat. *Sauve qui peut* became the order of the day.

The French artillery, released from duty at last and suddenly tearing into 3,000 jammed carriages, created confusion enough; Colonel Grant made matters ten times worse by rashly sending his Hussars pellmell into the town on top of the fugitives and in advance of the Allied infantry. Never would Kennedy forget the sight: royal coaches and generals' coaches inextricably mingled with baggage-wagons; the finest horses, mules, bullocks and donkeys he had ever seen; ladies' pet monkeys and parrots – 'in short, Noah's Ark'. The King, he heard from Joseph's captured servants, had abandoned his berline, leapt on a horse and dashed out of the town only five minutes before the 18th Hussars arrived. 'How unlucky I was,' lamented Kennedy, 'not having caught Joseph.'

King Joseph's coach, as a matter of fact, had already been stopped by Captain Henry Wyndham of the 14th Light Dragoons and Lieutenant Lord Worcester of the 10th Hussars. They discharged their pistols into the coach's near-side window and out sprang the Intrusive King on the other side, extruded yet again but still a free man. Either the British did not recognize him or his escort was too quick for them – or possibly it was the magnetic contents of the coach that held back his pursuers.

From among the treasures inside, Wyndham's Dragoons acquired Joseph's lordly silver *pot de chambre*, which they christened 'The Emperor'. Their successors still use it at mess functions for drinking toasts in champagne, after which the pot is placed ceremoniously on the drinker's head.

Meanwhile the 18th Hussars and Spanish peasants quickly joined in the fun. Treasure chests and ladies' bandboxes flew open and the ground was covered as if by magic with doubloons, dollars, watches, jewels and trinkets. 'Where did it all come from?' asked Kennedy. 'The whole wealth of Spain and the Indies seemed to be here.' Most of it had indeed been pillaged from the Spanish people, and who could blame them for grabbing some of it back, ably assisted by their Allies? Many of Grant's brigade never got back on to the road at all.

Joseph's captured coach fared little better at the hands of the 18th Hussars, a detachment of which Wellington put on to guard it. Inside were quantities of state papers and love-letters (for Joseph's regal intrusions were occasionally directed towards boudoirs), but above all a collection of priceless canvases, the property of the captive Spanish King, Ferdinand VII. The pictures were probably saved from the sentries' attentions by being roughly rolled up; but it was thought that some state documents were purloined,* and certainly a corporal stole the gold ends from a marshal's baton which he found in an ornamental case of blue velvet embroidered with thirty-two gold eagles. The rest of the baton was promptly stolen from him by a drummer in the 87th. Next day (22 June) the 87th proudly presented their share of the trophy to Wellington; whereupon the 18th Hussars sent along the engraved ends, 'to undeceive him about the 87th'. Thus the whole of Marshal Jourdan's baton – for such it was – came into Wellington's hands. He in turn was to present it to the Prince Regent, whose ecstasies over the victory had been unparalleled.

Wellington's feelings in the hour of victory and the days immediately following were something less than joyful. As usual after a battle, his mood was set by the losses not the glory. The Allied casualties at

---

* Wellington forwarded a selection of Joseph's state papers to Lord Bathurst with the frank remark that as Bathurst's office was 'a sink of papers' he would be glad to have these 'really curious' documents back again for his own files (*Despatches*, vol. XI, p. 76, 3 September 1813). The present Duke of Wellington has returned the private letters from Joseph's wife and daughters ('*Mon cher petit papa*', etc.) to France.

Vitoria – just over 5,000 against the French 8,000 – were not exceptionally heavy. But the success, though breathtaking in one respect, fell short of hopes in another. The world had seen nothing like Wellington's booty since the days of Alexander the Great. Among the masses of captured equipment were 151 cannon, just on two million cartridges, immense quantities of ammunition and 100 wagons: according to Wellington himself, everything 'except one single carriage and one single cannon'.[15] The great haul of guns sent Wellington's thoughts back to Assaye, and he wrote to his old friend of Indian days, Sir John Malcolm:

I have taken more guns from these fellows . . . than I took at Assye [sic], without much more loss. . . . The two armies were nearly equal in numbers, but they cannot stand us now at all.[16]

Nevertheless Wellington's aim of capturing Joseph's army as well as his armament and loot did not succeed. The initial pursuit up the Pamplona road on the evening of the battle had to be called off after five miles. Broken ground unsuitable for horses and torrential rain provided obstacles which only a cavalry commander of exceptional ability could have surmounted. There was no such man on Wellington's staff.

Some critics then and since have blamed Wellington himself for not getting the best out of his staff. William Tomkinson, for instance, asked himself after Vitoria why Wellington's army was always so deficient in pursuit. He saw the answer in distrust and jealousy. 'Lord Wellington may not like to entrust officers with detachments to act according to circumstances, and I am not quite clear if he approves of much success, excepting under his own immediate eye.'[17]

William Bragge got nearer to the truth. As a cavalry officer himself, Bragge kept his ears open to the nuances of regimental discussion and recognized the nauseous mixture of arrogance and incompetence in too many of his superiors. At the same time there is a hint that his brusque Commander-in-Chief had perhaps not found the best way of handling such touchy material. Bragge gave a brilliant picture of three stages in a vicious circle:

At present the Minister or Duke of York order out a batch of Generals, who . . . have neither Talent or Experience.

Stage two soon followed:

Some blunder is committed, Lord Wellington speaks his mind, the Great Man is offended at being crossed, and never bothers to exert himself or act upon his Judgment again.

The last stage was seen in the retreat from Burgos and again at Vitoria:

Here I think commences a slackness which is quickly felt throughout the whole Machine, occasions incalculable Mischief and has induced Lord Wellington to call this 'God Almighty's Army' a thousand times.[18]

If Wellington had never called the army by any worse name than that, no one would have objected. He was soon to pounce on a pithier phrase.

The exhausted infantry, some of whom had marched twenty miles since dawn, were allowed by Wellington to spend the night after the battle in rest. Unfortunately they did not do so. A tremendous, night-long bacchanalia developed out of the first lootings in Vitoria. The surrounding fields, lit up by flares and enlivened by wine, women and song, soon looked more like a fairground than a soldiers' camp on the eve of a vital pursuit. Regular auctions took place, as after Ciudad Rodrigo and Badajoz, but now on an altogether more splendid scale. This time the happy auctioneers were able to dress up in the bemedalled uniforms of French generals, and besides the high quality of the goods for sale there was a copious supply of money. The whole of the French army's pay had arrived in Vitoria shortly before the battle. It was reckoned that five million dollars were on the field, of which only 100,000 reached Wellington's military chest. 'No officer dared to interfere.'[19] One officer blatantly described how he himself had joined with, instead of restraining, the soldiers. The wagon of the French General Villatte was discovered stuffed with money and church plate. After a few 'awkward' moments the officer decided to take his share, later counting it out in a church belfry. He was able to send £250 home, buy a second horse and keep a nice balance. Privates Wheeler and Costello were encouraged by their officers to 'make merry', though Wheeler was warned at all costs to keep sober in case of having to march 'at any moment'.[20]

To march at any moment was precisely Wellington's idea, but one doomed to disappointment. His aide-de-camp, Colonel Staveley, recorded an ironic scene between the Commander-in-Chief and himself on the night after the battle.

'Tell Murray,' said Wellington to Staveley, speaking of the quarter-master-general, 'I shall march the army off myself in the morning.'

'At what hour?' asked Staveley.

'When I get up.'[21]

When Wellington got up his army had only just begun to go to bed. Even the Light Brigade admitted to being so heavy with raw meat and flour that they could not march.

Virtually unhindered by a pursuing force, King Joseph managed to get 55,000 men safely over the Pyrenees and back into France, leaving Wellington to compose the kind of acidulated document that too often had to form the postscript to his triumphs.

It is quite impossible for me or any other man to command a British army under the existing system. We have in the service the scum of the earth as common soldiers –

and what with proposals in Parliament for reforms and soft-hearted officers in the field, it was impossible to keep 'such men as some of our soldiers are' in order.[22]

The fatal phrase, *scum of the earth*, had long been and was to remain a favourite of Wellington.* He was to rub in his point to Stanhope in 1831 during one of his many arguments about flogging.

'Do they beat them in the French Army?' asked Stanhope.

'Oh, they bang them about very much with ramrods and that sort of thing, and then they shoot them.'[23]†

But the reason why the British Army needed the terror of the triangle as an ultimate deterrent, whereas the French did not, was because the French was an army of conscripts and the British of volunteers:

The conscription calls out a share of every class – no matter whether your son or my son – all must march; but our friends – I may say it in this room – are the very scum of the earth.

Wellington then went on to analyse the volunteer material:

People talk of their enlisting from their fine military feeling – all stuff – no such thing. Some of our men enlist from having got bastard children – some for minor offences – many more for drink . . . and it really is wonderful that we should have made them the fine fellows they are.

Wellington struggled hard, as has been shown, to improve his soldiers' conditions and to collect officers who could inspire obedience. He tried again soon after Vitoria to raise the level of recruits by making the Government pay allowances to soldiers' families, especially the

* See the Mary Anne Clarke affair.

† William Bragge referred on 6 May 1812 to 'my Cat of eight Leathern Thongs taken out of a French trumpeter's Kit at Llerena. It is a worse Instrument than ours and will be sent to Mr Whitbread if I have the good Fortune to bring it to England.' Clausel admitted he shot fifty soldiers to death on the retreat from Salamanca (Oman, vol. VI, p. 7).

Irish whose wives at present 'went not upon the parish but upon the dunghill to starve'.

When he used phrases like 'scum of the earth' or 'very worst members of society' he was not being vindictive but descriptive: stating the harsh sociological facts as he saw them. Of course he was wrong. Not nearly such a large proportion of the Army was 'scum' as he implied. Many 'fine fellows' came into it for adventure or patriotism who needed no baptism of fire or flogging. Young William Lawrence, the Dorset ploughboy who ran away into the Army, regarded his plunderings as pranks: the bayoneted pig hidden under the train of the Blessed Virgin Mary in a chapel till the hunt died down; the half-strangled cock stuffed under his cap which suddenly crowed on parade. Nor could the theory be defended that the really licentious soldiers became better disciplined or less brutal by being more brutally punished. As Tom Morris, the articulate private in the 73rd Foot pointed out, 'Once flog a man and you degrade him for ever, in his own mind; and thus take from him every possible incentive to good conduct.'[24]

Wellington saw no point in punishing a soldier at all except as a deterrent. But to treat a man purely as an 'example' was to deprive him of his human rights; and this the new century would increasingly reject. 'It was fortunate for Britain that Wellington was at once a great humanitarian and a great disciplinarian,' wrote G. M. Trevelyan.[25] But the two vital principles were not always reconciled in him. And when things went wrong, as after Burgos and Vitoria, the principle of order fought down the claims of compassion.

He himself felt that the sacrifice he made in popularity was repaid in the ultimate perfection of his army. On 21 November 1813, five months to the day after Vitoria, he was able to call the army which he had so often described as the worst that ever left England, 'the most complete machine for its numbers now existing in Europe'.[26] Years later he said to Lady Salisbury, 'I could have done anything with that army. It was in such perfect order.'[27]

Even with this army in its supposedly unregenerate state, Wellington had carried off at Vitoria one of the greatest strategic triumphs in British history. To do so he had marched 400 miles in forty days, in itself a victory of logistics that Fortescue celebrated with no less a salute than an epigram: 'Wellington's supplies were always hunting for his army; Joseph's army was always hunting for its supplies.'[28]

Public rejoicing at home reached a pitch surpassed only by the tumultuous revelling on the battlefield. William Wellesley-Pole described to Arthur how the Prince Regent had commanded him to take a principal share in organizing the most 'splendid and magnificent' fête ever held in England. In return for Marshal Jourdan's baton the Prince Regent raised Wellington to the exalted rank of field marshal, and set about personally drafting him a letter of congratulation and designing the first British baton, adorned with lions instead of eagles.

You have sent me among the trophies of your unrivalled fame, the staff of a French Marshal, and I send you in return that of England.[29]

The Duke of York rather unnecessarily added that he would have recommended Wellington to the rank of field marshal earlier (it had been mooted after Salamanca) but for 'the spirit of jealousy' which it would have aroused.

Wellington's soldierly reply to the Prince Regent showed he felt more than ever that he had been 'retained for life'.

I can evince my Gratitude for your Royal Highness's repeated favours only by devoting my life to your service.[30]

Even Kitty had to bear her share of the glory. She was the star at a party of Lady Templetown's, where Fanny Burney met her. 'Her very name,' wrote Fanny to her father afterwards, 'electrified me with emotion.'[31]

Europe's celebration was as unprecedented as the British baton. For the first time in history a *Te Deum* was sung in St Petersburg Cathedral for the triumph of a foreign army. Beethoven composed *Wellington's Victory* in honour of the battle of Vitoria, complete with trumpets, cannon, marching feet and snatches from 'Rule Britannia', 'Malbrouck s'en va t'en Guerre' (the original air of 'For He's a Jolly Good Fellow'), and 'God Save the King'. The alliance of Prussia, Russia and Sweden against France was joined by Austria, and on 16–19 October 1813 the European campaign against Napoleon was crowned by the victory of Leipzig, to be known as 'the Battle of the Nations'.

A certain prophetic sense seemed to have inspired the Portuguese Government when, out of the blue, they created Wellington '*Duque da Victoria*' just two months before the battle.

Napoleon, exasperated by the defeat in Spain which he characteristically described as 'ridiculous', ordered the grand extrusion and replaced Joseph by Soult.

The old kite was of course no longer expected to chase the leopards into the sea – that historic mission now looked a trifle bizarre – but only across the Ebro. With Europe united against him, Napoleon could not win. Wellington's problem was what came next, on the other side of the mountains.

17

Champagne and Coffee

'Here I am, sitting on the sand, and surrounded by a dozen little girls: one is mending my foraging cap, the rest singing "*Viva Wellington*".'[1]

The writer was Colonel Augustus Frazer of the Royal Horse Artillery, the date 30 June 1813. He was waiting at a beach near San Sebastián for ammunition to be landed. San Sebastián and Pamplona were the last two pockets of resistance in Spain, but they were enough to keep Wellington behind the Pyrenees. Until he knew the result of Napoleon's latest confrontation with the Grand Alliance, he could not risk invading France without a secure line on the Spanish frontier. That meant capturing the two fortresses, San Sebastián by storm, Pamplona by starvation.

There is a sense of anti-climax about the battles of the Pyrenees, despite Wellington's perfected skill and his troops' courage. Salamanca and Vitoria are behind; Waterloo casts its shadow before; Spain seems if not a backwater, at any rate 'the greatest of "side-shows" '.

Only in so far as the battles of the Pyrenees sharpen the silhouette of the man about to enter France, need they be fought again in detail here.

The first attempt at storming San Sebastián took place on 25 July 1813. Though there were as many as 100 engineers and sappers in Wellington's force and a strong siege-train, the engineer-historian, John T. Jones, regretted that the operations should have still been 'irregular': not enough science, not an effective enough blockade by the Royal Navy, too much talent in the French Governor, Emanuel Rey, and too little control by the amiable old British commander, Graham, over his subordinates. Doubts and arguments, wrote Napier, seeped through to the troops, 'abating that daring confidence which victory loves'.[2]

Wellington, the supreme inspirer of confidence, was pacing up and down in a graveyard. Why he chose this place is not known, except that it was in Lesaca, his headquarters on the River Bidassoa which ran northwards into the Bay of Biscay, forming the boundary between Spain and France. At 11.30 am they brought him the appropriately gloomy news. The assault upon San Sebastián had failed. He at once galloped over to the city, ordered the siege to be changed into a blockade and reached Lesaca again that evening – to receive disquieting rumours of gunfire in the mountain passes of Maya and Roncesvalles above Pamplona.

With the evocative name of Roncesvalles and the faint thunder of battle rolling down the valleys, came the insistent echoes of Roland's horn in 'that Chivalric ground'. Lord Dalhousie, however, who actually commanded a division not far from Roncesvalles, was undisturbed by echoes chivalric or otherwise. He sent Wellington a bland assurance that the French attack in the passes, though heavy, had been repulsed. Wellington warned Graham to stand by, ordered up reinforcements from Pamplona and went to bed. It had been a long day. It was to be a short night.

Soult with overwhelming force had invaded the passes above Pamplona at dawn on 25 July. By the morning of the 26th, both passes were evacuated. Cole's 4th Division, supported by Picton's 3rd, retired on Pamplona. Posted originally in an extremely strong position above Roncesvalles, where the ancient monastery still claimed to harbour Roland's bones, Cole had been ordered by Wellington to hold on until the last possible moment. He did not do so. An eerie mist suddenly blotted out the battlefield on the afternoon of the 25th. Cole dreaded being cut off. The point was that the only commander on whom the army could invariably rely was Wellington.

Picton, looking more eccentric than ever in his top hat and with an umbrella for a whip, felt equally lost without Wellington and could give Cole no encouragement to stay.* Wellington afterwards confessed that his daring scheme for attacking such widely separated fortresses as Pamplona and San Sebastián at the same time was 'one of the greatest faults he ever committed in war'. He also told the Prime Minister: 'There is nothing I dislike so much as these extended operations, which I cannot direct myself.'[3]

His chance to resume personal direction came in the small hours of 26 July, when he was roused from two or three hours' sleep by a message revealing the truth about the situation. He at once rode over

---

* Umbrellas were officially banned by Wellington on the battlefield, though he allowed all sorts of other odd personal equipment.

the mountains towards Pamplona, issuing orders as he went to his reserves, the 6th and 7th Divisions. The news he received along the route was so bad that he finally dashed ahead of his staff and, accompanied only by Fitzroy Somerset, galloped into a village not ten miles from Pamplona – Sorauren. Here he found his army drawn up by Cole and Picton on a steep ridge with the French in the act of taking up position on the heights opposite. There was only a moment in which to issue new directions to the approaching 6th Division, which was clearly in imminent danger of being cut off.

'The French are coming!' shouted the Spanish villagers signalling frantically up the road. Wellington, who had dismounted at the grey stone bridge over the River Lanz, seized his writing materials and resting them on the parapet scribbled thirteen lines of redirections to his quartermaster-general, Murray.

'The French are coming! The French are coming!' Fitzroy Somerset snatched the note from him, vaulted into the saddle and raced at full speed out of one end of Sorauren as the French light cavalry entered the other. Wellington, now quite alone, prepared to join his embattled lines above the village. He put his thoroughbred into a gallop and he flew up the scorching hillside between spicy box bushes. O'Toole's Caçadores knew who it was the moment they caught sight of him.

'*Douro! Douro!*' they cried, and the British regiments joined in with 'Nosey! Nosey!'

Wellington took his stand dramatically on the highest point of the ridge, opened his telescope and calmly surveyed the unpleasing visage of Marshal Soult opposite, which had been pointed out to him by a double agent. The act was partly to complete the reassurance of his agitated 'children', partly to make the naturally cautious Soult ask himself what all the cheering was about. Had reinforcements arrived? While Soult paused and considered (he took a siesta) Wellington's vital 6th Division would be making its way to Sorauren, as redirected by Somerset, through the hills.

'Who could sleep at such a moment?' exclaimed General Clausel in an agony of impatience. When Soult was awake again a colossal thunderstorm broke over the battlefield and washed out the rest of daylight. But at midnight there were grand illuminations in Pamplona, ready for the French victors.

They never came, for Soult had lost his chance. Next day, 28 July 1813, the omen of the thunderstorm was fulfilled and it was Wellington who won a resounding victory: the first battle of Sorauren. The French columns found that they could no more capture 'Cole's Ridge', as the great hill came to be called in honour of the 4th Division's heroic stand, than they had been able to storm Bussaco; while the 6th, led by Pakenham, suddenly swooped out of the mountains and delivered what was almost another Salamanca stroke against the French flank.

'The 28th was fair bludgeon-work,' wrote Wellington. 'I escaped as usual unhurt,' he told William; 'and I begin to believe that the finger of God is upon me.'[4] William was horrified to hear of his brother's narrow escape on Sorauren bridge and felt that the finger of God could be overworked. Wellington himself had to admit afterwards to Larpent that it had been touch and go. 'Why, at one time it was rather alarming, certainly, and it was a close run thing.'[5]

The fighting at Sorauren burst out again on 30 July, after a day of utter exhaustion when not a shot was fired. At the end of the second battle every French division had been beaten and forced to retreat, Foy's by mere goat-paths into France.*

'We have had some desperate fighting in these mountains,' wrote Wellington to the War Minister of the battles of the Pyrenees as a whole, 'and I have never known the troops behave so well.'[6] The Spanish regiments had defended 'Spanish Hill' with the utmost valour, and as for the Portuguese, they were now well known to be 'the fighting-cocks of the army'.

On 31 August 1813, Soult's counter-offensive came to an end with a failed attempt to dislodge the Spanish army from the heights of San Marcial above San Sebastián. The battle of San Marcial is famous for being a single-handed Spanish victory under General Manoel Freire, thanks to Wellington's psychological insight in refusing to reinforce the Spaniards when he could see that the day was theirs: 'Look . . . if I send you the English troops you ask for, they will win the battle; but as the French are already in retreat you may as well win it for yourselves.'[7] They went on to do so in fine style as he had foreseen.

The incident does not bear out the suspicions of certain British officers that Wellington always made sure of getting the credit for every success himself.

That very morning of 31 August San Sebastián fell (though General Rey withdrew his troops up Monte Úrgull, and into a sea-girt castle

---

* The exact site of the two battles above Sorauren used to be easily identified by the pilgrimage chapel of San Salvador in the valley between the two armies. Today it is a small heap of stones overgrown with brambles. The bridge, however, on which Wellington wrote his famous despatch is still exactly the same, and is a favourite picnic spot for the people of Pamplona.

above the town, where he held out until 9 September). The horrors, both accidental and deliberate, which attended its capture were never surpassed during the Peninsular War – unprecedented anxiety and 'senseless laughter'[8] amounting to hysteria before the count-down; slaughter in the breaches so ghastly that there were not enough officers left alive when the town was entered to control their maddened troops; a sack more murderous than Badajoz and a fire that eventually razed the town. William Napier suggested that Wellington could have cured his troops of pillaging after Vitoria by giving immediate rewards of prize money to the 'valourous' and shooting looters on the spot. But this would not have stamped out pillaging nor civilized the minority of savages in his army. The truth is that the public at home, while rightly recoiling from the age-old barbarities of siege warfare, expected their soldiers to perform in ways which made an unpleasant reaction inevitable. 'The indescribable *something*' in the faces of soldiers just before an assault, already noticed by William Grattan at Ciudad Rodrigo and Badajoz, resulted from the total suppression of human feelings such as pity and terror. They burst out afterwards in a degraded catharsis of terrorism and drink.

Anti-British elements in the Spanish and Irish press accused Wellington of burning down San Sebastián on purpose, in order to deal a blow at Spain's commerce with France. The charge was utterly false. Wellington had always refused to add to the horrors of war by ordering a bombardment. At San Sebastián he specifically forbade it, pointing out to Graham in a Wellingtonian understatement that it would be 'very inconvenient to our friends the inhabitants, and eventually to ourselves'.[9] 'I do not know how long my temper will last,' he fumed to Henry.[10] It had to last as long as the cause needed him, for he was retained for life.

In 1925 Queen Victoria Eugénie of Spain opened a cemetery in a flower garden on Monte Ürgull, facing the Atlantic, to commemorate the English soldiers who fought for Spain in 1813 and 1836. A stone was inscribed in Spanish and English.

> England has confided to us their honoured remains.
> Our gratitude will watch over their eternal repose.

Gratitude is not, nor can it be, the currency of international affairs. The only flowers growing in the garden today are wild garlic, and of the English gunners forming a large group of heroic statuary, four out of six have lost their heads.

The next push into the Pyrenees had to wait for over a month. Wellington was determined neither to anticipate victories in Germany, Catalonia and Pamplona nor to overdrive his exhausted army.* He himself had appeared inexhaustible – until lumbago struck him after Sorauren. William Maginn, a Peninsular diarist, noticed that his fifteen fine chargers had been reduced to skin and bone by all his riding. 'He was like a centaur,' said his courier, 'in seeming part of his horse, and he slept as soundly in his saddle as if in his bed.'[11] A visitor to Lesaca during the blockade of San Sebastián commented on how little he talked or drank of his excellent wine; not even a toast with his guests.[12]

By 8 August he was only just getting about again; but quite apart from illness, he intended to go forward at the correct pace dictated by circumstances, as he told William, 'notwithstanding the Clamour of our newspapers, & even of the Govt. . . . at our inactivity during the Winter'. He had heard this sort of clamour almost every year since the war began and he bore it stoically and stubbornly.

One piece of good news arrived from William in February 1814 to counter-balance some of these vexations. King Joseph's pictures, which he had shipped back to England on 5 October 1813, turned out to be masterpieces. William had shown them secretly to the President of the Royal Academy, who declared that a Correggio and a Giulio Romano ought to be framed in diamonds – it was worth fighting the battle of Vitoria for them alone. Lord Mulgrave, master-general of the Ordnance, added that Arthur must certainly keep them all himself as trophies of war.[13] Wellington knew only too well how this kind of talk would go down with the public. The pictures were not to be exhibited, he ordered William, until those belonging to King Ferdinand had been returned to him. 'The good natured World would accuse me of stealing them.' All the same it was a most agreeable surprise – 'I believe I was born with *Fortunatus'* cap on my head'.[14] Later, King Ferdinand performed one of his rare acts of generosity in asking Wellington to keep them, and they are now at Apsley House and Stratfield Saye.

Wellington's army crossed the River Bidassoa into France on 7 October 1813. As Bragge put it, they had 'infringed upon the Sacred Territory' at last.[15]

---

* Oman described Wellington's decision not to pursue Soult on 2 August as his 'grand refusal' and Napier wrote somewhat sententiously: 'Had Caesar halted because his soldiers were fatigued, Pharselia [*sic*] would have been but a common battle.'

Everything went like clockwork. There was the requisite thunder-storm the night before; local shrimpers whispered to Wellington that the Bidassoa estuary was just fordable at very low tide and proved correct; and Soult's 'impregnable' right flank was turned by an army apparently marching through the sea. The only fault with the clockwork was that it made the clock go too fast. Soult's fortified lines on the *massif* of La Grande Rhune, above the village of Vera, fell next day so smoothly to the Allies that Wellington's gallant officers expected to clear the next river-lines – the Nivelle, the Nive and the Adour – as if they were riding in a giant steeplechase.

It was here that a newcomer, the youthful, amusing and dandified Welshman, Ensign Rees Howell Gronow, saw the creator of this great army for the first time.

He was very stern and grave-looking; he was in deep meditation . . . and spoke to no one. His features were bold and I saw much decision of character in his expression. He rode a knowing-looking thorough-bred horse. . . .[16]

Gronow had not mistaken the decision in Wellington's character. He decided not to advance further while Pamplona still held out. This the indomitable garrison continued to do until 31 October, when they finally emerged like skeletons from their tombs on resurrection morning. Now at last, on 10 November 1813, Wellington was ready for the next move: to force the line of entrenched mountains above the river Nivelle.

Before the battle Harry Smith remembered Wellington sitting on the turf at the summit of La Rhune mountain, surrounded by his Light Division commanders – Alten, Colborne, Kempt – his eyes glued to his telescope and his ears alert to useful ideas on the coming assault, which was to take place against the Petite Rhune opposite. He explained that the French would not dare to concentrate their defence as he would concentrate his attack.

'Now I see it,' said Colborne. He and his fellow-officers began to get up and go.

'Oh, lie still,' said Wellington. So the group settled down again round him on the mountain top, and had the instructive experience of hearing him dictate his exact plan of attack to his quartermaster-general, Murray. The episode is significant. That intimate, informal gathering on La Rhune preserves the memory of a Wellington who was not always the cold, uncommunicative leader of legend.

'Remember: at four in the morning,' said Wellington to Larpent, as they rose from dinner on the evening of 9 November 1813.[17] Next day Larpent, standing high up on La Rhune, was able to follow the fall of one French redoubt after another by the advancing glint of the Allied bayonets.

The battle of the Nivelle was remarkable for personal valour: for William Napier storming the topmost fort at the head of the 43rd, with the Light Division's famous 'stern shout'; for John Colborne bluffing a strong French garrison into surrender – 'You are cut off. Lay down your arms.' 'There, Monsieur, is a sword which has ever done its duty' – and for Wellington suddenly appearing at the head of this or that column, his presence signified by cheers which were invariably described as 'electrifying'.[18]

By the Nivelle action he demonstrated his ability to drive Soult eventually from any and every position. If there had been more daylight and less mud, 'I should have given Soult a terrible squeeze.'

He had just heard the news of Leipzig from a sulky French prisoner whom he dined, wined and finally examined on the evening after the battle. Where were Napoleon's present headquarters?

'My Lord, there are no more headquarters.'

In a flash he realized that this was confirmation of the Leipzig rumours: Napoleon had been defeated and pinned behind the Rhine by the combined armies of Europe. 'I saw my way clearly to Bordeaux and Paris.'

At the very moment, however, that he was politely entertaining a French officer, his Spanish soldiers were horribly pillaging a French village – Ascain. His way forward to Bordeaux was suddenly less clear. If these Spanish marauders raised the countryside against him, as the French had earlier raised the Spanish guerrillas against themselves, his cause would be lost. As early as July 1813 he had made a moral appeal to his Spanish troops not to plunder the 'peaceful inhabitants of France': it would be 'unmanly and unworthy'. Now that it had happened he did not blame the hungry Spaniards. But if he could not blame them he could send most of them home. This he promptly did. It meant fighting the rest of the war with numbers inferior to Soult. He accepted the disadvantage in return for the increasing friendliness of a delighted French peasantry.[19]

There was a new proclamation against plundering and the bulk of his army, including Morillo's crack Spanish corps which was retained, were licked into shape by Pakenham, who as head of the reorganized military police went about, said Schaumann, 'like a raving lion'.[20]

223

Wellington roared also when necessary. There were fierce orders against keeping horses in churches or grazing mules in vineyards. After Nivelle he met Colborne whoe valiant 52nd had rewarded themselves with some French pigs and poultry.

'Though the Brigade have even more than usually distinguished themselves, we must respect the property of the country.'

'I am fully aware of it my lord . . . in the very heat of action a little irregularity will occur.'

'Ah, ah! stop it in future, Colborne.'[21]

Colonel Augustus Frazer believed that no army had ever behaved better than the British army, even in its own country, and put it down entirely to Wellington's 'wholesome regulations'. Sergeant Lawrence thought the Nivelle proclamation 'much to the credit of our noble commander'.[22]

The rain unfortunately could not be sent back to Spain with the unreliable Spanish regiments. As early as 2 September William Napier was writing to his wife about 'General *Rain*'. 'More, more rain!' lamented Larpent in his journal.[23] Yet again Wellington had to wait for a month before he could carry another of Soult's great river-lines, that of the Nive, and invest the city of Bayonne.

Wellington's own part during the protracted struggle on the Nive has raised a query. Why did he not follow his usual practice of taking over personally during the critical moments? There is no obvious answer, but it has been suggested that he wished to give his two senior generals, Hope and Hill, the experience of independent command.[24] If so, he was only doing for them what he had done for General Freire and his Spaniards at San Marcial, and incidentally refuting another hostile myth which had grown up during the early difficult stages of the Peninsular War. The episode of La Rhune proved that he was not always secretive; the battles of San Marcial and the Nive showed that he did not insist on winning every victory himself.

No doubt the growing perfection of his army helped to produce this new leader: 'There appears to be a new spirit among the officers . . . to keep the troops in order,' he wrote cheerfully on 21 November 1813. If Wellington and his army had stayed together even longer than they did, it may be that he would have forgotten he ever called them scum, and they that he ever seemed hard, cold and autocratic.*

* There were some reported backslidings on both sides. On two occasions Wellington was said to have spoken so sharply to staff officers who had made mistakes that each of them, Colonel Sturgeon and Major Todd, deliberately got himself shot in a skirmish. Even F.J. Hudleston, however, no admirer of Wellington, admits that the similarity between these two stories casts doubts upon the second, which was related by G. R. Gleig at the age of ninety.

His winter headquarters were at St Jean de Luz. There are many testimonies to the delectable change from poverty-stricken Spain to fertile France. Arthur Kennedy's tribute, given in a hitherto unpublished letter to his mother on 15 December 1813, is in the typical vein of a young officer.

Meantime allow me to say I am about to *attack the enemy* in the following advantageous *positions*. A boiled knuckle of veal on the right, a roast shoulder of mutton on the left. . . . Each flank covered with a bottle of champagne and sort of claret, not forgetting some Irish potatoes, my usual attendants. The whole commanded by a most civil landlady who . . . probably expects to carry me by a *coup de main*.[25]

Arthur Shakespear, who had had the privilege of seeing the Commander-in-Chief scratch his foot before Salamanca, was now permitted to lend this inveterate rider a horse. Wellington had come up from St Jean de Luz to inspect the 'Galloping Third' Dragoons, and the steep road had left Copenhagen exhausted. He told Shakespear he was never carried better.[26]

Such high good humour in the Commander-in-Chief prompted Shakespear to ask for promotion.

His Grace made no promise, but that day fortnight upon return of letters from England I was gazetted! . . . I attributed my good fortune entirely to having supplied the *Great Man* with a comfortable horse! We played at whist that evening & I won 30 shillings from his Grace!

When not on horseback to review troops, Wellington hunted his foxhounds for his health in the mountains above the Bay. He wore the sky-blue Salisbury coat presented to him by his old admirer, Lady Salisbury, a black cape and the boots he had designed himself for comfort and convenience after many experiments.

The army had its own experiments. Congreve's rockets were given a trial against cavalry. It was agreed that they would have scared the horses stiff if only they had gone near them.[27]

The political problem of how to regard Napoleon was not unlike that of the rockets. Wellington called him 'the grand disturber'. Yet he felt that once peace had been made the Emperor might still be the best available ruler for France, provided he behaved as he promised. Most of the Allied army, however, took the simpler view of Pakenham that the grand disturber must be 'dethroned and Decapitized [*sic*]'.[28] During this period of uncertainty Wellington had the doubtful pleasure of entertaining the Bourbon Duke of Angoulême, nephew of Louis XVIII, in his camp. Wellington's delicate task was to prevent a premature rash of white cockades – the royalist badge – in the towns he conquered. Otherwise the civil inhabitants, of whom Wellington constantly thought, might find themselves in serious trouble if the grand disturber came out on top. 'But if you cannot make peace with Buonaparte in the winter,' he wrote to the Cabinet on 10 January 1814, 'we must *run* at him in the spring. . . .'[29]

Wellington insisted that one last pressing but sensitive problem must be solved before he could run at Bonaparte – finance. A letter marked 'Secret and confidential' from the Chancellor of the Exchequer, N. Vansittart, to the Commissary-in-Chief, J. C. Herries, shows that by 11 January the solution was in sight, thanks to Nathan Mayer Rothschild. Vansittart explained to Herries that since it was essential for Wellington to get more specie than the Bank of England 'or any other usual channel' could obtain, it had been decided by the Prime Minister and himself to employ Mr Rothschild 'in the most secret and confidential manner' to collect up to £600,000 sterling in French coin on the Continent.

Upon consideration of the magnitude of the objects in view, of the dispatch and secrecy which it requires and of the risks which may be incurred, it is not thought unreasonable to allow Mr. Rothschild a commission of Two per cent. . . .[30]

Before the end of January Bathurst informed Wellington that 'our Jew' had been successful in Paris and the army would now get a good remittance. All the omens were favourable. The password for the month at the Tower of London was 'Wellington'.[31]

On 14 February 1814 Wellington's spring running began.

Between the middle of February and the beginning of March, Soult was driven remorselessly back. There was no need for Wellington to stop and storm Bayonne. He by-passed the city, leaving Sir John Hope to seal up its 17,000-strong garrison by crossing the River Adour at its perilous estuary on a bridge of boats. How were the engineers to get planks for the rafts? Cut up the siege-gun platforms, said Wellington brusquely. Then what about the platforms? Cut down trees from the pine forests when they were needed. Above all, get on. This was the same Wellington who had made them chop up wagons for scaling-ladders at Ciudad Rodrigo. He also showed himself the same man whose fondness for personal excursions had nearly landed him in captivity before Talavera, Salamanca and Sorauren. While examining the Adour he ran into a detachment of French *vedettes* and had to gallop for it.[32]

A few days after Hope's feat on the Adour, Wellington and Hill turned Soult's left wing successively on the rivers Joyeuse, Bidouse and Gave d'Oloron. This 'great game', as Oman calls it, was halted briefly when Soult faced the Allies on the River Gave de Pau at Orthez. Wellington sat down on a stone under an umbrella kindly provided by a passing officer to keep off the drizzle, and wrote out his battle-orders for Orthez, while waiting for the 3rd Division to come up.[33]

Next day, 27 February 1814, he was up long before dawn and after all was ready he snatched a moment's sleep wrapped in his short white winter cloak.

'Call me in time, Murray.'

After the quartermaster-general had roused him he triumphantly swept the demoralized French out of their strong positions, though error and ill-luck as usual prevented him from organizing a comparable pursuit. The pursuit was also hampered by an accident to Wellington himself, the nearest he ever came to being incapacitated by a wound.

He was riding with his Spanish liaison officer, General Alava, who suddenly called out that he had had a 'knock' on his bottom. Wellington could not help laughing. Next moment he was knocked himself: a spent bullet struck his sword-hilt driving it violently against his thigh and cutting the skin – a punishment, said Alava afterwards, for laughing at him.[34] As they laid him out on the grass, not knowing the extent of his wound, the same thought occurred to them all. 'Good God! Who is to get the army out of the country?' The wound was extremely painful and prevented him from galloping about in his usual carefree way for at least a week. Toughness carried him through, and by the end of March he had forced Soult into the fortified camp of Toulouse and reached his last river-line, the Garonne.

Accompanied by only two of his staff, Fitzroy Somerset and Colonel Alexander Gordon, he reconnoitred its bank. His very plain uniform and oilskin cover over his cocked hat luckily prevented a French sentry from recognizing the Allied Commander-in-Chief. After an informative conversation the two parted on the best of terms. Wellington's information on the political situation was not so easily come by.

Rumours were flying about during the first week of April that Napoleon's defensive action had collapsed and that the Allied armies of Blücher and Schwarzenberg were in Paris. What could Wellington believe? There were persistent reports that Napoleon was dead – of wounds, of poisoning, of the gravel. The conference between Allied statesmen and Napoleon's General Caulaincourt at Châtillon, where Castlereagh was wrestling mainly with his colleagues to achieve the peace terms that suited Britain, was said to be dissolved, leaving France in a state of insurrection. (On the contrary, though the negotiations with Napoleon had indeed collapsed, Castlereagh had won his own case with the Allies, and the future 'Quadruple Alliance' came into being with the signing of the crucial Treaty of Chaumont, 9 March 1814 backdated to 1 March.) 'Don't believe anything you hear in France,' wrote Wellington to one of his officers.[35]

Scepticism, however admirable, was not a policy. The essential fact on which he could have formed one – that as a result of the Treaty of Chaumont the Allies had triumphed and entered Paris on 31 March – did not reach him by 7 April, though the Horse Guards somewhat feebly hoped it would. 'I earnestly hope they may still have arrived in time to prevent another action,' wrote Torrens. Hope was not the means by which they brought the good news from Ghent to Aix. By the 10th, Easter Sunday 1814, Wellington had ordered 'another action' – the assault on Toulouse.

This was the closest-run thing of the whole Peninsular War. Wellington described it as 'a very severe affair'.[36] Freire's Spaniards and the 4th, 6th and 3rd Divisions were all desperately mauled, the last because Picton disobeyed orders and pushed forward when Wellington instructed him to feint. Nevertheless Soult was driven out of the town, though with only 3,200 casualties to the Allied 4,500, so that the French proclaimed themselves the victors.

On 12 April 1814 Wellington rode into Toulouse at the head of his army. Napoleon Bonaparte had already fallen – from the roof of the Town Hall, where his statue had been hurled to the ground and smashed. His eagles were gone and workmen were busily chipping the letters N and B from the municipal stonework.

An hour after Wellington's entry into Toulouse, while he was dressing for a dinner he was to give in the Prefecture, Colonel Frederick Ponsonby galloped in from the royalist town of Bordeaux.

'I have extraordinary news for you.'

'Ay, I thought so. I knew we should have peace; I've long expected it.'

'No; Napoleon has abdicated.'

'How abdicated? Ay, 'tis time indeed.'

Suddenly the penny dropped.

'You don't say so, upon my honour! Hurrah!' The Commander-in-Chief, still in his shirt sleeves, spun round on his heel snapping his fingers like a schoolboy.[37]

In the middle of the grand dinner Colonel Cooke brought in the official despatches and latest news. He had left Paris at midnight on 7 April. King Louis XVIII had been restored, there was a constitution, and the Emperor had abdicated on the 6th. He was granted by the Treaty of Fontainebleau a pension of two million francs for himself and more for his family. He was destined for Elba.

At last Wellington's political acrobatics were over and there was no more need to suppress the white cockade while still fighting the tricolour. He called for champagne and gave the toast of His Majesty Louis XVIII with three times three. General Alava at once sprang up and proposed, '*El Liberador de España!*' In a moment everyone was on his feet acclaiming the liberator in English, French, Spanish, Portuguese and German. The cheering and shouting went on for ten minutes. 'Lord Wellington bowed, confused,' noted the observant Judge Advocate-General, 'and immediately called for the coffee.'[38]

'Glory to God and to yourself,' young Lord Burghersh had written to Wellington on 7 April 1814 from Paris; 'the great man has fallen.'[39] For Wellington, the rest of 1814 promised to be a perpetual struggle between glory and hard fact, the champagne and the coffee.

On the evening after the dinner in Toulouse all was indeed heady effervescence. White cockades were ordered for Wellington's theatre party and he stood up in his box between Picton, Freire, Alava and the Mayor while the audience lustily cheered the new order. At one point a man in black entered another box, between tall wax candles, and read aloud the constitution. Then they began again cheering appropriate lines in the appropriate play about Richard Coeur de Lion.

In London Mme D'Arblay (Fanny Burney), sitting beside her dying father in Chelsea, watched the fireworks shooting up from the building in whose Great Hall Arthur Wellesley had stood his trial in 1808. It seemed to her that Dr Burney was sceptical about Napoleon being a prisoner on a British brig-of-war. He gave a little shrug of incredulity and died during the rejoicings.

But there were few during that gay springtime not prepared to write off the scourge of Europe. A punning anagram appeared in April in the London press:

'ABLE' no longer human kind to curse,
'ELBA' proclaims his exile in reverse.

Lord Byron published a contemptuous 'Ode to Bonaparte':

'Tis done – but yesterday a king!
And armed with kings to strive –
And now thou art a nameless thing
So abject – yet alive!

The champagne continued to flow, with a visit on 21 April from a queer figure in dirty overalls below but plastered with crosses and stars above. It was no less an emissary than Castlereagh's half-brother, Sir Charles Stewart, bringing an offer of the Paris Embassy.

Wellington's reaction was predictable. Since he could not serve in the Government owing to Liverpool's breach with his brothers Richard and William, and since he must serve somewhere, it had better be Paris. He wrote to Castlereagh by return, accepting

a situation for which I should never have thought myself qualified. . . . Although I have been so long from England . . . I feel no objection to another absence in the public service. . . .⁴⁰

Still the champagne popped and fizzed: Stewart told him privately that they were going to make him a Duke. It was not unexpected, for many people had mentioned it after Vitoria. When he wrote to his brother Henry a month later about Spanish affairs his letter ended with a casualness that was completely candid: 'I believe I forgot to tell you that I was made a Duke.'⁴¹ To his countrymen he was henceforth *the* Duke.

Henry Wellesley, a diplomat himself, approved of Arthur's new career. 'After all you have come through,' he wrote, 'you will find diplomacy very pretty amusement.'⁴²

His soldiers were reassured to learn towards the end of April that their hero would be going to Paris for the triumphal entry after all. On the way to Paris he stopped at Cahors where the thirty-nine-year-old French General Foy was still convalescing from a serious wound received in the Pyrenees; he had reluctantly gone over to the Bourbons on 16 April. Deeply touched by the way Wellington sought him out, Foy wrung his hand again and again. Afterwards he put on paper his impressions of the hero:

Lord Wellington speaks French with difficulty. [Foy may have mistaken Wellington's abrupt manner for language problems.] He is slim, of medium build: he has an aquiline nose. His countenance is full of distinction, simplicity and kindness; just as one pictures our great Turenne.[43]

Foy had begun by writing, 'Nous avons beaucoup parlé batailles,' as if the battles were all over.

Within a year the two of them would be hard at it again. Someone heard Napoleon murmur as he left Fontainebleau for Elba that when the violets returned next spring he too would be back. . . .

Wellington rode a white horse into Paris on 4 May, in time for the parade of Allied troops before Louis XVIII, having been gazetted Duke of Wellington on 3 May 1814. There was a great shoving and whispering among the spectators when they heard that the Duke of Wellington was coming. Emperors and Kings craned their necks to catch the first glimpse of him. Young John Cam Hobhouse, friend of Byron and the Radicals, who was travelling on the Continent, had what he called 'an insatiable desire' to see 'our great man', and risked many kicks and prods to get to the front of the crowd.

'Oh, for God's sake, let me see him!' exclaimed another English visitor, frantically elbowing his way past Hobhouse: 'I know you will excuse me, sir, for this; but I must see him!'[44]

Hobhouse described him as 'the curiosity of curiosities', riding between the half-brothers, General Stewart and Lord Castlereagh, in a plain blue frock-coat, white neck-cloth and top hat. One of his young Irish soldiers who was watching the procession noticed a double contrast between the glittering clothes but sullen expression of the wall-eyed King of Prussia and his own hero's plain coat but far-seeing eagle eye and aquiline nose, the stamp of talent. 'In all he seemed the Roman of old – save in pomp.'[45] Everyone was pleased and Larpent commented when he heard about it, 'This is quite like him'. It was also politic. He knew that he was to be Ambassador and did not wish to enter Paris as a red-coated conqueror.

Champagne again – cascades of diamonds, uniforms loaded with fur and frogging, a firmament of stars – for all but the new Duke. At a party of Lord Aberdeen's (whose younger brother, Colonel Alexander Gordon, was Wellington's aide-de-camp) an old friend found him quite unspoilt by success: 'gay, frank, and ready to converse' instead of resorting to the 'silence and reserve' which so often went with new dignities. When someone pointed out that Wellington was never opposed to Bonaparte in person, he answered instantly:

'No, and I am very glad I never was. I would at any time rather have heard that a reinforcement of forty thousand men had joined the French army, than that he had arrived to take the command.'[46]

It was felt that he showed true liberality in repeating this opinion after Bonaparte had fallen.

After only a week of fizz and sparkle (3–10 May) Wellington again called for the coffee – and answered Castlereagh's call to visit Madrid and knock some sense into King Ferdinand's reactionary advisers. On the road between Paris and Madrid, near Toulouse, Wellington and Soult passed in the night. Soult woke up while the horses were changed and prowled round Wellington's carriage, training his spy-glass on his sleeping conqueror inside.[47]

The reactionaries in Spain had brought back the regime's ancient glories with a zeal that shocked even the Tory Cabinet, and rendered Wellington's mission of 24 May to 8 June abortive. All the liberal reforms of the Cortes were reversed.

From Madrid Wellington travelled to Bordeaux, the chief embarkation centre for the Peninsular soldiers. Here the atmosphere was not all champagne. What was to be their future? Johnny Kincaid spoke for most of the younger men when he described their astonishment at peace: they had been 'born in war, reared in war, war was our trade'.[48] In this atmosphere of relief touched with anxiety, Wellington issued his farewell Order to the troops on 14 June 1814. There were four terse paragraphs written in the third person, all notably lacking in champagne; indeed only the last paragraph sounded more than purely formal. It ran:

4. Although circumstances may alter the relations in which he [the Commander-in-Chief] stood towards them, so much to his satisfaction, he assures them that he shall never cease to feel the warmest interest in their welfare and honor; and that he will be at all times happy to be of any service to those to whose conduct, discipline and gallantry their country is so much indebted.[49]

Simple brevity was natural to Wellington, and because he would have liked this mode of thanks himself, he believed that others would find it equally acceptable. They did not. In 1814 soldiers were accustomed to the rhetoric of 'glory', 'lustre' and 'immortal fame'. Wellington's notorious Order was unlucky in saying both too little and too much. The champagne of more lavish praise might have heartened the croakers. At the same time his promise to serve them raised quite unreasonable hopes. Even intelligent officers like Tomkinson believed that Wellington had it in his power to keep the Peninsular army together. A time was coming when the Duke would lament as keenly as anyone the dispersal of his model army.

Not only was the army broken up but the camp-followers also. Tomkinson saw no reason why the Portuguese and Spanish women who had suffered, marched, cooked, washed, danced, loved and plundered for the soldiers should not go home with them. The quartermaster-general, however, was only concerned with how to shake off these ministering angels most easily. As the British transports weighed anchor and the wind filled their sails, the last sound in the ears of Wellington's departing heroes was the wailing of women abandoned on the French shore.

Wellington himself stopped in Paris for one more heady draught before returning home. On his first night, 19 June, he was invited to what he called 'a grand party' at Clichy where the amazing Mme de Staël had been holding 'soupers' three days a week since May in her reconstituted salon.* Acknowledged as Europe's most brilliant eccentric and the voice of liberalism returned to France, she had been aghast at her first nightmare vision of Prussians and Cossacks encamped around the church of St Denis where lay the ashes of the French Kings. But the Duke of Wellington was another matter. He was the liberator. He was her hero. As if aware of all that the moment contained and of the many enthralling encounters to come, he approached her with the gallantry due; indeed it was one of those rare occasions when his latent histrionic talents found expression. He went down on one knee.

The tone of the evening changed somewhat, however, when the Abbé de Pradt, whom Chateaubriand referred to as 'the mitred mountebank' was called on for a speech. (As Archbishop of Malines, Pradt had been employed under the Empire and in 1814 became an unofficial member of the government team – people said, in order to make sure of Talleyrand having a foursome at whist.)

'We owe the salvation of Europe,' declared the Abbé, 'to *un homme seul*!' Before Wellington had time to summon a blush, as he himself related, the Abbé placed his hand on his own heart and added, '*C'est moi*!'[50]

No such misunderstanding occurred when the Duke reached the other side of the Channel. Waiting for him was a crowd frantic with joy. His arrival coincided with the state visit to England of the Allied

---

* Germaine Necker, Baronne de Staël-Holstein (1766–1817). She emigrated to England in 1793, returned to Paris 1795, and was banished by Napoleon.

Sovereigns, but it was he whom the people wished to see most. On 23 June 1814 he heard again the hoarse din of 'hurrahs' after five years of '*vivas*'; his carriage was mobbed at Dover and cheered all the way to London, with its occupant sitting up straight and stiff inside. If you once encouraged the mob to give tongue they might hiss you next time.

At Westminster Bridge there was a move to take out his horses so that his countrymen might pull him themselves to his house in Hamilton Place, Piccadilly, lift him out and deposit him, amid acclamation, in the Duchess of Wellington's arms. He was too quick for them. He galloped on alone.

18

See the Conquering Hero

With Wellington back on his own door-step, it is appropriate to pause and look at the man who had won the Peninsular War.

He was just forty-five, in the pride of manhood: lean, springy, his hair still brown, his eyes whether frozen over or sparkling as blue as ever, his laughter when it came an even more abandoned whoop, like a man with the whooping-cough, and his profile impressively Roman. To his passionate admirers nothing seemed beyond him. Lady Anne Barnard, sister-in-law of Colonel Barnard, was one who had thought the Regent would want him as Prime Minister. She realized that the ten thousand new things to be settled would require 'a different ability', but of this she understood he had displayed 'a great deal in India'.[1] Lady Anne rattled on about converting his sword into a plough-share. What sort of blade would it make? Uncomfortably sharp?

Wellington had certainly acquired the reputation for sharp repartee. He had never suffered fools gladly; as Commander-in-Chief he did not see why he should suffer them at all. The history of a Peninsular anecdote illustrates this. In 1811 the Prince of Orange accompanied by his English tutor, Mr Johnson, joined Wellington's staff. At dinner one day Wellington is said to have described a moment of danger when he was caught like a rat in a bottle, going on to explain the Indian conjuring trick in which muskrats were sucked into bottles by means of a vacuum created inside. The Prince's tutor raised his eyebrows.

'Either the rats must be very small or the bottles very large.' Next moment he regretted his attempt to score.

'On the contrary, Sir, very small bottles and very large rats.'

Wellington's retort was exaggerated by his critics after his death to prove that he was both offensive and stupid. Yet it showed nothing worse than caustic wit.

It must not be supposed, however, that all of Wellington's sharpness was cultivated. Some of it would have been regarded by him as a falling away from his own ideal of 'no asperity'. In personal interviews, as in letters, his explosive temper was generally controlled, but when it burst out, as Lord Ellesmere recalled, it was 'awful'.[2] He did not intend to make Sir Charles Stewart cry, nor to send the Spanish General Abisbal reeling from his presence pale as a ghost, faint, and clinging to the banisters. Most of the time he quelled the instinct to lash out by speaking in stern monosyllables.

On the closely related allegation that he was obstinate and above either taking advice or giving explanations, Peninsular opinion differed. The Judge Advocate-General, Larpent, recognized the inconvenience sometimes caused in different departments by Wellington's 'great secresy [sic]', but found him easier to work with than he had been led to expect:

I like him much in business affairs. He is very ready, decisive and civil. He thinks and acts quite for himself: with me, if he thinks I am right; but not otherwise. I have not, however, found what I was told I should, that he immediately determines against everything that is suggested to him.[3]

Good reasons for his reserve, connected with security, have already been advanced. It cannot be denied, however, that there was some failure in communication. Wellington certainly did not want to create 'mysteries', as an early letter to an Anglo-Indian officer shows:

Remember, that what I recommend to you is far removed from mystery: in fact, I recommend silence upon the public business upon all occasions, in order to avoid the necessity of mystery upon any.[4]

The 'mystery' arose despite himself and was not dispelled by his growing contempt for the press and public relations. Yet he would need good public relations even more as a statesman than as a soldier.

Unavoidable ignorance of home politics between 1809 and 1814 was another handicap. There had been economic distress from 1810–11, a threat of class war between the Luddites and mill-owners in 1812, rising prices and dear food in 1813.

As for the march of ideas, he had come home from India in 1805 having missed the French revolutionary ferment; similarly he returned from the Peninsula with little or no knowledge of what Professor Asa Briggs calls 'the new morality' in England.[5] What he had seen of it, as represented by dissenting preachers in his army, he did not like. Instinct told him, correctly, that the new morality would burst the old bottles. He criticized the Cortes to his brother Richard for 'having abolished the Inquisition, which if they had left it alone would have died a natural death', and added, 'they are casting a longing eye towards the landed properties of my Cousins and Grandees'.[6] It was half a joke, but like all Conservatives he feared the inexorable law of progression by which one thing leads to another.

If agitation and declarations of human rights did not appeal to him 'accommodation' was a benign star which he could recommend as a pilot. He wrote on 20 September 1809:

Half the business of the World, particularly that of our Country is done by accommodation, & by the parties understanding each other.[7]

Wellington's belief in accommodation was typical of his pragmatic mind. He had the English taste for improvisation and flexibility, highlighted by a constitution that was not written down. The coming months were bound to land him among the exponents of constitutional charters, commissions and carefully defined rights.

With accommodation went a certain permissiveness for which his army was grateful. He did not fuss about their clothes. 'There is no subject of which I understand so little,' he wrote emphatically in 1811. An officer could wear high-heeled boots, a light blue frock-coat with lace and a green velvet waistcoat with silver Spanish buttons like Captain Adair in 1812; or a totally glittering £300 outfit like Stapleton Cotton's, which earned him the nickname of 'Lion d'Or' and a place in *Vanity Fair* as 'Sir George Tufto, KCB'; or an old red nightcap at a pinch like Picton. When ordering a general's coat to be made for himself in Lisbon he worried over the fit but nothing else: 'Only let it be sufficiently large about the sleeves & shoulders.'[8]

This permissiveness was part of the distinction he drew between true discipline and nagging. It ranged him on the side of the Shorncliffe boys and (later) Desert Rats, against what he called the Russian Emperor Alexander's 'military discipline madness'.

Standards of food varied as much as clothes among him and his staff. 'Cole gives the best dinners, Hill the next best,' he once said, 'mine are no great things, and Beresford's and Picton's are very bad indeed.'[9] He could appreciate good food when set before him, contrary to some reports, but as a soldier he had neither time nor inclination to order it.

Over money Wellington was still the man who had surprised his brother Henry in India by caring for it so little. Throughout the war his affairs were left in William's hands, assisted by Lord Liverpool. He rarely mentioned them in letters, his only strongly expressed wish being for an estate in Somerset, the land of his ancestors. Honours came more plentifully the less one thought about them.

Notwithstanding the numerous favors that I have received from the Crown, I have never solicited one; and I have never hinted, nor would any one of my friends or relations venture to hint for me, a desire to receive even one. . . .[10]

On the intellectual side, university education held a magic for him that would have seemed plainly nostalgic if he had ever experienced it – which he never did. Instead, it was a might-have-been that glowed with a vividness brighter than reality. He wanted all officers to attend a university before joining the Army, and said so later on to Kitty's nephew, John Hamilton:

You can afford the money and time for two educations [military college and Cambridge]; avail yourself of these advantages, be educated first, as if for the pulpit or the bar, and then you will have a double chance of making a first-rate soldier. I would give more than I can mention that I had had a university education.[11]

Wellington's idea of a university looked back to the eighteenth century, though he was to battle with modern problems when he had sons of his own at college, and still more when he became Chancellor of Oxford University. Ideally his officers were all gentlemen, and gentlemen still approximating to the cultivated all-rounder of an earlier age who studied the past in his college library and the present on his European tour. He always said he was against promotion from the ranks because rankers could not hold their drink.[12] His correspondence with William about young candidates for commissions was conducted on a semi-humorous basis. When he offered William the nomination to a cornetcy in the Blues in 1813, provided his candidate was a '*Gentleman*' this time, William replied suavely that he had the very thing, 'a *raal* gentleman' – sending along yet another of his protégés with a name that today is not quite legible but looks suspiciously like Byrne, Boyne or Doyle.*

But behind the banter was a deep region of feeling which Wellington himself had not fully explored by the end of the Peninsular War. His own want of a university education probably came home to him only after his military career was over, since he was a 'first-rate soldier' without it.

Speaking for the Peninsular army, Sir Charles Oman made the sombre and sweeping assertion that Wellington was 'a thankless master to serve'.[13] Oman did not like him and allowed himself to be unduly

---

* Wellington's full stipulation to his brother was: 'But he must be *a Gentleman*: and he ought to have something to live upon besides his Pay. I am afraid that your Protégés are generally of a different description!' (*Raglan MSS*, no. 60, 5 October 1813).

influenced by occasional expressions of dissatisfaction in contemporary books, diaries or letters. A striking example occurs in an unpublished letter from Arthur Kennedy, who felt sore about the disgrace of the 18th Hussars at Vitoria for months afterwards:

A man gets no thanks for getting his head broke now-a-days. . . . This has been amply verified with us, never did a Regiment lose so many officers with so little thanks from the 'Head Butcher' as he literally is.[14]

A more recent historian who accuses Wellington of 'ingratitude' is the Spanish professor, Dr Jesús Pablón. He finds Wellington's Vitoria despatch unfair to the Spanish Generals Longa and Morillo who 'bore the brunt of the battle'. (They fought magnificently in the northern and southern sectors respectively, but the 'brunt' was also in the centre.) The fact was that Wellington took immense pains to be accurate and fair, and within the limits of his battlefield knowledge he succeeded. Napoleon used Wellington's despatches, which he read in the English papers, rather than his own generals' reports as sources of exact information.

Quite apart from regiments like the 18th Hussars which had misbehaved and could not be praised, it was literally impossible for Wellington to mention *by name* all the units and officers who distinguished themselves in every battle, quite apart from the civil departments which Dr James McGrigor had very reasonably insisted, ever since Badajoz, should also get their names into despatches.

'Is it usual?' Wellington had asked, the devotee of regularity fighting inside him with the apostle of accommodation.

'It would be the most essential service,' replied McGrigor firmly.

'I have finished my despatch – but, very well, I will add something about the doctors.'[15]

With the steady augmentation of his army the problem increased. Yet failure to name names continued to cause offence. Even William Napier, Wellington's ardent admirer, criticized him on these grounds. 'I don't like Lord Wellington's despatch about the Little Rhune,' he wrote to his wife after the battle of the Nivelle; 'I don't want to brag, but the best thing done on the 10th November, 1813, was the attack of the 43rd Light Infantry [Napier's regiment], and he has not done us the honour to mention our names.'[16]

That Wellington did realize what he owed to his troops is shown by his many tributes to his 'fine fellows', especially the infantry. But his stern front and curt battle-orders belied these kind feelings. Hindsight suggests that he might have got over some of his difficulties by taking a leaf out of the French book and making more use of medals and decorations. Colonel Harvey Jones, RE, who was taken prisoner at San Sebastián, was struck by the innumerable crosses of the Legion of Honour distributed to the garrison after every sortie.[17] Wellington, as has been shown, thought the British were above such things. He was mistaken. Time would show how much.

If he did not lavish praise on his soldiers, he inspired them with unique confidence. By 1813 his own self-confidence had a mystical streak. Long before Waterloo he was talking about 'the finger of God' protecting him. He spoke almost reverentially of the confidence which he in turn transmitted to his subordinates.

When I come myself, the soldiers think what they have to do the most important since I am there . . . and they will do for me what perhaps no one else can make them do.[18]

His soldiers were able to express the confidence he gave them less subtly. One of their favourite stories was of a new major-general visiting his headquarters and demonstrating that whichever way the French moved they would have Wellington in a cleft stick.

'Then what would you do?'

'Give them the most infernal thrashing they have had for some time.'[19]

In contrast to Wellington's robust attitude were innumerable examples of human diffidence, among the most poignant being General Clinton's agonized wish to avoid a large, independent command: he feared responsibility; he knew he would have a nervous breakdown.[20] Wellington's nearest approach to a breakdown had been long ago in India when responsibility was suddenly withdrawn from him and he caught the Malabar itch.

Taking him all in all, William Napier had no doubt when he came to write his *History of the War in the Peninsula* that this man's greatness as a leader touched the heights of genius:

The History I dedicated to your Grace, because I have served long enough under your command to know why the Soldiers of the Tenth Legion were attached to Caesar.

The Duke of Wellington returned home with the authority of character. He spurned the decorations of authority – the large staff, sentries, gold braid, cock's feathers – but was no leveller either. He walked alone. That phrase was still, as in India, one of which he entirely approved. When writing in June 1813 to his friend Sir John Malcolm (now home from the East) he advised him to stand for Parliament. 'I likewise recommend you not to fix yourself upon Lord Wellesley or any other great man. You are big enough, unless much altered, to walk alone. . . .'[21]

So was the Duke of Wellington.

This was the man whom London idolized. Kitty idolized him too. When she kissed his trophies after Salamanca with the ecstatic cry, 'Mine! my own!', it was obvious whom she clasped in her arms. There was no reason to think, however, that he saw her reflection behind the laughing eyes and flattering lips of the ladies in Spain. A great favourite with 'the fair ones',[22] Larpent hinted that he objected to being watched and plagued by aides-de-camp in his house at Toulouse because he was having an affair with the owner's wife. Going back a little to the middle of the war, an aristocratic Spanish lady in French-occupied Madrid was said to have regularly supplied him with secret information. As she was also believed to detest both sides equally, longing to see 'the English hanged in the Frenchmen's entrails', she may not have been the same aristocratic lady whose brief but affectionate note has survived among Wellington's papers. Dated *Madrid 11 de enero*, it was a letter of thanks, from 'La D[uquesa]. de S[an]. C[arlos].' to Wellington for sending her the 30,000 *reales*. She promised to repay them '*pronto posible*' and signed herself his '*apasionada Amiga*'.

Going back still further to 1809, there is a curious entry in Lady Sarah Napier's journal in which she deplores the retreat after Talavera, quoting as its immediate causes the failure of Spanish faith and English commissaries. She goes on to ask –

Whose fault is that? Why the Commander-in-Chief to be sure . . . who publickly keeps a mistress at head-quarters, does not give all the attention to the care of his army & disgusts his army, who lose all confidence in him.'[23]*

This sounds like Whig gossip at a time when hostility to Wellington was at its keenest. The admiration of Sarah Napier and her sons for him ever afterwards was as remarkable as this solitary attack.

Whether or not he had one or more mistresses during his five 'bachelor' years in Spain without any leave or wife, is irrelevant to the main fact: that his private life created no scandal of the dimensions

* There was gossip about Wellington and a 'Lady A.C-ham' around 1809.

which did so much damage to Richard's career. In Kitty's eyes a *chevalier sans peur et sans reproche* had returned to her at last.

Beside her, at 4 Hamilton Place, were the two little Cheam schoolboys he had last seen as babies of two and one; Arthur now seven and become 'Douro' through his father's victories, and Charles aged six. Every time Lord Liverpool or William Wellesley-Pole wrote to Wellington about his sons it was always to report that they were 'much improved'. Their father had no means of judging even now whether they were improved or not. At forty-five it might be said that he was becoming a parent for the first time.

Was Kitty improved? Her taste in clothes had not improved. While he was away she often passed the time in sewing homemade slippers and hats. She had a passion for 'little girl' muslin dresses which she wore, however inappropriately, on the grandest occasions. As this was June it is more than likely that the Duchess was in muslin, looking ridiculously young with her *retroussé* nose and pale skin untouched by rouge – a contrast to the flamboyant Spanish beauties to whom Arthur had become accustomed.

In her own mind, on the contrary, the improvement she had noticed in herself three years earlier was still being maintained. When Arthur wrote to her enquiring whether or not she felt equal to joining him in Paris and assuming the duties of British Ambassadress, her answer was surprisingly firm:

4 Hamilton Place, June 13th, 1814.

My dearest Arthur – I have received your letter of the 26th from Madrid in which you permit me to decide for myself with respect to accompanying [you] to Paris or not from the moment I heard of your acceptance of the appointment I had no other thought than that of going with you. . . . I have no hesitation in deciding to go, no other wish than to go. . . . I may venture to add that you shall *never* have reason to regret having allowed me on this subject to decide for myself.[24]

Arthur kept Kitty's letter among his papers, the first one to be preserved since 1807. He may have felt that some day he would need to convince a tearful and inadequate Ambassadress that she had brought it on herself. During these weeks of wild celebration Kitty was observed driving in her famous husband's carriage through the swarming streets of London, her head buried in a book. She was extremely short-sighted, and though several of her husband's staff wore spectacles, convention did not permit wives to do so. Lest she should fail to recognize a face in the crowd she kept her eyes down.

For him all doors were thrown wide open, from Almack's to the

House of Lords. Almack's Club, devoted since the peace to introducing fashionable dances like the waltz into English ballrooms, represented the very summit of London society. Practice of the new steps took place daily at Devonshire House. Its six patronesses were paragons; indeed, to the foreign visitors and returning soldiers, England seemed to be full of incomparable women, whether of the *ton* or not. Arthur Shakespear described the ecstasy of his German comrade-in-arms, Baron Decker, on arrival: '*What beautiful womens! I have not seen* such fine things in all my life! I shall not *sleep* tonight!'

On 28 June 1814 Wellington took his seat in the House of Lords and was thanked by the Speaker of the House of Commons on 1 July in language that matched the occasion:

When the will of heaven, and the common destinies of our nature, shall have swept away the present generation, you will have left your great name and example as an imperishable monument ... serving at once to adorn, defend and perpetuate the existence of this country among the ruling nations of the world.[25]

The Opposition were in a fix. Henry Brougham had particularly asked Creevey to note in September 1813 that he predicted Wellington's defeat and retreat from the Peninsula before Christmas. How completely he had been proved wrong in six months. Perhaps poor Samuel Whitbread, who was to die by his own hand a year later, discovered the most generous way out. He protested that Parliament's grant to the hero was not munificent enough, and got it raised from £300,000 to £400,000, making in all half a million. Speaking at a dinner of the Artists' Benevolent Society Whitbread contrasted Wellington's care for the Spanish art treasures with Napoleon's plundering. At the great Thanksgiving ceremony in St Paul's Cathedral, 7 July, he had carried the Sword of State, riding in the Prince Regent's carriage drawn by eight cream-coloured horses and sitting in the Cathedral on the Prince's right, with the Sword of State before him. He was painted by Sir Thomas Lawrence standing in front of St Paul's with the sword resting on a pedestal. The Duke, who had a very strong wrist, insisted on holding the sword upright, though Lawrence said it would make people feel tired.

His Duchess was the only English lady to be presented personally to the Tsar (by the Prince of Orange). But when the Duke paid an almost royal visit to the Salisburys at Hatfield to receive the freedoms of Hertford and St Albans, he managed to pass rapidly from pomp to informality. Kitty's old friend, Mrs Calvert, watched him reaching across the park paling to shake hands with as many people as possible, while the crowd roared its approval. 'His modesty and unaffected simplicity of manner are quite delightful.'[26] At the Prince Regent's Carlton House ball, Wellington made a revealing remark to the twenty-seven-year-old heiress Lady Shelley, as they sat together and watched his young aides-de-camp dancing.

'How would society get on without all my boys?'[27]

How would Wellington get on without them? They were still his 'champions', as they had been ever since India when Mrs Gordon used to tease him about them. With the end of the war this *jeunesse dorée* would no longer gather automatically, under orders, at his table. He would need the right hostess to keep them round him.

In the whirl of pleasure and business Wellington did not forget his Peninsular friends. Dr James McGrigor had been recommended for a knighthood. After breaking the good news, Wellington volunteered to present him at the levée where he would receive the accolade. Unfortunately Wellington was summoned by Castlereagh to discuss politics at his home at North Cray in Kent on McGrigor's great day. He therefore arranged for Lord Bathurst, the War Minister, to present McGrigor instead. The day came. Suddenly Wellington appeared from nowhere.

'I thought it as well to place you under Lord Bathurst; you are a shy fellow, and might not have found him out.' Then he hurried off to North Cray.

McGrigor, now 'Mac' to the chief who had once 'Sirred' him in a blaze of anger, was greatly touched but not surprised. 'There was in this act of the Duke,' he wrote, 'a benevolence of character of which I have observed many other instances, and which those only who had been much near him could know.'[28]

At last the summer 'craze', as Sarah Napier called the vast pilgrimages from all over the country to see Bonaparte's conquerors, drew to an end. The distinguished visitors had been the first to go: the Tsar, whom most people adored though one teenager, Maria Capel, found him '*horridly* Pink & Pudding-like';[29] the King of Prussia, the Tsar's poodle; and silver-haired seventy-two-year-old Marshal Blücher, who was voted the favourite with the crowd. When the ladies of Dover were all clamouring for one of those silver locks he had bowed and smiled: 'Ladies, were I to give each of you just one hair I should have none left.'[30]

White's Club had laid on the most dazzling as well as the gayest event of all: a *bal masqué* at Burlington House on 1 July in honour of Wellington. Two thousand people were present, among them the Duke's future wayward friend, Lady Caroline Lamb, who on this occasion hid Sir Lumley Skeffington's red Guard's coat and 'gesticulated' at Byron with her green pantaloons.[31] Lord Byron scowled back in the guise of a monk. In the Duke's honour, balloon ascents were made outside Burlington House. Spectators' tickets, half a guinea each. And J. W. Croker sought forgiveness for an impertinent letter the year before, by helping to persuade the committee of the Wellington Fund in Dublin to build a Wellington pillar which should be the highest in the world – '*stupendously* high' – beating Napoleon's in the Place Vendôme by some fifty feet.*

'It's a fine thing to be a great man, is it not?' said Wellington with a smile to Lady Shelley, as the London crowds respectfully made way for him.[32] But when the female despots of Almack's Club (as Gronow called its patronesses) turned him away for wearing trousers instead of knee-breeches, the great man meekly obeyed orders and left.

The time came at the beginning of August 1814 to think of taking up his diplomatic post in Paris. On the way there he inspected the frontier fortresses in the Low Countries. In Belgium the Duke found 'many advantageous positions' for defence, including the high road from Charleroi to Brussels, where it entered the Forest of Soignes.[33] Here stood the village of Waterloo.

A comedy was put on for him in Brussels named *John Bull*, but at the last moment he was too busy to attend, so that his fourteen-year-old aide-de-camp, Lord William Lennox, had the strange experience of entering Wellington's box without him, to the strains of 'See the Conquering Hero Comes'. Possibly the hero's absence from a play with that title was his first exercise in diplomacy, the profession that Henry had recommended as 'a pretty amusement'.

Pretty women as well as pretty amusements abounded. To Wellington, Brussels hummed with low feminine voices. One set whispered against the other, 'the Ladies in the Park' (as the aristocratic set were called who lived in the centre of Brussels) against the less fine ladies outside. Lady Caroline Capel, sister of the eloping Lord Paget (now Uxbridge), found Brussels the most 'Gossiping Place' she had ever known. The dangerous but delightful town released Wellington after a relatively short spell. But not for long.

---

* (*Croker*, 7 October 1814.) The Wellington Monument in Phoenix Park beat the Vendôme pillar by 306 feet to 44 metres. For once Wellington's victory was not a close run thing.

19

The Grand Disturber

The British Ambassador to the Court of the Tuileries, His Grace the Duke of Wellington, KG, whose titles alone occupied sixteen lines of close print in his letter of instructions, entered Paris on 22 August 1814. With his usual foresight he had already secured a home for the Embassy as suitable as it was romantic. The Hôtel de Charost in the rue du Faubourg St Honoré came into the market as a result of Napoleon's banishment to Elba. It had belonged since 1800 to his second sister, the beautiful and amorous Princess Pauline Borghese. Wellington bought the mansion, arranging for the total price of 870,000 francs to be paid by instalments – 'the number as great as possible'. He moved in before the end of his first week. Its spacious garden ran down to the Champs-Elysées, gay by day and quiet at night. Wellington's diplomatic successors, down to the present day, have had increasing reason to thank him for this truly Elysian property.

He was formally received at the Tuileries during his first week by the Duchess of Angoulême. King Louis XVIII had returned from Hartwell Manor and the deep green elms of Buckinghamshire, huge and helpless as a stranded whale. When walking about was absolutely necessary he could just drag along his gout-tortured limbs, one throbbing agony from head to toe. Wellington afterwards told Stanhope he was 'a walking sore, a perfect walking sore', even his head exuded a humour.[1] However, Mme de Staël divined a respectable intellect inside the sore head and predicted 'a king very favourable to literature'.[2] His Most Christian Majesty fancied himself as a Voltairean.

The Ambassador's duty was to hunt amicably with the royal family while hammering away at King Louis to abolish the slave trade in his colonies – an international reform on which British opinion was set. Between the French devotees of the slave trade and its dedicated British opponents, Wellington was the ideal intermediary. He himself naturally regarded the trade itself as 'horrible', but deprecated the violence with which his countrymen were accustomed to argue without consideration for the prejudices or feelings of others'.[3] Having missed the impact of the new morality by being abroad, he was almost as astonished as the French by the fervour it had generated.

He immediately made himself master of what he called 'the new crusade'. By September 1814 the great apostle of abolition, Thomas Clarkson, announced that the Ambassador needed no more help from him so far as knowledge went, since he had studied all the voluminous literature sent him by William Wilberforce, Zachary Macaulay and himself, including his own *History of the Abolition of the African Slave Trade by the British Parliament*.[4] While reading this famous book Jane Austen had said that she was in love with the author. Whether or not Wellington loved Clarkson, he maintained throughout the confidence of the British activists. His own intermediary was General Colin Macaulay, who was with him in Paris and had also been with him at Seringapatam.

On the other side, he could well understand Louis XVIII's difficulties. In the new Constitution, his Chamber of Peers (copied from the British House of Lords) was full of men who had money or friends in the French colonies worked by slave labour. Nothing would convince French opinion that the British campaign was humanitarian. They believed it was an attempt to throttle their French commercial rivals.

In face of these suspicions, Wellington's advice to his own Government was sensible and conciliatory: to create a public opinion in France as Clarkson had done in England by means of books and pamphlets. This was where the formidable Mme de Staël came in again, to assist and fascinate Wellington with her intellect and ardent spirit. The bond between them was not physical. She was the devoted attendant and mistress of John Rocca, a dashing horseman of twenty-eight who was dying of tuberculosis. She had met Wilberforce in England during her exile from Bonaparte's tyranny, and now assisted Wellington by translating English anti-slave-trade propaganda into French. 'If we can get those who read on our side, who are very few in numbers,' he wrote whimsically to a fellow-diplomat, 'we shall do a great deal of good.'[5] Provided, of course, there was no inflammatory anti-French reading matter published in the British newspapers. Wellington relied on Wilberforce to keep the subject out of the press as long as necessary, and his confidence was not misplaced.

As a result of this patient generalship he prevailed upon King Louis to promise abolition of the French slave trade in five years, and was congratulated by Wilberforce on his 'bloodless victory'.[6] It still remained for Lord Castlereagh to put across abolition internationally, at the Congress of Vienna.

After the days of bargaining came the break for hunting parties. *La chasse* with the Bourbons was an affair of almost medieval splendour and quaint, vicarious prowess. The Duke of Angoulême, an unreliable shot, was always attended by a keeper who fired his gun the moment his master took aim, and cried as he himself killed the stag, '*Monsieur tire à merveille!*'[7] Wellington once, in compliment to his hosts, wore the traditional fancy dress complete with gold lace, jackboots and a hunting-knife. He refused, however, to submit his horse to the indignity of trappings, but planted himself and his glorious breeches firmly on a plain English saddle.

After the hunting the concerts, assemblies, dinners, theatres and balls. Wellington paid his court to the duchesses of the *ancien régime* and the reigning beauties of the new. Chateaubriand was amused to see the Imperial ladies showing the returned dowagers of the Faubourg Saint-Germain the way around the Tuileries. Paris, he noted, was full of piquant contrasts in ancient and modern: the old Duke of Havré in powdered wig and back-cane ambling along as Captain of the Lifeguards, his head wobbling on his shoulders, while Marshal Victor 'limped in the manner of Bonaparte';[8] the Tuileries, once so 'clean and soldierly' under Napoleon, now reeking with the domestic odours of breakfast.

Wellington was amazed by the fat King's addiction to delicacies. When dining *en famille* he would tip a whole dish of strawberries on to his own plate, without offering any to the ladies.

'Queen Anne,' interjected Stanhope to whom Wellington later told this story, 'related that William III did exactly the same with fresh peas.'

'I hope it is not a Royal custom,' said the Crown's retained servant, laughing heartily.[9]

Foremost among the beauties were the little Duchess of Duras, who in a year or so was to be one of Chateaubriand's 'Madams', and the gentle Juliette de Récamier – *la belle Julie* – extending her long fingers to Wellington from her Empire sofa. Her gesture was friendly rather than seductive, for she had just become involved with Benjamin Constant, Mme de Staël's literary friend, and was destined in 1817 to supersede Claire de Duras as Chateaubriand's 'Arch-Madam'.

A beauty less remote than Mme de Récamier was the famous contralto who had followed Napoleon's eagles from the Milan Opera

House at the beginning of the century. Radiant, forty-year-old Giuseppina Grassini was as gracious to Wellington now as she had been formerly to Napoleon. In return Wellington was to keep a portrait of La Grassini in his room, balanced by a print of Pauline Borghese, with Pope Pius VII between them. When the Count of Artois paid a call on Wellington and saw the strange trio he threw up his hands in horror:

'Exactly like Our Lord between the two thieves.'[10] Mme de Staël had roughly the same idea when she wrote to her hero, 'Why expose the Pope to a situation of this sort?'

Then there was Talleyrand's niece Dorothea, who publicly declared her worship of Wellington. Dorothea was to act as hostess for her uncle in Vienna when the peace conference assembled there in September. Her blue-black eyes, said Sainte-Beuve, were always burning with 'an infernal fire' which turned night into day.

Of the marshals, Wellington met Ney almost at once, out hunting in the Bois. Marshal Soult was instantaneously recognizable as a result of the telescopic examination at Sorauren; but it was December before the Duke and Massena were brought together at a party. The marshal looked very old. After they had quizzed one another for some time through lorgnettes as if before a parlour version of Bussaco, Massena advanced.

'My lord, you owe me a dinner – for you made me positively starve.' Wellington laughed.

'You should give it to me, Marshal, for you prevented me from sleeping.'[11]

Apart from celebrated natives, Paris was packed with English visitors, eager to see the world after a decade of enforced insularity. Some of them were full of spice and charm. Charles Arbuthnot, a Secretary of the Treasury and Henry Wellesley's staunch ally during his divorce, had brought over his second wife, Harriet, whom he had married that January, though twenty-four years his junior. Harriet Arbuthnot was a first cousin of Wellington's favourite Burghershes. She too was to be a favourite.

By October the Duchess of Wellington was ready to join her husband as planned. Kitty's frame of mind on leaving England was not auspicious. Maria Edgeworth received a letter from her postmarked Deal, just before she embarked. 'The whole of her letter,' noted Maria, 'was full of her children and of sorrow for leaving them'.[12] The sorrow and tears became a flood when Kitty discovered the situation in Paris. To begin with, her husband was universally lionized while she was totally incapable of making any show. Then there was the gossip.

Kitty was not too short-sighted to see La Grassini on the Ambassador's arm. What she did not see her friends told her about. Everyone talked in Restoration Paris.

Lady Bessborough, married to the head of the great Whig family of Ponsonby, wrote to her ex-lover Granville Leveson-Gower on 13 November 1814:

The Duke of Wellington is so civil to me, and I admire him so much as a hero, that it inclines me to be partial to him, but I am afraid he is behaving very ill to that poor little woman; he is found great fault with for ... the want of procédé and publicity of his attentions to Grassini.[13]

There is nothing which could be called proof that Grassini was the Duke's mistress after having been Napoleon's. If she was, it appears to have been a distinction that she shared with the actress Mademoiselle Georges, aged twenty-seven in 1814, whose real name was Marguerite Josephine Weimer. She was seen in all her glory by John Cam Hobhouse at the *Comédie Française* that April: 'very large but with a fine face and strong lines with expressive action, so as now and then almost to remind me of Mrs Siddons'. Mlle Georges lived until 1867 and used to boast of having enjoyed the protection of both Wellington and Napoleon — '*Mais M. le duc était de beaucoup le plus fort.*' Meanwhile Wellington continued to arouse the unbounded enthusiasm of women. As was his way, he made no bones about it when people questioned him. After the great days in Paris were over a lady asked him if it was true that he had received all that female adulation?

'Oh yes! Plenty of that! Plenty of that!'[14]

Women and slaves were not the whole of the Ambassador's cares. Two royal personages caused him some anxiety. The Prince of Orange loved his newly acquired capital of Brussels, but not its native society. Belgium had been united by the peace treaties to Holland under the single rule of his father, King William I of the Netherlands. Wellington was deputed to point out to the Crown Prince that he entirely neglected the Belgians, confining his attentions to the English colony. His mentor admitted that his English education had given him that 'natural inclination';

but a Person in your high situation must get the better of his inclinations ... for the sake of the higher Interests committed to his charge. [England would be glad to see] a marked preference in favour of your new subjects.*

* (*Hague Royal Archives*, 12 December 1814.) Lady Caroline Capel provides independent testimony on this subject All the Prince wanted, she wrote to her mother, was 'a little snug *English Party*', where he could say just what he thought (*Capel Letters*, p. 66).

There was also the Princess of Wales. A private letter reached Wellington from the Prime Minister. The Princess might be coming to Paris. The French Court could not receive her as Princess of Wales, separated as she was from her husband. On the other hand, things should be made as agreeable as possible for her at the British Embassy, 'in order that she may have no inducement to return to England'.[15] Fortunately for Wellington, the Princess went elsewhere.

A minor concern over which Wellington did not lose much sleep was the site for his ducal home, to be built with the money presented by the nation. Benjamin Dean Wyatt, who had been his clerk in India and Ireland, was in charge. Born a member of Britain's most prolific family of architects, Wyatt now set out to purchase an estate to be 'a lasting Memorial' of the country's 'Gratitude and Munificence'. By the end of 1814, however, no sufficiently splendid mansion had been found. There were certain recurring obstacles. Chief among them was the proximity of an even more stately home which would outshine otherwise suitable sites. Blenheim Palace was particularly tiresome in this respect. Several attractive houses in Oxfordshire had to be turned down because Blenheim's superlative magnificence would have invited odious comparisons between the nation's gratitude to Marlborough and to Wellington. Where was Wyatt to find a place within reach of both London and a good pack of hounds, not too much enclosed like pretty Somerhill in Kent nor cut in half like so many parks by that ever-present menace, the turnpike road?

Wellington himself took it all calmly. He reckoned on laying out £100,000 over four years, which should build him, as he informed William,

a very fair house, & as magnificent as it ought to be. After having built it I shall not be a very rich Man; but I hope to do pretty well; that is to say if I am not ruined at Paris.[16]

The Duke was thinking of his entertaining as Ambassador, and the many expensive items he had to buy. A large array of uniforms was fortunately not among them. He always wore his scarlet field-marshal's uniform with gold-embroidered velvet collar, ribbons and orders (which included the Golden Fleece, Garter, Bath and Peninsular medal), white stock and white breeches. He was presented with the usual gift of ambassadorial silver on arrival. But apart from the handsome silver 'campaigning set' made for him in Lisbon, he had brought little but glory with him from the Peninsula. And so throughout the autumn of 1814, beginning on 22 September, bills were coming in from the famous Sèvres china factory for a splendid tea and coffee set. The Duke's taste led him to choose a white ground decorated with garlands '*de fleurs et de fruits polychromes et or*'. By 20 December he had laid out over 5,000 francs on the Sèvres service and another 1,500 francs in August 1815 – a considerable sum for those days.

Nevertheless, despite his fears expressed to William, he was not destined to stay long enough in Paris to be 'ruined'.

'Everything goes well here,' he reported on 15 September 1814. A fortnight later his tone had begun to change: 'I think we are getting a little unpopular in the town but I don't think that circumstance is of much importance.' On 4 October he had to admit a state of 'constant uneasiness', caused by the two extremes of disbanded Bonapartists and disappointed royalists who had expected a golden age.

The truth was that the Government of Louis XVIII had already degenerated into 'paternal anarchy', a kind of benevolent muddling which many people found worse than Napoleon's efficient tyranny. The French Army was Bonapartist to a man. Soldiers no doubt wore white Bourbon cockades on their shakos but at the bottom of each haversack was treasured a crumpled tricolour. Greedy old Louis they called '*le cochon*', and in playing cards they referred to the 'pig' of hearts or spades instead of the king. Those Bonapartists who frequented cafés rather than barracks sang the Marseillaise and shouted '*Vive l'Empereur*' quite openly. At the end of October some Bonapartist bullets actually whistled past Wellington and the Duke of Angoulême during a review on the Champ de Mars.

If he could have seen his friend General Foy's diary for these days his anxieties would not have abated. The Bourbons were, wrote Foy, and would long remain '*les très humbles valets de l'Angleterre*'. He was invited by Wellington to a soirée at his house where there would be dancing –

a famous reunion. I shall not go. . . . Lord Wellington and the English are held in horror by everybody. Even the Bourbonists are beginning to come out against them.

Suddenly the unfortunate general's bitterness caused by divided loyalties overflowed:

We who were lately masters of Europe, to what servitude are we reduced? . . . *O Napoléon où est tu?*[17]

Napoleon, as Foy had just heard, was very gay and active on Elba, thinking seriously of regaining his crown. If Foy, an honourable man who liked Wellington personally, felt like this, the Ambassador was clearly in trouble.

By November the British Cabinet were thoroughly alarmed for their Ambassador's personal safety. King Louis's scarcely established Government might be overthrown by an army of hungry ex-servicemen on half-pay. The Duke of Wellington might be seized. No longer referred to as the Duke, incidentally, but as 'Monsieur Villainton' in the hostile French press. He must quit Paris.

Various face-saving posts for him flitted through Lord Liverpool's agitated mind. A mission to the Congress sitting in Vienna to tell the British plenipotentiary, Lord Castlereagh, about the Netherlands' defences? Or the chief command in North America? He could 'give Jonathan one good thrashing' and then bring the unpopular American war to an end.

Wellington, however, would not go to America unless positively ordered to do so; and then only if absolutely free to negotiate. He had long been opposed to the war. Mme de Staël's passionate advocacy of peace with America did not make him any more favourable to continued hostilities. *The Times*, which was not over-friendly to Wellington, described on 14 October a startling scene in which she had 'pronounced an oration' in the presence of the Ambassador against the burning of Washington by his countrymen. This was 'a challenge to his Grace,' declared *The Times*, 'to prove that the sword is not his only weapon.' It had to credit him, however reluctantly, with yet another victory. 'The Duke of Wellington did all that Bonaparte himself could do – he silenced her.'[18] Nevertheless her influence grew.

She was asked to his autumn balls. 'Lord Wellington treats me with great distinction,' she wrote to a friend, 'and I am proud of it.' She even made a hit with Kitty, as Maria Edgeworth testified. Kitty had avoided meeting Mme de Staël when in London in case the Bourbon Court, to which she was about to become Ambassadress, declined to receive the colourful exile. When on the contrary the French Court proved welcoming, an encounter between the two women took place in which Kitty's curious combination of bluntness and timidity for once scored.

'. . . Madame la Duchesse, so you did not want to make my acquaintance in England?' challenged the woman whom Byron called the greatest mind of her times. Maria heard that she had swept up to Kitty in full fig, her eyes flashing with indignation; and since she foamed at the mouth when angry, at least according to Gronow, Kitty may have had to face that hazard also. Kitty stood her ground and replied firmly, 'No, Madame, I did not want to.'

'. . . Madame, why not?'

'It's because I was *afraid* of you, Madame.'

'You *are afraid* of me, Madame la Duchesse?'

'No, Madame, I am not afraid of you any more.' Germaine threw her glorious arms around the little duchess.

'Ah, I adore you!'[19]

Lord Liverpool's letters, meanwhile, became more and more excited. Let Wellington make sure there was always a Bourbon prince resident in the south of France, to raise the standard there in case of a Paris coup. (A standard was soon to be raised there, but not the King's.) Let Wellington slip away quietly or he might be recognized and stopped on the road. The sooner Lord Liverpool heard of his having landed at Dover the better.[20]

As the panic grew so did the Duke's phlegm. He had agreed in September that owing to 'the daring class of men' operating in Paris against the King's party, he ought to be moved. At the beginning of November he was hardening against it: 'I entertain a strong opinion that I *must* not be lost but . . . I don't like to be frightened away.' He had noticed that the King and royal family were remarkably well received at the *Comédie Française* on the 16th. Why assume an English tragedy to follow?[21] On the 24th he indignantly told William there was not a word of truth in newspaper stories that he was ill-treated by the marshals, who wanted the King to arrest him.

Still however it is necessary to withdraw me; but all I beg is that it may be done handsomely.[22]

As in Portugal, he was determined not to go out by the back door.

At last in December the solution was found. HM Government implored Castlereagh, Leader of the House, to return immediately to his place on the front bench for the new session, thus giving the Duke an excuse to take over his work in Vienna. Lord and Lady Fitzroy Somerset would hold the fort, assisted, if that was the word, by the Duchess of Wellington, until the Ambassador returned. There was to be no Congress of Vienna for Kitty.

Wellington had got his way. His departure from Paris was put off till 24 January 1815, after the rumours of his impending 'flight' had died away. His transfer was not to be to America. The Treaty of Ghent between America and Britain was signed exactly a month before he left, on 24 December 1814.

There was a tragic postscript to the American peace. Sir Edward Pakenham, already in America while the negotiations were taking place, was cut off from the good tidings of success. On Christmas Day 1814 he took over command of the British army which had been sent out to give 'Jonathan' his thrashing. On 8 January 1815 he was defeated and fell on the battlefield of New Orleans, hemmed in between the bayous and the Mississippi with a bullet through his spine.

The death of Kitty's favourite brother was another nail in the coffin of her married happiness. Wellington had always been attached to him, and the facial likeness between Ned and Kitty was strong. Ned on his side understood Kitty's temperamental difficulties: he once wrote about the failure of her domestic philosophy to keep her calm. This sympathy for Kitty, together with his hero-worship of Wellington, might have smoothed the path between them, growing daily more rough.

At Vienna Wellington already had an enviable reputation as a diplomat. Talleyrand later told Gronow:

He never indulged in that parade of mystification which is generally employed by Ambassadors: watchfulness, prudence and experience of human nature, were the only means he employed. . . .[23]

Wellington's principle of 'no mystery-making', not successfully practised in the Peninsula, had triumphed in Paris. The change must have been deliberate, showing his different conception of authority when in the hands of a civil and a military leader.

The Congress had assembled in September 1814. After a fortnight's bickering in October between the big five powers – Russia and Prussia, Austria, Britain and France – Castlereagh gave Wellington a first, sour report:

I send you under flying seal the result of our discussions, not progress; for progress we have not made. . . .[24]

A veteran wit, the Prince de Ligne, who at eighty odd was frolicking among the Congress visitors, put the same thing more brightly: '*le Congrès ne marche pas, mais il danse*'.

The Tsar's semi-mystical attempt to base the peace of the world on a Europe united by Christian principles – the Holy Alliance – was marred by his own terrestrial ambitions. Poland had been partitioned out of existence in 1795 and the Tsar proposed to re-establish the unity of that region by swallowing Poland whole and compensating dispossessed Prussia with independent Saxony, while Austria helped herself in Italy. Was there any combination that Britain could put up against the Holy Alliance, strong enough to thwart the Tsar and eventually produce a firm peace? Talleyrand persuaded Castlereagh and Wellington that there was. Britain's policy must be armed mediation, supported by Austria, France and the Netherlands against Russia and Prussia. This was where Wellington, while still in Paris, had first made his mark on the Congress. At the beginning of November he persuaded Louis XVIII to order Talleyrand (whom Castlereagh had hitherto found as personally difficult as Churchill found de Gaulle) to cooperate 'in every way' with Britain against Russia's Polish plan. By early December a compromise was reached over Poland, by which the Tsar got the Duchy of Warsaw but not the whole.

Wellington reached Vienna on 3 February 1815, after a dash across Europe which his two companions, young Lennox and Colonel Fremantle, found exciting but arduous. Though their entirely cold meals consisted of such delicacies as *foie gras* washed down with the best claret, sleep was limited to precisely four hours each night. Only the Duke undressed and dressed. The other two slept in their clothes before hot German stoves and presented themselves each morning bleary-eyed and crumpled to the spruce 'Beau'. His personality did not disappoint expectant Vienna.

'What have you done, gentlemen?' he asked his colleagues on arrival.

'Nothing; absolutely nothing,' replied Prince Metternich.[25]

According to Talleyrand, Wellington at once got the creaking machinery into rapid motion, while all the time maintaining 'his usual unassuming and nonchalant air'. A modern French writer, J. A. Chastenet, sees Wellington at the Congress as 'always alert and phlegmatic'. This rare combination of opposites has also been picked out by a recent British Prime Minister, Asquith, as a lucky possession of his own. In his case he described it as 'energy under the guise of lethargy'.[26] It might be seen in a wider context as a peculiarly English syndrome. If so, it was first launched upon an amazed world in Vienna as a counter-irritant to merry-making under the guise of peace-making.

Wellington's own straightforward methods were in marked contrast to those of his two closest colleagues, Talleyrand and Metternich.

'With nations, depend upon it,' he assured his friends in old age, 'the only way is to go straight forward without stratagems or subterfuges.' The very appearance of the brilliant Frenchman, on the contrary, was contorted: with his crippled leg and monkey face, he was a byword for chicanery, not least because he had managed to remain Foreign Minister of France under the Republic, Consulate, Empire and Restoration. In answer to an enquiry as to what Talleyrand was like, Wellington replied, 'Like Old Brag, but not so clever' – Old Brag being Scindiah's unprepossessing envoy in 1803.[27] A time was to come when he would change his opinion of this intelligent if devious statesman. In England Metternich was considered almost equally slippery, and Lord Liverpool specifically warned Wellington against his *finesse* & trick'.[28]

Yet the three had this in common: they were all 'Europeans' seeking the magic point of 'just equilibrium', which by definition was world peace. It depended on checks and balances between all the European states, rather than on a monolithic Continental system such as Bonaparte had run. Within this formula there were of course differences. In the end it was Castlereagh's concept which was adopted and later became known as the 'Balance of Power'. All three, however, were agreed that the 'just equilibrium' must be achieved through sovereigns, not through peoples, and through legitimate sovereigns at that. To Wellington also the smoky torch of legitimacy, handed on to him by Castlereagh who had received it from Talleyrand, seemed a manifestation of that principle of order and 'regularity' which he had always revered. A cosmopolitan by training and taste, it is questionable whether he was ever as much at home in the Mother of Parliaments as at the Congress of Vienna. He enjoyed himself in the splendid Viennese mansion allotted to him, while avoiding the scandals that surged and broke all round him, acting as a tonic to many a jaded statesman. Talleyrand's niece Dorothea had two sisters, Pauline and Jeanne, who were the mistresses of Congress personnel (Jeanne of its Secretary-General), while Dorothea's other sister Wilhelmina, Duchess of Sagan, lived in turn with the English chargé d'affaires, Prince Metternich and the new English Minister, Sir Charles Stewart. Dorothea herself was relatively discreet, falling in love only with a Count Clam.

A mild optimism began to supervene at Vienna, initiated by Castlereagh's remark to the Tsar after the American peace: '*Il commence l'âge d'or.*' Each individual settled down to promoting his own pet reform. J. W. Croker's contribution to the golden age was a uniform, international thermometer, which at the beginning of March he had high hopes of the Congress adopting. A golden age for the Africans would surely dawn when Wellington had persuaded Congress to denounce the slave-trade as unworthy of Christian civilization.

A golden haze seemed also to hang over Elba. The Emperor's ambition was said by his official warder, the British Commissioner Sir Neil Campbell, to be peacefully sinking to its close. 'I begin to think that he is quite resigned to his retreat,' wrote Campbell to Lord Castlereagh as early as 17 September 1814.[29] The haze, or Sir Neil and the French Ministry of Police, was dense enough to obliterate various facts and rumours emanating from the island. In December secret information reached the French Government that Bonaparte, knowing all about the quarrels inside the Congress, had remarked, 'I see it will be necessary to take the field again.' They ignored it. Naturally they knew they had not paid Bonaparte's grant and he was consequently in financial straits, and that he feared assassination, kidnapping and imprisonment on St Helena. Here were four good reasons for escape. None was taken seriously.

On 16 February 1815 Campbell courteously told his prisoner he was going to the mainland of Italy that day for an interview with the Austrian Minister. (Sir Neil's mistress, Signora Bartoli, was also on the mainland, at Leghorn.)

'Will you come back by the 28th?' asked the Emperor.

'Why the 28th?' Bonaparte explained that Princess Borghese was giving a ball on that day, to which Sir Neil was invited. The British Commissioner promised to be back in time.

Four days before this significant interview, a letter postmarked Calais was sent to Wellington by a Mr John F. Schrader, reporting an extraordinary conversation he had just had with his friend Mrs Wallace, wife of General Wallace and close associate of the Radicals Horne Tooke and Sir Francis Burdett.

'You very well know I am a friend to Bonaparte,' Mrs Wallace had begun. She went on to explain that she had crossed the Channel expressly to visit Bonaparte on Elba, for a particular reason.

'I can tell you my friend, most, most confidantly [sic] that his stay at Elba is but of very short duration!!! He will soon, very soon be King of Italy!!!'

Her breathless communication was received by Schrader with a smile.

'You have no occasion to smile – I have it from the best authority . . . and I am prodigious impatient to see him before he makes his Exit!!'

Schrader, convinced at last there was 'something very mysterious in this lady's journey', felt it his duty to get in touch with Wellington at the Congress.[30] Neither Mrs Wallace nor Schrader's letter can have reached their destinations at Elba or Vienna in time. The grand disturber got his sister Pauline to put forward her ball three days, after which he completed his preparations for escape. These included the sealing off of the island from the outside world. Not a fishing boat was allowed to put to sea. On 26 February 1815, supported by 1,200 soldiers, six small ships beside his own, and Pauline's jewels voluntarily contributed, he boarded the brig *Inconstant* at nightfall for France, while his loyal Elbans stood singing on the quay in the glow of coloured lanterns. As his vessel began to move a stupefied silence fell.

It was not till nine days later, on 7 March 1815, that the news reached Vienna. Three days earlier, however, the French telegraph system had conveyed it to King Louis in Paris.

The King's gouty fingers fumbled agonizingly with the envelope. After he had got it open and read it he sat with his head in his hands. At last he turned to a Minister.

'Do you know what this telegraph contains?'

'No, Sir, I do not.'

'Well, I will tell you. It is revolution once more. Bonaparte has landed on the coast of Provence.'[31]

At Vienna, a hunt in the park at Schönbrunn was arranged for 7 March. But when Wellington's horse was brought round to his house he sent it back to the stable. He had just heard that another horse had bolted. At first it seemed to him that they would return it to its stable almost as easily. He at once had his colleagues informed. They are said to have burst out laughing.

Talleyrand's elaborately powdered *coiffure* was being performed for him as usual in his bedroom, while his niece Dorothea sat on the end of the bed discussing the afternoon's rehearsal of a comedy in the Metternichs' house. Suddenly a message from Prince Metternich himself was brought in.

'Read it,' Talleyrand ordered her casually, still occupied with his *toilette*. 'It's probably to tell me the time of today's meeting of the Congress.' Dorothea opened it.

'Napoleon has escaped from Elba! Oh, Uncle, what about my rehearsal?'

'Go ahead with it.'

Talleyrand and Wellington were soon in unusually animated discussion.

'He'll go anywhere you like to mention,' said Talleyrand jauntily, 'except France.' Wellington did not disagree. Like many others, he thought Bonaparte would land in Italy.

Lord Castlereagh wrote at once from London to Wellington offering the choice of continued diplomatic service in Vienna or command of an army in Flanders.

Tsar Alexander, like Wellington himself, saw no choice. He laid his hand on the Duke's shoulder. 'It is for you to save the world again.'[32]

20

Where is Nosey?

Bickerings, billings and cooings at the Congress abruptly ceased. They got down to work. In the past the *Morning Chronicle* had derided them:

> We learn from high sources a project is made,
> How Vienna's grand Congress the Christmas will spend.
> Since public affairs have so long been delayed
> They may very well wait till the holidays end.

Now the holidays had ended with a bang. Who could tell when Europe would be on holiday again?

The Congress soon learnt that Bonaparte had arrived in France on 1 March – with the violets, as he said he would. His standard was raised at Fréjus on the Golfe Juan. He was marching on Paris. Marshal Ney, who had promised King Louis to bring back Bonaparte to Paris in an iron cage, decided to join his returned master.

There had been many jokes at Court about the iron cage. 'I would not like such a bird in my room,' the King had remarked with a grimace.[1] Someone suggested a home for it in the Jardins des Plantes. There was now little danger of the bird being caught.

On 13 March 1815, the Congress declared Napoleon an outlaw:

Napoleon Bonaparte, by again appearing in France with projects of confusion and disorder, has placed himself beyond the protection of the law [*hors la loi*] and rendered himself subject to public vengeance [*vindicte publique*].

Wellington's name appeared on the list of signatories and created an uproar among the Opposition. Whitbread interpreted the word *vindicte* as an incitement to assassination: Wellington was morally Bonaparte's murderer. A letter to William Wellesley-Pole, however, showed Wellington unrepentant: *vindicte* meant 'justice' not vengeance. As for the Radicals calling him personally an assassin day after day in the House of Commons while he was serving abroad, instead of moving a regular vote of censure – this struck him as vindictiveness personified.[2]

He was serving abroad in no easy conditions. Napoleon entered Paris on 20 March 1815 without a shot being fired in anger. Indeed the only blow struck on Louis XVIII's behalf was said to have been by an old woman selling chestnuts. When she shouted '*Vive le Roi*' a man roared back '*Vive l'Empereur*' – and she hit him on the head with her ladle.

The Emperor was carried shoulder-high into the Tuileries with his eyes shut and a sleepwalker's smile on his face. The Hundred Days had begun.

In the last hours of the night before, Louis XVIII had fled from his capital to a commodious house in the Netherlands at Ghent, with a garden into which he could be wheeled.

An announcement on 25 March of a formal alliance between the European powers to re-cage the eagle followed the extraordinary news from Paris. Wellington was appointed Commander-in-Chief of the British and Dutch-Belgian forces in Flanders. All military dispositions were agreed by the Congress before the end of the month. Five million pounds sterling were advanced by Castlereagh as subsidies – his *âge d'or* had begun with a vengeance – plus another million or so in lieu of the 150,000 troops which Britain was pledged but unable to provide. Pressed by Wellington, the Government applied to the Rothschild brothers for assistance, and on 14 April a letter passed from Nathan in London to James in Hamburg:

. . . Brother Solomon [in Vienna] will ere this comes to hand have visited Bruxelles to meet Mr. Herries [the Government's Commissary-General] on the business of the new subsidies. Mr. H. leaves here tomorrow morning with one of the Lords of the Treasury by request of the Duke of Wellington solely for this object.[3]

By 11 May the first instalment of the Russian subsidy was arranged and others were in train. Moreover, on 4 April, the same day that Wellington himself reached Brussels from Vienna, Nathan Rothschild had despatched the first consignment of bullion and coin for his army: three ingots valued at £3,053 15s. 6d. On 1 May twenty-eight ingots at £27,958 19s 1d. were sent and by 13 June (five days before Waterloo) the total had risen to over a quarter of a million pounds in ingots and specie. Nathan Rothschild wrote to Herries on 11 May to inform him of the successful operation so far, due to raising the exchange rate. Herries had found the franc standing at 17.50 when he was in Paris on 1 May 1814. 'By proper management, I was able to raise it to fr.22.'

Wellington's work in Vienna was finished by 29 March. All the ladies kissed him good-bye and he set off for Brussels in his carriage with Lennox and Fremantle as before. The final act of the Congress was not signed until 9 June, but when it was, a clause appeared declaring the slave-trade to be unworthy of Christian states – a tribute to Wellington's pertinacity. Louis XVIII's promise to Wellington, however, that France would abolish the slave trade in five years' time had meanwhile been made to look rather meagre by Napoleon. He abolished it forthwith.

This act was only one item in an impressive scheme of liberal government that the Emperor now held out to the Allies as a reason for laying down their arms and leaving him to reign, constitutionally, in peace. Castlereagh was not prepared to take the risk. Nor was Wellington, for he like Liverpool regarded 'Boney' and all Bonapartists as 'Jacobins', i.e. revolutionaries, at heart.

When the Commander-in-Chief reached Brussels on 4 April 1815 he was looking for what he called a 'third term' between the Bonapartists and the elder branch of the Bourbons. Wellington thought he saw the 'third term' in the Duke of Orleans, son of Philippe Egalité, a Bourbon of the younger branch, who was indeed to be King of the French but not till 1830. What was Castlereagh going to do about it? In a secret reply dated 16 April 1815 Castlereagh turned down Wellington's 'third term': the King must be supported at least 'for the present'.[4]

Twenty-eight of the Hundred Days had now come and gone. Wellington's political path had not become any less stony. The most decisive campaign of his life was to be based on a negative, though a stupendous one: no deep devotion anywhere towards the dispossessed monarchy but implacable hatred for the grand disturber of Europe. With the nations once more lying in the track of the hurricane there was only one possible answer: *Non ultra*.

The Bourbons were not the only royalties to give Wellington concern. His closest allies, King William I of the Netherlands and his eldest son, sometimes known respectively as the Old and Young Frog, caused (and suffered) much heart-burning. The difficulty of getting the Netherlands fortresses garrisoned drove Wellington to distraction. What could you expect when all the King's Dutch officers had been in the French service and he was surrounded with ex-French officials, all passionately keen 'to get us out of Antwerp and Ostend'? Fanny Burney noticed how careful Wellington was not to offend foreign susceptibilities. At a concert for the benefit of Madame Catalani at the end of April he was 'gay even to sportiveness', applauding everything she sang –except 'Rule Britannia'. To this he listened in silence and when his officers shouted for an encore, crushed them with a look. Nevertheless, King William was not appeased. At length on 3 May he bowed gracefully to the inevitable and appointed Wellington Commander-in-Chief of all the Dutch–Belgian forces in the Netherlands. Wellington's proposal to mix the Dutch–Belgian forces with British stiffeners, as he had done in Portugal, which the King had hitherto bitterly resisted, was also accepted. In Wellington's words, 'all the youth and treason of the army' was no longer in one corps. He explained to Bathurst, 'the screw with which I have operated upon the king is to threaten to make the real state of my relations with them known to the public. . . .'[5]

The poor Prince of Orange winced under the side-effects of the screw. On the same day (5 May) that Wellington wrote home more cheerfully, the Young Frog complained to the Old Frog of having to endure '*des moments pénibles à cause de la mauvaise humeur du Duc*. . . .' He himself had already been thrown into great ill-humour over his supersession as Commander-in-Chief of the British–Netherlands forces by Wellington. Nevertheless 'Slender Billy', his affectionate nickname in the Peninsula, had written with dignity to the Duke while still in Vienna,

I will be happy to give over to you although I can not deny that I would under the present circumstances do so with much reluctance to any body else.[6]

The Duke was in constant terror of his impetuous young colleague beginning the war before the other Allies were ready. Some of them might not be ready for a considerable time, if at all.

Russia would have to leave security forces behind in Poland, Prussia in Saxony and Austria in Italy. From Portugal Wellington had hoped for 25,000 of his splendid 'fighting cocks' under their experienced general, Beresford. But most of them were disbanded, it seemed, and in any case the Portuguese government were by now extremely tired of British officers and proposing to show them all off the premises.

Beside Beresford, other great Peninsular names were missing from his new staff. Sir George Murray was in Canada. Sir Edward Pakenham was dead and Wellington wrote to Ned's brother, Lord Longford, during these critical weeks again bewailing his loss. Sir Lowry Cole, Kitty's old flame, was tied up with his marriage to Lord Malmesbury's daughter; in congratulating him Wellington wished that he could 'bring every thing together as I had it when I took leave of the army at Bordeaux, and I would engage that we should not be the last in the race. . . .' Sir Stapleton Cotton, now Lord Combermere, wrote offering to command the British cavalry as in Spain but it appeared that the Prince Regent and Duke of York had promised this plum to Lord Uxbridge (Paget the eloper). Wellington was annoyed, but not because of the Paget–Wellesley divorce. His only objection to the appointment was that he had worked with Combermere in India and throughout the Peninsular War but with Uxbridge never. Uxbridge's cavalry actions, though brilliant, were confined to a brief period under Sir John Moore.

'I imagine you must have heard much of the talent of Sir Hudson Lowe,' wrote Sir Henry Torrens hopefully from the War Office of the intended quartermaster-general.[7] Wellington had, and considered him downright stupid. For one thing, the Duke could not bear hesitant answers.

'Where does that road lead to, Sir Hudson?' he had once asked in his abrupt way, and when Hudson began fumbling with his map Wellington muttered, 'Damned old fool!' One astute general, knowing his chief's quirk, made a point of giving a prompt answer to a question whatever the state of his own ignorance.

'How many rounds of ammunition have we?' Wellington would rap out.

'Four hundred and twenty' would come back pat, a figure that could be adjusted if necessary afterwards.[8]

So it was not surprising that Wellington insisted on having Lowe replaced by Sir William de Lancey, a Peninsular colleague, though not a patch on Murray.

Two grand personages who tried in vain to make their way on to Wellington's staff were the Dukes of Cumberland and Richmond. The former was choked off by his royal brother, the Prince Regent, after declaring his wish on 25 March to serve under 'Field Marschall [sic] the Duke of Wellington'. Richmond's disappointment caused the Horse Guards immense embarrassment until Wellington promised to 'co-operate in setting his mind at ease'.[9] In the end Wellington was allowed a large number of trusty generals who were also old Peninsular hands.

Among the younger officers from Wellington's old army to return in time from America was Harry Smith of the Rifles. He and his men had seen the burning of Washington and, accustomed to Wellington's 'humane warfare', were horrified. On his way home, Napoleon's escape from Elba had been conveyed to Smith with British phlegm by the skipper of a merchantman in the Bristol Channel.

'Any news?'

'No, none.' Then, as the distance widened between the two ships there was a sudden halloo. The skipper remembered.

'Ho! Bonaparte's back on the throne of France.'[10]

Wellington had been clamouring all through April for every man the Government could lay hands on but by the beginning of May he was still profoundly dissatisfied. All he asked for were 40,000 British infantry, 15,000 cavalry, 150 guns and staff of his own choosing. All he got were 30,000 British soldiers of all arms, only 7,000 of them veterans, and four pages of apology from the Duke of York on 5 May for having appointed staff officers without consulting him first; but as they had already 'indulged in expensive equipment', the Duke of York did not think it fair to countermand them.[11]

The Duke of York's letter crossed with a dignified statement from Wellington to the Horse Guards. He was not satisfied but – 'I think it much better that this correspondence upon the Staff should cease'.

Perhaps it was the irritation caused by an unexpected proposal from his favourite gun-maker, John Roebuck of the Carron Company, that provoked him to his last and most famous (or should it be infamous?) outburst. On 6 May Roebuck offered to send him some of his new, twenty-four-pounder iron 'carronades', as ordered for the East India Company, instead of the usual brass $5\frac{1}{2}$-inch howitzers. The new ones, Roebuck added, were particularly good with Colonel Shrapnell's 'destructive shells'. The Commander-in-Chief replied witheringly: 'I do not consider this to be a proper period to alter the equipment of the army or to try experiments.'[12] The guns that Wellington really needed, had repeatedly asked the Horse Guards to order and never received, were Napoleon's own favourites, the formidable twelve-pounders which the Emperor called his 'beautiful daughters'. Two days later Wellington let fly to Lord Stewart who was still in Vienna. Making use again, as was his habit, of an adjective he had previously found serviceable when applied to the unregenerate Peninsular army of 1810, he wrote on 8 May 1815:

I have got an infamous army, very weak and ill equipped, and a very inexperienced Staff. In my opinion they are doing nothing in England. They have not raised a man; they have not called out the militia either in England or Ireland....[13]

The handling of the militia question suggested that it was the Government rather than Wellington's army who were both infamous and idiotic in their dilatory cussedness, springing from fear of the Opposition. A legal scruple was allowed to tie the helpless hands of

Bathurst for several precious weeks, since the militia in Ireland, for instance, could not legally be called up for duties which would free the regulars except 'in time of war or insurrection'.[14]

What state was Britain in between March and June 1815? Clearly not at peace. While various ways of partially circumventing the militia law occurred by degrees to the British Government, a similar impasse was allowed to develop over veterans at the end of their service: these men 'must necessarily be discharged' – unless retained by authority of a Royal Proclamation.[15] It took another month to get the proclamation through. Thus Wellington's army remained 'very weak', as he said, in veterans and very dependent on Continental recruits, some of them mercenaries who were Bonapartists at heart and others totally untrained boys. 'Monseigneur!' wrote the commandant of Ath in the Netherlands to the Commander-in-Chief five days before Waterloo, 'Having in the Brigade of the Hanoverian Reserve many soldiers who have never fired a shot' – please send powder and cartridges to 'exercise' them.[16]

If Wellington wanted more veterans, his veterans had all along asked for Wellington. 'Where is Wellington? Surely we shall not be led to battle by that boy?' murmured the first arrivals in Belgium, aware that Slender Billy was still their titular commander. 'Wellington is the man that must lead us on,' declared Wheeler (now a sergeant) of the 51st. 'He is looked to by the remnant of the old Peninsular army, an hundred times a day. . . .' When at last a General Order announced that the Prince of Orange had surrendered his command to the Duke, all the Peninsular veterans went mad with joy.

'Glorious news! Nosey has got command! Won't we give them a drubbing now!'[17]

Kitty was not among the civilians in Brussels impatiently awaiting Wellington's return; she had gone home with the first rush from Paris. In London, however, she did her bit to keep up morale. At a party given by the master-general of the Ordnance she countered the many expressions of anxiety with, 'Ah! wait a little, *he* is in his element now; depend upon him'. Lady Caroline Capel in Brussels felt that *he* could not arrive too soon. Another civilian family to be much fortified by his coming were Thomas Creevey, his wife and two step-daughters, the Misses Ord. Creevey was amazed at Wellington's casualness and sang-froid over Napoleon. The most famous meeting between Wellington and Creevey took place in the Park a few weeks before Waterloo. Creevey asked the Duke what he would make of the coming battle.

'By God! I think Blücher and myself can do the thing.'

'Do you calculate upon any desertion in Bonaparte's army?'

'Not upon a man, from the colonel to the private . . . inclusive. We may pick up a marshal or two, perhaps; but not worth a damn.'

'Do you reckon upon any support from the French king's troops at Alost?'

'Oh! don't mention such fellows! No: I think Blücher and I can do the business.'

Just then a British infantryman came in sight, peering about at the Park and its statuary.

'There,' said Wellington, pointing to the small scarlet figure, 'There, it all depends upon that article whether we do the business or not. Give me enough of it, and I am sure.'[18]

In those words Wellington made atonement, raising the common soldier – 'the scum of the earth' – into the embodiment of British tenacity.

For all Wellington's confidence, it was soon apparent that he could not put complete trust in another vital section of his army – the Intelligence. The great Colquhoun Grant (*Granto el Bueno*) had returned to direct this department. But as long as Britain was 'neither at war nor at peace' Wellington was not allowed to send cavalry patrols to investigate French-held territory. So there was uncertainty, even contradiction in the intelligence that reached him.

On 9 May Wellington passed a report to the Prussian frontier troops at Charleroi that Bonaparte was setting out from Paris that day. Two days later an agent informed him that Bonaparte had already reached Lille on the 8th. By the 12th, however, Wellington was half inclined to believe that far from having left Paris Napoleon would never venture to do so, that his power was crumbling, and all the frontier movements were defensive. Two or three weeks later, on the contrary, the Prince of Orange sent Wellington an account from the French newspaper *Moniteur* of Bonaparte's magnificent demonstration in Paris (the so-called *Champ de Mai*) on 1 June. On 6 June British intelligence was unanimous that Bonaparte was approaching the frontier towards Lille. When Lady Georgiana Lennox told Wellington that her mother, the Duchess of Richmond, was planning a picnic to Tournai or Lille for the 8th, he warned her off:

'You'd better not go. Say nothing about it, but let the project drop.'[19] (Napoleon was still in Paris.) Meanwhile messages continued to fly between the British and Netherlands' headquarters with insistent orders by Wellington for securing the fortifications at Mons, Ath and Antwerp. He probably feared treachery more than attack by Napoleon. Indeed on 13 June he reverted to the view that Napoleon's departure from Paris was 'not likely to be immediate'.[20] (Napoleon had left Paris the day before.)

A danger to Wellington's army more serious than his unreliable intelligence had been caused from the start by international politics.

King Louis's precipitate flight from Paris on 19 March had one ludicrous side-effect. All the secret French Foreign Office documents fell into the hands of Bonaparte, who had the satisfaction of publishing them. As a result, the xenophobic Prussian general, Gneisenau, was disgusted to read the terms of the secret Treaty of 3 January 1815 which had been directed against his own country (though as much against Russia).

Fortunately the veteran Marshal Blücher, Gneisenau's chief, was of radically different material. Uncouth, illiterate and belonging very much to the period before the sweeping reforms in the Prussian Army (1807–14), he was essentially a soldier's soldier: brave, loyal and utterly unimpressed by his own numerous defeats. When appointed to his 1815 command he was said to be suffering from mental disturbance, as in 1811, during which he believed himself to be pregnant of an elephant. Wellington liked and admired him.

'He was a very fine fellow, and whenever there was any question of fighting, always ready and eager – if anything too eager.'[21]

Nevertheless there was much jealousy and ill-temper among Prussian officers, wrote Wellington to Bathurst on 4 April, and he was sending his trusted friend, Colonel Hardinge, as liaison officer to keep Gneisenau 'sweet'.[22]

Sweet or sour, the Prussians were in no mood to share either headquarters or lines of communication with Wellington. While the British communications ran back westwards and northwards to Ostend and Antwerp, Blücher's lines moved in the opposite direction eastwards through Liège and Aachen into Germany. Between the two armies there was thus a joint or hinge represented by the area on either side of the great paved *chaussée* running due north from Charleroi to Brussels. Napoleon had his eyes on the hinge. Wellington had one eye on the hall door.

By training and experience Wellington had learnt to keep his eye at certain times on the exit rather than on the ally or associate. In the Peninsula he had faced every kind of unpleasantness with his Spanish allies rather than risk his hall door at Lisbon. In northern Europe there was the special position of Belgium causing him to watch the North Sea exits with a peculiarly, though as it turned out, unnecessarily suspicious eye. Belgium had belonged to France by conquest for over twenty years. The perils that Wellington was constantly guarding against in Mons, Ath, Antwerp and Tournai, of a *coup de main* from within, were things he had not usually needed to consider in the Peninsula. In the Netherlands he completely trusted neither the Belgian fortresses nor the Dutch–Belgian regiments, particularly since Bonapartist broadsheets had begun flooding into Belgium.

> The Eagles which have led us so often to victory
> have reappeared. Their cry is always the same:
> glory and liberty!

– or even better, glory and loot!

> You will receive the rewards with which the
> genius of France ever knows how to honour
> courage.

If national pride had caused King William to keep the Netherlands troops and fortresses under his own control as long as possible, national security forbade Wellington to weaken his vital network by moving left away from them and towards the Prussians, before he was forced. That he might be so forced was always on the cards. Indeed, he had met Blücher on 3 May at Tirlemont, half-way between Brussels and Liège, to agree upon a joint strategy. The agreed plan involved Wellington in closing up eastwards to his left in case of an attack on the central hinge. It was for his Prussian allies, however, to warn him of the first sign of such an attack.

They failed to let him know that on the night of 13–14 June advanced Prussian patrols under General Zieten had seen the twinkling lights of innumerable camp fires in the direction of Beaumont, a few miles from the frontier on the French side of the River Sambre.

The eagles had reappeared with the swiftness and silence of night birds.

21

Humbugged, by God!

From 7 June the total security measures which Napoleon knew so well how to impose had sealed off his frontiers along the Sambre, Rhine and Moselle. As at Elba before his escape, fishing boats were forbidden to move. Every stage coach was finally immobilized, every document intercepted – apart from the false information which his agents continued to circulate more industriously than ever in places like Ghent and Mons. On 12 June at 3.30 am Napoleon left Paris. By the 14th he had concentrated the Army of the North, 122,000 strong with 366 guns, in a space of eighteen square miles around his headquarters at Beaumont. Here he gave the army its Orders of the Day for 15 June.

Soldats! He recalled the glorious anniversaries of Marengo and Friedland, both fought on 14 June. *Soldats!* He reminded them of other victories where the defeated enemy had been three to one, six to one. . . . (With their 122,000 against the combined Anglo-Dutch and Prussian forces of 210,000, the odds were once more heavily against him. But Napoleon had no intention of facing his two enemies combined. The hinge or joint between them was the single, weak spot at which he would drive, forcing the two halves apart and defeating each separately.) *Soldats!* They were asked to remember their own 'frightful' sufferings in English prisons, as also the millions of Poles, Italians, Saxons, Belgians 'devoured' by the princely enemies of the people. They would have to endure forced marches, battles, perils. For every true Frenchman the moment had come to conquer or perish.

Among the more subtle perils not mentioned by the Emperor were suspicions of political treachery. The monolithic faith for or against Napoleon finally died on the dissecting table at Vienna. Treason was in the air and surreptitiously caused Wellington as well as Napoleon to make mistakes. Napoleon underestimated the betrayal- neurosis among his French soldiers. More dreadful even than the cries of the wounded and dying at Waterloo was to be the nihilistic screech of the survivors, '*Nous sommes trahis*' – we are not defeated but betrayed.

Wellington on 13 June was still waiting for the incontrovertible sign that Napoleon had marched. Everything, apart from that essential knowledge, was ready. He had even received from his boot-maker, Hoby, two pairs of 'Wellington' boots specially ordered for the campaign.

The last boots you sent me were still too small in the calf of the leg & about an inch & half too short in the leg. Send me two pairs more altered as I have above described.

The great Hoby of St James's Street prided himself not only on his boots but also on his preaching – at a Methodist chapel in Islington. On hearing the news of Vitoria he is said to have remarked complacently, 'If Lord Wellington had had any other boot-maker than myself, he never would have had his great and constant successes; for my boots and prayers bring his Lordship out of all his difficulties.'[1] The Duke certainly needed all that Hoby could do for him now.

Personally Wellington was more convinced than ever that Bonaparte would take the course he himself would have chosen: a sweep round the Anglo-Dutch right flank to cut them off from the sea. This favourite strategy, known to Napoleon himself as *la manoeuvre sur les derrières* or the advance of 'envelopment', had already been employed by him thirty times since 1796, half of them with spectacular success.*

Wellington, it is constantly said, ought to have realized that Napoleon could not possibly adopt the 'envelopment' strategy, since in doing so he would automatically drive the Anglo-Dutch and Prussian armies together and thus present himself with a single enemy of double his size. This argument was of course perfectly well known to Wellington but he rejected it. In his view Napoleon's chances were against his permanently separating two such generals as Wellington and Blücher – as indeed turned out to be the case, though it was a close-run thing.

Having made his analysis, Wellington continued to canton his new forces, as they arrived in a steady stream, over what he believed to be the threatened areas west of Brussels. In case of need they could be transferred into more easterly positions – with speed but not at a moment's notice. Ninety-three thousand men were ready to march. Only a third were British.

* See D. Chandler, *The Campaigns of Napoleon*, pp. 162–72 and Appendix B. Famous victories in which Napoleon used this manoeuvre included Ulm, Jena, Eylau, Friedland, Wagram.

Meanwhile he carried on with simple but effective psychological warfare against those in Belgium showing Bonapartist sympathies.

What occupation conveyed to the foreigner a maximum sense of leisurely confidence and English phlegm? The game of cricket. On 12 June he compensated one of the pretty Lennox girls, the sixteen-year-old Lady Jane, for the forbidden expedition to Tournai by taking her to watch a cricket match at Enghien. Cricket was not the army's sole distraction. On the occasion of a grand cavalry review it was hard to decide which was more memorable – the splash of scarlet uniforms at the time or of pink champagne afterwards. Resplendent officers were not discouraged from partnering the daughters of aristocratic English visitors or Belgian families of the *ton* at many parties and balls, not a few of them given by Wellington himself. Caroline Capel was one who spotted Wellington's deliberate policy of inculcating confidence. His niece, Emily Somerset, who was expecting her first baby, had been persuaded to stay and have it in Brussels. As for his own next moves, he successfully convinced everybody that his silence about them was due to his well-known secrecy, rather than to the fact that he did not yet know them himself. 'Nobody can guess Lord Wellington's intentions,' wrote Caroline Capel on 11 June. 'In the meantime he amuses himself with Humbuging [*sic*] the Ladies.' 'The Duke of W—' she wrote primly to her mother, 'has not improved the *morality* of our Society, as he has given several things [i.e. parties] and makes a point of asking all the Ladies of Loose Character. Every one was surprised at seeing Lady John Campbell at his House, and one of his Staff told me that it had been represented to him her not bein [*sic*] received for that her Character was more than suspicious.'

' "Is it, by —," said he, "then I will go and ask her Myself." On which he immediately took his Hat and went out for the purpose.'[2]

Lady Frances Wedderburn-Webster was another of the 'Loose Characters' on whom Brussels society cast an alert but disapproving eye. One incident in her much discussed relationship with Wellington was witnessed by a twenty-year-old subaltern, Basil Jackson. He happened to be sitting in the Park with an 'elderly' Belgian lady when 'a very great man' walked past them. Next moment a carriage drove up and a young lady alighted. She was joined by the very great man. Jackson and his friend stood up to see better and watched the couple until they 'descended into a hollow, where the trees completely screened them'. The little drama concluded with the arrival of another carriage containing an agitated female sleuth, identified by Jackson as old Lady Mountnorris, 'who went peering about for her daughter, Lady F.W.' The green hollow, however, kept its secret.[3]

Imagination would no doubt fill the blank in this Restoration comedy with the seduction of Lady Frances Webster by the Duke of Wellington under the nose of her mother Lady Mountnorris – but for the inconvenient fact that Lady Frances was expecting a baby in a few weeks' time.

So it was to be business and pleasure as usual during those last days of suspense. Reports of French activity behind the frontier kept arriving at Wellington's headquarters but none of them yet showed that enemy troop movements had ceased in front of Mons, key to the shortest, straightest route to Brussels. Until Wellington was sure there was no threat to the Mons road he could not answer the Prussians' anxious questions as to where he would concentrate his army. His own uncommunicativeness was matched by Gneisenau's. Having been told nothing of the camp fires seen by Zieten on 13–14 June, Wellington was similarly kept in the dark about an audacious intention of Blücher to concentrate at Sombreffe and fall back no farther than Fleurus – both recklessly advanced positions – in case of sudden attack on the Prussian outposts at Thuin and Charleroi.

Long before dawn on 15 June Napoleon began his advance into Belgium. Though his commanders were prevented from keeping to their timetables, he was able to drive the Prussians out of Charleroi with the help of the Imperial Guard at 11 am and to watch his army entering the town at noon. He sat in a chair outside the *Belle-Vue* inn. Later it was observed that the *petit Caporal* was fast asleep. Meanwhile, a crucial message from Wellington's trusted chief of Intelligence, Sir Colquhoun Grant, giving the true direction of Napoleon's advance and laying once for all the Mons ghost, started on its precarious journey to Brussels. It was intercepted by the witless Hanoverian cavalry officer, General Dörnberg, who had served as a colonel in Prince Jerome Bonaparte's army, deserted to the English in 1813 and become a general. Dörnberg returned the vital letter to sender with the remark that far from convincing him of Napoleon's advance, 'it assured him of the contrary'.[4] The luckless Grant rode with his letter like a madman to deliver it to Wellington personally but thanks to Dörnberg it was too late. When Grant arrived the battle of Quatre Bras was in full swing.

Without Grant's essential information, Wellington can hardly be blamed for continuing to interpret the important but still inconclusive reports of French activity according to his previous analysis. The main new reports were three in number.

About 3 pm, nine hours after Napoleon's start, the Duke received his first. A Prussian officer covered with dirt and sweat galloped into Brussels with a much delayed despatch sent by General Zieten from Charleroi at 8 or 9 am. Zieten's 1st Corps had been attacked and the Prussian outposts driven in at Thuin. Now Thuin, though a great deal nearer to Charleroi than to Mons, was nevertheless close enough to Mons for Wellington's right shoulder to give him another twinge.

Then came a second message: the Prince of Orange announced that the Prussians had been pushed out from the village of Binche; what's more he had heard gun-fire around Charleroi with his own ears.

Wellington acted quickly. Feint or not, it was clearly time to alert his troops. He ordered his whole army to collect at their various divisional headquarters and be ready to march at a moment's notice. The orders went out between 5 and 7 pm. The 20,000 troops of the reserve, including Picton's division, were to remain in Brussels under Wellington himself; the cavalry were to collect at Ninove under Lord Uxbridge. When the rest of the army moved to take up their prearranged positions between Grammont and Nivelles, under Lord Hill and the Prince of Orange respectively, it was clear that the balance had automatically shifted somewhat farther to the west of Brussels, i.e. away from Blücher, than otherwise. While the Mons–Ath–Ghent line in the east would be as closely watched as before, nothing whatever would be found nearer to the centre – the crossroads at Quatre Bras – than some of the Prince of Orange's Nassauers at Nivelles, seven miles away.

Napoleon's build-up of a phantom strategy by false intelligence was successful indeed, when it deceived one of his enemies into inclining outwards even before the wedge was driven home.

Fitzroy Somerset was one of those who could not understand why there was no definite order to march following the 'stand to arms'.

'No doubt we shall be able to manage those Fellows,' he said to his chief. Wellington was firm.

'There is little doubt of that, provided I do not make a false movement.'[5] By a 'false movement' Wellington meant a move which, if it turned out to be wrong, could not be rectified.

At 10 pm his Prussian liaison officer, General Müffling, arrived with the third important message so far that day. It was from Gneisenau, to say that Blücher had concentrated on the east–west *chaussée* at Sombreffe, only twenty-five miles from where they were sitting. What was Wellington going to do? Wellington replied that the main attack might still come through Mons.

'For this reason I must wait for my advice from Mons before I fix on my rendezvous.'

Towards midnight the Duke's carriage drew up at Müffling's house. Wellington had received the long awaited despatch – his report from Mons. The yes-no question as to whether the attacks round Charleroi were feints or not was answered. The answer, surprisingly, was no.

'I have a report from General Dörnberg at Mons that Napoleon has moved on Charleroi with all his force, and that he, General Dörnberg, has nothing in his front.'

So that was it. The other way round from what he had guessed. The activity around Mons had been the feint, that at Charleroi the real thing. Wellington quickly assured Müffling that he had already issued fresh orders to the troops, this time to concentrate on Nivelles and Quatre Bras – to the *east* at last.

'The numerous friends of Napoleon who are here,' continued the Duke, 'will be on tiptoe; the well intentioned must be pacified; let us therefore go all the same to the Duchess of Richmond's ball, and start for Quatre Bras at 5 am.'[6]

The most famous ball in history was the climax of Wellington's psychological warfare which always involved 'pleasure as usual'. The question of holding it or not had first come up in May.

'Duke,' said the Duchess of Richmond one day, 'I do not wish to pry into your secrets. . . . I wish to give a ball, and all I ask is, may I give my ball? If you say, "Duchess, don't give your ball," it is quite sufficient, I ask no reason.'

'Duchess, you may give your ball with the greatest safety, without fear of interruption.'[7]

Since those dignified ducal exchanges circumstances had altered more radically than Wellington even now supposed. That very afternoon there had been a close-run thing, though a small one, at Quatre Bras. Prince Bernhard of Saxe-Weimar had brilliantly occupied on his own initiative the empty crossroads at Quatre Bras and had easily driven off French skirmishers unsupported by artillery; next morning, however, Marshal Ney himself rode forward to reconnoitre and but for shoulder-high rye that concealed the true weakness of the Prince's position, Ney might have ridden straight through into

Brussels. Neither Ney nor Wellington knew anything of the crisis that had come and gone. All Wellington knew was that the Prince of Orange, who was now dancing at the ball, had reported all quiet on the Nivelles–Namur *chaussée* earlier in the day.

It has often been asked why Wellington did not cancel the ball at 3 pm or at any rate did not ride out to Quatre Bras at midnight to see for himself what was on the other side of the hill. Apart from Wellington's extreme sensitivity to the chances of a Belgian stab in the back, his place was in Brussels. Having at last redirected his whole army towards Quatre Bras, nothing more remained for him to do there that night. He was personally to lead out the reserve in the morning. Orders had still to be distributed among officers in Brussels and personal interviews held. Why not under the convenient camouflage of a ball? This was to be Wellington's explanation to his friends during later post-mortems of Waterloo, and it is confirmed by Lord Fitzroy Somerset's own brief statement: 'As it [the ball] was the place where every British officer of rank was likely to be found, perhaps for that reason the Duke dressed & went there.'[8]

Morale-building, duty, convenience – they all played their part in getting Wellington to the ball. And the Irish devil in him wanted to go. He would go; and see 'those fellows' damned.

Wellington's decision gave Byron his chance to include Brussels in Childe Harold's Pilgrimage and Thackeray to make Becky Sharpe roll her green eyes and flaunt her pink ball dress in a perfect setting.

> There was a sound of revelry by night,
> And Belgium's Capital had gather'd then
> Her Beauty and her Chivalry – and bright
> The lamps shone o'er fair women and brave men . . .

The ballroom, situated on the ground floor of the Richmonds' rented house in the rue de la Blanchisserie, had been transformed into a glittering palace with rose-trellised wallpaper, rich tent-like draperies and hangings in the royal colours of crimson, gold and black, and pillars wreathed in ribbons, leaves and flowers. All the ambassadors, generals and aristocrats were present as well as dashing young officers like Arthur Shakespear of the Light Dragoons and Captain Pakenham of the Royal Artillery – Sir Charles Stuart, General Alava, the Mountnorrises and Wedderburn-Websters, the Capels, Grevilles and Mrs Pole. The rear was brought up by the diplomat Mr Chad, Wellington's surgeon Dr John Hume and his chaplain the Reverend Samuel Briscall.

Wellington arrived 'rather late'. In the ballroom those officers whose regiments were at any distance were already beginning to slip quietly away. The seventeen-year-old Lady Georgiana Lennox was dancing. She immediately broke off and went up to Wellington to ask whether the rumours were true. Wellington replied, as she thought, very gravely, 'Yes, they are true, we are off tomorrow.'[9] As this terrible news (Georgiana's words) rapidly circulated, an excited buzz arose from all the tables and elegantly draped embrasures. The Duke of Brunswick felt a premonition of death and gave such a shudder that he dropped the little Prince de Ligne off his lap.[10] Some officers flew to and fro saying their good-byes and departed, others clung so desperately to the loved one's hand or to the champagne bottle that when the hour struck there was no time to change and, like the heroine of *The Red Shoes*, they had to march in their dancing pumps.

One guest, Lady Dalrymple-Hamilton, who sat for some time beside Wellington on a sofa, was struck by his anxious expression beneath the assumed gaiety: 'Frequently in the middle of a sentence he stopped abruptly and called to some officer, giving him directions, in particular to the Duke of Brunswick and Prince of Orange, who both left the ball before supper.' But even the lady on the sofa did not suspect the degree of drama with which the Prince of Orange's departure was attended.

Shortly before supper, as Wellington stood with Lady Charlotte Greville on his arm, a despatch had been brought in by Lieutenant Henry Webster from Quatre Bras for the Prince of Orange. The Prince handed it unopened to Wellington. The message, dated about 10 pm that night, announced the repulse of Prussian forces from Fleurus less than eight miles as the crow flies from Quatre Bras. As soon as Wellington had read this grim piece of news he recommended the Prince to miss supper and return straight to his headquarters in the field.

'Webster!' he called to the Prince's aide-de-camp, 'four horses instantly to the Prince of Orange's carriage. . . .' After other instructions now made necessary had been delivered in whispers or scribbles, Wellington proceeded to the supper-room.

Hardly had he sat down before the Prince of Orange reappeared and whispered something to him for several minutes. Wellington looked incredulous but said nothing except to repeat that the Prince should go back to his quarters at Braine-le-Comte and to bed. Wellington kept up an animated and smiling conversation for twenty minutes more, when a lesser man would have fled the moment he heard the Prince's news. A notable Belgian aristocrat, the Marquise d'Assche, who sat next to the Duke of Richmond and opposite the Duke of Wellington at supper, did not relish the English nonchalance. Painfully conscious that her brother was somewhere out there where the cannon had been booming at dusk, she looked across at the Duke with a jaundiced eye. His own *placement* was agreeable: Georgy Lennox on one side, who received from him a miniature of himself painted by a Belgian artist, and Frances Webster on the other. 'I would willingly have throttled him,' recalled the Marquise d'Assche, 'from the impatience which his phlegm caused me, and the ease of his conversation with Lady Withesburne [*sic*] to whom he paid ardent court.'

At last the necessary interval was up and Wellington turned casually to the Duke of Richmond.

'I think it is time for me to go to bed likewise. . . .' The party rose and moved into the hall. As Wellington was saying good-night to his host he whispered something in Richmond's ear – the last recorded and most celebrated whisper of an evening remarkable for its undertones.

'Have you a good map in the house?' He needed to discover the exact implications of the almost incredible message verbally passed on to him at the supper table by the Prince of Orange. The written message which the Prince had received from his headquarters at Braine-le-Comte was dated 15 June 1815, '10½ pm' and signed by Baron Jean de Constant Rebecque, the Prince's chief-of-staff.

The enemy, de Constant Rebecque reported, were said to have pushed up the *chaussée* towards Brussels as far as Quatre Bras. 'It has been my duty,' he continued, 'to take upon myself to instruct General de Perponcher to support his second brigade [Prince Bernhard's] by his first. . . .' De Constant Rebecque added that he had ordered all other units at or near Nivelles to stand by in readiness.

First a threat to Fleurus; now, a few minutes later, to Quatre Bras. Napoleon was forking right and left up the roads like a streak of lightning. No wonder Wellington was incredulous, or so the Prince of Orange imagined. For he wrote later across the original of de Constant Rebecque's despatch, that he had given the news it contained to the '*Duc de Wellington qui ne voulut pas le croire*'.

De Constant Rebecque's action was in fact a vital sequel to the march on Quatre Bras of Prince Bernhard during the early afternoon, which had temporarily precluded Ney from occupying the crossroads himself. But Ney's vanguard had withdrawn no further than Frasnes, only two miles south of Quatre Bras. Ney was now in charge of Napoleon's left wing as Grouchy was of his right, and they would almost certainly advance simultaneously up the Frasnes and Fleurus roads at dawn on the 16th. Therefore around 8pm de Constant Rebecque had decided on his own initiative to reinforce Quatre Bras that night. What his despatch did not reveal was that Wellington's earlier order to concentrate at Nivelles had arrived when Perponcher's two brigades were already beyond it. To obey would have meant marching back again, away from the guns. Rebecque showed the order to Perponcher in silence. Perponcher looked at it with the sightless eye that common sense prescribed. The two tacitly agreed to ignore it and to pursue their plan of strengthening Wellington's position at Quatre Bras, the crossroads which were now literally the crux.

Once Wellington knew the full truth he acted with decision. Orderlies again scoured the country; Brussels was awake. He had guessed wrong but not irretrievably. Like a great fighter he was still on his balance, though tipped the wrong way. Now he righted himself.

The Duke of Richmond took him into his study next to the ballroom and spread out a map. Wellington looked at it wryly:

'Napoleon has *humbugged* me, by God! he has gained twenty-four hours' march on me.'

'What do you intend doing?'

'I have ordered the army to concentrate at Quatre Bras; but we shall not stop him there, and if so, I must fight him *here*.' Wellington passed his thumbnail over the map just south of the Waterloo position. Then he left the scene of his acute discomfort, avoiding for once the hall door.

The party hardly looked like a ball any longer. Guests were scurrying rather than drifting away. Georgiana Lennox went out to help her brother Lord March, another of the Prince of Orange's aides-de-camp, to pack. Wellington returned to his hotel for under two hours' sleep, between 3 am and 5 am on the morning of 16 June. He was interrupted by the arrival of yet another delayed despatch describing the Prussian position. 'I cannot tell the world,' he said afterwards, 'that Blücher picked the fattest man in his army to ride with an express to me, and that he took thirty hours to go thirty miles.' He also remarked later that anxiety never kept him awake.

'I don't like lying awake, it does no good. I make a point never to lie awake.'

So he slept soundly through the rising clamour of bugle calls, bagpipes, drum-beats, hammering, shouting, neighing, barking, crying. In the Park Picton inspected his division at 4 am and soon his green-jacketed riflemen and kilted Highlanders went swinging out of the Namur gate for Quatre Bras, the Highlanders marching so steadily that the black plumes on their bonnets scarcely quivered. It was only an hour or two earlier that some of their sergeants had been dancing reels for the amusement and education of the Duchess of Richmond's Belgian guests. Captain Johnny Kincaid, still with his 95th Rifles, spent the early hours either asleep on a Brussels pavement or advising agitated civilians to 'keep themselves perfectly cool'. Sir Augustus Frazer, commanding the Horse Artillery as in the Peninsula, received an early report that Wellington was moving at 6.30 am to Waterloo – or so Sir George Wood thought, who commanded the Artillery. Frazer could not find the odd-sounding place on the map and remarked disgustedly that this was 'the old story over again'. He sent to de Lancey, the quartermaster-general, to learn 'the real name'. Captain Cavalié Mercer, commanding 'G' Troop of Frazer's Horse Artillery, woke up with a jump to find himself abruptly ordered to proceed to Enghien 'with the utmost diligence'. The rush and bustle, the sounding of the 'boot and saddle' followed by the 'turn-out' and parade, were in Mercer's words 'animating and soul-stirring'.[12] Twenty-seven-year-old John Haddy James, however, assistant-surgeon to the 1st Life Guards and no veteran, found the trumpets sounding 'to horse' at 2 am, the sudden confusion and the troops' sardonic humour somewhat daunting.

'I don't think I shall go to bed now,' shouted a Hussar, rolling up drunk to answer the call to arms.

'Belike you will be put to bed with a shroud this night,' said a Life Guard, who overheard him, 'and know nothing about it.'

Frederick Ponsonby, colonel of the 12th Light Dragoons, met one of his captains, William Hay, and said ruefully,

'You were lucky not to go to the ball, I am quite knocked up . . .'[13]

Wellington was up at 5.30 am and out giving orders.

By 8 am Brussels was returning to serenity and the quiet clip-clop of donkeys bringing in their loads of cauliflowers and strawberries for the civilian population. Lady Dalrymple-Hamilton, who had left the ball at 2.30 am and watched from her window the Highlanders passing at four, was woken at eight by her maid.

'Oh my lady, get up quick; there he goes, God bless him, and he will not come back till he is King of France!'[14]

It was Wellington at the head of his staff riding off to Quatre Bras.

22

Quatre Bras:
The Knotted Rope

The Duke trotted into Quatre Bras on 16 June 1815 at 10 am. The scene at the crossroads, twenty-one miles from Brussels and twelve from Charleroi, was hardly less quiet than the city he had left behind. He was not surprised, for a reassuring despatch from the Prince of Orange was in his pocket.

Near Frasnes, June 16, 1815
7 am

My dear Duke – I am just arrived. The French are in possession of Frasnes, near *Quatre Bras* . . . but not as yet in force. . . .[1]

In fact Ney's force at Frasnes, only two miles away, already outnumbered the Dutch–Belgians at Quatre Bras by nearly three to one in men and seven to one in guns; but the rolling, wooded country concealed the two armies from one another.

The Prince went on to inform Wellington that he had immediately sent for one of his Dutch–Belgian cavalry brigades from Nivelles and at the same time ordered his sharp-shooters to cease fire, which had the desired effect of further tranquillizing the enemy.

At 10.30 am, after having heartily approved the Prince's disposition of his exiguous force, Wellington dictated a memorandum for Blücher: the Anglo-Dutch reinforcements would reach Genappe and Nivelles by noon; he would wait at Quatre Bras until they arrived. An hour or so later he realized that his memorandum had been guilty of wildly optimistic predictions. His reinforcements would reach him nothing like so soon. He therefore decided to ride the six miles over to Blücher, concert their joint plans and incidentally put the picture right.

About 1 pm Henry Hardinge, Wellington's young attaché with the Prussians and as such Müffling's opposite number, saw a small party approaching Blücher's headquarters on horses with cut tails. Guessing they were English he rode out to meet them. A few minutes later Wellington and Blücher were together climbing the windmill of Bussy

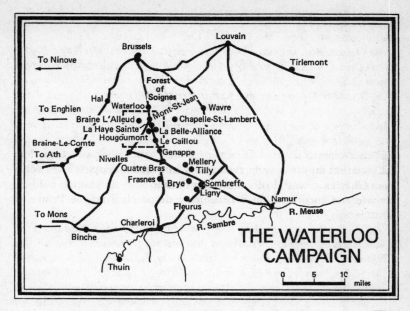

THE WATERLOO CAMPAIGN

on a ridge behind Ligny. At the top they opened their telescopes. The sight revealed to Wellington was alarming.

Napoleon was clearly visible among his staff. He too had his telescope out; indeed, the three generals may at that historic moment have been looking at one another. Napoleon's 68,000 infantry and 12,500 cavalry confronted Blücher across the Ligny brook. Blücher, it is true, commanded 84,000 Prussians; but they were drawn up on forward slopes with no cover from the enemy's imminent cannonade. Wellington muttered to Hardinge,

'If they fight here they will be damnably mauled.' Then he faced Blücher and Gneisenau and said the same thing more tactfully.

'Everybody knows their own army best; but if I were to fight here, I should expect to be beat.'

'My men like to see their enemy,' replied Gneisenau with annoyance. A forward position was in fact taken for granted by Continental armies, and the magic of the 'reverse slope' was Wellington's alone. The discussion ended with Wellington giving the suspicious Gneisenau a pledge of support, though a qualified one.

'Well! I will come, provided *I am not attacked myself*.'[2] He then started to ride back. As he neared the crossroads at 2.20 pm nine cannon-shots sounded in threes at regular intervals in his rear. It was the signal for Napoleon's advance. The battle of Ligny had begun.

At Quatre Bras the lull was over. Since just before noon Ney's 20,000 men of his IInd Corps had been on the move. The thick dark columns shouted, sang, drummed and stamped their way up the Brussels road. The Prince of Orange's force had increased to sixteen guns and 8,000 men, but it was still as slender as Slender Billy himself. And behind the IInd Corps was Ney's Ist Corps under d'Erlon with 20,000 more men and guns to match. By 2.30 pm the main obstacles to Ney's capture of the vital crossroads, including the hill and farm of Quatre Bras, had fallen. It remained only to clear the large wood of Bossu. That done, Quatre Bras would be his. Next morning at 7 am Ney would be precisely where Napoleon hoped, insisted and positively foretold – in Brussels.

As Wellington galloped up, the resilient young Prince did his best to break the bad news cheerfully. At that instant there was a roar of *'Vive l'Empereur!'* A powerful voice began chanting the famous jingle that had spurred French soldiers all over the world to gain and glory: *'L'Empereur récompensera celui qui s'avancera!'* Wellington did not need to hear it twice.

'That must be Ney going down the line. I know what that means: we shall be attacked in five minutes!'[3]

The time was 3 pm. Wellington had returned after an absence of several hours to find the battle of Quatre Bras not only begun but in a fair way to being lost. Could even he retrieve a situation so desperate? The only other question worth asking was why Ney, with overwhelming force since morning, had not won hours ago.

It is true that if Ney had done for Napoleon what Rebecque did for Wellington the Allies might have been swept out of Quatre Bras by noon. By that high standard Ney no doubt deserved some of the epithets which have since been hurled at him – lethargic, slow-witted, shell-shocked. Napoleon, however, was at least as culpable. His first orders of the day did not reach Ney until 11 am, nor did they convey a clear-cut sense of urgency. Ney was not to march forthwith but only to be ready to march as soon as his reserves reached him. General Reille, meanwhile, proved to be no less lethargic than Ney himself. Expatiating to Ney on the 'blind' country around Quatre Bras, Reille suggested waiting, as ordered, for d'Erlon.

'This is going to be a battle as in Spain,' he hinted darkly, 'where the English only showed themselves at the last moment.' But Ney's blood was up at last. Having been beaten in the Peninsula by

Wellington's brains he was not going to be beaten at Quatre Bras by his mere reputation. Without waiting for d'Erlon he ordered the attack.

Nevertheless Reille's healthy respect for Wellington continued to prevent the French attack from turning into an avalanche. While Wellington was hurrying to the battlefield his reputation was there already, fighting for him.

Once on the spot, Wellington met the crisis at the crossroads with an immediate and daring counter-stroke particularly aimed at the captured farm buildings on his left. At all costs he must play for time and keep in his hands the *chaussée* linking Quatre Bras to Ligny. The weakness of his line was partially concealed by the standing corn which in those days the farmers grew to a height of five or six feet for the straw. Behind him Picton's 8,000 men had come up from prolonged 'cooking' at Waterloo, though they still had to be deployed. Behind Picton were the Brunswickers in their black uniforms – in mourning for the Duke of Brunswick's father, killed at Jena. Behind them were the Nassauers from Ussingen, the Hanoverians, Halkett's brigade, the Guards . . . Time was on his side.

By the time Ney was ready to launch his second, far more massive assault, Picton's division was in action and the pattern of Quatre Bras was beginning to emerge. Time and time again Wellington's thin line was destined to receive the furious onrush of cavalry preceded by a cannonade and stinging swarm of sharpshooters; every time something would give way for lack of ammunition, cavalry support or guns, and there would be imminent risk of a breakthrough or envelopment of one or other of his flanks; always some contingent which had received its marching orders from him the night before would come up in the nick of time – each new arrival a *deus ex machina* to save him from destruction.

Ney also had his share of divine apparitions, but in his case they took the form of confused messages emanating from Napoleon and sailing down on a cloud which formed part of the fog of war. It is this dramatic contrast that still gives Quatre Bras the power to move today – on Wellington's side a steady build-up from the most desperate weakness (7,000 troops) to superiority (26,000) and on to absolute supremacy (36,000); on Ney's, no increase whatever on his original 20,000 men but constant depredations on his temper and judgement. Looked at another way, Ney's *deus ex machina* should have been Count Drouet d'Erlon; thanks to counter-orders from Ligny, d'Erlon was to be the god who never descended. Ney's bitter experiences were the bones of the battle and imposed its shape.

At 4.15 pm the voice from Ligny first spoke to Ney; that is, for the first time since the battle of Quatre Bras began. A 'definitive' despatch dictated by Napoleon to Soult at 2 pm ordered Ney to destroy immediately any force in his front (i.e. Wellington) and then to swing right and envelop '*un corps de troupes*' which Grouchy was on the point of assaulting at Ligny.

This message, far from conveying to Ney the fact that *un corps de troupes* meant the whole Prussian army and that Grouchy therefore required reinforcements, simply impressed Ney with the burning need for reinforcements of his own. He sent an urgent message to d'Erlon at Frasnes. Let him lose not a moment in bringing up the Ist Corps.

Wellington had held or driven off Ney's onslaught on his left and centre but a body of young, raw Dutch–Belgian troops in Bossu wood gave way. The Duke of Brunswick, sent to support them, was beaten back and both Netherlanders and Brunswickers broke and fled. Brunswick, with the badge of a death's-head already grinning on his cap, was hit by a ball in the stomach while trying to rally his countrymen. He died that evening. He was the brother of Princess Caroline of Wales.

On the battlefield, the defeated Netherlanders continued in head-long flight from Ney's Chasseurs, leaving havoc in their train. First, Wellington and Fitzroy Somerset who were up in front had to gallop for their lives, Wellington skimming a bank and ditch lined with Picton's Gordon Highlanders.

'Ninety-second, lie down!' he shouted as he sailed over the retracted *chevaux de frise* of bayonets. 'On a worse horse,' commented Fitzroy, 'he might not have escaped!'[4] Nor if he had been a less athletic rider.

The flight of the young Netherlanders, many of them mere boys, had no permanent effect; indeed it put the veteran 92nd on their mettle. Wellington's opponent, moreover, was about to be visited again from on high, a visitation far more devastating to Ney and valuable to Wellington than all the volleys of British infantry so far assembled. A message from Count d'Erlon disclosed that he and his 20,000 men had been halted just short of Quatre Bras on the pencilled order of Napoleon's aide-de-camp, La Bédoyère, and marched off to Ligny.

Ney was beside himself. He could not know that Napoleon only needed d'Erlon on the Prussian flank to fell the staggering giant with a blow from which he would never recover. All Ney knew was that one mad stroke had suddenly halved the threat to Wellington. Before he had recovered from the shock he was called on again in an Imperial order dated 3.15 pm to look sharp, finish off the business at Quatre Bras

and fall on Blücher's rear. This time the divine voice, as interpreted by
Soult, added to its instructions a solemn warning and exhortation: 'The
fate of France is in your hands.' At the same instant Wellington, as if
supernaturally guided, threw the newly arrived Hanoverian division
into the attack.

Ney could bear no more. If the fate of France was in his hands, so was
the fate of his corps commander, d'Erlon, or soon would be. He ordered
d'Erlon to return forthwith. A speeding aide found the Ist Corps about
to enter the Ligny battlefield. D'Erlon took the easy way out. He turned
round and began, like the noble Duke of York, marching back again.

As the savage fighting at Quatre Bras reached its climax
Wellington's strokes, always controlled and effective, were countered
with a fury that was sometimes crazy, sometimes sublime. At 5 pm his
infantry were submitted to a sudden, fantastic onslaught of cavalry led
by Kellermann, the brilliant negotiator of Cintra. A frantic Ney had
launched him with the watchword, 'The Fate of France is in your
hands' and the staccato commands, 'Crush them. Ride them down.'
Kellermann dashed in with his single brigade and before Wellington
knew where he was he had a few daredevil French squadrons for the
first time in possession of his crossroads.

Then came the reaction. Without immediate support, Kellermann
was at the mercy of a raking musket-fire from the 30th and 73rd of
Halkett's brigade, and the usual assortment of 'delicacies' (grape and
canister) from a hidden battery. Ensign Macready (brother of the
famous actor) and some others of the 30th had got left behind by their
regiment in the early morning dash for Quatre Bras. As they now
panted up, a crowd of wounded from a regiment that had suffered
severely, the 44th, cheered and called out faintly:

'Push on old three tens – pay 'em for the 44th – you're much wanted,
boys – success to you my darlings.' A Gordon Highlander, bleeding to
death from a severed arm, gasped out to Morris of the 73rd:

'Go on, 73rd, give them pepper! I've got my Chelsea commission.'[5]
Wellington himself saw to it that the volleys of his Gordon
Highlanders were lethal.

'92nd, don't fire till I tell you!'[6] He allowed the huge French
Cuirassiers to come pounding up to within thirty yards of his steady
square.

'Fire!' Riders and horses dropped or fled. A British ball got
Kellermann's charger but the quick-witted general managed to seize
two of his troopers' bits and run off the field between them. Still the

French cavalry came on. As fast as a column was beaten off another was rallied and reformed for a new attack. Wellington's old 33rd, having withstood the fire of a French battery from Bossu wood, succumbed to a cry, 'The cavalry are coming!' and instead of getting into square, melted away. But as ever at a critical juncture reinforcements came up, this time the Guards.

Suddenly a fourth apparition, Soult's staff officer, Major Baudus, appeared to Ney with the news that Napoleon now attached little importance to his doings at Quatre Bras but much to the arrival of d'Erlon at Ligny. It was the end for Ney. His face turned as red as his hair and speechless with rage he turned his back on Baudus and rushed on foot – his second horse had just been killed under him – to rally his faltering columns.

Wellington's crisis was over, once the Guards and fresh Brunswickers had brought up his ever-growing force to 36,000 men and seventy guns. 'It was now his turn to attack,' writes Houssaye, '– and to attack with certainty of success, as was his wont.'[7] The tone of Houssaye's last phrase, implying that a greater than Wellington would have taken a chance earlier, will be familiar to Wellington's successors in the British Army.

At 6.30 pm the Allied bugles sounded the advance.* The Guards had the honour of clearing Bossu woods, over which hung a great cloud of black smoke. They succeeded, though with severe losses, 'not perhaps going about it', according to Fitzroy Somerset, 'as a Rifle or Light Corps would have done'. Ensign Batty, who went into Bossu wood with the 1st Foot Guards, wrote: 'The trees were so thick, that it was beyond anything difficult to effect a passage. . . . Our loss was most tremendous. . . .'[8]

The Guards had approached Quatre Bras in the later afternoon, as their assistant surgeon, John Haddy James, recalled. The interesting sight of Germans marching along with outsize packs and sacred music could not keep James's eyes from a sinister cloud to the south – a solid pyramid with a perfectly flat base. 'It was the canopy which the combatants had formed for themselves.' The marchers of the German Legion, including Edmund Wheatley, arrived just too late. Most of the cavalry missed the battle also. Like Arthur Shakespear and William Hay, they had long distances to cover, Hay fifty-two miles. When he

---

* Bugles not trumpets were used on the battlefield, since trumpets, being several feet long, were too cumbersome to carry.

and his colonel, Frederick Ponsonby of the 12th Light Dragoons, at last reached the scene of carnage, Ponsonby immediately made for a dead Frenchman's cuirasse, punctured in three places.

'I wanted to find out if these cuirasses were ball-proof or not; this plainly shows they are not.'[9]

One thing Shakespear, like Ponsonby and Hay, was in time to see: his first vision of the famous Cuirassiers. Six of them were lying dead close together at the corner of Bossu wood. That was how Wellington remembered them when he later gave his opinion that these armour-plated champions (partly Saint Denis and partly a tank) were not worth it. At a party in the Admiralty in 1826, someone asked the Duke whether the Cuirassiers 'had not *come up very well at Waterloo*?'.

'Yes, and *they went down very well too*,' replied the Duke with his whooping laugh. After the 92nd gave them a couple of volleys at Quatre Bras, he explained, they could not get up but lay sprawling and kicking in their cuirasses and jackboots 'like so many *turned* turtles'.[10]

By 9 pm Dr James's solid pyramid had faded, darkness was falling and the battle was over. Sergeant Robertson and his Gordon High-landers turned to their sombre and respectful task of removing the wounded and burying as many dead as possible – 'especially the officers'.[11] In every sense the battle had been a draw. The heavy casualties were almost equal: 4,800 Allied losses (exactly half of them British) and only a few hundred less French. It was perhaps that slight balance in Napoleon's favour that made him claim a victory, for there was no other justification. Both sides were back to start at nightfall, Wellington holding Quatre Bras, Ney in Frasnes. As far as objectives went, each had prevented the other from achieving his aim. Wellington checkmated Ney's advance to envelop Blücher; Ney prohibited Wellington from sending Blücher help.

D'Erlon's imbecile promenade, caused by Soult and Napoleon, contributed to the draw in its own way. Not a shot had been fired by his veterans on either battlefield all day.

Wellington was not the man to underestimate the help he had received from d'Erlon. Writing to one of the Ponsonbys some time later, he said that Napoleon's greatest disaster during the Hundred Days was his failure to persuade Berthier to rejoin him. If his skilful chief-of-staff had been there to interpret the voice, instead of the bumbling Soult, d'Erlon would have got somewhere, there would have been no Waterloo and Napoleon would have lasted much longer.

Berthier, however, having refused to fight for Napoleon, had fallen out of a window on 1 June 1815. In choosing Soult as a substitute Napoleon picked the wrong man.

Firing in the direction of Ligny ceased about 9 pm also. As Wellington and his staff trotted back the three miles to Genappe where supper and beds were awaiting them at the *Roi d'Espagne*, he cheerfully assumed Blücher had repulsed the enemy.

'Blücher is a damned fine old Fellow,' he said to Fitzroy as they rode along side by side.[12]

So he was, even finer than Wellington guessed. At that moment Blücher was lying in a cottage crammed with wounded at Mellery, unknown to the rest of his army, battered, bruised and dosed up to the eyes; in fact 'damnably mauled'.

Napoleon had relentlessly burnt and blasted the exposed Prussian columns, until the Ligny stream flowed red like a river in hell. Blücher led a last gallant cavalry charge; its failure was complete. His horse was killed, and he was twice ridden over. Only the presence of mind of his aide-de-camp, Nostitz, who threw a cloak over his medals, saved him from being recognized and taken prisoner. 16,000 of his Prussians were casualties, as against 12,000 French, while 8,000 more of his 'children', as he called them, were streaming over the dark fields towards home. Gneisenau had taken over.

Something of this reached Wellington's ears when he entered the inn at Genappe. He found an agitated young captain there, brother of Henry Hardinge whose left hand had been shot off at Ligny. Captain Hardinge was looking for a surgeon; though he could not be sure, he thought there had been a Prussian defeat.

Wellington, always optimistic, hoped that young Hardinge's gloomy report was due to his anxiety over his brother. His actions, however, showed no complacency. He was not in bed until nearly midnight but rose again at 3 am, galloped straight back to Quatre Bras and sent Gordon, his ADC, to Ligny to find out the worst.[13]

In Brussels, meanwhile, the booming of the guns had brought large crowds on to the ramparts towards the evening of the 16th. Lady Charlotte Greville's house became a centre where news of Quatre Bras was disseminated. At night young Major Hamilton rode in to tell them about the day's two most dramatic events: Brunswick dead and Wellington nearly captured.

It is probable that Wellington was not averse to accounts of his narrow escape being circulated. Despite Vitoria and Orthez there had been persistent, malicious rumours since May 1814 that 'he had not over-exposed himself to danger' in the Peninsula.[14] His many raw troops at Quatre Bras had now seen for themselves what sort of a man this 'Nosey' was.

The crossroads were chilly at 6 am on 17 June 1815, as Wellington waited for Gordon's return from Ligny in a draughty hut made of branches. '92nd, I will be obliged to you for a little fire.'[15] His Highlanders lit one for him and were much pleased with his enthusiastic thanks.

It was nearly 7.30 am when Gordon returned, his horse in a lather and his news so grave that he preferred to whisper it to his chief. Wellington appeared totally unmoved. He gave Gordon some quick orders and turned to Captain George Bowles.

'Old Blücher has had a damned good licking and gone back to Wavre, eighteen miles. As he has gone back, we must go too.'

For a brief moment he could not help wondering how his retreat would appear to the Opposition.

'I suppose in England they will say we have been licked. I can't help it; as they are gone back, we must go too.'[16]

Few of Wellington's staff could at first find Wavre on the map. They imagined it, reported Fitzroy Somerset, to be only a little in the rear of Ligny, never dreaming that Blücher could have fallen back so far. Müffling soon disillusioned them. '*Ma foi, c'est fort loin!*' he exclaimed.

Together he and Müffling debated the next move. Was a renewed challenge to Napoleon by the combined Anglo-Dutch and Prussian armies still possible? They agreed that it was. Wellington would retire level with Wavre and await a further report from Blücher.

Exactly how bad the Prussian affair had been was not known to Wellington until much later, if ever. When Gneisenau stood in the moonlight on the night of the 16th and ordered, 'Retreat on ... Wavre',[17] his options were wide open. From Wavre he could indeed keep in touch with Wellington – or strike off obliquely through Louvain to his home bases in the north-east. Wellington rightly hailed the Wavre decision as crucial. 'It was the decisive moment of the century,' he wrote after Waterloo.[18] But the moment was Blücher's. The indomitable old man, partially resuscitated, was discovered during the night by Gneisenau at Mellery. Blücher and his quartermaster-general demolished Gneisenau's arguments for parting company from Wellington. It was not the least of Blücher's victories.

Next morning, 17 June, Blücher summoned Hardinge and embraced his *'lieber Freund'*, despite Hardinge's amputation and his own highly spiced condition. *'Ich stinke etwas,'* he said, apologizing for the results of last night's medicinal debauch on gin and rhubarb flavoured with garlic. Before setting off for Wavre he bathed his bruises in brandy and fortified his stomach with a generous *schnapps*. Then, fit for anything, he rode out with his men, sending ripples of good humour all down the line.[19]

It was 8 am when Wellington finished his business in the hut. He came out and for an hour paced up and down alone in front of his 'splendid Mansion' (as a Highlander called the hut), his left hand behind his back and in his right a switch which he sometimes gave a ruminative chew. The same observant Highlander calculated that his Grace was travelling at a speed of $3\frac{1}{2}$–4 miles an hour. He and Müffling had just settled themselves on the grass when at 9 am the first personal message of the day arrived from Blücher. Old Marshal 'Vorwaerts' had gone backwards but was in great heart. What did Wellington intend?

Wellington intended to retreat – to stand – to fight. A year ago he himself had reconnoitred the open ground in front of the Forest of Soignes and the village of Waterloo. His engineers had been surveying the ridges to the south of Waterloo during the past weeks. That was where he had put his thumb on the Duke of Richmond's map. That was where he would defend Brussels – if Blücher could support him 'even with one corps only'.

The retreat began an hour later at 10 am, Wellington sending ahead his quartermaster-general, de Lancey, to mark out the army's positions. Not everyone was happy to surrender the ground so heroically fought for the day before. Picton was surly to a degree, and later denounced the 'Waterloo' position as one of the worst ever chosen. Only his servant knew that he had had two ribs broken at Quatre Bras.

Wellington covered his army's retreat with a strong screen of cavalry and artillery, including a few of the Congreve rockets that had given him so little satisfaction in the Peninsula. He had been at his most characteristic when the question of using these rockets was first mooted. Major Edward Whinyates, to whose troop they belonged, was sharply forbidden to take with him such poor substitutes for guns. One of Whinyates's superior officers, however, dared to plead his cause with Wellington.

'It will break poor Whinyates's heart to lose his rockets.'

'Damn his heart, sir; let my order be obeyed.'[20] After the big bark the Duke had promptly relented and allowed Whinyates to bring 800 rockets to Quatre Bras. Here they were, ready to prove themselves.

At intervals during the morning, Wellington rode forward and swept the Frasnes and Namur roads with his telescope. The French were so strangely quiet that for a moment an odd thought struck him: perhaps Ney like himself was retreating after all.

At Ligny and Frasnes also there was, if not a retreat, an unaccountable pause. Napoleon, tired and torpid despite seven hours' sleep, had begun the day badly by dictating one of his obscure messages to Ney who received the impression that Saturday 17 June was to be a day of rest and revictualling – apart from the occupation of Quatre Bras.

Should this prove impossible, you must report at once all details and the Emperor will move in your direction. . . .[21]

Ney's men were out requisitioning their breakfasts as usual, and Wellington was still at Quatre Bras, in force; its capture did indeed seem '*impossible*', unless the Emperor should arrive, as promised, with help. The Emperor, however, remained in a curiously detached though unusually agreeable mood. Suddenly at 11 am he awoke, as only he could, to the needs of the day. Marshal Grouchy was packed off with 33,000 men to shadow Blücher, having been earlier slapped down with the remark – 'I will give you orders when I judge it to be convenient.' By noon Napoleon was at length advancing along the east–west *chaussée* to join Ney in the day's long-postponed attack. They were too late. At 1 pm a stray camp-follower brought astounding news from Quatre Bras. The village was empty. Wellington had flown.

Napoleon turned to d'Erlon and said with acid emphasis in front of Ney:

'*On a perdu la France.*'

It was Wellington's own cool, even carefree behaviour that had set the tone for the retreat. Anxious officers were cheered to see him sitting on the grass between reconnaissances, laughing over the tittle-tattle in the London newspapers. Once he lay down in his cloak and slept for a few minutes with the gossip columns of the *Sun* shading his face. General Alava joined him from Brussels in an apprehensive state. Was he still the same imperturbable Wellington who had never failed in Spain? The great man's first words to him set his mind at rest:

'*Etiez vous chez Lady Charlotte Greville hier soir?*'[22]

When the Duke added that his defence of the new position at

Waterloo would give those fellows the devil of a surprise, Alava knew for certain all was well.

Waiting about for one's turn to retreat was an unpleasant experience, thought the Guards' young surgeon, John James. Just then Wellington and his staff trotted past. His smile and 'air of calm put heart into us all'.[23]

When the order was given for the Guards to move off, Wellington felt that the testing operation was almost over.

'Well, there is the last of the infantry gone,' he said briskly, 'and I don't care.'[24]

The time was 2 pm. He turned abruptly to the commander of his rear-guard, Lord Uxbridge.

'No use waiting. The sooner you get away the better. No time to be lost.'[25] And indeed something bright and shiny was beginning to emerge from the *chaussée*. Wellington thought it was bayonets. Uxbridge said lancers. Sir Hussey Vivian handed Wellington his own spy-glass. It was lancers. In a few moments the vision became vast and awe-inspiring: billows of startlingly white dust rolling through the vivid green trees, and marching columns glittering in the rays of a sickly sun that was fast being swallowed up by the inkiest, most pendulous thunder-cloud that Captain Mercer and his troop of horse-artillery had ever seen. An ominous wind rushed down from the north-west. A deep shadow had already swept over the British rearguard. To complete the 'ballet of war',[26] as Colonel Taylor of the 10th Hussars called it, a single, dark horseman whom Mercer at once recognized as Napoleon himself, stood silhouetted for an instant against the still brilliant fields to the south.

Suddenly there was a violent detonation and sheet of flame as the British guns opened. A second later the swollen storm-cloud, blasted by the concussion, burst apart with a flash and a roar like a gigantic battery, reducing the man-made cannonade to a whisper. Even Wellington, who knew the rains in India, had never seen such a storm. Others spoke of a tropical drenching, tubs, pitchers and walls of water.

'Captain Mercer, are you loaded?' yelled Uxbridge through the din.

'Yes, my lord.'

'Then give them a round as they rise the hill, and retire as quickly as possible.' Turning to Colonel Frederick Ponsonby of the 12th –

'Light dragoons, threes right, at a trot, march!' William Hay, who was in the leading squadron, had always been taught to lead on steadily, but it was utterly impossible when the word was constantly piped from behind, 'Faster, faster in front.'[27]

Faster and faster they flew, firing and galloping, until many had safely squeezed through the dangerous bottle-neck of the single Genappe street – for Uxbridge dared not take his cavalry off the paved road into the surrounding fields. They had suddenly become a quagmire.

'Make haste! – make haste! for God's sake, gallop, or you will be taken!' shouted Uxbridge more vehemently than ever. However, the water-logged ground prevented the French from exhibiting their usual cross-country agility, and fighting on 17 June petered out in skirmishes and artillery duels where Major Whinyates's rockets played a picaresque part. The first rocket demolished a French gun and its crew, but all the rest either shot vertically into the air or wriggled sideways, one turning to the right about and chasing Captain Mercer up the Brussels road.

Captain (later General) Mercer's rip-roaring story of the retreat – 'a confused dream' – 'wild' – 'all blunder and confusion' – makes such good reading that it may have misled Houssaye into calling the retreat a 'mad flight'. It was no such thing. After the first rush through Genappe, Uxbridge noted that 'the retreat was conducted at a walk'. Fitzroy Somerset did not disagree. Wellington, he wrote, 'proceeded leisurely towards Waterloo. . . .'[28]

Napoleon had started too late and the weather did not forgive.

By the late afternoon of the 17th Wellington was approaching the ridges in front of Waterloo where he meant to do battle next day. On the first of these ridges stood the inn of *La Belle-Alliance*, to the right of the road.

At this point Lord Fitzroy Somerset enters the story with a most interesting but unforeseen disclosure about Wellington's strategy, forming part of his account of the Waterloo campaign apparently written in 1816:

. . . on arriving near to La Belle Alliance He [the Duke] thought it was the position the Qr. M. Genl. would have taken up, being the most commanding ground, but He [de Lancey] had found it too extended to be occupied by our Troops, & so had proceeded further on & had marked out a position.

So much has been written about Wellington's inspired choice of the crossroads on the Mont-Saint-Jean ridge for his Waterloo battle-ground, that it is hard to believe this was not his first preference. Yet

Somerset was close to Wellington and had long been renowned for his truthfulness, exact execution of his master's orders and accurate echo of his master's voice. The *Belle-Alliance* site would certainly have meant a much larger battlefield, though one not lacking in essential features such as reverse slopes, a good lateral road to the right (facing south) and tracks off to the left. Moreover, Wellington had made a point of not fortifying *à la* Torres Vedras whatever site he selected, for this would have given the show away to Napoleon. It is possible that his passion for preserving the elasticity and secrecy of his plans kept his colleagues as well as Napoleon in the dark.

The *Belle-Alliance* position having been left to Napoleon (though of course in reverse, facing north instead of south) Wellington went on to climb the ridge at Mont-Saint-Jean, quietly entering his headquarters in the village of Waterloo. He soon found, however, that his opponent was determined not to be kept in the dark any longer. The Emperor ordered some batteries to begin firing and the English incautiously made reply, thus revealing their position. Wellington began the evening in a raging temper.

Another, less successful attempt made soon afterwards by Lord Uxbridge to extract information probably tried the Duke's temper almost as much; this time his practice of giving short answers in order to preserve self-control was successful. Lord Uxbridge, who would be his successor as Commander-in-Chief if the finger of Providence were unexpectedly withdrawn, wished to know before he went to bed something of the great man's strategy. The Duke listened to him in formidable silence. At the end of the recital he briefly asked,

'Who will attack the first to-morrow, I or Bonaparte?'

'Bonaparte.'

'Well, Bonaparte has not given me any idea of his projects: and as my plans will depend upon his, how can you expect me to tell you what mine are?' Then he got up, put his hand on the general's shoulder and said encouragingly:

'There is one thing certain, Uxbridge, that is, that whatever happens, you and I will do our duty.'[29]

Only a leader of moral grandeur could afford to preach such pragmatism.

In later years he used to dwell lovingly on the pragmatic theme, with special reference to his method of defeating the French marshals:

They planned their campaigns just as you might make a splendid piece of harness. It

19 *The Duchess of Wellington, by Sir Thomas Lawrence, 1814.*

20 *Princess Pauline Borghese, Napoleon's sister. When asked by friends about the pose she said it was quite all right as the studio was well heated.*

21 *Madame de Staël.*

22 *Giuseppina Grassini.*

25 Right *Napoleon escapes from Elba. A hostile cartoon: his steed, Liberty, bleeding from bit and spurs, is led by folly and the Devil, and manures the ground with his medals; his eagle, with a peacock's tail, flies ahead bearing 'General Peace'; but Death marches behind with a scythe and a placard: 'I am going to follow him to Mont St Jean'.*

23 *Prince von Blücher, Field Marshal of the Prussian forces, a sketch from the life when on his visit to London, June 1814, by Major-General Birch Reynardson.*

26 Right *the Duchess of Richmond's ball, 15 June 1815. The guests, with Wellington in the centre, receive news of Napoleon's advance against the Prussians.*

Fleurs du printems si chères aux français,
Vous nous rendrez notre gloire et la paix.

24 *Napoleon's favourite flower. He always said that he would return from Elba with the violets of spring. This bouquet conceals the faces of the Emperor, the Empress Marie-Louise, and their son the King of Rome. The caption reads 'Flowers of spring so dear to the French, You will give us back our glory and peace.'*

RETOUR DE L'ILE D'ELBE, IL RAMENE LA LIBERTÉ !.....

27 *Copenhagen, Wellington's chestnut charger, painted posthumously by B.R. Haydon. The Duke always said it was a good likeness.*

28 *Battle of Waterloo, 18 June 1815, by Sir William Allan, now in the Royal Military Academy Sandhurst. The twin of this picture, showing the field from the French side, is in the Wellington Museum and was admired by the Duke. 'Good – very good,' he said; 'not too much smoke.' Wellington is seen here on the left in his civilian dress and small cocked hat.*

29 *Waterloo, late afternoon. Congreve rockets show up as the sun begins to sink. On the left is La Belle Alliance, in the centre La Haye Sainte with the Observatory above, built for Napoleon but not used, and on the right Wellington's Tree. An infantry square has formed near the tree, front rank kneeling to fire, and Wellington is galloping beyond it. Hougoumont flames on the horizon.*

30 *Wellington orders the general advance. We see a column of Highlanders on the left, with some puffs of smoke from Prussian cannon in the hills behind; the Duke by his tree with the remnants of his staff; the long, flattened cornstalks; La Haye Sainte with its gateway on to the road.*

31 *Meeting of Wellington and Blücher at La Belle Alliance.* 'Mein lieber Kamerad!' *exclaimed Blücher;* 'Quelle affaire!' *The artist George Jones was right to imply that their kiss was exchanged from horseback, but Wellington recollected the scene as having taken place nearer to Genappe.*

32 *The Duke of Wellington writing his Waterloo despatch. Sir Alexander Gordon is lying dead in Wellington's camp-bed next door. By the Duke's favourite niece, Lady Burghersh, 1839.*

33 'A Wellington Boot,
or the Head of the Army'.

34 'Portrait of a Noble Duke'. In this
cartoon the lines on his forehead are
made by Vittoria [sic], Salamanca
and Waterloo; his upper lip is a sentry
box; his eyes and teeth are cannon; his
eyelashes bayonets, his ears a drum and
the line of his jaw a curved sword.

**DESCRIPTION SERVICE, &c. of *Thomas Atkins, Private,*
No. 6 Company, 1st Batt. 23d Regt. Foot.**

Where Born	Parish of Odiham, Hants.
When ditto	1st January, 1781.
Height..............	5 Feet 6½ inches.
Complexion	Fair.
Hair...............	Light Brown.
Eyes...............	Hazle.
Face...............	Oval.
Marks..............	Scar above left eye—Mole on right cheek.
Former Service in other, and what Corps.....	Surrey Rangers from 25th May, 1802, to 18th February, 1804—Corps disbanded. 4th Regt. Foot from 5th July, 1806, to the 16th August, 1815—Limited Service, discharged.
Attestation in present Corps..............	10th May, 1815, for Unlimited Service.
Bounty	£7. 7s. Received, Thomas Atkins, his ×mark.
When, where, and by whom paid	On being attested at Salisbury, by A. F. Recruiting Officer .... On intermediate approval at Taunton, by A. I. District Paymaster .... On final approval at Bristol, by A. K. Paymaster ....

and Adjutant

1st Batt. 23d Regt. of Foot.

Deal, 24th June, 1815.

Com. Officer

1st Batt. 23d Regt. of Foot.

Printed by W. Clowes, Northumberland-court, Strand.

35 'Small-Book' or Pay-Book showing the name Thomas Atkins on first specimen page. The owner was Private Thomas Fisher of the 14th Foot. Note that 'Thomas Atkins' is assumed to be illiterate and makes his mark x. Thomas Fisher does likewise in the manuscript pages which follow.

36 Wellington as Master-General of the Ordnance, 1819. Ladies watch him exercising his 'hobby-horse'. 'Bless! what a Spanker!' says one. 'I hope he won't fire it at me.' 'It can't do any harm,' replies her friend, 'for he has fired it so often in various Countries, that it is nearly worn out!'

The Master of the Ordnance Exercising his Hobby

looks very well; and answers very well; until it gets broken; and then you are done for. Now I made my campaigns of ropes. If anything went wrong, I tied a knot; and went on.[30]

The rope had broken and been knotted several times already since the Waterloo campaign began, and there were still loose ends. He went to bed, according to Fitzroy Somerset, between 11 pm and midnight. He was still waiting to hear officially that Blücher was going to knot them together. The final Prussian arrangements for support had in fact been made just as his talk with Uxbridge finished.

At 11 pm Blücher received confirmation from Müffling that Wellington was actually in position to give battle at Mont-Saint-Jean. Could he now expect at least one Prussian corps? After a last session with Gneisenau, Blücher summoned Hardinge and told him triumphantly,

'Gneisenau has given in! We are going to join the Duke.'

Then he showed Hardinge the draft of his despatch in reply to Wellington.

Bülow's [IVth] Corps will set off marching to-morrow at daybreak in your direction. It will be immediately followed by the [IInd] Corps of Pirch. The Ist and IIIrd Corps will also hold themselves in readiness to proceed towards you.[31]

Next day Blücher repeated these lavish promises – double what Wellington expected – in a despatch written about 9.30 am to Müffling: ill as he was, he had made up his mind to lead his troops himself against Napoleon's right wing. Rather than miss the battle, he added later, he would be tied to his horse.

Meanwhile Wellington at Waterloo either did not sleep when he had the chance (an unheard of procedure for him) or someone or something woke him before 3 am, for at that hour he was up again, writing letters.

Beginning with Houssaye, it has been universally assumed (though never proven) that the 'something' was Blücher's messenger bringing the despatch of 11 pm. The distance between Blücher's headquarters, near Wavre, and Waterloo was fourteen miles. Though the roads were poor and the night execrable, a Prussian officer who did not lose his way should have reached Waterloo by 2 am – as all the books say a Prussian officer did. The evidence of soldiers who were close to Wellington, however, told a different story.

Both Fitzroy Somerset and Müffling stated that Blücher's despatch arrived much later next morning, Somerset at 6 am, Müffling at 9 am. Somerset wrote:

About six o'clock the Duke got on Horseback; on the way to the front of the Line, He met a Prussian Officer who came from Blücher, in consequence of the Duke having the night before, sent to Him for one or two Corps of Prussians to support Him. Blücher promised to do so.[32]

Houssaye, on whose account all others rest, brusquely dismisses Müffling's evidence as 'wrong'. Fitzroy Somerset's he had not seen, since it is now published for the first time. These two may yet turn out to have been nearest the truth. If so, this is how things went.

Wellington was waiting at Waterloo at least up to 1 or 2 am, probably longer, on the 18th for Blücher's despatch – but not in growing anxiety. He relied on Müffling's arguments delivered on the 17th that Blücher was still strong enough to support him and would not let him down. In this case, Houssaye's castigation of Wellington for waiting at Waterloo until the small hours instead of writing off Blücher and organizing a further retreat, is unjustified. 'Fortune had favoured him,' wrote Houssaye sternly and not overpleased with the goddess, 'but he had nevertheless remained too long expectant.'[33] If Houssaye could have been convinced (by Somerset's evidence) that Wellington was to remain 'expectant' for yet another four hours, he would no doubt have felt still less warmly about the Child of Fortune. But whether the official confirmation arrived at 2 am, 6 am or 9 am on Sunday 18 June, makes little difference to the real point at issue. Was Wellington a lucky gambler? Or a strategist whose security was factually if not formally guaranteed?

For whatever reason, Wellington rose between 2 am and 3 am, according to Somerset. He had been called at the same time the night before. As the rain swished and gurgled round the rambling hostelry in which he was quartered and drummed on the small chapel opposite he pulled up his armchair to the two candles on his table and began to write. It was important to explain to persons in authority how to avoid putting too much strain on the rope and its knots. First, the Ambassador, Sir Charles Stuart, must be firm with the English population of Brussels during the coming crisis. Wellington warned Stuart that Napoleon might turn his right flank at Hal, in which case he would have to retreat and uncover Brussels. (There was no mention of his left flank being turned, showing that he counted on the Prussians here.) He continued to Stuart:

Pray keep the English quiet if you can. Let them all prepare to move [to Antwerp], but neither be in a hurry or a fright, as all will yet turn out well.*

* The author possesses this letter.

Next, the Duke of Berry must also be ready to move the French royal family to Antwerp but not a moment before the enemy had actually entered Brussels.

The instant Wellington's letter was received the Duke of Berry fled. Then there was a personal letter to Lady Frances Webster.

Waterloo, *Sunday morning, 3 o'clock* June 18th 1815

Mr dear Lady Frances,

. . . We fought a desperate battle on Friday, in which I was successful, though I had but very few troops. The Prussians were very roughly handled, and retired last night which obliged me to do the same to this place yesterday. The course of the operations may oblige me to uncover Bruxelles for a moment . . . for which reason I recommend that you and your family should be prepared to move to Antwerp at a moment's notice.

I will give you the earliest information of any danger that may come to my knowledge; at present I know of none.[34]

So far the knotted rope held.

23

Waterloo: The Finger of Providence

Prologue

For the third night running the Duke had hardly any sleep. What he had was sound and dry. When he met his landlady next morning she was in tears over her danger. He slapped her cheerfully on the back:

'I answer for everything, no French person shall suffer to-day except the soldiers.'[1]

To the majority of his army bivouacking in the open, the night of 17 June 1815 had demonstrated all the suffering of war and none of its grandeur. The rain poured down ceaselessly, the ground became quaking mud.

Captain William Hay, Sergeant Edward Cotton and Ensign William Leeke, just seventeen years old, were three who believed in prayers before battle. Strength to do his duty was all Hay asked; Leeke, who was to grow up into an argumentative clergyman, thought there should be compulsory prayers for victory; Cotton, who later became a Waterloo guide, began his story with the injunction:

> Kneel, warrior, kneel; to-morrow's sun
> May see thy course of glory run.[2]

If the army had knelt it would have been to pray for the rain to stop.

The redoubtable 52nd 'Light Bobs', whom Leeke had joined five weeks earlier, were encamped in soaking corn to the west of the Brussels road. All night long tethered horses kept breaking loose and galloping down the hill to the château of Hougoumont and then back again, making Leeke dream he was in a cavalry charge.

Below, in the Hougoumont enclosures, Private Matthew Clay and some of his comrades in the 3rd Foot Guards were sleeping on the side of a wet ditch that ran beside the orchard. Back along the ridge thousands upon thousands of bedraggled soldiers lay in their sodden lines, each under his dripping blanket, yearning for the rations that were still on the commissariat wagons, grinding their way out from Brussels through the ruts and pools of the Forest of Soignes.

Some of the regimental doctors, in view of their likely work next day, felt particularly unhappy at the army's 'disastrous state'.[3] An assistant-surgeon, John Smith of the 12th Light Dragoons, was bivouacked without food, wine or water but warmed by a row of bonfires placed on the Ohain road behind the crest of the ridge, and fed with furniture and farm implements from the village of Mont-Saint-Jean. The glow was watched with pleasure from across the valley by Napoleon. He had been haunted by the fear that the leopards would elude him after all by fleeing to their ships. Now he knew they were still there. Surgeon Smith fell asleep in a drain by the roadside, and as the night wore on the water gradually rose through his bundle of straw until he seemed to be lying at the bottom of a leaky boat.

If the Allies were miserable so were the French. Thanks to Napoleon's late start on the 17th, his soldiers were still taking up their positions long after darkness had fallen. Napoleon's famous '*grognards*' (old hands) grumbled as only they knew how, blaming the weather and their rationless state on treachery. Rather than lie down in seas of mud some of the soldiers slept on their horses' backs. Not a good preparation for uphill charges next day.

For the civilians, the night before Waterloo was hardly more pleasant. Fanny d'Arblay and an English friend had failed to make their escape from panic-stricken Brussels on Saturday owing to the implacable heroics of Wellington's military commandant, who refused to issue passports.

'It is not for *us*, the English, to spread alarm, or prepare for an overthrow.' He complained also of the Bourbons' tameness.

'We want blood, Madam! What we want is blood!'

Cowed by the dreadful soldier's thunder, Fanny tottered home. At 6 am on Sunday she was awakened by loud thumps and her friend calling, 'Open your door! There is not a moment to lose!'

Fanny's friend had received instructions to rush on foot to the wharf and go by barge to Antwerp. But when the two ladies arrived they heard all was lost: Wellington had commandeered every barge for the wounded and Boney was marching on Brussels.[4]

'The Horrors of that night are not to be forgot,' wrote Caroline Capel from a rustic retreat outside the city: rumours that Wellington was defeated – their courtyard full of 'poor wounded drenched soldiers and horses' – Mr Capel resolved to move again though unable to get a conveyance to Antwerp – Caroline, expecting a baby, in despair –

This has indeed come upon us like a Thief in the Night – I am afraid our Great Hero must have been deceived for he certainly has been taken by surprise.[5]

Among the wise virgins to reach Antwerp before the 'tumult, terror and misery' of a refugee avalanche, was Miss Charlotte Waldie.[6] She arrived with the first crash of the thunderstorm and had to listen at midnight to a sinister hammering in the hotel room next door. The nails were being driven into the Duke of Brunswick's coffin. At dawn on the 18th she too heard the dismal refrain that all was lost. But instead of preparing to flee, she told herself firmly that Wellington had been despaired of once before, in Portugal. She clung to the thought of Torres Vedras.

On Sunday 18 June at 6 am Wellington rode out from Waterloo village on his chestnut horse, Copenhagen, the thoroughbred that had carried him at Vitoria, the battles of the Pyrenees and Toulouse. His appearance was a tonic to the troops. Setting off along the ridge to inspect the positions taken up the night before, he began with Clinton's division on his extreme right and then moved back towards Hougoumont.

'Now Bonaparte will see how a general of sepoys can defend a position,' he said to Müffling.[7] Soon afterwards he ran into the usually exuberant Harry Smith who had sent his Juanita to Brussels and needed cheering. The sight of the Duke so 'animated' on his noble horse, so cool and clear in his orders, so hawk-like in his watch upon the enemy, struck Smith as 'delightful'. Wellington had extra loopholes made in the orchard wall and further work done on the garden wall and the rampart behind it. A battalion of Nassauers posted on the edge of the Hougoumont fields began to feel uncomfortably close to the gathering French. Finally they made off.

'Do you see those fellows run?' said Wellington to General Vincent, the Austrian attaché on his staff. 'Well, it is with these that I must win the battle, and such as these.'[8] Then he galloped over and rallied them. When a few irreconcilables aimed shots at him as he rode off, he took no notice. It was only afterwards that he remarked how different the history of Europe might have been if one of 'those fellows' had been a better shot.

Some of his orders at Hougoumont were made on General Müffling's advice, who feared that this vital bastion on the army's right flank would prove untenable. Wellington reassured him.

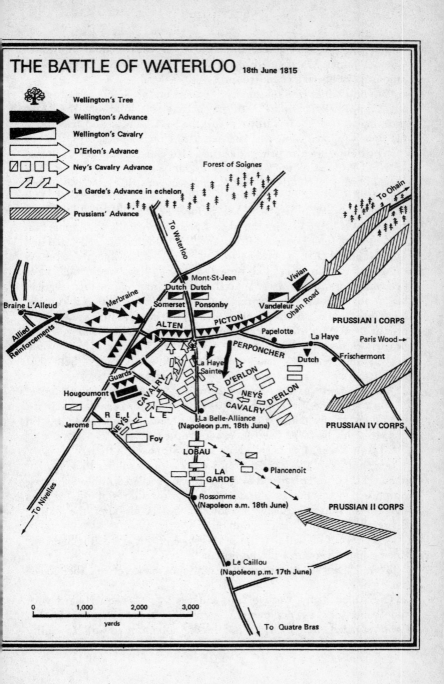

THE BATTLE OF WATERLOO 18th June 1815

Wellington's Tree
Wellington's Advance
Wellington's Cavalry
D'Erlon's Advance
Ney's Cavalry Advance
La Garde's Advance in echelon
Prussians' Advance

Forest of Soignes

To Ohain

To Waterloo

Mont-St-Jean

Dutch   Dutch

Somerset   Ponsonby

Vivian

Braine L'Alleud

Merbraine

ALTEN   PICTON

Vandeleur

Ohain Road

PRUSSIAN I CORPS

Allied
Reinforcements

Papelotte

La Haye

Paris Wood →

PERPONCHER

Frischermont

La Haye
Sainte

Hougoumont

Guards

CAVALRY

D'ERLON

Dutch

NEY'S   D'ERLON
CAVALRY

PRUSSIAN IV CORPS

Jerome

REILLE

NEY'S

Foy

La Belle-Alliance
(Napoleon p.m. 18th June)

LOBAU

To Nivelles

LA
GARDE

Plancenoit

Rossomme
(Napoleon a.m. 18th June)

PRUSSIAN II CORPS

Le Caillou
(Napoleon p.m. 17th June)

0   1,000   2,000   3,000

yards

To Quatre Bras

'Ah, you don't know Macdonnell. I've thrown Macdonnell into it.' Colonel James Macdonnell of Glengarry and his Foot Guards were among Wellington's crack troops.

'But how will it be if the enemy advances on the Nivelles road . . . on the English right wing?'[9] Müffling's hint was followed, the Duke ordering an *abattis* to be thrown across the Nivelles road and drawing in his right wing at Braine l'Alleud closer to Hougoumont.

Why did he not also bring back the IIIrd Corps under the eighteen-year-old Prince Frederick of the Netherlands ten miles away, at Hal? Daylight showed clearly that the French were massing for a frontal, not a flank, attack.

Müffling said it was because Prince Frederick's corps became 'superfluous' once Wellington knew Blücher was going to support him with more than one corps of Prussians.[10] Wellington himself noted in a memorandum of 1842 that he had sent a 'small detachment' to Hal. As things turned out this 'small detachment' of 17,000 men would have been far from superfluous at Waterloo. Three interrelated ideas were in his mind: he was still harping on the political effect of a turning movement against Brussels; he needed a large reserve in case he had to retreat from Mont-Saint-Jean; he mistakenly credited Boney with a healthy respect for 'that article', the British infantry, which would prevent him risking a head-on clash. Wellington always held that Napoleon ought to have gone for the Allied right.

About a mile to the east of Braine l'Alleud was the village of Merbraine, where Ensign Leeke was now eating his breakfast; at least, he had just received his ration of one biscuit and was putting a mess-tin of soup to his lips when an officer interrupted –

'Master Leeke, I think you have had your share of that.'[11]

Sergeant Tom Morris of the 73rd was too old a soldier to be caught like Leeke. He and his friend Sergeant Burton settled down to their grog ration which was pleasantly augmented by the shares of Quatre Bras casualties. Why not keep part of this bonus for after the battle? suggested Burton. Tom was dubious.

'Very few of us will live to see the close of this day.' But Sergeant Burton had a veteran's premonitions.

'Tom, I'll tell you what it is; there is no shot made yet for either you or me.'[12]

The Allied army, formed into squares like a chequerboard with spaces between for deployment, seemed to those who like Ensign Gronow gazed along the ridge to form one solid human wall. In reality the 'wall' was built of remarkably heterogeneous material. One brigade in particular, Bylandt's Dutch–Belgians, stuck out like a sore thumb. When the rest of the army were ordered to lie down behind the crest, Bylandt's men stood forward prominently in front of the ridge, looking 'very well', as Sergeant Dickson observed, but an easy target for French guns. Bylandt, as a Continental soldier, did not understand what Houssaye calls Wellington's 'very peculiar tactics'.[13] His men were not trained to await the nerve-racking advance of an invisible enemy lying down. Along the rest of the front the weak units of the 'infamous army' were intermingled and aligned with the veterans.

Wellington's staff was by now swollen into a jingling, glittering cavalcade, some forty strong, which included such determined camp-followers as the elderly Duke of Richmond and his injured fifteen-year-old son. Wellington tried in vain to send these two home.

'William, you ought to be in bed. Duke, you have no business here.'

The two simply moved off towards Picton's division farther along the ridge. Beside his staff proper there were the foreign commissioners and also a swarm of aides. 'They all seemed as gay and unconcerned,' said Gronow, 'as if they were riding to meet the hounds in some quiet English county.'[14]

From every part of the line came the same comments. Surgeon James saw Wellington go by as smart as if 'riding for pleasure'. Almost the same words as James had used after Quatre Bras came to him again: 'the very sight of him put heart into us all. . . .'[15] When the smiling Duke and his staff passed, Cotton was proud to observe that his leader required no glistening cascade of white cock's feathers to give him distinction; only the four cockades of Britain, Spain, Portugal and the Netherlands on a low cocked hat worn as usual 'fore and aft'. (Bonaparte's hat was no more gaudy than Wellington's but worn square.) The Duke was in his comfortable civilian clothes: white buck-skin breeches with tasselled top-boots and short spurs; a white stock, blue coat over the gold knotted sash of a Spanish field-marshal and his blue cape which he put on and off fifty times in the day. 'I never get wet when I can help it.'[16]

When he needed a command-post there was one available – the elm tree which stood at Mont-Saint-Jean in the south-western corner of the crossroads. As he stood by the 'Wellington Tree' his army was spread along the ridge on either hand, in front the infantry supported by artillery, the cavalry behind. Hougoumont, surrounded with fruit trees and woods, lay in the valley below him to his right, but hidden by rolling cornfields. Straight in front of him stood the white-walled farmhouse of La Haye Sainte a quarter of a mile down the Brussels high road which bisected the battlefield. With its garden, barn and dovecote over the gateway into the *chaussée*, it formed a bastion corresponding to Hougoumont, though not so strong.

Not far away Captain Mercer of 'G' Troop, Royal Horse Artillery, spent a soaking night, though no one disturbed him by complaining. The 'Johnny Newcomes' who might have complained were afraid of being laughed at by the old Peninsular hands. Towards morning Mercer made a fire under a friend's umbrella: 'We lighted cigars and became – comfortable.' Across the road Johnny Kincaid bivouacked against the wall of a cottage inside which his commander, Sir Andrew Barnard, was asleep. In the morning Kincaid brewed a huge kettle of sweet tea which he shared with the bigwigs as they passed up and down the *chaussée*. A cup went to the Duke. Another old soldier across the road from Mercer was Sergeant Wheeler of the 51st. He was happy to think that the enemy were just as badly off and that it had rained before Fuentes, Salamanca and Vitoria. 'It was always the prelude to a victory.'[17] He might have added that it had rained all night before the battle of Agincourt exactly four hundred years ago.

On Wellington's extreme left, roughly level with La Haye Sainte, stood the bastions of Papelotte farm and La Haye, defended by Prince Bernhard's Nassauers. Here among a group of officers belonging to Sir Hussey Vivian's cavalry, Arthur Shakespear found himself making 'a good stewing' in the middle of the night out of two old hens and a sack of potatoes. Arthur Kennedy had been jumped on by a horse while asleep under a hedge the day before and was feeling extremely sorry for himself. Nevertheless, his confidence was unbounded. They would soon be in Malplaquet, he felt sure, and this man who led them was 'our modern Marlborough'.[18]

Wellington's intense activity, deliberately showing himself everywhere and heartening all who saw him by his habitual calm and unusual geniality, contrasted in every way with Napoleon's morning performance.

At 8 am the Emperor, attended by Soult and others of his staff, breakfasted at the farm of Le Caillou off crested silver plate. He had been relieved to see the Allied army still on Mont-Saint-Jean at dawn.

'Aha, now we've got them – those English!' But he postponed the hour for getting them from soon after daybreak, as originally designed, until 9 am and finally until 1 pm; officially in order to let the ground dry. This delay was his first blunder of the day, mainly due to contempt for Wellington as an opponent and disbelief in the Prussian powers of recuperation. What was the hurry to get those English?

'We have ninety chances in our favour and not ten against.'

Marshal Soult, who knew a good deal more than Boney about Wellington, felt uneasy. He advised the immediate recall from the eastern flank of Grouchy's 33,000 men, to reinforce Napoleon against Wellington. The Emperor jeered.

'Just because you have been beaten by Wellington, you think he's a good general. I tell you, Wellington is a bad general, the English are bad troops, and this affair' – here Napoleon glanced towards the plates which had just been cleared from the breakfast table and replaced by maps – 'this affair is nothing more than eating breakfast.' Soult looked grim.

'I earnestly hope so.'

Somewhat unwisely the Emperor next asked Reille, who had also experienced defeat in the Peninsula, what he thought of Wellington's army.

'Well posted,' replied Reille, 'as Wellington knows how, and attacked from the front, I consider the English infantry to be impregnable' – Napoleon began to look black – 'owing to its calm tenacity and its superior aim in firing.' Reille hastily got on to the French advantages: 'If we cannot beat it by a frontal attack, we may do so by manoeuvring.' The Emperor interrupted with a bark of incredulity and turned his back on Reille. His brother Jerome had just arrived from the *Roi d'Espagne* inn with a piece of gossip about a junction between Blücher and Wellington.

'Nonsense,' snapped the Emperor. 'The Prussians and English cannot possibly link up for another two days after such a battle,' and he went on to demonstrate how Grouchy would deal with what remained of the Prussians while he himself, after a cannonade and cavalry charge, would march straight at the English with his Old Guard.

It was now 10 am and he at last drafted a reply to a vital despatch from Grouchy that had been lying about since he first read it six hours earlier. Grouchy announced his intention of following the Prussians towards Wavre in order to keep them away from Brussels and Wellington. This was Napoleon's chance urgently to redirect Grouchy away from Wavre and towards Waterloo. Instead, he ordered,

His Majesty desires you will head for Wavre in order to draw near to us. . . .

– in the circumstances a plain contradiction, since Wavre lay north of Grouchy and east of Napoleon ('us'). Grouchy was also to 'push before him' the Prussians who were marching in 'this direction' – an operation which, taken literally, would mean Grouchy pushing the Prussians towards Wellington – and reach Waterloo 'as soon as possible'.[19]

In this verbal fog Grouchy was to discover only three luminous words: 'Head for Wavre.' They were to prove fatal.

Not until 9 am when the baggage was ordered to the rear did some of Wellington's soldiers realize that a battle was definitely to be fought that morning. From one end of the ridge to the other men were still cleaning their weapons and drying their scarlet tunics. Humourists in the ranks noticed that their white belts were already dyed blood-red.* The quickest method of cleaning weapons was to shoot them off into the air. Such waste of ammunition was to bring its nemesis later, particularly to the brave German riflemen in La Haye Sainte. Now the popping all along the plateau anticipated cheerful hours ahead. Crack riflemen expected to achieve one aimed shot a minute with their Baker rifles, for as long as required. The best musketeers would fire three or even four volleys in the same time (though really accurate only up to a range of 100 yards) with the sturdy 'Brown Bess' which had served the army almost unaltered since 1759; no comparable Continental weapon equalled it. When Wheatley had finished his cleaning at 10.30 am he was allowed to lie down and rest, which he and the King's German Legion thankfully did. The popping had died away and there was no music or singing.

The Earl of Albemarle's sixteen-year-old son could not help wishing it would begin. He remembered his father once telling him about a conversation between himself and Henry Pearce, the Game Chicken, on the eve of a prize-fight.

'Well, Pearce, how do you feel?'

'Why, my Lord, I wish it was *fit*.'[20] Young George did not feel much like a Game Chicken except in that one way – he wished the fight was fought.

For those with steady nerves there was plenty to watch on the slopes

---

* The same thing happened on 18 June 1965, when the 150th anniversary of Waterloo was celebrated on the battlefield. There was a torrential downpour just as the commemoration service began and in a few minutes all the white belts were red.

opposite during the last hours of suspense. As Napoleon's regiments arrived they were deployed with a portentous display of power and noise. Their headgear alone made them shine like gods and showed from what a variety of peoples the conqueror had drawn his might. There were Lancers in red shapkas with a brass plate in front bearing the imperial N and crown and a white plume eighteen inches long, Dragoons with brass casques over tiger-skin turbans, Carabiniers all in white with tall helmets of a classical design, Grenadiers of the Old Guard in massive, plain bearskins towering above powdered queues and earrings of gold. Against the dark, menacing background of the Imperial Guards' long blue coats thousands of pennants fluttered and uniforms flaunted brilliant facings.

Wheatley noticed a new English recruit staring as if in a trance, the muscles on his round, chalk-white face quivering. Yet all this display was absorbing, even exhilarating to the British veterans. A thrill of excitement shot through Sergeant Cotton at the thought that two such noble antagonists as Wellington and Napoleon were to meet at last. Kincaid listened with interest to the soldiers' shouts of '*Vive l'Empereur!*' as they filed past Napoleon, who had moved forward to a command-post at Rossomme, and to the *rub-a-dub* and *tantarara* of their drums and trumpets.

Napoleon was about to order the cannonade. He had at last brought into line 71,947 men with 246 guns in support. Opposite him were Wellington's 156 guns and 67,661 men: a total of nearly 140,000 men and over 400 guns, not to mention 30,000 horses, all crammed into under three square miles. Wellington had seen a mass of troops squeezed into a small space at Assaye; never anything like this.

At 11.25 am the French guns opened up with an ear-splitting roar. Within a few minutes the shredding mists were thickened and deepened into a poisonous fog of black smoke, as the Allied gunners replied with their cannon grouped between the regiments along the edge of their hill, many in embrasures cut in the hedges of the Ohain road. The French bombardment was particularly heavy on Welling-ton's right in the direction of Hougoumont. Violent as it was, however, the attack on Hougoumont was planned only as part of a diversionary operation to weaken Wellington's centre by forcing him to draw away reinforcements. Over on the left wing, Prince Bernhard of Saxe-Weimar and his Nassauers were dealing with a similar though less determined demonstration against Papelotte and La Haye. Wellington had stationed himself above Hougoumont beside the Guards before the action began. He was thus in a key position to direct Hougoumont's defence.

Sergeant Wheeler was surprised by the intensity of the attack: 'grape and shells were dupping [sic] about like hail, this was devilish annoying.' Then the bugles sounded to lie down and Wheeler and the 51st gladly did so.

While the cannonade boomed and belched at Waterloo its reverberations travelled over the low hills and disturbed Marshal Grouchy, who had just reached the strawberry stage of a late breakfast. He and his staff went into the garden and put their ears to the ground. General Gérard was emphatic:

'We ought to march to the guns.'

Grouchy objected.

'A rearguard affair.'

Again Gérard listened:

'The ground trembles under us.'[21]

Smoke could now be seen in the west and a tetchy dispute developed in which Grouchy, the more he was pressed to follow the sound of the guns the more he resolved to follow Napoleon's orders – 'head for Wavre'. In the end Grouchy won the argument – and Napoleon lost. For if Grouchy had turned half left instead of butting on ahead he must have cut the Prussians' line of march.

*11.30 am: Hougoumont**

The Guards by whom Wellington was standing when the struggle for Hougoumont opened were part of the Prince of Orange's Corps. Wellington began by giving all his orders through the Prince. When 'things got on', as Fitzroy Somerset noted, the Duke gave his orders direct.[22] At Hougoumont things got on fast and furiously.

Prince Jerome, Napoleon's youngest brother, who was in command of the attack, saw a unique chance for glory and snatched at it greedily. Four splendid regiments of veterans, protected by swarms of skirmishers, were launched against the château. They fought their way through the woodlands, out into the orchard and up to the château walls. Here a stream of bullets through every loophole brought them down in heaps. From inside the Hougoumont buildings, Nassauers, Hanoverians and Guards under Macdonnell poured their volleys into the besiegers. At the same time Wellington ordered Bull's battery of

---

* The times given for the acts or phases of Waterloo are approximate.

howitzers, which he had himself led into position close to the back of the château, to begin the delicate task of firing shrapnel over the defenders' heads into the besiegers beyond. He knew he could trust the gunners to make no mistakes. Their fire allowed the Allied infantry in front to counter-attack, recapture the orchard and even some coppices. Hougoumont was once more secure.

Jerome now summoned fresh infantry, against General Reille's advice, to support him in another bull-headed assault. Napoleon did nothing to stop him.

At first there was a savage moment of success. A gigantic subaltern stove in a panel of the great north door and, followed by a handful of wildly cheering men, dashed into the courtyard. Pandemonium broke out. The defenders slashed and hewed at the invaders in desperate hand-to-hand duels. But the real thing was to prevent any more of the enemy from entering the yard. Five powerful Coldstreamers – Macdonnell, three other officers and a sergeant – threw themselves bodily against the huge door and slowly, slowly, by main force pushed it back against the pressure outside. This done, they dealt with the invaders.

'The success of the battle of Waterloo depended on the closing of the gates of Hougoumont.' So said Wellington afterwards.[23]

Among the heroic five was Henry Wyndham, who had opened the door of King Joseph's coach at Vitoria. Now he shut a door to more purpose.

Jerome's obsessive reaction to this second repulse was to throw in even more battalions, this time drawing on Foy's fresh division. With extraordinary confidence and economy, Wellington replied by sending down only four extra companies of the Guards. Though they could not hold the woods, the balance of Hougoumont was restored for the third time. Still Jerome would not let go. The affair, begun as a feint, was destined eventually to suck from Napoleon's main army the best part of two divisions to one brigade of Wellington's.

It was now 1 pm, time for Wellington to move from the spot where he had played his masterly hand since 11.30 am. Hougoumont could be reasonably regarded as impregnable, though it was never out of his thoughts. Other sectors of the battlefield were far from impregnable. It was towards one of these that the Emperor was about to direct his great push under Ney. Wellington put spurs to Copenhagen and the chestnut horse carried him up over the rolling cornfields to his command-post at the crossroads of Mont-Saint-Jean. Before the second act could begin, however, there was an unexpected flurry off-stage.

The Emperor, still on his high bank at Rossomme, surrounded by his staff, decided on a sweep of the distant hills with telescopes before they were blotted out by smoke.

Immediately they all saw it. The black line over by Chapelle-Saint-Lambert on the edge of the wood. A cloud shadow? A row of trees? Napoleon knew at once it was soldiers, and in a few minutes that it was the vanguard of Bülow's IVth Corps. He revised the odds. 'This morning we had ninety odds in our favour.' They had shortened but – 'We still have sixty against forty. . . .'[24] And to make sure that they did not shorten any more he sent off in support of Grouchy two cavalry divisions and Lobau's whole VIth Corps. That meant well over 50,000 men (counting those at Hougoumont) tied up and nine hours of daylight used up; for it was already half past one. Napoleon, Grouchy and Jerome had made serious mistakes. Could d'Erlon and Ney redeem them?

1.30 pm–3 pm: The Infantry Defeated

Ney's advance had been heralded by a renewed cannonade, beginning at 1 pm. 'One could almost feel the undulation of the air from the multitude of cannon-shot,' wrote Wheatley. A battery of no less than eighty-four guns, twenty-four of them Napoleon's twelve-pounders, was ordered to soften up the enemy's left-centre and centre aligned on the high ground to either side of the crossroads. Unfortunately for Napoleon, the ground was already too soft. Many cannonballs buried themselves. Most of Wellington's troops in any case had taken cover on the reverse slopes; only Bylandt's exposed Dutch–Belgians suffered heavy losses.

At 1.30 pm Napoleon moved to his most forward post at *La Belle-Alliance* and ordered the advance. Ney passed on the word to d'Erlon, and d'Erlon's magnificent corps of 16,000 men began their march towards the plateau of Mont-Saint-Jean. As Wheatley watched them approach a chill ran along his spine. These 'gloomy bodies' gliding down the slopes opposite, 'disjointing then contracting, like fields of animated clods . . . had a fairy look and border'd on the supernatural in appearance.'

The formation of d'Erlon's divisions added to their daunting look: three out of the four drawn up in dense phalanxes, 200 files wide and twenty-four to twenty-seven deep. Yet the men who had fought and conquered at Bussaco could have told them it would not do. Their firepower was restricted to the first two ranks and the whole so tightly packed that they could not deploy.

Nevertheless their first onslaught was worthy of the *Grande Armée*. The Germans defending La Haye Sainte were driven from the orchard and garden into the farm buildings and there isolated. It was thanks only to the German Legion's valour that La Haye Sainte was isolated, not overrun.

On swept d'Erlon's infantry, having driven out Prince Bernhard's men from Papelotte and La Haye, and forcing the 95th Rifles from a nearby gravel pit. Then they crashed into Bylandt's light brigade, already badly shaken by the cannonade. A few wild shots were all the Dutch–Belgians managed. With every one of their officers above the rank of major either killed or wounded, they were withdrawn according to some accounts, according to others they broke and fled. Whichever it was, the survivors retired in disorder, booed by the Cameron Highlanders as they passed. Throughout the rest of the battle they camped in the Forest of Soignes. At least, as Wellington himself conceded, none of his foreign troops deserted to the enemy.*

The situation on the crest was critical. But Picton's division of splendid infantry were only waiting to spring up and fight. Picton gave the word. His Peninsular commanders, Pack and Kempt, dashed forward.

'92nd, you must advance!' shouted Sir Denis Pack to the Gordons. 'All in front of you have given way.'[25] His brigade had been reduced to 1,400 by the fighting at Quatre Bras, but the Gordons, Black Watch and 44th flung themselves with bayonets on 8,000 French, while Kempt's brigade poured in volleys at close range. Sir Thomas Picton led Kempt's front line himself.

'Charge!' he roared, waving his sword. 'Hurrah! Hurrah!' Then to Kempt as the Gordons staggered under the weight of d'Erlon's mass,

'Rally the Highlanders!'[26] Those were his last words. A bullet pierced his famous top hat, worn to protect his eyes, and struck him on the temple. He fell off his horse stone dead.†

* The behaviour of Bylandt's light troops is still a matter of controversy. Two distinguished historians, F. de Bas and Count de T'Serclaes de Wommerson (*La Campagne de 1815 aux Pays Bas*, vol. II, pp. 142–6) have put the Dutch–Belgian case: that the brigade was ordered to the rear after appalling casualties. They attribute the story of *lâcheté* – cowardice – to Siborne and upbraid Houssaye for resurrecting it in his *1815 Waterloo*. Fortescue, however, who greatly admired the Dutch–Belgian historians and re-examined the whole question, came to the sad conclusion that the broken brigade did indeed flee and failed to return.

† The hat, with a bullet-hole near the junction of crown and brim, is in the National Army Museum

Suddenly the Gordons were aware of huge grey horses thundering down on top of them with wild, exultant greetings.

'Hurrah, 92nd! Scotland forever!'

Wellington had seen from his tree that Picton's counter-attack must be overwhelmed by sheer numbers without immediate support. Lord Uxbridge therefore ordered a double advance of the Union and Household Brigades of heavy cavalry.* He personally led forward the Life Guards. As the sixteen-year-old John Edwards, field-trumpeter to Somerset, raised his bugle ready to sound the Charge – ten compelling blasts climbing in threes to the long, insistent G – the excitement was unbearable. Suddenly a martial-looking civilian, whom some Irish troopers recognized as the Duke of Richmond, popped up from behind the hedge and found himself shouting.

'Go along, my boys! now's your time!'[27] It was enough for the Inniskillings. They took wings. Lord Uxbridge, who should have remained behind to throw in the reserves when necessary, was drawn irresistibly into the first line and led the charge of the Household Cavalry himself. 'To Paris!' shouted Colonel Fuller as the Royals charged.[28]

In they went like a torrent shaking the very earth, or so it seemed to Captain Hay. The Life Guards and King's Dragoons smashed up against Travers' Cuirassiers like a wall, and the sound of British swords on French breastplates reminded Sergeant Robertson of a thousand coppersmiths at work. Big men on big horses everywhere bore back the lighter French until they turned and fled. The French horses were blown. All had galloped uphill; some had carried sleeping troopers on their backs all night. The British horses were not only fresh but fierce, as Corporal Dickson realized when his Rattler, one of a long line of giant grey horses with flowing manes and heads down, dashed at the sunken Ohain road.

I felt a strange thrill run through me, and I am sure my noble beast felt the same, for, after rearing a moment, she sprang forward, uttering loud neighings and snorting, and leapt over the holly hedge at a terrific speed.[29]

Now Dickson's 'strange thrill' swiftly became in all of them an ungovernable frenzy. To swarm over the valley was nothing. Up they thundered on the other side, on and on, deep into the enemy lines. Buglers sounded the Rally – the imperious, staccato call that was

---

* The Union Brigade was so called from its combination of English, Scottish and Irish regiments – Royals, Scots Greys and Inniskillings. In the Household Brigade were the Life Guards, King's Dragoon Guards and Blues.

meant to halt and gather the men. No one listened. Two eagles were captured and fifteen guns in Napoleon's great battery disabled, while the French gunners sat on their limbers and wept. Rattler went as mad as her master, biting and tearing at everything in her way, until she dropped down from her many wounds, apparently dead.

'Those terrible grey horses, how they fight,' said Napoleon back on his mound. Then he watched with equal interest the moment of retribution.

Dickson saw all at once that the whole valley behind them was flooded with French troops. They were cut off.

'Come on lads; that's the road home!' Dickson was lucky to burst through into his own lines on a riderless horse – even to find a chastened Rattler waiting for him there. Out of 300 of his comrades, 279 failed to return and sixteen out of twenty-four officers. Young John Edwards survived, together with his bugle, which now hangs among the battle honours in the Household Cavalry Museum at Windsor. Beside the bugle is a bullet extracted from the leg of that Captain Edward Kelly who had led so gallantly at Genappe. Three horses were shot under him in the great Waterloo charge before he himself fell. 'My dearest dear love,' he wrote to his wife next day. He was alive. But there was little joy. 'All my fine Troopers knocked to pieces. . . .'[30]

How did Wellington's account stand? D'Erlon's first great attack had been defeated but at a fearful cost: 4,500 British and Dutch–Belgian infantry dead and 2,500 cavalry, a quarter of the whole. Though Wellington personally welcomed back the Life Guards with a lift of his cocked hat and a warm, 'Guards! I thank you,' next day the Household Cavalry were to receive warnings against impetuosity mingled with his renewed thanks. Uxbridge never forgave himself for losing control. Yet Uxbridge's fault was endemic in British cavalry. It cannot have surprised Wellington.

On the positive side, no cavalry had ever before routed so great a body of infantry in formation. As the village clocks at Mont-Saint-Jean struck three, not a live Frenchman was to be seen on the ridge. Papelotte and the gravel-pit had changed hands again and the bastion of La Haye Sainte stood firm. So did Hougoumont.

Hougoumont had received such a terrible visitation at 3 pm that the peasants universally believed it was saved by a miracle. Haystack, outbuildings and château were all set on fire by howitzers, the wounded of both sides burnt to death in the barn and the horses in the stables. Wellington sent over a parchment slip of instructions, which still survives.* They were to hold on as long as possible but without endangering lives from falling timbers. Suddenly the flames stopped abruptly in the chapel, at the foot of the cross.

At the same time (3 pm) Napoleon learnt that his own miracle was not to happen. Grouchy was not heading for Waterloo. Napoleon came forward from Rossomme to *La Belle-Alliance* and sharply ordered Ney to take La Haye Sainte now – before the Prussians arrived.

Wellington had just had his first glimpse of the Prussian vedettes, at about 2.30 pm. Never had he watched a troop movement with such desperate concentration.

The time they occupied in approaching seemed interminable; both they and my watch seemed to have stuck fast.[31]

3.45 pm–5 pm: The Cavalry Repulsed

With possession of La Haye Sainte, Napoleon could hardly fail to break Wellington's centre. It was Ney's duty to take it. Left to decide for himself how it should be done, Ney thought of a positive horde of light cavalry. The preliminary cannonade must match the cavalry in volume and terror.

'We had nothing like this in Spain, Sir,' said a white-faced sergeant-major to his superior officer as the tempest of metal tore into the Allied ranks.[32] Wellington's lighter and fewer artillery blazed away in reply but the infantry had much to endure. Though all could lie down, many could not escape the varieties of death that came whistling out of the smoke. 'Never had the oldest soldiers,' wrote General Charles Alten of the King's German Legion, 'heard such a cannonade';[33] indeed it was the mightiest that the world had so far known.

Part of the Allied line was drawn back by Wellington a hundred yards. This partial withdrawal looked to Ney like a retreat. It was the moment to send 4,500 horsemen into what he firmly believed would be a pursuit. On his side Wellington realized that the unbelievable was about to happen. Ney was going to attack his still unbroken infantry with light cavalry alone.

The supernatural impression of the French army's earlier advance, felt by Wheatley, was caught independently by Victor Hugo in

---

* Four of these Waterloo slips have survived, written in pencil on asses' or goatskin which could be wiped clean and used again. They are now in the Wellington Museum, Apsley House.

describing Ney's cavalry attack.* He called it 'a prodigy' crawling over the battlefield in two columns, 'undulating and swelling like the rings of a polyp'; through rents in the vast veil of black smoke the cuirasses could be seen, 'smooth and shining as the hydra's scales'. To most of the British, however, this mounted host was as beautiful as the sea – and as helpless, when it dashed itself against a wall of rock.

'Prepare to receive cavalry!' The order rang out along the ridge and Wellington's infantry formed into squares. The artillery he instructed to go on firing until the very last moment and then to make a dash for the nearest square, bowling along with them one wheel from each immobilized gun. The squares were ready and resolute when the third act of Waterloo began.

Up through the deep, sucking mud pounded the French, laughing all at once to see abandoned cannon and British gunners running away. Exclamations of delight broke from Napoleon's watching staff:

The English are done for! . . . Their general is an ignoramus . . . look! They are leaving their guns.[34]

Now the squares were only thirty yards away. Pistols cracked, sabres flashed and with blood-curdling yells the French horsemen gathered themselves together to overwhelm the enemy. Next moment volleys of musketry lashed men and horses at close range with a fiery hail; horses crashed on their riders, riders toppled and reeled, riderless horses plunged into the mêlée to increase the disorder, tumult and din.

Wellington's veterans had not fought for five years through the Peninsula for nothing. The front ranks knelt, the butt ends of their muskets resting on the ground and *chevaux de frise* of bayonets lacerating the French horses. Above the sharp knives two deadly lines of muskets fired and reloaded and fired again. Inside the squares all was horror: patches of blood-stained ground reserved for field-hospitals; piles of dead. To the outward eye the squares were unmoved: wasted, no doubt; but every time a red-coat fell, his comrades dragged him inside the square and closed the ranks. Whenever Wellington saw an opening he ordered his cavalry to counter-attack.

At last Ney called off his shattered columns to reform. Immediately the Allied artillerymen sprang back to their guns and fired into the enemy's backs. Why were those guns not disabled? Wellington's 'captured' batteries stood ready to shoot down yet more brave

---

* *Les Misérables* was first published in 1862, Wheatley's contemporary diary in 1964.

horsemen when they charged again. He turned to his aide-de-camp, Colonel James Stanhope, and asked the time.

'Twenty minutes past four.'

'The battle is mine; and if the Prussians arrive soon, there will be an end of the war.'[35]

He had heard the first Prussian guns on the fringe of Paris Wood.

The idea of another series of charges tried the Emperor hard, indeed he condemned Ney for launching the first wave an hour too soon. But 'the bravest of the brave' must be supported, even though the day's events had injected a dose of frenzy into his admirable courage. A huge addition of 5,000 heavy cavalry was ordered forward under Kellermann, the last of Ney's reserve.

Wellington, meanwhile, galloped up and down strengthening his line and encouraging his men. Numbers of his 'young gentlemen' had begun to lose hope, though his Peninsular officers like Andrew Barnard never doubted the Duke would win. 'We had a notion,' said Barnard afterwards, 'that while he was there nothing could go wrong.'[36]

When Ney's second wave of attacks was launched, still head-on and now so tightly packed that many horses were lifted bodily from the ground – no manoeuvring, no mobile artillery, no foot soldiers – then at last the Duke realized Napoleon had never done him the honour of studying his tactics in the Peninsula. His British infantry, the best in the world, were to be pulverized like any Continental militia before 1814.

'Damn the fellow,' he said turning to Barnard, 'he is a mere pounder after all.'

> On came the whirlwind – steel gleams broke
> Like lightning through the rolling smoke.

That was how Sir Walter Scott imagined it afterwards. At the time the men in the squares simply said, 'Here come these fools again!'[37]

A demented Ney was seen through a rent in the fog beating an abandoned British gun with his sword. His fourth horse had been killed under him. For brief, frozen moments the squares and horsemen seemed to be aimlessly intermingled, incapable of deciding what to do next. At other times a whole blanket of fog would rapidly roll away disclosing some unexpected peril only a few yards off. Horace Seymour, one of Uxbridge's aides, was riding along with Wellington when the fog vanished in this way and the two of them escaped capture only by 'a very sudden run'. Here, there, everywhere the Duke was seen.

Wheatley of the King's German Legion saw him waving his hat to 'beckon' the Horse Guards forward. Gronow of the Foot Guards saw him sitting 'perfectly composed' on Copenhagen, though very pale; Morris of the 73rd saw him addressing General Halkett just as the Cuirassiers arrived, when he promptly took refuge in the 73rd's square; Mercer saw him waiting for 'G' Troop to arrive on the ridge above Hougoumont, where the air was like a furnace and full of an infernal humming.

'Ah! that's the way I like to see horse-artillery move,' said the Duke as 'G' Troop galloped up.[38] His warm approval reflected anxiety about the western end of his line, which Mercer had come to support.

'I'll be damned if we shan't lose this ground if we don't take care,' he said to Fitzroy Somerset, who agreed that the troops were 'much thinned'.[39] Some of them were also unsteady. However, there was no one who could restore a shaky battle-line like the Duke. He made the Guards move left towards Halkett's badly mauled brigade, and sent for Adam's and Mitchell's reserves from across the Nivelles road. Adam's brigade he formed four deep – a useful compromise between lines and squares which could hold an extensive area in relative safety.

Hardly had he crowned the crest with these fresh troops when, between 5.30 and 6 pm, Ney made a new attack with a mixed force at last, of 6,000 cavalry and infantry – a development which Wellington had foreseen. The Allied squares, though shrunk, stood firm from above Hougoumont to La Haye Sainte, positively welcoming the renewed charges as a relief from the cannonade. The French columns, unable to make an impression, were mowed down by the Allied artillery and raked with fire from Maitland's Guards and Adam's Light Brigade. The thirty-one-year-old Frederick Adam, riding at Wellington's side, heard him say half to himself, 'I believe we shall beat them after all.'

Nevertheless the Duke's cavalry, without the sorely missed 'heavies', were not altogether effective at this stage, especially as the Cumberland Hussars from Hanover left the field. Composed entirely of decorative 'young gentlemen', this body had never contemplated action. As they wheeled to fly, Horace Seymour grabbed their colonel by the collar. With an anguished bleat that he couldn't trust his men, the colonel tore himself away and raced with his regiment to Brussels, shouting that the French were at their heels. The regiment was afterwards disbanded and its colonel cashiered.[40]

Time and the Prussians marched on. The sturdy little man at the

Belle-Alliance command-post knew that his chances were down to ten to one against – his line regiments hammered, his cavalry squandered, one army on his front, another on his flank. He rode to and fro before *La Belle-Alliance* among the shot and shell, sizing up Wellington's position. Then he decided to seize that one chance. *Coûte que coûte*, Ney must take La Haye Sainte.

6 pm–6.30 pm: La Haye Sainte Lost

There were 376 of them at La Haye Sainte, all King's German Legion, under a British officer, Major George Baring. They had begun the day with sixty rounds each; they were down to four or five. Why were their desperate demands for ammunition not answered? This is one of the unsolved puzzles of Waterloo. Long afterwards Wellington thought the trouble had been a lack of communication. However, it is probable that the ammunition was nonexistent. There were rumours that a wagon bringing supplies had overturned and gone up in smoke.

La Haye Sainte went up in a storm of fire. Ney, raging with frustration and resolved as never before to do or die, led out a combined force of infantry, cavalry and guns. After their last cartridge was spent the King's German Legion defended the farmhouse with bayonets. 'But now they flocked in,' wrote an eighteen-year-old British survivor, Lieutenant George Graeme. Forty-one men besides Graeme and Baring were the only survivors from La Haye Sainte. General Charles Alten and the Prince of Orange had made one attempt to relieve the farm. It was little short of disastrous. Alten ordered an attack in line by two battalions of the King's German Legion and when their colonel, Wheatley's friend Christian Ompteda, pointed out the fearful danger from French cavalry, the Prince, in a highly tense state, enforced Alten's order. Edmund Wheatley went down in Ompteda's catastrophe. He had been standing in his square alternately taking a pinch of snuff and a pinch of Southey – *But 'twas a famous victory* – when he realized it was all set for a famous defeat. Then he was knocked senseless. He came to, but the colonel was lying on his back beside him with a hole in his throat and he himself was a prisoner of the French.[41]

Now that Wellington's bastion had fallen his centre was at Ney's mercy. The marshal did not fail to press home his advantage. He sent a vast cloud of skirmishers all over the terrible slopes – Wellington had not the heavy cavalry to subdue them – and rushed a battery up to within 300 yards of Wellington's line, changing the bastion of La Haye Sainte into a nest of sharp-shooters. Fitzroy Somerset, riding close beside his chief, lost his right arm. His left arm and Wellington's right were actually touching at the time. Nothing between them but the finger of Providence.

The Duke was running short of aides-de-camp. It was said that once or twice he was reduced to using stray civilians to carry his messages – a traveller in buttons from Birmingham, a small Londoner on a pony who turned out to be a commercial traveller for a City firm.

'Please, Sir, any orders for Todd and Morrison?'

'No: but will you do me a service? Go to that officer and tell him to refuse a flank.'

His raw, second-line battalions could not be relied on. 'Little specks,' said Hay, were all that remained of the veteran squares under Pack, Kempt and Halkett.

'Well, Halkett, how do you get on?' asked the Duke, white in the face but unmoved as marble.

'My Lord, we are dreadfully cut up; can you not relieve us for a little while?'

'Impossible.'

'Very well, my Lord, we'll stand till the last man falls.'

One hopeful gunner with a good view of Napoleon suggested a quick way out.

'There's Bonaparte, Sir, I think I can reach him, may I fire?' The Duke was aghast.

'No, no, Generals commanding armies have something else to do than to shoot at one another.'[42]

Mercer's beautiful troop was a wreck: horses heaped up dead on top of smashed guns and gunners, Mercer himself deaf and confused by cannon-fire. Harry Smith and Kincaid (and no doubt hundreds more) wondered whether this battle would be the exception where everyone was killed. To Wheatley, being hustled by his captors down the road to Charleroi, the little squares seemed to be entirely engulfed by foes.

The hands of Wellington's watch had crawled on to 6.30. As he looked at it yet again someone said they heard him say,

'Night or the Prussians must come.'[43]

6.30 pm–7 pm: The Pause

The signs that the Allied centre was crumbling were apparent to Ney.

He sent the Emperor an urgent appeal for reinforcements to deliver the *coup de grâce*. Napoleon hesitated. Fourteen battalions of the Imperial Guard were still untouched. How should he use them? This was Napoleon's crisis. He decided to reinforce the clamouring Lobau, and turned down Ney.

'Troops? Where do you expect me to find them? Do you expect me to make them?'[44]

In these words he threw away his chance of victory.

With Ney rebuffed a lull supervened. Only Napoleon's artillery continued to bombard the ridge. No pause was ever used by Wellington to more purpose.

Three things had to be done: the gaping hole in his centre plugged and the waverers there steadied, his line to right and left reorganized and every man persuaded not to seek relief in wildly hitting back but to stand and hold fast a little longer. All the reserves Wellington could lay hands on were brought up to the centre.

'Go you and get all the German troops you can to the spot,' he ordered Captain Shaw, 'and all the guns you can find.'[45]

Five fresh battalions of Brunswickers, in their extreme youth and terror, at once gave way. It was a bad moment and could be overcome only by direct personal effort. Wellington himself rallied both Brunswickers and Nassauers, with the gallant assistance of officers like Canning, Gordon and the Prince of Orange. As a result, Canning fell dead and Gordon mortally wounded; the Prince of Orange was struck on the left shoulder and carried off. He made an honourable exit from a field where he had shown consistently high courage, if not always an equal degree of judgement.* With another crisis surmounted, the secondline battalions were back in position and the gap filled.

But for Müffling, however, the Prussians might have been deflected from the battlefield at the last moment. A Prussian staff officer informed General Zieten that Wellington was withdrawing. Though on the edge of Wellington's battlefield Zieten turned round and marched back towards Blücher. Müffling dashed after him.

'The battle is lost if the Ist Corps does not go to the Duke's rescue.'[46]

Zieten again changed direction and started back.

All along the battered ridge Wellington pursued his charmed course,

---

* British historians have tended to treat the Prince of Orange's errors more harshly than those, for instance, of the heavy cavalry. That a royal youth of twenty-three should be a corps commander at all was a fault of the system, not of the Prince.

reining in Copenhagen wherever the tension was greatest to speak a word of caution or encouragement.

'Are we to be massacred here? Let us go at them, let us give them *Brummegum!*' the men shouted at him, brandishing their bayonets.

'Wait a little longer, my lads, you shall have at them presently.'[47]

To their officers he said, 'Hard pounding, this, gentlemen; try who can pound the longest.' Once there was an echo of *Henry V*: 'Standfast . . . we must not be beat – what will they say in England?'[48]

7 pm–9 pm: The Crisis

A royalist deserter galloped melodramatically into Wellington's lines with a breathless message. The Guard were coming.

Napoleon himself led out his 'Immortals' – Grenadiers and Chasseurs of the Middle Guard, supported by all d'Erlon's and Reille's remaining contingents: a total force of 15,000 men. Riding on his white charger, he took the Grenadiers as far as La Haye Sainte and there handed them over to Marshal Ney. The excitement was at fever pitch. '*Vive l'Empereur!*' they roared again and again in an ecstasy of pride, joy and gratitude. A damaging rumour that Prussian troops had been seen was promptly transformed for their benefit by the Emperor's magic into wonderful news. He ordered La Bédoyère to announce the arrival of Grouchy. Soon the false, heartening words were winging down the lines: '*Vive l'Empereur! Soldats, voilà Grouchy!*'

And now the fog of war again intervened, as at Quatre Bras, to obscure certain aspects of the final clash. Ney struck out diagonally from the Brussels *chaussée* in echelon, but shortly afterwards the Guard formed two separate columns, whether by Ney's order or accidentally is not clear. Nor has the exact number of the Guard battalions to attack the ridge of Mont-Saint-Jean ever been agreed. It was probably five. But the effect of the Allied fire was clear and unforgettable. As soon as the Guard began to emerge out of the smoke, British and KGL gunners cut their first swathes with double-shotted guns. Lieutenant Pringle of the Horse Artillery remembered how the Guard 'waved' at every successive discharge like corn blown by the wind; but not a man retired. They closed ranks and came on steadily towards death the reaper.

Then it was the turn of the Allied infantry to watch mesmerized a race of giants breasting the plateau. The Guard's leading officers waved their swords and Ney, blackened with smoke and without a horse for the fifth time, marched on foot up the reeking slopes. Wellington's men marked the ranks of long blue overcoats, 6,500 strong, broadened by huge epaulettes and packs containing ceremonial dress for the victory march into Brussels.

Wellington stood in the right-centre of his position with the 1st Foot Guards of Maitland's brigade, all of whom he had ordered to lie down behind the Ohain road. At least one young soldier in that *élite* corps, Ensign Gronow, couldn't help recalling that his French opposite numbers were 'the heroes of many memorable victories'. Leeke in the 52nd managed to concentrate on the rhythm of the drum-beats in that awful advance: 'the rum dum, the rum dum,' they seemed to say, 'the rummadum dummadum, dum dum.'

Wellington still had the Guards lying down when he noticed signs of confusion on his left.

'See what's wrong there – ' he shouted, unaware that he was continually sliding the tube of his telescope in and out. An assistant quartermaster-general dashed away to question Halkett, who before he could answer was shot in the mouth and carried off; nevertheless his 30th and 73rd were rallied while the Duke himself galloped over and brought back into position two battalions of Brunswickers who were actually in flight. Vandeleur's cavalry backed him up, as Vivian's had done earlier, by refusing to let them get through to the rear.

The Duke wheeled again and returned to Maitland's concealed Guards. The advancing French were only sixty yards from the Ohain road. They could see nothing opposing them but the Allied guns. There was dead silence behind the ridge. Then Wellington alerted Maitland.

'Now, Maitland, now's your time!' The enemy still came on and had covered another twenty yards when the Duke gave his final commands:

'Stand up, Guards!' Up sprang 1,500 men as if out of the ground, bringing the startled French to a momentary halt.

'Make ready! Fire!' The long lines of British muskets, 400 in the first of four ranks and a full half of the total force able to bring their fire to bear, lapped the enemy at twenty yards in a stream of bullets. Down crashed three hundred of the Guard at the first volley. Their close formation prevented them from deploying and they began to give way. The 1st Foot Guards were suddenly looking at the backs of long blue overcoats.

'Now's your time, my boys,' called out Colonel Lord Saltoun.[49] They charged with their bayonets; their opponents dispersed. By the time they had returned to the ridge, another British regiment had stepped in dramatically to despatch the Imperial Guard.

Well aware of Wellington's mind and methods from hard-fought Peninsular actions, Colonel Colborne of the 52nd was one who did not hesitate to strike without orders when he saw the need. Wellington had himself brought up Adam's Light Brigade, of which the 52nd formed a part, to lie in wait for the Chasseurs. Now Colborne sprang forward out of the concealing corn, wheeled his thousand men to the left, brought his right shoulder round until the regiment was standing parallel to the French. General Adam galloped across to find out what the Colonel of the 52nd was up to.

'What do you intend?'

'To make that column feel our fire.'

'Move on.'

The 52nd were already pouring volley after volley into the French left flank. Unable to deploy, the Chasseurs recoiled under this violent, totally unforeseen attack. In a moment Colborne's bayonets were flashing and his men driving the enemy in a slanting line south-eastwards across the field. Wellington at once followed up with all available bayonets; he had personally ordered the 95th Rifles to charge before Colborne's action began. Kincaid remembered how he himself and his fellow-riflemen began cheering when the Duke appeared. As usual he stopped them:

'No cheering, my lads, but forward and complete your victory!' Both Uxbridge and Colin Campbell, one of the Duke's surviving aides-de-camp, were alarmed by the risks he was running and begged him to move away from such exposed positions. He said much the same thing to each:

'So I will when I see those fellows driven off.'

When Colborne, finding himself far out in front of his supports, prepared to call a temporary halt, he heard the Duke's voice at his side:

'Well done, Colborne! Well done! Go on. Never mind, *go* on, *go* on. Don't give them time to rally. They won't stand.'[50]

As the relics of d'Erlon's and Reille's columns, already demoralized by their earlier defeats, realized the appalling truth, a cry of horror went up such as Napoleon's army had never heard before:

'*La Garde recule!*'

Something told Wellington that their splendid harness had snapped, and unlike his own contrivance of much-knotted rope, once broken it could not be mended. The finest army in the world stopped in its tracks, pennons still fluttering, the sun twinkling slyly on lances and breastplates – the setting sun. Down in the valley Hougoumont still flamed and still held out.

'You see, Macdonnell has held Hougoumont!'[51] With this triumphant salute to Müffling, the Duke gathered up Copenhagen's reins and galloped with Uxbridge towards the crossroads. The finger of Providence was pointing at his tree.

Half an hour or more of daylight remained, for it was not yet 8 pm. Wellington's army was down to some 35,000 men, but all proven in defence and now only anxious to prove themselves in attack. The French army was shaken but not routed. Napoleon still held some of the Old Guard in reserve; the Young Guard were in Plancenoît, where they were to remain until the battle was over. As Wellington's telescope swept the eastern hills for the hundredth time, it showed him something that Sergeant Robertson of the Gordons noticed a few minutes later: 'something extraordinary' going on. The enemy's extreme right was under a cross-fire – was turned – was in flight. At that instant – somewhere about 7.30 pm – an aide-de-camp from the Duke himself came spurring down the Highlanders' rear.

'The day is our own! The Prussians have arrived!'

Then the Highlanders and all other regiments who were near fixed their eyes impatiently on the focal point – the Duke of Wellington standing in his stirrups at his command-post by the tree, a sudden ray of the setting sun throwing into relief the unforgettable but indescribable expression on his face. This was the decisive moment. Every soldier knew it. Some advised only limited action. The Duke knew better.

'Oh, damn it!' he exclaimed. 'In for a penny, in for a pound,' and taking off his hat he waved it three times towards the French.[52] In a flash his signal was understood. Three deafening cheers of relief and exultation burst out as the foremost regiments, led by Vivian's and Vandeleur's light cavalry, swooped on to the plain.

The Duke put spurs to Copenhagen and plunging through the mêlée, called on each regiment to charge under whatever officer had survived to lead it. Standing amid billows of smoke he caught sight of Harry Smith. Smith had been stupefied by the sudden silence of the guns, knowing that one side must have retreated – but which? A hearty 'British shout' had given him the answer. Then came the Duke's urgent voice:

'Where are your people? . . . Tell them to form companies and move on immediately.'

'In which direction, my lord?' Smith had completely lost his bearings in the fog. Wellington pointed, 'Why, right ahead.'

One of the last cannon-shots to rake the fields below La Haye Sainte flew over Copenhagen's neck and smashed into Uxbridge's right knee.

'By God! I've lost my leg!'

'Have you, by God?' Wellington lowered his telescope and supported his gallant second-in-command until others came to carry him away. Then he galloped on.[53]

Now Frederick Adam was galloping with him, and they both saw the group of enemy infantry and artillery rallying on a hill opposite. It was one of their shells that had brought down Uxbridge.

'Adam, you must dislodge those fellows,' ordered the Duke in his staccato way. Adam's brigade did their work and the French cannonading ceased for good. Now Sir Hussey's voice rang out.

'18th! you will follow me.'

'To hell!' they roared back. All three Hussar regiments, the 18th, 7th and 10th, charged furiously down the hill, the 18th capturing a French battery at *La Belle-Alliance* and the other two breaking a square of the Guard, though with terrible loss. Even the dead inflicted wounds, for the countless swords and bayonets sticking up all over the fields cut the fetlocks of the horses.[54]

The Highlanders above La Haye Sainte rushed down upon the farm and gravel-pit, 'like a legion of demons', driving the French before them and mingling with the first Prussian soldiers on the Brussels road. A Prussian band began to play 'God Save the King' and the English responded with 'Nun danket Alle Gott'.

At the heart of the struggle was still the Duke, urging Copenhagen over the blood-soaked cornfields and splintered hedges. Above him the Congreve rockets streaked ever more brightly across the darkening sky.

This time it was Colonel Felton Hervey who tried to make him go back.

'We are getting into enclosed ground, and your life is too valuable to be thrown away.' But again the Duke had a reason, if the opposite one from before, for staying where he was.

'Never mind, let them fire away. The battle's won; my life is of no consequence now.'[55]

The numb horror with which Napoleon's army had first watched the Guard give way was rapidly passing into panic. Which were the fatal words that started the rout? '*Nous sommes trahis*' – the spectre of treason ushering in Blücher instead of Grouchy? Treason has been called the 'heart-cry of the Hundred Days'.[56] Or '*Sauve qui peut*' – the fear that in another moment there would be no more army to serve, and therefore it was already time to say, 'Every man for himself'?

Napoleon, pale but resolute, formed the reserve of his Old Guard into squares to stem the torrent. It was impossible. Yet even their failure was magnificent and at least one British soldier watched in awe as a Guard's regiment, amid the bedlam that surrounded them, stalked majestically from the field. Posterity has been no less impressed by the language with which their general, Cambronne, received the Allies' invitation to surrender. Scarcely majestic, it could not be misunderstood.*

Napoleon just had time to spring into his *berline* and reach Genappe before he was overtaken by the Prussians. Out he jumped and on to a horse, his escort of Red Lancers keeping off the mass of fugitives until he had forced his way through Quatre Bras and Frasnes and arrived in Charleroi at 5 am next morning.

Among the treasures captured by the Prussians in Napoleon's handsome dark blue and gilt carriage with vermilion wheels were close on a hundred pieces from a splendidly appointed travelling-case, a million francs' worth of diamonds and a cake of Windsor soap. The carriage was presented to the Prince Regent, exhibited in London and then lost sight of, until picked up for a song by the owner of Madame Tussaud's waxworks. There it was destroyed in the fire of 1925. *Sic transit* . . .

It was 9 pm on 18 June 1815 and nearly dark when Blücher and Wellington rode forward to greet one another on the Brussels road between *La Belle-Alliance* and Rossomme.

'*Mein lieber Kamerad!*' cried the old hero, leaning forward from his horse to kiss Wellington; '*Quelle affaire!*' That was about all the French he knew, said the Duke long afterwards. But when they were both in Paris a year or two later and the Duke came to visit him, he spoke of the dreadful elephant that had again made an appearance, in French:

'*Je sens un éléphant là,*' he said, pointing to his stomach. This last

---

* ' "*Merde!*" Historians sometimes translate this as "The Guard dies but never surrenders." '
(C. J. Herold and Professor Gordon Wright, *The Battle of Waterloo*, p. 138). Cambronne denied to his son that he had ever used the obscenity.

pregnancy seemed peculiarly ironical since the elephant, he believed, had been fathered on him by a French soldier.[57]

Also ironically, Wellington and Blücher could communicate only in the language of their common enemy – France. War, like Blücher, was a little mad.

'It was the best night of my life,' said Gneisenau after pursuing the French to Frasnes.

For Wellington it was the worst. As he silently walked Copenhagen back to Waterloo, the moonlit fields on either side of the *chaussée* were littered with the dead and dying, with horses, weapons, helmets, caps, belts and feathers. Here and there the sinister shadow of a robber bent over a corpse. Wellington's total losses were close to 15,000. The French lost 25,000 in killed and wounded, the Prussians over 7,000. Altogether between forty and fifty thousand dead and wounded men lay on that small stricken field. Here Major Ramsay had been killed, there Whinyates wounded. Nine generals had all in the end joined the melancholy procession of wounded to the rear. It was true that there were lucky ones: Frederick Ponsonby, desperately wounded first by French sabres and then by Polish lances, ridden over by the Prussians, robbed, used as a musket-rest by a *tirailleur* and as a place to die on by a mortally wounded soldier, and later found still alive by a British infantryman who mounted guard over him till morning; and Sergeants Morris and Burton of the 73rd.

'Out with the grog, Tom: didn't I tell you there was no shot made for you or me?' Sergeant Burton had his own ideas about the hand of Providence. He and Tom Morris were two out of the seventy surviving men from their battalion of 550.

There were also dauntless characters who though desperately wounded had not felt the finger of death: Lord Uxbridge, whose pulse never changed when his leg was amputated and who next morning joked with the Marquise d'Assche when he arrived on a stretcher at her hotel:

'Well, Marquise, you see I shan't be able to dance with you any more except with a wooden leg.' And Fitzroy Somerset who called out to his surgeons:

'Hallo! don't carry away that arm till I've taken off my ring' – the ring given him by Wellington's niece Emily at their marriage.[58]

It was too soon after the terrible events of the day for Wellington to feel even a gleam of comfort. Nevertheless, life must go on. After dismounting at 11 pm outside his inn at Waterloo he gave Copenhagen an approving pat on the hindquarters. Copenhagen lashed out and nearly inflicted the wound that Wellington had miraculously escaped on the battlefield. Copenhagen had Arab blood from his dam and was a grandson of the famous racehorse Eclipse. After his death the Duke would say:

There may have been many faster horses, no doubt many handsomer, but for bottom and endurance I never saw his fellow.[59]

Supper was a subdued meal. Wellington had just seen his favourite aide-de-camp, Alexander Gordon, whose smashed leg Dr Hume had amputated on the battlefield two or three hours before.

'Thank God you are safe,' whispered Gordon. The Duke told the wounded man about the victory and then said encouragingly, 'I have no doubt, Gordon, you will do well.' But his young friend felt the finger of death and could not answer; he was carried on Wellington's instructions to his own bed.

Müffling dropped in about midnight with the news that Blücher was speaking of the 'Battle of *La Belle-Alliance*'. Wellington said nothing for he had already decided to call the battle as usual by the name of his headquarters, Waterloo. He looked up anxiously each time the door opened. Could it be one of his missing young men? When hope had vanished he held up both hands and said, 'The hand of Almighty God has been upon me this day.'

He drank one toast only, in a glass of wine with Alava – 'To the Memory of the Peninsular War'. Then he got up, quickly lay down on a pallet and was fast asleep.[60]

While the Duke was still sleeping the wounded Prince of Orange wrote at 2 am from Brussels to his parents at The Hague. His letter was as usual in French.

Victoire! Victoire!
  Mes très chers Parents
We have had a magnificent affair against Napoleon today . . . it was my corps which principally gave battle and to which we owe the victory, but the affair was entirely decided by the attack which the Prussians made on the enemy's right. I am wounded by a ball in the left shoulder but only slightly.[61]

The Prince's bullet-torn jacket was preserved at the Soestdijk Palace. Wrapped in tissue paper inside a painted box and enclosed in a silver casket are the splintered fragments of bone which, weeks after the battle, were still working their way out of his shoulder.*

* The Prince's Waterloo relics are now in the Royal House at The Hague.

An hour after the Prince had begun his Waterloo letter, the Duke was woken by Dr Hume. For once the Beau had been too tired to wash. He sat up in bed and stretched out his hand to the doctor. Hume took it and held it while he told the Duke that Alexander Gordon had just collapsed and died in his arms. Then he recited the long list of casualties which had come in since midnight. It was even more shocking than Wellington had suspected. Dr Hume felt tears dropping on his hand and looking up from the list he saw them chasing down the Duke's face, making furrows in the sweat and grime. As Wellington brushed them away with his hand he said in a broken voice,

'Well, thank God, I don't know what it is to lose a battle; but certainly nothing can be more painful than to gain one with the loss of so many of one's friends.' Wellington dressed and began his despatch to Lord Bathurst, the War Minister – the renowned but controversial 'Waterloo despatch'.[62] The stupendous event, the titanic endurance, the blaze of glory, the oceans of blood deflected him not an inch from his accustomed brevity and restraint. His 'description of troops' was reduced to a minimum. The Horse Artillery were not mentioned by name, nor any of the Hussar regiments, nor Colborne and his victorious 52nd. A reference to bravery found its way into the text only once (over the Guards at Hougoumont) as did steadiness (the infantry at Quatre Bras) and glory (when Picton fell) but there were four mentions of distinguished or highly distinguished conduct and five of gallantry or the utmost gallantry (the Brunswickers at Quatre Bras and the Guards at Hougoumont again).

Every sentence was scrutinized for praise or neglect of individuals or regiments. Lord Uxbridge's sister, Caroline Capel, called it 'odious',[63] while one Waterloo officer, William Leeke, busied himself for over half a century in trying to convince the world that the 52nd alone and singlehanded had repulsed the Imperial Guard and won the battle of Waterloo. The omission of Colborne's name from the despatch was certainly an error on Wellington's part; it was said that when he asked for Colborne's report, that great and good soldier was seeing to his wounded and could not be found. Wellington himself may have come to regret his reticence. Sir Winston Churchill told Field-Marshal Montgomery that a friend once asked the aged Duke whether, if he had his life over again, there was any way in which he could have done better. The Duke replied, 'Yes, I should have given more praise.'[64]

Who won the battle of Waterloo? Wellington refused to discuss it. When Colonel Gurwood, editor of the *Despatches*, tried to pin him down, he said impatiently,

'Oh, I know nothing of the services of particular regiments; there was glory enough for all.'[65]

This left the field open to claims (beside those already mentioned) ranging from Sir Hussey Vivian to the Prussian army – and of course Napoleon, as some of the monuments erected and literature sold on the battlefield today make clear. In the case of the Prussians nothing could have prevented national rivalries, but the Duke at least paid them an unqualified tribute in his despatch:

I should not do justice to my own feelings, or to Marshal Blücher and the Prussian army, if I did not attribute the successful result of this arduous day to the cordial and timely assistance I received from them. The operation of General Bülow upon the enemy's flank was a most decisive one. . . .[66]

Those who believe Napoleon's campaign entitled him to the moral victory are usually concerned to prove that his total genius as a man was greater than Wellington's. This grand question, like other important comparisons, must be left until the end of the Duke's life. At Waterloo, Wellington's firepower served him better than Napoleon's, his lines better than Napoleon's columns, his generals better than Napoleon's marshals, even though he had not selected or welcomed all of them.

Manoeuvres give a battle its cachet. In one sense no one was to blame for the absence of manoeuvres at Waterloo. Napoleon had to strike quickly. There was not time for a typically Napoleonic sweep through the difficult, waterlogged country on his right, and Wellington was prepared for him – over-prepared – on his left. Nevertheless, without risking lengthy sweeps, Napoleon could have fought a battle, as Reille suggested, of movement. That Waterloo became a pounding-match was his responsibility. Weary and still dispirited, Wellington described it to Beresford on 2 July 1815:

Never did I see such a pounding match. Both were what the boxers call gluttons. Napoleon did not manoeuvre at all. He just moved forward in the old style, in columns, and was driven off in the old style.[67]

Napoleon's contempt for the 'Sepoy General' had always served him ill and at Waterloo it ruined him. Wellington did not make the mistake of despising his opponent.

Rather than admit that Wellington routed Napoleon, people sometimes suggest that neither was at his best. This was true of Napoleon's health which may have affected his tactics, but not of his strategy. Indeed, Wellington himself told Charles Greville in 1820 that 'Bonaparte's march upon Belgium was the finest thing ever done – so rapid and so well combined'.[68] Nor was it true of the Duke's tactical and personal achievements on the battlefield, which far outshone Napoleon's. He *was* the battle, as countless eye-witnesses felt:

. . . his entire concentrated attention, exclusive aim, and intense thought were devoted impartially, imperturbably and grandly to the Whole, the All.[69]

Before 5 am on Monday morning the Duke started off with his unfinished despatch for Brussels.

Some twenty years on, in 1836, a new generation in the shape of young Lady Salisbury tried to recapture from the Duke the flavour of victory. If he could not feel triumph on the field itself as he strenuously assured her, it must have come to him on the way back to Brussels.

'But now!' she urged, 'while you were riding there! Did it never occur to you that you had placed yourself on such a pinnacle of glory?'

The Duke might have replied, with Johnny Kincaid, that it was the most uncomfortable heap of glory he ever had a hand in.[70] He was more matter of fact.

'No. I was entirely occupied with what was necessary to be done.'[71]

Napoleon had not yet been scotched, the Allied army had to be reorganized, and there was still the despatch to finish. The Duke went up to his hotel room in Brussels and sat down at the open window, pen in hand. There was a crowd round his door among whom he recognized Mr Creevey.

'What news?' called Creevey, for the accounts in Brussels were still confused.

Wellington called back, 'Why, I think we've done for 'em this time.' Creevey looked incredulous.

'Come up here,' said the Duke, 'and I'll tell you all about it.'

Wellington at once began to fire off his views in what Creevey now knew to be his natural way – short and blunt, with a succession of quick monosyllables; but without a spark of joy.

'It has been a damned serious business. Blücher and I have lost 30,000 men. It has been a damned nice thing – the nearest run thing you ever saw in your life.'*

---

* *Creevey*, p. 142. Wellington's rough figures, given less than twenty-four hours after the battle, are too high. They should be between 22,000 and 23,000 for his own and Blücher's combined casualties at Waterloo. Many of those reported to Wellington as missing were afterwards found to have gone back with the wounded but later rejoined their units.

Then the Duke let his thoughts play on the battle, on the crises at Hougoumont and above La Haye Sainte, on the endless watching for trouble, galloping towards it, rallying the waverers under shot and shell – and under the finger of Providence. It had all hung on the thread of one life. At last he burst out,

'By God! I don't think it would have done if I had not been there!'

He did not tell Creevey about the finger of Providence at Waterloo, though he did bring it in at the end of a note written that same day to Lady Frances Webster: 'The finger of Providence was upon me, and I escaped unhurt.'[72]

His brother William, who had already heard about the finger at Sorauren, was given an insight into that other force on which Arthur had depended at Waterloo – the British infantry:

. . . It was the most desperate business I ever was in. I never took so much trouble about any Battle, & never was so near being beat. Our loss is immense particularly in that best of all Instruments, British Infantry. I never saw the Infantry behave so well.[73]

Within a few weeks his view that victory was almost as bad as defeat had grown into something like a revulsion from war itself.

'I hope to God that I have fought my last battle,' he told Lady Shelley. 'It is a bad thing to be always fighting.'[74]

His hope was to be fulfilled. But would it be easy, even possible, to set aside for ever the trade in which he had shown his incomparable genius, and yet remain the nation's servant, retained for life? He was a hero for life. That would not make it any easier. It meant beginning again at the top.

Personal problems, also, would have to be solved in the limelight. As a soldier he had scolded or promoted his young men in the secluded villages of Portugal or the Pyrenees. Now it would be young women, and his headquarters an opera box.

'My die is cast.' He had said it in 1808 when he gave up politics for soldiering. Now the hero of Waterloo was about to reverse the decision. Creevey and others would think it a foolish gamble for a hero to take. But he had never felt a hero, not even on the morning after Waterloo, as young Lady Salisbury, cross-questioning him in 1836, was at last to be convinced.

'I cannot conceive,' she persisted, 'how it was that you did not think how infinitely you had raised your name above every other.'

'That is a feeling of vanity,' he said simply. 'One's first thought is for the public service.'

'But there *must* be a satisfaction, and a lasting one, in that feeling of superiority that you *always* enjoy. It is not in human nature it should be otherwise.'

'That is true . . .' he conceded. 'But when the war is over, and the troops disbanded, what is this great general more than anybody else?'

Try as she would she could not get him to tell her what it was like to be a hero. He only kept saying that carpenters and shoemakers and farmers could all beat him on their own ground.

'I feel I am but a man.'[75]

He probably did not remember he had used those very words to a friend twenty-three years earlier, in 1813, after his triumphal entry into Cádiz.

I ought to have somebody behind me to remind me that I am 'but a man'.

They stood for what was almost his hair-shirt, but worn as naturally and comfortably as his civilian clothes on the battlefield.

24

End of an Occupation

Boney's beat! Boney's beat!
Hurrah! hurrah! Boney's beat.

Highlanders shouted and stamped out the compulsive rhythm as they brought their wounded into Antwerp from Waterloo early on Monday morning, 19 June 1815. No one behind the lines suspected the titanic scale of Wellington's victory. The Highlanders did their best to convey it.

The nameless dead of Waterloo lay out under the burning June sun, a growing horror to man and beast. Carriage-horses approaching from Brussels would scream at the smell of corruption. On the Monday and Tuesday piles of dead horses began to be collected for burning. Some were swollen to monstrous size so that the soldiers could hardly lug them to the bonfires. The human dead went into great pits or were burned by peasants protected with handkerchiefs and using the longest possible pitchforks.

On the day after Waterloo the Duke spent many hours visiting the wounded. Among them young Colonel Frederick Ponsonby had been appallingly mauled and left on the field for dead. When he recovered as if by a miracle, the Duke felt bound to keep a friendly eye on him for the rest of his life, which included lending him a large sum of money.[1] William Verner of the 7th Hussars was another young officer who needed a personal visit from the Duke to recall him almost from the grave. 'You are not nearly so bad as you think,' said the Duke briskly. At the end of a month Verner had neither hair on his head nor flesh on his bones, but he was on his feet.[2]

The time had come for Wellington to complete the overthrow of Bonaparte. He left Mont-Saint-Jean to join his army at Nivelles. It was Tuesday 20 June. All around him the grass was white with scraps of paper – letters home, laundry bills, muster rolls, memoranda and love-letters shed by the dead and wounded of both sides. On his left as he rode off stood the elm tree that had been his command-post above the field of battle. Ripped and battered by gunfire, it was to be felled in 1818, and twenty years later, in the year of Queen Victoria's coronation, made into two chairs, one for Her Majesty and the other for the Duke.

Long before his chair was carved, honours had been lavished upon him by the crowned heads of Europe. If there was still any doubt as to who had won the battle, Tsar Alexander 1 of Russia set it at rest. He presented a diamond-hilted sword to the man whom he named 'Conqueror of Waterloo'.[3] Kings would henceforth call him '*Mon Cousin*', for William 1 of the Netherlands had created the Duke a prince – Prince of Waterloo.

The crown meanwhile had slipped from another head, that of Napoleon Bonaparte, Emperor of the French. He abdicated in favour of his son.

Wellington crossed the border into France on 21 June, three days after Waterloo. It was a moment of triumph. Nevertheless, the follow-up after a victory had never been his favourite operation. Indeed he was later to inform an agreeable young friend in the diplomatic corps, Philip von Neumann, that there was nothing worse than a battle won except a battle lost. To which the Austrian replied with that pleasing mixture of tartness and flattery learnt in his profession, that the Duke could not make the comparison because he had never lost a battle.

Up till the 20th only one man in London had received the news of Napoleon's defeat. An agent of Nathan Rothschild, the banker, arrived from Ostend on that evening bringing his employer a garbled account in a Dutch newspaper of a resounding Allied victory. Next morning Rothschild's newspaper was in the hands of the British Cabinet. The Prime Minister, Lord Liverpool, did not believe it. The Cabinet sat on it. Throughout Wednesday contradictory reports agitated London. William Wellesley-Pole heard that there had been a terrible defeat. Other rumours were of victory. Bets were laid in the London clubs, many of Brooks's Whigs backing Napoleon for a win. According to one legend, Rothschild had withheld the good news from the Cabinet until early afternoon, standing by his accustomed pillar in the Stock Exchange on the Wednesday morning with a glum face and buying up cheap the funds which he had deceitfully depressed. This of course was a fabrication, though one apparently believed by Wellington. Not until evening did Lord Liverpool discover that Rothschild's news was true.[4]

Henry Percy, one of the Duke's very few aides-de-camp to come through Waterloo without a serious wound, brought the news to the Cabinet twenty-four hours after it was known to Rothschild.

He had left Brussels for Ostend on the 20th, Wellington's despatch folded inside a purple velvet sachet given to him by a dancing-partner at the Duchess of Richmond's 'Waterloo Ball'. Still in his blood-stained uniform, he had had to row to the Kent coast after becoming becalmed. From Broadstairs, which he reached about 3 pm on the 21st, he dashed to London with two captured French eagles, their banners fluttering from the windows of his chaise-and-four. A noisy crowd followed the eagles, some demanding information, others shouting, 'Wellington's safe!' The battle had not been a Trafalgar.[5]

Arrived at Harrowby's house in Grosvenor Square, Percy presented the despatch. Lord Harrowby's fourteen-year-old daughter Mary, roused from sleep by the uproar (the time was 11 pm), tiptoed to the head of the stairs and was transfixed by the sight of a dusty young soldier plunging into her father's panelled ante-room with a cry of 'Victory! victory!'. Here Wellington's despatch was opened. Then Lord Harrowby read it aloud to the milling crowd under his windows, while Percy galloped off to lay the eagles at the Prince Regent's feet.

Only a single account of Waterloo would do for Wellington – his own official despatch. He discouraged research into the campaign, including the hypothetical question of an Allied retreat, an issue which nagged the Duke.

'Pray, what would your Grace have done,' asked a Waterloo commander, Frederick Adam, one day at dinner, 'if the French Guards had not been dispersed?'

'Oh, I should have retired to the Bois de Soignes and given battle again next morning.'

'But if you could not have done that?'

'It could never have been so bad as that you know,' retorted the Duke, ruffled. He got up and ordered the coffee.[6] In the days of 1814 he had ordered the coffee to cut short an embarrassing flow of compliments. Now the coffee was used to short-circuit a painful recall of that 'close-run thing'.

Adam's needling concerned the physical difficulties of retreating through a forest. An answer was given by the Duke ten years later at a dinner given by his niece's husband, Edward Littleton: he could have retreated if he had wanted to but did not want to. 'I never contemplated a retreat on Brussels. My plan was to keep my ground till the Prussians appeared, and then to attack the French position, and I executed my plan.'

There had been a time in August 1815 when Croker hoped to write 'a full history of Waterloo' under the Duke's guidance. The Duke, however, did not want a history. 'The history of a battle is not unlike the history of a ball. . . .' Individuals might remember particular incidents, but 'no individual can recollect the exact order in which, or the exact moment at which, they occurred, which makes all the difference as to their value or importance'.[7]

Many years later when a baronet, Sir Watkyn Williams Wynn, began asking him in a pronounced Welsh accent whether he had had a good view of the battle, Wellington cut him short – 'I generally like to see what I am about.'[8]

There was also the unknown lady who made a disastrous conversational gambit.

'Is it true, Duke, that you were surprised at Waterloo?'

'No, Madam, but I am now!'[9] Yet Wellington himself had declared at the Duchess of Richmond's ball, 'Napoleon has *humbugg'd* me, by God.'

Wellington solved his problem with a typical slash at the knot. If he could not stop the historians he would not read their histories.

The great man, meanwhile, prepared to occupy Paris. At times there had seemed a disagreeable prospect of his having to storm some of the French fortresses on the route. However, Napoleon had left for Rochefort on the south-west coast of France, disregarding the excellent advice of his Minister of the Interior, Lazare Carnot, that he should flee to America – 'From there you will again make your enemies tremble' – and the Bourbon royal family were about to enter their capital in the wake of Wellington's army, 'with the baggage', as it was scornfully noted. Wellington proposed to ride in on his bright chestnut, Copenhagen, decked with gold and silver trappings. Madame D'Arblay, the novelist Fanny Burney, who was married to a member of Louis XVIII's bodyguard, wrote to her husband in ecstasy, 'Immortal Wellington! *Vive! vive! vive!*'

Other ladies more dazzling than Fanny were soon to gather round him: Lady Shelley, Mrs Arbuthnot, Lady Frances Wedderburn-Webster, Lady Caroline Lamb, Lady Charlotte Greville and Madame de Staël, not to mention the singers Grassini, Catalani and their sisterhood – all the beauty and seductiveness of Paris to which he was now coming not, as in 1814, a mere ambassador, but to be the country's only effective prince – Prince of Waterloo. It took him four months before he was ready to receive into this galaxy his own sad star, Kitty, Duchess of Wellington, still waiting in England.

At the same time, Paris meant problems as well as parties. There was also the private soldier to be christened. The Prince of Waterloo may have found time during the first weeks after victory to invent the Tommy.

A military paper had been submitted to him suggesting a typical name for a private. The Duke crossed out the entry and substituted the name of a veteran in his old regiment, the 33rd Foot. Private Thomas Atkins had been with him during the wretched retreat towards Antwerp in 1794. At one tense moment he ordered his 33rd, held in reserve, to form open lanes and let the crumbling first line through to the rear, then fill the gap themselves – a grim manoeuvre. Though they succeeded, Thomas Atkins was one who fell, to become immortal after Waterloo.*

Wellington's humane hope was to arrange the capitulation of Paris without further fighting. He succeeded, though at the cost of misunderstanding and future trouble.

At first there was nothing but profound relief. 'It is true, thank God!' wrote Wellington's artillery commander at 2 pm on 3 July. 'Paris has surrendered. . . .' The provisional government under Fouché agreed to withdraw the French army of some 100,000 men to the left bank of the Loire while all disputed articles in their proposed terms of surrender were dropped except for Articles XI and XII. Through these articles Fouché intended to protect the public monuments and those inhabitants of Paris who by reason of their functions during the

* The above version of the well-known story seems on balance to be the most probable. The RAMC Historical Museum, Aldershot, possesses an original pay-book with the name Thomas Atkins at the top of its specimen page and the date 24th June 1815 at the bottom. The Duke cannot have chosen the name as late as 1843 while Warden of the Cinque Ports according to the usual version, since there is an actual entry in this pay-book (following the specimen pages) as early as 1825. The fact that 24th June 1815 was given as the specimen date on the title page raises the strong likelihood that the Duke changed the name to Tommy Atkins on the proof copy soon after this date. (See A. L. Kipling, *Bulletin of the Military Historical Society*, February 1957; Fortescue, *History of the British Army*, vol. xii., fn. p. 568; *Cornhill Magazine*, June 1915, pp. 755–6; *Winter's Pie*, Christmas 1912, pp. 38–40. I am greatly indebted to Maj.-Gen. A. MacLennan, OBE, Curator of the RAMC Museum, for his kindness, and to Mr Dineen, RUSI, for his tracing of documents.

Hundred Days might find themselves in danger. The key sentence in Article XII ran:

The inhabitants, and in general terms all persons who are in the French capital at this moment, will continue to enjoy their rights and liberties. . . .

This was ambiguous. Who was an 'inhabitant'? Would it prohibit King Louis from punishing traitors? When the Convention of Saint-Cloud was ratified on 4 July Wellington had no thought whatever of interfering in a future French civil government. His mind was occupied, as always after a battle, with protecting civilians from military excesses.

As far as the Prussians were concerned, Marshal Blücher saw nothing wrong in reprisals – though when some of his troops entered his own quarters in search of loot the old man expostulated, '*Mes enfants, c'est trop.*' 'He is a famous old fellow,' the Duke told Lady Shelley, 'though he don't quite stop his troops in plundering.'[10]

The difference between British and Prussian ideas had become evident as soon as the two armies left Waterloo. Wellington not only forbade pillaging but ordered his men to respect every inch of the French countryside, crossing the cornfields in single file. 'The impression towards him and his army is indescribable,' wrote Castlereagh from Paris.[11] But the Prussians remained unabashed after indulging in rape and murder on a savage scale. 'England has never been overrun by French armies,' one of them explained, 'or you would act as we do. The French acted a cruel part in Prussia . . . they taught us a lesson we are now come to France to put into practice.'[12]

Though Wellington could not prevent all excesses, he did frustrate Blücher's intention to blow up the bridges of Austerlitz and Jena and Bonaparte's pillar in the Place Vendôme, contrary to Article XI of the Convention which protected public buildings. The story of how Wellington 'kept the bridge' of Jena was rather more Horatian (in the sense that he had several assistants) than his admirers admitted. Talleyrand was in fact the first to get wind of its imminent destruction by Blücher. But when his government protested under Article XI, Blücher replied that the bridge had already been mined and he very much hoped that M. de Talleyrand would be standing on the parapet. King Louis then declared himself willing (though perhaps not quite able) to jump off it, if the Prussians so wished. Wellington promptly posted a British sentry on the bridge. He was amused to hear afterwards that the Prussian engineers, fuses in hand, had requested his sentry to remove himself, to which this stolid Britisher replied, 'Not until I am relieved by the corporal.'[13]

As for Napoleon, having failed to get a guaranteed safe passage to America from Rochefort, he decided on 13 July to throw himself on the mercy of Britain's Prince Regent.

Your Royal Highness.... I have ended my political career and come, like Themistocles, to seat myself at the hearth of the British people. I put myself under the protection of her laws and address this entreaty to Your Highness as the most powerful, the most steadfast and the most generous of my foes.

Bastille Day, 14 July, was his last day on French soil. On the 15th Themistocles donned his green uniform of the Chasseurs of the Guard, inspected the weeping French sailors who were to row him to Captain Maitland's ship, *Bellerophon*, and sailed for Plymouth to see what his assault on British hearts would achieve.

No British Bastille was ready to fall. True, the Prince Regent's first reaction had been favourable. 'Upon my word, a very proper letter: much more so, I must say, than any I ever received from Louis XVIII.'[14]

But on most Tory ears the 'Themistocles' passage grated, and for every radical, like John Cam Hobhouse, who found the whole letter 'very good', there were a hundred citizens longing to have the suppliant hanged. The British Cabinet's choice was St Helena.

Napoleon Bonaparte was carried away on 7 August 1815 to a rock in the South Atlantic where, unexpectedly, he founded a new empire, and in the timeless worlds of literature and thought reigned over far more hearts than ever he had conquered as Emperor of the French.

See Paris and live!

Wellington, as usual on his small chestnut, with a plain red coat, one star and no feathers, 'looked nothing as compared with the rest,' wrote George Keppel. Yet every neck was 'on the stretch' to see the hero, and all throats ready to bawl, 'Vive Wellington!'[15]

Dapper young Captain Gronow noticed a female riding-habit at the Duke's side on 25 July 1815. This was the day of the grand review on the plains of Saint-Denis, the rider being Frances Shelley, wife of Sir John Shelley, Bt. At the end of the complicated manoeuvres the Austrian general, Prince Schwarzenberg, paid Wellington a heartfelt compliment. 'You are the only man who can so well play at this game.'

Beautiful Lady Shelley seemed to Gronow to be playing another game. How 'strange' that the Duke should allow her to cavort around him, mounted on one of his horses. Certain French ladies insinuated that she was indecorous.[16] But the Duke continued to lend her a horse whenever she wished. On occasion it would be Copenhagen. It amused him to see her coping with another Waterloo hero. 'I believe you think the glory greater than the pleasure in riding him!'

Lady Shelley was what Dr Johnson used to call a 'rapturist'. Her enthusiasm for Wellington – 'How I adore that great man!' –sometimes bored him. She watched his face at manoeuvres. Why did it stiffen when his soldiers took off their hats to him and shouted? 'I hate that cheering. If once you allow soldiers to express an opinion, they may, on some other occasion, hiss instead of cheer[ing].' Then he relaxed. 'However, I cannot always help my fellows giving me a hurrah!'

She watched his face in his own house. Would he not dislike peace and quiet after the military life? Surely he would never settle down?

'Oh! yes I shall, but I must always have my house full. For sixteen years I have always been at the head of our army, and I must have these gay fellows round me' – with a glance at his aides-de-camp.

On a different point he showed a lack of taste, she thought, in picking up some tiny, dusty French child from the boulevards and eating something horrible it offered him. How could he bear to touch the uninteresting little creature? Frances Shelley much preferred the delightful picnics when his friends would sit on a grassy bank while Colonel James Stanhope (uncle of the Duke's future 'Boswell') recited Byron's *Childe Harold*, Catalani, Grassini and Tom Moore sang, or Kemble talked about Shakespeare and Walter Scott about Mme de Pompadour. Scott told Frances that Wellington was the only man who had ever made him feel awed and abashed.[17]

Then there was the sensational press report on Wellington and Lady Frances Wedderburn-Webster. That Wellington was attracted to this unusual girl (pretty, pious, married at seventeen to a self-confessed libertine and Byron's inamorata though not his mistress) is proved by the fact that he wrote brief notes to her both on the morning of Waterloo and on the day after. That he was her lover is highly unlikely, though the contrary cannot be proved. He had been introduced to her for the first time shortly before the battle and at this date she was seven months gone in pregnancy. It might be argued that in the hectic atmosphere preceding Waterloo anything could happen, that the tensions unwound in Frances Webster's company. 'I am but a man,' he had said of himself. The argument, such as it is, does not stand up to the contrary statement that Wellington was soon making to his closest friends, such as Alava.

The *St James's Chronicle* reported:

The husband has laid his damages at £50,000 which it is said the fortunate lover offered to pay; but this affair was too notorious for composition or the party injured had too much sensibility to be content with wearing 'gilded' horns.

Two days later the newspaper followed up with a spread-as-you-deny paragraph.

Several of the public prints have in some particulars gone too far in their insinuations ... and have blamed a 'crim.con.' and magnified damages in their usual sweeping way. ... We may moreover ask, if the rumour of a criminal connection at an antecedent period, while subsequent to it the wedded parties lived & appeared together ... be sufficient grounds for an action at law?

Predictably, an unctuous denial followed.

We are rejoiced to learn from good authority that there is not the least foundation for a story of criminal intercourse on the Continent. ...

But a later paragraph reinstated the scandal.

A very beautiful woman of Irish extraction is said to be a party in the amour at Brussels which has made so great a noise on the Continent.

The public soon heard that Captain Wedderburn-Webster, instead of instituting proceedings against his wife for adultery, intended to combine with Lady Frances in bringing a (successful) joint action for libel against the *St James's Chronicle*. Whether or not Webster at first contemplated a divorce action is not known. But by the early autumn of 1815 Wellington had convinced him there was no ground for divorce. The Duchess of Wellington was sent for in October, which may have been part of the same operation. Certainly there was a note of relief in Lord Liverpool's letter to Castlereagh announcing the fact.

The Wedderburn-Websters pass dismally from history. By 1828 the family were in financial trouble, owing to Webster's extravagance, and periodic entreaties reached the Duke for patronage. His polite but steady refusals were understandable.

Then there was the problem of returning the works of art that Napoleon had looted, without hurting French feelings. This was to prove impossible. Was there a solution that Wellington overlooked? It seems unlikely. His troubles derived from the very nature of loot. Loot is not subject to an ethical code. Wellington later defined it as 'what you could lay your bloody hands upon and keep'.[18] In 1815 he had to be satisfied with such morsels of comfort as a letter from Pope Pius VII. His Holiness was delighted to hear that the Vatican treasures were being restored and 'with unexampled generosity' England was paying for the transport.[19]

Napoleon had made the Pope pay the cost of abduction.

Far worse than the 'arts' controversy was that of the 'traitors'. Under the so-called White Terror, Generals Ney and Lavalette, and Colonel de La Bedoyère were arrested. Wellington did not intervene. When Ney and La Bedoyère were shot (Lavalette escaping in his wife's clothes) Wellington was widely accused of a punitive peace.

On 20 November 1815 the Second Peace of Paris was concluded with France. Though Richelieu was deathly white as he signed for France, afterwards writing, 'all is finished . . . I have put my name to this fatal treaty!', the peace treaty was fatal only to vindictive Prussian hopes. Minor border adjustments were made; French fortresses were dismantled but not seized; there was to be an indemnity of 700 million francs; and France was to be occupied for a minimum of three and a maximum of five years by 150,000 Allied soldiers, fed at French expense and commanded as from 22 October by the Duke of Wellington. Even an army of occupation was not necessarily fatal to future international harmony. But behind the peace terms stood the ominous 'Holy Alliance'. Through this innovation the Duke feared being drawn into perpetual intervention.

The Holy Alliance was the precious brainchild of Tsar Alexander I. Announced at a grand review, it was signed for a start by himself, the Austrian emperor and the Prussian king on 26 September – a combination of mystical dilettantism inspired by the Tsar's personal priestess, Madame de Krüdener; of near-Messianic crusade for a Christian brotherhood of rulers and nations; and of political ambition to extend Russia's influence by sweeping under her wings all Christian nations, including Britain's maritime rival, America. Neither Britain nor America signed. Castlereagh described how he and Wellington had reacted to the invitation: 'The Duke of Wellington happened to be with me when the Emperor called, and it was not without difficulty that we went through the interview with becoming gravity.' In fine, it was 'sublime nonsense' – something idealistic and imprecise from which the first British instinct was, and still is, to sheer off.

A second innovation was produced by Castlereagh in a firm

tightening of the Quadruple Alliance. He had come to the conclusion that a permanent conference of the four ambassadors at Paris was required during the occupation, not to interfere unnecessarily in the four occupied zones but to keep an eye on France for any signs of revolution. In the short run, his five-year plan for nannying France – for such it soon seemed to be – could only damage the popularity of Wellington and his four-pronged army of occupation. If anything went wrong he would be blamed. If it succeeded it would only be for the benefit of Castlereagh and the politicians. Would he not show common prudence and stay out? But no – his friend, Sir John Malcolm, recorded:

He is confident that his opinions may do good, and cannot do harm; & he is ready to encounter all the abuse that can be poured upon him, rather than show the prudence which fights more about personal character than public interests.[20]

Increasing hostility towards the occupation inevitably affected Wellington's popularity. It was further damaged by the discontents of soldiers after a war. On one side, the Commander-in-Chief's ineffable glory blazed forth. At regimental feasts his name in laurel leaves would appear level with the Duke of York's.

On the other side was an angry suspicion on the part of the common soldiers that like their Peninsular comrades they would not get even one medal. In 1815 Wellington hoped he had scotched that serpent by ordering an identical silver Waterloo medal for all officers and men alike. Sergeant Robertson praised the Duke's decision: 'As we had all shared equally in the dangers of the day, we should all partake alike in its glories.'

Many officers, however, were dissatisfied with the glories in which Wellington invited them to partake. Colonel Lygon, for example, rejected the Cross of the *Second Class* of the Order of St Vladimir as degrading.

'Won't Colonel Lygon accept it?' said the Duke. 'Well then, give it to Colonel Somebody-else, who will.'[21]

The politics of occupation, meanwhile, did not improve. In France it was felt that the feeding of the hundred and fifty thousand would require a miracle. Then Pozzo di Borgo, for Russia, came up with the miracle. What could be easier than to reduce the army of occupation? Let the Duke of Wellington send home thirty thousand men forthwith.

The Duke was in a dilemma. Though personally not unfavourable, a 'Red' disturbance provoked by the 'White Terror' of Artois and his Ultras indicated the dangers of premature evacuation. On the other hand the Russians were playing for French favour. Must he stand aside and let them win? It was crucial to decide whether or not the French people were basically loyal to the occupying forces. He decided they were, if only to be saved from the 'White Terror'. In such a climate it might well be both politic and generous to reduce the army of occupation.

This would mean going to England for discussions and incidentally for the change of air his health needed. On 24 June he wrote privately to the War Minister suggesting a visit to Cheltenham. The public did not know that the Duke had already decided by the 24th to go home. So when a startling event occurred next day, they thought he had been driven out by a gunpowder plot.

On 25 June he gave a great ball in his Parisian mansion, rue Champs Elysées, in honour of the royal princes. It was noted that the princes left early. In the small hours a part of the basement was found to be on fire. Gunpowder, cartridges and shavings had been pushed through the bars of the area window, shattering the iron and setting the floorboards alight. Footmen quickly put out the flames and the host made light of the incident. Nevertheless most people interpreted it as a Royalist crime, and Wellington's nonchalance as an attempt to hush up his quarrel with the Ultras.

Crowds visited Cheltenham during July to watch the Great Duke strolling in public with his wife and two sons. Kitty wrote happily about various improvements in her hero. He was 'considerably better both in looks & spirits since his arrival in England', and had more time for his boys. 'I say with delight they are as fond of and as familiar with their noble & beloved Father as if they had never been separated from him. They accompany him on his walks, *chat* with him, play with him. In short they are the chosen companions of each other. . . .'[22]

In private, the rivalries between his admirers such as Lady Jersey, Lady Shelley and Mrs Arbuthnot, which for years were to be a bizarre feature of his social life, made a brief beginning. 'You are all Syrens!' he wrote to Mrs Arbuthnot. 'You the Principal: & want to keep me from where I ought to be'[23] – namely, in the City of London, discussing the financial plight of France. There was also Lady Caroline Lamb, who needed protecting from herself. His object was to see Caroline reconciled to her husband, William Lamb.*

---

* William Lamb, 2nd Viscount Melbourne (1779–1848), Prime Minister 1834 and 1835–41. Married in 1805 Lady Caroline Ponsonby, who died in 1828.

Giving good advice to pretty women with problems was becoming one of the Duke's pleasures. Gossip reported that Lady Kinnaird was about to leave her husband, while Lord Holland in his memoirs observed cryptically that she was 'living in intimacy' with the Duke of Wellington. Was this in reality another attempted reconciliation between a husband and wife? If so, it would strengthen the conclusion that Wellington's endeavours (like Gladstone's towards the end of the century) were all too likely to start up rumours of affairs with the very women he was trying to help.

In a similarly conciliatory mood he had written to Richelieu from Cheltenham on 18 July that the British Government would be very sympathetic to a cut of thirty thousand in the occupation troops.

Hardly was he reinstalled in France than it appeared that his own attitude to concessions had become one of opposition. This seemed surprising, considering that while he was in England Louis XVIII had, with his approval, sent the diehard *Chambre Introuvable* packing, and the subsequent elections had produced a more moderate Chamber. Yet the Duke's reception of these political improvements was nonetheless cautious. Troops could not be reduced before the end of the season. After all, the new deputies had not yet been put to the test by a vote on the indemnity. Would they pay up?

So disgusted was Richelieu by this reversal of policy that he felt Wellington must have been given fresh instructions in London, 'for it is impossible for me to raise the least doubt upon the straightforwardness and integrity of his character'.[24] Bad news from the French countryside had indeed shocked everybody, Wellington included. The harvest was a failure; distress and consequently disaffection were widespread. In these circumstances Wellington did not feel justified in making more than a minimal concession over troops. He brought down the army, which had risen to 157,886 men, to a strict 150,000 Altogether, the general report on the French situation that he submitted to the Cabinet on 11 December was grim in the extreme. Since his return from England he had noticed a great change for the worse: 'There is a general cry throughout France against the occupation, and as usual, particularly against England.' In face of such hostility no reduction was possible. 'I must find matters in a very different state at Paris . . . to alter this opinion.'[25]

A fortnight later this opinion had been altered. He made a dash to England for one day's emergency meeting with Castlereagh on 26 December. What or who had intervened?

A gradual revolution had in fact been taking place once more in Wellington's ideas, though, as was his way, it had not yet been openly expressed. Due in part to his own realization that things could not go on as they were, the credit for this change was also due to Mme de Staël.

Already suffering from her last illness, Germaine de Staël had reached Paris in October 1816, equally opposed to Bonapartists and ultra-Royalists. For this reason the Duke had called her 'one of us'. By 1816, however, she too condemned the occupation, having become a vehemently patriotic champion of 'France for the French'. The Duke at first refused to accept this development:

I cannot help observing that you still call yourself *French* in spite of being one of us. I reclaim you; we think too highly of you to let you go in this manner. . . . I recognise the battle-fields on which we shall meet when I have the pleasure of arguing with you once more.[26]

But when they met and argued in Mme de Staël's salon that autumn, or continued the argument in a great duel of letters, it was the woman of brass, as the British thought of her, who slowly but surely converted the man of iron. While their verbal antagonism was as keen and well-matched as ever in December 1816 – she urging him to withdraw every Allied soldier forthwith, he standing pat on conference decisions – the French crisis was sharpening the edge of her arguments, not his.

On the day the Duke arrived in England (26 December) William Napier was passing on the Paris gossip to his wife at home. The French, he heard, could not pay the indemnity and Mme de Staël predicted it would be paid in gold the first year, in silver the second and the third in *lead*. 'She certainly belongs to the brazen age herself.'[27]

Brazen or not, she certainly knew how to phrase an appeal. 'You must become the greatest man, not of our time, but of all times,' she had written to Wellington – 'and give us back France.'[28]

Wellington was back in France before the new year, 1817, had begun. His volte-face about a reduction in the occupying forces was complete. On 9 December 1816 he had declared that a substantial troop reduction was impossible. On 9 January 1817 he notified the permanent conference of the four ambassadors, 'I confess, however, that my opinion has altered. . . . I would propose' – a reduction of thirty thousand men to begin on 1 April 1817. He had realized that only the reduction could give Richelieu that 'moment of popularity' his Government so desperately needed.[29]

Moreover, a contract with Baring Brothers and Hopes for a first loan to the French Government was about to be signed – on 10 February. This great step forward made further advances possible. It had needed all Wellington's persuasiveness to get the other Allies to accept the idea of a loan handled by British bankers, though at this date the preeminence of Barings in floating long-term loans was unchallenged. 'There are Six Powers in Europe,' Richelieu said in 1818, 'Great Britain, France, Russia, Austria, Prussia and Baring Brothers.'

With the troop reductions, Mme de Staël's fervent hope of a free France was half realized. She devoted the last four months of her life to working on her powerful friend for a total end to the Occupation, and on 7 May she dictated an appeal as flattering as it was inspiring: 'The conviction has spread that you sincerely intend to do good to poor France and, in fact, to conquer is not enough, one must build in order to be the first man of modern times.'[30]

Wellington replied on the 16th regretting that her need to dictate curtailed the flow of her ideas: 'It would be a great pity if your continued weakness were to deprive us of them for long.' Despite the tease, Wellington cherished her and during a visit to Paris from his HQ at Cambrai in June he called on her daily. 'Such compassion,' wrote her great friend, the poet Schlegel, 'well becomes a hero.'[31] Her deathbed conversion to Catholicism astonished the Duke. 'The truth is that she was terribly afraid of Death . . . I doubt however the ability of any Priest to convince her that there is a better world than this, or that if there is she will go to the best place in it.'[32] When she died on 14 July 1817 he felt she had at any rate made this world a better place.

Politics, however, were as usual not prospering. A despatch from the Cabinet dated 1 December 1817 showed that they now intended to drag their feet over ending the occupation. Popular impatience in France to get rid of foreigners, wrote Bathurst to the Duke, did not inspire him with a corresponding wish to leave. Bathurst in fact felt that the Cabinet had learnt from events at home how to silence popular discontent.

The booming wartime economy had collapsed in poverty and suffering. There were petitions by marchers, riots in Spa Fields and elsewhere; 'gag' laws; hangings.

What did Wellington make of it all? In 1817 his predictions were sombre – until Metternich congratulated him on England's extraordinary good luck in having a really bad riot. 'The effects of such violent crises,' wrote the Continental statesman, 'always turn in favour of the good party.' Wellington promptly passed on Metternich's opinion to that high Tory, Mrs Arbuthnot, but with a characteristic flavouring of irony: 'I did not know of all the advantage that could be derived from the operations in Spa fields. . . .' Left to himself in December 1816 he had blamed the upper classes as well as the lower orders for the country's distress, particularly the gentry who indulged a 'rage' for spending money on foreign travel which ought to have given employment at home.[33]

Unlike politics, the Duke's personal affairs were flourishing. His two sons were still young enough to give him nothing but pleasure. His Duchess caused little trouble to him, though plenty to herself. It was perhaps as well that Kitty was by no means always with her husband. 'The Duke is here,' wrote Lady Granville from Paris, 'his Duchess is at Cambrai and his loves are dispersed over the whole earth.' If some of them were 'flirts' rather than 'loves', Kitty nevertheless felt it deeply and wept while she worshipped. Her friends encouraged her; indeed Maria Edgeworth heard from Lady Bathurst that she had been more hurt by her friends than her enemies, 'and more by herself than by both put together – but still if she does not quite wash out his affections with tears, they will be hers during the long autumn of life'. As if to confirm this, the Duke said to his sister-in-law, Mrs Wellesley-Pole, 'After all *home* you know is what we must look to at last.'[34]

Kitty's autumn was to be brief but her life was not always sad.

On Waterloo Day, 18 June 1817, took place the state opening of London's new Waterloo Bridge. A 'Waterloo Fair' was held on the river bank, and the Thames itself was almost hidden by bobbing wherries as the Admiralty barge, with its quota of Waterloo heroes, approached Rennie's magnificent bridge, hung with Allied flags. At 3 pm began the salute of 202 guns in memory of the number captured by the British at the battle, followed by a procession on foot over the bridge with Wellington and Anglesey immediately behind the Prince Regent and the Duke of York. The sun shone all day.

Another happy event was Wyatt's discovery at long last of a site for Wellington's 'palace'. There had been many disappointments. Ravishing Uppark in Sussex had too steep a drive for the Duke's horses. Miserden in Gloucestershire seemed the last hope by May 1817, though the Duke did not like its proximity to a fashionable spa: '*I am not desirous of placing myself so exactly within a morning's ride of Cheltenham.*'[35]

He was saved by an offer from the 2nd Lord Rivers in July 1817 of

Stratfield Saye House in Hampshire. Wyatt was enthusiastic: 'I feel no hesitation in saying, that the estate possesses great beauty & dignity; & is capable of being made a princely Place.'[36] The happy state of the tenantry, fine carriage drives through splendid plantations, magnificent park and prospects made it by far the handsomest estate hitherto proposed. Pope's lovely River Loddon – 'the nymph Loddona' – glided through it. At the end of 1817 the nation bought Stratfield Saye for £263,000 and presented it to Wellington.

Stratfield Saye was to be the Duchess's beloved home for the rest of her life. It was partly due to her affection for it that the Duke never proceeded with the grandiose plan conceived by Wyatt for rebuilding it on higher ground at a cost of £216,850 15s. 3d. Wyatt's dream of something really sublime – not 'a Confectioner's Device' like Blenheim but a dome copied from the Pantheon and a circular colonnade from St Peter's; state rooms not an inch smaller than those at Hatfield; vaulted and groined arches in the basement; Italian marble, Portland and Bath stone, the best stock brickwork and £4,000 worth of gilding – all this and more was to remain forever a paper palace, exquisitely drawn, plainly framed and hung up in a passage of the old Stratfield Saye.

Kitty had little interest in visionary state rooms or indeed in the more spacious of the apartments already existing. She moved into a small bedroom at the top of the house in the north-east corner (her husband preferred the south-west corner of the ground floor) and her sitting-room next door, which faced the lawns sloping down to the river and the deer park rising beyond, was reassuringly like the old day-nursery at Pakenham Hall in Ireland.

By the beginning of 1818 Wellington feared that the Army of Occupation might be drawn into clashes with both Bonapartists and ultra-Royalists. If the occupation ran its full term of five years this would be certain.

Indeed, Wellington's own life was twice in danger from assassins. The second attempt, by one of Napoleon's veterans named Cantillon, failed, it was said, because he was in too great a hurry to get his reward. Others, less friendly to the Duke, said it was because he aimed too high, thinking Wellington was *un grand homme*. Bonaparte was to reward him handsomely. In his will he left the would-be assassin 10,000 francs, for had not Wellington assassinated the martyrs La Bedoyère and Ney?

At last, on 1 October 1818 the Congress of Aix-la-Chapelle met to end the occupation. With Wellington and the Tsar both in favour of evacuation, no time was lost in reaching agreement on this issue. The army was to be out of France by 30 November, the indemnity having been reduced to 265 million francs. Now, however, began a tug of war between the Congress system of the Tsar and his 'Holy Allies' on one side, and British interests as represented by Wellington and Castlereagh on the other.

For Castlereagh and Wellington, the 'Concert of Europe' was intended to take concrete shape only on specific issues like the occupation. They still regarded the Quadruple Alliance, extended into a Quintuple Alliance, as the lynchpin of peace, for it was through this instrument that the Powers controlled France, the revolutionary seedbed of Europe. Their belief did not prevent them from sponsoring King Louis for the Congress; but for a Congress which was to involve no general supervision of everybody by everybody and no limitation of national sovereignty such as the British Opposition dreaded. Banish the thought of an international Cossack force keeping order in Hyde Park! The Tsar's proposal for a *garantie générale* or 'general alliance' was rejected at Aix-la-Chapelle.

In the end Metternich found a compromise and both sides believed they had won.

Alexander I might glitter in Europe for the present and seem to hold out the most seductive hopes for the future; Britain had only one hero – the Duke of Wellington. And his conduct as soldier, administrator and financier over the past three years gave him a position in Europe also which no other Englishman had ever held. He returned to England at the end of 1818 with the batons of six foreign countries in his knapsack.

The Duke was to make his London home in an imposing mansion at Hyde Park Corner, formerly the property of his brother Lord Wellesley – Apsley House. In order to assist Richard's finances Arthur had offered the generous sum of £42,000 for Apsley House without at first disclosing that he was the purchaser. He quickly made some savings. A nightwatchman was to be shared with the neighbours at only 3s 6d a night each. But the treasures inside Apsley House soon required more than this part-time Cerberus to guard them.

In the hall to start with stood Canova's gigantic nude statue of Napoleon, bought by Britain from the Louvre and presented to Wellington by the Prince Regent. When a British visitor told Canova that the globe in Napoleon's hand looked too small, the sculptor replied, 'Ah, but you see Napoleon's world did not include Great

Britain.' In London's Hyde Park a colossal statue of Achilles was promised by 'the ladies of England' costing £10,000 and using 36 tons of metal from guns captured at Salamanca, Vitoria, Toulouse and Waterloo; in Dublin's Phoenix Park the first stone for Smirke's granite pillar had been laid on 18 June 1818.

Prize money from Waterloo was distributed in June 1819. To Wellington £60,000 (he gave back two-thirds of his share to the Treasury); generals £1,250 each, subalterns £33, sergeants £9, privates £2 10s.

Loaded with material honours, the Duke also brought home a medley of verbal tributes from the most varied well-wishers. For Northern France, the Prefect felt that he must thank the Duke for his troops' discipline. For himself and the ladies, Metternich said, 'He's one of the men I love best in the world, and if I were a woman' – he was speaking to Lady Shelley – 'I'd love him better than all the world.'[37] For himself and his family, Thomas Creevey expressed astonishment and gratitude that such a character as the Duke should exist.

Shortly afterwards Creevey had an unexpected glimpse into the Duke's future. He happened to be in the Hôtel d'Angleterre in Brussels where Lady Charlotte Greville was staying. Wellington came in, saw Creevey, and asked if he had any news from England.

'None but newspaper news.'

Creevey's brief answer was an attempt to draw the Duke, for the papers were full of reports that he was to join the British Cabinet as Master-General of the Ordnance. But Wellington was markedly uncommunicative.

'Ho!' he replied, 'Ha!' Nevertheless he did not contradict the reports and his Radical friend deduced they were true.

He had indeed accepted that post in the Cabinet – on his own terms.

25

Westminster Warriors

Not a few of Wellington's friends deplored his change of career. Why politics, party politics, Tory politics? General Alava, his faithful Spanish ally and a liberal, told Creevey he never was more sorry for an event in his life: 'The Duke of Wellington ought never to have had anything to do with politics.'

The great man himself was prepared to make some concessions to this feeling. The Duke of Wellington must not be let down by the Master-General of the Ordnance. A compelling manifesto was therefore sent to the Prime Minister stating his own conditions of service. He must be a servant of the country first, of party second. Tories might come and go; the Duke could well go on for ever.

His dislike of factiousness in politics dated from the Peninsular War.

The experience which I have acquired during my long service abroad has convinced me that a factious opposition to the government is highly injurious to the interests of the country; & thinking as I do now I could not become a party to such an opposition. . . .[1]

Lord Liverpool, with his usual good sense in man-management, recognized the 'special circumstances' of the Duke's position.

Wellington's luck has often attracted attention. He was lucky to fight in India with a brother as Governor-General and in the Peninsula with a friend as War Minister. He was lucky to stop fighting during his prime, while he looked taller than his five feet nine inches, while his complexion was still as fresh as a young man's, his forehead romantic and his expression like a Roman hero's, apart from the mouth. The painter Haydon called it 'a singular mouth like a helpless infant learning to whistle!'[2] The truth was that active service had early destroyed Arthur Wellesley's back teeth, a single stroke of ill-luck that was largely responsible for his 'wretched' utterance in Parliament.

Nevertheless Arthur, having fought his last battle at forty-six, was lucky to enter the Cabinet at forty-nine, a perfect age in his case. But

355

there the luck ended. He struck the unhappiest year in nineteenth-century British history for his first as a peacetime politician.

'Mischief and embarrassment' were the two names under which the Duke had learnt to recognize the new enemies of postwar Britain.[3] By 'mischief' his Tory colleagues meant political agitation and by 'embarrassment' economic distress. Repressive measures had reduced the mischief in 1817 to a trickle, while improved trade mitigated the embarrassment during the following year. But in 1819 embarrassment and mischief returned, in that order, with a vengeance.

The harvest of 1818 had been bad and yet a stringent, unreformed Corn Law was still in force. Peel attacked the great postwar problem of cash and by the 1819 Act for the resumption of cash payments caused prices to fall. Corn and cash – these were two out of the three spectres that were to haunt politicians for a generation. (The third spectre, Catholics, soon completed the intractable trio.) Mob brutality, said Lord Palmerston, was typical of the times. A matching brutality was the savage penal code.

'Orator' Hunt, a leader of the Lancashire weavers, had called a Reform meeting for 16 August 1819 to be attended by industrial unions from the cotton districts of Lancashire. Since Reform meetings were not yet illegal the Cabinet warned magistrates not to disperse the crowds unless they proceeded to felony or riot. If that happened, there was a force of constables and specials commanded by Captain Nadin, as well as the Manchester Yeomanry Cavalry and Colonel L'Estrange's 15th Hussars and 31st Foot, while the Northern Command as a whole was under Wellington's friend General Byng, named by him for valour at Waterloo.

By noon on that fine Monday morning up to eighty thousand men, women and children had converged on St Peter's Field after hours of orderly marching with garlands and the usual Reform banners – 'Suffrage Universal', 'Vote by Ballot'. Perhaps the Saddleworth Union struck a sinister note with its black flag inscribed 'Equal Representation or Death'; but on the reverse was 'Love' beneath two clasped hands. Four hundred police already on the field met with no hostility from the crowd. The crowd's vast size, however, struck terror into the heart of 'Miss' William Hulton, the young, blue-eyed chairman of the magistrates.

Hunt had scarcely spoken for twenty minutes to a silent multitude before there was a confused murmur at the top of the field and a wave of pressure towards the hustings. From a window 'Miss' Hulton had read the Riot Act to those who could hear it and ordered Nadin and his police to arrest Hunt. Nadin looked at the warrant and then at the vast concourse between him and the hustings. He told Hulton the job couldn't be done without the military.

'Then you shall have military power,' exclaimed Hulton, '& for God's sake don't sacrifice the lives of the Special Constables. . . .'[4]

It was not their lives that were in danger.

At once the blue and white uniforms of the yeomanry were seen moving into the crowd. Hunt promptly called for three cheers, meaning that the reformers would stand firm and continue their meeting. Some of those with sticks raised them to cheer, some hissed the troops, but nothing was thrown. The yeomanry, brandishing their sabres, advanced under Captain Birley (afterwards known as Hurly-Burly) and at once became engulfed.

'Good God! Sir,' shouted the horrified Hulton at his window to Colonel L'Estrange, 'don't you see they are attacking the yeomanry? *Disperse the meeting!*'

Those three fatal words were the flash-point of Peterloo. Having spoken them, Hulton turned his face away from the window.

There is no unbiased evidence that Hulton was right and that the crowd attacked first. All the testimony of impartial observers agrees that the yeomanry, a body of forty unskilful horsemen, were ordered to squeeze one by one into a crowd two thousand times their number – but were not attacked. 'Not a brick-bat was thrown at them – not a pistol was fired during this period,' said *The Times* reporter, a man 'about as much a Jacobin . . . as is Lord *Liverpool* himself'. But from the moment a Waterloo bugle sounded the charge and the 15th Hussars went to the rescue of the yeomanry, all was changed: 'Swords were up and swords were down,' wrote another impartial eye-witness, Edward Stanley, a clergyman and father of the future Dean of Westminster. Hunt and all the platform party including journalists jumped down, Hunt's hand grazed by a sabre.

Not only Hunt and the reform leaders but also *The Times* correspondent were arrested by Nadin – 'Oh! oh! you are one of their writers' – while in a whirlwind of wrath the yeomanry turned on the people with a wild shout: 'Have at their flags!' Suddenly there was a roar and a rumble like low thunder. Every narrow exit was blocked by a terrified stampede. Samuel Bamford tried to rally his contingent: 'Stand fast, they are riding upon us; stand fast.' His exhortations were drowned in screams – 'For shame! Break! break! They are killing them in front and they cannot get away. Break! break!'[5]

But the people could not break. Mounds of trampled victims began to pile up on the blood-stained grass. In ten minutes it was over. Silence fell and the August sun beat down on a thick, motionless cloud of dust. Then a light breeze lifted the dust-cloud to reveal something ominously like the aftermath of Waterloo, except that among the torn caps, hats, shoes, ripped-up banners and broken shafts was a wreckage of shawls, bonnets and children's clothes.

The aftermath of Peterloo was a political struggle between the two sides

The official letter of thanks sent to the magistrates seemed to many an act of gratuitous callousness; but Wellington was one of the thirteen ministers who believed that unless magistrates were supported in their hour of crisis they would never again do their duty. The Government hoped to prosecute the leaders for high treason but evidence only of 'misdemeanour' could be marshalled, for which Hunt was given over two years in prison and Bamford one. An unfortunate woman who had been wounded and lifted into Hunt's carriage went down in Tory mythology as 'Hunt's concubine' –

> His mistress sent to the hospital her face for to renew,
> For she got it closely shaven on the plains of Peter-Loo.

General Byng awaited the Radicals' next great meeting of 1 November with calm confidence. It passed off without a revolution. Nevertheless the Government clamped down on the whole country their retaliatory Six Acts, against the press, drilling and arms, and 'seditious' public meetings. The Acts did not prevent a dramatic plot, known as the Cato Street Conspiracy. Its ringleader, Arthur Thistlewood, planned to murder the Cabinet. He and his friends were betrayed by an informer and hanged, their heads being exposed in the City.

Social issues in 1820, however, were suddenly swept from the board by a new affair. It obsessed the whole population, and yet was incapable of adding one crumb or halfpenny to the diet or wages of a single workman in Westminster, where the farce was played.

The question seemed simple. Should Queen Caroline of Brunswick be allowed to take her place beside her husband George, now King George IV, on the throne of England? The pair had been virtually separated ever since their only child, Charlotte, was conceived in April

1795. The Prince was out of love with Caroline at first sight. She left his roof for her own convivial house in Blackheath and, after the peace of 1814, for a rackety life on the Continent. Why could she not stay in Italy, leaving her husband to the pink-and-white Lady Conyngham, known as the Vice-Queen?

Because Caroline was a political pawn and always had been. While her husband was hobnobbing with the Whigs, who were so devoted to her interests as the Tories? Tory George Canning became her slave at Blackheath, Tory Lord Eldon sat on her right hand at dinner; but when the Prince Regent backed the Tories in 1812, their Whig and Radical opponents automatically discovered that the Princess's cause was their own.

Queen Caroline landed at Dover on 5 June 1820, entered London on the 6th and was given a rapturous welcome, stage-managed by the radical Alderman Matthew Wood. The Tories put up Wellington to negotiate a compromise settlement with Henry Brougham, her Attorney-General, by which in return for £50,000 a year she would live abroad and allow her name to be omitted from the Liturgy. Alderman Wood, however, decided that Caroline need concede nothing. Two nights running the mob stoned Sidmouth's house, almost catching him, Wellington and Eldon as they arrived in Sidmouth's carriage at the very moment the attack began.

'Let me out; I must get out!' cried Sidmouth to the Duke.

'You shall not alight,' the Duke shouted back, never ashamed to beat a tactical retreat; and to the coachman, 'Drive on!' The carriage, with one pane of glass already broken, was saved by the Duke's decision.[6]

While the Queen stood pat on her privileges the Government examined their secret weapon – a green bag containing eyewitness accounts of Caroline's behaviour abroad, collected by the Milan Commission in 1818. By 24 June the Wellington–Brougham talks had broken down, and on 5 July the Prime Minister introduced in the House of Lords the notorious instrument by which George IV hoped to obtain his freedom: a 'Bill of Pains and Penalties' to deprive Her Majesty of all her prerogatives, and to dissolve the Marriage between his Majesty and the said Queen.'

Mounting hysteria filled the pause of forty-three days between the first and second readings of the bill (5 July–17 August). In London the problem of law and order caused the Duke such vivid anxiety that his mind began to play with the possibility of a major reform. No proper police force as yet existed, the burden of controlling mobs fell on the military and the Guards gave every sign of siding with the Queen. His Majesty, very gouty and 'in a terrible temper'[7] according to Wellington, cowered in Carlton House while the mob screamed 'Nero!' under his window. One battalion of Guards mutinied.

It was this last awful event which brought forth a seminal memorandum from the Duke. The emergency, he stated, had produced chaos in the Guards' conditions of service: 'nobody knows who is on or off duty, all the troops are harassed, and the duty is ill done after all' – for which they were savagely punished. How could 'these unfortunate troops' be rescued from their predicament? His answer was historic:

In my opinion the Government ought, without loss of a moment's time, to form either a police in London or a military corps, which should be of a different description from the regular military force, or both.[8]

Eight years later, with Peel as Home Secretary but under the Duke's leadership, 'a police of a very different description' from anything before, even with a different name – 'Peeler' or 'Bobby' after Robert Peel – would be formed.

On 17 August 1820, however, it was still the Guards on whom peers had to rely for a passage into the House through a milling crowd around Parliament Square. Everyone expected the worst. The actors in the opening scene of the 'trial' nevertheless reached their House safely on 17 August, though one of them only after an unpleasant experience. As the Duke entered Parliament Square a mob broke into hisses causing his horse to shy. An extraordinary double event: 'The Duke of Wellington – will England credit it? will the world believe it? – was hissed!' (*Morning Post*) and not only hissed but undoubtedly 'taken by surprise', a back-handed cut at his Waterloo strategy.

Now began the deployment of the craziest bill-cum-prosecution in history. The Queen wore black artificial ringlets and a white veil over her face, which nevertheless showed through as red as brick-dust. The unqueenly manner in which she lolled in her chair provoked Lord Holland, though her supporter, into a ribald joke: 'Instead of sleeping with Bergami [her majordomo], she sleeps with the Lords.' Small wonder if Caroline shut her ears to some of the green bag's sleazy evidence: the masked ball when Bergami helped her into three indecent costumes, their giggling at fig-leaves on the garden statues, her garment found in his bed. When her livery servant, Teodoro Majocchi, suddenly appeared as a witness against her, she gave a piercing shriek variously interpreted as 'O Teodoro!' 'O *traditore*!' or just 'O!' and fled from the Chamber.

Her counsel, Brougham, his eyes blazing and nose wrinkled, made short work of Majocchi, whose evasive refrain of '*Non mi ricordo*' – 'I don't remember' – became the ironic motto of the mob.

'Well, Creevey,' said Wellington to this keen ally of Queen Caroline after a particularly bad display by the foreigners, 'so you gave us a blast last night.'[9] Creevey heartily agreed, pointing out that foreigners would never be believed in England. 'Oh, but we have a great many English witnesses,' interposed the Duke, '– officers.' Though the officers were unable to give evidence of actual adultery, their description of behaviour on board their ships helped to dispel any lingering doubts that adultery had in fact been committed.

The mob turned out to be good-humoured, except towards the bishops, the Prime Minister and Waterloo heroes. Liverpool lost his nerve and could speak in the House only after dosing himself with ether. Lord Anglesey they hissed and in return, according to Lady Granville, he made them speeches about his duty. She failed to record what may have been his most notable speech, when the mob one day demanded a tribute to their idol. 'God save the Queen,' he obliged, '– and may all your wives be like her.' An equally persistent tradition gives the famous retort to Wellington, for whom the roughest treatment was reserved. A climax was reached on 28 August when a hostile mob tried to unhorse him, and *The Times* reported 'considerable difficulty' before he got clear.[10]

Attendance at the trial was compulsory for all peers except the over-seventies, minors, Catholics, those serving abroad or exempted on grounds of sickness or compassion. Otherwise an absentee was fined £100 for each of the first three days and £50 for every subsequent one. Two hundred and sixty peers sweated out the hot August weeks on the bank of the stinking Thames, their physical discomfort surpassed only by their mental wretchedness. By September some were ailing, among them the Wellesley brothers. Richard complained of suffocation, while Arthur developed a feverish cough with touches of his old enemy, rheumatism. On 10 November, the third reading was carried by a mere nine votes. Lord Liverpool immediately withdrew the doomed bill.

The Government soon got their revenge. Queen Caroline was outside Westminster Abbey on the day of her husband's coronation. The sight of her on foot, jostled by the rabble, frantically but vainly rushing from door to door, evoked nothing but catcalls from the spectators. Even the Whig Lady Jersey had deserted her, for the two Jersey boys as well as the Duke's sons were holding up the royal train, inside.

Emily Cowper thought the King looked at death's door and was only kept alive, apart from sniffing Lady Alicia Gordon's vinaigrette, by the smiles of the Vice-Queen. But it was the Queen who died. Caroline succumbed on 7 August to inflammation of the bowel brought on, it was thought, by a broken heart.

Wellington had just witnessed the dissolution by death of a disastrous marriage. His own married life, though it differed utterly from the King's in being a union of well-meaning rather than monstrous incompatibles, was also going through a tempestuous phase. Indeed during the worst year, 1821, he too felt that he could not live under the same roof as his wife.

Maria Edgeworth drew an appealing picture of Kitty on St Patrick's Day 1819, when she called for the first time at Apsley House. A slight figure whose grey curls and wan skin made her look older than her forty-seven years came towards Maria with a smile of singular sweetness, picked up some shamrocks from a bowl and murmuring in French, 'You are worthy of them', pressed the national emblem into Maria's hand. 'Nothing could be more like Kitty Pakenham,' wrote the delighted novelist, 'former youth and beauty excepted.' As Wellington's ex-aide-de-camp Lord William Lennox wrote of the Duchess, she was 'amiable, unaffected and simple-minded. . . .' She was also 'generous and charitable'.[11] It was these last two qualities which were to be so nearly her downfall.

Mistress of a large establishment in Hampshire, Kitty's pious concern was chiefly for her servants and the poor. The kind of managerial genius which a future great hostess like Lady Palmerston (Emily Cowper) displayed found no place in Kitty's make-up. Yet this was what her husband expected. He asked for a commissary-general and was given a domestic chaplain.

The trouble began at the time of the Cato Street Conspiracy, when the accused men tried to justify their attempt on the Duke's life by citing his alleged harshness to the masses, as reflected in his treatment of his wife. This legend, the Duke held, Kitty had started up herself by her '*foolish* conduct'. He wrote to her angrily on 19 April 1820,

... that you & your family have complained of my conduct towards you without Reason; that your whole conduct is one of watching & spying [on] me, and that you have employed my own Servants in doing so. ...[12]

It was probably on 4 May 1821 that he received from Kitty a letter containing the names of persons to whom he had not given charity. Next day, 5 May, he returned her a rocket:

I have given all that I chuse to give. Upon this point I cannot help observing upon your mode of enquiry into my Transactions from Servants and other Underlings. It really makes my life a Burthen to me. If it goes on I must live somewhere else. It is the meanest dirtiest trick of which any body can be guilty.[13]

The Duke suspected that his wife was criticizing him for not giving enough to charity. The second part of his letter to Kitty went further. He hinted that Kitty's system of espionage was motivated by suspicion not only about his charities but also about his private life:

Yet do or say what I will you cannot avoid adopting some dirty way of trying to find out something which if it could [be found out] & you did find it out would give you the greatest uneasiness.

The Duchess replied on 10 May with four large indignant pages.

I ... thought you would have been gratified to be assured that I ... am neither indifferent nor inattentive to the wants, the comfort or the characters of those about us. You may judge then of the bitterness of my disappointment on receiving the letter which I am now answering ... I am as incapable of any mean or dirty action as you are yourself —

— and if he had time to study her character he would find this out for himself.

With respect to the suspicion so clearly expressed in your [letter] that I cannot misunderstand it, I never had, I have not such a thought[;] dismiss then from your mind so hateful a suspicion. I do not deserve that you should harbour it ...

Kitty concluded with a request and a hope, both forcefully stated,

... that I may not again be subjected to offensive accusations for which there is positively no grounds whatever.

I hope this subject so painful to you and so injurious to me now be dismissed forever.[14]

Kitty's hope was not to be gratified. Her letter reached Arthur at the worst possible moment, during a harrowing family crisis. His niece, the beautiful Lady Worcester, daughter of his only sister Anne, had suddenly been taken ill and died at Apsley House on 11 May.

That same day both Kitty and Arthur wrote notes which crossed.

Kitty offered to come up instantly from Stratfield Saye but also warned Arthur not to overtax Martha Baxter, the housekeeper, whose health was delicate; Arthur returned to the charge:

I don't care what your object was. If you are to continue to ask & obtain information of what I do from any Servant or dependant of mine or anybody else excepting myself I'll not live in the same House with you.[15]

This peal of thunder was not calculated to improve Kitty's health. On Monday 9 July she decided it was unlikely she would survive the night. Accordingly she sorted all her unpaid bills, placed them in Martha Baxter's reliable hands and returned to Arthur his two lethal letters of 5 and 11 May, together with a farewell note:

. . . I hope that I forgive you. I would and I am sure I could have made you happy had you suffered me to try, but thrust from you I was not allowed, for God's sake for your own dear sake for Christ sake do not use another woman as you have treated me never write to a human being such letters as those from you which I now enclose they have destroyed me.

God in heaven bless you my husband and bless and guard and guide you and my Children.[16]

Kitty survived; but in this same July Europe heard of Napoleon's end.

A Parisian party was in full swing when the death that had taken place at St Helena on 5 May 1821 became known. Wellington and Talleyrand were there to hear the chorus of startled cries.

'What an event!'

'No, it's not an event any more,' corrected the cynical old diplomat, 'now it's only *an item of news.*'[17]

George IV, expecting to hear from a courtier that Queen Caroline had died, found it was only Napoleon.

'It is my duty to inform Your Majesty that your greatest enemy is dead.'

'Is she, by God.'[18]

Naturally the mourning for Napoleon could easily be turned into renewed abuse of his conqueror, as indeed it was by various romantic spirits from Byron downwards:

Victory was never before wasted upon such an unprofitable soil, as this dunghill of Tyranny, whence nothing springs but Viper's eggs.[19]

Wellington's own immediate reaction to the news, as reported by Mrs Arbuthnot on 4 July 1821, was characteristic of the light but half deferential tone in which up till now he habitually spoke of his great rival. 'The Duke of Wellington called on me,' wrote Mrs Arbuthnot, '& said, "Now I think I may say I am the most successful Gen[era]l. alive." '[20] Ever since 1814 the Duke had expressed unstinted admiration for Napoleon's generalship. 'I used to say of him,' he often repeated, 'that his presence on the field made the difference of forty thousand men.'[21] This was somewhat warmer than Napoleon's own slighting remarks about the 'Sepoy General'. There was in fact nothing insensitive or ill-natured in the Duke's comments on Napoleon – until the publication of the codicil to the Emperor's will, with its spectacular legacy to Cantillon the assassin. Then indeed the Duke's tone changed. In 1831 he said of Napoleon's written works, 'scarcely once has he tripped into truth'.

The death of Napoleon may have reminded George IV that he had never seen Waterloo, for he ordered Wellington to parade towards the end of September 1821 as historian and guide.

The royal visit to Waterloo went off without a hitch. 'His Majesty took it very coolly; he never asked me a single question, nor said one word, until I showed him where Lord Anglesey's leg was buried, and then he burst into tears.'[22] It may have been this martial experience that was responsible for one of George IV's numerous fantasies, namely that he himself had led the Germans' great charge at Salamanca disguised as General Bock.

'Was not that so?' he would shout to the Duke down the dinner-table.

'I have often heard Your Majesty say so,' his Grace would reply.

After so many conducted tours of Waterloo the Duke had long since learnt to control his own tears. Only once was he said recently to have registered intense feeling, and that was on technical grounds concerned with the correct understanding of the battle. When he saw the monumental Lion Mound erected by the Dutch he burst out:

'They have spoiled my Battlefield.'[23]

Kitty's next clash with a distinctly 'Iron Duke' came in January 1822. She wrote to him that, economize as she might, her personal allowance of £500 a year was insufficient. Would he increase it to £670? Arthur refused. For a lady of her rank £500 was generous; only princesses had more.

Kitty was no fairy-tale princess but she was still queen of charity. Indiscriminate charity was what she finally had to admit had run away with her allowance:

I believe I may have given away money very injudiciously, perhaps sometimes [Kitty conscientiously corrected 'sometimes' to 'often' in her fair copy] to spare myself the pain of refusing. . . . I will from this time only retain as permanent Pensioners those who are so very old & friendless that they must perish without my assistance – [24]

– a retired miniature painter with an idiot daughter and only £20 a year who had once taught Kitty drawing, a disabled dancing master, the Wellesley boys' wet-nurse, now abandoned by her husband. The sums allowed by Kitty to this poor flotsam and jetsam of great houses were then added up (wrongly, of course; she made the total £216, £9 too little), and after promising in future to stick to her £500 allowance, she bravely asked Arthur to clear her of debt – 'I am ashamed to say of £200. . . .'

The air was cleared also. She resumed her old practice of addressing her husband in letters as 'My dearest Arthur', having for a time adopted his own brusque style of doing without a beginning. By May 1822 she was willing to abandon even a little of her personal puritanism for his sake. After a rapturous morning on the river at Eton with her two sons, rowing and eating mutton chops, she returned to Apsley House windblown and happy – and promptly ran into her husband. He gazed at her dishevelled locks, as she noted, with wonder. Then he lifted them in his fingers and said very gently:

'Had you not better do something with them, had not you better? They are so very grey! had you not better?'

'I feared you hated everything approaching a wig.'

'Oh, no. I am sure you would look better.'

Kitty rushed off to the hairdresser and came home looking 'within a trifle' as young as her niece Kate, to whom she recounted the whole adventure.

Less than two months later, Wellington suddenly poured out to Mrs Arbuthnot the whole story of his unhappy marriage.[25] First, bitter complaints of their incompatibility – 'he had repeatedly tried to live in a friendly manner with her' – 'she did not understand him' – 'might as well talk to a child'. Next, her obstinacy – 'thinks herself so excessively clever that she never stirs even to accommodate herself to him' – (what about the wig?) – '& never for an instant supposes that when their opinions differ, she may be the one in the wrong' – (what about the debts?). Then his own thwarted domesticity – 'nothing would make him so happy as to have a home where he could find comfort' – and Kitty's failure as a hostess.

The last charge was fully justified. Arthur, however, was neither fair to Kitty in his earlier charges, nor accurate in his self-analysis. Eulogies of a quiet home life were all very well; but the women with whom he could have been happy – Lady Charlotte Greville, Lady Shelley, Mrs Patterson the American, Mrs Arbuthnot herself – attracted him by their social graces rather than by their domesticity. Wellington's ideal life was an army mess and his ideal family the military 'family' of his aides-de-camp. Though he thought the opposite, he would not have been the easiest of men to live with as a husband.

Nevertheless an impression emerges from Wellington's tirade of 27 June 1822 that the worst between him and Kitty was over. It was vexation recollected in tranquillity. Mrs Arbuthnot finally arrested the flow of grievances by saying he was a fool to have married her.

He agreed cordially in my abuse of him & I could not think him a greater fool than he did himself. He seemed quite *soulagé* after having made me this confidence, & seemed quite glad to have someone to whom he could say anything.[26]

If Mrs Arbuthnot brought him comfort, the Duchess had her own consolations.

The young loved her – from secretaries to the large brood of her adopted children, though Douro and Charles were her 'first *earthly* consolation', as she freely admitted to her sister. She spoilt them, let them bully her and now and then forgot their needs.

When the Duke was severe with his sons it was because, as he once told Mrs Arbuthnot, he was afraid that they might develop the traits he disliked in their mother. His feelings for his younger son were clouded by Charley's breezy indolence, a quality that the Duke prophesied would ruin even the *jeunesse dorée* in a gritty postwar world, and which drew from him periodic mutterings. Douro was an entirely different character, thought Napier, 'very much resembling the Duke without his *devil*'. For '*devil*' read genius in all its manifestations, including demonic energy and fire, and you have the Wellington–Douro problem in a nutshell, a problem that has beset many a famous father of a promising eldest son. How bring him up without either false pride or a destructive sense of inferiority?

Mrs Arbuthnot was once described by the Duke to her husband as 'a pattern of *sensible* women; for she makes the whole world do whatever she pleases!'[27] Did she want Wellington for her lover, and succeed in her desire?

Peel thought so. The man responsible, however, for disseminating the belief that the Duke and Mrs Arbuthnot were lovers was that arch-gossip, father of at least one illegitimate child and bachelor diarist of genius, Charles Greville. In 1824 Mrs Arbuthnot received anonymous letters accusing her of a love affair with the Duke. Wellington at once recognized the writing as Greville's.

The letter of 11 April 1824 was discussed frankly in her journal:

Mr. Arbuthnot & I have been greatly annoyed by another anonymous letter accusing me of being in love with the Duke of Wellington, of being always in *holes* and *corners* with him.[28]

Wellington, Harriet and Charles Arbuthnot fumed together over this outrage, particularly the '*holes* and *corners*' phrase.

However, we have agreed that in public we will not talk much together, but go on just the same in private. The anonymous writer would be surprised if he knew how amicably we three had discussed his amiable letter.

If Greville was maligning Mrs Arbuthnot – and the whole tone and temper of her journal leave no room to doubt that he was – he had stronger reasons for accusing Wellington. Somewhere about the year 1820 the Duke was certainly involved in a passionate love affair with Lady Charlotte Greville, mother of Charles Greville. Two hitherto unpublished letters, or rather parts of letters, unsigned and virtually undated, prove that Charles Greville had indeed had cause for alarm. Charles Greville senior wrote to his wife Lady Charlotte:

. . . with respect to Charles, living in the world as he does, & quick & clear sighted as he is, if you had reflected but a moment it would have occurred to you that he could not be blind to your conduct with the Duke of Wellington. But it did not follow that he must know, or even suspect, the degree of intimacy which had subsisted! . . .[29]

On 'Friday 17th' an affectionate and clever letter was sent off by Lady Charlotte to her son Charles in which, while not admitting that anything immoral had actually happened, she agreed that a change in behaviour might be necessary. All ended happily except that Charles Greville junior was to take his revenge. Three days after the great Duke died, Greville dedicated a long passage in his famous diary to the Duke's '*liaisons*', especially with Mrs Arbuthnot. The relevant Greville diaries were first published in 1887 and Mrs Arbuthnot's not until 1950, so that Greville's revenge had a free run for over half a century.

Wellington had first stayed with the Shelleys at Maresfield, Sussex, in October 1819. He was to inform Mrs Arbuthnot three months later: 'The shooting has been excellent; but I have shot worse than usual.'

This was a formidable boast if his usual style was that displayed at Lady Shelley's, where he began by peppering a dog, went on to a keeper's gaiters and reached a climax with the bare arms of a cottager hanging out her washing at an open window.

'I'm wounded, Milady.'

'My good woman, this ought to be the proudest moment of your life. You have the distinction of being shot by the great Duke of Wellington!' The Duke had always thought Lady Shelley rather a goose. He quickly produced a sovereign.[30] It was said that in private he himself took these shooting accidents lightly. 'Bird shot never hurt anyone.'[31]

It was 12 August 1822. Lord Castlereagh, Wellington's friend and Harriet Arbuthnot's idol, was about to attend the new European Congresses of Vienna and Verona. Driven out of his mind, however, by blackmailers falsely accusing him of a homosexual crime, he cut his own throat. Wellington was summoned back from his annual inspection of the Dutch fortresses to attend the Congresses in Castlereagh's place. 'Poor Human Nature!' he wrote to Harriet, 'How little we are after all!'

There is no doubt that the death of Castlereagh resulted in a new relationship between the Duke and Harriet Arbuthnot. Her passion both for friendship and for political discussion, which before had been mainly ministered to by Castlereagh, now found its outlet in Wellington. 'He has promised to fill the place of the friend I have lost.'[32]

There was a corresponding change in the Duke's own feelings. He found himself needing 'the *sensible* woman' as much as she needed him. Up till August 1822 Mrs Arbuthnot had been only the first among equals in that brittle circle of female adorers whose pleasure was to invent rivalries, victories and defeats in the game of winning the great Duke's favour. Wellington had entered into the fun. Mrs Arbuthnot he had nicknamed '*La Tyranna*', the jealous guardian of his engagement-book.

Though it would be quite wrong to suggest that after August 1822 *La Tyranna* finally triumphed over her rivals and made him fall in love with her, she did receive one uniquely self-revealing letter in which the old *badinage* had a different sound and the reticence had vanished. On 13 September he wrote just before leaving England again:

I hope you will think of me sometimes, and whenever you think of me wherever I may be, you may feel certain that my thoughts and wishes are centred on you, and my desire that every action of my life may please you. God bless you

Your most devoted and affectionate Slave.[33]

What did he really feel for her? 'The Duke's feelings,' write the editors of *The Journal of Mrs Arbuthnot*, 'may be described in Landor's words, "There is a middle state between love and friendship more delightful than either, but more difficult to remain in." ' For the Duke, his performance on this tightrope was rendered less difficult by Harriet Arbuthnot's own qualities. He recognized that she was neither imaginative nor romantic. When the famous dancer Maria Mercandotti suddenly gave up her career to marry a wealthy *arriviste*, Harriet applauded and the Duke wrote: 'You are right *au fond* in preferring gold to Love! But then . . . you have no *Romance* in your composition! You look to realities; and imagine nothing!'[34]

A deeply conventional and faithful wife, Harriet had no taste for dalliance but a consuming interest in political drama. She was probably the only woman who refused to meet Lord Byron when the prince of romance himself asked for an introduction.

Who would step into the dead man's shoes? Surely not George Canning – brilliant, iconoclastic, consumed by '*a love of undoing*' – or so it soon appeared to Wellington and the Arbuthnots in the course of many a ruffled confabulation. As Charles Arbuthnot was to declare: 'They might as well try to amalgamate oil and vinegar as the Duke & Mr Canning.' Yet it was Canning whom Wellington had to force upon the King.

As far as the Duke was personally concerned, he liked Canning no more than the King did. But the Duke was a man on his own; making up his own mind, occasion by occasion, about what was for the public good at any given time. And at this time the public interest seemed to demand a Tory Government tinctured with Canning's brand of liberalism rather than the alternative, a Whig Government tainted by the Radicals. Canning it must be, and it well became the country's 'retained servant' to tell the King so.

The Duke had made a crucial intervention in British politics at their most sensitive point. It was to set a pattern for the future. Here and now, however, another duty of the greatest intricacy confronted him. He was to take Castlereagh's place at Vienna and Verona, where in contrast to the Congress of Aix-la-Chapelle he would find the autocrats grown more autocratic, the oppositional movements more active and Metternich the man in control.

Moreover, instead of pulling steadily in double harness with Castlereagh as in 1815 and 1818, he would be continuing the policy of a ghost, and a ghost who had quitted a world grown hostile and vehement. At least Castlereagh had been Foreign Secretary, with all the punch of that great office behind him. Behind Wellington was Canning, a new Foreign Secretary, seen as the exponent of a new word which Peel memorably designated 'odious but intelligible' – the word 'liberal'.*

The conference instructions drawn up by Castlereagh for himself were taken over unchanged by the Duke. They sounded forthright enough: preservation of the European 'system' by maintaining strict British neutrality in all internal disputes abroad. But against the background of upheavals in Spain, Portugal and Greece it seemed exceedingly doubtful whether the late maestro himself, for all his expertise in conducting the Concert of Europe, could have succeeded in preserving harmony and peace.

The explosion in Spain was the most dramatic. It had been sparked off by mutinies in regiments earmarked to fight against Spain's rebellious colonies in South America, but it swiftly became a successful onslaught against the despotism of Ferdinand VII. When the King was forced to accept the liberal constitution of 1812, Spanish ultra-Royalists appealed to the Holy Alliance for help.

The French assembled an army along the Pyrenees to prevent the constitutional infection (as well as yellow fever) from spreading into France. Should that army invade Spain? Since the French Ultras were pressing for invasion and wanted to stage their intervention as a mandate from their Holy Allies, the question to be thrashed out at Vienna and Verona, with Wellington's participation, was whether or not to grant that mandate. The scales, however, were already tipped against peace. The Congress of Verona had been convened for the purpose of letting the French Ultras deal with the Spanish people as Metternich had already dealt with the Neapolitans – by forcible suppression. Clearly the Duke would need to be all eyes and ears when he arrived on the Continent, particularly if he was to fulfil the high

---

* The word 'liberal' had come into usage from the Spanish *liberales*, the opponents of Ferdinand VII.

hopes of his admirers. Creevey relied on him 'as the only man who, on this occasion, could keep those Royal Imbeciles and Villains of Europe in any order'.[35]

Unfortunately his hearing had been damaged on 5 August when, as Master-General of the Ordnance, he was present at a review of howitzers and accidentally got too near an explosion. His left ear was to remain stone deaf for the rest of his life.

Though Vienna was a frost, his arrival at Verona created a stir. Every lady longed to be seen promenading on the hero's arm. Byron wrote in his *Age of Bronze*:

> Proud Wellington, with eagle beak so curled,
> That nose, the hook where he suspends the world.[36]

Into the midst of all this fine feeling Nosey, with soldierly precision, dropped his bomb, for it is agreed that his bleak refusal to approve the proposed invasion of liberal Spain created as much consternation in the Congress as if he had hurled a bombshell at the Holy Allied feet. It was his ineluctable duty to oppose the war which everyone but Britain wanted. There was perhaps some consolation in the British press reports from Verona.

It is certainly the manly firmness of the Duke of Wellington in opposing propositions which he considers to be at variance with the interests of his country, which is thought one of the greatest obstacles to an early conclusion. The Noble Duke is resolved to maintain his ground to the last. . . .

This was the *Courier*, writing on 5 November. *The Times* followed up on the 12th with the remark that war was 'only stopped or suspended by the influence of the Duke of Wellington'.

And in the evenings at any rate he could play cards with the ex-Empress of the French, Marie-Louise, telling her genially that he would pay his debts in *napoléons*. On the 18th he gave a musical party with his niece Priscilla Burghersh as hostess and Marie-Louise as guest of honour. As he led in the ex-Empress many people asked themselves how she felt, leaning on the very arm that had laid her late husband low.

He was not back in London until December. There was still 'something very extraordinary' about his head despite cuppings and blisters; but the Emperor of Austria had given him riding-horses at Verona if not the imperial confidence, and his general health seemed improved. Even in politics he detected 'a breeze everywhere for Peace' among moderates, though Ultras and Jacobins in all countries wanted war.

In the last effort to avert the invasion of Spain he sent out Fitzroy Somerset to urge upon the Spanish moderates a less extreme constitution than that of 1812. Alas, Fitzroy wrote back that the grandees were not the patriots they had been in 1808 and would rather welcome a French invasion; General Alava, that pillar of the moderates, had grown very grey and melancholy.

Then should Wellington adopt Canning's plan and himself lead a forlorn hope, a mission to Madrid? All his friends expostulated.

The date being now the end of February 1823, it was too late to play any card great or small. On 6 April a French army under Louis XVIII's nephew, the Duke of Angoulême, crossed the Pyrenees and by the autumn had restored Ferdinand VII to absolute power.

The Quintuple Alliance was as dead as Castlereagh – given the *coup de grâce* by the very Bourbons in whose aid it had been invented.

As a result the Duke found himself isolated in a grim no-man's-land between two fires. On the right, the Continental Ultras derided '*la politique Britannique*' at Verona, calling non-interventionist Britain 'an abettor of anarchy', sneering at the Duke's 'narrow patriotism'. On the left, a British mob howled outside the French embassy in London where Wellington was attending a ball, and demanded to know why the Peninsular hero had not saved Spain again.

Wellington could only resort in Parliament to his party's perennial defence in such circumstances: how could the Opposition claim to stand both for keeping the peace and putting down aggression? On this occasion, 24 April 1823, a few sentences from his speech give the dry, pungent flavour of his style at its best:

And here I must call upon the noble Lords opposite, and ask them to state to me whether, at the commencement of these negotiations [at Verona], they would have adopted measures of war or of neutrality for the basis of their future proceedings? As yet (your Lordships will have remarked) they have not declared whether they mean peace or war. Their argument would lead to the alternative of war, but they still seem to lean to pacific measures. I call upon them, therefore, to adopt the one line or the other.

But the Opposition had its perennially convenient way out of this dilemma: by using firm language they would have stopped aggression without provoking war.

In the first few months of 1823 it seemed that Verona had damaged Wellington in many eyes, including, sometimes, his own. The King blamed his intransigence:

He had the great, great disadvantage of being incapable of flexibility or of making a diplomatic approach. He sets about a question like a battery of cannon.

Why had the Alliance suffered such damage at Verona? the Duke asked himself. Was it Castlereagh's death or his own behaviour? Yet he thought he had done his duty.

Wellington was right. He had done his duty, and what seemed a lack of finesse to the King and the Ultras was in fact loyalty to Canning. That loyalty, however, was by no means reciprocated. In the Commons' debates on the invasion of Spain Canning used Wellington as his scapegoat and the Opposition, dazzled by the new Foreign Secretary, were only too delighted to accept this solution.

The truth was that the agonizing paradox of the Duke's position only gradually dawned on his circle. 'He was put with his back to the wall,' said the King in March, now complaining of Wellington's treatment at Verona.[37] Back to the wall, yes; but not a solid wall or a wall he could lean against; rather, a crumbling wall, undermined by Canning's subterranean works.

Wellington did not know that Canning's private instinct had been against sending any British delegate whatever to Verona, and that even Liverpool called the Duke too 'Continental'. He did not yet know of Canning's jubilant comment on the European breakdown: 'So things are getting back to a wholesome state again. Every nation for itself, and God for us all.' Nor of Canning's new policy, defined in terms of strictest patriotism: 'For *Europe* I shall be desirous *now and then* to read *England*'; 'for "Alliance" read "England", and you have the clue of my policy.'[38]

Patriotism was no alien concept to the Duke either. But in Canning he was confronting a kind of virulent, insular, ambitious and highly popular patriotism which has its practitioners in every age. He himself remained both by training and conviction a cool, sophisticated European.

Would the Duke, leading spokesman for the old European system based on co-operation between legitimate monarchs, find it possible to march into such a brash new world? Could he 'amalgamate' with vinegar?

26

The Canning Factor

'Amalgamation' of Wellington and Canning was not yet in question. Up to the early summer of 1823 the oil appeared to float effortlessly on top once more, in both Court and Cabinet. Canning knew as little about the King as the man in the moon, or so Mme de Lieven deduced from his intensive questioning, whereas Court circles were aware that His Majesty's true feeling for the Duke was 'more like Love than anything else!!'[1] Some members of the Cabinet confidently relied on the Duke's authority and good temper to keep Canning in order and give the Alliance the kiss of life.

By mid-summer, however, Canning had begun to exert noticeable influence over Lord Liverpool. The Court was alarmed. 'The King is very jealous of Mr Canning,' reported Wellington to Mrs Arbuthnot on 19 August.[2] In fact George IV was secretly corresponding with the Continental courts, besides intriguing with his Keeper of the Privy Purse, Sir William Knighton (known as 'the Accoucheur' from his previous profession), to get Lord Liverpool supplanted by the Duke. Canning suppressed the King's Continental correspondence by threatening to expose it in Parliament, while Wellington himself dealt firmly with the plot to put him in Liverpool's place after banishing Canning.

By mid-October he had at last convinced the Accoucheur that he would 'not be the means of tripping up Lord Liverpool, as in fact I should never afterwards be of any use to myself or to anybody else'. Canning, moreover, was beginning to find his own way to the King's heart – through patronage. As early as January 1823 he had given a government job to the favourite's son, Lord Francis Conyngham (now known as 'Canningham'), as a result of which the King had been observed walking about with his arm round the Foreign Secretary's neck.[3]

At the same time Wellington believed by the end of the year that his own policy duel with the Foreign Secretary was going fairly well.

Though the feeling in Downing Street was hostile to the Allies, he had wrung 'a sort of engagement' from No. 10 not to do any mischief while ministers were away over Christmas.

The long-awaited Cabinet meeting to decide the King's Speech for 1824 was 'very stormy', but the Duke felt that his own interventions had succeeded. There would be no insulting attack on France for her aggression against Spain; no proposal for recognition of the revolted Spanish colonies. But on 23 July Canning bounced back, to score a resounding victory on South American trade against Wellington's tenacious arguments in a divided Cabinet. The Duke's disgust at his defeat was unbounded.

A few months later the Duke had to concede Canning's greatest triumph so far: Cabinet agreement to full and formal recognition of the South American republics. At the meeting on 15 December all other contestants had fallen away, leaving the Duke and Canning to fight it out in single combat. Canning stumbled away exhausted but victorious. 'I am really quite knocked up with it,' he wrote to Lord Granville. 'The fight has been hard, but it is won. The deed is done. The nail is driven. Spanish America is free; and if we do not mismanage our affairs she is English. . . .'[4]

This was the refrain of Canning's nationalistic anthem: Spanish America *English*. The New World *ours*. It grated on Wellington's ears, and indeed he often had cause to remind Canning that other powers besides Britain had a right to legitimate influence in Europe and elsewhere. Canning's foreign policy, however, was creative in its own way. As he was to say in Parliament in 1826:

I resolved that if France had Spain it should not be Spain with the Indies. I called the New World into existence to redress the balance of the old.

The House was electrified. Golden phrases, golden as the Indies themselves if not altogether meaningful or modest, seemed to pour from the orator. To others he was too clever by half. A pedestrian style sounded more trustworthy.

It was probably on 11 October 1825 that a personal blow struck Wellington. A letter from Mrs Patterson, one of the three lovely Caton sisters who visited Paris from America after the war, announced that she was going over to Ireland to marry, of all people, Richard.

In order to understand the violence of the Duke's reaction to this news it is necessary to recall his peculiar relations both with Richard Wellesley and Marianne Patterson. Lord Wellesley had first forfeited his brother's esteem during the Peninsular War by allowing his womanizing and indolence to injure a potentially brilliant political career. After Waterloo, Wellesley was jealous of and opposed to his brother in politics. His first wife, a French actress, after long being separated from him, had died in 1816. Marianne Patterson, on the other hand, had been the Duke's romantic ideal during the years after Waterloo and until she returned to America where her husband Robert Patterson died. So when Arthur heard that Mrs Patterson was to marry the Marquess Wellesley he lost his head and dashed off a furious letter in the hope that he might save her at the eleventh hour from a fate worse than widowhood.

What were the facts about this Marquess, this Lord-Lieutenant of Ireland, this Knight of the Garter whom Marianne was to marry? The ever-present Mrs Arbuthnot listened aghast to the Duke's summary of his 'very indiscreet' letter:

... Ld Wellesley was a man totally ruined; when he quitted Ireland, which he must soon do, he wd not have a house to take her to, or money to keep a carriage; that he had not a shilling in the world, &, moreover, was of a most jealous disposition, a violent temper & that he had entirely worn out his constitution by the profligate habits of his life.[5]

Mrs Arbuthnot tried in vain to console her distracted friend ('I have never seen the Duke more annoyed') with the suggestion that the rich and beautiful Marianne was no better in her own way than Lord Wellesley: 'I told him . . . that it was pretty well for the widow of an American shopkeeper to marry a Marquis. . . .'

No less stunned by the news was the sister of the late 'American shopkeeper', Betsy Patterson-Bonaparte.

'I married the brother of Napoleon the conqueror of Europe,' she said bitterly*; 'Mary has married the brother of Napoleon's conqueror.' One of the most curious links in history had indeed been forged.

Wellington was soon writing to Mrs Patterson, 'that a wise man would hold his tongue', and had recovered enough to send the Lord-Lieutenant good wishes on his marriage.[6] Lord Wellesley's ménage, past and future, was one aspect of an Irish scene that daily engaged more and more of the Duke's attention.

* Napoleon annulled the marriage.

377

Though the Duke rarely declared emotional feelings for any subject or person explicitly, apart from the constitution and monarch, he was deeply and emotionally committed to Ireland. The strength of this feeling was shown by the amount of time he gave throughout his life to research and writing on possible solutions for Ireland's problems.

The Catholics had been stirred by the winds of change blowing both in Ireland and England. Wellington saw their point only too well. How could the British Cabinet recognize Simon Bolivar's bid for emancipation from Spain in South America while rejecting Daniel O'Connell's claim for Ireland?

Daniel O'Connell had founded the Catholic Association on 10 May 1823, thus screwing up the agitation to an unheard-of pitch. This burly Kerryman, himself a Roman Catholic and proprietor of a small estate, was gifted with a huge voice capable of carrying to ten thousand people, and a lawyer's brain astute enough to devise a form of Catholic association which did not actually contravene the law. A Catholic 'rent' of 1d per month was levied by O'Connell on the Irish masses, raising as much as £22,700 that year for the emancipation campaign. It was paid with patriotic pride. Soon an immensely powerful new force was thrown behind the rent – the Irish clergy. Catholic priests became treasurers of their local branches and the pennies were collected at the church doors on 'Rent Sundays' after Mass.

Throughout his life Wellington regarded the formation of political societies, whether Catholic or Protestant, radical or constitutional, with instinctive disfavour. Why should the incomparable British constitution be submitted to these excrescences? They were either dangerous or superfluous. He was therefore fiercely hostile to the Catholic Association. But with its inception in 1823 he was also eager to withdraw from the ultra right-wing Constitutional Association which he had reluctantly joined in 1821, for the purpose of hauling seditious scribblers into court. This egregious society, after coming under heavy fire in Parliament, dissolved itself, to the Duke's relief, in 1823.

All this time the Duke was pursuing his researches into the Irish question, impeded as usual by a flow of uninvited suggestions. A Mr Richard Keene, for instance, was anxious to offer a tract of empty country in Mexico for 'drawing off' the surplus Irish population. The increasing violence in Ireland was reported to him from many Irish sources, among them an old colleague Lord Clancarty, who had retired from the foreign service after offending the King of the Netherlands:

We are in even a worse state [wrote Clancarty], than immediately prior to the Rebellion of 1798. As to the local government [Lord Wellesley's], deprived as it is of all patronage, and without the means of exerting force, what can it do?[7]

Force was a solution that the Duke did not dismiss. Impressed by a book by a Captain Noel which argued that the conquest of Ireland had never been 'perfected', he felt that 'unless measures can be discovered to quiet that country we shall have to compleat the Conquest'.[8] This was in April 1823. Two months later 'conquest' or conciliation seemed even more essential because of fissures in the British Cabinet.

The prematurely aged Prime Minister (he was a year younger than Wellington) was irritable, ill and speaking of resignation. He could not face remedial measures for Ireland, particularly if the Home Secretary Peel resigned on the issue, as he threatened to do. Wellington saw Peel, urging him to act '*manfully*' at the head of Irish affairs (Peel had said he was 'sick of the job') and forestall a Catholic rebellion. 'I fairly scolded him,' he reported to Mrs Arbuthnot. But he felt he had made no impression except to prevent Peel from resigning without warning him first.[9]

Wellington's own mind continued to move forward along the two parallel paths of force and reform. First, suppression of the Catholic Association. 'If we can't get rid of the Catholic Association,' he wrote to Peel on 3 November 1824, 'we must look to a civil war in Ireland sooner or later.' As Master-General of the Ordnance it was his duty to warn Bathurst, Secretary for War and the Colonies, to increase the army in Ireland, though hoping that Peel's new 'Constable Acts' might enable the Government to keep the peace through a police force rather than soldiers. On the other hand, further correspondence with Dr Curtis, his friend from Peninsular days, now Roman Catholic Primate, showed him that force was not enough. The fact of Catholic clergy contributing and collecting funds for the Association radically altered the position. Was there no way of pacifying Ireland by bringing back her clergy to the side of law and order?

In this atmosphere of controversy Wellington began the new year, 1825, by drafting his own peace policy for Ireland. He spent all February reading the Irish reports, writing his paper and intermittently relaxing on his real tennis court. He was also heartened by the passage of an Unlawful Assembly Act on 9 March, ostensibly aimed at both Orange and nationalist factions, but which caused the dreaded Catholic Association, now known to Protestants as the 'Popish Parliament', to wind itself up. He did not know that it was to be a case of 'The Association is dead! Long live the Association!' For a new Catholic association was to arise in July from the ashes of the old. His answer, meanwhile, reached after tireless consultations and delving into his own Continental experience, involved what was known as an 'Erastian' solution, after the Swiss sixteenth-century theologian who had worked out a scheme for the co-ordination of Church and State, with the secular State on top. His version of Catholic emancipation required a Concordat negotiated in Rome.

'Having settled these measures at Rome,' concluded the Duke, 'they should be recognized by Parliament, and the same Act should repeal every law imposing any disability upon a Roman Catholick.'

Half-way through his analysis the Duke had made a significant plea for reaching a settlement now – now, at a time of 'external peace and of internal tranquillity'. Britain was prosperous. Agriculture had recovered in 1824, commerce was booming. Let a settlement be negotiated from strength and not left to be 'extorted from our fears'.

At a Cabinet meeting on 24 April the Prime Minister suggested a talk with Wellington about his 'Catholic' paper. The very next day, 25 April, a speech was made in the Lords that temporarily blew the idea of a settlement out of the sky.

The Duke of York, heir to the throne, was gouty and dropsical but still, in Thackeray's words, 'a man, big, burly, loud, jolly, cursing, courageous'. This man pledged himself in ringing tones to defend the Coronation Oath and Established Church, 'whatever might be his station in life, so help him God!' George IV was older and sicker than York. It seemed like a renewal of George III's hysterical pledges against Catholic emancipation from a man soon to occupy the throne.

The Orange party was ecstatic, Wellington aghast. He dashed off a note to Arbuthnot on the 26th:

There never was such folly. It must render all parties more eager to decide the question at an early period and on the wrong grounds!! It appears to me as if the finger of God was on this family . . . and they were being driven mad.[10]

There had been a time when the Duke thought the finger of God was laid benignly upon himself. Now it was a vengeful finger, incidentally destroying his own careful and complicated plan for emancipation. When he called at 10 Downing Street for a verdict, the Prime Minister could see nothing in his document but difficulties. The cerebrations of Erastus had gone down before the bellowings of York.

On 10 May Burdett's Relief Bill passed its third reading in the Commons, but by only 248 to 227 votes. Enormously relieved, the Tory peers refused to give it a second reading by a resounding majority of 48 (178 to 130). It was said that certain peeresses had locked up their 'Catholic' husbands before the vote was taken, and Tory toasts were drunk to 'The Glorious 48!'.

The Duke of York's oration forced even Wellington off course. He shelved his ideas for emancipation and a Concordat with the Vatican in favour of a snap election, since the country seemed to have swung so far against the 'Catholics' as to offer the chance of a solidly 'Protestant' Parliament being elected for the first time in years – a prospect he could not but welcome. Even if Lord Liverpool decided against an election – as he did – Wellington's conditions for emancipation scarcely obtained after the spring of 1825. Where was the economic 'tranquillity'? The better off suffered from speculative mania. 'Englishmen, who were wont to be sober, are gone mad,'[11] wrote Lord Eldon of the railway speculators. 'The banks are breaking in all directions,' noted Harriet Arbuthnot almost gleefully, enjoying a bust as much as a boom. The workless who had no money with which to speculate were maddened by clear acts of God, a bad harvest and a hard winter.

When Canning proposed a Russian mission on Christmas Eve 1825 Wellington jumped at it. 'Never better in his life', 'ready to start in a week' – such expressions of alertness convinced Canning that the selection of anybody else would have injured the Duke's health far more than all the frosts of Russia.[12] For this was intended to be far more than a courtesy visit.

Events in Eastern Europe had reached a critical point where the Sultan of Turkey might exterminate the Greeks or alternatively the Emperor of Russia decimate the Turks. At the same time Canning saw in these dangers the ideal opportunity for finishing off the old European system and reassembling the pieces under Britain's lead. His policy was to offer British mediation between Russia and Turkey, and Turkey and Greece. It will be noticed that the success of this policy depended on certain nicely adjusted tensions. Too much bellicosity at St Petersburg would precipitate war; too little would give the British mediator no chance to mediate.

It was curious that Canning should have chosen the Duke for such an exercise in brinkmanship. He had been criticized after Verona for inflexibility and Canning can hardly have expected him to change overnight from a lion into a fox. Some people thought Canning simply wished to get the Duke out of the way.

Wellington charmed the new Tsar Nicholas and negotiated the secret Protocol of St Petersburg, by which Britain should mediate between Turkey and Russia to obtain qualified Greek independence. On his resumption of British politics, however, at the beginning of May 1826 the Opposition, with Canning's tacit support, dubbed his mission a failure. Personally, the Duke was divided between pleasure at being back among scintillating friends and distaste for home affairs in their continuing disturbed state.

There had been machine-breaking in the North during April with a thousand power looms smashed in one week, followed by a drought. These things forced the Cabinet to promise some relaxation of the Corn Laws even at the cost of fury on the farms. Except in Ireland, however, quarrels within the Whig party saved the Government from disaster in the 1826 election. At Waterford, Ireland, O'Connell's Catholic forces won a stunning victory. Whereas in Wales a sharp Radical challenge to the Tory Marquess of Worcester –

> Shall the sons of Newport free
> E'er to Worcester Bow the knee? –

resulted in the labourers' knees still remaining bowed, in Ireland thousands of peasants known as '40s-freeholders' straightened their backs and voted for the first time against their landlords.

The Irish poor, in fact, were in the plight customary during a bad season. Here Wellington showed an understanding of the country superior to the *laissez-faire* economists who argued in abstract terms. He believed that the systems of land-tenure and labour were responsible for recurrent famines, rather than the size of the population. He and Peel (Home Secretary) discussed the impending disaster on 20 August. Next day, obsessed with the potential horror, he wrote to Peel picturing a situation in which a million Irish would have to be fed by the State. He also described to Harriet the difference between his and Peel's reaction:

. . . I was astounded by the magnitude of the calamity. [Peel] was quite cool & quiet; and said in answer to my observations that we should lose one third of the Population, 'that is the natural course of this great excess of Population'.

Wellington showed his disagreement with Peel in the rest of his letter to Harriet:

It is not true that the Population of Ireland is too great. If the working classes were paid in Money instead of Land & were in the Habit of coming upon the markets for their food, instead of [raising it in potato patches] to pay the rent of which they mortgage their Labour, this misfortune would not have been felt in the same degree or indeed at all.

His solution was neither emigration nor Peel's 'natural course', i.e. death, but a market economy in Ireland to raise the standard of living. Meanwhile, the 'natural course' of change was at work in Britain.

The Commander-in-Chief of the British Army, HRH the Duke of York, died on 5 January 1827.

The royal funeral, on 20 January, made sure that as many other people as possible were soon dying also. It took place at night in St George's Chapel, Windsor, with nothing on the flagstones to relieve the rising damp. On returning to Stratfield Saye during the small hours of the 21st Wellington was taken violently ill.[13] Next day Peel, a guest in the house, tried to reassure the Duchess by telling her that before this attack Wellington had looked stouter and heartier than for years.

'That is the effect of age,' said Kitty tremulously. 'People about his time of life get larger.'

'His face is larger.'

'I am so short-sighted I cannot remark his features, I can only judge by the colour, and when I look at *that precious face*, it seems to be very pale.' She burst into tears, filling the deeply uxorious Peel with mingled pity and aversion – aversion from those who found it in their hearts, as he told his wife, to usurp Kitty's place. This hit at Mrs Arbuthnot was followed by an even fiercer denunciation of the Duke: 'What wickedness and what folly to undervalue and to be insensible to the affection of a wife!'[14]

While Wellington was recovering from his illness, however undeservedly in Peel's eyes, others were less lucky. The fatal toll of the funeral night was said to have been two bishops, five footmen and several soldiers; while many took to their beds. Canning and his friend Huskisson, both in poor health, caught chills which they never completely threw off. As for the Prime Minister, he had been too unfit to attend the macabre event; on 17 February he was found unconscious from a paralytic stroke. In Lord Liverpool was removed the untiring, placatory influence that so long had enabled the old aristocracy to absorb this and other shocks.

The succession of Wellington to the command of the army was a foregone conclusion. The King no doubt had entertained an intoxicating vision of himself in that post, but it was quickly dissipated by his ministers. Lord Londonderry questioned whether the Duke's new office was compatible with his becoming in due course Prime Minister –'However, there never was a Wellington before; and never will be again' – and to a Wellington all things were possible.[15]

His main task was how to effect drastic military economies – the country's emphatic postwar demand – while maintaining the army's efficiency. Cuts had been made already. Why was not the late Commander-in-Chief given a military funeral? The answer in Wellington's opinion was obvious: they had not enough soldiers in England to bury a field-marshal.

Other difficulties were connected with the late Field-Marshal's active life. As one of his executors, Wellington heard from the Accoucheur that all the secrets of HRH's debts were to be 'placed in your Grace's bosom', including claims rising out of a legion of mistresses. '*This morning* another female friend presented herself,' wrote Knighton jocularly on 31 May to the Duke, 'with a Bond for a thousand pounds: so that you will see that the disbanded Troops are rather numerous!'[16]

If there were not enough officers in England of the rank to bury a field-marshal, there were certainly not enough to discharge his debts, though Londonderry suggested they should do so by a 'voluntary' whip-round among officers of all ranks – a plan that the Duke at once vetoed. It was for Parliament to pay up.

However, with Liverpool politically dead, a bigger question arose. Would there be enough men in England willing to raise a field-marshal to the highest office in the State? Four years of struggle between Wellington and Canning had reached their climax.

Excitement began to build up the moment Lord Liverpool's condition was known. All the Opposition newspapers backed Canning for Prime Minister. The King was torn by doubts. Could the new Government, like the old, contain both Wellington and Canning? Or was it a case of either/or? William Ponsonby, a Whig in the know, analysed the crisis for his sister Caroline Lamb on 20 February:

Everything continues in an extraordinary state & great anxiety is felt to know what will be the consequence. Lord Liverpool is alive, but that is all, & Canning far from strong. His party & the Duke of Wellington's, having been long held together by Lord Liverpool alone, must sever.[17]

Throughout March political fever continued to mount as the committed supporters of each side went into action. Accusations of intrigue flew between the two camps. It was a testing time for both champions: Canning because of physical pain from rheumatic fever, Wellington because he always hated political manoeuvres, particularly in his own interest. He felt too much the master to need them and too much the servant to use them.

One of the turning-points in the great race was 5 March. During the afternoon and evening the Government's two 'buggaboos', as Canning called corn and the Catholics, came before the Commons with results not calculated to strengthen Wellington. Canning pleased the moderates of all parties by introducing a liberalized Corn Bill; and a bill for Catholic emancipation was defeated. Paradoxically this reverse to 'Catholic' Canning got the King off the hook. For it drove that particular buggaboo from the stage at least until the next session. No insurmountable obstacle now stood between the 'Protestant' monarch and a 'Catholic' Prime Minister.

As Wellington saw it, he was in the race neither to destroy Canning's career, nor for himself, but to reconstruct Liverpool's masterpiece – the old, old Government of 1812 that had struggled uphill to Waterloo and gone downhill ever since. He was content to serve under any acceptable Prime Minister – say Peel – who was not a 'Catholic'.

21–25 March: Wellington now faced a serious menace to his cause from a group of Tory peers. Led by the Dukes of Newcastle and Rutland, they tried to press a 'Protestant' premier (obviously Wellington) upon the evasive King. The annoyance of this Tory pressure-group was to be ably exploited by Canning.

28 March: Lord Liverpool's resignation was placed in the King's hands.

10 April: Stalemate faced the King. Neither Wellington nor Peel would serve under Canning; Canning would serve under no one but a puppet. King George could not do without Canning, in the sense that no Tory Government could be formed from which Canning was excluded, but he could well do without the advice of high and mighty Tory peers like Newcastle and Rutland. It was said that Canning had won during an audience when he touched the King's pride:

'Sir, your father broke the domination of the Whigs; I hope your Majesty will not endure that of the Tories.'

'No, I'll be damned if I do.'[18]

So the Duke was beaten at last. On the afternoon of 10 April the King commissioned his Foreign Secretary to prepare a plan for the reconstruction of the Government. For Canning, these curiously chosen words held no ambiguities. He was Prime Minister.

When the bolt fell Wellington was strangely sceptical. 'It was said in the House of Lords yesterday afternoon that Mr Canning had been appointed Minister,' he wrote on the crucial 10 April 1827, 'but I have no reason to believe the Report to be true up to this moment, half past two.'[19] So, with the rumours already discounted, he saw no finality in a terse circular letter received from Canning that evening. It simply informed him of Canning's commission from the King to make 'a plan' for the reconstruction of the ministry and trusted that the Duke would continue to be a member of it. There was no visit from Canning; no offer to elucidate any obscurities such as other colleagues received; just the bare invitation. Wellington was not flattered.

However, he decided to elucidate the main obscurity forthwith. Who was to be Prime Minister? Before the Duke could answer Mr Canning's 'obliging proposition' he wished to know 'who is the person whom you intend to propose to His Majesty as the head of the Government?'

Canning drafted a shrivelling reply and sent it to the Duke.

My dear Duke of Wellington,

I believe it to be ... generally understood that the King usually entrusts the formation of an Administration to the individual whom it is His Majesty's gracious intention to place at the head of it. . . .

Deeply insulted and suspicious, the Duke resigned. And not only did he resign the Ordnance but also his position as Commander-in-Chief. While the former, being a Cabinet post, could be justified on political grounds, the latter could not, since Wellington himself held that command of the army was non-political. His dramatic dual resignation, therefore, was personal.

Peel's advice to defend himself in Parliament had untoward results, The Duke rose on 2 May to explain that he had resigned because the Government had shifted towards the 'Catholics'. It was led in the Lords by the 'Catholic' Viscount Goderich (formerly Frederick

Robinson) while on the Woolsack appeared another 'Catholic', the Whig Sir John Copley, created Lord Lyndhurst; in the Commons Huskisson and Palmerston, as Canningites, still sat on the front bench, but the many vacancies were perforce filled by 'Catholics'.

Moreover, in his anxiety to disprove allegations of personal ambition he was lured into a memorable statement proving that it was 'totally out of the question' for him to be Prime Minister:

... a situation for which I am sensible that I am not qualified; and to which, moreover, neither His Majesty ... nor any wished to see me called. ... My Lords, I should have been worse than mad if I had thought of such a thing.

How long would Canning remain as premier? His popularity was enormous, his health wretched. Of his two major domestic concerns, Catholics and corn, Catholic emancipation was relegated to a future session, while argument about the details of the Corn Bill had ended in complete misunderstanding between the Government and the Duke. The inventive Sir Robert Wilson announced that instead of the Duke being admired for Wellington boots he would be execrated for a 'Wellington loaf' – odious symbol of the starvation inflicted upon the people by keeping up the corn duties.

Nevertheless, apart from the Corn Bill's fiasco in the Lords – it was withdrawn after an amendment by the Duke – he maintained something like an independent role during Canning's 'Hundred Days'. If any human agency was responsible for Canning's collapse it was the leader of the Opposition, Lord Grey. His personal tirades against the Prime Minister so worked upon Canning's excitable temperament that his physician, Dr Farr, told the Duke after his death, 'It was Canning's temper that killed him.'[20] On 3 August Wellington heard that Canning was desperately ill with a stoppage of the bowel and had a blister covering his whole stomach. 'He had no relief.' In the same bedroom at Chiswick House where Fox had expired twenty years earlier, Canning died on 8 August, exactly a hundred days after he had first faced Parliament as Prime Minister.

In Canning a giant had died. A few days before his death the Duke had held forth to the Grevilles on Canning's astonishing talents, fertility and inexhaustible resources – 'the finest speaker he ever heard' – yet able to take criticism. It was only when thinking of the future that the Duke's forebodings got the better of his magnanimity. 'I send you the bulletin from Chiswick this morning,' he had written to Mrs Arbuthnot on 7 August: 'In short he will be dead in a few Hours; after having done as much mischief in four Months as it was possible for a Man to do God knows how it is to be remedied.'[21]

By whom was the 'mischief' to be remedied? That was the real question. Wellington had no illusions about his own chances. They were no more than fifty-fifty. On the 10th, he received the news that Goderich was to be Prime Minister and an effort made to keep together the Canningite coalition. By the 14th hope of any post was almost abandoned but on the very next day came the letter from Windsor.

My dear Friend

  I write for the purpose of again offering to you the command of my army, and I sincerely hope that the time is arrived when the country will no longer be deprived of . . . your high talents.

  Always, with great truth, your sincere friend,

G.R.

It is to be noted that Wellington was invited to resume his position at the Horse Guards, not his Cabinet office. Nevertheless he immediately sent on the King's letter to Peel and after a prompt and most favourable verdict replied, 'I accept.'

'Goody' Goderich was honest and liberal, but fate had dealt him a cruel blow in 1826 when his daughter Eleanor died aged eleven. Two months after her death he was asking to retire to the Lords in order to save his wife from long evenings alone. Tears were henceforth never far from his eyes, and he was crying as he kissed hands on 9 August and again as he haggled over his Cabinet ministers; 'blubbering fool,' said the King behind his back. His middle-of-the-road Cabinet, with William Huskisson as Leader of the Commons, was the right one for the times.

If the King was not altogether displeased to have a weak Prime Minister for a change, the Ultras were now set on getting King Arthur back into the field. They invited him to some of their northern estates, where under cover of private hospitality he might make a royal progress among the people. The experiment was variously rated. Walter Scott felt that the great Duke had demeaned himself by this manoeuvre. The Duke's own accounts paid light-hearted tribute to his endurance: 'passed through a *very heavy* fire at York'.

Not long after the Duke's return south an event occurred to give the Cabinet a jolt from which it never recovered. On 20 October 1827 Admiral Codrington took pity on the Greeks and sent the marauding Turkish fleet to the bottom of Navarino Bay. To the Whigs nothing so glorious had happened since Byron died at Missalonghi. To Wellington and the Tories it was the shocking first fruits of Canning's four months' 'mischief'.

King George IV and his brother William, the Lord High Admiral, put their heads together and decided to give Codrington the Grand Cross of the Bath before a scandalized Wellington could stop them. Afterwards the King is said to have repented sufficiently to observe: 'I send him the ribbon but he deserves the rope.'[22]

'The Ministers are frightened to death at the scrape they are in,' wrote Mrs Arbuthnot gleefully; 'quite at *sixes and sevens*, some for peace, some for war, and all despised and derided by everybody. . . .' At last on 8 January 1828 Lord Goderich, dissolved in tears as usual (the King lent him his handkerchief), dissolved the Government also. Before 8 am next morning, 9 January, a note was delivered at Apsley House from the Lord Chancellor. While the Duke was still dressing Lyndhurst arrived in person to sweep him off to Windsor. The call had come. He was to be Prime Minister.

'Arthur,' said the King sitting up in bed with a turban nightcap on, 'the Cabinet is defunct!'

How did his own case stand, now that he had been hoisted to the top of the greasy pole?

In correcting a wax impression of his profile which was to go on a snuffbox, Kitty showed that his physical style in 1828 was vital and lapidary as ever.

The Hair grows rather *up* from the forehead, being naturally inclined to curl, it never lies flat and covers very little of the forehead, which is rather broad, open & beautiful. The nose is hardly large enough but from the Eye to the nostril . . . it is too thick, it should be very fine indeed. . . . The jaw from the ear to the chin requires to be rather more square.[23]

Though this uppish hair was turning from grey to white, Mrs Arbuthnot snipped off two locks for Lady Shelley as a keepsake, one of which was still brown.

His mastery of unyielding subjects like finance seemed very English; from England too came his attention to detail and concentration; from Ireland doubtless his 'devil', as once noticed by William Napier, part devilry, part genius.

His devil expressed itself sometimes in secretiveness, sometimes in cutting repartee, both habits established during his military career. Lord Holland found him 'very close and his designs quite impenetrable'.

Occasions when he exhibited his other peculiarity, the crushing retort, were no doubt multiplied by the wit and inventiveness of his contemporaries; but the celebrated exchange between the Duke and some minor official from a government office is authentic.

'Mr Jones, I believe,' said the official blandly, accosting the great man in Pall Mall and mistaking him for the secretary of the Royal Academy. The world-famous profile froze.

'If you believe that, you'll believe anything.'

Wellington's first ten years at home had not taught him to speak the language of Tory politics with fluency. Moreover, he remained impervious to the political exigencies of the House of Commons all his life; hence his imperfect understanding of Peel and his trials, so courageously faced. Far less had his experiences given him a taste for the incantations of the Whigs. It is almost superfluous to add that he was out of step with the famous 'March of Intellect', 'March of Mind' or 'Spirit of the Age', whose tireless tramp through the press and public meeting-places had begun the movement for 'liberality' and swept along even Tories in its train. Goderich, for instance, was according to the Duke of Rutland an advocate of 'the march of mind, and a parcel of mischievous and infernal trash'.

Wellington based his antipathy to the press on long personal experience. As Irish Chief Secretary he had several disagreeable brushes with Dublin newspapers in 1808. The traditionally 'bought' Irish press cost the Government under his direction £20,000, whereas a 'free' press in Dublin went either bankrupt or berserk.[24] The extraordinarily unfettered British and French press gave him no more confidence than the Irish as time went on. By the 1820s England had sprouted a new crop of often scurrilous journals – the *Age*, the *Beacon*, the *Satirist*, *Nimrod*. Wellington was soon calling all journalists with monotonous irony 'the *Gentlemen*'.

As for the 'mob' who could not read, but whose leaders read aloud inflammatory articles to their henchmen in public taverns – they represented Britannia at her worst, worse even than the arch-fiend of revolution, France. 'Rely upon it,' he wrote in 1826, 'that with all our civilization and advantages, we are the nation in Europe the least disciplined and the least to be trusted in a situation in which we are not controlled by the strong arm of authority and law.'[25]

The Duke was a suppressed introvert, whose record as a man of action showed the brilliant externalizing of all his talents and genius – perhaps the perfect human syndrome. Hence the external man's willingness to retreat, while the man within remained inviolate and unbeatable; hence the resolution to make persuasive parliamentary speeches when his inner self could be expressed only in music, for ever barred to him since the burning of his violin. Sir Walter Scott described his method of debate as 'slicing the argument into two or three parts, and helping himself to the best'. It sounded both dry and boorish. Yet his table-talk, as Scott also testified, was remarkable for 'the sweetness & *abandon* with which it flowed'.

It was the existence of these natural springs that made him a sociable man, despite the more uncompromising qualities. In the 1820s he became a founder-member of clubs like the Athenaeum and the Oriental, both started in 1824, and Crockford's gambling club, 1827 – the last for companionable reasons, though enemies said it was in order to blackball his son Douro.

Though the Duke was so convivial, it is not altogether surprising that the club stories about him emphasize the iron rather than the charm.

'Very well, think what you are about,' he is supposed to have said to the Kildare Club, Dublin; 'but if you let in the bishops, mind your umbrellas.'

The Dutch school of painting was the one that the Duke liked beyond all others. What was it that attracted the Duke? We are told that the Dutch masters stood for 'the practical social application of the philosophy that things must be made to work'.* Wellington too was that kind of pragmatist. He might be an aristocrat himself, but the Britain he hoped to guide as Prime Minister was populated by growing numbers of workers in factories, shipyards and mines. Here in a hundred future Coketowns were not a few men already 'slaves of an iron-handed despotism'; nor did a man like Cobbett find that all was beauty on his rural rides.†

Such was the picture, such the chiaroscuro of lights and shadows; and while many admired, others wanted to upset the quivering balance. Was the restless 'Spirit of the Times' a true time-spirit or a mere errant fashion? This insistent question, confronting as it does every statesman in his day, now rang its challenge in the Duke's ears.

* Kenneth Clark, *Civilisation* (London 1970).
† Dickens, *Hard Times* (London 1854); Cobbett, *Rural Rides* (London 1830).

27

Prime Minister

The difficulties of forming a general staff were caused by Whitehall sending out the wrong men, not by officers arguing about their postings. 'I say to one go, and he goes.' Forming a Cabinet was the opposite. The Prime Minister would say to one come and he would come – and argue.

Peel at any rate must come. In an unexpectedly high key the Duke summoned his right-hand man:

My dear Peel, I entreat you to come to town in order that I may consult with you . . . everything is open to all mankind, excepting one person [Grey].[1]

That was to be another trouble. Far too many of mankind were open to invitation, and political aspirants required delicate handling.

He managed to impress Peel at their first meeting (10 January) with his friendliness and tact, though immediately afterwards he was writing to Mrs Arbuthnot that 'between ourselves Peel is not easy to deal with'.[2] The future Leader of the House had in fact ruffled Wellington in three separate ways. Through shyness Peel's manner had been cold; he hinted clumsily that the Prime Minister would have to cease being Commander-in-Chief; and he himself insisted on having Canningites with speaking talent in the Cabinet to strengthen his control over a difficult House of Commons.

The Duke misinterpreted Peel's craving for Canningites as due to lack of stamina in facing the Opposition ('Mr Peel, whose fault is not being courageous in the H of Commons, wishes to surround himself with all the speakers,' echoed Mrs Arbuthnot in her journal)[3]; and Peel's insistence on parliamentary orators meant further restriction on the Prime Minister's choice of former associates.

The Ultras had gone out with him in April 1827; they expected to come back with him in January 1828. But like every Prime Minister the Duke had to harden his heart against the claims of auld lang syne, writing again and again the letters which began, 'Nothing has given me more pain . . .'. The search for eloquent speakers was a serious matter and brought the Duke up against one of the more disagreeable episodes of his political career.

Charles Arbuthnot fully expected to be a Cabinet minister, since he regarded himself as a member of the Duke's '*private* Cabinet when we were all out together'. But he was a non-speaker. As such Wellington merely reallocated him to his old 'Woods and Forests' without a seat in the Cabinet. Poor Arbuthnot thought for a time of refusing to serve, because of 'the sneers & remarks of everyone', while Harriet wailed from Woodford, 'I can't bear it all.' The Duke, as he continued to stand firm, groaned that he was risking 'the break-up of the only private & confidential Relation I have in Life'. When the Arbuthnots eventually caved in he declared that he had got a better night's sleep than for weeks.[4]

On the principles agreed with Peel, room could not be found in the Government for either Richard or William, his brothers, a situation which the press gleefully exploited. Plagued alike by importunities and remonstrances, Wellington stood knee-deep in red boxes and green bags, gesticulating fiercely to Croker: 'There, there is the business of the country, which I have not time to look at – all my time being employed in assuaging what gentlemen call their *feelings*.'[5]

He was a dog with a canister tied to its tail; he was 'very unhappy and uncomfortable'; he would nevertheless push on, alone:

I must work for myself and by myself; and please God however I may suffer I shall succeed in establishing in the Country a strong Govt.; and then I may retire with Honour.[6]

Was it a coincidence that he had again chosen images so often used during his early days in India: the tormented dog, and walking or working alone? Perhaps the same vision thirty years later of a great country hitherto misruled and relying upon him to evoke order out of confusion produced the same response.

By 20 January he had assembled his 'strong' Government, or at least the strongest he was allowed by the conflicting pressures of his own party, the Canningites and the King. Cabinet ministers sitting in the Commons consisted of three Tory 'Protestants' – Peel as Leader and Home Secretary – and three Canningite 'Catholics' – Lord Palmerston as Secretary at War and Huskisson in charge of the Colonies. When an ultra-Tory reproached the Duke for taking Huskisson, the Whigs' favourite, he is said to have replied, 'Oh! he is a very good bridge for rats to run over.'

In the Lords were four more 'Catholic' Cabinet ministers – the brilliant but opportunist Lyndhurst as Lord Chancellor, the 'fanciful' and near-mad Dudley as Secretary of State for Foreign Affairs (Lord Redesdale made a neat pun on this strange man's job: *Ses affaires lui ont été toujours étrangères*) and two able Tory newcomers, Aberdeen and Ellenborough as Chancellor of the Duchy and Lord Privy Seal respectively. Only two 'Protestant' peers returned to office, Bathurst to be Lord President and Melville to the Board of Control (India). It was a Cabinet of thirteen counting the Duke, and the score was seven to six in favour of the 'Catholics'.

Hardly had they settled in before all the Duke's colleagues, banding themselves together as twelve good men and true, gave their unanimous verdict for the Prime Minister resigning his post of Commander-in-Chief. As they expected, he was 'strongly excited' against this move though hardly in a position to resist, having himself suggested less than a year before that command of the army was incompatible with the premiership.[7]

On 22 January Wellington's first Cabinet dinner took place at Apsley House. Everyone was scrupulously polite but with the courtesy, noted Ellenborough, 'of men who had just fought a duel'.[8] Only a little over a year later one of the diners was to do just that. Already there was some sort of mental duel going on between Wellington and Peel.

The sad fact was that though they admired and depended on each other's outstanding gifts, their temperaments clashed. Wellington had long known that Peel was really a liberal, and a liberal whose hidden instincts put a brake on his party political attack, making him cautious and sometimes dejected. Though as remote from party factiousness as Peel himself, Wellington received no disturbing signals from alien systems of thought, as Peel did, and so could go into action in a state of either euphoria or exasperation but very seldom of melancholy. Peel shied away from the ebullience conferred by blue blood and the adulation of women. Wellington had no prejudices whatever against the red blood of the northern merchants to whose class Peel belonged, indeed he prized it; but in Peel's case he felt that water had got into the wine.

All in all, he missed in Peel the 'high tone' that Queen Victoria was later to miss in Gladstone. This alleged weakness of his second-in-command was summed up for Mrs Arbuthnot on 7 April:

The truth is that Peel is afraid of the Opposition, his colleagues and his supporters. He is afraid to place himself on high ground.[9]

Despite the tensions between liberals and reactionaries the Duke's Government introduced two long-overdue reforms during their first two months. Repeal of the Test Acts was the heaviest blow to religious bigotry for fifty years; while the Corn Law was the longest step towards free trade since Waterloo. The Duke of Wellington may not have led the vanguard; but he was marching with the spirit of the times.

Far more divisive were the problems set by two corrupt boroughs, though again a Cabinet compromise was hammered out: Penrhyn's voting rights should be transferred *in toto* to Birmingham and East Retford merely merged with Bassetlaw. But the Cabinet had not reckoned with the House of Lords. When the Penrhyn transfer bill came up to them they took preliminary steps towards killing it. This had repercussions on the fate of East Retford, now before the Commons. If the Lords would not transfer Penrhyn to Birmingham, why should not the Commons let Birmingham have Retford's votes? Huskisson felt himself pledged to *one* transfer at least. On 19 May neither he nor Palmerston went into their own Government's lobby on the East Retford bill but sat tight in their seats and were counted with the Opposition minority. Peel, Leader of the House yet totally unprepared for a front-bench sit-in, was flabbergasted.

It was Wellington's turn to be flabbergasted, though not quite so unpleasantly, when at 10 am on 20 May he received from Huskisson what he and Peel agreed was a letter of resignation.

Huskisson, with his fatal gift for doing the wrong thing in an emergency, had picked up a pen at 2 o'clock that morning and still fevered by the previous night's events conscientiously made bad worse. 'I owe it to you,' he told Wellington, '. . . to lose no time in affording you an opportunity of placing my office in other hands' – in order to prevent any appearance of ministerial disunity on however 'unimportant' a question.

Huskisson did not intend to resign. His ill-conceived letter was meant as an *amende honorable* for his demonstration of the night before. Sensible rather than 'honourable' action, however, was required on that hectic Tuesday, 10 May. Huskisson had admittedly not been at all sensible. Was it sensible of the Prime Minister to write him an extremely stiff answer?

Your letter of two this morning, which I received at ten, has surprised me, and has given me great concern. I have considered it my duty to lay it before the King.

395

The Duke had had enough of Cabinet crises and he was not going to look a gift resignation in the mouth. When Lord Dudley came round to No. 10 and explained in person that Huskisson's letter was 'a mistake', the Duke said: 'There is no mistake, there can be no mistake, and there shall be no mistake.' And with this triple affirmation the high priest of firmness slipped out of No. 10 and strolled about in Birdcage Walk, just in case Huskisson should make the mistake of calling.

The last phase in the 'Battle of Retford' came on 26 May when the Duke appointed in Huskisson's place an old Peninsular officer who was now commanding the forces in Ireland, Sir George Murray. Out went all the Canningites in a body; in came more military men, more Tories like young Colonel Maberly and gallant Sir Henry Hardinge minus the arm he had left behind at Ligny. Field-Marshal the Duke of Wellington would soon have his wartime staff complete, sneered the Whigs.

The man at No. 10 cared little about the Opposition's criticism of his reconstructed Cabinet: 'all the women are with us,' he repeated gaily after sitting between Lady Cowper and Lady Conyngham at dinner. His crony appointments would produce more loyalty than brains or balance for Peel's team in the House of Commons; but loyalty was what he felt the team needed.[10] It never struck him, as he went on taking his airings in Birdcage Walk, that he himself had become the bird in the cage. Through Huskisson's clumsiness and his own willingness to walk alone he was caught in a cageful of nothing but Tories.

By the end of May 1828 the Duke had some right to feel a 'miserable wretch'. It had been a month of incessant challenge, crucial developments overlapping one another or even occurring on the same day. While the Cabinet had chosen 8 May to begin their protracted arguments about the Corn Law, the Commons had selected it to give a vital vote on Catholic emancipation. For the first time since 1826 the 'Catholics' were successful, Sir Francis Burdett obtaining for his phoenix-like bill a majority of six.

An almost equally important decision on Ireland had been reached by the Cabinet six days before. On 2 May they decided not to renew the 1825 Act against the Catholic Association. This placatory gesture accorded with the advice of Lord Anglesey. If this 'irritating and provoking' act, wrote the Lord-Lieutenant, were quietly allowed to lapse, the extreme Catholic and Orange movements would probably lapse also. 'If, however, we have a mind to have a good *blaze* again' – the Duke should re-enact it.[11]

The last thing Wellington wanted was a good blaze, despite the impression he had given when William Lamb, then Irish Chief Secretary, first suggested dropping the repressive act. 'He looked staggered,' wrote Lamb, '& with that air, which he always has, of a man very little accustomed to be differed from or contradicted, & changed the subject.'[12] Yet he had long been considering how to satisfy the Irish Catholics without imperilling the Union, as reference to his past attitudes makes clear.

'I don't like the Catholick question,' he had written to his brother William, for instance, in 1812. Ireland had always been inclined to separate from Britain. 'It is a Natural Wish in every people to become Independent of their numerous & more powerful neighbours.'[13] While himself serving as Irish Chief Secretary he had been 'astonished' to find how far both Protestants as well as Catholics had become separatists. It was only the religious divisions which kept Ireland for the Empire, by turning the Protestants into a privileged garrison, afraid of the Catholics. 'Abolish the distinction, & make all Irishmen alike and they will all have Irish feelings; which tend towards Independence & Separation.' Catholic emancipation would inevitably lead to repeal of the Union unless there were political safeguards. But safeguards were available. 'Provided the crown appointed the Catholic Bishoprics as it does in Spain and Portugal,' Wellington thought it might even be best to go the whole length of disestablishing the Irish Protestant Church. In conclusion he denounced politicians for not having 'thought deeply enough upon this great question of Ireland and Britain'. It might be that his brother Richard was the person to settle it, 'upon the largest principles'.

Taking this and his plan of 1825 together, it is clear that the Duke had looked facts in the face. He was prepared for almost any innovation except an Irish breakaway.

Peel was a statesman who had also 'thought deeply' about Ireland. But his formative years as Chief Secretary (1812–18) left an indelible impression of permanent danger from that quarter. Emancipation to him ultimately spelled separation, with all its historic perils.

Why did the Duke cast yet another vote against Catholic emancipation in June 1828? This was in line with a frosty remark he had made on 24 April:

... there is no person in this House whose feelings are more decided than mine are with regard to the subject of the Roman Catholic claims; and until I see a great change in that quarter, I certainly shall oppose it.

So oppose it he did when Burdett's bill came up from the Commons; and his speech on 10 June made sure of its being defeated by a substantial majority. He had wound up with a fervent plea that these perpetual discussions and agitations should cease – 'then it might be more possible to discover the means of doing something'. However, it was clear that his whole tone had mellowed already.

Part of the credit was due to Peel, whose advice before the speech had been as sensible as his own position now become illogical. The Prime Minister, he had argued, was free to leave the door open for Catholic emancipation because of his own relatively moderate record in the past. But Peel himself felt that he had been too extreme an anti-Catholic to support the Duke except from the back benches, once the door was opened wide. Some 'great change' would be needed to prevent Peel's bizarre resignation. In fact the 'great change' was not a month away.

Daniel O'Connell announced on 24 June that he himself, a Roman Catholic, would stand against Vesey Fitzgerald at a by-election in Clare. The news was stunning. Up till this moment Wellington's candidate had seemed invincible. Indeed O'Connell had finally come to his dramatic decision precisely because the Catholic Association could not find a single candidate of the Protestant religion to oppose Fitzgerald on their behalf. The beauty of it was that while the law forbade a Catholic to *sit* in Parliament it did not forbid him to *stand*. But no one had made use of this legal magic until Daniel O'Connell presented himself at Ennis, the county town of Clare, on nomination day, 30 June 1828.

Polling began next day. It was exactly three weeks since Wellington's plea in the Lords for no more agitation. An age seemed to have passed since then, turning the whole Catholic world upside down. Every pulpit was a tribune, boasted the nationalist Sheil, as the peasant voters responded with grave and orderly enthusiasm to the heart-cry of their priests. For five days the disciplined processions set out at 8 am and marched to the polls carrying green leaves, green banners or shamrocks in golden wreaths, while onlookers cheered and further coach-loads of clerics came in from all over Ireland to harangue them at every corner.

It might well become open rebellion, warned Anglesey, and he could see no solution but to invite Messrs O'Connell, Sheil and all the rest of the nationalists into the House of Commons. 'It occurs to me,' he added with a temerity which shook Wellington, 'that if O'Connell can force himself upon the House and thus establish the Catholics, it would probably be a most fortunate event.'[14] Two days later, on 4 July, Wellington and Peel were actually facing this 'most fortunate event' in the form of a threat by O'Connell to thunder at the doors of Westminster. Next day at 11 am the great Dan was carried shoulder high to the Court House of Ennis and there declared elected by 2,057 votes to 982. Such a victory against the odds seemed fit to stand alongside one of the Duke's own coups.

The incredible session ended on 28 July 1828 with the Duke exhausted and Princess Lieven blaming it on himself: 'He will do everything himself: he is in everything, business, balls, and visits – in a word, he wishes to be the universal man.'[15] Mrs Arbuthnot looked forward to 'comparative repose' for her 'worn out' hero. But once more pacing with him up and down Birdcage Walk, she heard the whole story. He had been racking his brains for a fortnight over the Irish dilemma. Parliament insisted on conciliation first and coercion if necessary afterwards, believing in Catholic emancipation as a cure for agitation; he could not dissolve Parliament in order to get a more 'Protestant' one as long as the 40s-freeholders could outvote every 'Protestant' candidate in Ireland; yet this Parliament would not vote for the abolition of the 40s-freeholders until he had pledged himself to Catholic relief. Between them they had him in a vice, or at any rate running round in a vicious circle like a squirrel in a cage. The somewhat awestruck Harriet saw exactly what he meant when he said solemnly, 'This state of things cannot be allowed to continue.'[16]

If there was a point in time when the Duke opted for Catholic emancipation, this was it.

Not for a moment did either of them contemplate his resigning the cage to Lord Grey. That would have been putting His Majesty into the hands of the Opposition. Besides, a statesman does not resign twice.

Two days later, 31 July, the Duke of Wellington began a 'break for freedom'.[17] He put the last touches to a secret plan for Ireland, about which no one knew except the Chancellor, the Home Secretary and the Arbuthnots. Next day he was to present it like a pistol at His Majesty's head. Between that July and the following November the Duke was to fight behind the scenes round after stormy round on behalf of Catholic emancipation. The King was passionately anti; the bishops understandably anti; Ernest Duke of Cumberland, the King's influential brother, furiously anti; Lord Anglesey (the eloper, known as One-Leg after Waterloo) impossibly pro; Peel pro by conversion but pledged to resign as soon as his side won. As the year 1828 drew to an end, trouble was still piling up at Windsor, Phoenix Park (Anglesey was eventually recalled), Lambeth Palace and, worst of all, in the Home Office. Peel's pledge to resign still stood and the Duke could no longer buoyantly contemplate walking alone. His feelings about Peel now never fell below smouldering heat and were often inflamed. What disasters would not occur if Peel failed to urge the King to follow his Prime Minister's advice on Ireland? Towards the end of the month, however, his alarm was subsiding, after the most cordial conversation with Peel since the Government was formed. 'I cannot say that he will stay with us. But he has taken my paper away to read it; and I am not without hopes that he will stay.'[18] By 12 December there was another hopeful sign. Peel was showing interest in the date for the opening of Parliament (5 February 1829).

Yet January found Peel back on the resignation tack and Wellington exasperated by his changes of mind. 'It now appears that his real difficulty is that I am the [Prime] Minister,' he wrote bitterly to Harriet on the 7th. Peel had told him the difference between him, Wellington, and Canning was that emancipation had been forced upon Wellington by the circumstances of the times, whereas Canning had taken it up '*con amore*'. But it struck Wellington that if he had been forced, it was by Peel. 'He is *the* person who has forced me forward in the Question.'[19] Wellington himself on the other hand felt it morally impossible to force Peel.

Next day he interviewed Peel again. Still no decision. Would he resign or not? 'God knows what we shall do!' he groaned to Harriet on the 10th. 'Every body says *you must settle it*. If I answer will you support me? I receive a reply which renders all support useless.' Peel was with him again on the morning of the 12th. 'I am nicely worsted,' he confessed afterwards to Harriet, though the interview was to be resumed at 10 o'clock that night.[20]

Suddenly all was transformed. Rather than place Catholic emancipation and the whole Government in jeopardy by resigning, Peel had spontaneously conceded that it was his duty to stay. He brought round what the Duke called 'a vy. satisfactory paper' and the day's 'communications' were the best ever. The King also had apparently come round. When Peel and other members of the Cabinet visited him at Windsor on the 15th he was in 'remarkably good humour with his Ministers'[21] and showed his *finesse* by asking Peel how he could demand a sacrifice from the King and not make one himself. This clinched the matter for the sensitive Peel. It also meant that stage three had begun. The King had given his consent for the Cabinet to take up the Catholic question.

Next day Mrs Arbuthnot received a jubilant note: 'Peel will stay with us. . . .' The pact was ratified in writing on 17 February as if by high contracting parties. The Prime Minister formally stated to the Home Secretary, 'I do not see the smallest chance of getting out of these difficulties if you should not continue in office',[22] and Peel formally replied that he would continue. It was a double triumph, for Wellington's patience and Peel's public spirit.

On 25 February, the Duke drove confidently to Windsor to discuss Catholic relief with the King. Expecting to find him 'very tranquil', he was astounded to be received with a mixture of frivolity and hysteria. The King could not have behaved worse. Mesmerized by the brother he loved and dreaded, the wretched man was 'backing out of the Catholic question'.[23] Wellington drove home in a rage, leaving his Sovereign to the comfort of fantasies about abdication and the polishing of his latest epigram:

'Arthur is king of England, O'Connell is king of Ireland, and I suppose I am Dean of Windsor.' He had left out Cumberland, the lord of misrule.[24]

The decisive battle was now on, and Thursday 26 February was a day of resentment but resolve for both the Duke and Peel. They agreed that the Duke must return to Windsor next morning and bring matters to a head. Either the King must back them or the Cabinet resign. It appeared next day that the King was not only apostasizing but trying to corrupt as many other Tory voters as possible. The Duke found a Cumberland plot in existence to make the Royal Household vote against the Relief Bill. The five hours which he spent with the King were profoundly painful to both. Wellington could not help pitying the poor old man, whose tears flowed fast for his Protestant conscience. (Cumberland had persuaded him he was betraying it.) But as the committed leader, Wellington explained again that he could not retreat. The King capitulated. Dissolving at last in a flood of assurances and more tears, he gave his trusted Arthur authority to make the Household vote straight, and try to make Cumberland go back to Germany. The traditional royal kiss at parting was bestowed with an arm around Arthur's neck.

But on Wednesday 4 March the dauntless three – Wellington, Peel and Lyndhurst the Lord Chancellor – were summoned to Windsor. There they found the King drained of his usual spirits but filling up with brandy and water preparatory to refusing his consent to the bill. All three resigned on the spot. How would the King form a new Government?

With the help of Lady Conyngham and Knighton the King quickly realized the enormity of what he had done. Hardly had the Duke reached Lord Bathurst's house with the crazy news, before a royal letter of retraction was chasing after him along the Windsor road. 'My dear friend,' it began:

As I have found the country would be left without an Administration, I have decided to yield my opinions to *that* which is considered by the Cabinet to be for the immediate interests of the country. Let them proceed as proposed with their measure. God knows what pain it costs me to write these words. G.R.[25]

At 11 am on Thursday 5 March the Duke called on the Arbuthnots to tell them 'it was *all set to rights again*'. Harriet was relieved; nevertheless the Duke's situation still seemed to her unenviable. It could not be pleasant to hear that the Sovereign accepted the advice of his Government only because 'he can't get another'.[26]

That the Duke suffered inordinately from this latest unpleasantness may be doubted. He was a realist. Only two years had passed since the King preferred Canning to him. And after all, as Peel truly but tactlessly pointed out, the Duke himself had not taken up Catholic emancipation '*con amore*'. In certain moods he accepted the policy of Catholic emancipation for much the same reason as the King accepted his Government – because he couldn't get another.

The great debate on 5 March in the Commons was preceded by a burst of excited speculation about the Government's fate. Had the King bundled them out? 'I rise as *a minister of the King*,' began Peel, deliberately killing the speculation at a blow; and in the four hours of brilliant argument that followed, Peel converted the excitement into the wildest enthusiasm. The anger and despair of Protestant fanatics like Sir Charles Wetherell, the Attorney-General, were correspondingly fanned. As the debates on emancipation proceeded Wetherell was to work himself into such passions of oratory that he would unbutton his braces and allow his waistcoat to ride up and his breeches to fall down, his 'only lucid interval', according to the Speaker, being between those two garments.

Fortunately the Duke was able to take five days' respite from the

Lords, for on the 7th he was prostrated by such an appalling cold that he had to be bled and temporarily excused himself from argument as 'a sick man'. Something tremendous in the way of tension and reaction was needed to make Wellington plead illness.

Back in his place on 10, 13 and 16 March he answered the accusations of Winchilsea, Eldon and the rest that he was establishing Popery, subverting the Constitution and forcing the King to violate his Oath. As usual Winchilsea roared as if he were addressing a mob in the open on a windy day.[27] It was on the 16th, a Monday, that there was a more remarkable development. A letter appeared in the *Standard* from Lord Winchilsea announcing that he had cancelled his subscription of £50 to King's College, London, because the Duke of Wellington was associated with its foundation.*

The audience had been profoundly stirred when the Duke, as Prime Minister, took the chair at the opening of King's College on 21 June 1828. Flanked by three archbishops and seven bishops, he had reaffirmed the place in education of religious teaching. University College in 'Godless Gower Street' had decided, after much controversy, to get on without it. So King's College was the Establishment's ringing answer to the unbelievers.

Lord Winchilsea, like the Duke, had seen salvation in a new London college based on the King's faith. But what if emancipation brought Roman Catholics not only into the King's hitherto faithful Parliament but into his college also? The possibility of this double infiltration suddenly struck the not very bright Winchilsea and he saw it all as a plot laid by the Duke. King's College was a *blind*, a *cloak* under which Wellington had betrayed Westminster.

Blind, cloak . . . Such words in the *Standard* seemed to the Duke to put the struggle on an entirely new footing. They attributed to him 'disgraceful and criminal' motives.

He wrote to Winchilsea on the 16th and again on the 19th giving him a chance to retract and apologize. But Winchilsea refused to apologize unless the Duke stated publicly that he had not contemplated Catholic emancipation when he inaugurated King's College.

'I cannot admit that any man has a right to call me before him,' replied the incensed Duke on the morning of Friday, 20 March, 'to

---

* Wellington was the proprietor of ten shares of £100 each and donor of £300. King's College was left with heavy debts from the effects of Winchilsea's cancellation and those Ultras who followed his example.

justify myself from the charges which his fancy may suggest.' At 6.30 pm the Duke issued a formal challenge:

I now call upon your Lordship to give me that satisfaction for your conduct which a gentleman has a right to require, and which a gentleman never refuses to give.

The seconds, Sir Henry Hardinge and Lord Falmouth, had already arranged for a duel to take place at 8 am next morning.[28]

The Duke's doctor, John Hume, was surprised to receive a request from Hardinge on the Friday night to attend a duel between unnamed 'persons of rank and consequence' and to meet Hardinge at his house at 6.45 am on Saturday for instructions, bringing with him a case of pistols. Their carriage stopped at a crossroads half a mile beyond the river. Next moment he was astonished and shocked to see Hardinge riding up with the Duke of Wellington.

The party proceeded into Battersea Fields. Hume carried the pistols under his greatcoat and hid them beneath a hedge. They waited about.

At last Winchilsea and his second arrived. The party moved forward into the field, but catching sight of some farm-workers, made for safer ground. Hume then loaded his two pistols for the one-armed Hardinge and almost had to load Falmouth's also, since Winchilsea's second was shaking so much with cold and the effect of Hardinge's reproaches.

'Now then, Hardinge,' called the Duke, 'look sharp and step out the ground. I have no time to waste.' Hardinge hastily marked out the Duke's position with his heel and then stepped out twelve paces towards a ditch where Winchilsea was standing. Again the Duke called to him.

'Damn it! don't stick him up so near the ditch. If I hit him he will tumble in.' Finally the two pistols were in the principals' hands and cocked.

'Then gentlemen, I shall ask you if you are ready,' said Hardinge, 'and give the word fire without any further signal or preparation.' There was an instant's pause. 'Gentlemen, are you ready? *Fire!*' Winchilsea kept his right arm glued to his side. The Duke noticed, and instead of hitting Winchilsea's leg fired wide. Having stood the Duke's fire, Winchilsea now felt that honour permitted him to apologize for the *Standard* letter. Falmouth produced a draft apology which he read aloud to the Duke.

'This won't do,' said the Duke in a low voice to Hardinge; 'it is no apology.' For though the word 'regret' appeared the word 'apology' did not. Hume promptly pencilled the words 'in apology' and initialled them, 'J.R.H.'. This the Duke accepted. He bowed coldly to the two peers and touched the brim of his hat with two fingers. 'Good morning, my Lord Winchilsea; good morning, my Lord Falmouth' – and cantered off the field. It had been a good morning, he felt, for a Prime Minister.

He had been living, he said, for quite some time in such an atmosphere of calumny that he had seized upon Winchilsea's 'furious letter' as a heaven-sent opportunity to dispel the miasma. The magic worked. In consequence of the duel moderate 'Protestants' had come forward to remonstrate with the extremists. Men were ashamed at having believed lies. 'The system of calumny is discontinued.'

Put briefly, the gesture of the duel was delivered to extremists in language they understood. This showed Wellington's instinctive knowledge of his wild men. It also showed once again the dramatic sense which lurked in the Iron Duke. With a sweep of his cocked hat he had cried 'Farewell Portugal!' in 1813; he waved it again in 1815 to start the Waterloo charge. This man in 1829 found it not unnatural to scatter the past and salute the future by cocking a pistol.

On the 31st the Duke moved the bill's first reading in the House of Lords, allowing an interval of only one day before he opened the debate on the second reading on 2 April. Speaking slowly, with folded arms and no notes, he was forceful but not vehement, and entirely free from his usual hesitations. His speech contained the most moving and effective passage he ever delivered. He had described Ireland as on the brink of civil war and was appealing to noble lords who argued that he could have put down O'Connell's Catholic Association by means other than concession. By force.

But, my Lords, even if I had been certain of such means of putting it down, I should have considered it my duty to avoid those means. I am one of those who have probably passed a longer period of my life engaged in war than most men, and principally in civil war; and I must say this, that if I could avoid by any sacrifice whatever, even one month of civil war in the country to which I was attached, I would sacrifice my life in order to do it.

The 'Great Captain's' simple, sincere and direct plea for peace went straight to the nation's heart. He wound up on 4 April with a good-tempered reminder to noble lords that even as a soldier his services had not always been approved; that nevertheless

I rendered them through good repute and through bad repute, and that I was never prevented from rendering them by any cry which was excited against me at the moment.

Nor would he be prevented now.

Catholic relief obtained a majority of 105, 217 voting for it and 112 against. Wellington had predicted a 'very substantial' majority, meaning about 50; the Ultras told the King it would be only 5. The size of the majority stunned everyone. 'Really it seems like a dream!' wrote the generally unimpressionable Ellenborough. Agitation would end in England and tranquillity dawn in Ireland. But Ellenborough's first thought was, 'This will quiet Windsor.' Far from it. The result of the second reading on Windsor was an outburst of royal passion which tried even the Duke's monumental patience. Aberdeen reported on the 6th that the King in his paroxysms talked of a disgraced Parliament and a revolutionary people – Wellington's name he did not deign to mention. Wellington's corresponding anger with the King took Mrs Arbuthnot's breath away.

He abused him most furiously, said he was the worst man he ever fell in with in his whole life. . . .[29]

Next day, 10 April, the Prime Minister moved the third reading of the Relief Bill. He expressed gratitude to the Tories who had stuck to him and warmly thanked the Whigs: 'I had no right to expect the cordial and handsome support they have given me.' Then he congratulated everybody on having brought the measure to its final stage and confidently awaited the vote. The House divided: Contents, 213; Not Contents, 109. Majority, 104. Running into Lord Dungannon, a prominent Whig, outside the Chamber, the Duke said gaily, 'Well, I said I would do it, and I have done it handsomely, have I not?' The gaiety was short-lived.

The Royal Assent was extracted rather than given on 13 April and among the 109 Not Contents were men who had been the Duke's close friends. When he went down to the House on the 13th his cold had returned in force. He left the Chamber with his cloak drawn tightly round him. 'His anxious wish, I may say determination,' Mrs Arbuthnot had written with her usual percipience towards the end of March, 'is to draw the Tories round him again. . . .'[30]

One penalty of being a reformer was having to go out into the cold. The full impact of Wellington's party problem, however, was yet to be felt. But for a long golden moment national thankfulness flooded all party bounds, giving Wellington a lustre which some thought outshone Waterloo. The endearing Duke of Sussex who, with the late Duke of Kent, represented the royal left wing, said his laurels had changed into olive, a change into greater glory. There was a deep conviction that where so many statesmen had tried and failed none but the great Duke could have steered the country into its religious haven. 'He is the only Man living,' wrote Colin Campbell to Kitty, 'who could have carried the measure, & he has saved his Country from a Civil War by his firmness & manliness.'[31] Wellington's vast prestige, combined with his vigour and courtesy in the lengthy debates, undoubtedly won over many waverers. Princess Lieven put his personal vote in the great Lords debate at 150. He also commanded an army of hero-worshippers outside Parliament, among whom was numbered the thirteen-year-old Charlotte Brontë. Never could she forget Papa opening his newspaper and reading aloud the drama of the debate:

. . . the anxiety was almost dreadful with which we listened to the whole affair; the opening of the doors; the hush; the royal dukes in their robes and the great Duke in green sash and waistcoat; the rising of all the peeresses when he rose; the reading of his speech – papa saying his words were like precious gold; and lastly the majority – in favour of the Bill.

A few months later, on 28 July, Charlotte began writing a magical tale called 'The Search After Hapiness [sic]', in which it transpired that happiness depended on living under the benign rule of a great 'military King' – the Duke of Wellington.

Or as Lord Clarendon explained cynically to Macaulay, the Whig MP and famous historian, the Duke only had to say, 'My Lords! Attention! Right about face! Quick march!' and the troops would obey.

A change was detectable in the Duke's own feelings also. Quoting his great speech, Ireland was the country to which he was 'attached' in more than one sense. Why should he not revert to Anglo-Irish custom and spend part of the year (and of his money) there? His brother Richard was trying to sell the last of the family estates. After his great victory the Duke began negotiating with Richard's agent to buy them. Perhaps he too might share some of 'the peace, the happiness and the prosperity' which, in his speech, he hoped he had brought to the country of his birth.

The Duke expected to reap the benefits of his triumph in a firmer political position. For a time he did so, though the immense international prestige which Princess Lieven had predicted for whoever carried Catholic emancipation was not always visible. When young Dr Wiseman, the future Cardinal, illuminated the front of the English College at Rome with the mystic words '*Emancipazione Cattolica*', the Italians stared up in deep perplexity.

At home, however, the Duke's Government was seen to be a reforming one, and enthusiasts like Jeremy Bentham and Robert Owen (who offered him a socialist plan to recast the whole of his domestic and foreign policy)[32] rightly assumed that he had not exhausted his appetite for change. 'Head it, Duke!' cried Bentham, sending him the prospectus of a new Law Reform Association drawn up by himself in magnificent Gothic lettering and even more Gothic language. Though Jeremy got no more out of his hero than the usual 'Compts.' and thanks, his high hopes were not unreasonable. For Catholic emancipation had been quickly followed by another historic reform.

The creation of the Metropolitan Police force was in every sense the child of Peel's foresight and labour. As Home Secretary he had worked for years at penal reform as well as at the police. Nevertheless Wellington's call for an absolutely new kind of police in 1821 must not be forgotten, nor the active support he gave to Peel in 1829. He introduced the Metropolitan Police Bill himself in the Lords in June, after Peel had done the same in the Commons on 15 April, just two days after Catholic emancipation became law.

'In one parish, St Pancras,' said the Duke, 'there are now no fewer than eighteen different establishments . . . not one of which has any communication with another. The consequence is that the watchmen of one district are content with driving thieves from their own particular neighbourhood into the adjoining district.' This ludicrous beating of game which was never brought down represented only one aspect of an utterly inefficient and often corrupt system, if system it could be called. Leaving out the City which managed its own affairs, less than 350 men protected the million and more inhabitants of London. Some of these were parish constables, some special constables, some watchmen. Their duties were defined by a series of statutes, but lack of personnel as well as total deficiency in organization prevented them from being carried out. Crime was annually increasing.

For the first time in the history of Parliament a Select Committee had reported (July 1828) in favour of a single streamlined police force for the metropolis, under the Home Office. Peel's bill, based on this report, was passed on 19 June 1829. Within eight weeks the two Police

Commissioners had recruited their new force, with headquarters at Scotland Yard.

The Duke well understood, though he did not share, the ingrained British fear, not only among the criminal classes, of a centralized police force. It smacked of arbitrary power. In a year's time the London mob were calling them 'raw lobsters' in contrast to their hard-boiled scarlet colleagues, for they hated the blue-uniformed police even more than the red-coats. But the public christened them 'bobbies', a sure sign of incipient warmer feelings. As for the Duke, by November 1829 he was already congratulating Robert Peel on the entire success of the new force. 'It is impossible to see any thing more respectable.'[33]

The same could not be said of the militant Irish. A habit of violence was not easy to break. Moreover the Government were to blame for alienating O'Connell. Instead of admitting him to Parliament forthwith, they compelled him to stand again under the new Catholic laws. He denounced the mean spirit of the Ascendancy and Union, and swept in unopposed. As Creevey said, the Beau was immortalized by his measure apart from this 'one damned thing'. In July and August proclamations were issued against Orangemen (Protestants) and Ribbonmen (Catholics) respectively.

Nevertheless Wellington's reward from Catholic emancipation was substantial. Ireland as a whole was quieter at the end of 1829 than it had been for two years, and the Duke was studying a hopeful thirty-page memorandum from his friend Maurice Fitzgerald, the Knight of Kerry, on how to cure Irish unemployment through more public works and less absenteeism. Everyone who could afford it left Ireland for part of each year, wrote Fitzgerald; perhaps it was his eloquence that gave Wellington the idea of travelling in the opposite direction, to acquire his brother's estates.

He felt calm and confident enough about Ireland that autumn to answer some unusually bizarre advice from wellwishers with perfect good temper – a suggestion for silencing all Irish political meetings by pensioning off five leading Orangemen and five leading Catholic orators at £2,000 per annum each; and a request from Valentine Blake of Galway to be created a peer, descended as he was from a Knight of King Arthur's Round Table and willing as he would be to serve the modern 'King Arthur' in a similar capacity.

Notwithstanding Wellington's successes the session had ended on 24 June with lugubrious feelings among his friends. Without his legendary good luck, part of which consisted in the Opposition's chronic internal disputes, they did not believe that the Government could survive. Sir Henry Hardinge reckoned that in losing the Canningites and Brunswickers (Ultras) the Duke had forfeited at least fifty parliamentary votes. There were continual discussions about how to gain an access of strength. It was hoped that Lord Rosslyn, a Whig, would bring over some fellow Whigs when he consented to enter the Cabinet. Nobody followed him. Nor could the Duke 'coquette' – to quote Hardinge – with the Whig leader himself, Lord Grey, because of the King's personal animosity. Wellington indeed laid the ultimate blame for his Government's weakness on the two royal brothers, King George and Duke Ernest. 'Dearest Ernest' was generally understood to have sworn not to leave his brother's side until he had turned out the present Minister. 'He *keeps the pot boiling*,' said the Duke ominously to Harriet; but she stoutly refused to believe that Cumberland would ever get the King actually to dismiss Wellington. 'I don't believe the King *dares*.'[34]

By September the Duke had recovered sufficiently from a dose of ill-health to enjoy the continuing battle with the King. 'He is now quite fat enough,' reported Harriet on the 12th; 'looks strong & muscular & his face, instead of being pale and wrinkled, looks quite full & florid' – like her portrait of him by Lawrence, though Peel, who had stayed with him at Stratfield Saye on the 3rd, thought his walk had lost its elasticity: 'He seems feeble and drags one leg after the other as if he was weak.'[35] On the 15th Mrs Arbuthnot found him roaring with laughter over a caricature of himself in *The Times*. The artist had portrayed him reading a passage from that newspaper to the King which ran: 'We have to announce on undoubted authority that a serious difference has arisen between a great personage & his prime minister.'

More than one jealous grievance against Wellington indeed afflicted the King. His wish to visit Paris was vetoed owing to the political situation ('Poor king!' said Cumberland, 'I knew it! He can never do what he likes.') Yet a week or two later Wellington had a spree in the north, receiving the freedom of Doncaster, going to the races and attending a most successful ball. 'Lady Londonderry fainted under the weight of her finery,' he told Harriet, 'before I arrived.'[36]

The Duke's September tour had not been without its political interest. 'Distress' was a sad and sinister word which had begun to feature more and more often in discussions on the state of the country. Not that the 1828 harvest had been immoderately bad. But the spring of 1829 heralded nothing remotely cheerful. Lord Sefton, a fervent Whig, wrote to Creevey in April: 'The Beau's troubles are not over yet.

The distress in the country is Frightful. Millions are starving, and I defy him to do anything to relieve them.'[37]

Over sixteen million people now inhabited Britain and an appallingly large number of them could reasonably be described as starving. The postwar depression in industry that followed Waterloo had prompted the bolder spirits to organize, and to air their grievances at Spa Fields or Peterloo. But agitation simply resulted in political repression by 'gag acts'. A decade passed and acute distress was by no means confined to the great industrial towns, where beneath the bustling surface groaned an underworld of sweated labour, unemployment, squalor and disease. The countryside, also in a wretched state since the fall of agricultural prices after Waterloo, was working up for a doomsday explosion. Over the years tens of thousands of peasant proprietors had left their homes to swell the city ant-heaps, drawn by higher wages or driven by the 'enclosures' policy, often applied to common land. (The Duke had refused to enclose a common near Stratfield Saye when his agent recommended it.) Weekly wages in the country for those who had stayed behind could sink in places as low as three or four shillings. But the nadir in 1829 was reached in industrial Yorkshire. A wage reduction provoked strikes and rioting in Barnsley while in Huddersfield, though there was no violence, an investigating committee of employers informed the Government that thirteen thousand workers in fancy goods were earning 2½d a week.

He could see no remedy in any of the nostrums suggested by Opposition and friends alike – Huskisson wanting free trade; others, including some Tories, arguing for reform of the banks, parliamentary reform, a coalition, economies. The Duke was deeply sceptical; at the same time he resented criticism of his own inactivity. Intensely irritated by the moans of great landowners at the state of agriculture, he wrote, 'I hear of nothing but complaints from all quarters. But somehow or other we do not see any Man refuse himself any gratification or Luxury.' He would not believe that the Dukes of Norfolk, Rutland or Beaufort had reason to grumble until they ceased giving huge parties in their castles or at the races.[38]

A major reform in the army was obstinately rejected by Wellington himself. Corporal punishment had come up regularly since Waterloo. Even his friend Sir Henry Hardinge wanted a switch to the reformed Prussian system in 1829, but Hardinge failed to shake him. As long as Britain had an empire Wellington believed that her battles would be fought abroad in horrible colonial climates; so long, her soldiers could not be conscripted as in Prussia; only 'the scum of the earth' would volunteer for such unpleasant service; 'the scum' must be controlled ultimately by corporal punishment. This view of human nature had a superficial realism that influenced Wellington for many a long year to come.

Was he correct even on the main question of consolidation versus advance, 'quiet' versus 'novelty'? The answer must be no. He had mistaken the spirit of the times. Discontent in autumn 1829 was not, as he supposed, the subsiding groundswell of Catholic emancipation but the sign of oncoming storms.

He saw out his great year of 1829 in an ambivalent mood. 'I should say that matters were looking upwards,' he wrote to the Duke of Rutland on 3 December. Revenue was keeping up, arrears of taxes falling. Whether or not the reports of distress were exaggerated, the country was improving everywhere. In agriculture, manufacture and commerce, in building of houses, roads and bridges, progress in the last few years had been 'astounding'.[39]

Sometimes he would feel over-confident. 'If Lord Grey opposes us he will destroy himself in the opinion of all the Quiet People in the Country.' At other times it was he himself who was going under. 'If I do not get some relief I shall be destroyed. . . .' But he dared not delegate: 'I feel myself to be situated as I was in the Command of the Army; without resource excepting in my own Mind and knowing that where I was not myself to give directions matters would go wrong.'[40]

It was Charles Arbuthnot, whose home was temporarily out of bounds to the Duke because of press innuendo, to whom the Duke poured out on 13 December the most eloquent of his tales of woe:

I certainly admit that I am anxious to quit office. Till I became First Lord of the Treasury I never had a dispute or a difference with any body; excepting the Scum of the Earth, who defrauded the Publick or who would not do their Duty. In my Office I am necessarily put in Collision with every body. The King the Royal family every Nobleman & Gentleman in England, every foreign sovereign, every Ambassador or Foreign Minister.

Apart from Clarence, not one of the royal family spoke to him.

Then I am obliged to keep every thing and every body in order and in His Place; and I have a quarrel open with Mr Huskisson and Lord Anglesey; and another ready for Lord Combermere; and all for what?

How could the Duke paper over all these cracks? In the old days a prime minister would have used patronage. But it had been the Duke's own policy to abolish every sinecure as it fell in.

I have nothing to give to any body excepting Smiles and a Dinner; and I cannot excuse myself, or write and answer in a hurry or make any mistake without giving offence!! I should be more than Man if I did not feel the Misery of my Position.[41]

And Wellington, in his own words, was 'but a man'.

Even his faith in the great Hoby, maker of his Wellington boots, withered during this December month of trials. 'I shall be very much obliged to you,' he told Charles Arbuthnot, 'if you will write me the direction of the Man who makes your Waterloo boots.' Mr Hoby had made him a pair which left him lame.

Then why did he not resign in favour of Peel? A letter to Peel was duly drafted but never sent. How could the Duke in truth hand over to this strange, austere man, so full of absurd new schemes of reform? Yet if he had served under Peel in 1820 instead of waiting four years, he would have saved himself from an impending disaster.

Meanwhile, with the death of George IV on 26 June 1830, the Duke became the late King's executor and guardian of many royal scandal-sheets. Through him, for instance, the fact that Cumberland 'more than once attempted to violate' the person of his sister Princess Sophia was kept dark for over 140 years. In 1835 another box of letters, this time between the Prince and Princess of Wales (George and Caroline) was brought to the Duke and burnt. They 'would have been most agreeable food for the Radical Revolutionaries of the present time'.[42]

The Duke was now to face the 'Radical revolutionaries' of 1830 unencumbered at least by royal scandals.

28
Reform

King William IV, formerly Duke of Clarence, wanted to make Wellington happy, as indeed he wanted to make all his subjects happy: 'he is an immense improvement on the last unforgiving animal,' wrote Emily Eden in her famous welcome to the new reign. 'This man at least *wishes* to make everybody happy. . . .'[1]

The general election of 1830, necessitated as usual by a new reign, began after the prorogation of Parliament on 23 July and proved to be the Opposition's chance for demonstrating that they, at least, had not been made happy. Some of them had expected Grey to enter Wellington's Cabinet once the late King's objections had died with him. Others had hoped a new reign would mean a new ministry. George Seymour was convinced that during the first debate in the Lords after the announcement of George IV's serious illness Grey, from having been a consistently moderate opponent, had suddenly changed. The Duke did not miss the signs, for he wrote to Peel that he expected more 'active opposition' from Grey in the future.[2] Nor did it escape Seymour's notice that Grey's change of tactics coincided with a petition to the Lords on reform. Not merely reform of the laws governing agriculture, commerce, finance or poverty but the reform of Parliament itself.

This was Reform with a capital R. Away with rotten boroughs! Votes for the great cities! An end to the land-owning magnates' monopoly of the franchise! Parliamentary reform was ready to take over from all other battle-cries. Grey had advocated it as long ago as 1793; several Reform Bills had been introduced quite recently and killed, including John Russell's in February 1830; outside the House Thomas Attwood and Francis Place were able radical politicians. Reform became the Opposition's inspiration. But if the whole country was to take fire, reform must somehow be blown up to truly gigantic dimensions – the healer of every social sickness and panacea of all ills, for which the people hungered. Electioneering was not yet over, with the borough votes cast but 40 county seats to come, when in Paris occurred the blow-up (a favourite word of Wellington's) which was afterwards labelled the French Revolution of the 'Three Glorious Days', or 'July Days'. It succeeded in firing hundreds of thousands of Britons and in revolutionizing much of Europe.

Within three days, 26–28 July, the commercial classes of France succeeded in abolishing a reactionary King (Charles x) and government and installing Louis Philippe as King of the French – and in particular of the French bourgeoisie.

The hopes roused by the Three Glorious Days lived on in Britain. 'What a glorious event this is in France!' wrote Palmerston.[3] As Henry Brougham rampaged around Yorkshire and Henry Hunt around Lancashire on their election campaigns, the message got home. If the French could achieve the Parliament they wanted, so could the English. For France, the 'Limited Liability Revolution'; for England, reform.

Though the Duke utterly failed to appreciate the dynamism of reform, the overall election results were not stark enough to destroy his optimism. He still had a majority. But he had to gloss over the fact that the country squires, who had come to represent an important part of public opinion, were ratting. Peel, Ellenborough and Lyndhurst were despondent, the last telling Princess Lieven that all but the Duke now recognized the crying need for Cabinet reinforcements.

At the Kentish village of Lower Hardres, not many miles away from Walmer Castle where the Duke as Lord Warden of the Cinque Ports was restoring his vital energies, a group of labourers destroyed a theshing-machine on 28 August. This was an early case of machine-breaking in what soon became a major tragedy for the poor. Desperate agricultural workers felt they could not face another winter like the last, with machines taking away their employment on the threshing-floor just when they needed it most.

A day or two before the outbreak of Kentish machine-breaking, the rocket of revolution had exploded for the second time, exactly a month after take-off. The Belgians suddenly decided to be a Dutch province no longer. They would achieve independence, either absolute or leaning towards France.

This was a colossal challenge. Was France to begin once more at Antwerp? Yet the last thing Wellington wanted was to fight France again. Fortunately for his pacific designs the new French ambassador appointed to London by Louis Philippe was Talleyrand. He might be received in England with shrieks of horror from right, left and centre: 'varlet' to Eldon, 'monster' to Cumberland, 'really hardly human' to Harriet Arbuthnot; reptile, death's-head, prince of darkness. To the Duke he was a diplomat of perfect probity and matchless skill when it came to warding off an international situation which they would both regard as calamitous. It was due mainly to Wellington and Talleyrand together that an armistice was arranged between Belgium and Holland, with a five-power conference to follow. Europe owed Wellington a debt of gratitude. He had resisted the warmongers and showed once again that he preferred the olive to the laurel.

Early in August the Duke had asked permission of William IV for leave of absence from 6 to 20 September. He wished to visit Lancashire for the opening of the Liverpool–Manchester railway. Dutifully he hoped it would not 'derange HM's projects'.[4]

The Duke's own projects in the north went far beyond railways. The new parliamentary session was to open on 2 November. He would feel the pulse of northern industry, perhaps strengthen it, and possibly strengthen also his Government in ways that 'Black Billy' Holmes, the party agent, was already exploring.

So on the 15th the large ducal party clambered gaily into the first coach, a sprightly gilt affair standing at Liverpool station, and settled down under its scarlet velvet awning, edged with tassels and draped pelmets of gilded wood, for the joy-ride to Manchester. The awning would save its passengers from being burned by flying sparks, as had happened the year before when Creevey first rode in a train and a pelisse, gown and cheek had been holed. Entering into the spirit which had prompted Creevey to call his journey 'a *lark* of a very high order', the Duke was suitably impressed with the cheering crowds along the embankments, as well as with the iron horse's breakneck speed. It averaged sixteen and sometimes travelled at thirty miles an hour, so that he could not read the figures on the mileposts along the track. As for the crossing of two trains going in opposite directions, a diversion which was frequently staged for the Duke's amusement – 'It was the whizzing,' he gasped, 'of a cannonball.'[5]

After an hour's activity the iron horse reached Parkside at 11.30 am and stopped to be watered. The passengers must not descend on to the track, warned the directors of the company. 'Black Billy' Holmes, however, had been assigned the congenial task of presenting a distinguished fellow-traveller to the Duke at this moment of general euphoria: none other than Huskisson who, as MP for Liverpool, was riding in the directors' carriage. It was intended to be the beginning of a grand political *entente cordiale*. The Duke and Huskisson had met less than a year ago at Lord Hertford's, so there was no personal difficulty.

Eyewitnesses said that Huskisson had already grasped the Duke's hand when a loud shout went up. 'Stop the engine! Clear the track!' The *Rocket*, Stephenson's prize-winning engine, was dashing towards them, eager to show its paces. Caught between the lines, about a dozen strolling passengers made for safety. But Huskisson, heavily built and enfeebled since the Duke of York's funeral, could not make up his mind whether to run for his own carriage or scramble for the Duke's. As once before a muddled decision had cut short his ministerial career, so now it terminated his life. The *Rocket* struck him as he stumbled, flung him down, ran over his leg at the thigh and in Croker's words 'crushed the limb to a jelly'. Lady Wilton distinctly heard the crunching of the bones. Croker, an enthusiast for the new railways, explained to his patron Lord Hertford that such an accident could have happened as easily in the Strand if a man slipped from the kerb while the stagecoach was passing. The Duke did not take this philosophical view.

Perhaps it was the tragic utterance of Huskisson – 'It's all over with me; bring me my wife and let me die' – or the piercing shrieks of poor Mrs Huskisson; or the roaring of a loudhailer to stop their train; or the cries from carriage to carriage to know what had happened; or the screams for surgical aid; or the tourniquet applied unavailingly by Lord Wilton; or the news of Huskisson's agonized death at 9 pm – perhaps it was a combination of all these horrors which prejudiced the Duke for ever against railways. He was later to find added reasons for disliking them, but his friend Gleig always believed that Huskisson's death had really done it.

The sudden removal of this formidable political character would plainly weaken the Duke's Government. It left the Canningites without a shepherd who could be relied upon to lead them, if anywhere, back into the Tory fold, and necessitated attempts to whistle up Palmerston for high Cabinet office.

That the Duke was sceptical about such political manoeuvres can be taken for granted. It is more surprising to find him equally sceptical about the increasingly dangerous state of the disturbed southern counties. No one ever doubted the possibility of trouble in the north, and with a wave of industrial strikes the Duke was sending more troops to the garrison towns; indeed Lord Francis Leveson-Gower was glad to get him out of Lancashire – 'The spirit of the district was detestable.' In Manchester there was even a threat to assassinate the Duke, and though he commented on it in somewhat oracular style – 'I never neglect and never believe these things' – he did not fail to take the north seriously. It was different in the south.

'The Gentlemen in Kent, so bold in Parliament, are terrified out of their wits with the burning of a few cornstacks and the breaking of a few threshing machines,' he wrote contemptuously to Mrs Arbuthnot on 15 October. But the truth was that hardly had the Duke returned home before the outbreaks in the countryside entered a new, more violent phase. In October incendiary fires, rick-burning and machine-breaking all occurred together. At Ash in Kent, a village considerably nearer to Walmer than Lower Hardres, a local magistrate and overseer had his property completely destroyed for 'unfeeling conduct' towards the poor. (The Oxenden family of Canterbury, however, were known for their compassion and as a reward had only one shaft of their threshing-machine sawn off.)

The rioting spread. The Duke of Wellington was disgusted when Lord Camden, another Kent landowner, sent him a terrified letter implying that everything was lost unless he satisfied the people by strengthening his Government with reformers. Not for the last time the Duke privately commented, 'I am more afraid of terror than I am of anything else.'[6]

A no less terrified and far longer letter than Camden's arrived from a Mr James Hamilton in Dublin, describing the whole of Connaught and Munster as depots of anarchy and rebellion, while O'Connell's party were all incendiaries. Would the Duke please return forthwith to his command of the army and bring it with him to Ireland? 'Alas! My Lord, that the Necessity ever existed for your descending . . . to mix yourself with English Politicks.' The Duke replied curtly that his correspondent should descend from opinions to facts:

The Duke begs leave to observe to Mr Hamilton that he misapplies his own time as well as the Duke's by writing invectives against any Men or Parties. That which is desirable is to state facts shortly and clearly and how and where the Evidence can be procured. The Duke can assure him that it is not worth while to state his opinions.[7]

Under which heading did the need to woo Palmerston and other reformers come? Was it a fact – or merely the opinion of a lot of frightened ministers?

Wellington had already expressed his private views on reform in no uncertain terms. A distinguished acquaintance, Sir James Shaw, had asked him on 17 October if he could not introduce moderate reform as 'an act of grace & justice'. The Duke replied flatly:

Not only do I think Parliamentary Reform unnecessary but that it would be so injurious as that Society, as now established in the Empire could not exist under the system which must be its Consequence.

Then came the punch-line, even more significant on 2 November than when he wrote it on 17 October:

I shall therefore at all times and under all circumstances oppose it.[8]

The night of Tuesday 2 November in the House of Lords. Debate on the Address. Earl Grey had wound up for the Opposition and the Duke of Wellington rose to wind up for the Government. He wore his familiar white stock with the plain silver buckle behind and quiet, well-cut dark clothes. For once nobody said he looked worn or ill.

There seemed little to expect in the way of sudden drama, judging by what had gone before: a King's Speech preaching firmness at home and abroad, coupled with conciliation; the usual attempt by the irreconcilable Winchilsea to make capital out of the distress; Grey paying a handsome tribute to the Duke's extraordinary ascendancy and introducing reform only towards the end of his speech as a remedy for distress.

Even then Grey admitted that he personally was not tied to any particular measures of reform – a hit at the radical Brougham who, in another place, was clamouring for universal suffrage, the secret ballot and annual parliaments. So far so good. There was an atmosphere of which no prime minister could complain.

Wellington began as graciously as Grey. He congratulated the noble Earl on many of his sentiments and sincerely regretted that he could not assent to them all. However, some considerable time spent in differing from Grey on Portugal, Holland and Ireland seemed at last to give an edge to the Prime Minister's oration. When he reached the outrages in Kent and Sussex he roundly denied that they were caused by distress, since greater distress in the past had produced no outrages. Were they then due to evils resulting from the recent disturbances in France? And if they were, was this country to be protected from similar revolution only by reform? The noble Earl Lord Grey had been candid enough to admit that he was 'not prepared with any measure of reform'. His Majesty's Government, declared the Duke, speaking more vibrantly than hitherto, 'is as totally unprepared as the noble Lord'. Suddenly he was launched into his great onslaught on Parliamentary reform. That at least was prepared.

Nay, I, on my own part, will go further, and say, that I never read or heard of any measure . . . which in any degree satisfies my mind that the state of representation can be improved. . . .

Both sides were now listening with rapt attention as the Duke, entering upon his peroration, moved from the imperfections of reform to the perfections of the present system. His voice rose, his tone became challenging. He was pushing himself further, further, further – towards what?

I am fully convinced that the country possesses at the present moment a Legislature which answers all the good purposes of legislation, and this to a greater degree than any Legislature ever has answered in any country whatever.

The Government benches began to look uneasy, the Opposition incredulous.

I will go further and say, that the Legislature and the system of representation possess the full and entire confidence of the country. . . .

What of the packed reform meetings, the Birmingham and other political unions, Brougham's election walkover in Yorkshire, the largest county in the whole of England? But the great Duke was sailing into the empyrean and no one could save him.

I will go still further, and say, that if at the present moment I had imposed upon me the duty of forming a Legislature for any country, and particularly for a country like this, in possession of great property of various descriptions, – I do not mean to assert that I could form such a Legislature as we possess now, for the nature of man is incapable of reaching such *excellence* at once, – but my great endeavor would be, to form some description of legislature which would produce the same results.

The face of Lord Aberdeen, the Foreign Secretary, who was sitting next to him, looked more like a tragic mask than usual. For the Duke even now had not finished. The special excellence of the present system, he emphasized, consisted in its being heavily weighted in favour of the landed proprietors.

Under these circumstances, I am not prepared to bring forward any measure of the description alluded to by the noble Lord. And –

further, further, further –

I am not only not prepared to bring forward any measure of this nature, but I will at once declare that ... I shall always feel it my duty to resist such measures when proposed by others.

The Duke sat down. He had said exactly what he meant. In this age of reform, no scheme of his own and damnation to anyone else's.

There was not an immediate uproar as there would have been in the Commons. Only a brief stunned silence followed by a rising murmur of bewilderment. The Duke noticed and turned to Aberdeen.

'I have not said too much, have I?'

Aberdeen's long lugubrious face became still longer as he thrust forward his chin in a gesture reserved for extremities.

'You'll hear of it,' he warned.

George Seymour was aware of a friend convulsively grasping his arm.

'That He should have taken the Bull of Reform by the Horns at such a moment!'

As the House emptied someone outside asked Aberdeen what the Duke had said. The Foreign Secretary, having heard the bell toll for the Government, replied hollowly,

'He said that we were going out.'[9]

What had come over the Duke? Why did Grey's very moderate references to reform have such a catastrophic effect? No one could understand. The House got the impression that he had unaccountably lashed himself into a fury and Brougham in his memoirs recalled that it was the Duke's autocratic tone as much as his matter that had shocked the peers. Lord Granville charitably suggested that his defiant delivery and whirling words were all part of his inexperience as a speaker, leading him to exaggerate.

The Duke's uncompromising language was not only premeditated but almost a repetition of what he had written about reform to Shaw only a fortnight before – 'I shall therefore at all times and under all circumstances oppose it.' No doubt his raptures over the constitution, though extremely inopportune, would not have sounded quite so fulsome to his contemporaries as they do today. Men still vied with each other in extolling the British constitution as if it were quasi-divine. Wordsworth described its sublime principles as 'archetypes of the pure intellect'. But the Duke's paean of praise sounded defiant rather than lyrical. The further question is, then, why not the brilliantly urbane manner in which he had conducted the debates, for instance, on Catholic emancipation?

Partly because, as has been seen, he was trying to reassure the Ultras by beating a big drum; some of them had even flirted with the idea of reform. But the figure of Lord Palmerston must also be again invoked. And not only because of what Palmerston had demanded on 1 November – reform – but because of what Wellington had offered – a place in the Cabinet. (But not enough additional 'Liberal' places for Palmerston to accept.)

The Duke was suffering on 2 November from guilt. His vehemence was partly self-flagellation. All along he had felt intuitively it would be wrong to take in the 'Liberals' when the Government had a majority without them and had won an election only three months before. Peel, however, was adamant. When the manoeuvres failed, and failed in a fashion so humiliating, he could only kick himself. The one step he regretted having taken in autumn 1830, he told Lady Salisbury two years later, was 'making an overture to Lord Palmerston to join him with the Canningites'.[10] Often and often had he said in the past that a reputation for manly, straightforward dealing was his great asset. What was he doing, playing Palmerston's sibylline game? It had made him fall from grace. At all costs he must climb back. In doing so he was to climb out.

Less subjective but equally relevant was the Duke's attitude to reform itself. This also contributed largely to the débâcle, seeming as it did to give his emotions a rational base. He saw parliamentary reform as the next stage before revolution: 'Beginning reform,' he told Mrs Arbuthnot, 'is beginning revolution.'[11] That he himself had given the country a taste for Tory reform through his Test Acts, Corn Laws and Catholic relief did not strike his political imagination. All his life the first French Revolution had been vividly present to his imagination. For him, its destructive ideas had never been modified. They had merely been kept at bay, by British arms and British institutions. In a year like 1830, who would exchange an English borough, even a 'rotten' one, for a revolutionary commune? Not he. Looking at France's '*Journées Glorieuses*' in July, his final reflection was that Britain should be 'more and more satisfied with its own institutions'.[12]

A Radical like Cobbett would no doubt discover a few more rotten boroughs on his rural rides as bad as Old Sarum, where a grassy mound, bare of all human habitation, was represented in Parliament. Votes for mounds but not for Manchester? The Duke remembered instead the number of pocket boroughs which had stuck to him, when the Ultras defected, and helped him to push through his great 'imperial measure', Catholic emancipation. He regarded them as an independent element in Parliament with a wider outlook than most. They were ready to consider the Empire as well as home interests. This element must be reassured as to its future safety in Tory hands.

The question finally resolved itself into one of fundamentals. Why did the Duke's mind work in this way? Why did he equate the 'March of Intellect' with what he now called the 'March of Insurrection'? There is no room for argument here. His most fervent admirers from Sir William Fraser onwards have agreed that he was totally lacking in political imagination. Battlefield imagination, yes; it was his forte. A favourite carriage-game often played with Croker as they bowled along the English roads together was to guess what kind of terrain lay 'on the other side of the hill'. Croker was always astounded by the Duke's accuracy. His guesses seemed to be inspired. Not so in politics. If genius is an infinite capacity for taking pains, imagination may be defined on a similarly practical level as an infinite number of past experiences projected forward in a sudden flash. The Duke's mind was already formed when he entered high British politics. After a dozen years he had not yet learned to divine the lie of the land. Was it surprising that on some of his political excursions he wrongly guessed that revolution lay on the other side of the hill?

The effect of the Duke's speech was prodigious. Wild rumours circulated in the City. Had he acquired secret information of some conspiracy emanating from abroad? Funds fell four points. Bets were laid among the Whigs on his resigning immediately or becoming a reformer before the end of the week.

Among the hundreds of offensive letters came the Duke's first personal experience of 'Captain Swing'. This legendary character was really nothing but a name, though a marvellously potent name standing for the unknown leader or leaders of the rioting agricultural labourers; the true King Ludd. No one had ever seen 'Swing' for certain, though he was believed to ride about in a gig setting fire to hayricks with a strange blue spark. After threatening notes on 3 and 4 November, came the first death threat, on the 8th:

Parliamentary Reform in a full and fair representation of the people or Death!!! Mark this thou Despot. Swing.

So serious did the risks of mob violence appear, that the presence of the King and his ministers at the Lord Mayor's Day dinner at the Guildhall was cancelled.

The greatest test of all was still to come. After the double shock to public confidence of the speech and the cancellation, what were the Duke's chances of surviving the new session? The Duke 'at last convinced himself', according to Harriet Arbuthnot, writing in her journal on 15 November, that for Peel's sake there *must* be a Tory–Liberal alliance. Peel could not go on any longer in the House of Commons alone.

On that very morning, 15 November, a gale which was suddenly to sweep through the Commons and flatten the Government to the ground began to blow.

A meeting of ultra-Tories chaired by Sir Edward Knatchbull resolved to cast a bold, revenge vote against the Government that evening. There was to be a debate on the Civil List, a minor affair, the grand collision over Brougham's Reform Bill being scheduled for the following day. The collision came twenty-four hours earlier than expected.

Sir Edward Knatchbull seconded a motion by Sir Henry Parnell, an Irish MP and kinsman of the future Irish patriot, that a commission should look into the Civil List accounts. Goulburn, for the Government, refused. The vote was taken in a packed House, from which many anti-Government MPs were excluded through lack of space. Members, swarming together and buzzing like wasps round an overripe plum, waited for the Speaker to declare the result: 233 for Parnell and Knatchbull, 204 against. A Government defeat by 29 votes. There was an exultant roar, despite the Whig leaders' tactful order that their rank and file should not cheer. They need not have worried. Peel's purgatory was over and he longed to join in.

The Duke was entertaining the Prince of Orange to a large dinner in the Waterloo Gallery at Apsley House when a note was sent up to him giving the news and saying that Peel, Goulburn and Arbuthnot were waiting to see him downstairs. With a whispered word to Harriet alone the Duke went down.

Peel was still radiant with relief. All three insisted that the Prime Minister must hand in his resignation to the King next morning. It would be Brougham's radical bill which occupied the field for the future, by right of conquest. To accept defeat on the Civil List was surely to place the country's fate in Grey's more tender hands? Reluctantly the Duke agreed. He and his ministers went to St James's Palace shortly before 1 pm on Tuesday 16 November – the third dramatic Tuesday in a row. Their resignations were accepted by His Majesty with tears.

To fall from power three months after an election victory needs some doing. How did the Duke achieve it? In one sense he was his own executioner; in another, the country forced him to meet his political Waterloo. From 1830 onwards the British people were resolved that something radical should happen.

After nearly three years at the top the general shape of his statesman-ship was firmly blocked in. To begin with, it was always obvious that he had once been Europe's most successful soldier. He brought to his civil office both the strength and weakness of his past: the great soldier's devotion, acumen, resolution, calm, steadfastness, courage and readi-ness to take responsibility at all times, but especially when he judged the safety of the State or of innocent lives to be at risk. There is also no doubt that the authoritarian nature of military command had left its indelible stamp. Even the devoted Mrs Arbuthnot commented more than once on his 'savage' rages when contradicted – rages for which he made quick reparation with a stronger than usual application of his charm. Less than five years were to pass before he was explaining to Lady Salisbury the difference between Cabinet ministers and his staff officers, to the formers' disadvantage:

One man wants one thing and one another; they agree to what I say in the morning, and then in the evening up they start with some crochet which deranges the whole plan. I have not been used to that in all the early part of my life.

It is possible to feel sympathy for the Duke when the 'crochets' of Huskisson and Peel are recalled. His complaint, however, was followed by a less engaging account of how he did things, so to speak, in the army:

I have been accustomed to carry on things in quite a different manner; I assembled my officers and laid down my plan, and it was carried into effect without any more words.[13]

That treatment had been good enough for an old general like Erskine, as blind as a beetle and not very sober; but it was not good enough for Peel.

Half in jest he would often subscribe to the image of himself as an Iron Duke determined to get his own way. He was once staying with Lord Hertford for a shoot at a time when there was trouble with the Portuguese constitutionalists. 'These gentlemen little know this iron hand,' he said, 'and it will never allow them to do what it does not wish.' (The iron hand had accidentally just winged a keeper.)[14]

The habit of deluging political leaders with advice was another trait of British democracy not found in the army. 'I have come to the conclusion that the English are the most officious people that I have yet met with,' he wrote after nine months of the premiership – but he answered every letter personally, 'to a degree which is not only unprecedented,' said Greville, 'but quite unnecessary, and I think unwise, although certainly it contributes to his popularity'.

Despite his enormous correspondence, the Duke had not learned to communicate. He distrusted the press, often with good reason. Nevertheless papers like *The Times* were increasingly listened to and no statesman in 1830 could afford to speak to 'the *Gentlemen*' in Wellington's tone of voice. Disraeli was also to observe failure of communication in regard

to those unconstitutional speeches, full of naivete and secret history, which the Duke of Wellington was in the habit of addressing to the peers when his grace led the house of lords. . . .[15]

As for 'the mob', or 'mobbikins', as Maria Edgeworth called the smaller groups of demonstrators, Wellington was beginning to show a touch of the Coriolanus-type hero towards them. Charlotte Brontë, whose happy obsession with her great Duke did not diminish with the years, published her novel *Shirley* in 1847, and called one chapter 'Coriolanus'. Her fictitious hero, Robert Moore, a harsh but dynamic and lovable mill-owner, has something of Wellington in him. Always referring to the poorest of his work-people as 'the mob', he is nonetheless a great man. But why this fault? Charlotte turns to Shakespeare's *Coriolanus* for some possible answers:

> Whether was it pride,
> . . . whether defect of judgment,
> . . . or whether nature,
> Not to be other than one thing, not moving
> From the casque to the cushion but

> Even with the same austerity and garb
> As he controlled the war?

'*From the casque to the cushion.* . . .' If Wellington in fifteen years had not made the transition, the presumption was that he would never fully make it. Yet his entire lack of pride, his far from defective judgement, and above all his abhorrence of cruelty were arguments on the other side.

The integrity of public life, even in its most secret corners, was always scrupulously observed by him. When Talleyrand's nephew was imprisoned in 1829 for huge gambling debts incurred in England, everyone except the Duke implored the French ambassador to obtain diplomatic immunity for the delinquent by taking him into the French embassy. Wellington was prepared to pay the debts himself rather than have the diplomatic service discredited.

Those who obtained pensions through the Duke were more often the young or the old than the powerful – his two secretaries and seventy-four-year-old Miss Sarah Ponsonby, survivor in 1829 of that inimitable, romantic partnership, the Ladies of Llangollen.

Notwithstanding the two most remarkable innovations of Wellington's premiership (Catholic MPs and the New Police) there has always been a tendency to see him as a modernizer *malgré lui*. Professor Turbeville, who has many penetrating and generous things to say, at the same time gives him a curious label: the well-known, 'None go so far as those who do not know whither they are going.' Wellington, however, had contemplated a new police force and Catholic rights for years. In each case he knew where he was going and got there. Over parliamentary reform he thought he knew where the reformers were going, namely towards the revolution, and got it wrong. His mistake was to bar that road and go nowhere.

In those years of misery a new lead was vital. Never mind if parliamentary reform could not by itself cure 'distress'; at least it could give the cause of the distressed more punch in Parliament. To argue as the Duke did that Britain's over-all wealth was increasing, even if certain unfortunate individuals on 2½d a week were destitute, was to fail to see the trees for the wood. With all the criticism, some justified and some not, no one ever accused him of opposing parliamentary reform for selfish reasons. He never consented to be a borough-monger himself, pointedly rejecting the additional offer of a borough when he was extending his estate at Stratfield Saye. Proprietors who constantly added to their bag of boroughs for the sake of the money he considered detestable. The conviction that as Prime Minister he had acted only for the public good, as he saw it, gave him his incomparable strength. A 'nest of corruption' as denounced by Captain Swing might or might not exist in Downing Street or other inviting sites along Whitehall. Nobody ever thought the nests were built or feathered by Wellington. It was this incorruptibility together with his shining honesty of purpose which made him a towering political leader, and caused so many of his countrymen to feel he could never be replaced.

'If people think I like this station,' he had said to Colin Campbell soon after becoming Prime Minister, 'they are mistaken. The nation has rewarded me and over-rewarded me. My line is to command the army, but if I think I can do any good by being Minister, I am willing to . . . do what I can.'[16]

Like many a wife before and since, Kitty was not sorry that her husband had become a fallen minister. From her sickbed at Stratfield Saye she pencilled her thoughts to her sister Elizabeth Stewart in Ireland:

My Bess, depend upon it, the Duke having found it advisable to Resign . . . was the direct Hand of that God who has ever protected him in the more evident though not more real dangers of Battle.

Everybody saw that the Duke's health was altering, that his countenance was acquiring a drawn and fallen look, his figure to shrink, and many other appearances that precede the breaking up of a constitution from over work.

He was fallen and looked fallen. But, added Kitty, 'Thank God he has resigned in time. . . .' Here at Stratfield Saye his friends assured her his looks were already beginning to mend. Not that he was resting – 'You know dear Bess, that unlike others of the name of Wellesley, the Duke cannot be idle. . . .'[17] He had left London for his country home on a mission. Wherever his presence as Lord-Lieutenant was needed to pacify the countryside he would appear.

For 'Captain Swing' had reached Hampshire.

Samuel Rogers, the poet and financier, remembered the Duke sitting over the Arbuthnots' fire and outlining his post-resignation plans.

'I will go down into my County,' he said, 'and do what I can to restore order and peace.' Nor were politics to be neglected. 'And in my place in Parliament, when I can, I will approve; when I cannot, I will dissent, but I will never agree to be leader of a faction.'[18] For the sake of principle he would fight reform but not for party. Meanwhile there were many other duties of a public or personal nature to occupy every hour of his day and exorcize any remaining signs of a fallen minister's particular demon, the aching void.

'He has literally been hooted down by the people,' wrote Cobbett on 20 November 1830. This harsh travesty of the Duke's defeat was nonetheless a true picture of the next eighteen months. Indeed, the sixteen years of active politics still before him were never to recapture a sense of 'bright confident morning'. The world was changing around him. He was the last of the national leaders who saw themselves primarily as servants of the Crown. His fall paved the way for party chiefs and the party system as we know it.

In Peel's opinion Wellington had been misled by females of the most 'mediocre' kind. 'No man has any influence with him,' he said speaking of the Duke's fatal declaration against reform; 'he is led by women; the foolish ones envelop him with incense, and he has fallen a victim to this weakness and to his own vanity.'[19]

One of the 'mediocre' females to whom Peel referred, Mrs Arbuthnot, naturally took a different view of the Duke's fall. She felt he himself was to blame for refusing to admit more talent in his team. Soon Harriet was more sorry for herself than for him. With his reading, riding and county affairs he was 'much happier out of office', but politics for her had lost their savour. 'I shall write very seldom now, I dare say, in my book.' She broke off her first entry for 1832 in the middle of a sentence. An '&' was left hanging in mid-air, as if to symbolize her disenchantment with the unfolding drama of Whig politics.[20]

'Everybody seems to be charmed,' wrote Lady Granville of the new regime.[21] And well they might be, for Grey had something for everyone. His Government found room for Whigs like Althorp, son and heir to Earl Spencer, and Lord John Russell, younger brother of the Duke of Bedford; Radicals like Brougham and the 1st Earl of Durham, Grey's son-in-law; Canningites like Goderich, Melbourne and Palmerston; and the Tory Duke of Richmond. The spectacle of Brougham, idol of the 'rabbleocracy', sitting on the Woolsack had a special charm. Radical Lord Sefton invited him and the Grey family to dinner one night and after the port preceded the Lord Chancellor out of the room carrying a fire-shovel for the mace.[22]

Once the new ministers were installed Parliament adjourned till February. Harriet Martineau, the extraordinarily plain and deaf but enthusiastic radical historian of the period, spoke of the year beginning with November 1830 as 'Year I of the People's Cause'.[23]

On 1 March 1831, Lord John Russell, Leader of the House of Commons, rose to introduce his great Reform Bill.

Suspense but not undue alarm was the mood of the House as Lord John began. How many rotten boroughs were to be purged? Some peers hoped for no more than a dozen. Wellington expected about thirty. But with at least two hundred Commons' seats – one-third of the whole – controlled by a hundred great landowning peers, Russell was determined to administer to Parliament a really strong purgative. No more should a notorious borough-monger like the Duke of Newcastle own *nine* constituencies, their members being known as his 'ninepins'. Nor should Parliament, at least, hear again such words as Newcastle had used after evicting tenants for voting the wrong way – 'Have I not the right to do what I like with mine own?'

Disfranchisement of enough pocket boroughs would enable Russell to enfranchise the large towns, thus satisfying the two main objects of popular fervour. The third object, a fairer property qualification for the vote, would be achieved by extending the franchise to all £10 householders in the boroughs and £10 leaseholders in the counties. There would then be a new total of half a million upper- and middle-class male voters. A marvellous advance? With not a working-class voter or a woman of any class among them? When it is asked how people not very different from ourselves could have allowed boroughs like Old Sarum and behaviour like Newcastle's to exist as long as they did, the reply must be that a race of totally voteless women lingered on well into our own century.

Russell read out his list of doomed boroughs and the whole House reeled with shock, some in ecstasy, others in agony. He had kept his secret on Parliamentary reform as successfully as the Duke had once kept his on Catholic relief. There were to be sixty wholly disfranchised. Tories writhed and squirmed on their benches. Radicals felt their cup of joy was overflowing when they suddenly heard Russell adding that forty-six more boroughs were to be partially disfranchised. After the number of MPs had been reduced from 658 to 596, the large towns were to get 42 of the disposable seats.

'I have kept my word with the nation,' wrote the well-satisfied Prime Minister, Grey, to the stupefied Princess Lieven. London buzzed with speculations. 'What is said now? How will it go? What is the last news? What do you think?' The Duke prophesied that if the bill went through, 'a shake will be given to the property of every individual in the country'.[24]

For some time before the bill he had blamed Peel for persuading him to resign in November 1830. ('I confess that I regret my consent to the resignation more than I do any Act of my Life.') Now he felt that if only Peel had refused to give the bill a first reading the moderate Whigs would have combined with the Tories to oust the Government. Instead, Peel had made an eloquent speech pointing out that Old Sarum existed even in the sacred year of the Glorious Revolution, 1688, and that a whole string of dazzling young men from Pitt to Grey himself had first entered Parliament through gates now declared rotten and unhinged. After which the bill had been read a first time. With the second reading almost upon them, the Duke desperately foretold the absolute destruction of government 'by due course of law'.[25]

But in the Commons each side expected victory, as at 3 am on 23 March 1831 the vote was taken on the second reading. There was dead silence followed by a storm of Whig shouts, cheers and even weeping when the Speaker announced a Government majority of – one. Wellington could have been forgiven if he had regarded his nephew as that one, for 'Wicked William' had voted with the Whigs against his uncle's cause. The brilliant young Whig MP, Thomas Macaulay, observed the havoc on the Tory benches. Peel's jaw dropped and Herries, taking off his tie, looked like Judas preparing for the 'last operation'.

Next day the Duke went down to the Lords and made his first speech on the bill. It lasted only two or three minutes, but his concluding words were effective.

I possess no influence or interest of the description which will be destroyed by the measure now proposed; but I am an individual who has served His Majesty for now nearly half a century –

and he could not but feel it his duty to say that,

from the period of the adoption of that measure will date the downfall of the Constitution.

No one could doubt his sincerity; nor that he was correct in forecasting the end of a constitutional machine powered by the aristocracy.

As the Duke saw things, the committee stage of the bill, reached on

18 April, would give the country time to 'come to its senses'. The Commons he felt were doing so when they voted in committee more than once against the Government. There were moments now when the Duke was hopeful. He had written to Lord Falmouth on 3 April: 'The King of this country is (thank God) still a tower of strength.'[26] Unfortunately the tower was about to be occupied by the enemy.

What was Lord Grey to do? Defeat in committee meant subsequent destruction of the bill. In the spirit of the times, the Prime Minister decided on a *coup d'état*. William IV should descend like a *deus ex machina*, dissolve Parliament and enable the Whigs to accumulate an unbeatable majority at a general election.

The King at first jibbed and scribbled on a scrap of paper,

> I consider Dissolution
> Tantamount to Revolution.

But when on 22 April he heard that a Tory peer, Lord Wharncliffe, proposed to pre-empt his royal right to dissolve by putting down a motion against it the very next day, the Sailor King swung round into the teeth of the gale and ordered his royal equipage forthwith. And if his cream ponies could not be groomed in time for him to drive to Parliament in state, he would go in a hackney coach. Lord Albemarle, Master of the Horse, was called from a late breakfast to prepare for His Majesty's sortie.

'Lord bless me! is there a revolution?'

'Not at this moment, but there will be if you stay to finish your breakfast.'[27]

Lord Albemarle buckled to, the crown was rushed from the Tower and the King's robes from the painter Sir William Beechey's studio in Wimpole Street, the cannon boomed and King William rolled down in his coach to dissolve Parliament, where a revolution 'by due course of law', as the Duke would have said, already seemed to be in progress.

Bawling rather than debating occupied both Houses. In the Lords the Ultras were rampant, Mansfield shouting abuse and Londonderry brandishing a whip at Richmond while five peers clung to his coat-tails. What was all the hubbub? asked the King of the Lord Chancellor.

'If it please your Majesty,' replied Brougham smoothly, 'it is the Lords debating.'[28]

Next door Peel, in an ecstasy of denunciation, his auburn hair blazing like Ney's at Waterloo, refused to give way even when Black Rod was banging on the door, though his scorching periods had long been punctuated by gunfire signalling His Majesty's approach. Finally the King put an end to this bedlam by 'taking Parliament by storm' (in Buckingham's outraged words to Wellington), his crown as wobbly and crooked on his head as the Sword of State was stiff and straight in Grey's hand. Some saw it as the sword of an executioner.

The Duke of Wellington that day was not in his place in the House of Lords.

Kitty was dying. He had rushed up to town earlier in the month, to spend unbroken hours at her bedside. Otherwise he would have been happier at Stratfield Saye. 'I feel growing upon me a desire to live out of the World,' he had written to Mrs Arbuthnot. 'The truth is that this Reform Question breaks me down as it will everything else. . . .'[29] Now it was Kitty who was to leave the world.

'She is better certainly,' he told Harriet on 9 April; 'but she is still very unwell; and I shall not go out of town again.' Two days later he wrote sombrely: 'It is impossible to calculate upon the duration of her life.'

Maria Edgeworth believed that Kitty's last illness was cancer. It may have been cholera, though the family records throw no light on the subject. By January Kitty had seemed already very near her end when her old friend visited her at Apsley House. Maria marvelled at the contrast between the waxen figure resting on a high white sofa-bed and the glittering array of her husband's trophies which surrounded her in the spacious ground-floor room. Following her friend's gaze, Kitty raised herself up so that she too could see the magnificent china and golden shield of Achilles.

'All tributes to merit – there is the value!' she exclaimed; 'and pure! pure! – no corruption – ever *suspected* even. Even of the Duke of Marlborough that could not be said so truly.'

Despite Maria's dislike of Wellington, she could not help rejoicing that Kitty's enthusiasm still fed on her hero's glory. 'I hope she will not outlive the pleasure she now feels, I am assured, in the Duke's returning kindness,' Maria added. 'I hope she will not last too long and tire out that easily tired pity of his.' The hope, however uncharitably expressed, was realized, and three months later the Duke's last vigil began.

His wife and the old order were slipping away together. When he heard that more and more country gentlemen were becoming alarmed at the Reform Bill, he felt no surprise. 'They are right. Their order will be annihilated even sooner than any of them expect.' It was the same when they told him that people were cutting down their establishments in preparation for 'the expected Storm'.

'They are very right. If the Bill passes we shall have it.'

In the ground-floor room Kitty clung to a hand that was no longer iron. Once she ran her fingers up inside his sleeve to feel if by chance he was still wearing an armlet she had given him long ago.

'She found it,' said the Duke to a friend, 'as she would have found it any time these twenty years, had she cared to look for it.' How strange it was, he reflected sadly, that two people could live together for half a lifetime 'and only understand one another at the end'.[30]

The end came on 24 April, two days after King William dissolved Parliament. The Duke and his sons immediately went down to the country, black edgings were ordered for his writing-paper, Apsley House was shut up and nothing remained but for the small coffin to make its journey to Stratfield Saye for burial in the family vault. Before the hearse was ready 'the expected Storm' broke.

The Lord Mayor of London ordered illuminations on 27 April in honour of the dissolution. From Westminster to Piccadilly there were sparkling pyramids of candles in the fine sash-windows of the wealthy. But not in all. A roistering reform mob marched up Piccadilly, breaking the windows of those who showed by their dark fronts that they regarded the dissolution as a black day for Britain.

Apsley House was in darkness because of the Duchess's passing rather than Parliament's. But the Duke would certainly not have illuminated for reform even if he had been at home. Stones smashed immense quantities of his new plate-glass on the ground floor. When the crowd pulled up the railings on the Piccadilly side the Duke's servant fired two blunderbusses over their heads (though loaded with gunpowder only). At once the crowd, who were out for a lark rather than a riot, turned their attention to fresh windows and pastures new in Grosvenor Square.

I think my Servant John saved my House [wrote the Duke] or the lives of the Mob – possibly both – by firing as he did. They certainly intended to destroy the House, and did not care one Pin for the poor Duchess being dead in the House. . . .

The reformers in this unreformed Parliament swept home to a tremendous election victory. With a Whig-Radical-Irish-Scottish majority of 140 against them, the Tories were utterly routed. According to the Duke, it had been achieved by sheer terrorism. 'I confess that I am much more alarmed about Terror,' he wrote to Charles Arbuthnot, 'than I am about Reform. It is not to be believed how far it goes, and what it has done.'[31]

September came and with it the King's coronation. A loud spontaneous cheer went up for Wellington as he took the oath and the shout which the Whigs then tried to raise for Grey was far from triumphant. But there were to be triumphant majorities for Grey's bill in the Commons.* Suddenly the Duke found his static policy untenable. If the enemy would not withdraw he must plunge to the attack. For the next eight months he was to struggle in a breathless mêlée hardly less stubborn than the eight hours of Waterloo.

The Tory decision to oppose the terrible bill in the Lords had been taken at Apsley House on 21 September in an atmosphere of solemn tragedy. It was turned to farce by Lords Eldon and Kenyon, who came in 'drunk as porters' from a dinner at the Duke of Cumberland's and ranted furiously. (Lord Kenyon apologized to Wellington next day for the effects of HRH's punch.[32]) The second reading debate was more memorable, however, for Lord Brougham's advocacy of the bill than for the Opposition's resistance. His emotion carried him to heights of oratory which all agreed were 'superhuman'. So was his intake of negus. George Seymour said that he drank like a preacher regularly turning his hour-glass.[33] Though roaring drunk by the end, the final scene was wildly exaggerated in the account given by Tory Lord Campbell: how Brougham fell on his knees before the Duke's squares and having pleaded with them to retreat was unable to regain the Woolsack without assistance.

The Duke had begun too loudly for a speech that consisted of cannister-shot rather than 12-pounders: that the new, elected members would be mere delegates instead of independent-minded MPs; that the people wanted universal suffrage, so if the Government's self-confessed policy was to please the people, why not really radical reform?

If the Duke's shots were not very damaging, his troops needed no mighty cannonade to strengthen their resolution. They voted down the bill on 8 October by a thumping majority of forty-one. Twenty-one out of the twenty-three bishops opposed the bill. Because these twenty-one by changing their votes could have given the Government another

---

* Young Mr W. E. Gladstone, a student at Oxford, went to hear the Reform Bill debate and could find no vacant stool or chair in the Chamber, only an iron railing which gave him occasional 'cutting repose'. (Gladstone Papers, p. 96.)

majority of one, popular opinion saddled them with defeat of the Second Reform Bill. '*The Bishops have done it*,' declared the militant free-thinker Richard Carlile; 'it is the work of the Holy Ghost.'

Immediately the pent-up people broke into every kind of retaliation, legal and illegal. On the morning after the defeat Wellington's particular foe, the *Morning Chronicle*, came out with borders as black as his own writing-paper. His effigy and that of Cumberland were burned at Tyburn (Marble Arch), while the Bishop of Exeter's was thrown on a diocesan bonfire on 5 November along with Guy Fawkes and the Pope. John Russell told the agitator Attwood, some thought rashly, that the voice of the nation could not be drowned by 'the whisper of a faction'.

Apsley House was stoned for the second time in one year, on 12 October. This time the Duke was at home. In broad daylight the stones came hurtling through the plate-glass windows for fifty minutes before the police arrived on the scene. One narrowly missed the Duke's head as he sat at his writing-table and broke a glass-fronted bookcase behind him; another cut through the canvas of Lady Lyndhurst's portrait by Wilkie, hanging on the wall. The garden was full of stones, though the stone-throwers themselves were kept outside the railings by the sight of armed men posted round the house. Having withdrawn to the Park, the mob circled menacingly round the Achilles statue but found it too heavy to overturn. 'It is now five o'clock, and beginning to rain a little,' the Duke wrote to Mrs Arbuthnot from his beleaguered citadel, giving her a blow-by-blow account of the affair; 'and I conclude that the Gentlemen will now go to their Dinners!'[34] Thank God for his new shutters even though Lord Grey, riding past a few days before, had taken them as a personal affront.

The Duke had been well prepared and he got off relatively lightly. In Derby anti-reformers' houses were wrecked; in Nottingham the castle belonging to the Duke of Newcastle was burned down; in Bristol the worst catastrophe since the Gordon Riots of 1780 took place, due to an incredible combination of evils. Provocative authorities insisted that the hated Wetherell's entry as City Recorder should not be postponed; timid magistrates delayed the action of the military; a humane but ineffectual colonel lost his nerve during the crisis and committed suicide during his court martial; and thieves out only for plunder joined the reformers' demonstration. Half the city centre was destroyed, hundreds of demonstrators were killed and wounded by the soldiers and many drunken pillagers burned to death in the cellars of houses they themselves had set on fire. Madame Tussaud's famous waxworks, which she had just brought to Bristol, narrowly escaped destruction; and Wetherell himself was said to have got away only by donning the disguise of a wash and a clean suit.

On the propaganda front, pamphlets and broadsheets with the theme, 'What ought to be done with the Things called "Lords"?' spread over the great towns. The answer was, Down with them. 'No Lords!' Better to die a republican of the *cholera morbus* than survive that plague, a slave of lords.

The Duke was in constant touch with Fitzroy Somerset and other officers over military support for the police. His aim was to create security without alarm, and a suggestion for removing the display guns from Walmer Castle received the cold reply that since there was no ammunition no one would steal them.[35] A secret report from Melbourne of an impending attack on Dover Castle was similarly discounted. But when a partly fictitious story of arms being sold by a London dealer to the Birmingham Political Union reached the Duke, he rushed headlong into the fray. On Guy Fawkes' Day he warned the King about this conspiracy, so reminiscent of the July Days in Paris, and was gratified when the Government squeezed out a proclamation against armed unions.[36] Of far more importance, however, to the Duke's subsequent actions than the Birmingham affair was the secondary purpose of his letter to the King.

This purpose was to let His Majesty know that if he wished to escape from the thraldom of the Whigs, the Duke of Wellington would 'assist him to do so'. The retained servant was ready once more to serve the King as Prime Minister. However, 'our poor King', as the Duke now called him, was not yet ready to throw over Grey.[37]

Nor did the Duke feel sure of Peel's support. 'I did pretty well with him while we were in office, but I cannot manage him at all now,' he wrote to Lady Salisbury on 21 November. 'He is a wonderful fellow – has a most correct judgment – talents almost equal to those of Pitt, but he spoils all by timidity & indecision.'[38]

The bill's second reading in the Lords passed by no more than nine votes, despite the support of converts among the bishops. The prospect for Grey was bleak. What could happen in committee but defeat? On Monday 7 May the Lords duly defeated the third attempt at a Reform Bill and the May Days began. Only a creation of Whig peers, it seemed, would enable the people's will to prevail.

With King William playing the part of Charles x in his subjects' imagination, by refusing to create peers as Charles had refused to withdraw the Ordinances, the July Days of France seemed in a fair way to reproduce themselves in Britain. Wellington would of course be Polignac, the reactionary French leader. Radical agitators had often equated the two in the past and now the Duke was to give them some excuse for doing so again.

The May Days raced past like the mileposts he had watched from the Liverpool–Manchester train. Close at hand, the flying shapes of Throne and Parliament with King, Cabinet and Opposition merged in remorseless struggle; in the background, the people roused to a passion of petitions and monster meetings, secret conspiracies and broad radiant dreams.

7 May: 150,000 Birmingham Unionists sang their hymn, 'We will, we will, we *will be free!*'

8 May: Grey demanded the creation of at least fifty peers.

9 May: The King refused a mass creation, Grey walked out and the King, through Lyndhurst, commissioned the Duke to form a government. At the same time the Duke must bring in the extensive measure of Reform to which HM considered the country since the dissolution was entitled. 'The King appeared to think all this day,' wrote the courtier George Seymour, 'that he had done with the Whigs . . . for the next forty years.' There was heavy enrolment in the political unions.

10 May: The Duke complained privately at the King's tying him down to a reform programme.[39] And well he might. The King had set him an impossible task. Nevertheless, as HM's retained servant he wrote with quixotic loyalty in reply to Lyndhurst's approach, 'I am perfectly ready to do whatever his Majesty may command me.'[40] Not so Peel, who was in closer touch with reality. In the interests of consistency and public confidence, he declined not only the premiership but any office whatever. He could not repeat on reform his performance over Catholic emancipation. While the Duke negotiated undeterred for support elsewhere, the news of Grey's fall reached the provinces. Liverpool Stock Exchange closed. Business everywhere faltered. Placards appeared in windows, 'No taxes paid here till the Reform Bill is passed.'

11 May: Reform leaders from far and near met at Francis Place's house in London to plan resistance to a Wellington ministry.

12 May: Revolutionary arrangements for barricading Birmingham, Manchester, etc., were put in hand. Funds continued to drop despite Rothschild's efforts to hold them firm. A brainwave came to Place and he wrote out his famous poster: 'To Stop the Duke Go for Gold.' Other things, however, might stop the Duke first. Only his veterans, Hardinge and Murray, seemed eager to serve. This was Saturday. 'Well, we are in a fine scrape,' he told Croker, 'and I really do not see how we are to get out of it.'[41] Right through until Monday he continued his anxious interviewing and succeeded in finding a Chancellor of the Exchequer in Alexander Baring. Greville wrote in his diary, 'The town is fearfully quiet.' It was what the Duke had called at Waterloo the dreadful pause.

13 May: The Scots Greys were ordered to rough-sharpen their sabres; not all were prepared to use them. A meeting was being organized for the next day on the field of Peterloo, where rough-sharpened sabres had been employed thirteen years before. These facts, together with a widely quoted and sinister remark of 'Wicked William's' about his uncle having 'a way' of keeping the people quiet, convinced reformers that there was to be a *coup d'état* by the Duke.

14 May: With a run on the Bank of England already begun, Parliament met. There were wild rumours that Wellington was to be assassinated on the way there and his niece Priscilla begged him to go incognito in her carriage. 'I could no more go to the House of Lords in your Carriage after such Reports,' he said, 'than I could crawl [on] all fours.' Hobhouse, one of the Whig ex-ministers, told Taylor, the King's secretary, that Wellington's only chance was to 'try what another dissolution would do'.[42] Perhaps Hobhouse was right. At any rate, there was no chance whatever for the Duke to head a government with the present House of Commons. The violence was extreme. One after another the MPs flayed him for opposing reform, destroying Grey and then resurrecting the very bill which he had killed. When the Whig Lord Ebrington called it 'gross public immorality', all was over with the Duke. Three times Alexander Baring tried to speak and was drowned by uproar. The fourth time he proposed that ex-ministers should resume their seats on the Government front bench and carry the bill. He would rather face a thousand devils, he told the Duke that evening, than such a House of Commons.

15 May: The Duke informed the King that he could neither form a government nor find support in the Commons. His retreat was absolute. When a group of Ultras urged him to call a peers' meeting and think again, he answered stiffly that he had not acted for their sake but for the King's. Meanwhile Grey, recalled to Windsor, adjourned the House till the 17th, while he set about bringing the King to heel.

17 May: Grey confronted the King with a ruthless dilemma. HM must either promise to create peers or face the possibility of insurrection. He crept out of the dilemma with the help of the Duke, who promised to abstain from further opposition to the bill and make his friends do likewise. But the Duke would not disclose his promise in Parliament. Such a public admission, he considered, would amount to condoning Grey's coercion of the King. Instead he eased his conscience by delivering an apologia in the House for his recent conduct, which shocked and misled by its angry tone. Nevertheless, there was one sentence which deeply moved his hearers and rang in their ears as long as he lived:

If I had been capable of refusing my assistance to His Majesty – if I had been capable of saying to His Majesty, 'I cannot assist you in this affair' – I do not think, my Lords, that I could have shown my face in the streets for shame of having done it – for shame of having abandoned my Sovereign under such distressing circumstances.

In the streets. . . . If the Duke had shown his face in the streets at that moment he would have felt the pressure building up again. For no one guessed he was making his farewell speech on reform. Every reformer thought he had double-crossed them again. One of them proposed to assassinate him, he was warned. 'The Duke knows of old,' he replied, 'that assassins and those who employ them are not the boldest of mankind.'

18 May: Britain as near as it had ever been to revolution – so much all agreed. The *Morning Chronicle* announced 'the eve of the barricades'. But Grey and Brougham were at Windsor extracting a written guarantee from the King to create peers if necessary, and the Duke, backed by a hundred other Tories, kept his promise to abstain. Both Houses met and Grey announced victory. The Duke was not without his share in it.

On 4 June the bill was read a third time in the Lords by 106 votes to 22.

37 *Wellington in 1818. The Duke commissioned this portrait as a gift for his godson, Lord Arthur Russell, and kept a stock of engravings to give to friends who asked for a picture.*

39 *Short-sighted Kitty sketching.*

38 *The Library at Stratfield Saye, sketched by Catherine Pakenham (Kitty), Duchess of Wellington.*

40 *Wellington, 1824. Portrait painted for Peel by Sir Thomas Lawrence. The artist began by putting a watch in the Duke's hand, as if he were waiting for his Prussian allies, but the Duke expostulated, 'That will never do. I was not "waiting" for the Prussians at Waterloo. Put a telescope in my hand, if you please.'*

41 Below *Wellington, 1827, as Achilles sulking in Apsley House, after he had refused to serve under Canning. The Achilles statue is seen in the Park outside. His baton, as Commander-in-Chief, lies broken and a sarcastic letter from George IV reads, 'His Majesty accepts the resignation of his Grace the Duke of W-ll-ngt-n with the same regret that it is communicated.'*

42 Below right *'Killing Time'. Wellington eyeing a lady in the street. An unsigned print probably by 'HB' (John Doyle) though it is not among his collected works and may have been withdrawn. Harriette Wilson, the 'demi-rep', published her Memoirs in 1825, containing a number of stories about Wellington.*

43 *Wellington, 1829. 'Leaving the House of Lords – through the Assembled Commons'. The mob yells 'No popery – No Catholic ministers' as Wellington gallops home after a debate on Catholic emancipation.*

44 *The duel, 1829. Wellington challenges Winchelsea on 'the field of Battersea' over Catholic emancipation. The Prime Minister wears a priest's robes and rosary, with the head of a lobster, symbol of a scarlet-uniformed soldier. He says, 'I used to be a good shot but have been out of practice for some years.'*

TAKING AN AIRING IN HYDE PARK
A PORTRAIT
Framed but not yet Glazed

45 'Framed but not yet glazed'. Wellington looks through his broken windows at Apsley House.

46 Lord Grey's defeat of Wellington. The GREY gander seizes the WATERLOO cock's tail feathers in his 'Reform' BILL and cocked hat in his foot, with the words, 'I will teach you my Bill is a match for your spurs any day my Dunghill.'

THE WATERLOO COCK BOLTING FROM THE GREY GANDER

47 *'A Sketch in the Park'.*
Wellington and Mrs Harriet
Arbuthnot.

48 *'A Celebrated Commander on the Retir'd List'. Wellington*
relaxed and elegant.

49 'Wellington musing on the Field of Waterloo'. Imaginative scene painted by
B.R. Haydon in 1839, showing the Lion Mound and monument to Sir A. Gordon
in the background. 'They have spoilt my battlefield', said the Duke when he first saw
the Mound in 1821. Count D'Orsay, who himself painted the Duke in 1845, touched
up Copenhagen's hind quarters, but after he had left the studio Haydon obliterated his
work with the words, 'This won't do – a Frenchman touch Copenhagen.'

50 Reform of the Corn Laws, 1846. Wellington and Peel as sheep leading the flock
through a gap in the hedge of 'Protection' into the pasture of 'Free Trade'. John Bull
looks on in hilarious surprise.

51 *The Wellington statue being transported from Wyatt's studio to its position in front of Apsley House. 'The awful apparition to a gentleman whilst shaving in the Edgware Road.'*

52 *Sketch by C.R. Leslie, formerly in the possession of John Murray the publisher. When a French friend asked Murray why he chose to have the Duke's back view Murray replied: 'I like it because it is the point of view you Frenchmen never saw.'*

53 *'The First of May' by Franz Winterhalter, 1851. The birthday of Queen Victoria's son Prince Arthur and of Wellington who, as godfather, is shown giving the Prince a casket. In fact he did not present the casket, which belonged to the Queen and was introduced into the picture by Prince Albert for effect. Prince Arthur was ragged about it when he grew up.*

54 *Wellington with his grandchildren in the library at Stratfield Saye. From left to right: Henry (afterward 3rd Duke), Mary (Lady Mary Scott), Arthur (4th Duke), Victoria (Lady Holm Patrick). The miniature was painted by R. Thornburn for Angela Burdett-Coutts in 1853, though the Duke's head may have been taken from life the year before and copied here. Miss Coutts had wanted the Duke at breakfast but the 2nd Duke suggested the breakfast-table would be a 'terrible stumbling block'. Would she not prefer him opening his letters in the library before breakfast 'and giving as he did the covers to the children'?*

55 *The funeral procession passing Apsley House. On the right is the Decimus Burton Arch surmounted by Matthew Cotes Wyatt's statue.*

That Wellington's volte-face of May 1832 did not prove his end was due to his remarkable character being recognized for what it was. After the first shock, there were few who believed that he had acted for the sake of power or party advantage rather than loyalty to that Sovereign in whose person he saw the country embodied.

On a more practical level, rigid consistency had never been the Duke's creed. He would no more hesitate to alter his course in politics than in battle he would refuse to change his tactics. For the purposes of war, he had his simile of the rough-and-ready harness made of rope, which might break but could be knotted and used again. His policies had certainly snapped during the May Days. He tied one knot on the 10th for the King's sake and on the 15th had to untie it. But life was not finished, and a fighter may have to knot, knot and knot again.

Back in March 1831 the Duke had made one of his fiery resolves against the Reform Bill. 'I certainly never will enter the House of Lords from the time that it passes.'[43] John Wilson Croker, MP, his close comrade-in-arms during the reform struggle, may have known of this dramatic decision. At any rate, two months after the bill passed he wrote to Wellington declaring his own firm determination not to stand for the reformed Parliament. At great length he explained that it was a '*usurpation*', a new version of the Long Parliament, a means of subverting 'the Church, the Peerage & the throne'. No doubt Croker expected a pat on the back from Wellington. But the Duke meanwhile had begun to get a grip on the ravelled rope. In reply to Croker's four pages he drafted four lines.

My dear Croker,
    I have recd. your letter.
    I am very sorry that you do not intend again to serve in Parlt.
    I cannot conceive for what reason.

In the Duke's eyes it was never impossible to serve.

29

The Duke on Elba

A brief but fervent reaction in the Duke's favour resulted from his having been mobbed on Waterloo Day 1832.* He sensed nonetheless a continuing personal hostility and felt himself banished to an Elba of his own. The situation produced occasional glooms, particularly as he had no intention of returning like Napoleon with the violets of spring.

However, when a question of emigration arose in his own family circle the Duke came down against it. His wife's favourite niece, Kate, had married the Rev. William Foster, a Church of Ireland clergyman who quoted their famous uncle's views about reform and was therefore disliked by his parishioners. Should he emigrate for his family's sake?

'Is not your duty to remain at your post and hope for better times?' asked the Duke in reply. 'Make every exertion, every sacrifice, to enable you to do justice by everybody, including your family; but I confess that if I was in your situation I would not quit my post.'[1]

Croker noted that it was the death of his wife and mother in the same year which partly accounted for his low spirits; yet the world said he had no feeling for either. And why did he not marry again?

This question was actually put to him by the bold and devoted Kate Foster. His reaction, she wrote, 'puts a final answer, not only to the supposition that there were grounds, but even to the idea that there *ever could be* grounds for believing such a step could enter his contemplation'. It was not for lack of opportunities that he failed to select 'from the brightest of England's fair treasures, one who would consent to share his high position and the glories of his name'. No, said Mrs Foster, her aunt remained 'his only chosen bride beyond the grave!'[2]

Allowing for Mrs Foster's sentimental prose, there is still little doubt that the Duke maintained a special feeling for Kitty as his wife. Though not logically definable, this feeling belonged to the whole body of his

---

* The iron shutters on Apsley House – his *visage de fer* – he felt were amply justified.

ideas on life in general as it should be lived: on loyalty, on duty, on what was proper, on the right order of things. It was of the essence of his being..

Kitty's single-minded devotion also contributed to her final victory: 'With all my heart and soul I have loved him straight on from the first time I knew him (I was not then fifteen) to the present hour.'[3]

The first reformed Parliament was elected in 1833. Only one seat in the towns had been carried by the Conservatives without an expensive and 'bloody contest' – Peel's at Tamworth.[4] In Winchester they had the 'advantage' of a Political Union, explained the Duke sarcastically to Harriet, which intimidated voters by physical outrage. 'In truth the Revolution is effected.' If 'Revolution' meant the Whigs winning 320 seats with a substantial leaven of Radicals, and the Conservatives only 150, the Duke was right. They asked him what he thought about the remodelled Parliament, when for the first time he surveyed the new MPs from the Peers' Gallery. Think of them?

'I have never seen so many bad hats in my life!'[5]

Hats could be a sign of social status. When the Duke was Prime Minister one of his self-appointed advisers had seen salvation in a graduated hat tax. Not much tax would have been raised from the middle-class hats now submitted to his inspection. Old Cobbett was present for the first time, looking like John Bull up from the country. But Orator Hunt, the owner of a bad white hat symbolizing revolution, had lost his seat.

The Duke, in agreement with Peel, decided not to harass Grey's Government until another was fit to take its place. To do so earlier would have been contrary to all his principles: 'Our course in the House of Lords,' he had announced in the previous December, 'ought to be very firm and uncompromising, but very moderate' – an example of what has since been called the politics of the extreme centre. They must attend assiduously and argue every point, 'but avoid dividing except upon occasions of great importance'.[6] The great occasion did not arrive until June 1833. Meanwhile a low-profile leader again had to face ultra-Tory criticism.

Cumberland badgered the Duke to call immediate party meetings, some large to gratify the inconspicuous members, some '*smaller* meetings of the GREAT GUNS' to initiate action. But the greatest gun of all refused to fire. The last thing he wanted was to stoke up the party fires at Apsley House. Lord Londonderry's hopes that the Duke's health would stand up to the 'perilous trials' ahead were deliberately extinguished. There were to be no perilous trials. It was no good the House of Lords holding fierce debates until they were 'opportune'.[7] Similarly, all suggestions that he should create constitutional associations to counteract the political unions were snubbed. 'I feel a great disinclination to recommend to any class of the King's Subjects,' he wrote to a Devon farmer, 'to associate or combine for any purpose which is not . . . recognised by the Laws and by the Government of the Country.' Gleig was told more brusquely, 'It is very easy to turn the Society with the *best* Name and rules and regulations to the worst purposes. . . .'[8] Such an attitude could never satisfy a busy character like Gleig, far less Cumberland.

Nor was Wellington as yet friendly with Peel, though their cautious and moderate policies exactly coincided. The sulphurous fumes of the May Days were still in their garments. In public no doubt they each congratulated the other on having taken the course he had chosen, Wellington for serving the King, Peel for not serving. But the contradiction could not be agreeable to either. Wellington met Peel in February at the Carlton Club. Peel did not speak to him and after dinner sat reading by one of the fireplaces while the rest of the company conversed around the other. The Duke suspected Peel was jealous, though why? 'I have repeatedly told him I would not stand in his way.'[9]

The King's Speech of February 1833 at once showed the Duke that during the coming session he must give the Government qualified support on more than one subject. The 'great occasion' for a full-scale attack would nonetheless arise – Ireland.

From the Speech it appeared that the Government's policy on Ireland was two-edged: repression and concession. Repression meant a Coercion* Bill to restore law and order. Where O'Connell called the Speech 'brutal and sanguinary', the Duke found nothing to criticize. Concessions, however, that hit the Irish Protestant Church could and must be opposed. Admittedly six million Catholics were required by law to pay tithes in support of eight hundred thousand Protestants. Grey planned in the course of this Parliament to abolish ten redundant Protestant bishoprics, to phase out Protestant clergy who had no parishioners and lastly to commute the tithes, appropriating surplus

---

* Coercion was the method of putting down political disturbances by replacing the ordinary law of the land with a special act which introduced an element of force.

income derived from the streamlined new system to lay purposes. In all, a sweeping programme, a 'great occasion' indeed.

How could the Duke applaud concessions, and such concessions, to Catholic peasants who were taking the law into their own hands, refusing to pay any tithes whatever and murdering the police who distrained on their cattle? Besides, 'Lay Appropriation' (of tithes) was an attack on Church property. The men who seized Church property one day would seize yours and mine the next. Was it not the first step towards repeal of the Union? "It will put an end to the Protestant Interest in Ireland; and if the Connection is to be maintained it must be by the Bayonet.'[10]

It would be July, however, before the first Irish Church Bill reached the Lords. With growing confidence in his policy of the extreme centre, Wellington suddenly felt able to divide against the Government in June. Even Greville was impressed by the return of his crowd-magnetism. As they rode through St James's Park on 19 May hats were lifted to him and people stood up. 'I like this symptom,' wrote Greville, 'and it is the more remarkable because it is not *popularity*.' It was a much higher feeling – 'great reverence'. The Duke's surprise attack on the Government, an attack upon Lord Palmerston's foreign policy in Portugal during the debate of 3 June, was to try the people's reverence very hard. The Duke beat the Government by seventy-nine to sixty-nine votes. Dismay and indignation in the Whig ranks. What did the Duke think he was doing? Grey called it a vote of censure intended to overthrow his Ministry. The Duke denied any such intention, so the Ministry was not overthrown.

Exhilarated by the derring-do of June, the Duke rough-sharpened his sabre for the Irish Church Bill in July. He and Peel were still in accord over preserving the Whigs as long as the only alternative was a Radical coup. But short of actually destroying Grey, the Duke felt no inhibitions about brinkmanship. He went down to the House on 11 July and proceeded with great vehemence to pour out the thoughts he had collected from sheaves and sheaves of historic notes on Ireland covering three centuries. 'I consider the Bill utterly inconsistent,' he summed up, 'with the policy of the country since the period of the Reformation.'

The Duke's speech had the worst possible effect. Inflamed beyond endurance, the High Tory peers called a secret meeting at Buckingham's house two days later and resolved to turn out the Ministry on the Irish Church Bill, even if Peel refused to join in forming a new Tory Government. This was mutiny. One of their number, Lord

Strangford, got cold feet and warned the Duke at 8 am next morning to tackle the rebels at a party meeting already scheduled for the following day in Apsley House. 'If something be not done, I fear (from the language held last night,) that we shall again witness *a split*, worse than that of 1829.'[11]

The Duke acted promptly. On Monday 15 July he steadied all but the irreconcilables at the party meeting, arguing that for the Church's own sake the bill must go to committee. He did not intend to oppose the second reading. Four days later, 19 July, his bugles were publicly sounding the 'Recall' to his over-excited troops. 'It appears to me absolutely impossible,' he declared in the House, 'that the Church of England established in Ireland can continue to exist for a day if some measure of this description is not passed to relieve it from its present unfortunate situation.' He admitted that had he been asked to establish the Protestant Church in Ireland for the first time in 1833, he might not have found it necessary to have three archbishops and twenty-two bishops to two thousand clergy – 'but they are there' – and he could not vote for their withdrawal or contemplate a scene where a Catholic bishop might occupy the palace, 'and probably use the very furniture', of the Protestant bishop. At the same time he could not vote against it.

The Ultras, foaming with rage when he abstained, ignored his bugle-call and though outnumbered by 158 to 96 dug in their heels & voted 'Not Content'.

Though the Duke had saved the bill, the crisis had been partly due to his earlier tactical error in exciting the heavy cavalry beyond recall. It was a mistake which he would never have committed on the battlefield. Peel was determined that it should not happen again on the floor of the House. He wrote to the Duke next day making it clear that their joint strategy of pricking rather than puncturing the Government must not itself be punctured in the Lords. The Duke agreed with all Peel's points, explaining only that it was hard for the Lords to realize all of a sudden that they no longer counted. 'The true sense of the position will be inspired at last,' he added grimly, 'when they will become more manageable.'[12]

After the excitement had subsided the Duke was able to please the ruffled bishops by helping to vote down the Jews and Dissenters in their respective attempts to enter Parliament and the ancient universities. Unlike many of his followers who had left long ago for the grouse moors, he stuck out the session to its end, proposing reasoned amendments to the Bank Charter bill on 26 August. Not everyone admired his zeal.

Grey spoke irritably of his 'strange conceit' in appearing to understand every question better than all the world besides and thereby often cutting 'a sorry figure'.[13] Listening to the Duke's indistinct enunciation and looking down on so many bald heads (not his) and trembling limbs – Lord Eldon on someone's arm, Lord Holland wheeled in – the radical Lady Morgan, the Irish novelist, would have liked to see the House of Lords abolished, 'barrier against progress' as it was, manned principally by the aged and infirm.[14]

Notwithstanding these strictures, the Duke had achieved his difficult task of bringing their lordships safely through the session in a state verging on sanity. Neither so badly demoralized by retreats as to make no contribution, nor so dementedly euphoric over successes as to invite condign punishment, their House had avoided the head-on collision with the Commons that the King above all dreaded.

The King had a further reason for being grateful to the Duke. One of those delicate assignments from royalty, which the Duke knew so well how to handle, had helped to keep him in London when others left.

The secret of Mrs Fitzherbert's marriage to the late King had lain dormant with her papers for nearly two years. By the spring of 1832, however, she had begun to regret that her letters were accessible to Sir William Knighton, one of George iv's executors and a man she loathed. Supported by King William, who loved her and also detested Knighton, she requested the other executor, Wellington, either to hand over her letters or destroy them. Knighton refused point-blank to betray his 'sacred Trust'[15] to George iv by handing over any letters, and even the Duke was much alarmed at the possibility of this explosive material afterwards being wormed out of a frail old lady and published. The lie that Charles James Fox had so audaciously told the House – that the Protestant heir was *not* married to a Catholic – must never be nailed.

The Duke began, therefore, by suggesting to Mrs Fitzherbert, with King William's approval, that all the letters and documents exchanged between her and George iv (she possessed his to her) should be destroyed in the presence of a third party. This time it was she who refused. The Duke was baffled, until he discovered that she really wanted to preserve only one love-letter, her marriage certificate and a few other documents of that kind. He devised a solution satisfactory to all. Two peers, Lord Albemarle, the Master of the Horse, and Lord Stourton, her Catholic relative, were appointed by her early in August 1833 to act with the Duke and Knighton. The four agreed to destroy all the papers except those precious few, which should be sealed and locked up in Coutts's bank.

Then followed one of the great letter-burnings in history. The Duke and Albemarle met at Mrs Fitzherbert's house in Tilney Street off Park Lane on 24 August, and for several industrious hours fed Mrs Fitzherbert's drawing-room fire with the records of a long-dead passion. 'I think, my Lord, we had better hold our hand for a while,' said the practical Duke at last, 'or we shall set the old woman's chimney on fire.'[16] Next day the burning was completed, poor Mrs Fitzherbert collapsed and the Duke retired to Stratfield Saye.

The Professor of Poetry at Oxford, the Rev. John Keble, had asked the Duke in March 1833 to be sculpted by the famous Francis Chantrey. Keble and some university colleagues wished in this manner to express their sense of his noble loyalty to the King during May last. Unexpectedly touched, the Duke replied that though no one had approved of his conduct then but himself, he would gladly sit to Mr Chantrey or anyone else they liked.*

The next thing he heard was that Lord Grenville, Chancellor of Oxford, was gravely ill and *he* would be nominated to succeed him. The Duke was overwhelmed. That the golden plum of academic honour should be offered to him, the backward boy who had been sent by his mother and eldest brother to the barrack square instead of an Oxford quadrangle, and afterwards had removed his own two sons and sent them to Cambridge! He could not resist writing to Harriet Arbuthnot: 'What will Lord Wellesley say?'

Sir Robert Peel was deeply hurt. He still had his following in Oxford but others did not like the way he had refused to serve the King in May 1832. In any case most of Oxford wanted a peer. Though the Duke wrote pressing his own disqualifications and Peel's claims, they wanted *him*.[17] He was elected Chancellor on 29 January 1834.

The boyish pleasure came bubbling out when he described to Harriet the first installation ceremony of 7 February at Apsley House and how well he had understood the Latin. 'This shows what attention to a Language for a few days will do.'

His triumph at the Installation of 11–13 June in Oxford was a high

---

* Normally he would skirmish with artists, once complaining that he had been painted in every position except standing on his head.

Tory carnival, a Tory 'Three Glorious Days'[18] – Peel absent but Newcastle, Wetherell, Winchilsea and Eldon there in force, the latter wildly cheered because 'he never ratted!' The Duke, robed in black and gold, stood outwardly unmoved among the scarlet doctors and bewigged bishops as the surges of enthusiasm rolled round him and the stamping feet raised a huge cloud of dust. Wellington himself had to raise his hand to bring the shouting to a close. Two false quantities in his Latin oration did not upset the Duke's poise, though they may have shown what attention to a language for only 'a few days' could do. One of his future tips on public speaking was never to use Latin.

On the last day of the carnival he called at the colleges to render thanks. Mrs Yonge, wife of a Waterloo officer, pushed forward her son Julian, aged four, and daughter Charlotte, eleven, to shake hands. To the immeasurable pride of Julian's family, the Duke kissed him. But afterwards Julian's friends, if they wanted to tease him, would say,

'Show us the place where the Duke bit you.'[19]

The intoxication of Tory Oxford gave Wellington's political position a lift at the right moment. Grey's Government had entered an agonizing final phase.

Grey wound up the Ministry on 8 July 1834, after resignations over a period of six weeks from 'right', 'left' and centre. Of the two major subjects before this Parliament, the coercion of Ireland and the Poor Law, Coercion had brought down a British government. It was not to be Ireland's last achievement in this line.

Having sent for Lord Melbourne after Grey's resignation, King William prorogued Parliament on 15 August in a mood of dynamic despair brought on by Russell's Tithe Bill. The country seemed to share his intense irritability. 'There exists a general uneasiness about something, nobody knows what, and dissatisfaction with everything,' wrote the Duke on 5 October to the King's brother Cumberland now abroad.[20] Later that month the Houses of Parliament were burned to the ground, through a load of old rubbish – used Exchequer tallies – having set fire to a chimney. 'Sweep!' shouted opponents of the Climbing Boys Bill* ironically, as they watched the blaze and drew their own moral; but was it not rather a portent that the first reformed Parliament would never sit again, either in that building or any other?

Soon afterwards Providence seemed to hear the King's cry.

---

* The bill of 1834 forbade 'climbing boys' of under ten from sweeping chimneys. The Duke supported the bill

Melbourne announced to him that the lynchpin of the House of Commons, Lord Althorp, had suddenly been removed from his position as Leader. His father, Earl Spencer, had died on 10 November and Althorp would succeed to the Lords. This was made by Melbourne to sound like the end. If King William persisted with the Whigs, it would mean his having the terrible Lord John Russell himself for leader in the Commons. He summoned Melbourne to Brighton and on 14 November told him that he need not trouble to reconstruct his Government. But he accepted Melbourne's very civil offer to summon his successor – handing him a letter addressed to the Duke. The King, sure of release, was very affable to his former gaoler. That the dismissed Prime Minister had a substantial majority in the Commons did not worry him. Nor that he would go down to history as the first king who had deliberately set out to be a constitutional monarch, and the last who had succeeded in dismissing a government supported by the popular vote. A curious paradox.

The Duke of Wellington was in Hampshire about to go hunting when the King's summons reached him at 8 am next morning. He hurried to Brighton as soon as his carriage was ready. His sudden arrival took all but the King completely by surprise. The Court had been told nothing about the crisis. With the delivery of *The Times* newspaper, however, it became clear that HM's confidential interview with Melbourne was no longer a secret in London, and indeed had been leaked by Brougham to *The Times* with a punch-line of his own invention: 'There is every reason to believe the Duke of Wellington has been sent for. The Queen has done it all.' Holding out the obnoxious passage to his 'retained servant', the King exclaimed,

'There, Duke! You see how I am insulted and betrayed . . . will your Grace compel me to take back people who have treated me in this way?'[21]

The Duke was too old a hand to feel sure that His Majesty had not got himself, by premature action, into a constitutional jam. Nevertheless, what could he do but go to the King's rescue? His willingness to waive his own doubts about the constitutional issue, moreover, gave him the whip-hand over the King on another matter. Peel must be Prime Minister, not himself.

Peel happened to have left England on 14 October for a long holiday abroad; 'just like him,' muttered the Duke, feeling that he must have known about the King's state of mind and ought to have stayed at his post.[22] A lesser man than the Duke might have been tempted to exploit the situation and accept the King's offer. But it was one of the Duke's greatest hours. He had promised Peel not to stand in his way or thwart the country's need for a prime minister in the Commons. Peel must be recalled at once. The Duke declined to form another Wellington administration. Meanwhile as caretaker, he would keep the King's Government going single-handed, until Peel arrived to appoint his own Cabinet.

The Duke's nominal eminence was dazzling: First Lord of the Treasury, Secretary of State for the Home Office, Foreign Affairs and War. The date was 15 November 1834, exactly four years to the day since his fall. If Elba were followed by no more than the prescribed hundred days, they would be a hundred days to take his mind off a tragic personal loss.

Mrs Arbuthnot, for twenty years his dearest friend and confidante, had died of cholera just over three months before.

July 28th, 1834.

My dear Mrs. Arbuthnot,
 I have received your Note and am delighted to learn that you are better. . . .[23]

It was the Duke's last letter to Harriet and the end of a most unusual, subtle and successful essay in triangular friendship.

On the evening of 2 August, while staying with the Salisburys at Hatfield, he received an express from Sir Henry Halford, Mrs Arbuthnot's doctor:

My dear Lord duke! . . . my amiable friend was taken from us at six o'clock this morning. Did not suffer but wandered when was conscious. . . .[24]

The Duke threw down the fatal paper and flung himself on to a sofa. Then he walked about the room for a few minutes almost weeping aloud before he went to his room. Next morning he left at 8 am to be with Charles Arbuthnot.

The first letter from the stricken husband to the Duke was written in a pathetically shaky hand immediately after this visit (5 August) and explained much of their previous relationship.

I am very glad you came to me instead of writing to propose it; for had you, I must have said no. There was no one I so much dreaded seeing for the first sad time – She had no friend to whom She was so much attached as She was to you. . . . I believe I may say that you never had such a friend before & you will never have such a one again. As for myself I without murmur feel the conviction that life to me is from this day a blank. . . .

I am writing all my thoughts to you, for we were *three*, & you will understand – O my dear Duke you feel for me I know – you feel for yourself also –

He then went on to describe his utter dependence on her.

I got into agitations & anxieties which made me unfit for everything; but she relieved me from all troubles . . . all my income was paid in her account – I even went to her for mere Pocket Money – It was my delight & joy to feel that I had such a guardian angel – [25]

In the Duke, Arbuthnot found his new guardian angel, as he never ceased to declare: a guardian who handled his business affairs, got him through a protracted nervous breakdown and took him to live in his house.

That the Duke 'felt for himself' also, to quote Mr Arbuthnot, needs no stressing. Mrs Arbuthnot's special gift lay in devoting herself exclusively to whatever subject occupied her at the moment – her estate and garden, her stepchildren, society, politics. She was a person to be uniquely missed. Nevertheless, young Lady Salisbury, to whom he turned for the next four years, believed the loss of Mrs Arbuthnot to be no more than that of a sincerely loved friend, whatever liaison may have existed in the past. Her death, however, was to expose him to the advances of another woman.

The Duke returned to Apsley House one day in 1834 to find a letter waiting for him from a Miss Jenkins, dated 15 January. It was about his soul. He acknowledged it immediately on the 18th, making one or two blots on his reply and dating it '1833', which Miss Jenkins thought betrayed his agitated feelings.[26] On the anniversary of Kitty's death, 24 April, she therefore delivered a bible at Apsley House with St John, Chapter III, verse 5 marked in pencil: 'Except a man be born again . . . he cannot enter into the kingdom of God.'

The Duke did not answer. Four months later, however, (27 August) the death of Mrs Arbuthnot prompted him to thank the bible lady whose name he had misread as *Mrs* Jenkins. She informed him that she was single and invited him to call. He answered her summons on 12 November 1834 after carefully explaining that he was not in the habit of visiting young ladies with whom he was not acquainted. It was just three days before the royal summons arrived from the King. The extraordinary interview that followed was described by Miss Jenkins in her diary. But first, who was she?

Anna Maria Jenkins, aged twenty and blessed with charms as imperious as her piety, was the orphaned only child of middle-class parents living with a companion, Mrs Lachlan, on a slender income in Charlotte Street. Hitherto her claims to fame had consisted in bringing a murderer named Henry Cooke to a condemned-cell repentance the year before. Now she asked the Lord, what next? 'Greater things than these', came the 'precious' reply. She realized in a flash that this could mean only one thing. The Duke of Wellington must be given 'a new *birth* into righteousness. . . .'

Both of them were struck dumb by the sight of the other: Anna Maria by the Duke's 'beautiful silver head', the Duke by the lustrous young beauty where he had expected an elderly, spinsterish 'Saint'. An arrow had certainly pierced him. He could not speak, so Anna Maria planted a bible between them on the table and raising her lovely hand in the manner which had been so successful with poor Cooke, began to read aloud, '*Ye MUST be born again. . . .*'

The Duke suddenly got his voice back and seizing the uplifted hand in his, repeated over and over again with mounting energy – 'Oh, *how* I *love* you! *how* I *love* you!' Astonished by the vehemence of his expression, Anna Maria asked who made him feel thus. He had the presence of mind to reply, 'God Almighty!'

The Duke was in the midst of intense political preoccupations when they met again on 23 December. He spoke rapidly. 'This must be for life! This must be for life! . . . Do you feel sufficiently for me to be with me a whole life?' The lovely young evangelist deceived herself into misunderstanding his proposal and replied demurely, '*If it be the will of God*'.[27]

After he had gone she began to feel doubts and on 10 January 1835 wrote that he had seemed to forget he was speaking to a virtuous woman. They had better part. By return came a short note repeating his proposal and agreeing that since she could not answer yes, her decision was entirely correct.

Two days later, 12 January, fire and brimstone descended on his 'beautiful silver head'. Oh, that this letter might sink into his rebellious soul: for the Lord alone could 'make crooked things straight'.

The crooked thing again replied by return. Showing himself a better politician than on other occasions, he evaded the issue of whether he had proposed to seduce or marry her and answered a question in the affirmative that she had not asked: yes, he was strongly impressed with veneration for her virtues, attainments and sentiments.[28] So ended the first act of a play which was to continue with intervals until the last year in the Duke's life. When she told him that his being the *Duke of*

Wellington meant nothing to her, since she had never even heard of Waterloo (the second fact was true), he believed her. 'I know it, I know it and I respect you for it.'[29] What he did not know was that once she had decided it was better for him to marry her than to burn, she would never stop trying to become the Duchess. There was indeed a gap of five months in 1835. But when Anna Maria again raised the torch of salvation, his irresistible instinct to answer letters, his courtesy, his loneliness, his pleasure in feminine society, his humble gratitude to a young girl whose apparent interest was in his soul rather than in his dukedom, forced him to respond.

Sir Herbert Maxwell, one of his biographers, robustly writes it all off as 'twaddle'.[30] But the Duke had more to him than common sense. He could suffer and grope for consolation. Life without Mrs Arbuthnot had to answer for life with Miss Jenkins: the calls, the tiffs, the tracts received and the notes sent – all 390 of them. With Mrs Arbuthnot alive, he would not have needed to write more than the first.

There was, however, one advantage in Mrs Arbuthnot's dying at the precise moment when she did. Politically, she had not always been a good influence, particularly in her contempt for Peel. Lady Salisbury now saw in Peel the country's gift from God – a *Dieudonné*.[31] With turbulence and unrest feared for the future, it was vital that Wellington should see this also. At any rate, his conduct as caretaker through the delicate three weeks and more of waiting for Peel was strikingly magnanimous.

Though it was mid-November, London pulsated, carriages bowling to and fro, crowds thronging the streets, clubs humming with political guesswork. What would the Duke do? What would the new Government be? Would it be the rule of 'Humbug' [old Toryism] or of 'Humdrum' – 'an Enlightened-Spirit-of-the-Age Liberal-Moderate-Reform government'? Disraeli, who imagined these pertinent questions in his novel *Coningsby*, also imagined the Duke's answer. 'Nothing could be pumped out of him. All that he knew, which he told in his curt, husky manner, was that he had to carry on the King's government.'[32]

In fact from 15 November until 9 December 1834 the Duke put into operation his own original method of caretaking. He took care of everything himself. He was everybody from Prime Minister downwards, holding five major and three minor offices. People laughed delightedly or groaned with anger to see the determined figure 'roving' about Whitehall, now at the Home Office, his HQ, now at No. 10, a turn in the Foreign Office, a spell in the Horse Guards or Colonial Office and back to the Home Department. The advantage was that government proceeded regularly, but nothing else. No appointments, no decisions, no policy, no legislation; all free and ready for Peel to do as he liked. Only one exception was permitted, the Chancellorship, of which the seals were *lent* to Lyndhurst. It must be admitted that this was a brief paradise for the Duke also. He was one of those who believed passionately in government and coolly in legislation. Now it was his duty to act strictly as he felt.

The Whigs' astonishment had been great – 'kicked out' by the King, as Greville put it, 'in the plenitude of their fancied strength, and utterly unconscious of danger'.[33] As soon as they had got their breath back they used it to denounce Wellington. Not Caretaker but Dictator, was the cry. 'His Highness the Dictator,' Grey wrote indignantly to Princess Lieven, 'is concentrating in himself all the power of the State, in a manner neither constitutional nor legal.'[34]

It did not wash. The people knew their Duke well enough by now to acquit him of personal ambition. A few raised the cry, 'Reform in danger!' but most enjoyed the engaging absurdity of the situation and the current jokes. 'At last we have a united government,' said one wit. 'The Cabinet council sits in the Duke's head and the Ministers are all of one mind.' The Duke laughed with them, and enjoyed referring in later years to his brief period of 'Dictatorship'.

Seriously, he no longer doubted that the King had the constitutional power to dismiss ministers as he had dismissed the Whigs. (Whether he had been wise to use it was debatable.) 'I may be constitutionally responsible for enabling the king to carry on a Government without the aid of his popular Ministers,' admitted the Duke.[35] But that was his only personal involvement. If the King was within his rights, so was the Duke in serving him.

At the same time as the Duke defended his action, he showed exceptional enthusiasm in getting the party organization going, ready for Peel's return and a probable general election. Forgetting his usual aversion from such activities, he congratulated two East Anglian magnates on holding a Conservative dinner in Ipswich and 'entreated' them to stir up all their friends, while an indirect offer from the *Standard* to support his caretaker Government was actually described as candid and fair.

He naturally found no difficulty in turning a deaf ear to the siren or importunate voices of strangers and friends. To the gentleman from Bedford Square, for example, who advised 'a Radical reform' with Disraelian seductiveness: 'The natural allies of the nobility are the common People. Do not, therefore, fear them. They will rally around you to a man. . . .' Or to Lord Londonderry, who urgently demanded the Paris embassy for himself. 'I have not given a single office,' answered the Duke calmly. 'I don't propose to give one. . . .'[36]

There was one anonymous writer who was not snubbed. This man congratulated the Duke on shedding no blood, causing no tears, persecuting no one for former opinions, yet saving the State from anarchy.

Anarchy was in the news. A few months later the great Whig Duke of Bedford, master of Woburn's incalculable wealth, said the nation's choice was now between anarchy and despotism, and he preferred anarchy.

'I can tell Johnny Bedford,' commented the Duke, 'if we have anarchy, I'll have Woburn.'[37]

Peel brought the Duke's 'despotism' to an end by landing at Dover on 9 December, after a dash home across Europe from Rome, where he had been eventually located. He saw the King that same day and with his usual ill luck was able to offer nothing but a display of 'awkward' manners in response to His Majesty's glowing welcome. Peel turned immediately to Cabinet-making. The Duke slid gracefully out of his seven redundant skins, retaining the office of Foreign Secretary; Lyndhurst stayed on as Lord Chancellor, while Peel was Prime Minister and Chancellor of the Exchequer. There were other worthy men in Peel's Cabinet, but not the two he needed to give permanency to his Government – Stanley and Graham.

These two Canningites had left the Whigs but were as yet unable to make the further transition to the Conservatives. They both refused to serve. Without them the fort which Wellington had held might turn out to be built on sand. Perhaps, indeed, Wellington had held the fort a shade too scrupulously. There had been a moment when the royal secretary passed him two letters containing personal appeals to Stanley and Graham from the King. But to ask for their services at that juncture would have meant the Duke's breaking his trusteeship and compromising Peel's liberty of action. His Majesty's letters went into the Duke's pocket. In any case, the Duke could see nothing to keep Peel and the former Canningites apart, now that reform, slavery, the China trade and Stanley's own Irish Bill were 'irrevocably settled'.[38]

The Duke's final words on the Stanley–Graham affair illustrated the contrast between his personal sensitivity and his failure to discern the nuances of parliamentary debate. He heard afterwards from the diehard Lord Wilton that Stanley had been chiefly put off by a speech of the Duke's last session in which he again denounced reform and all its works, including Stanley's.

'I don't believe that I was the real difficulty,' reflected Wellington. 'If I should have thought that I was, I should have been too happy to have gone out of the Way.'[39]

A Stanley for a Wellington? Peel's was not an easy task.

Despite their failure with the Canningites, the Duke and Peel set out bravely to educate the Tories into becoming true Conservatives. It was Peel's first ministry and the choices before his party were still the same three which had faced them since the Duke's crash in 1830. To step back out of the reform flood and try to rebuild on the old Tory rock; to go forward with the (voteless) people under the phantom aegis of a paternal aristocracy; or to become a reforming party hardly distinguishable from the Whigs. Except that Peel's and Melbourne's names were not very amenable to a semantic marriage, the last choice faced Peel with the risk of becoming 'Pelbourne'. Yet this was the choice he made. Moderate reform.

He had returned from his holiday to find everybody expecting an election. He duly called one and prepared for the occasion by a distinctly liberal programme named, from his own constituency, the Tamworth Manifesto.

Having in mind the Duke's return from his political Elba in November 1834, the Ministry in which he now sat as Foreign Secretary might well be called his Hundred Days. Certainly it lasted little longer. From the dissolution of Parliament on 28 December 1834 to Peel's resignation on 7 April 1835 was exactly one hundred days. Its interest, however, rarely lay in the Duke's performance as Foreign Secretary, though one of the Foreign Office clerks later paid him a handsome tribute. Charles Scott, younger son of Sir Walter, in comparing foreign secretaries under whom he had served, described the Duke as 'one by himself "superior and alone" – of the fewest words but those few always straight to the point and doing the business to be done at once – in writing minutes or directions of any kind – short and full and *clear* . . . so simple that almost any one would think "I could have written that" – till he tried. . . .'[40]

The Duke found many old European problems already settled by Palmerston, though not always according to his taste. But if the Duke could not make much impact on foreign affairs, neither could Peel on the statute book. No memorable reforms marked his first premiership. His was a minority Government, harried, thwarted.

The interest of this ministry lay primarily in its being the stage on which the new Wellington–Peel partnership opened. In the Commons, Peel's hand rocked the cradle of Conservatism and should therefore have ruled his world. But there was the shadow of the Lords. Even Wellington was not always willing or able to protect the young party growing up in the other place from its wicked uncles, Londonderry, Newcastle, Cumberland, Buckingham and the like. As Lady Granville put it later, the poor Beau had to 'seesaw' between Peel and the Ultras.[41]

After continuous opposition on his Irish Tithe Bill, a despairing conviction swept over Peel that he could carry on a minority Government no longer. He summoned the Duke to Whitehall Gardens on 24 March 1835 and told him so. The Duke strongly objected, begging Peel to hold on at all costs. What he described as 'a dreadful scene' ensued.[42] The scene achieved little or nothing. for next day, 25 March, Peel announced his intention of resigning in a circular letter to the Cabinet. The Duke again implored Peel to fight on or at least to wait for defeat on an issue which the country would recognize as crucial.

'But surely,' interposed Lady Salisbury, to whom the Duke was telling this story, 'does he not see that his own reputation must be sacrificed if he gives way without absolute necessity?'

'I don't know. He has very bad judgment on these points,' said the Duke, thinking of his own forced resignation in 1830; '– and some people are so wonderfully sensitive. But I think he'll stay.' Nevertheless the Duke could not forget the way Peel's face had worked during that 'dreadful scene' of 24 March – his awful agitation and features 'twisting in a thousand ways', while he himself sat as coolly as possible telling him not to resign. But Peel saw his chance for release in the Opposition's attack on his Irish Tithe Bill and in the steady re-appearances of that old Whig sin, Lay Appropriation (of Tithes), introduced by the inveterate sinner, Lord John Russell. This was an issue on which even the Duke agreed Peel might resign.

The first critical debate came on the night of 2 April. Lady Salisbury told the Duke that Lord Lyndhurst had offered to send her the result at the earliest possible moment next morning.

'I am quite satisfied to have it when the newspapers come in at 10 o'clock,' said the Duke. 'If I could do any good by having it before, I would; but as I can't, I had just as soon wait.'

'You always look at these things coolly,' said Lady Salisbury. 'Now! you never lie awake with anxiety?'

'No, I don't like lying awake – it does no good. I make it a point never to lie awake. . . .'[43]

It was the temperament which had carried him calmly through the last anxious hours before so many victories. Now it prepared him for defeat. He read in his newspapers on 8 April that Peel, after defeats three days running, had lost again on 7 April by twenty-seven votes. This was Peel's fighting finish. He resigned on the 8th. The Hundred Days were over and the Duke had held office for the last time.

The Whigs' debonair and leisurely leader, Lord Melbourne, was by temperament no reformer. In his opinion good seldom came of interference. The earnest violence of the age of reform made no appeal to his easy-going, careless, cynical geniality. Nevertheless, he had one heavyweight reform ready for the 1835 session – a Municipal Corporations Bill powerful enough to clear the ground of feudal debris and lay the foundations for the city and town councils of today. For the first time councillors were to be elected by the ratepayers. What would the House of Lords say?

There was scarcely a moment of controversy which did not result in an Apsley House meeting. It was the peers against Peel, who backed the bill, if not against the people. The Duke was active again on his seesaw.

By the spring of 1837 Lord Melbourne's defeat seemed to be at hand. One half of the country found his measures insufficient and the other half extreme. William IV longed to get rid of him. Old, asthmatic and devoutly supported by his reactionary German spouse, he had been since 1832 'a true King of the Tories'. Some people had pinned their hopes to June 1836 when Mrs Norton's husband cited Melbourne in a divorce case. There had been eager speculation on the result if the suit succeeded.

'Would Melbourne resign?' Greville asked the Duke.

'O Lord, no! Resign! Not a bit of it. I tell you all these things are a nine-days wonder . . . it will all blow over and won't signify a straw.'[44] In any case the suit failed.

Now in 1837 the pressure on Melbourne was political. The battlefields were perforce the old ones, Irish Tithes and Municipal Corporations with a little new skirmishing for the Whigs over Church rates and property. But if the terrain was familiar, the tactics were not. Nothing quite like them had been seen since Wellington and Marmont twisted and coiled round one another for week upon week before the Battle of Salamanca, each trying to drive the other into a fatal position. That Melbourne's resignation was coming no one doubted. 'Is not the probable resignation of the Government the great Question of the Day?' wrote the Duke to Peel in March.[45] But for another two months both sides went on with their sterile yet intricate manoeuvres leading, it was hoped, to the enemy's eventual humiliation and defeat. Suddenly Providence intervened to give one side the victory.

When June arrived the 'true King of the Tories' was desperately ill. He died on 20 June, thus cutting the serpentine knots.

Awaiting the event at Kensington Palace was his successor, the young Princess Victoria, her fair hair neatly braided into a small coronet. Her blue eyes like bubbles on a clear stream searched for the happiness that had so far eluded her youth; but would she find it with the Tories? Lord Melbourne's romantic personal aura and unruffled kindness seemed on the face of it more likely to attract the King's niece.

On the King's instructions Wellington had held the Waterloo banquet as usual, feeling he dared not disobey his Sovereign's last command; but he gave the royal toast with deep melancholy. Afterwards he still had time to do two necessary things before the new reign began. He took his annual 'rent' for Stratfield Saye to Windsor, a small tricolour flag fringed with gold, symbolic of his gratitude to Crown and people for the honours they had done him. The old King buried his face in its folds, happy at having lived long enough to see the sun of Waterloo set on 18 June 1837.

30

Pillar of State

Surely the young Queen's first act would be to send for the Duke? On Waterloo Day 1837 Lady Salisbury bet 5*s* on its happening. But there were rumours of radical and other influences at Kensington Palace. 'I shall lose,' she added.[1]

Lose she did. The Duke was not sent for. He felt no surprise. A week before the accession he had heard that 'Radical Jack' Durham was hastening home from the Continent to establish Victoria as a radical Queen. He thought it not unlikely that 'the transfer of the Crown to the Head of a Young Lady of eighteen years' would go to that young head, making her choose the Radicals 'and the Race for Popularity!'

Soon he and everyone else realized that it was not the Radicals but her Whig Prime Minister for whom the Queen had fallen headlong; her dear, wise, witty Lord Melbourne. The Duke was simply an old hero whom her Mama had entertained now and then at Kensington. For his part he followed the current stories from well outside the magic circle. 'She is surrounded by Whigs and Whiglings male and female,' he wrote in July; 'and Nobody knows any thing excepting Gossip'[2] – gossip about the Queen's dislike of her mother the Duchess of Kent, her loathing for Sir John Conroy, the Duchess's majordomo, and her devotion to the foreign lady, formerly her governess, the Baroness Lehzen.

At the Queen's first Privy Council on 21 June the Duke told Greville 'that if she had been his own daughter he could not have desired to see her perform her part better'. Her part at a Hyde Park review, however, he decided must not be to caracole between himself and Lord Hill. He had been privately consulted by the Court about her wish to ride on a horse instead of in a carriage with her ladies. The Duke reported back to Windsor on the '*unsuitableness*' of her being attended on horseback 'by men *only*'. What a target she would present to the caricaturists by surrounding herself with 'such youths as Lord Hill and me'. She was trying to do a Queen Elizabeth at Tilbury, he suspected; but as there was no threat of an Armada in 1837, what was the point?[3]

This was the first clash between the old hero and the young girl. The girl won. In August she was prancing between the two venerable 'youths', thin bent Wellington and 'old Fatty Hill', as Creevey called the Commander-in-Chief.

There were other signs that the little Queen intended to ride a high horse. At a Buckingham House banquet on 19 July the Duke of Wellington was the only Tory present, and he had not been admitted in his own right. 'Chancellor of Oxford' was on his place-card. 'It is curious that she should not be able to venture to invite the Duke of Wellington to dinner excepting as Chancellor of Oxford,' he wrote to Arbuthnot next day. 'I keep the Card as a real curiosity.'[4]

The statesman whose beloved name appeared so frequently in the Queen's journal that it soon had to be shortened to 'Lord M' made a poor impression on the electorate. At the general election there were ominous demands from the left that Melbourne should repeal the Corn Laws and push radicalism further by introducing the secret ballot, frequent parliaments and universal suffrage. But the Leader of the House, John Russell, in his new role of 'Finality Jack', refused any further extension of the franchise.

On Melbourne's right, the Tories made overall election gains of thirteen, leaving the slim Whig majority further attenuated. Tories were returned *en masse* for the English counties, a result that compensated them for defeat in Ireland. Foreseeing this situation, the Duke was delighted to have persuaded the gentlemen of Northamptonshire, of whom Arbuthnot was one, to hand over their election fund to Dublin. Behaviour as handsome as it was rare, he wrote, 'There is nothing so selfish as the collection of money for the purposes of an Election.'[5] Altogether the Tories were in good heart. The Duke particularly liked the story of the Tory candidate at Canterbury.

'Sir,' said a man he was canvassing, 'I would as soon vote for the devil.'

'But, Sir, if your friend should not stand,' pursued the Tory candidate, 'may I then hope for your support?'

The Conservatives of the day, Wellington argued, would no doubt support Melbourne when he deserved it; but soon they would have passed from the stage. (The Duke was now sixty-eight.) Their successors, having been alienated by Whig measures, a Whig Court and the exclusion of their caste from government by the Reform Bill, would refuse to give a future Whig government the support which 'good sense' dictated.[6]

This was the Duke despairing of the future. Fortunately these moods never made him any less assiduous in helping the present.

His decision to stand alone, pursue a straightforward course and wait for a fair stand-up fight (to use a few of his favourite expressions) involved him in all the old problems of leadership over again. Canada, where insurrections had broken out in both the Upper and Lower Provinces, proved to be this major new issue.

On 18 January 1838 the crisis was debated in the Lords. The Government were on the mat. In a happy state of suspense the Opposition peers waited for the great Duke to pulverize Melbourne for the disgraceful inadequacy of the armed forces in Canada. But the Duke said to the House exactly what he had privately said to Lord Melbourne, namely, that in this context he could not blame him.

Collapse of Conservative hopes. Lord Mahon rushed from the Carlton Club saying that the Duke had floored the coach. Lord Londonderry declared that the Duke's speech had stopped Ellenborough and Aberdeen from making 'mince meat' (his favourite dish) of the Government. Aberdeen agreed that but for the Duke's fatal intervention the Government might have fallen. Angry Lord Wharncliffe was reminded of Wellington's anti-reform speech and thought he had again gone further than he meant, 'not having a perfect use of his weapon when he speaks'. Peel climbed into his pulpit and wagged a cold finger at Wellington. He was risking the unity of the party.[7]

The Duke sizzled with resentment. He told the shocked Lady Salisbury that he did not care sixpence about the party turmoil. He had done the right thing.

By February he had helped to restore his popularity by preaching preparedness: 'There is no such thing as a *little War*,' he said, 'for a great Nation.'* In his own mind, however, contempt for the party zealots only deepened when there was a move to join with the Radicals in a vote of censure on Melbourne's Colonial Secretary, tabled for 7 March. It was temporarily thwarted by Peel, but the dreaded conjunction between Conservatives and Radicals happened at last on 7 May. The Whigs, at loggerheads with the Jamaican planters, asked Parliament to

---

* This famous remark was first made to Fitzroy Somerset on 5 January by letter. The Duke repeated the words in Parliament on 16 January and again on 2 February, afterwards explaining to Sir Willoughby Gordon by letter what he meant: namely, a great nation's interests were so wide that they were bound to touch the interests of other nations at many points. (Maxwell, vol. 11, p. 319; *Wellington MSS; Speeches*.)

dissolve their House of Assembly. At once both Conservatives and Radicals raised an outcry. Caught in this crossfire, the Government survived with a majority of only five votes. For a party already staggering, this was a fatal fall. Melbourne resigned next day.

The Duke realized something of what it would mean for the Queen to lose her Whig ministers. 'I have no small talk,' he said, 'and Peel has no manners.' But he could not foresee the depth of the Queen's misery at the changes, or the kindly foolishness of Melbourne's plan for alleviating it. He advised her to keep at least the ladies of her Household unchanged. The distraught young Queen snatched at this straw. Beleaguered as she already felt by the Hastings set, how could she open her palace gates to them and their like as Tory ladies-of-the-bed-chamber? Five votes in the Commons blew up the Flora Hastings scandal into the Bedchamber Plot.*

Queen Victoria has described with inimitable panache her deplorable but highly diverting victory over Wellington and Peel combined. Let Wellington give the story from his angle, as he told it to Greville three months later.

The Queen saw him for twenty minutes in the Yellow Closet on 8 May. Coached beforehand by Melbourne, she began by asking him to be Prime Minister. He explained that his years and deafness were prohibitive. Peel was her man.

'But what am I to do if he proposes appointments that are disagreeable to me?'

'Fight upon the details as much as you please,' advised the shrewd tactician, 'but make no conditions as to principles, and depend upon it, there will be every disposition to consult your wishes and feelings in every respect.' She agreed. Then she said:

'You must promise me to be Secretary of State for Foreign Affairs.'

The Duke again demurred. This was the same constitutional error which her late uncle, William IV, had tried to perpetrate in 1834. He did not think much of the Queen's political education, but gently told her that the Prime Minister must make his own appointments. Once more she agreed.

'Will you desire him to come to me?' She must write to Peel herself.

Would he then tell Peel she was writing? He would.

The first interview left the Duke 'excessively pleased' with HM's

---

* Lady Flora Hastings, the unmarried lady-in-waiting of Victoria's mother, was cruelly suspected by Victoria and Melbourne of being pregnant by Conroy, when in fact she was dying of a tumour.

docility and frankness. Peel reported himself perfectly satisfied by his own subsequent interview. When the Queen brought up her Household he promised that no changes should be made without her agreement. But if he was satisfied, she was distraught. She wept passionately after the two interviews. Lord M. had warned her she would find Peel close and stiff. He had in fact minced and shuffled like a dancing-master. But the dancing-master should not send *one* of her ladies – not Baroness Lehzen above all, her beloved friend and Conroy's enemy – off the floor.

Next day Peel returned to the palace in 'perfect security' of a tranquil arrangement. Instead the Queen catapulted her famous stone into the middle of Goliath's forehead. She must retain *all* her ladies.

'All?'

'All.'

'The Mistress of the Robes and the Ladies of the Bedchamber?'

'All.'

Peel was suddenly unnerved. He fell back on the obvious remedy. The Duke must see her next day. She consented; but this time the Duke told Greville she was not only in high passion and excitement but extremely naive and girlish.

'Well, I am very sorry to find there is a difficulty,' he opened.

'Oh, *he* began it and not me,' she retorted. 'It is offensive to me to suppose that I talk to any of my ladies upon public affairs.'[8]

'I know you do not . . . but the public does not know this,' he answered. He went and fetched Peel from the room next door, where he was waiting, close and stiff.

Where the Duke had failed Peel was powerless, though never before had the Duke seen him 'so gentle and conciliatory'. On 10 May everyone knew that Peel had thrown up his commission. Melbourne stood by the Queen as the Duke had stood by the King five years before. He reconstituted his Whig Government. To see the two old Tories, Wellington and Peel, looking very much put out at her ball on the 10th, gave 'Little Vixen', as Creevey had once affectionately called her, immense pleasure.

Greville and his Establishment friends did not try to hide their feelings of disgust. The pillar of state had been overthrown. There was something peculiarly shocking in 'this mere baby of a queen setting herself in opposition to this great man, the decus and tutamen of the kingdom'. It was all a terrible 'Scompiflio'.*[9] Someone rounded off the

---

* Greville found relief in bizarre language. *Decus et tutamen* (glory and guardian) were on the 'Crown' coins of 1688. 'Scompiflio' was an Italian word for confusion or disorder.

affair with a good, simple Tory joke: 'One has often heard of the country going to the dogs – but never before of a country going to the bitches!'[10]

The Duke further angered the Queen by insulting, in her eyes, Prince Albert. He voted for an allowance of £30,000 instead of £50,000; and he opposed the Prince's precedence over the royal dukes. It was only at the last minute that she invited 'the Old Rebel' to her wedding. The Duke commented drily: 'I hear that our Gracious is very much out of Temper.'[11]

The Duke's first speech in the House after the return of Melbourne to office, on 14 May 1839, struck his friends with dismay. It was not only the subject-matter – he spoke of 'anomalous influences' at the Palace – but the delivery. This was a good deal more anomalous: the emphasis on unimportant words, the whispers alternating with shouts, the 'drop by drop' pace, the swaying on his feet. But nothing happened this time. By July he was telling Lady Douro, his elder son's wife, he was very well and could continue the session for another twelve months if need be. He was also telling Lord Aberdeen with angry sarcasm what he thought of his leaving early for Scotland: 'With all my heart be it so! I will not desire anybody to *stay*! I have before now stood; and I can *stand alone*!'[12]

Then came 15 October. Young Lady Salisbury died, that perfect confidante of the Duke's who had rivalled Mrs Arbuthnot for good sense. Just over a month later, on 19 November, he had a stroke and was found by his valet lying on the floor of his room at Walmer. He recovered consciousness after three-quarters of an hour and then his sight and speech. He had been starving a cold the week before and also hunting. When he felt the attack coming on he had tried to 'walk it off'. After a few days he insisted that he was quite well and got to the Privy Council on the 23rd for the Queen's declaration of marriage. She looked round for him kindly and was glad to see him there.[13] But everyone noticed that his mouth and right arm were still slightly affected.

By Christmas the after-effects had disappeared. In this year, however, he first developed his beast-of-burden theme. He declined a Pitt Club dinner in April with the words:

Every Animal in the creation is allowed some relaxation from Exertion . . . except the Duke of Wellington. All that the Duke can say is this: that if such relaxation is not allowed him; he must take the Liberty of giving it to Himself.[14]

After Lady Salisbury's funeral he coined his half-ironic, half-serious phrase about being a costermonger's donkey. Lord Mahon had suggested his resting:

Rest! [he echoed] Every other animal – even a donkey – a costermonger's donkey – is allowed some rest, but the Duke of Wellington never! There is no help for it. As long as I am able to go on, they will put the saddle upon my back and make me go.[15]

The real truth was that he needed neither carrot nor stick to make him go; just sense of duty.

Three months later, in February 1840, he was smitten again, first with giddiness in the House of Lords and soon afterwards with another seizure while riding over to Lady Burghersh in Harley Street. He could not read her door number and only just reached home with his groom holding the reins of both horses. This time Croker predicted the end of the Duke's public life, Lady Palmerston (formerly Emily Cowper) thought he would not last long, and M. Guizot, the French ambassador, recognized in his empty and extinct eyes a sign that 'the soul, about to depart, no longer bothers to show itself'.[16]

Miss Jenkins offered to come to Apsley House and nurse him. He replied frostily: 'The Duke is much obliged to Her. He is quite well. He has no reason to believe that he will have occasion to trouble Her upon any object whatever.' At which Anna Maria swotted him with a text. 'Let NOT Him that girdeth on his harness *boast himself* as he that putteth it off. I Kings, XX. II.' In August he told her that he would write no more. Whether he wrote again or not depended not on him but on the Lord, she retorted. No more letters, the Lord decided, for four years.[17]

Meanwhile Sir Ashley Cooper, the Duke's neurologist, was amazed by the completeness of his recovery. He resisted a spell at Bath or Auschowitz but agreed to take fluid magnesia for his stomach recommended to the army and navy after hard drinking and for 'Irritability of Pregnant Females'.

The forties were upon them. What would the Duke offer to the Tories in the way of leadership? Precious little. 'If the House of Lords act wisely,' he wrote curtly to Croker, 'they will not be in a hurry to attack the government. I can say no more. . . .' The peers wanted him to say a great deal more. Even Peel was beginning to think like an activist. At the end of January the Duke did indeed admit to Lady Wilton, his new confidante, that there was 'a screw loose in the machine' – the Government machine.[18] But he still preferred offering a screwdriver rather than summoning the demolition squad. By August his bipartisanship had been carried so far that he jokingly looked forward to attending Whig Cabinet dinners. This was all very difficult for a renaissant Tory party which meant to win and win soon. But when French ambitions in the Middle East threatened war, Wellington's was the name to conjure with.

In the event of war, the King of Prussia asked him in 1840 to command the armies of the German Confederation. 'Mine is a most extraordinary Position,' reflected the Duke truthfully. Here he was at nearly seventy-two, still the greatest warrior-name in Europe. He must remember to be humble, he told Lady Wilton, or he would have the Soothsayer after him, sending him a 'Memorandum' like the one he had sent Caesar. 'Beware!'

The Ides of March, 1841, brought Wellington nothing worse than fears and forebodings. His professional expertise told him that in these perilous times his country was not adequately armed: 'We are not and are not likely [to be] in a state to defend ourselves. . . .'[19]

For the Whigs, things were desperate. They did indeed get through March and even as far as June, but always in a hubbub of old and new cries which they could neither appease nor ignore. Corn and sugar duties were assailed with peculiar ferocity. The Duke heard of a meeting in Salford where a Tory speaker had put Free Trade before all political parties. 'The gentleman was prepared to be Tory, Conservative, Whig, Radical or Chartist – (Hear) – to accomplish this great object – (Loud cheering).' The minds of both leaders, Peel and Russell, were stretched and harassed by the new situation, but Russell was in the hotter seat.

Two years earlier, when the writer Samuel Rogers had remarked to Wellington upon the host of Conservative talent in the Commons against one talented Whig, Russell, the prompt answer came, 'John Russell is a host in himself.' Now the host had literally dwindled to one. At 3 am on 5 June 1841 the Government were defeated on a vote of confidence by 312 to 311 – one vote. All the good hats flew up into the air and the bad hats were crammed down on anxious faces. Would their leader resign? Not Melbourne. He decided to wait till Parliament was prorogued and then try his luck, as the Queen wished, at the polls. It would at least give her a few more weeks of his company.

Raikes said it was just like the Whigs not to go out like gentlemen.

'They will only go out,' said the Duke, 'when compelled by the police.'[20]

They were compelled by the people.

Wellington's 'Elba' and his 'Hundred Days' had taught him much about the age of reform. Meanwhile he had learnt – and taught others – almost as much from his Chancellorship of Oxford.

'Let these boys loose,' said the new Chancellor of Oxford University, astonished by the joyous bedlam at his installation in June 1834 – 'Let these boys loose in the state in which I saw them, and give them a political object to carry, and they would revolutionize any nation under the sun.'[21]

Curiously enough it was not the boys of Oxford who were to be let loose during his first stirring decade of office. These young men of good family, a large proportion of whom would enter the Church, chose to show the indiscipline of youth in private extravagance and debts. Various attempts by the University to introduce stiffer laws against student luxury received short shrift from the Duke. A quarrel with Christ Church over his own son Charles had taught him a lesson. By 1838 he believed that better discipline in the home was the answer. Not that he disapproved of college discipline – far from it – but 'the liberal World of the day' insisted on fewer rules, not more. Therefore to a complaining parent the Duke offered his own solution: 'If a Youth is not fit to be treated immediately as a Man under the Discipline of a College in the University, he should be kept in his Father's House or at a private tutor's till he becomes sufficiently ready.'[22] He had little sympathy with those who could not keep order in their own house. When he heard that the flogging headmaster of Eton, Dr Keate, boasted of having subdued an insurrection among his boys, the Duke expressed nothing but contempt:

'You might as well talk of an insurrection in a fishpond. The fish might just as well talk of an insurrection.'[23]

Only once during the Duke's tenure at Oxford did the boys break loose. It was at a public degree-giving in the Sheldonian Theatre. A deafening uproar earned the four ringleaders a grand total of twelve years' rustication. But on this occasion, 1845, the small fry behaved no worse than the big fish. They were mainly barracking a don who had hired private detectives to pry into their rooms. The big fish, the professors, fellows and tutors, joined in, raising a hubbub that wrecked the bestowal of an honorary degree upon Mr Edward Everett, the American minister and a *Unitarian*.

Here was the clue to the turbulent Oxford of the thirties and forties – religion. The Christian theologians were the ones to be let loose. Within the fold there were wild bleats and battle-cries, sheep biting sheep to right and left, and coming away with great lumps of wool in their teeth.

The Duke's Oxford was less like its descendant of today than any other institution with which he had to deal, for the majority of its dons were in holy orders. Parliament, the army – changed as they are, he would still know them if he returned. In Oxford he would no longer find the prevailing wind of clerical draperies swishing round every corner and softly nudging one another at every high table, nor the rings of white clerical collars singing together in planetary harmony or discord.

There was a violent upheaval over the appointment by Melbourne of a Whig Evangelical as Regius Professor of Divinity. Dr Renn Dickson Hampden, though no soul-mate of the Duke, must be 'made the best of'; schism in the church would be worse. Particularly as this mere College Hampden was swiftly followed by the High Church 'Tractarians', another potential schism that the Duke handled equally adroitly. Apart from Low and High Church attempted 'revolutions', the reforming spirit which Wellington always dated from 1830 was unlikely to bypass Oxford and Cambridge. He was not surprised therefore when the radical 3rd Earl of Radnor raised the question in 1835 of reforming some of the Universities' statutes with a view to admitting dissenting sects.

As a pillar of Church and State the Duke was opposed to reform in this direction. He automatically decided to defend Oxford against an aggressive Parliament. At the same time, as a sensible man he could not but agree that one of the conditions for admission to the University, namely 'subscription' to the Thirty-Nine Articles, was indefensible. How could a callow youth of seventeen be expected to understand and subscribe to such intricacies? On this matter, he urged, Oxford must accept reform. Either the ancient statute must be altered 'to suit the altered Circumstances of the times', or, if kept unchanged, explained away by a new statute: 'We shall not long be able to resist some alteration, and I earnestly entreat the University to make it themselves.'

The House of Lords defeated Radnor's bill. Undeterred, he struck again in 1837 on a wider front. He proposed an enquiry into the college statutes of Oxford and Cambridge through which, as interpreted by

College Visitors, the individual colleges ultimately controlled entry into the Universities. The Duke made his own enquiries. It appeared that College Visitors were no safeguard against ancient abuses. Some colleges had statutes drawn up centuries ago which restricted candidates for scholarships to 'founder's kin' or a county of England whose supply of eligible young men had long since dried up. His answer to Oxford was a trumpet call for reform:

The Colleges have but one course to follow. That is to look into their own Affairs, and to put them in order themselves. Let each of them which has a Visitor and the Power of Legislation consider its Statutes, repeal all that is anomalous and obsolete, and frame a code suitable to the University and to the times.[24]

When some colleges leapt to the conclusion that the Conservative success in the 1837 election would save them from the need to reform at all, the Duke wrote sternly:

There is not in Oxford a Gentleman who dislikes innovation and change so much as I do. But I live in the World, I know the Times in which and the Men with whom I live. Even the best Friends of the University ... will not support the existing order of things.[25]

In the course of his first seven years as Chancellor, 1834–41, the Duke had spoken often and often about the spirit, circumstances or symptoms of the times. When he returned to political power in the summer of 1841 as a member of Peel's cabinet, the University and its colleges were not yet reformed.

The battle had nonetheless enabled him to see the spirit of the times in a new light. By contrast with some of the college's obscurities, it seemed a spirit to be tolerated, even fostered. The lesson was a valuable one for the next five years with Peel.

31

Rightabout Face!

What was to be the Duke's position in the new Government? The 1841 election had given Peel a Conservative majority of ninety-one. It also gave him the opportunity to form a superlatively strong Cabinet, including five prime ministers past, present and to come. The Duke had clarified his own requirements well in advance of victory. 'The truth is that all that I desire is to be as useful as possible to the Queen's service,' he wrote to Peel on 17 May 1841, ' – to do anything, go anywhere, and hold any office, or no office, as may be thought most desirable. . . . I don't desire even to have a voice in deciding upon it.'[1] But in case Peel wished to know his opinion, he gave it: the best thing would be for him to continue in the Cabinet as Leader of the Lords but for the first time without office. He would thus be free to deal with any trouble-spots.

Thanks largely to the Duke, the Palace was no longer a trouble. His personal success with the Queen was of great use in dispelling any Whig miasma that might remain. As early as August 1840 she had shown him incipient favour. He sat next to her at dinner. 'She drank wine repeatedly with me,' he reported; 'in short, if I was not a milksop, I should become her Bottle Companion.' Six months later the milksop (he concentrated on iced water these days) was invited to stand proxy for the Queen's father-in-law, the Duke of Saxe-Coburg-Gotha, at the Princess Royal's christening: 'I must be in favour to be thought of as a Beau Père!' In 1842 he had lent Walmer Castle to the Queen and her young family for a blast of sea air. There was only one untoward event when her postilions failed to negotiate the Castle entrance. 'She Stuck in it, and was obliged to get out of the Carriage.'[2] Even in old age the Duke was accustomed to drive himself and his guests at breakneck speed along the narrow lanes of Walmer. Sometimes they trembled; they never stuck.

And then, in January 1845, the Queen conferred the most daunting favour of all by inviting herself to stay at Stratfield Saye House. The

Duke was for once staggered by a problem of logistics. How fit HM and all her train into a gentleman's residence which, though undoubtedly the most comfortable, was not the largest in the world? He put these points tactfully to HM. 'She smiled and continued to be very gracious, but did not give a Hint of postponing the Visit.'

By dint of many ingenious makeshifts culminating in a proposal to harbour any high sheriffs, mayors and corporations who might turn up, in the tennis court, an unexpected success was made of the visit. 'I thank God!' he wrote to Lady Wilton afterwards, 'the visitation is concluded. I have just now returned from attending Her Majesty on Horseback to the Borders of the County.'[3] From Queen Victoria's journal it appears that he not only saw her off the premises but attended almost every step she took, showing her to her room, fetching her for dinner, helping her generously to pudding, talking to her confidentially on the sofa in the hearty tones of the deaf and lighting her up to bed. Prince Albert had a go at tennis when there were not too many spectators and, according to Florence Nightingale, was also 'taught to miss at billiards'.[4] The Peels were staying in the house and the Queen noted that Albert had talks with the Prime Minister.

The whole visit, like the rest of the Duke's work with the Queen, was invaluable to Peel. Only one question arose. Was it possible that the Duke had succeeded almost too well in impregnating the shy and sensitive Peel with his own enthusiasm for the Crown? If the Duke had a hand in firing Peel with excessive chivalry, he would have something to answer for at the end of the year.

A great experiment had been planned to begin in 1842. It rested on two things: a united party and a breakthrough in legislation. At long last Peel and Wellington were leading a combined force of Conservatives like themselves, former Canningites like Stanley and Ultras like Buckingham. And whither was this united force to march? Into Peel's promised land: a land of financial stability and economic growth; a land where the revenue which had fallen under the Whigs would rise again, where manufacturers would get cheaper raw materials and so increase production and employment, where consumers would get cheaper food and so buy more manufactured goods; to be precise, a land of tariff reform and income tax.

Peel had watched the horrors of the winter. Thousands had to be fed by charity. In Paisley alone £600 a week was needed to keep the people from starving. Yet charity was a wretchedly haphazard net in which to catch the unfortunate. There was the ghastly story from the Anti-Corn Law League of a hand-loom weaver in the midst of his family found dead at his loom. Peel exclaimed passionately, 'Who was the relieving officer? Why did he neglect his duty?'[5]

The League and the Chartists raged. The League could count on additional support in the Commons, their leader Richard Cobden becoming a member. Peel's aim was to get the economy going and let the people save themselves, first from starvation and then from Chartism. To Wellington, Chartism was a greater menace than misery. Nature had made him a keeper of order rather than a creator of laws. Peel's imaginative genius for law-making was something he respected but could not imitate.

When Parliament met in 1842 the great experiment was announced. Duties on corn and meat were to be lowered while the tariffs on a mass of other products would be reformed or removed. To make up for loss of revenue, a three-year experimental income tax was to be imposed for the first time on a peacetime Britain: 7d in the £ on all incomes over £150 per annum.

Even a cynic like Greville was impressed by Peel's vision and competence. 'One felt all the time he was speaking,' wrote Greville of his great financial exposition on 12 March, ' "Thank God, Peel is Minister".' Others felt the opposite. Fat old Buckingham, unable to forget his promises at agricultural dinners to maintain the Corn Laws, had already resigned as Lord Privy Seal. Lord Hardwicke left the Queen's Household. Wellington said roundly that Buckingham and Hardwicke had been fools. 'Both will be the ridicule of the whole nation.'[6]

While the mass of Conservative protectionists gulped and swallowed the changes, the Whig and Radical out-and-out free traders declared Peel's tariff reform to be an insult and his income tax a crime. They had denounced the latter when Castlereagh tried to maintain it after Waterloo and they denounced it again now. Harriet Martineau, the radical author, who carried two hearing-aids, one long and one short to scoop up radical wisdom from far and near, wrote:

There is something transcendently disgusting in an Income Tax, which not only takes a substantial sum immediately out of a man's pocket, but compels him to expose his affairs to a party [the Tax Collector], that he would by no means choose for a confidant.[7]

Nevertheless the tax collector worked away, the revenue in time began to float and even become buoyant, and in 1845 this 'criminal' miracle measure was re-enacted for another three years.

Ireland had temporarily lost the limelight. Plenty of disagreeable rumours were abroad in 1842 such as the report of fifty thousand Americans coming to the assistance of Irish rebels. The undeniable facts, however, were not reassuring. After the defeat of the Whigs, O'Connell and his surviving Irish MPs renewed their demand for repeal of the Union. They developed a powerful repeal programme, with a repeal 'Rent' target of £3 million, non-payment of landlords' rent and over forty monster meetings to destroy 'spinning-jenny Peel' and 'Wellington the old Buccaneer', the two defenders of the Union. The Duke's informants, mainly Government spies, Protestant parsons and Orange peers, reported frequent use among Nationalists of the sinister phrase, 'When the Day comes'.

According to the Government, O'Connell's 'Day' was planned for 8 October, with a monster meeting at Clontarf near Dublin. 'The Duke for Ireland' was not a slogan which attracted Peel though the Duke was again Commander-in-Chief. That great gun must not speak unless there were a mutiny or actual rising. But if the Duke could not go to Clontarf, O'Connell and his million men should not go there either. At the last minute the Cabinet issued a proclamation banning the Clontarf meeting. Six days later, on the 14th, Daniel O'Connell was arrested and condemned by a packed jury to a year's imprisonment and a fine of £2,000. Though the House of Lords later quashed the sentence by four to one, it is said that the six months which O'Connell served in prison began his break-up. When the next lethal blow struck a million of his countrymen, he too was dying.

Peel sent his dire news to Wellington on 15 October 1845. The Irish potato crop was a failure. A strange potato disease had already appeared in the south of England that summer and in North America three years earlier. The difference was that English and American potatoes were food; Irish potatoes were the only food. Loss of a potato crop anywhere meant suffering; in Ireland it meant dying. Lord Wellesley had once found his Irish marquessate, given as a reward for his services in India, a pitiful thing, a mere 'gilt potato'. To the Irish peasant his potato was truly gilded with the blessing of life itself. When his potato turned black, then indeed life in Ireland would be a pitiful thing.

The tone of Peel's letter to the Duke conveyed a sense of emergency. He had already told the Home Secretary and Lord-Lieutenant just what he was considering – complete repeal of the Corn Laws in order that cheap grain might enter famine-stricken Ireland: 'The removal of impediments to import is the only effectual remedy.'[8] Perhaps because the Duke was leader of the landed aristocracy who lived and moved and had their being in the Corn Laws, Peel did not yet mention to him their repeal.

Throughout November Peel consulted, but far from pushed, his Cabinet colleagues. Then with Lord John Russell's recent public conversion to free trade ringing in his ears, he sent a definitive memorandum on 29 November. It made little attempt to convert the doubters, and its pedantic tone greatly irritated opponents. 'Shall we modify the Corn Law, shall we maintain it, or shall we suspend it for a limited period?' was Peel's routine formula, followed by his own recommendation of suspension.

The Duke's answer to the memorandum was the most important and forthright Peel received. He was against repeal of the Corn Laws but was more against a split. While unconvinced by Peel's arguments, he promised faithfully to support Peel's action. Reluctantly a majority of the Cabinet took the same decision. Two stood out. Lord Stanley and the Duke of Buccleuch stuck to protection.

Stanley's opposition finished Peel. With this leading figure in the Lords vociferously against him and his Cabinet colleagues in the Commons lukewarm, he felt his mission to repeal the Corn Laws hopeless. On 6 December his resignation was accepted by the Queen at Osborne. He had behaved with absolute honesty towards his colleagues but without the slightest magnetism. From the Duke, however, he had not concealed his acute suffering in reaching the momentous decision on corn, above all his anguish for Ireland. 'I cannot doubt,' wrote the Duke soon afterwards to an incredulous Croker, 'that which passed under my view and frequent observation day after day. I mean Peel's alarm at the Consequences to Ireland of the Potato Disease. I never witnessed in any case such Agony!'[9]

The Queen sent for Lord John Russell, but could he form a ministry? What became known as the 'Ten Days' of waiting for Russell, between 10 and 20 December, were spent by Wellington in writing enormous letters to his bewildered friends.

From these it is clear that the Duke envisaged no break-up in the Conservative party, but varying degrees of opposition to Russell's Free Trade measure. Such a solution was not to be.

'Another *coup de tonnère* this morning!' wrote Lord Mahon excitedly to the Duke at 2 pm on Saturday 20 December. 'Lord John Russell's attempt to form a government is over!'

The Duke had already that morning received a hurried scrawl from Peel. After having accepted, Lord John had declined to form a government and Peel was summoned to Windsor:

I am going to the Queen – I shall tell her at once, and without hesitation that I will not abandon her – whatever happens. I shall return from Windsor as her Minister –[10]

The Duke was delighted with Peel's breathless promises of loyalty. Lord John Russell had failed because of fierce opposition by his colleagues to having Palmerston again as Foreign Secretary.

The Prime Minister replied to his Sovereign's appeal with a happy oblivion of colleagues surely unique in the annals of Downing Street.

'I want no consultations, no time for reflection. I will be your Minister, happen what may. I will do without a colleague, rather than leave you in this extremity.'[11] Stanley was the first to resign, but two days later a euphoric Peel rejoiced to inform the Duke that he had persuaded Bucchleuch to remain in office and Gladstone to enter the Cabinet as Colonial Secretary: 'a good beginning'.[12] It was a good beginning of the end.

'The Duke says, "rotten potatoes have done it all; they have put Peel in his d—d fright"; and both for the *cause* and the effect he seems to feel equal contempt.'[13] So wrote Greville at the time when illusory hopes were rising. Nevertheless the Duke spent the whole interval between 20 December and 27 January, when Peel was to address Parliament on repeal of the Corn Laws, in trying to quell with his indefatigable pen the Tory mutineers and doubters – Redesdale, Beaufort, Croker, Salisbury, Rutland; some of them with three, four and five letters apiece. Redesdale was told that the Queen had to choose between Peel and Cobden, Russell having failed her. 'We are very sick!' he said honestly. 'God send us a good deliverance.'

Redesdale refused to help send it. He resigned as whip and sent the Duke a scorpion of a message on Christmas Day: 'Better that we should go into opposition than cut our throats.' Of course we must examine everything, retorted the Duke. 'But I do not at once declare against a Man who says to his Queen, Happen what may, I will stand by you. . . .' It was Peel's duty 'to rescue the lady from Cobden'.[14]

Croker, a more damaging critic because a contributor to the *Quarterly*, attacked the Duke's attitude with increasing vehemence: 'Whatever broke you upon the *10th* Decr. was equally in force when you reunited on the *20th*. This is *my guess* but I don't ask *yours*.' Croker's guess was right. Corn had split them then and still did. He passionately urged his Grace to give up the key of his Cabinet boxes and let Peel face the music. 'But – ' continued Croker, 'then you ask Where is a Government to be found? I reply – Let Peel answer *that*. Let him make a Government of *those who agree in his opinions*.' The voice of the Duke's old friend had become uncommonly rasping, especially about the Cabinet key. There was only one possible answer for the Duke to make: 'I am the retained Servant of the Sovereign of this Empire.'[15]

It was a pleasanter duty to write pages and pages for Lord Salisbury's guidance on Ireland, discussing public works, a market economy and imported maize, with a copy and covering letter for the Duke of Rutland. He reminded Rutland encouragingly of their Sunday morning walks when 'you and I generally take the same view of political Questions'. His message for all of them now was to have patience until Peel spoke in the new year. As long as Peel enjoyed the Queen's and the public's confidence he must be supported. 'A good Government is more important than Corn Laws.'[16]

Parliament met at last. On 26 January Wellington extolled in the Lords a Prime Minister who next day was to shine magnificently in the Commons. Showing Peel in the light of what the Duke afterwards called 'a warm-hearted enthusiast', he based his leader's claim to support on that leader's own support for the Queen. Pleased with his idea, he drew Lady Wilton's attention to the pleasure it had also given Sir Robert:

You will be amused by my representing Him to the House a warm-hearted Enthusiast! He is much pleased with what I said, has written to me, and Lady Peel has called upon me this morning, and in tears assured me that what I said had the same Impression upon Him as what I said upon Talleyrand in the House of Lords some years ago had upon *Him!**[17]

For the next four months, while the slow course of politics contrasted with the gathering disaster in Ireland, Wellington followed his path of

---

* When the Duke, in September 1831, said no man's character, public or private, had ever been so much belied as Talleyrand's, the old sinner wept. He added, according to Lady Salisbury, '*C'est le seul homme qui a jamais dit du bien de moi*' – 'He is the only man who has ever spoken a good word of me.' (Burghclere, p. 331, 17 December 1851.)

duty: in public fanatically loyal to Peel, in private deeply disturbed about the party. 'I am very apprehensive that a great Mistake has been made,' he wrote to Lady Wilton on 9 February, 'though we are not told.'[18] Not told . . . There again was the old trouble of Peel's deep-seated inability to communicate. 'At all events,' he continued, 'I am certain that a Party mistake has been made, and that if we continue to be a Government we shall be without support.' Resignations were in fact pouring in. Despite this, the Duke expected the Commons to carry Corn Law repeal. Of the Lords he was profoundly doubtful.

The least he could do, therefore, was to try to win over Lord Stanley (later Derby), since he was the focus of disaffection in the Lords. Admired as 'the cleverest eldest son for a hundred years', Stanley happened also to be one of the wealthiest. In these two capacities he was a natural cynosure for anxious Conservative eyes. It was he who on 18 February tackled Wellington on Peel's leadership. Peel had 'completely dislocated and shattered the great Conservative party in both Houses'; he would never lead a united party again and there was no other leader in the Commons. But there was still the Duke. Though even his 'great name and influence' would not carry Peel's Corn Bill through the Lords, he was the party's natural leader. Stanley's personal tribute to the Duke would consist in repelling all entreaties by the Ultras to lead a faction against him.[19]

So far so good. Stanley already neutralized by reverence was something. The Duke, however, hoped for his conversion. He replied next day, agreeing that Peel's influence was probably diminished for ever but demolishing the idea of himself leading the party, or even continuing to lead the Lords, in a typically curt and unexplained aside:

It is not easy to account for my being in the situation which I have so long filled in the House of Lords. Its commencement was merely accidental.

Finally he invoked a pair of powerful new arguments calculated to sway Stanley. First, he had always used his influence to prevent a collision between the two Houses; repeal of the Corn Law would get its second reading in the Commons – it did so, eight days later, on 27 February – and must not be frustrated by the Lords. Second, his policy would prevent conflict not only between the two Houses but between two classes, the rich and the poor. The great landed proprietors had a personal interest in protection which could not be concealed.

Here the Duke was probably influenced by Arbuthnot who, as a landowner himself, saw the class issue most vividly: 'The Corn Laws are considered as a class monopoly,' he had written to Peel from Stratfield Saye on 8 January 1846, 'and are thus most detrimental to the aristocracy, and to the landed interest.'[20]

While offering these new thoughts to Stanley, the Duke allowed himself a familiar peroration:

I am the servant of the Crown and People. I have been paid and rewarded, and I consider myself retained. . . .[21]

The Duke failed to convert Stanley. Two or three weeks later, on 8 March, he was elected leader of the protectionist peers. But at least the Duke was instrumental in keeping him quiet except in debate for another four months.[22] And if the Duke did not entirely succeed with Stanley, he may have more than half converted himself – to free trade. Arbuthnot was already a convert. There were many winter evenings in 1846 when the two old friends sat together over the fire, talking . . .

Spring came hysterically to the Commons, bursting out in ardent Government striving, violent Ultra execrations and a rush of sap to Young Ireland and Young England – the former a rival to O'Connell, the latter a defunct Tory hybrid reborn in 1846 as the creation of Lord George Bentinck's will-power and Disraeli's oratorical genius.

Disraeli's virulence against Peel had been rising. At the third reading of the Corn Bill, in the middle of May 1846, the invective surpassed itself in what Disraeli called afterwards 'my great speech', torturing Peel, enchanting the Opposition and more than once drawing wicked laughter from all sides of the House.

It was inevitable that Peel's changes of front, first on the anti-Catholic laws in 1829, then on protection in 1846, should prove a sitting target. In circumstances suggestively parallel he had twice been elected to preserve a principle which he then proceeded to abandon. He and Wellington had trounced the 'Catholics' on emancipation and the Leaguers on corn, only to steal their policy when in power. 'His life has been a great Appropriation Clause,' said Disraeli (shouts of laughter and cheers). 'He is a burglar of others' intellect.' A halt would be called to 'this huckstering tyranny of the Treasury bench (loud cheers) – these political pedlars that bought their party in the cheapest market, and sold us in the dearest. (Enthusiastic cheers)'.

The pedlars nonetheless got their majority of ninety-eight for repeal of the Corn Laws on 15 May 1846. Within a fortnight the bill was before the Lords for the second reading.

Stanley, living up to his romantic label, showed himself a true 'Rupert of debate'. In replying to Stanley, it was not a counter-stroke by cavalry that the Duke hoped to produce, but the familiar impregnable square. He began by briefly recapitulating the obligations he had felt in December last – his double duty to Peel and the Queen. Then he entered his square.

My Lords, it is not necessary that I should say more on that subject. I am aware that I address your Lordships at present with all your prejudices against me for having adopted the course I then took – a course which however . . . if it was to be adopted tomorrow, I should take again.

I am in Her Majesty's service – bound to Her Majesty and to the Sovereigns of this country by considerations of gratitude of which it is not necessary that I should say more to your Lordships.

Perhaps he ought not to be connected with any party. 'Be it so, my Lords, be it so, if you think proper.' But if he never addressed them again he would give them this advice. Let them remember that he once before made them change their vote. What was the position this time? A bill had come up from the Commons, passed by a majority there and recommended by the Crown. If it were rejected, the Lords would stand alone.

He had spoken for some eight minutes. Suddenly the pace changed. The square had formed into line and it was time for the advance:

Now that, my Lords, is a situation in which, I beg to remind your Lordships, I have frequently stated you ought not to stand; it is a position in which you cannot stand, because you are entirely powerless; without the House of Commons and the Crown the House of Lords can do nothing. You have vast influence on public opinion; you have great confidence in your own principles but without the Crown or the House of Commons you can do nothing – till the connection with the House of Commons is revived, there is an end of the functions of the House of Lords.

In fact it was rightabout face, as Lord Clarendon had once said over emancipation, rightabout face with Peel or nothing. 'Attention, my Lords! Rightabout face! quick march!'

At 4.30 am on the morning of 28 May 1846 the 'Contents' to the number of 211 marched out to record their votes, while only 164 'Not Contents' remained with their feet firmly under their seats: a majority of 47.* It was not the last speech the Duke was to make to their lordships, but it was in many ways the finest. In a matter of fifteen minutes he had routed Stanley and shown them clearly what they most needed to see – themselves.

* The present procedure of both sides going below the Bar to vote was not adopted until 1857.

As the Duke left the House in the bright light of the summer morning some early workers collected to hear the result. When they saw him they cheered with relief and gratitude, crowding round the old warrior.

'God bless you, Duke!'

'For Heaven's sake, people, let me get to my horse!'[23]

He was right not to celebrate. Retribution came to his party in less than a month.

In Ireland, agrarian crime had followed in the wake of hunger and destitution. It was feared that desperate peasants would kill the landlords whose rent they could not pay. Peel introduced yet another Coercion Bill. At the beginning of the year he had had the support of almost all MPs but the Irish. Now it was different. Now it was revenge.

Young Ireland and old Dan, young Dizzy and Bentinck, case-hardened Whigs and inveterate Tories – but especially the old ultra-Tories – combined against the political 'pedlars' who they believed had sold their party to the highest bidder, to the anti-Corn Law mob.

Peel and the Duke both saw defeat coming on coercion, and everything happened as the Duke feared. The Corn Bill went through the Lords and Coercion was beaten in the Commons a few hours later.

'They say we are beaten by seventy-three,' whispered Graham into the Prime Minister's ear, as he waited on the Treasury bench after the vote.[24] Peel did not speak or even look round. He merely stuck out his chin, as politicians do in anger, and as Aberdeen had done sixteen years earlier after the Duke's speech on Reform. Then, as now, the Government had been brought down by ultra-Tories taking their revenge. Now, as then, the Prime Minister had made a mistake. What was Peel's?

A last-minute tactical error? Ought he to have brought forward Coercion before Corn, to make sure of both? But the Opposition were out to get him by then and would have got him somehow. Was he broken by Disraeli's philippics, as Canning had been by the old Tories? He certainly had little fight left in him by June. Or was it the mistake of allowing Lord John Russell to manoeuvre him into introducing controversial legislation – Corn Law Reform – with a split party? – the 'poisoned chalice' of Disraeli's suitably Borgia-like phrase. Peel had been under no necessity to accept. He could have insisted on leaving the chalice in Russell's hands.

But what if Peel was in fact under a psychological necessity, a glorious compulsion to accept? There was the Queen. There was that 'movement of enthusiasm'. The Duke had been the first to recognize it and indeed had participated in it. If that was the mistake, the poisoned chalice had been handed back by Queen Victoria herself to her two servants, now both 'retained'. Fortunately the draught injured neither of them, at least with posterity. Each has survived with his reputation for courage and patriotism enhanced.

But the old political party of Pitt, Liverpool, Canning, Wellington and Peel was poisoned beyond recovery.

The new Prime Minister, Russell, tentatively offered Wellington and other Conservatives places in the Government. They all declined. At the same time Wellington pledged himself to support the Whigs wherever possible. Similarly when the Queen repeated a request of last December that he should continue as Commander-in-Chief, he accepted with the proviso that he should no longer act as a party leader in the Lords.

Command of the army from 1842 onwards had undoubtedly given the Duke a much-needed lift. His renewed vitality took everybody by surprise. 'Nothing is more extraordinary than the complete restoration of that vigour of mind which for the last two or three years was visibly impaired,' wrote Greville on 19 March 1843. 'His speeches this session have been as good if not better than any he ever made.'

Yet Wellington must bear a heavy responsibility for the army's unpreparedness to face the Crimean war, since he was Commander-in-Chief for ten out of the twelve preceding years. The failure of this former master of detail and miracle of foresight was due to a variety of causes. He was old. He suffered from a historical hangover, shared by many other people, which made him see the British Army as an anomaly:

It is an exotic in England; unknown to the old constitution of the country; required only for the defence of its foreign possessions; disliked by the inhabitants, and particularly by the higher orders, some of whom never allow their families to serve in it.[25]

This 'exotic' must therefore be careful not to obtrude itself upon the notice of Parliament or the public with Prussian-type plans for its own advancement. It should be seen as little as possible and heard not at all.

There was also the national drive for economy ever since Waterloo, which prevented him from saving the Royal Waggon Train from disbandment: one of the gravest losses to Crimean soldiers.

Again, his innate conservatism affected his thought on all subjects, from the officer class to specialized and scientific training. His lifelong conviction that officers should begin with an all-round 'gentleman's education' like civilians, before attending one of the military colleges, was admirable within its assumptions; and Wellington College, the public school founded in his honour, was a most fitting memorial to him. Nevertheless Wellington, even within the assumptions of the time, tended to overvalue the 'gentlemanly' side of an officer's education compared with the technical, which he sometimes feared might attract the wrong kind of candidate. This applied especially to the artillery and engineers.

In straightfoward infantry training he was not an innovator like Sir John Moore. Nor, if he had lived in the next century, would he necessarily have been the first general to insist on the revolutionary tank. Nelson was not interested in a new gun sight offered by the Admiralty for trial and report. Wellington brought his genius to preparing and fighting a battle with an unbeatable combination of action and character. But once the hero himself has departed, his legacy of 'steady troops', despite everything at the Alma or Balaclava, is easily forgotten, while the deplorable examples of top-ranking officers like Cardigan are vividly remembered as an all but lethal bequest. Having remembered them, no one can doubt that the old Duke should have retired earlier, taking not a few of his generals with him. As his descendant, the 7th Duke, has written with understanding and pungency:

The incompetence shown during the Crimean War is often with some justification laid at his door. No man should ever cling to a job when he is too old, and no one will ever tell him when that moment arrives.[26]

Finally there was a paradox. The very intensity of his obsession with the country's defencelessness during his last ten years forbade him to risk inventions and new ideas where old, tried methods were available.

1848 was the Year of Revolution.

Louis Philippe was driven from the throne in February. So ended what Tocqueville called his 'usurping dynasty . . . the most selfish & grasping & exclusive of Plutocracies'. A few days later a letter arrived for the Duke from Lamartine, the French romantic poet turned revolutionary leader, hoping for his Grace's approbation of this very liberal revolution. After all, the English Constitution was 'the most ultra of liberal republics, having a hereditary Sovereign Magistrate, as chief'. The Duke replied that he hoped France would be happy. No comment on Britain's advanced liberal republic. 'Very judicious,' wrote Russell.[27]

Hardly were the royal fugitives from France installed in their traditional asylum, England, before the European revolutions of March began. Prince Metternich had to run from Vienna in a disguise and was seen for three hours in London by the Duke.

'What does he do?' asked the invalid Mr Chad whom the Duke was visiting.

'Oh he perorates.'[28]

The Duke himself was too busy to perorate. '*We are living in Strange Times!*' he wrote to William Spicer, a West Country friend. 'However, I hope that we may be able yet to preserve the general Peace, although it appears probable that we alone of the Nations of the earth may . . . be saved from Wreck and Destruction!'[29] According to his information, the appointed day for 'wrecking' England was Monday 10 April. Feargus O'Connor,* Nottingham's MP since 1847, proposed to direct yet another tidal wave of Chartism on Parliament, by means of a petition with five million signatures and a vast meeting on Kennington Common to launch its processional journey to Westminster. A National Assembly on the French model would then replace Parliament until the Charter became law.

The Commander-in-Chief, saying he felt as well as twenty-five years ago, rose to the challenge with a mighty effort of mind and body which gradually instilled courage into all who worked with him. During the week before the crisis Lord Campbell, Chancellor of the Duchy, did not at all like the look of things: 'Many people believe that by Monday evening we shall be under a Provisional Government,' he wrote to his brother. The Duke tried personally to calm him.

'Lord Campbell, we shall be as quiet on Monday as we are at this moment, and it will end to the credit of the Government and the country.'[30]

In the Cabinet room on the eve of operations Campbell listened enthralled to the Duke's Council of War. As in 1830, all the soldiers were to be kept out of sight but so disposed that ten thousand could be assembled at any danger-point in a matter of minutes. Lady

---

* O'Connor's father had been the last tenant of Dangan, Wellington's old Irish home.

Palmerston afterwards understood from her husband, also present, that this arrangement was to prevent them from fraternizing with the mob.[31] The Duke, however, did not fear fraternization. It was to prevent provocation. As he laid out and explained his maps and plans, Campbell marvelled at his quickness and precision. Thomas Macaulay, another Cabinet minister, told Campbell he had never seen such an interesting spectacle; he would remember it to his dying day. In this thin, silver-haired old man they could all see the boundless spring and energy which had won Waterloo.

Cannon were placed on the bridges and all government offices in the Whitehall area garrisoned and provisioned. Prince Albert wanted a mass removal of the Tower guns out of harm's way but the Duke would have none of it: 'Considering that the Guns have thus been kept in security upon former occasions of the Disturbance of the Peace of the Tower by Mobs, it appears to the Duke to be best to leave *well* as it is.' Special constables to the number of two hundred thousand were enrolled, presumably one to each of the expected Chartist demonstrators. (The Duke had written to Lady Wilton on the 5th, 'I am up to the Eyes in arrangements for the reception of the Chartists on Monday to the amount of 200,000.') Among the specials were Prince Louis Napoleon, Bonaparte's nephew, and Charles Greville, with all his Privy Council clerks and messengers, their ground-floor rooms barricaded with the Council registers. The democratic Lady Palmerston was enchanted by the 'higgeldy piggeldy' mass of volunteers – peers, commoners, servants and workmen, all united 'to stand by our constitution'. In fact the Duke found many of the workmen, though willing to defend their allotted buildings, unwilling to attack the mobs. 'We think like them.'[32]

Before leaving London on 8 April at her ministers' request, the Queen asked Wellington if there was really any danger.

'None, Madam, if I am allowed to proceed with my precautionary measures.'

Then the great day dawned, and suddenly it was clear that all these preparations had been made to deal with far fewer Chartists than predicted bearing rolls of signatures of which only 1,975,496 were genuine. Among the forged names that of the Duke of Wellington appeared no less than seventeen times. By 9 am Feargus O'Connor had already lost heart. The Duke, as yet unaware of this, was at the Horse Guards at 10 am, where he proposed to stay until it was time to go down and meet the petitioners at Westminster. At 1 pm he heard the procession had been formed on Kennington Common. At 1.45 pm an officer announced that the petition was trundling over Vauxhall Bridge in a cab, O'Connor having been talked out of his procession by Sir Richard Mayne, Chief of Police, in the nearby Horns Tavern. The Chartist MP, gigantic in stature but no more than human in spirit, had gladly folded up his long limbs among the scrolls, agreeing with Mayne that it would be foolish to march and get his toes trodden on or pockets picked. The petitions were delivered by cab.

'I consider the heart of the Affair broken,' wrote the Duke from his office to Lady Wilton.[33] He ordered his troops back to barracks. By 3.30 pm it was raining. 'In short the War is over,' continued the Duke, 'and the Rain will probably keep the Town quiet this night.' He left for the House of Lords at 4.30 pm, well pleased that the Monarch, though evacuated to Osborne with a newborn baby, was still on her throne.

'It must have been a happy day for him,' the Queen wrote to him in the third person on the 12th. 'It is a pity he is not 59 instead of 79. Such Men are indeed now valuable in these days.'[34]

The Young Irelanders had been expected by the Duke to rise on the same day as the Chartists. Blood-curdling reports of their speeches had arrived, all proving that they had abandoned the voting-booth for the pike. Whereas the old O'Connellite cry had been 'Register, register, register!' Young Ireland proclaimed, 'Arm, arm, arm!' Should the whole world be free, they asked, and Ireland remain a slave? The Duke thought he saw clearly what they wanted: 'to deprive the Queen of her crown! and to establish a republick!'[35] Forgetting who had first said it, their favourite quotation was, 'Trust in God and keep your powder dry.' For those without powder, pikes were selling on the streets at 2s 6d to 4s 6d well polished.

Two days before the 10th the Duke was dreading a far worse fate for Dublin than for London:

As there are few of the Police armed with Staves in Dublin the Mob must be dealt with there by Fire Arms! . . . There will therefore possibly be great slaughter of the Insurgents! This is heart-breaking![36]

But spasmodic violence never concentrated into the single flame of revolution. Inexorably the leaders were rounded up and transported. The potato blight meanwhile struck yet again, but no signs of permanent cure for Ireland's desolation occurred to either Whigs or

Tories. The Whigs tried to punish the landlords for past sins by forcing them to bear, through the rates, the cost of salvaging the poor. Instead the landlords evicted their paupers, thus condemning the second half of the century to orgies of mutual hatred.

Conservative policy up to 1846 had been less parsimonious and doctrinaire than Whig. Nevertheless Peel and Wellington went out of office 'without having accomplished anything to make the Irish people better able to meet the calamity that lay ahead of them'.[37] The Duke, indeed, at times saw no solution at all or only a solution that would be too slow. Somehow 'the anomalous state of social life in Ireland' – the landlord–tenant relationship – must be changed.

I entertain no doubt that no Improvement can be effectual in Ireland till the Reform in contemplation will take place in the common social Relation between employer and Workman![38]

For lack of that 'Reform' probably at least two million Irish were lost, one million by emigration and one by famine.

Also worthy of note are the population figures for the Duke's two native islands at the beginning of the century and at the end of his life. When he died the population of Ireland was fast shrinking back to what it had been when he was a young man in Dublin; England's had more than doubled.

Much personal happiness compensated the old Duke for the political confusion abroad and at home during his last years. He found solace more and more in the reflected gaiety and hopes of a younger generation, represented among others by Angela Burdett-Coutts.

Grand-daughter and heiress of the immensely wealthy banker, Thomas Coutts, and daughter of Sir Francis Burdett, the Duke's old radical antagonist, 'Miss Angela', as the Duke almost always addressed her in the 842 letters he wrote her, was born in 1814. This plain but strong-minded young woman lived at No. 1 Stratton Street at the corner of Piccadilly, not far from Apsley House, and there was continual visiting between No. 1 Stratton Street and 'No. 1 London', as the Duke's house was now reverentially called. Miss Angela's conscientious desire to use her enormous wealth charitably gave her a common interest with the Duke. They shared the Victorian fervour for rescuing prostitutes, the Duke in particular becoming almost lyrical once Miss Angela had aroused his compassion. A typical outpouring was sent to her on 30 March 1849:

My young Lady fills her letters with assurances that she does all the good things which I have enjoined; in return for all the Money I have given her and paid for her! at the same time demanding more. . . . But her letters are not to be compared to those of my Irish girl who is going to Australia! . . . She is a character such as a Heroine in a Romance or Novel personified! and I feel the same interest in her fate, as I should in the story of such a one . . . and her letters to me are models of modesty, humility. . . . [39]

They were almost certainly models of duplicity. Of the Duke's large clientele of unmarried mothers who gave birth at suspiciously frequent intervals before receiving their passage-money to the Antipodes, few ever left Lambeth or Charing Cross; indeed many of them were the same person, and that a man. But when the Mendicity Society exposed a fraud, it was the Society whom the Duke heartily disliked, not the impostor: 'An Officer from the Mendicity Society called on me and gave me such a scolding, as I have never had before in my life!'[40]

From the Duke's letters to Miss Angela – most of them non-political – many racy trifles emerge concerning his last years: that he had thought of being trained to sing as a consolation in his deafness but was too much occupied; that in order to prevent colds he wore the finest Bengal muslin next to his skin and carried a bottle of vinegar and rose-water in his pocket, to rub himself each time he changed his clothes (usually three times but sometimes seven times a day); that he dreaded the draughts of Windsor – 'I don't know where I have been more uncomfortable';[41] that he was once caught up when waltzing under a stranger's petticoat – 'She was very well looking and must have been very much surprised to find a veteran with grey Hair under her Cloaths'.

There were many signs of a touching affection for one another. The Duke's pale grey writing-paper still carries the stains here and there of pressed rose leaves, geraniums or verbena sent to his young friend. One small envelope contains a tiny bow of pure white hair tied with a few brown strands. Another, labelled on the outside in Angela's hand, 'Duke of Wellington's favourite Poplins', is filled with small patterns of material: gold shot with pink (6s), gold and purple (4s 9d), checks of lilac, grey and deep violet (ditto), shot purple (3s 6d), fawn shot with rose (5s 9d). The colours the Duke preferred were gay and warm; no greens, blues, black or white.

The warmth flowed into words when Angela was abroad in October 1847:

My Dearest! for so I must call you! your constant recollection of and kindness to me, charm me; and I must express what I feel for you! . . . we think aloud! and the thoughts of the one are imparted to the other! this is the charm of our existence.[42]

Were these the words of a lover? On 6 February of that year he had written her a temporizing letter which suggested nevertheless that an emotional crisis was impending.

I am sensible of your kindness and confidence my dear Miss Angela! and of the admirable good sense and goodness of heart which induced you to write me your letter of last night. You are right! there can be no Secrets between us on such Subjects! . . . The subject is now exactly as it ought to be between us! and as every other is; one on which either can think aloud!

By the following evening, however, Miss Angela had decided that the subject was far from being exactly as it ought to be between them. She proposed marriage to the Duke on 7 February 1847 and received a refusal, she being thirty-two and he seventy-seven. He wrote to her next day:

My Dearest Angela,
I have passed every Moment of the Evening and Night since I quitted you in reflecting upon our Conversation of yesterday, Every Word of which I have considered repeatedly.

But he could not change his mind. His first duty to her was that of friend, guardian, protector.

You are Young, My Dearest! You have before you the Prospect of at least twenty years of enjoyment of Happiness in Life. [As Baroness Burdett-Coutts, Angela was to live to be ninety-two, marrying at sixty-seven a man less than half her age.] I entreat you again, in this way, not to throw yourself away upon a Man old enough to be your Grandfather, who, however strong, Hearty and Healthy at present, must and will certainly in time feel the consequences and Infirmities of Age.[43]

Nevertheless their mutual affection was strong enough to defy critics like Greville, who spoke of the Duke's 'strange intimacy' with Miss Burdett-Coutts as one of the 'lamentable appearances of decay in his vigorous mind'.[44]

The Duke's friendship with other young women and his persecution by an ageing spinster were noticed with even more spleen. There was Mrs Jones of Pantglas, there were the Misses Hatton, and above all there was Lady Georgiana Fane, unmarried daughter of Lord Westmorland, who was the Duke's most heartless pursuer and like Miss Burdett-Coutts and Miss Jenkins never gave up hope of catching him. At one point it seemed likely that Lady Georgiana would sue him for breach of promise. But he kept his head and also, more surprisingly, kept his special liking for the 'Bardwell and Pickwick' passage in Dickens, which he used to read aloud.

Lastly, his own daughters-in-law. Charles had married Sophia Pierrepont, niece of Lord Manvers, in 1844 and to the Duke's joy produced many Wellesley grandchildren. Though the eldest, Arthur, died in infancy, to the Duke's great sorrow, Henry and Arthur Charles grew up to become 3rd and 4th Dukes respectively. Lady Charles's children made the platform at Walmer 'quite gay', as the Duke told Mrs Jones. To his elder daughter-in-law, Lady Douro (born Lady Elizabeth Hay), he was especially devoted, precisely it would seem because she was childless and unloved.

32

The Other Side of the Hill

Prolonged huzzas, fluttering of handkerchiefs and kisses blown by gloved hands greeted the Duke as he entered the Crystal Palace on 1 May 1851 and processed for three-quarters of an hour round the building towards the central point, accompanied by members of the Government, Opposition and other notables. One of the spectators, Lady Charlotte Guest, observed the contrast between the Duke's 'hearty cheer' and Russell's 'tolerably good one'. The Duke's cheer was indeed a double-barrelled salute, for he and Lord Anglesey supported one another, arm in arm, up and down and round the long aisles, all their family and political feuds long forgotten. That the two old heroes tottered in their walk only added to the crowd's affectionate enthusiasm.

When the sightseeing began someone remembered it was the Duke's birthday. More cheers; and a round of applause from each section he visited; wax flowers to amuse Lady Douro and heavy machinery to amuse himself. At the end of the dizzy afternoon he was whisked off to Buckingham Palace to give a birthday present to his godson Prince Arthur, one year old on the day that he was eighty-two. The Queen's favourite artist, Franz Winterhalter, painted a picture she greatly admired of the presentation. The Duke's only surviving comment on the picture characteristically concerned the unconscionable time he had spent on sitting. Counting the journeys to and from the Palace, Winterhalter's masterpiece represented three hours' lost time a day.

The Glass Palace, on the contrary, was soon drawing the old Duke like a magnet. 'Whether the Shew will ever be of any use to anybody may be questioned,' he wrote to Lady Salisbury at the end of the first week, 'but of this I am certain nothing can be more successful.' He went again and again and became so much a part of the 'Shew' that his final visit on 7 October almost ended in disaster. Unaware of the situation, he strolled in like anyone else. Suddenly eighty thousand Wellington worshippers were rushing down upon him from all quarters determined to touch him before it was too late:

Never did I see such a mob, or get such a rubbing, scrubbing and mashing . . . I expected at every moment to be crushed and I was saved by the Police alive![1]

A crowd of social duties still pressed upon him, though the ferocity of his complaints about them gradually faded. In August 1850 he had given away one of the brides at a double Pakenham wedding and signed the register of St George's, Hanover Square, for the thousandth time — or so he said. When he escorted another young relative, Prudence Penelope Leslie, known as 'Britannia', up the aisle, the bride heard him saying quietly,

'Left, right! Left, right!' She realized it was not to keep *her* in step but himself.*

Of the five Wellesley brothers and one sister, he and Gerald were the only two left. Richard had gone in 1842, Anne in 1844, William in 1845, Henry in 1846. He and Richard, to everyone's surprise, had become reconciled four years before the latter's death. Richard's son-in-law, Lord Hatherton, believed the old trouble had been jealousy, which made Wellesley 'a most difficult man to act with'. An extraordinary conversation about Arthur took place between Hatherton and his father-in-law on 12 March 1837.[2] Having been questioned regarding the Duke's faults of character, especially 'neglect' of his family, Lord Wellesley embarked on a review of all his four brothers' qualities.

'But you know,' he suddenly said to Hatherton, 'Pole [William Maryborough] and Lady Anne and I are Wellesleys, Arthur's father was Mr Gardiner.' (The Gardiners were a Meath family and this Mr Gardiner was possibly the Wellesley boys' tutor.) Hatherton then suggested that though Richard and Anne were clearly brother and sister in full blood, Arthur and Henry were not quite so much like one another.

'Oh! I believe Henry and Arthur have also different parentage,' said Lord Wellesley.

A man who could claim that his severe mother was an enthusiastic adulteress must indeed have been difficult to act with, particularly as there is not a shred of evidence to confirm his statement.†

---

* Told to the author by Mr William Cavendish-Bentinck, the bride's descendant.

† Professor A. Aspinall, an authority on the documents of this period, denies the rumour. (See also the life of the Marquess Wellesley by Iris Butler, *The Eldest Brother*.) From portraits all the brothers seem to have resembled one another, but Arthur was the one who chiefly inherited his father the Earl of Mornington's musical talents.

A perennial marvel seemed to have come to an end when Lord Palmerston was dismissed from Russell's Government for going behind his own ambassador's back over Napoleon III's *coup d'état*. The Duke described Pam's exit as a nine days' wonder and awaited with interest his next move. It was worth waiting for. Next February Palmerston gave Russell his famous 'tit-for-tat' by bringing down his Government. To the Duke there was a double relish in this event: Palmerston was primed by the Duke's arguments when he defeated Russell on a Militia Bill, and the defeat enabled Derby (Stanley) to give the country a Tory administration. Only one thing was not perfect. As the new Prime Minister read out the names of his Government the old Duke, wearing his white winter cape to keep warm, craned forward but still could not hear.

'Who – who?' he asked in a loud whisper. It was Sir So-and-So. 'Never heard of the gentleman!'[3]

He was to die under the 'Who – who? Government', but not before he had caused the Prime Minister a headache or two. Lord Derby once returned to the Duke a peculiarly illegible letter with the request that he would decipher it.

'It was my business to write that letter,' said the Duke with a smile, 'but it is *your* duty to read it.'[4]

On 1 May 1852 he celebrated his eighty-third birthday and the greetings and cheering in the streets awakened once more his warning interior voice, even though he acknowledged them with his familiar salute of two fingers raised to the brim of his hat. The voice spoke in Cromwell's remembered words, since there was an election on in Dover and his friends wanted him to use his influence on their behalf. 'They would readily pull me to pieces if convicted of exciting undue influence in the Election of Dover. Alas! we are but men!'

Lady Charlotte Guest found him a very unresponsive old man, hemmed in by huge crowds at a ball given at Apsley House on the 14th – 'he seemed almost asleep'.[5]

That spring the circuit judges had dined as usual at Stratfield Saye and Mr Justice Talfourd, once a famous reform MP, was surprised and delighted to see the Duke tuck into turtle soup, salmon, a patty, roast beef and 'a child's portion of apple tart and cream'. At his last Waterloo banquet his face, pink and smooth without a wrinkle, shone with pleasure. He refused to feel old. When a man one day helped him across Hyde Park Corner he ought to have been grateful but was not.

'I thank you, Sir,' he managed to say. Then the man perorated.

'My Lord, I have passed a long and not uneventful life; but never did I hope to reach the day when I might be of some assistance to the greatest man that ever lived.'

'Don't be a damned fool!'[6]

At last he escaped to Walmer from the hot July days where he had been 'stewed up' in drawing-rooms (though always careful to sit next to a handsome woman when there was music) and obliged to 'sneak along' the shady side of the street. The Sword of State had been carried by him for the last time at the Prorogation, when he confessed to finding it 'as heavy as a regimental firelock'.[7] His last visitors to Walmer – the Grand Duke and Duchess of Mecklenberg-Strelitz, gracious but a strain – departed on 28 August, leaving him to his reading, rides and walks; to his great lime-tree in the garden, of course 'the finest in the world', and his head gardener, Sergeant Townsend, a Waterloo veteran who suited the Duke admirably.

'Do you know anything about gardening?' the Duke had asked the unemployed soldier who came to his door at Stratfield Saye.

'No, Your Grace.'

'Then *learn – learn* and return here this day fortnight at the same hour. Take the place of gardener at Walmer Castle.'

'But I know nothing of gardening.'

'Neither do I, neither do I.'[8]

Sometimes during his solitary rides there would be a little hob-nobbing with country people, like the owner of Ripple Mill, who years afterwards recalled the knocking on the steps of his mill and the voice shouting up,

'That the miller? – come down and talk.'

Then the two would sit together in the rumbling, sweet-smelling mill while the soldier confessed to the miller that war was a horrible trade.* Many years later still, an old lady remembered as a girl opening the gate on the Upper Deal road for the Duke to ride through. Often he was fast asleep in the saddle and his horse would stop, wait and then continue gently along the road for home.[9] On the day after his foreign

---

* Told to the author by Mr John Mannering, descendant of the miller. There is another account of the Duke's hob-nobbing in the *Illustrated London News* (12 September 1846). When he was temporarily stranded near Plymouth, the guard of the stage-coach offered him a lift. 'No, I thank you . . . I'd rather walk; besides, I have company', pointing to a couple of navvies and a farmer with whom he had been deep in conversation.

royalties left Walmer, 29 August, he wrote jubilantly to Lady Salisbury of his good health:

I am always well, never fatigued, and I can do anything! I have none of the infirmities of old age! excepting *Vanity* perhaps!

. . . My deafness is accidental! If I was not deaf, I really believe that there is not a youth in London who could enjoy the world more than myself or could bear fatigue better! but being deaf, the spirit, not the body, tires! One gets bored in boring others, and one becomes too happy to get home![10]

To get home . . . He was nearly there now. He had made two attempts on 2 and 3 September to see old Croker, who was convalescing at Folkestone. Croker had been out the first time; quite a blow, since the Duke had tired himself by walking from the station, not realizing it was three miles up and down hill. Next day he went again, only to be teased by Croker for having failed to guess that yet more hills lay on the other side of Folkestone Hill. Mrs Croker looked puzzled and the Duke explained to her:

'All the business of war, and indeed all the business of life is to endeavour to find out what you do not know by what you do; that is what I called "guessing what was at the other side of the hill!" '

September was in its second week and the Duke still reading hard at his standing-desk, or dealing with letters at his cluttered table and laughing away over the answers he composed. On 12 September a particularly choice note arrived by hand. 'I had one this morning,' he wrote to Lady Salisbury, 'from a Madman who announces that he is a messenger from the Lord, and will deliver his message to-morrow morning Monday at Walmer Castle! We shall see!'[11]

Monday the 13th was his last full day.

The Charles Wellesleys arrived with his grandchildren. He had got up early at 5.30 am to look at his garden and was in high spirits for the rest of the day. Games with his grandchildren, venison for dinner; then up the Castle stairs for the last time, candle in hand, to the small irregularly shaped room with yellow curtains behind the ramparts. There was just the amount of furniture he needed: the wing armchair, his curtainless camp-bed with faded green counterpane, horsehair mattress and pillow covered in chamois leather, copper cans and washbasin in the cupboard, towel-horse, standing-desk, tables and bedside reading in a bookcase, including Jeremy Taylor's *Holy Living and Holy Dying*. He liked his camp-bed partly because it was his army one – only 2 feet 9 inches wide – and partly because the sight of it had amused Mary Salisbury. She asked him how he managed to turn over in such a narrow bed and he replied,

'When it's time to turn over it's time to turn out.'*

But on the morning of 14 September 1852 there was no need to turn out, for the messenger of the Lord had come for him. It was fifty-eight years all but one day since he fought his first action at Boxtel in Holland.[12] His valet, Kendall, had knocked on his door as usual at 6.30 am. An hour later a maid came running to say his Grace was 'making a great noise' and must be ill. Kendall rushed in half-dressed but his master was lying quietly.

'It is half-past seven o'clock, your Grace.'

'*Thank you*, where does the apothecary live?'

'At Deal, your Grace.'

'Send for him, I wish to speak to him.'

Dr Hulke the apothecary left his breakfast unfinished and reached Walmer at 9 am.

'I am sorry that your Grace is an invalid – what do you complain of?'

'I think some derangement' – passing his hand across his chest. The pulse was irregular but Hulke was not unduly alarmed and ordered an ammonia stimulant after some tea and toast. He told Lord Charles he would return at noon. As soon as the apothecary had gone Kendall asked the Duke if he would take a little tea.

'*Yes if you please.*'

Kendall underlined these words in the account he sent to Shackle, the Queen's footman who had originally come to Windsor from Stratfield Saye, because they were the last words his beloved master spoke. They did indeed seem to underline one side of the Duke's character: his courtesy and readiness to do his duty even if it meant drinking the hemlock. The tea was immediately followed by a fit, and then another and another.

He was no longer conscious when Dr Hulke hurried back at 9.45 am accompanied by his son. The two Hulkes plied him with the remedies which had been effective in the past – a mustard emetic and a feather to 'irritate the fauces [jaws]' while another manservant, Collins, assisted Kendall in applying mustard poultices to the Duke's body and legs.

* I have assigned the Duke's famous quip to this occasion on the strength of his letter to Mary Salisbury dated 27 August 1850. 'I slept in my little camp bed without curtains, which amused you so much! Indeed I think I liked it better for the notice taken of it.' (Burghclere, p. 83.) Douro quoted the quip to Henry Hobhouse in December of the same year, 1850, that is about four months later, if indeed the Duke's quip was first made to Lady Salisbury that August. (Broughton, vol. v., p. 266.)

Meanwhile the local doctor, McArthur, had been summoned; he took over the feather while the rest went on poulticing. There was no relief. Three grains of calomel were administered and the Duke becoming restless at about 2 pm, he was lifted into his wing-chair on Kendall's advice. Kendall felt sure this was what he wanted.

Sitting in his favourite chair he slowly sank. At 3.25 pm with Charles and Sophia beside him and his devoted servants and doctors around he died. The end was so quiet that Charles could not believe he had gone. Dr Hulke's son held up a mirror to his mouth. There was not a whisper of breath on the glass.

While the Duke was alive it had been the custom to strike the Lord Warden's flag flying over the Castle when he returned to London. His friends, watching his carriage vanish over the other side of the hill, would make their way sadly home feeling Walmer was an empty place.[13] Now the flag flew at half-mast and the whole country seemed empty. 'The greatest man that England ever knew is no more,' wrote Prince Albert's secretary to the royal family at Balmoral, confirming the news of the 14th received by electric telegraph; 'One can hardly realise to oneself the idea of England without the Duke of Wellington.' When the news was brought to the Balmoral schoolroom the Queen's niece, Princess Feo, looked up with swimming eyes: 'and what will become of the Aunt Victoria?'[14]

The Times in its leading article struck a rich philosophical note: 'The Duke of WELLINGTON had exhausted nature and exhausted glory. His career was one unclouded longest day. . . .' More realistic, the radical *Spectator* said that on one point there could be no doubt: 'As a Counsellor of his Sovereign, the great Duke is not to be replaced.' With this conviction added to the Queen's personal grief for her '*dear* & great old Duke of Wellington', she and the Prince decided to postpone the funeral until after Parliament met in November: 'Every Englishman shall have time and opportunity to take his humble part in it,' announced the Prince.[15] In fact time was needed not by the humble but by the proud: time to organize the most superb State funeral the nation had ever known.

As the day of the funeral approached, many shared the 2nd Duke's reservations (he would have preferred a private funeral). Lady Palmerston had never looked forward to her dearest but gouty Harry having to process for six or seven hours. She decided personally to ignore the whole thing. 'It seems to me so unnatural and so grating to one's feelings to make a festival of a funeral! It's like an Irish Wake.'[16]

Yet in the end it was neither like a wake nor anything else anyone had ever known before. After a wet blustery night the sun suddenly shone upon a million and a half people lining the route. They were packed together at windows, on rooftops, in trees, to watch the incredible cortège: great dignitaries of Church and State in their splendid coaches; marching bands with trumpets and kettledrums; officers carrying the Duke's standard, guidon, banners and bannerols, and eighty-three Chelsea pensioners who joined the procession on foot at Charing Cross; a black mourning coach containing Bluemantle and Rouge Dragon, their brilliant tabards worn over mourning cloaks; then the Duke's servants in another mourning coach, followed by representatives from the Tower, East India Company, Trinity House, Cinque Ports, Board of Ordnance, Oxford University; Prince Albert in a coach and six; Lord Anglesey carrying the Duke's British army baton and distinguished foreigners with the batons of their respective countries.

Now at last appeared the ducal coronet borne by Clarenceux King of Arms on a black velvet cushion, the pall-bearers in two mourning coaches, the band of the Grenadier Guards and – 'THE BODY, placed upon a FUNERAL CAR, drawn by twelve Horses, and decorated with Trophies and Heraldic Achievements. The Hat and Sword of the Deceased being placed on the Coffin.' The huge dray horses, borrowed from a London brewery, were caparisoned in black up to the eyes.

There followed the 2nd Duke in an immensely long mourning cloak, with his 'assistants', 'supporters', friends and relatives: Wellesleys and Pakenhams; Salisbury, Tweeddale, Raglan, Burghersh, Cowley, Smith, Worcester, Hamilton, Foster and two Arbuthnots. As the mourning coaches rolled out of sight all eyes turned towards the Duke's horse, led by John Mears, his groom. The reversed Wellington boots hanging on either side brought tears to many eyes including the Queen's. There was a subdued murmur in contrast to the profound silence that had greeted the coffin.

Inspired by Prince Albert, the car was 21 feet long by 12 feet wide and weighed 18 tons, while the coffin, though a foot longer than the Duke at 6 feet 9 inches, looked lost on its high perch. The creaking architectural mass on which it trembled was too much for even the six great wheels. They sank into the mud opposite the Duke of York's statue in Pall Mall, and the vast edifice moved again only after sixty strong men had been roped in to heave. The canopy was successfully lowered by machinery in order to pass under Temple Bar, but the mechanism for transferring the coffin to the bier at the west door of St Paul's failed to work for over an hour.

To be both monstrous and inefficient was too much. Prince Albert had chosen the 'abominably ugliest' of all designs, declared Carlyle, and Lady de Ros – Georgiana Lennox of Waterloo days – was positively appalled: 'The car! oh, so frightful! I can't describe it. I must leave it to the *Morning Post*.' Lady Morgan hoped they would have no more heroes to bury for a thousand years.[17] In the guns, plumes and martial trophies of Britain's last heraldic funeral, the evangelical Lord Ashley saw many signs of death but none of immortality.

All along, the Prince's guiding light had been 'that nothing should be wanting in this tribute of national gratitude'.[18] Nothing was wanting; except the simplicity that had been the hallmark of the hero.

As the coffin waited helplessly outside the Cathedral's open door a biting November blast whistled up the aisles, chilling those inside and forcing some with bald heads to put on handkerchiefs or even hats. Contrariwise, shafts of cheerful sunlight pierced the gloom, killing the intended theatrical effect of a cavernous cathedral soaring into utter darkness, while every spark of radiance was concentrated on the central point beneath the dome.

But when all this was said, there remained an experience for hundreds of thousands that was beautiful and unique. They wept as the catafalque passed by, showing that they did not need great art to mediate their feelings for the Great Duke. The sight of all the hats raised looked to one eyewitness like 'the sudden rising from the ground & settling again of a huge flock of birds'.[19] As the bier at length entered the nave a draught caught the feathers on his cocked hat, so that it seemed to stir. Thousands of pages turning over together in the hands of the vast congregation sounded like a drawn-out universal sigh. Six tall candlesticks stood round the coffin, three on either side, to be lighted again 112 years later for Winston Churchill. Some of the music had been composed long years before by the Duke's father.

Of the eight pall-bearers, Seaton, Maitland and Woodford had served the Duke at Waterloo and Hardinge at Quatre-Bras; Charles Napier and Gough had conquered in India, the former still tortured by his head-wound received at Bussaco; Combermere had constantly looked to the Duke for military, political and even domestic advice, Londonderry for military and political counsel which, however, he seldom took. Lord Seaton (Colborne of Waterloo) judged the sonorous reading of the Duke's titles and the throwing of the broken staff into the grave to be relics of heraldry "inapplicable to the present age'. But the playing of the Dead March as the coffin was lowered into the vault, followed by the singing of 'Man that is born of a woman', moved him to tears. 'I was very much affected, and thought I should have been obliged to sit down.'[20]

Suddenly, 'Sleepers awake' rang out, the Tower guns crashed and at the west door the trumpets sounded 'a wail'. It was over.

> Under the cross of gold
> That shines over city and river,
> There he shall rest for ever
> Among the wise and the bold.

' – I wonder how you could suffice,' said George Chad one day to the Duke, marvelling at his prodigies of achievement in India.

'I never should,' said the Duke, 'if I had not been very young in command.'[21]

Early advantages were not enough to account for all that the Great Duke had become since. In a scheme for a statue in St Paul's it was the Duke's 'chief virtues' which Prince Albert wished to see commemorated allegorically, rather than 'endless marble Bayonets, swords, cannon smoke, Shakoes & Drums'.*[22]

The Great Duke's chief virtues were not in dispute: the truthfulness, courage, honesty, fairness and simplicity; the prudence and foresight; the directness, straightforwardness, decision and realism that made him so extraordinarily sensible; the repeated proofs that personal ambition, after youth was over, had no power to move him and that all he responded to was service, duty and patriotism, on whose full tide he was carried forward.

To the Victorians, sense of duty was a major virtue not because everybody possessed it but because so many did not. Wellington set the

---

* The magnificent monument designed for St Paul's by Alfred Stevens was completed by John Tweed and originally placed in the Chapel of St Michael and St George. It had its allegorical virtues of Truth and Valour defeating Falsehood and Cowardice. When it was removed to the present position the equestrian statue on top was omitted, because Dean Milner objected to a horse in a church. About 1903 the equestrian statue was added but the whole was not completed until 1912. After a good deal of argument over where to put the funeral car, it was returned to St Paul's, where it could be seen in the crypt, in all its grandeur and misery. Today it is in the Stratfield Saye Museum.

style for the great public servant of the future, single-minded and incorruptible. The most admired couplet in Tennyson's 'Ode on the Death of the Duke of Wellington', already quoted, was in fact a verse paraphrase of what the Duke had often said himself:

> Not once or twice in our rough island-story
> The path of duty was the way to glory[23]

There was the French reviewer of his *Despatches* who complained of finding 'duty' on every page and 'glory' never. 'That,' said the Duke, 'is the difference between the French and English soldier; with the French glory is the cause; with us, the result.'[24]

'I will cling to the heroic principle. It can alone satisfy my soul.' So said Coningsby, the hero of Disraeli's novel.

Not much was known of the Duke's soul, despite Miss Jenkins. But an unsuspected interest in theology was confided to a few of his friends. Who would have thought he sat up half the night reading Keith's *Demonstration of the Truth of Christianity*? 'It is the most interesting Work upon any Subject that I ever perused.'[25] Or that he told Miss Angela a sensational book on the French Revolution would 'amuse' her less than Dr Wiseman's *Lectures on Science and Revealed Religion*?

The Duke's Christianity was tolerant. Dr Wiseman, a Roman Catholic, had become Cardinal-Archbishop of Westminster in 1850, thus causing Protestant England to smell the sulphur of 'Papal Aggression'. The Duke remained calm. To be sure, he found himself again regretting the Concordat which he had vainly proposed in the 1820s and which he believed would have prevented the present crisis. But he regretted even more the anti-Catholic hubbub. 'I hear nothing everywhere but the dangers of Popery,' he wrote scornfully. 'It is driving people mad. I have this day two letters foretelling the end of the World!'[26]

He deprecated shallow criticism of non-Christian religions. 'The whole army, while I was in India, except about 50,000 men, consisted of idolators,' he told Parliament in 1839, ' – but they were as good soldiers as could be found anywhere.' Not all missionaries, on the other hand, were good soldiers of Christ. 'I know . . . the little progress they make; and I know at the same time that their labors create a good deal of jealousy'.[27] Nevertheless, he defended missions in principle for the sufficient reason that Christ had ordered them.

'A soldier must obey orders,' he said to a man who was attacking missionaries.

'What do you mean?'

'It is orders to preach the gospel to every creature alive.'

Above all education must never be separated from religion, otherwise you would create 'so many clever devils'.[28]

Ultimately his Christianity focused upon the Lord's Prayer, in which he found 'the sum total of religion and morals', and upon the Christian virtue of forgiveness, with which he identified peace. When an army colonel asked Wellington how he could forgive and reinstate Sir Robert Wilson, a soldier who had intrigued so much against him, the Duke answered that he himself had done many things which required forgiveness '& he hoped God who was a God of Peace would forgive him'.[29] Forgiveness and peace were not perhaps the virtues most closely associated by the outside world with the Duke; certainly they were those most prized by him at the end of his life.

Peculiarities are not necessarily virtues but sometimes they give as much pleasure. 'Wyatt called, and we revelled in His Grace's peculiarities,' wrote the painter Benjamin Haydon in his diary for 30 September 1839. 'Wyatt informed me he always said when people tried to persuade him to do what he had made up his mind not to do, "The rat has got into the bottle – the rat has got into the bottle." ' Odd as the expression always sounded, it conveyed the special flavour of the Duke's obstinacy: the damned large rat at bay inside the damned small bottle, from which he could not be budged.

It was widely believed by contemporaries that the Duke 'never took anybody's opinion but his own', and that this obstinacy led him into making mistakes which he never rectified or even admitted. 'The Duke has strong sense, great resolution,' wrote Knighton in 1830, 'but being wrong he has no power of setting himself right either from the advice of friends or . . . his own reflection.' Fourteen years later, however, the Duke had so far conquered this weakness as to publish in the records of Pembroke College, Oxford, a mistake he had made as Visitor, precisely through listening to only one side of a question and then making up his own mind – wrongly. The mistake had been to veto the appointment of a Dr Jeune as Provost, on the representations of his rivals. The Duke recorded his mistake, he said, as 'a Memento of warning not only to myself but to others who may have similar Duties to perform'.[30] The rat had come out of the bottle.

In a wider context, the Duke cannot be exonerated of neglecting public opinion. Though his contempt for the press was mitigated in later years, the old fighter would be heard protesting to the end that he did not care a pin what 'the Gentlemen' said. This peculiarity was one which his circle either 'revelled in' or condoned. As Professor Brock has pointed out, the bigger the man the greater the blunders he is allowed to make by respectful colleagues.

From self-confidence were derived many of the Duke's other peculiarities. His secretiveness, which saw no advantage or pleasure in taking others into his confidence, remained with him from first to last, the wound of a deprived child which nonetheless went with the proud bow of Achilles. No phrase is more striking throughout his long life than the will to walk or stand alone. He once said that if the hairs of his head could talk he would tear them out and wear a wig.'[31]

Much of his domestic inventiveness sprang from a wish that he and his friends might be independent of doctors, coachmen, butlers, valets. Such was the finger-bandage which he could fix himself, the infinite variety of wet-weather equipment to prevent colds, the three pairs of bath gloves in linen and tweed, the fast self-drive curricle, the individual pots of tea on the breakfast-table, the purchase of an early safety razor and, before that, the regular journeys from the country to the one man in London who sharpened his razors so perfectly that he could always shave himself.*[32]

In old age he brushed his own clothes and wished he were 'strong enough' to clean his own boots. This, despite the protocol against such practices. A group of visiting diplomats were said to have protested to Abraham Lincoln when they caught sight of him polishing away under their windows at the White House,

'In England no gentleman ever cleans his own boots.'

'Indeed? Whose boots do they clean then?'

The Duke's attitude towards the 'lower orders' was certainly not peculiar to him. He was devoted to his own personal servants but had no wish to see a blurring of class edges. Ernest Bevin said a century later that the tragedy of the working class was 'the poverty of their desires'. To Wellington and his friends this was a mercy, not a tragedy. He wrote to Charles Arbuthnot:

---

* 'I am vastly amused by the Bloomer discussions!' he wrote when Mrs Bloomer invented her knickers, 'I understand them, being somewhat of a Taylor!' – but finally decided they were 'impossible'. (Burghclere, p. 208, 18 October 1851.) He was also, as no one needed reminding, more than somewhat of a bootmaker.

We have educated the lower orders. They now say why should they not associate with us? They wanted to resort to our private houses, our entertainments; have the run of our kitchens and dance with our wives and daughters. Alternatively, they would invite us to their public houses, to live with them. They would shortly afterwards discover that they are better qualified to be Legislators Ministers Generals Holders of Large Properties than we are.[33]

This diatribe, probably the most reactionary in tone that the Duke ever perpetuated, must be seen in context. It was written in 1832 at the height of the Reform struggle.

It is unnecessary to dwell again at length on the Duke and his women friends. In the prime of life he settled for clever women, but still with the emphasis frankly on what they could give to him. A snatch of dialogue recorded by Fanny Salisbury makes the point:

I asked him if he thought Ly Peel had any influence over her husband. 'No, she is not a clever woman – Peel did not wish to marry a clever woman.' I observed how extraordinary it seemed to me that a man of abilities should not wish to have a wife capable of entering into the subjects in which he took interest – 'and of anticipating one's meaning [interposed the Duke] – that is what a clever woman does – she sees what you mean.'*[34]

As he grew older the relations subtly changed. He found more pleasure in giving. From Lady Wilton, a hard woman, he received only a modest return for his friendship. Between himself and each of the Lady Salisburys a perfect interchange was established, despite the difference in age. His love for Angela Burdett-Coutts was the final stage, showing itself in the prodigal expenditure of thought and imagination on *her* interests, her talents, her future. Such a radiation of protective and eager devotion made his friendship irresistible.

'Transparent' is one of the adjectives that seems to have been made for Wellington. His contemporary and friend, G. R. Gleig, wrote at the end of his biography that if anyone was still in doubt about Wellington's character it was the biographer's fault, since no great man's character was ever 'more completely free from disguise'.

Yet there are opacities, mainly in the Duke's attitude to politics and

---

* Compare Dr Johnson on the actress Kitty Clive: 'Clive, Sir, is a very good thing to sit by; she always understands what you say.'

party. He put country above party. Did he, as critics have suggested, put himself above party also?

British politics claim to be grounded in a mature patriotism so that the eternal triangle of country, party and self cannot be dismembered or despised in any of its parts, however much they may war with one another at times. When the Duke saw himself as the Sovereign's retained servant he was linking two arms of the triangle – self and country – in a noble and honourable way. Moreover, he saved the party of the 'right' from disaster when he saved its major constitutional long-stop, the House of Lords. Without his reiterated commands to faceabout and retreat, the Lords might have been mown down and thrown like the proverbial grass into the oven.

Would that have been such a bad thing in the 1830s and 1840s? It would have saved much subsequent trouble, including the Parliament Act of 1911 to restrict their powers.

The answer must surely be that in the crucial years sandwiched between two European revolutions, 1830–48, the risk to British democracy would have been unjustified. The great landed and financial interests would hardly have surrendered their Upper House without attempting a counter-revolution. In those stormy times British democracy and the budding party system might well have vanished into the oven, along with the old constitutional House of Lords. By preventing the Upper House from dashing itself to pieces against the Commons, Wellington may have saved more than he knew.[35]

As for his putting himself above party, there was no admixture of personal ambition to this trait, which was in any case a limited one. Twice in his career – 1834 and 1839 – he made the *gran rifiuto* of supreme office. Few other British statesmen have refused the premiership once; only one more than once.*

How far was the great Duke aware that his sublime position above party and almost beyond politics could not be taken as an example by other statesmen? He was well aware. He may not have foreseen, as Disraeli did, how the British party system would develop, but he fully realized that his own stance, half within and half outside, was a political once-for-all, or at any rate, once in a century. 'This anomalous position' was how he described it to Lord Londonderry in 1846.[36]

Wellington's relations with the army were complex and unusual. As

---

* Lord Hartington refused in 1880 and 1886; Lord Halifax took steps in 1940 which prevented his being asked.

a disciplined body of men he was devoted to them, and they to him; not because he was *séduisant* in the way that people found Napoleon seductive, but for the trust he invited and never betrayed, for the guns he never lost and the armies he never threw away. Old soldiers who accosted him in the streets were rewarded with a sovereign from a stock kept ready in a special purse; it contained three when he died. Yet in the long bitter controversies over flogging he could not be brought to abandon that most abominable of deterrents. He still insisted before the Royal Commission on Military Punishments in 1836 that Prussian reforms were not suited to Britain, clinging to his old distinction between an army of conscripts drawn from every class and a volunteer force generally supplied by the lowest.

Ten years later, on 9 August 1846, the masters of Manchester Grammar School asked him his views on the subject, hoping they might have softened. He replied that he dared not yet do without flogging entirely, and people like them who lived in Manchester where the army was so often called in to disperse mobs ought to be thankful it was a disciplined army. In his last speech on flogging, however, delivered in the Lords two days later, he recognized that the change would come. Flogging was on the way out. Twenty years before, one soldier in fifty had been flogged per year; by 1844 the figure had dropped to one in 194.

'I hope I may live,' he said, 'to see it abolished altogether.'

His pathetic decline during the last ten years when he held the chief command has already been taken into account, together with its serious consequences to the Crimean soldiers. Nevertheless he gave to the Crimean army, and to every British army, a tradition of victory, a pride, a doggedness, an iron nerve even in the most unnerving conditions, without which they must have succumbed as in 1793–5.

It is usual to compare great commanders with their peers, in many ways a profitless task. With regard to the strategy and tactics of Wellington and Napoleon, 'their only common characteristic was an overwhelming tendency to be victorious'.[37] Comparisons between himself and Marlborough were often invited by Wellington's contemporaries, and though he deprecated them he was occasionally drawn into giving a view. 'I can conceive nothing greater than Marlborough at the head of an English Army,' he once told Lord Mahon.

He had greater difficulties than I had with his Allies; the Dutch were worse to manage than the Spaniards or Portuguese. But on the other hand I think I had more difficulties at home. He was all in all with the administration, but I supported the Government much more than they supported me![38]

When Mahon wished to publish this judgement, however, the Duke replied sharply:

I can't help thinking that if you avoid to make a comparison between living and dead persons you might as well not make me settle the comparison for you. I am convinced that you will see that you cannot publish what you propose without writing a History of the War and of the State of this Nation; and of Europe at each Period.

Lord Mahon hastily agreed.

In this always unreal exercise, Napoleon must be the key figure, since it was he who in his own day disputed with Wellington the supreme title. Everything was done by their respective nations to enhance their own hero and belittle his rival: the French chess set with Napoleon as white king and Wellington a mere black bishop, the English anagram of Arthur Wellesley, Duke of Wellington – 'Let well foil'd Gaul secure thy renown.'*

At their most magnanimous the rivals freely conceded one another's genius, Napoleon admitting during the voyage to St Helena that the Duke had everything he had, with prudence added; Wellington never deviating from his original dictum that Napoleon's presence on the field was worth forty thousand men. When asked who was the greatest general of the age, General Sir John Le Couteur remembered the Duke replying, 'In this age, in past ages, in *any* age, Napoleon.'[39]

Napoleon was more dazzlingly prodigal with men and material, Wellington more brilliantly economical. If the French Chasseurs could be made to perform miracles, so could the Scots Greys. Napoleon created his élitist gigantic Guard, Wellington his thin red line. Wellington's stroke was a battering-ram, according to William Napier, Napoleon's the onrush of a wave. The Prussian military writer, General Carl von Clausewitz, made a brave attempt to cut down both heroes to size over the Waterloo campaign. His strictures on Wellington added up to one argument: that the British general could have stood shoulder to shoulder with the Prussians at *any point* he cared to choose, without waiting to see where the French would strike, since Napoleon was bound to see him out in a head-on collision wherever he stood.

---

* The modern French mastery of the Waterloo battlefield shows signs of slipping. A traveller in 1971 who asked why there were no Wellington busts in the shops was told, 'He does not sell.'

This criticism was rightly rejected by the Duke when he read it in 1842. It virtually demanded of him second sight, as well as a crude view of Napoleon quite out of character, at least until after the bludgeoning and pounding of Waterloo.

Napoleon's total genius exerts a more powerful attraction on the world than Wellington's, partly because the Emperor was defeated and died in exile and partly because he chose the nations for his footstool and Europe for his throne. 'He was a glorious tyrant after all,' said Byron.[40] Despite wide experience of dictators, mankind prefers to lie prostrate in imagination at the feet of the world's masters, rather than turn to the honest and just men of history.

The great, idealistic impulses in the Emperor do indeed shine forth in splendour: those that made him give France the *code Napoléon*, establish national education and put a field-marshal's baton into the knapsack of every common soldier. But all the fine things he was going to do in the way of liberating the European peoples if he had won Waterloo were propaganda issued from St Helena after the time for doing them had passed. In his day it was felt that despite his constructive legacies to the French he had left them with a spoilt palate for constitutional government.

Wellington handed down to his fellow-countrymen a clear mandate to make constitutional government work. His total genius was less spectacular than Napoleon's, apart from the fact that he seldom used theatrical aids to communication. Napoleon, he once remarked, was 'a great man but also a great actor'. Speaking of General Montgomery in 1944, the Permanent Head of the British Foreign Office wrote, 'I don't believe he's a general at all, but just a film star.'[41] Wellington did not belong to this, in many ways effective, school of leadership. Did he also have to manage without the gift of intuitive genius?

In his Wellington Memorial Lecture, 1969, Lord Montgomery described the Duke as 'the best soldier our nation has produced for many a long day'. This said, he failed to find in him that 'inner conviction, which at times will transcend reason.' A moment comes for boldness. 'When that moment comes, will you soar from the known to the unknown? In the answer to this question lies the supreme test of generalship in high command.'

Wellington must be allowed to answer this challenge in his own words, as recorded by Frances Salisbury in her diary:

'There is a curious thing that one feels sometimes; when you are considering a subject, suddenly a whole train of reasoning comes before you like a flash of light; you see it all (moving his hand as if something appeared before him, his eye with its brightest expression), yet it takes you perhaps two hours to put on paper all that has occurred to your mind in an instant. Every part of the subject, the bearing of all the parts upon each other, and all the consequences are there before you.'[42]

Wellington the commander was restricted by the politicians as Napoleon never was, and his titanic tussle with Marshal Massena in Portugal put a stamp of defensiveness on his generalship that was belied by Salamanca, Vitoria and the Pyrenees. Before Waterloo itself he said, 'Now I will show the French how I can *defend* a position' – meaning that in the years before he had constantly been on the attack.

His political imagination could not compete with Napoleon's but its limitations did far less damage than his great opponent's boundless range. His temperamental objection to reminiscences, outside his official *Despatches*, had its advantages. In our over-all knowledge of the man, it adds almost as much as it takes away. What a character, who could be persuaded to write in the margins of contemporary accounts of his battles only the words 'True' and 'False'; or even merely the letters 'L.' and 'D.L.' – Lie and Damned Lie.[43]

In the halls of virtue rather than fame, the Duke makes an incomparably better showing. Goodness, in a Christian sense, did not enter into Napoleon's motivation. For the purpose of bestriding Europe it would have been foolish to choose compassion and humility as mounting-blocks. The two men's ideas of duty were radically different. Wellington's has already been examined; Napoleon wrote to his brother Jerome: 'Never forget that . . . your first duty is to me, your second is to France.'[44]

Wellington's sense of Britain's place in the world was essentially non-aggressive. 'A sort of fabulous Englishman,' he wrote after the Chinese Opium War, 'is not to be permitted to go about the world bullying, smuggling, and plundering as he pleases.'[45]

His sense of mankind's place linked him with another great soldier-statesman, George Washington, to whom he was indeed likened by the American minister, Edward Everett. 'I have always felt the Highest respect for the character of General Washington,' wrote the Duke to Everett in thanking him for the comparison.[46] Curiously relevant to the Duke's refrain, 'I am but a man', is the story of Washington riding through a small town and overhearing a girl of seven, brought out to see the hero, exclaim,

'Why, he is only a man!' The General swept off his hat, bowed and said,

'Yes miss, that's all I am.'

There is one last image which must be either fitted into or discarded from the Wellingtonian gallery – the Iron Duke. The iron in his make-up was often molten, but when it was cool it possessed an incomparable quality. Wellington showed the army that a man could have an iron constitution not because he had been born with one but because he had acquired it the hard way. Though some of his hardness belonged to the leader's stock-in-trade, it exhibited more than common resilience. He showed the world of politics that the stern Tory need not always be unbending or the silent Englishman always stern.

Nevertheless he had a defect that was popularly associated with the cold hard side of an Iron Duke. He was generally insensitive to the spirit of the times and lacked the political warmth and luminosity that imagination gives. Obsessed by the first French Revolution, he was adamant that reform threatened the constitution. He was therefore a reactionary in a revulsion from the liberal movements of Europe and in his affinity with the High Tories at home. The French Revolution, however, simply put a permanent edge on these feelings; it did not create them. He was not anxious to put the clock back, but like the aristocracy as a whole he found himself suited by things as they were. Change he disliked in his very bones. He accepted it only when he had to. At such times he was a pragmatist and did what was necessary and seemed to him right. With his pragmatism, however, the picture shifts again. He found it necessary to break with the French Ultras over constitutional government. He found it necessary to break with the British Ultras over Catholic emancipation, and despite reconciliations to give them more than one subsequent hammering. Thus he could behave as a man of iron towards reactionaries as well as radicals. For this steely impartiality even those who were most conscious of his defects had to give him credit.

Then the succeeding generations got hold of him. His arresting character, moulded by traditions and legends, or transmuted through the Brontës' genius into the Rochesters, Helstones and Moores (with just a touch of Heathcliff) was finally handed down to a later race of 'strong silent Englishmen' doing their imperial duty in pith helmets and at all times and everywhere keeping a stiff upper lip. That was not the Duke.

His iron was closer to reality: sometimes feared as men feared the 'iron-handed despotism' of the Industrial Revolution in Dickens's *Hard Times;* always honoured like the 'pillar of iron' in the *Book of Jeremiah;* once chosen by Teilhard de Chardin as the noble metal that gave him 'the feeling of full personality'. There were repressed and repressive elements in Wellington, but these did not prevent the full personality from breaking through. It was during the second half of his life that the process came to fruition. As a young man he had heard Pitt's unforgettable words, 'England saved herself by her exertions and will, as I trust, save Europe by her example.' He himself was soon to be honoured for his exertions and his example. But his glory lay also in the fact that he did not cease from mental fight even after he had received the ultimate acclaim and seen his physical battles become legends in his lifetime. No man ever rested less on his laurels. Sometimes mistakenly, always selflessly, he continued to serve. After Waterloo they called him the Great Captain. If he had fallen on the field it would have been as the Great Captain that he was remembered. He lived to become the Great Duke. In those two words his countrymen, going beyond rank and honours, have paid tribute to a hero and saluted the completeness of a man.

Select Bibliography

MANUSCRIPT SOURCES

Royal Archives, Windsor Castle.

Royal Archives, the Royal House, The Hague.

Wellington MSS. in the possession of the Duke of Wellington, K.G.

Raglan MSS. in the possession of Lord Raglan. For the correspondence of Wellington, his brother Lord Maryborough (William Wellesley-Pole) and Lord Fitzroy Somerset, afterwards Lord Raglan.

Confidential Memoranda of Admiral Sir George Seymour, in the possession of Mrs Freda Loch.

Letters of Captain Arthur Kennedy, in the possession of Sir Anthony Weldon.

Arthur Shakespear's journal, in the possession of the Countess of Albemarle.

Extracts from the *Notes Journalières* of General Maximilien Foy, in the possession of the Comte Sébastien Foy.

Longford MSS. in the possession of Mr Thomas Pakenham.

Archives of the House of Rothschild, London.

Archives of the Household Cavalry Museum, Windsor.

Public Record Office of Northern Ireland. For the Drenan MS, 1803, Oriel papers and Stewart Papers.

Pratt Papers, Kent County Archives. For 1795–6.

Lady Dalrymple-Hamilton's Diary, in the possession of Admiral Sir F. Dalrymple-Hamilton.

The British Library for the Wellesley, Peel, Aberdeen, Huskisson, Place and other manuscripts.

National Library of Ireland, for Wellington correspondence; letters of Maria Edgeworth to Lady Romilly: the Wellington Monument.

Irish State Paper Office, for Wellington correspondence.

West Sussex Record Office, for Maxse papers.

Surrey Record Office, for Goulburn papers.

Frances Lady Salisbury's Journal, in the possession of the Marquess of Salisbury.

Letters of Anna Maria Jenkins, in the possession of Rice University, Texas.

MSS copy of Lord Hatherton's diary, in the possession of Colonel R. J. Longfield.

Stewart papers, in the possession of Mr Michael Farrar-Bell.

Department of Western MSS, Bodleian Library, Oxford, for Dr Wynter's papers and Wellington correspondence.

Spicer letters, in the possession of Mrs Noel Tweddell.

A Tour of Waterloo 1815, in the possession of the Naval and Military Club.

Letters of Lord Wellesley and others, in the possession of Mr John Showers.

Letters concerning Wellington, in the possession of Lord Kenyon, Brigadier K. Thompson, Mr R. Boulind, Mr P. Skottowe, the Society for the Promotion of Christian Knowledge.

PUBLISHED SOURCES

Airlie, Mabell, Countess of: *Lady Palmerston and her Times* (2 vols., London, 1922).

Albemarle, George Thomas, Earl of: *Fifty Years of my Life* (London, 1877).

Aldington, Richard: *Wellington* (London, 1946).

Alington, Cyril, *Twenty Years of Party Politics – being a Study of the Development of the Party System between 1815 and 1835* (Oxford U.P., 1921).

Allan, General: Extracts from diary published by Lt. Col. J. G. O. Whitehead, *Army Quarterly*, October 1965.

Anglesey, Marquess of: *One-Leg, The Life and Letters of Henry William Paget, 1st Marquess of Anglesey* (London, 1961).

Annual Register.

Arbuthnot, Mrs P. S.-M.: *Memories of the Arbuthnots of Kincardineshire and Aberdeenshire* (London, 1920).

Arbuthnot: *The Journal of Mrs Arbuthnot*. Edited by Francis Bamford and the Duke of Wellington (2 vols., London, 1950).

Archer, Mildred: *Tippoo's Tiger* (Victoria and Albert Museum, 1959).

Aspinall, A.: *The Correspondence of Charles Arbuthnot*. Edited by A. Aspinall, Camden 3rd Series, LXV (London, 1941).

Aspinall, A.: *The Correspondence of George, Prince of Wales*, I 1770–89, II, 1789–94, III 1795–8, IV 1799–1804 (London, 1963–7), V 1804–6 (London, 1968).

Aspinall, A.: *The Diary of Henry Hobhouse 1820–1827*. Edited by A. Aspinall (London, 1947).

Aspinall, A.: *The Formation of Canning's Ministry, February to August 1827*. Edited by A. Aspinall, Camden 3rd Series, LIX (London, 1937).

Aspinall, A.: *Later Correspondence of George III*, III 1798–1801 (London, 1967), IV 1802–7 (London, 1968).

Aspinall, A.: *The Letters of George IV* (3 vols., Cambridge U.P., 1938).

Aspinall, A.: *Three Early Nineteenth Century Diaries* (Le Marchant, Ellenborough and Littleton, afterwards Hatherton). Edited by A. Aspinall (London, 1952).

Baldick, R.: *The Duel, A History of Duelling* (London, 1965).

Bamford, Samuel: *Passages in the Life of a Radical* (2 vols., London, 1844).

Barnard: *The Barnard Letters*. Edited by Anthony Powell (London, 1928).

Barnes, Thomas: *Parliamentary Portraits* (London, 1815).

Barrington, Daines: *Miscellanies* (London, 1781).

Barrington, Sir Jonah: *Personal Sketches of His Own Times* (2 vols., London, 1869, first published, 1827).

Bartlett, C. J.: *Castlereagh* (London, 1967).

Beatson, Lt.-Col. Alexander: *Views of the Origin and Conduct of the War with Tippoo Sultaun* (London, 1800).

Bell, H. C. F.: *Lord Palmerston* (2 vols., London, 1936).

Bennell, A. S.: 'Wellesley's Settlement of Mysore, 1799' (*Journal of the Royal Asiatic Society*, October 1952).

Bennell, A. S.: 'The Anglo-Maratha Confrontation, Factors in the Marquis Wellesley's Failure against Holkar, 1804' (*Bulletin of the School of Oriental and Asian Studies*, vol. xxviii, part 3, 1965).

Berry: *Journal and Correspondence of Miss Berry, 1783–1852*. Edited by Lady Theresa Lewis (London, 1865).

Bessborough: *Lady Bessborough and Her Family Circle*. Edited by the Earl of Bessborough in collaboration with A. Aspinall (London, 1940).

Best, G.: 'The Protestant Constitution and its Supporters, 1800–1829', vol. 18, 5th series, Royal Historical Society.

Bird, Anthony: *The Damnable Duke of Cumberland* (London, 1966).

Blake, Robert: *Disraeli* (London, 1966).

Blake, Robert: *The Conservative Party from Peel to Churchill* (London, 1970).

Blakeney, Robert: *A Boy in the Peninsular War* (London, 1899).

Blanch, Lesley: *The Game of Hearts, Harriette Wilson and her Memoirs* (London, 1957).

Blessington: *The Literary Life and Correspondence of the Countess of Blessington*. Edited by R. R. Madden (2 vols., London, 1855).

Bolitho, Hector: *The Galloping Third* (London, 1963).

Bowdler, C. Henry: *The Iron Duke's Dentures*, British Dental Journal, October 1968.

Bowring: *Autobiography of Sir John Bowring* (London, 1877).

Bragge: *Peninsular Portrait. Letters of Captain William Bragge*. Edited by A. C. Cassels (London, 1963).

Brett-James, Antony: *Wellington at War, 1794–1815. A Selection of his Wartime Letters edited and introduced* (London, 1961).

Brett-James, Antony: *The Hundred Days. Napoleon's Last Campaign from Eye witness Accounts* (London, 1964).

Brialmont and Gleig: *The Life of the Duke of Wellington* (2 vols., London, amended edition, 1862).

Briggs, Asa: *The Age of Improvement* (London, 1965).

Brontë, Charlotte: *Shirley* (London, 1849).

Brontë, Charlotte: *The Search after Happiness* (London, 1969).

Brougham: *Works of Henry Lord Brougham* (vols. 3–5, 'Statesmen of the Times of George III and George IV', London edition 1872–3).

Broughton, Lord (John Cam Hobhouse): *Recollections of a Long Life* (4 vols., London, 1911).

Bryant, Sir Arthur: *The Great Duke* (London, 1971).

Bryant, Sir Arthur: *The Napoleonic Wars* (3 vols., London, 1942–50).

Buchan, Susan: *The Sword of State: Wellington after Waterloo* (London, 1928).

Buckingham and Chandos, Duke of: *Memoirs of the Court and Cabinets of George III* (4 vols., London, 1853).

Buckingham and Chandos, Duke of: *Memoirs of the Court of George IV, 1820–1830* (2 vols., London, 1859).

Buckingham and Chandos, Duke of: *Memoirs of the Court and Cabinets of William IV and Victoria* (2 vols., London, 1861).

Burghclere: *A Great Man's Friendship. Letters of the Duke of Wellington to Mary, Marchioness of Salisbury, 1850–1852*. Edited by Lady Burghclere (London, 1927).

Burghersh: *The Correspondence of Lady Burghersh with the Duke of*

Wellington. Edited by Lady Rose Weigall (London, 1903).

Butler, J. R. M.: *The Passing of the Great Reform Bill* (London, 1914).

Byron's Correspondence: Edited by John Murray (2 vols., London, 1912).

Calvert: *An Irish Beauty of the Regency.* Compiled from the unpublished journals of the Hon. Mrs Calvert, 1789–1822, by Mrs Warrenne Blake (London, 1911).

Camden Miscellany: Some Letters of the Duke of Wellington to his Brother William Wellesley-Pole. Edited by Sir Charles Webster (vol. xviii, Royal Historical Society, 1948).

Capel: *The Capel Letters,* 1814–1817. Edited by the Marquess of Anglesey (London, 1955).

Castlereagh: *Despatches* (12 vols., London, 1848–1853).

Cecil, David: *Lord M. or the Later Life of Lord Melbourne* (London, 1954).

Chad: *The Conversations of the First Duke of Wellington with George William Chad.* Edited by the Seventh Duke of Wellington (Cambridge, 1956).

Chadwick, Owen: *The Victorian Church* (Part I., London, 1966).

Chandler, David G.: *The Campaigns of Napoleon* (New York, 1966, London, 1967).

Charles X and Louis Philippe: The Secret History of the Revolution of July 1830. By one of King Charles's officers. (London, 1839).

Chateaubriand: *The Memoirs of Chateaubriand.* Edited by Robert Baldick (London, 1961).

Chesney, R. E.: *Waterloo Lectures. The Campaign of 1815* (London, 1869).

Christophe, Robert: *Napoleon on Elba* (Paris, 1959; London, 1964).

Clark, George Kitson: *Peel and the Conservative Party 1832–1841* (London, 2nd edition 1964).

Clarkson, Thomas: *History of the Abolition of the African Slave Trade by the British Parliament* (London, 1808).

Cloncurry, Lord: *Personal Recollections of the Life and Times of Valentine (Lawless) Lord Cloncurry* (Dublin, 1849).

Cobbett, William: *History of the Regency and Reign of King George IV* (London, 1830).

Cobbett, William: *The Political Register.*

Cobbett, William: *Rural Rides* (London, 1853).

Colborne: *Life of Sir John Colborne, Field-Marshal Lord Seaton* by G. C. Moore Smith (London, 1903).

Colby, Reginald: *The Wellington Despatch* (Victoria and Albert Museum, 1965).

Colchester: *The Diary and Correspondence of Charles Abbot Lord Colchester.* Edited by his son (3 vols., London, 1861).

Cole: *Memoirs of Sir Galbraith Lowry Cole*. Edited by M. Lowry Cole and S. Gwynn (London, 1934).

Coleridge: *Unpublished Letters of Samuel Taylor Coleridge*. Edited by E. L. Griggs (2 vols., London, 1932).

Combermere: *Memoirs and Correspondence of Field-Marshal Viscount Combermere*. Edited by Lady Combermere and W. Knollys (2 vols., London, 1866).

Cooper, Duff: *Talleyrand* (London, 1932).

Cooper, Leonard: *The Age of Wellington* (London, 1964).

Costello, Edward: *Adventures of a Soldier* (London, 1952).

Cotton, Edward: *A Voice from Waterloo* (Brussels, 5th edition 1854).

Cox, Cynthia: *Talleyrand's Successor, Duc de Richelieu, 1766–1822* (London, 1959).

Creasy, Sir Edward: *Fifteen Decisive Battles of the World* (London, 1867).

Creasy, Sir Edward: *Eminent Etonians* (London, 1876).

Creevey, Thomas: *The Creevey Papers*. Edited by Sir H. Maxwell (London, 1904).

Creevey, Thomas: *The Creevey Papers*. Edited by John Gore (London, 1934).

Croker, John Wilson: *The Croker Papers, 1808–1857* (3 vols., London, 1884).

Croker, John Wilson: *The Croker Papers*, Edited by Bernard Pool (London, 1967).

Cruttwell, C. M.: *Wellington* (London, 1936).

Dalton, Charles: *The Waterloo Roll Call* (London, 1900).

D'Arblay, (Fanny Burney): *The Diaries of Madame D'Arblay*. Edited by her niece (7 vols., London, 1854).

Davis, H. W. C.: *The Age of Grey and Peel* (Oxford, 1929).

De Bas, Colonel F., and Le Comte J. de T'Serclaes de Wommerson: *La Campagne de 1815 aux Pays-Bas d'après les rapports officiels néerlandais* (3 vols., Brussels, 1908).

De Grey, Earl: *Characteristics of the Duke of Wellington* (London, 1853).

De Lancey: *A Week at Waterloo in 1815. Lady de Lancey's Narrative*. Edited by Major B. R. Ward (London, 1906).

Delany: *The Autobiography and Correspondence of Mary Granville, Mrs Delany* (2 vols., London, 1861).

Demeter, Karl: *The German Officer Corps in Society and State, 1650–1945* (London, 1965).

De Ros: *A Sketch of the Life of Georgiana Lady de Ros* (née Lennox) by the Hon. Mrs J. R. Swinton (London, 1893).

Dickens, Charles: *Hard Times* (London, 1854).

Disraeli, Benjamin: *Vivian Grey* (London, 1826).

Disraeli, Benjamin: *Coningsby or The New Generation* (London, 1844).

Disraeli, Benjamin: *Sybil or The Two Nations* (London, 1845).

Disraeli, Benjamin: *Lord George Bentinck: A Political Biography* (London, 2nd edition 1852).

Dixon, Pierson: *Pauline, Napoleon's Favourite Sister* (London, 1964).

Doyle, James Warren: *Letters on the State of Ireland*, 1825 (using the pen-name of 'J.K.L.', i.e. Bishop James of Kildare and Leighlin).

Eaton, Charlotte A. (née Waldie): *The Days of Battle, or Quatre Bras and Waterloo* (London, 1853, first published, 1816).

Eden: *Miss Eden's Letters*. Edited by her great-niece, Violet Dickinson (London, 1919).

Edgeworth, Maria: *The Absentee* (London, 1812).

Edgeworth, Maria: *Castle Rackrent* (London, 1800).

Edgeworth: Maria Edgeworth *Letters from England 1813-1844*. Edited by Christina Colvin (Oxford U.P., 1971).

Edgeworth: *The Life and Letters of Maria Edgeworth*. Edited by Augustus Hare (2 vols., London, 1894).

Edgeworth: *The Memoirs of Richard Lovell Edgeworth* (2 vols., London, 1820).

Egremont, Lord: *Wyndham and Children First* (London, 1968).

Elers: *Memoirs of George Elers, 1777-1842*. Edited by Monson and Leveson Gower (London, 1903).

Ellenborough, Lord: *A Political Diary 1828-1830*. Edited by Lord Colchester (2 vols., London, 1881).

Ellesmere: *Personal Reminiscences of the Duke of Wellington by Francis, First Earl of Ellesmere*. Edited by Alice, Countess of Strafford (London, 1903).

Ellison, The Rev. C. C.: *Riocht Na Midhe*. Records of Meath Archaeological and Historical Society (vol. iii, no. 4, Dublin, 1966; vol. iv, no. 1, 1967).

Elvey: *Life and Reminiscences of Sir George Elvey* (London, 1894).

Elvin, Charles: *History of Walmer Castle* (Privately printed, 1894).

Farmar, Hugh: *A Regency Elopement* (London, 1969).

Fitzgerald, Percy: *The Life and Times of William IV* (2 vols., London, 1884).

Fitzpatrick, W. J.: *Ireland before the Union, with revelations from the unpublished diary of Lord Clonmell* (Dublin, 1887).

Following the Drum: Edited by Sir John Fortescue (London, 1931).

Fortescue, Sir John: *History of the British Army* (vols. iv–x, London, 1906–20).

Fortescue, Sir John: *Wellington* (London, 1925).

Fox: *Journal of the Hon. Henry Edward Fox, 4th and last Lord Holland, 1818–1830.* Edited by Lord Ilchester (London, 1923).

Foy: *Vie Militaire du Général Foy*, by Maurice Girod de l'Ain (Paris, 1900).

Fraser, Sir William: *Words on Wellington* (London, 1899).

Frazer: *Letters of Colonel Sir Augustus Frazer* (London, 1859).

Frith, W. P.: *My Autobiography and Reminiscences* (2 vols., London, 5th edition 1888).

Fulford, Roger: *George IV* (London, 2nd edition, 1949).

Fulford, Roger: *The Life of Samuel Whitbread* (London, 1967).

Fulford, Roger: *The Royal Dukes* (London, 1933).

Fulford, Roger: *The Trial of Queen Caroline* (London, 1967).

Gash, Norman: *F.R. Bonham*, English Historical Review, (October 1948).

Gash, Norman: *Mr Secretary Peel, The Life of Sir Robert Peel to 1830* (London, 1961).

Gash, Norman: *Politics in the Age of Peel, A Study in the Technique of Party Representation 1830–1850* (London, 1953).

George, Eric: *The Life and Death of Benjamin Robert Haydon 1786–1846* (London, 1967).

Gibney, Dr: *Eighty Years Ago, or the Recollections of an Old Army Doctor.* Edited by Major R. D. Gibney (London, 1896).

Gladstone, W. E.: *The Gladstone Papers* (London, 1930).

Gleig, G. R.: *Life of Arthur Duke of Wellington* (London, 1889).

Gleig, G. R.: *Reminiscences of the First Duke of Wellington* (London, 1904).

Glover, Michael: *Legacy of Glory* (New York, 1971).

Glover, Michael: *Wellington as Military Commander* (London, 1968).

Glover, Michael: *Wellington's Peninsular Victories* (London, 1963).

Glover, Richard: *Peninsular Preparation* (Cambridge U.P., 1963).

Gordon, Sir A.: *The Earl of Aberdeen* (London, 1893).

Gower, Lord Ronald: *My Reminiscences* (London, 1883).

Gower, Lord Ronald: *Old Diaries 1881–1901* (London, 1902).

Granville: *G. Leveson Gower, First Lord Granville, Correspondence* (2 vols., London, 1916).

Granville, Lady: *Letters of Harriet Countess Granville 1810–1845.* Edited by her son, the Hon. F. Leveson Gower (2 vols., London, 1894).

Grassini: *La Chanteuse de l'Empereur par René Jeanne* (Paris, 1949).

Grattan, William: *Adventures with the Connaught Rangers* (2 series of 2 vols. each, 1847; edited by C. Oman and republished, 1902).

Gray, Denis: *Spencer Perceval* (London, 1963).

Greville: *The Greville Memoirs, 1817–60.* Edited by H. Reeve (8 vols., London, 1875–87), by L. Strachey and R. Fulford (8 vols., 1938).

Griffiths, Major Arthur: *The Wellington Memorial, Wellington and His Contemporaries* (London, 1897).

Gronow: *The Reminiscences and Recollections of Captain Gronow.* Edited by John Raymond (London, 1964).

Guedalla, Philip: *The Duke* (London, 1931).

Guest: *Lady Charlotte Guest, Extracts from her Journal 1833–1852.* Edited by the Earl of Bessborough (London, 1950).

Hamilton, John: *Sixty Years Experience as an Irish Landlord* (London, 1894).

Hamwood Papers of the Ladies of Llangollen. Edited by Mrs G. H. Bell (London, 1930).

Hare, Augustus: *The Story of My Life* (vols. 4 and 5, London, 1900).

Harris: *Recollections of Rifleman Harris* (London, 1829).

Haswell, C. J. D.: *The First Respectable Spy: The Life and Times of Colquhoun Grant, Wellington's Head of Intelligence* (London, 1969).

Hay, Captain William: *Reminiscences, 1808–1815* (London, 1901).

Haydon, B. R.: *The Autobiography and Memoirs of Benjamin Robert Haydon.* Edited from his Journals by Tom Taylor (2 vols., London, 1926).

Haydon, B. R.: *Correspondence and Table-Talk* (2 vols., London, 1876).

Haydon, B.R.: *Lectures on Painting and Design* (2 vols., 1846).

Hazlitt, William: *The Spirit of the Age or Contemporary Portraits* (London, 1825).

Hemlow, Joyce: *The History of Fanny Burney* (Oxford U.P., 1958).

Henderson, E. F.: *Blücher and the Uprising against Napoleon* (London, 1911).

Herold, J. C.: *Mistress to an Age, a life of Madame de Staël* (London, 1959).

Herrick, C. T.: *Letters of the Duke of Wellington to Miss J. Edited with extracts from Miss J's diary by Christine Terhune Herrick* (London, 1889).

Hickey: *Memoirs of William Hickey.* Edited by Alfred Spencer (4 vols., London, 1925).

Hidy, Ralph W.: *The House of Baring in American Trade and Finance. English Merchant Bankers at Work, 1763–1861* (Harvard U.P., 1949).

Hill, Constance: *Juniper Hall* (London, 1905).

Hill, Rev. Edwin Sidney: *The Life of Lord Hill* (London, 2nd edition, 1845).

Hobhouse, Christopher: *1851 and The Crystal Palace* (London, 1937).

Hobsbawn, E. J. and Rudé, George: *Captain Swing* (Harvard U.P., 1949; London, 1969).

Hodson, L. J.: *A Short History of the Parish of Salehurst* (1914).

Holland: *Lady Holland's Journal*. Edited by the Earl of Ilchester (2 vols., 1908).

Holland, Lord: *Further Memoirs of the Whig Party 1807–1821*. Edited by Lord Stavordale (London, 1905).

Hook, Theodore: *Life of Sir David Baird* (2 vols., 1833).

Houssaye, Henry: *1815: La Première Restauration – Le Retour de l'île d'Elbe – Les Cents Jours* (Paris, 1893).

Houssaye, Henry: *1815: La Seconde Abdication – La Terreur Blanche* (Paris, 1905).

Houssaye, Henry:*1815: Waterloo*. Translated by A. E. Mann, edited by A. Euan-Smith (London, 1990).

Howarth David: *A Near Run Thing* (London, 1968).

Hudleston, F. J.: *Warriors in Undress* (London, 1925).

Hudson, Derek: *The Forgotten King and Other Essays* (for Miss Jenkins) (London, 1960).

Hunt: *Memoirs of Henry Hunt from Ilchester Jail* (2 vols., London, 1820).

Hussars: *Memoirs of the 10th Hussars* (1891).

Hyde, H. Montgomery: *The Strange Death of Lord Castlereagh* (London, 1959).

Inglis, Brian: *Poverty and the Industrial Revolution* (London, 1971).

Inglis, Brian: 'Sir Arthur Wellesley and the Irish Press', *Hermathena, LXXXIII*, 1954.

Jackson, Lt.-Col. Basil: *Notes and Reminiscences of a Staff Officer*. Edited by R. C. Seaton (London, 1903).

James: *The Journal of Surgeon James*. Edited by Jane Vansittart (London, 1964).

Jeejeebhoy, J. R.: *The Duke of Wellington in Bombay, 1801 and 1804* (Bombay, 1927).

Jenkins, Roy: *Asquith* (London, 1964).

Jeune: *Pages from the Diary of an Oxford Lady, 1843–1862* (Mrs M. D. Jeune). Edited by Margaret Jeune Gifford (Oxford, 1932).

Jones: *Letters from the Duke of Wellington to Mrs Jones of Pantglas*. Edited by her daughter Mrs Davies-Evans, Century Magazine, December 1889.

Jones, Lt.-Col. Sir John T.: *Account of the War in Spain, Portugal and the South of France, 1808–1814* (3 vols., London, 2nd edition, 1821).

Jones, Lt.-Col. Sir John T.: *Journals of the Sieges in Spain, 1811–1814, with Notes and Memoranda relevant to the Lines, 1810* (London, 3rd edition, 1846).

Kee, Robert: *The Green Flag, A History of Irish Nationalism* (London, 1972).

Kelly, Christopher: *The Memorable Battle of Waterloo* (London, 1818).

Kincaid, Captain John: *Adventures in the Rifle Brigade* (London, 1830).

Kinsey, Rev. W. M.: *Portugal Illustrated in a Series of Letters* (Lisbon, 1829).

Kurtz, Harold: *The Trial of Marshal Ney* (London, 1957).

Lachouque, Henry: *Anatomy of Glory, Napoleon and his Guard*. Translated by A. S. K. Brown. (London, 1961).

Lamb, Lady Caroline: *Glenarvon* (3 vols., London, 1816).

Larpent: *The Private Journal of F. Seymour Larpent, Judge-Advocate General*. Edited by Sir George Larpent (2 vols., 2nd edition, 1853).

Lawrence: *The Autobiography of Sergeant William Lawrence*. Edited by G. N. Bankes (London, 1886).

Leeke, William: *The History of Lord Seaton's Regiment and Autobiography of the Rev. William Leeke* (2 vols., London, 1866, Supplement, 1871, 1st edition, Le Havre, 1850).

Lennox: *Life and Letters of Lady Sarah Lennox* (Napier). Edited by Ilchester and Stavordale (2 vols., London, 1901).

Lennox, Lord William: *Three Years with the Duke, or Wellington in Private Life*, by an ex-aide-de-camp (London, 1853).

L'Eveque, Henry: *Costumes of Portugal* (Paris, 1814).

Liddell Hart, B. H.: *Famous British Generals* (London, 1951).

Liddell Hart, B. H.: *Strategy, the Indirect Approach* (London, 1954).

Lieven: *Correspondence of Lord Aberdeen and Princess Lieven 1832–1854*. Edited by E. Parry Jones, Camden 3rd series, vol. LX (London, 1938).

Lieven: *Correspondence of Princess Lieven and Earl Grey*. Edited by Guy Le Strange (3 vols., London, 1890).

Lieven: *Lettres de François Guizot et de la Princesse de Lieven* (Paris, 1963).

Lieven: *Unpublished Diary and Political Sketches of Princess Lieven*. Edited by Harold Temperley (London, 1925).

Lieven: *Letters of Dorothea, Princess Lieven, during her Residence in London 1812–1834*. Edited by Lionel G. Robinson (London, 1902).

Lieven: *The Private Letters of Princess Lieven to Prince Metternich 1820–1826*. Edited by Peter Quennell (London, 1937).

Lincoln, L. J., and McEwen, R. L.: *Lord Eldon's Anecdote Book* (London, 1960).

Livermore, H. V.: *A New History of Portugal* (Cambridge U.P., 1966).

Londonderry and Gleig: *The Story of the Peninsular War* (London, 1827).

Long: *A Peninsular Cavalry General: The Correspondence of Lt.-Gen. Robert Ballard Long*. Edited by T. H. McGuffie (London, 1951).

Longford, Elizabeth: *Victoria R.I.* (London, 1964). *Queen Victoria: Born to Succeed* (New York, 1965).

Longford, Elizabeth: *Wellington: The Years of the Sword* (London and New York, 1969). *Pillar of State* (London and New York, 1972).

Lutyens, Mary: *Effie in Venice, Unpublished letters of Mrs John Ruskin written from Venice between 1849–1852*. Edited by Mary Lutyens (London, 1965).

Lynch, P. and Vaizey, J.: *Guinness's Brewery in the Irish Economy 1759–1876* (Cambridge U.P., 1960).

Macaulay, Rose: *They Went to Portugal* (London, 1946).

McGrigor: *The Autobiography of Sir James McGrigor*, late Director-General of the Army Medical Department (London, 1861).

Macintyre, Angus: *The Liberator, Daniel O'Connell and the Irish Party, 1830–1847* (London, 1965).

Malcolm: *The Life and Correspondence of Maj.-Gen. Sir John Malcolm*. Edited by J. W. Kaye (2 vols., London, 1856).

Malmesbury: *Letters of the First Earl of Malmesbury, 1745–1820* (2 vols., London, 1870).

Marchand, Leslie A.: *Byron: A Critical Introduction with an annotated Bibliography* (3 vols., London, 1957).

Markham, Felix: *Napoleon* (London, 1962).

Marshall-Cornwall, Sir James: *Marshal Massena* (Oxford U.P., 1965).

Martineau, Harriet: *A History of the Thirty Years Peace, 1816–1846* (2 vols., London, 1850).

Maxwell, Constantia: *County and Town in Ireland under the Georges* (London, 1940).

Maxwell, Constantia: *Dublin under the Georges, 1718–1830* (London, 1956).

Maxwell, Sir Herbert: *The Life of Wellington* (2 vols., London, 1899).

Medwin, Thomas: *Conversations of Lord Byron, Noted during a Residence with his Lordship at Pisa* (vol. I, London, 1824).

Mercer, General Cavalié: *Journal of the Waterloo Campaign* (2 vols., London, 1870).

Montgomery, Field-Marshal Viscount: *A History of Warfare* (London, 1968).

Monypenny, W. F. and Buckle, G. E.: *The Life of Benjamin Disraeli, Earl of Beaconsfield* (2 vols., London, 1929).

Moody, T. W. and Martin, F. X. (editors): *The Course of Irish History* (Cork, 1967).

Moore, D. C.: 'The Other Face of Reform', *Victorian Studies* 1961–2 (Indiana University).

Moore, Thomas: *A Selection from Tom Moore's Diary*. Edited by J. B. Priestley (London, 1925).

Morgan, Lady (Sidney Owenson): *The Wild Irish Girl* (London, 1818); *The O'Briens and The O'Flaherty's* (London, 1828); *Florence Macarthy* (London, 1839).

Morgan, Lady: *Autobiography, Diaries and Correspondence* (2 vols., London, 1862).

Morris, Thomas: *Recollections of Military Service* (London 1847, new edition by J. Selby, 1969).

Morton, Frederic: *The Rothschilds* (London, 1962).

Mudford, William: *The Campaign in the Netherlands in 1815* (London, 1817).

Müffling, Baron von: *A Sketch of the Battle of Waterloo* (6th edition, London, 1870).

Müffling, Baron von: *Passages from my Life*. Translated and edited by Philip Yorke (London, 2nd edition, 1853).

Namier, Sir Lewis: *Personalities and Powers* (London, 1955).

Namier, Sir Lewis: Essays Presented to Sir Lewis Namier. Edited by Richard Pares and A. J. P. Taylor (London, 1956).

Napier: *The Life and Opinions of Gen. Sir Charles Napier* by Lt. Gen. William Napier (4 vols., London, 1857).

Napier: *Passages in the Early Life of Gen. Sir George Napier*. Edited by his son Gen. William Napier (London, 1884).

Napier, Sir William F. P.: *History of the War in the Peninsula and the South of France 1807–1814* (6 vols., London, Cavendish edition, 1886).

Napier: *Life and Letters of Sir William Napier*. Edited by H. A. Bruce (2 vols., London, 1864).

Napoleon at Waterloo: Edited by Bruce Low (London, 1911).

Napoleon's Memoirs. Edited by S. de Chair (London, 1948).

Naylor, John: *Waterloo* (London, 1960).

Neale, Dr Adam: *Letters from Portugal and Spain* (London, 1809).

Neumann: *Diary of Philip von Neumann 1819–1850*. Edited by E. B. Chancellor (2 vols. London, 1928).

Newman, Aubrey: *The Stanhopes of Chevening* (London, 1969).

Nowlan, Kevin B.: *The Politics of Repeal, A Study in the Relations between Great Britain and Ireland 1841–1850* (London, 1965).

Old Soldier: *Life Military and Civil of the Duke of Wellington digested from the materials of W. H. Maxwell and re-written by an Old Soldier* (London, 1852).

Oman, Carola: *The Gascoyne Heiress, The Life and Diaries of Frances Mary Gascoyne-Cecil, 1802–39* (London, 1968).

Oman, Sir Charles: *A History of the Peninsular War* (7 vols., Oxford U.P., 1902–30).

Oman, Sir Charles: *Studies in the Napoleonic Wars* (London, 1929).

Pakenham Letters: Edited by the 5th Earl of Longford (London, privately printed, 1914).

Pakenham, Thomas: *The Year of Liberty: The Great Irish Rebellion of 1798* (London, 1969).

Palmerston: *The Letters of Lady Palmerston*. Edited by Tresham Lever (London, 1957).

Pange, Victor de: *The Unpublished Correspondence of Madame de Staël and the Duke of Wellington*. Translated by Harold Kurtz (London, 1965).

Parker, C. S.: *Sir Robert Peel* (3 vols., London, 1891–1899).

Peel: *The Private Letters of Sir Robert Peel*. Edited by George Peel (London, 1920).

Peninsular Sketches by Actors on the Scene. Edited by W. H. Maxwell (2 vols., London, 1845).

Percival, Victor: *The Duke of Wellington, A Pictorial Survey of his Life* (Victoria and Albert Museum, London, 1969).

Petrie, Sir Charles: *Wellington, A Reassessment* (London, 1956).

Physick, John: *The Duke of Wellington in Caricature* (Victoria and Albert Museum, London, 1965).

Physick, John: *The Wellington Monument* (Victoria and Albert Museum, London, 1970).

Picton: *Memoirs of Sir Thomas Picton*. By H. B. Robinson (2 vols., 1836).

Pirenne, Jacques-Henri: *Le Congrès d'Aix-la-Chapelle et L'apogée de l'influence russe après Napoléon* (Brussels, 1953).

Pirenne, Jaques-Henri: *La Sainte Alliance* (Brussels, 1961). *Great Britain and the Treaty of Ghent, Herdenking van de 150e Verjaardag van de Vrede van Ghent*, with Sir Charles Petrie and others (Brussels, 1965).

Plumb, J. H.: *The First Four Georges* (London, 1956).

Poynter, J. R.: *Society and Pauperism 1795–1834* (London, 1969).

Raikes: *Journal of Thomas Raikes, 1831–1847* (4 vols., London, 1856).

Redding, Cyrus: *Personal Reminiscence of Eminent Men* (3 vols., London, 1867).

Richardson, Ethel: *Long Forgotten Days* (London, 1928).

Ridley, Jasper: *Lord Palmerston* (London, 1970).

Roberts, P. E.: *India Under Wellesley* (London, 1929).

Rogers: *Recollections of Samuel Rogers*. Edited by W. Sharpe (London, 1859).

Rogers: *Recollections of the Table-Talk of Samuel Rogers*. Edited by A. Dyce (London, 1856 and 1887).

Rolo, P. J. V.: *George Canning* (London, 1965).

Ropes, John Codman: *The Campaign of Waterloo* (New York, 1892).

Rose: *Diaries and Correspondence of the Rt. Hon. George Rose*. Edited by L. V. Harcourt (2 vols., London, 1860).

Rose, John Holland: *A Short Life of William Pitt* (London, 1925).

Rose, John Holland: *William Pitt and the Great War* (London, 1911).

Russell, G. W. B.: *Collections and Recollections* (London, 3rd edition, 1898).

Salisbury: *A Great Man's Friendship. Letters of the Duke of Wellington to Mary, Marchioness of Salisbury, 1850–1852*. Edited by Lady Burghclere (London, 1927).

Saunders, Edith: *The Hundred Days* (London, 1964).

Schaumann, A. L. F.: *On the Road with Wellington. The Diary of a War Commissary in the Peninsular Campaigns*. Edited and translated by A. Ludovici (London, 1924).

Seymour: *Confidential Memoranda by Admiral Sir George Seymour* (Loch MSS).

Shaw-Kennedy, Sir James: *Notes on the Battle of Waterloo with a Memoir* (London, 1865).

Shelley: *The Diary of Frances Lady Shelley*. Edited by her grandson Richard Edgecumbe (2 vols., London, 1912).

Sherer, Moyle: *Recollections of the Peninsula* (London, 4th edition, 1825).

Simmons, J. S. G.: 'The Duke of Wellington and the Vice-Chancellorship in 1844'. Bodleian Library Record, V (1954–6), 37–52.

Smith: *Autobiography of Lt.-Gen. Sir Harry Smith*. Edited by G. C. Moore Smith (2 vols., London, 1901).

Smyth, Sir John: *In This Sign Conquer: The Story of the Army Chaplains* (London, 1968).

Spencer-Stanhope: *The Letter-Bag of Lady Elizabeth Spencer-Stanhope* (2 vols., London, 1912).

Stacton, David: *The Bonapartes* (New York, 1966; London, 1967).

Stanhope, Philip Henry, 5th Earl: *Life of Pitt* (vol. 4, London, 1879).

Stanhope, Philip Henry, 5th Earl: *Notes of Conversations with the Duke of Wellington, 1831–1851* (London, 1888).

Stanley: *Letters of Lady Augusta Stanley, A Young Lady at Court, 1849–1863.* Edited by the Dean of Windsor and Hector Bolitho (London, 1927).

Stapleton, A. G.: *George Canning, 1822–1827* (3 vols., London, 1831).

Stevens, Joan: *Victorian Faces, An Introduction to the papers of Sir John Le Couteur* (Jersey, 1969).

Stuart, D. M.: *Daughters of George III* (London, 1939).

Surtees, W. E.: *A Sketch of the Lives of Lords Stowell and Eldon* (London, 1846).

Tallon, Maura: *The Patriot Bishop of Kildare and Leighlin* (Dr Doyle) (Journal of the Kildare Archeological Society, vol. XIV.2.1966–7).

Temperley, H. V.: *Life of Canning* (London, 1905).

Thackeray, W. M.: *The Irish Sketch Book, 1842–1844* (first vol. published London, 1843).

Tollemache, L. A.: *Old and Odd Memories* (London, 1908).

Tomkinson, Lt.-Col. William: *The Diary of a Cavalry Officer in the Peninsular and Waterloo Campaigns, 1809–1815.* Edited by his son James Tomkinson (London, 1894).

Trench: *The Remains of the late Mrs Richard Trench* (Mrs St George) *being selections from her Journals etc.* (London, 1862).

Trevelyan, Sir G.M.: *British History of the Nineteenth Century and After* (London, 2nd edition, 1937).

Turbeville, A.S.: *The House of Lords in the Age of Reform, 1784–1837* (London, 1958).

Tussaud, John Theodore: *The Romance of Madame Tussaud's* (London, 1925).

Tussaud: *Catalogue of Pictures and Historical Relics* by W. Wheeler (London, 1901).

Twiss, Horace: *The Public and Private Life of Lord Chancellor Eldon* (3 vols., London, 1844).

Twiss, Richard, F. R. S.: *A Tour in Ireland* (London, 1775).

Victoria, Queen: *The Girlhood of Queen Victoria 1832–1840.* Edited by Viscount Esher (2 vols., London, 1912).

Victoria, Queen: *The Letters of Queen Victoria 1837–1861.* First Series, vol. I. 1837–1843, vol. II. 1844–1853. Edited by A. C. Benson and Viscount Esher. (London, 1907).

Vivian, Hon. Claud: *Richard Hussey Vivian, First Baron Vivian, A Memoir* (London, 1897).

Walmsley, Robert: *Peterloo: The Case Reopened* (Manchester U.P., 1969).

Ward, S. G. P.: *Wellington* (London, 1963).

Ward, S. G. P.: *Wellington's Headquarters, 1809–14* (Oxford U.P., 1957).

Waterloo. Account by a Staff Officer, Paris, 10 July 1815 (London, 1815).

Waterloo, The Battle of, by 'A Near Observer' (London, 1817).

Waterloo: by 'An Officer' (Pack's brigade), *United Service Magazine*, part II, 1841.

Waterloo Letters. A Selection from original and hitherto unpublished Letters bearing on the 16th, 17th, and 18th June, by Officers who served in the Campaign. Edited by Maj-Gen. H.T. Siborne (London, 1891).

Webster, Sir Charles: *The Congress of Vienna, 1814–15* (London, 1934).

Weiner, Margery: *A Sovereign Remedy, Europe after Waterloo* (London, 1971).

Weller, Jac: *Wellington in the Peninsula, 1808–14* (London, 1962).

Weller, Jac: *Wellington at Waterloo* (London, 1967).

Wellesley: *Diary and Correspondence of Henry Wellesley, 1st Lord Cowley, 1790–1846.* Edited by the Hon. F. A. Wellesley (London, 1930).

Wellesley: *The Indian Despatches of the Marquess Wellesley* (5 vols., London, 1836).

Wellesley, Lord Gerald, and Steegman, J.: *Iconography of the 1st Duke of Wellington* (London, 1935).

Wellesley, Muriel: *The Man Wellington* (London, 1937).

Wellesley, Muriel: *Wellington in Civil Life* (London, 1939).

Wellesley Papers by the Editor of the *Windham Papers*, (2 vols., London, 1914).

Wellington: *Despatches, Correspondence, and Memoranda of Arthur Duke of Wellington (New Series) 1819–1832.* Edited by his son (8 vols., London, 1867–1880).

Wellington: *The Dispatches of Field Marshal the Duke of Wellington during his various Campaigns.* Compiled by Lt.-Col. Gurwood (12 vols. London, 1834–8).

Wellington: *Supplementary Despatches, Correspondence, and Memoranda of Field Marshal Arthur Duke of Wellington, K.G.* Edited by his son the Duke of Wellington (Vols. I–XI, London, 1858–64).

Wellington: *A Selection from the Private Correspondence of the First Duke of Wellington.* Edited by the Duke of Wellington (The Roxburghe Club, London, 1952).

Wellington: *Speeches of the Duke of Wellington in Parliament*. Collected by Col. Gurwood (London, 1854).

Wellington Anecdotes: (2nd edition, London, 1852).

Wellington and His Friends: Letters of the 1st Duke of Wellington to the Rt. Hon. Charles and Mrs Arbuthnot, the Earl and Countess of Wilton, Princess Lieven, and Miss Burdett-Coutts, selected and edited by the 7th Duke of Wellington (London, 1965).

Wellington Studies: Essays by five Old Wellingtonians, edited by Michael Howard (1959).

Wellingtoniana: Anecdotes, Maxims and Characteristics of the Duke of Wellington by John Timbs (London, 1852).

Wheatley: *The Diary of Edmund Wheatley*. Edited by Christopher Hibbert (London, 1964).

Wheeler: *The Letters of Private Wheeler, 1809–1828*. Edited and with a Foreword by Captain B. H. Liddell Hart (London, 1951).

Whitehead, Lt. Col. J. G. O.: 'Wellington at Waterloo', Army Quarterly, October 1965.

Wilkins, W. H.: *Mrs Fitzherbert and George IV* (2 vols. London, 1905).

Williams, David: *John Frost, A Study in Chartism* (Cardiff, 1939).

Williams, Helen Maria: *The Present State of France* (London, 1815).

Willis, G. M.: *Ernest Augustus Duke of Cumberland* (London, 1954).

Willis, N. P.: *Pencillings by the Way* (2nd edition, London, 1850).

Wilson, Harriette: *Harriette Wilson's Memoirs of Herself and Others* (London, 1929).

With Napoleon at Waterloo and other unpublished documents of the Waterloo and Peninsular Campaigns. Edited by Mackenzie Macbride (London, 1911).

Woodham-Smith, Cecil: *The Great Hunger, 1845–1849* (London, 1962).

Young, Arthur, *A Tour in Ireland* (Dublin, 1780).

Young, Desmond, *Fountain of the Elephants*, Life of de Boigne (London, 1959).

Ziegler, Philip: *The Duchess of Dino* (London, 1962).

Ziegler, Philip: *A Life of Henry Addington, 1st Viscount Sidmouth* (London, 1965).

Ziegler, Philip: *William IV* (London, 1971).

References

Wellington's *Despatches* and *Supplementary Despatches* are abbreviated to '*Desp.*' and '*Supp. Desp.*' respectively. The word 'despatches' is spelt uniformly for the sake of clarity throughout this book, except in the Bibliography. Wellington's *Despatches, Correspondence and Memoranda (New Series)* is abbreviated to '*Desp.* NS'.

1 RETAINED FOR LIFE

1 Wellington MSS., 2 September 1843.
2 Barrington, Daines, 317–18.

2 ODD MAN OUT

1 Hamilton, p. 12.
2 Gleig, *Life*, p. 4.
3 *Etoniana*, No. 76, 11 November 1939, Diary of Miss Margaretta Brown.
4 *Hamwood Papers*, p. 1; MS of an unpublished book by K. M. R. Kenyon based on 100 letters from Miss Sarah Ponsonby to her cousin Miss Tigh.
5 Brialmont and Gleig, I. 6.
6 Ellesmere, p. 102.
7 Butler, p. 53.
8 Stanhope, p. 218.
9 *Wellingtoniana*, p. 7.
10 Maxwell, Sir Herbert, I. 5–6.
11 Wellington MSS., 15 November 1850.
12 *Hamwood Papers*, p. 72, 21 June 1788.

3 FOOD FOR POWDER

1 Morgan, *The O'Briens and the O'Flahertys*, II. 85.
2 *Hamwood Papers*, p. 152.

3 *Hamwood Papers*, p. 254, 17 July 1790.
4 Wellington MSS., 28 March 1790.
5 Wellington MSS., 8 May 1790.
6 Maxwell, Sir Herbert, I. 8.
7 *Private Correspondence*, pp. 1–2, Hon. A. Wesley to Hon. C. D. S. Pakenham.
8 Stanhope, p. 182.
9 Guedalla, p. 45.
10 Aspinall, *George III*, I. xv, 2 December 1794.
11 *Supp. Desp.*, XIII, 2.
12 Ellesmere, p. 161.
13 Stanhope, p. 182.
14 Stanhope, p. 111.
15 Guedalla, p. 51; Wellington MSS., 25 June 1795.
16 Pratt, U 840/C 121/1; 122/3; Wellington MSS., 30 September 1795.
17 Guedalla, p. 52, 15 September 1795.
18 Guedalla, p. 54; Wellington MSS., 5 and 16 June 1796.
19 Pratt, U 840/C 121/2; *Supp. Desp.*, I. 18; Hill, p. 42.

4 ASCENDANCY IN THE EAST

1 Wellington MSS., 9 March 1797, to General Cunninghame.
2 Hickey, I. 79 and 154.

3 Hickey, I. 190–1.
4 Wellington MSS., 17 April 1797, to Lord Mornington.
5 Wellington MSS., 11 April 1797, to General St Leger.
6 Wellington MSS., 20 May 1797, Lord Mornington.
7 *Supp. Desp.*, I. 17–18; Wellington MSS., 12 July 1797.
8 *Supp. Desp.*, I. 12–17; Wellington MSS., 27 July 1797.
9 *Supp. Desp.*, I. 17.
10 Hickey, I. 171–2.
11 Buckingham, II. 372, April 1797, Buckingham to Lord Mornington.
12 Aspinall, *George III*, II. 627, 3 October 1797.

5 TIGERS OF MYSORE

1 Hickey, I. 175.
2 *Supp. Desp.*, I. 86, 15 December 1798.
3 Wellington MSS., 19 and 21 October 1798.
4 *Supp. Desp.*, I. 151.
5 Beatson, p. 28.
6 *Supp. Desp.*, I. 187–8, 29 January 1799.
7 *Supp. Desp.*, I. 180–1 and 199, 20 January and 27 February 1799.
8 Hook, I. 157.
9 Wellington MSS., 20 March 1799.
10 *Supp. Desp.*, I. 202–3, 21–22 March 1799.
11 *Supp. Desp.*, I. 206–8.
12 *Desp.*, I. 24.
13 National Library of Ireland, 18 April 1799, A. Wellesley to Knight of Kerry.
14 *Supp. Desp.*, I. 209.
15 Indian Despatches of Marquess Wellesley, I. 522.
16 Hook, I. 187.
17 Elers, p. 103.
18 *Supp. Desp.*, I. 246, 14 and 19 June 1799.

19 Wellesley Papers, I. 121, Lord Wellesley to Pitt, April 1800.
20 *Supp. Desp.*, I. 461, 26 February 1800, to Colonel Agnew.
21 *Wellingtoniana*, p. 18.
22 *Desp.*, I. 37, 1 December 1800.
23 *Supp. Desp.*, II. 306, 19 December 1800.
24 *Supp. Desp.*, II. 325, 8 January 1801.
25 *Desp.*, I. 35–6, 6 October 1800.
26 *Supp. Desp.*, II. 364, 21 March 1801.
27 *Desp.*, I. 70, 18 February 1801.
28 Wellington MSS., 23 March 1801.
29 *Supp. Desp.*, II. 355, 10 April 1801, to Colonel Montresor.
30 *Supp. Desp.*, II. 408, 26 May 1801, to Henry Wellesley.
31 *Supp. Desp.*, II. 409, 15 June 1801, from Henry Wellesley.
32 *Supp. Desp.*, II. 501, 8 July 1801, to Henry Wellesley.
33 Hickey, IV. 267.
34 Wellington MSS., 7 July 1801, to Henry Wellesley.

6 THAT IS ALL INDIA

1 *Supp. Desp.*, II. 474–5, 20 and 27 June 1801, from and to Colonel Wilkes.
2 *Supp. Desp.*, II. 587, 21 October 1801, to Colonel Webbe.
3 Wellington MSS., 19 March 1802, to Hon. Basil Cochrane.
4 *Supp. Desp.*, III. 67, 8 February 1802, to Major Thomas Munro.
5 *Supp. Desp.*, III. 42, January 1802, to General Stuart.
6 Gleig, *Life*, p. 41.
7 *Supp. Desp.*, IV. 71–3, 97–8, 27 May 1803, to General Lake.
8 *Desp.*, I. 198.
9 Bennell, *The Anglo-Maratha Confrontation*, p. 125, Meyrick-Shawe to Malcolm.
10 *Supp. Desp.*, IV. 154, 17 August

1803, report to General A.
Wellesley.

11 Ellesmere, p. 138.

12 Oman, Carola, p. 239.

13 Pool, *Croker*, pp. 99–100.

14 Stanhope, p. 49.

15 *Desp.*, I. 387.

16 *Desp.*, I. 402.

17 Pool, *Croker*, p. 99.

18 Oman, Carola, p. 216.

19 *Desp.*, III. 330, 12 October 1803.

20 Chad, p. 20.

21 *Supp. Desp.*, IV. 184–7.

22 J. R. Jeejeebhoy, *The Duke of Wellington in Bombay, 1801 and 1804,* (1927).

23 Stanhope, p. 182.

24 *Ibid.*

25 Stanhope, p. 67.

26 *Supp. Desp.*, IV. 466.

27 *Supp. Desp.*, IV. 466.

28 *Desp.*, III. 188, 17 March 1804, to Major John Malcolm.

29 Hickey, IV. 22.

30 *Supp. Desp.*, IV. 492, 17 February 1805, to Major John Malcolm.

31 Elers, p. 166.

32 *Supp. Desp.*, II. 409, 15 June 1801, from Henry Wellesley.

33 *Desp.*, II. 345.

34 *Supp. Desp.*, IV. 507, 3 July 1805, to Major John Malcolm.

35 Stanhope, p. 57.

36 Stanhope, p. 49; *Times* review of *Despatches,* 5 March 1838.

37 Stanhope, p. 270; Ellesmere, p. 182.

38 *Supp. Desp.*, II. 567, 27 September 1801, to Commander-in-Chief.

39 *Supp. Desp.*, IV. 312, 7 January 1804, to Governor Duncan.

40 *Supp. Desp.*, IV. 504, 9 March 1805.

41 *Supp. Desp.*, II. 547–8, to Major Doolan.

42 *Desp.*, I. 521–2, footnote.

43 *Desp.*, I. 323, 21 August 1803, to Colonel John Murray.

44 Elers, p. 126.

45 Guedalla, p. 117.

46 Elers, p. 126.

47 Wellington MSS., 20 June 1807, from Major John Malcolm.

48 *Private Correspondence*, pp. 2–3, [1801], from Colonel M. Beresford.

49 *Private Correspondence*, pp. 3–4, August [1801], to Hon. Mrs Sparrow.

50 *Private Correspondence*, pp. 5–6, 7 May [1802], Hon. C. D. S. Pakenham to Hon. Mrs Sparrow.

7 MY DEAREST KITTY

1 Barrington, Sir Jonah, p. 177.

2 *Croker Papers*, II. 233, 1 October 1834.

3 *Supp. Desp.*, IV. 533; Wellington MSS., 21 December 1805, to Lord Wellesley.

4 *Private Correspondence*, pp. 7–8.

5 Calvert, pp. 66–7.

6 Wellington MSS., Memorandum by Mrs Catherine Foster.

7 Calvert, p. 67.

8 *Private Correspondence*, pp. 9–10, copy of letter from Hon. C. D. S. Pakenham to Sir Arthur Wellesley, sent to Hon. Mrs Sparrow, 5 November 1805.

9 Stanhope, *Pitt*, IV. 347.

10 *Supp. Desp.*, IV. 540.

11 *Supp. Desp.*, VI. 587, to Major John Malcolm.

12 *Desp.*, II. 616, footnote.

13 Guedalla, p. 129.

14 Mrs Arbuthnot, I. 169, 27 June 1822.

15 Edgeworth, Maria, I. 149–50, 13 April 1806; I. 150, 1 May 1806.

16 Edgeworth, Maria, I. 151, 23 May 1806.

17 Letter in author's possession.
18 Wellington MSS.

8 THE GILT POTATO

1 *Supp. Desp.*, IV. 587, 31 July 1806, to Malcolm.
2 Wellington MSS., 6 July 1807.
3 *Private Correspondence*, pp. 12–13, 18 and 25 July 1807.
4 *Supp. Desp.*, V. 108.
5 *Supp. Desp.*, V. 143.
6 *Supp. Desp.*, V. 68.
7 *Supp. Desp.*, V. 47.
8 Wellington MSS., 21 May 1807.
9 *Supp. Desp.*, V. 69, 1 June 1807.
10 Wellington MSS., 22 November 1807.
11 *Supp. Desp.*, V. 14–16, 26 April 1807.
12 *Supp. Desp.*, V. 120, 16 July 1807, from Secretary Trail.
13 *Supp. Desp.*, V. 98.
14 National Library of Ireland, MS. 4707.
15 *Supp. Desp.*, IV. 546–585, Memorandum written on board ship while returning to England, 1805.
16 *Supp. Desp.*, V. 125, 24 July 1807, to Duke of Richmond.
17 National Library of Ireland, MS. 8637.
18 Napier, Charles, I. 77.
19 Fortescue, *British Army*, VI. 66.
20 *Supp. Desp.*, VI. 12.
21 Wellington MSS., 7 December 1807.
22 *Supp. Desp.*, V. 139.
23 H. J. Barnes, *History Today*, 1967, 'Father Robertson in Denmark'; Oman, Sir Charles, *Napoleonic Wars*, 'Tales of the Secret Service', p. 125; Oman, Carola, p. 210.

9 MY DIE IS CAST

1 *Desp.*, IV. 4.
2 Wellington MSS., 25 June 1808, to General Charles Stewart.

3 *Supp. Desp.*, VI. 90.
4 *Supp. Desp.*, VI. 95, 1 August 1808, to Duke of Richmond.
5 *Supp. Desp.*, VI. 116, 16 August 1808, to Duke of Richmond.
6 *Ibid.*
7 Fortescue, *British Army*, VI. 231.
8 Raglan MSS. No. 3, 22 August 1808.
9 *Supp. Desp.*, VI. 123, 23 August 1808, to Duke of Richmond.
10 Cobbett, *Political Register*, pp. 481–502, 24 September 1808.
11 Raglan MSS. No 5; *Supp. Desp.*, VI. 138.
12 *Desp.*, VI. 143, 17 September 1808.
13 Stanhope, p. 244.
14 Granville, I. 339.
15 Pool, *Croker*, p. 96.

10 CINTRA AND CHARYBDIS

1 Gore, *Creevey*, p. 54.
2 *Supp. Desp.*, VI. 133, 12 October 1808.
3 Brett-James, *Wellington at War*, p. 137.
4 *Harriette Wilson*, pp. 51, 58–9.
5 *Harriette Wilson*, p. 60.
6 Mrs Arbuthnot, I. 378, 19 February 1825.
7 Elers, p. 57.
8 *Supp. Desp.*, V. 567, 12 March 1809.
9 *Supp. Desp.*, V. 575, 17 February 1809, and V. 579, 19 February 1809, to Duke of Richmond.
10 *Supp. Desp.*, VI. 210.
11 Wellington MSS., 2 April 1809.
12 *Supp. Desp.*, V. 634; Irish State Papers Office, 588/AAE/984/4, 'Public works in Ireland', No. 93, Memo undated.
13 *Harriette Wilson*, pp. 74–5.
14 *Harriette Wilson*, p. 78.
15 *Harriette Wilson*, p. 156.

11 THE HIDEOUS LEOPARD

1 Londonderry and Gleig, I. 303–304.
2 *Desp.*, IV. 247, 24 April 1809, to Frere.
3 Raglan MSS. No. 132 (I), 12 May 1809, to General Beresford.
4 *Desp.*, IV. 317, 18 May 1809, to Castlereagh.
5 *Creevey Papers*, I. 105, 4 September 1809.
6 *Desp.*, IV. 296, 11 May 1809.
7 Oman, Sir Charles, II. 363 and 300.
8 *Desp.*, IV. 352, 31 May 1809, to Castlereagh.
9 *Supp. Desp.*, VI. 343, 30 May 1809.
10 *Desp.*, IV. 344, 30 May 1809.
11 *Desp.*, IV. 385, 11 June 1809.
12 *Desp.*, IV. 394, 13 June 1809.
13 Raglan MSS. No. 13, 1 July 1809.
14 *Desp.*, IV. 496–8.
15 Stanhope, p. 46.
16 Wellington MSS. *Duchess's Journal*.
17 *Croker Papers*, I. 417, 27 April 1828.
18 Oman, Sir Charles, II. 505.
19 Fortescue, *British Army*, VII. 239.
20 *Croker Papers*, I. 433, 17 October 1828.
21 *Desp.*, IV. 508, 29 July 1809, to Castlereagh.
22 Brett-James, *Wellington at War*, p. 159.
23 *Supp. Desp.*, VI. 431, 3 December 1809, to Major Barclay.
24 Raglan MSS. No. 93, 22 August 1809, from W. Wellesley-Pole.
25 *Desp.* V. 156, 16 September 1809.
26 Ellesmere, p. 90; Gleig, *Life*, p. 443.

12 RETREAT TO PORTUGAL

1 *Desp.*, V. 8, 8 August 1809, to Castlereagh.
2 Napier, George, p. 169.
3 Burghclere, p. 107–10.
4 Brett-James, *Wellington at War*, p. 165, quoting John Scott's *Paris Revisited in 1815*.
5 Brett-James, *Wellington at War*, p. 176.
6 Wellington MSS., Duchess's Journal, 12 August 1809 and 29 January 1811.
7 Ziegler, *Addington*, p. 285.
8 Ward, *Wellington* p. 78.
9 Calvert, p. 144.
10 Raglan MSS. No. 24, 6 October 1809.
11 Raglan MSS. No. 25, 22 October 1809 (part to be found in Brett-James, pp. 173–4).
12 Calvert, p. 150.
13 Fortescue, *British Army*, VII. 330.
14 *Desp.*, V. 31, 2 August 1809, to J. C. Villiers.
15 *Pakenham Letters*.
16 *Desp.* V. 230–5.
17 Smith, Sir H., *Autobiography*, I. 38.
18 *Desp.*, V. 466, 31 January 1810.
19 McGrigor, p. 283.
20 Napier, William, *Peninsula*, p. xxiii.
21 *Desp.*, VIII. 148.
22 Raglan MSS. No. 28.
23 Incident related to the author by Lord Head, who heard it from Mr Duff Cooper.
24 Raglan MSS. No. 28, 4 January 1810; *Desp.* V. 391, 2 January 1810, to W. Wellesley-Pole.
25 Raglan MSS. No. 138.
26 *Desp.*, VI. 5–9, 2 April 1810.
27 British Museum, Add. MSS. 37415, Letter 57, to Lord Wellesley.

28 *Pakenham Letters*, 10 July 1810.
29 Guedalla, p. 196, quoting Lowry Cole MSS.
30 Long, p. 248.
31 *Supp. Desp.*, VI. 582, 29 August 1810.
32 *Supp. Desp.*, VI. 468, 9 January 1810, from Liverpool.
33 Raglan MSS. No. 34, 5 September 1810, to W. Wellesley-Pole.
34 *Desp.*, V. 392, 2 January 1810.
35 Brett-James, *Wellington at War*, p. 185, 26 January, and p. 189, 6 April 1810, to W. Wellesley-Pole.
36 Raglan MSS. No. 93, 2 August 1809.
37 Oman, Sir Charles, III. 233 and Fortescue, *British Army*, VII. 420.
38 Oman, Sir Charles, III. 272.
39 Kinsey, *Portugal Illustrated*.
40 *Desp.*, VI. 428, 18 September 1810.
41 *Desp.*, VI. 436, 22 September 1810; *Supp. Desp.*, VI. 609, 4 1810, Massena to Berthier.
42 Marshall-Cornwall, p. 36.

13 THEY SHALL NOT PASS

1 Oman, Carola, p. 208.
2 Napier, George, p. 142.
3 Raglan MSS. No. 35, 4 October 1810, to W. Wellesley-Pole.
4 *Supp. Desp.*, VI. 610–11.
5 Wellington MSS., 8 October 1810.
6 Wellington MSS., 13 October 1810.
7 *Pakenham Letters*, 9 November 1810.
8 Raglan MSS. No. 39, 11 January 1811. (This letter is published in part in *Supp. Desp.*, VII. 403, but with these passages omitted.)
9 Raglan MSS. No. 109, 7 December 1810.

10 *Supp. Desp.*, VI. 606, 4 October 1810 to C. Stuart; VI. 616, 13 October 1810, to Liverpool.
11 Wellington MSS., 6 January 1810, from Colonel Peacock.
12 *Supp. Desp.*, VI. 467, 5 January 1810.
13 *Desp.*, VI. 467, 6 October 1810, to C. Stuart.
14 Wellington MSS., 25, 27 December 1810, from General Craufurd.
15 Marshall-Cornwall, p. 231.
16 *Desp.*, VII. 195, 28 January 1811, to Colonel Torrens.
17 *Desp.*, VII. 211, 23 February 1811, to Liverpool.
18 *Pakenham Letters*, 16 March 1811.
19 *Desp.*, VII. 429.

14 THE KEYS OF SPAIN

1 *Desp.*, VII. 169, to C. Stuart.
2 *Supp. Desp.*, VII. 177, to W. Wellesley-Pole.
3 Grattan, First Series, I. 96.
4 *Desp.*, VII. 571, to Perceval.
5 Larpent, I. 86.
6 *Desp.*, VII. 533, 12 May 1811, to General Beresford.
7 *Supp. Desp.*, VII. 123, 15 May 1811, to W. Wellesley-Pole.
8 *Desp.*, VII. 558, 19 May 1811.
9 Ellesmere, p. 107.
10 Maxwell, W. H. *Peninsular Sketches*, I. 331.
11 *Desp.*, VII. 635, 8 June 1811, to Stuart.
12 *Pakenham Letters*, 5 July 1811.
13 Bragge, p. 8, 29 August 1811.
14 Wellington MSS., 18 December 1811.
15 *Supp. Desp.*, VII. 166, 25 June 1811; Raglan MSS. No. 114, 16 June 1811.
16 Royal Archives, 18640, 25 June 1811, to Colonel J. Willoughby Gordon.
17 *Pakenham Letters*, 20 August 1811.

18 *Desp.*, VIII. 225.
19 *Pakenham Letters*, 29 September 1811.
20 Wellington MSS., September 1812.
21 Wilkins, I. 131.
22 Robinson, *Picton*, II. 63; Maxwell, *Peninsular Sketches*, I. 240 and 249.
23 Smith, Sir H., *Autobiography*, I. 58; Grattan, Second Series, I. 306, quoting Gurwood, 1843.
24 Fortescue, *British Army*, VIII. 364.
25 Smith, Sir H., *Autobiography*, I. 60.
26 Fraser, Sir W., p. 181.
27 *Desp.*, IX. 1, 20 January 1812, to Lady Sarah Napier.
28 Wellington MSS., 19 February 1812, from Lady Sarah Napier.
29 Stanhope, p. 29.
30 Grattan, First Series, I. 193–4 and 144–5.
31 Fortescue, *British Army*, VIII. 400.
32 Fortescue, *British Army*, VIII. 405 (J. Stanhope MS.); *Pakenham Letters*, 27 June 1812; Stanhope, p. 9.
33 Oman, Sir Charles, V. 255, 7 April 1812, to Liverpool.
34 St Aubyn, G. R., *Wellington, Studies*.

15 GRANDEUR AND MISERY

1 Raglan MSS. No. 46, 29 April 1812.
2 *Desp.*, IX. 240, 18 June 1812..
3 *Supp. Desp.*, VII. 307, to Duke of Richmond.
4 Raglan MSS. No. 143, 29 June 1812; *Desp.* IX. 239.
5 *Desp.*, IX. 183, 28 May 1812.
6 *Pakenham Letters*, 9 May 1812.
7 Bolitho, pp. 108–10.
8 Tomkinson, I. 166.
9 Wheeler, p. 83, 24 June 1812;

Fortescue, *British Army*, VIII. 462.
10 *Desp.*, IX. 270, 3 March 1812, to General Graham.
11 Stanhope, p. 51; Glover, M., *Peninsular Victories*, p. 68.
12 Raglan MSS. No. 47, 29 June 1812.
13 *Greville Memoirs*, 2 February 1839.
14 Wheeler, pp. 85–7.
15 *Desp.*, IX. 299, 21 July 1812, to Bathurst.
16 *Desp.*, IX. 309, 25 July 1812, to General Graham.
17 Ellesmere, p. 159; *Greville Memoirs*, 2 February 1839; Grattan, First Series I. 242; Londonderry and Gleig, p. 266; Ellesmere, p. 108; Londonderry and Gleig, p. 266.
18 *Desp.*, IX. 395, 7 September 1812, to Colonel Torrens.
19 Bragge, p. 175, 25 September 1812.
20 Grattan, First Series, I. 244 and 246.
21 *Pakenham Letters*, 25 July 1812.
22 Combermere, I. 274.
23 Oman, Sir Charles, V. 473.
24 *Pakenham Letters*, 23 July 1812.
25 Napier, William, *Peninsula*, IV. 299.
26 Raglan MSS. No. 49, 25 August 1812.
27 Wheeler, p. 90.
28 Bragge, p. 72; *Supp. Desp.*, VII. 384, 17 August 1812.
29 McGrigor, p. 302.
30 Wellington MSS., *Duchess's Journal*.
31 Granville, II. 449.
32 *Desp.*, IX. 430, 20 September 1812, to General Maitland.
33 *Supp. Desp.*, VII. 443, 6 October 1812, T. Sydenham to Henry Wellesley.
34 *Desp.*, IX. 466, 5 October 1812.
35 Bragge, p. 45.

36 *Desp.*, IX. 566.
37 Ellesmere, p. 146.
38 McGrigor, p. 311.
39 Oman, Sir Charles, VI. 145–6.
40 *Greville Memoirs*, 18 November 1838.
41 Brett-James, *Wellington at War*, p. 247, quoting G. F. Burroughs.
42 Maxwell, Sir Herbert, I. 200, quoting Salisbury MSS., 1837.
43 *Desp.*, IX. 609.

16 VITORIA

1 *Blackwood's Magazine*, vol. 26, p. 925.
2 Wellington MSS., 23 January 1813, Wellington to an unnamed correspondent. (See Chap. 14, note 32.)
3 *Supp. Desp.*, VII. 566, 4 March 1813.
4 McGrigor, p. 327.
5 Gleig, *Subaltern*, p. 2.
6 Bragge, p. 46.
7 Wellington MSS., 26 March 1813.
8 Brett-James, *Wellington at War*, p. 245.
9 Larpent, I. 106, 4 April 1813.
10 Bragge, pp. 97–100.
11 Pool, *Croker*, p. 92; Ellesmere, p. 149.
12 Robinson, *Picton*, II. 195–6 and 208–10.
13 Smith, Sir H., *Autobiography*, I. 96–8.
14 Stanhope, p. 144.
15 Stanhope, p. 144.
16 Malcolm, II. 91.
17 Tomkinson, pp. 252–3.
18 Bragge, p. 89, 7 February 1813.
19 Schaumann, p. 381.
20 Oman, Sir Charles, VI. 443–4; Fortescue, *Following the Drum*, p. 93; Wheeler, p. 119.
21 Glover, M., *Peninsular Victories*, p. 127.
22 *Desp.*, X. 473 and 495–6.

23 Stanhope, p. 18.
24 Morris, pp. 119–20.
25 Trevelyan, p. 129.
26 *Desp.*, XI. 306, to Bathurst.
27 Oman, Carola, p. 266.
28 Fortescue, *British Army*, IX. 192.
29 Royal Archives, Windsor, 20699; *Desp.*, X. 532, 3 July 1813.
30 *Desp.*, X. 532, 16 July 1813.
31 D'Arblay, VII. 8, 24 August 1813.

17 CHAMPAGNE AND COFFEE

1 Frazer, Colonel Sir A., p. 176.
2 Napier, William, *Peninsula*, V. 195.
3 Maxwell, Sir Herbert, I. 331, quoting Lady de Ros; *Desp.*, X. 596, 4 August 1813.
4 *Desp.*, X. 602, 5 August 1813, to Lord William Bentinck; Raglan MSS. No. 56, 3 August 1813.
5 Larpent, I. 304, 24 August 1813.
6 *Desp.*, X. 591, to Bathurst.
7 Stanhope, p. 22.
8 Gleig, *Subaltern*, p. 34.
9 *Desp.*, XI. 33, 23 August 1813, to General Graham.
10 *Desp.*, XI. 186, 11 October 1813, to Henry Wellesley.
11 Bowring, p. 105.
12 Ward, *Wellington*, p. 90, quoting Eastlake.
13 Raglan MSS. No. 126.
14 Raglan MSS. No. 69, 20 February 1814.
15 Bragge, pp. 123–4.
16 Raymond, *Gronow*, p. 28, 15 October 1813.
17 Larpent, II. 27.
18 Moore Smith, *Colborne*, p. 195; Smith, Sir H., *Autobiography*, I. 135.
19 *Desp.*, XI. 275, 11 November 1813; *Desp.*, XI. 169, 9 July 1813; *Desp.*, XI. 306, 21 November 1813.
20 Wheatley, p. 31.

21 Smith, Sir H., *Autobiography*, I. 136–7.
22 Wheeler, p. 193; Frazer, p. 389; Lawrence, p. 177.
23 Napier, William, *Life*, I. 144; Larpent, II. 48.
24 Weller, *Wellington in the Peninsula*, p. 338.
25 Kennedy MSS.
26 Shakespear MSS.
27 *Desp.* X. 640, 14 August 1813, to Bathurst.
28 *Pakenham Letters*, 29 November 1813.
29 *Desp.* XI. 436, 10 January 1814.
30 Rothschild Archives.
31 *Supp. Desp.*, VIII. 547, 28 January 1813; Tower Records.
32 Larpent, II. 156; Gleig, *Life*, p. 236.
33 Smith, Sir H., *Autobiography*, I. 163.
34 Gleig, *Life*, p. 494; Larpent, II. 187.
35 *Desp.*, XI. 557–8, 7 March 1814.
36 *Desp.*, XI. 645.
37 Broughton, (Hobhouse), I. 190.
38 Larpent, II. 267.
39 *Supp. Desp.*, VIII. 726.
40 *Desp.*, XI. 668, 21 April 1814.
41 *Supp. Desp.*, IX. 100, 22 May 1814.
42 *Supp. Desp.*, IX. 74, 16 May 1814.
43 Foy MSS.
44 Broughton (Hobhouse), I. 112–13.
45 Blakeney, pp. 338–41.
46 Berry, III. 16, 11 May 1814, to Hon. J. W. Ward. (See also Samuel Rogers, *Recollections*, p. 197; Stanhope, pp. 9 and 81.)
47 Stanhope, p. 19.
48 Kincaid, p. 221.
49 *Desp.*, XII. 62, 14 June 1814.
50 Haydon, *Table-Talk*, II. 139.

18 SEE THE CONQUERING HERO

1 *Barnard Letters*, 2 December 1813, Lady Anne Barnard to her brother-in-law in the Peninsula, Sir Andrew Barnard.
2 *Desp.*, IV. 442, 27 June 1809, to Beresford; Ellesmere, p. 13.
3 Larpent, II. 161.
4 *Desp.*, III. 563, 28 June 1804, to Lt.-Col. Wallace.
5 Briggs, pp. 175–82.
6 British Museum, Add. MSS. 37415, letter 64, 3 September 1813.
7 *Desp.*, V. 163.
8 Wellington MSS., 13 September 1809, to Villiers.
9 Cole, p. 59.
10 *Desp.*, XI. 98, 10 September 1813.
11 Hamilton, pp. 19–20.
12 Stanhope, p. 15.
13 Oman, Sir Charles, II. 306.
14 Kennedy MSS., 30 January 1814.
15 McGrigor, p. 278.
16 Napier, William, *Life*, I. 165, 14 December 1813.
17 Jones, *Sieges*, II. 103.
18 Larpent, I. 285, 9 August 1813.
19 *Wellingtoniana*, p. 42.
20 *Supp. Desp.*, VIII. 219.
21 Malcolm, II. 91.
22 Larpent, II. 322; 295.
23 Lennox, Lady Sarah, II. 228.
24 Wellington MSS.
25 *Desp.*, XII. 69.
26 Calvert, p. 234, 27 July 1814.
27 Shelley, I. 67; 70.
28 McGrigor, p. 359.
29 *Capel Letters*, p. 36.
30 *European Magazine*, June 1814.
31 Marchand, *Byron*, I. 460.
32 Shelley, I. 71.
33 *Desp.*, XII. 129, 22 September 1814.

19 THE GRAND DISTURBER

1 Stanhope, p. 32.
2 Staël and Grand Duchess Louise, p. 168.
3 *Desp.*, XII. 77.
4 *Supp. Desp.*, IX. 228, Clarkson to Duke of Gloucester.
5 *Supp. Desp.*, IX. 277, 23 September 1814, to Villiers; *Desp.*, XII. 170.
6 *Supp. Desp.*, IX. 435, 16 November 1814.
7 Gleig, *Life*, p. 250.
8 Chateaubriand, p. 267.
9 George, *Anecdotes*, p. 312–13.
10 Stanhope, p. 125.
11 Granville, II. 516, 21 December 1814, Lady Bessborough to Lord Granville.
12 Edgeworth, Maria, I. 224, 13 October 1814.
13 Granville, II. 458.
14 Fraser, Sir W., p. 97.
15 Wellington MSS., 15 September 1814, from Liverpool.
16 Raglan MSS. No. 72, 26 September 1814.
17 Foy MSS., 26 October 1814.
18 Wellington and Staël, p. 6.
19 Edgeworth, Maria, I. 266.
20 *Supp. Desp.*, IX. 409, 451, 430.
21 *Supp. Desp.*, IX. 368, 422, 431, 435, 439.
22 Raglan MSS. No. 76.
23 Raymond, *Gronow*, p. 374.
24 *Supp. Desp.*, IX 345, 14 October 1814, from Castlereagh.
25 Raymond, *Grownow*, p. 374.
26 Jenkins, *Asquith*, p. 334.
27 Cobbett, *Talleyrand: A Spy*; Shelley, I. 121; Ziegler, *Duchess of Dino*, p. 76; Ward, p. 46.
28 *Supp. Desp.*, IX. 494, 23 December 1814.
29 *Supp. Desp.*, IX. 272.
30 Wellington MSS., 12 February 1815.
31 Brett-James, *Hundred Days*, pp. 3–4, quoting Col. Reiset's Journal, 5 March 1815.
32 Stanhope, p. 25; Neumann, I. 201.

20 WHERE IS NOSEY?

1 Gore, *Creevey*, p. 127, 3 April 1815, Bennett to Creevey.
2 *Desp.*, XII. 351–2; Raglan MSS. No. 81, 5 May 1815.
3 Rothschild Archives.
4 *Supp. Desp.*, X. 81, 16 April 1815, from Castlereagh.
5 *Supp. Desp.*, X. 167–8; 231.
6 Royal Archives, The Hague, no date.
7 *Supp. Desp.*, X. 69, 12 April 1815; 10, 31 March 1815.
8 Moore Smith, *Colborne*, p. 246.
9 Aspinall, *George IV*, II. Letter 541; *Supp. Desp.*, X. 83–4, 16 April 1815.
10 Smith, H., *Autobiography*, I. 200.
11 Wellington MSS., 5 May 1815.
12 Wellington MSS., 6 May 1815, from and to John Roebuck.
13 *Desp.*, XII. 358.
14 *Supp. Desp.*, X. 67, 11 April 1815, from Bathurst.
15 Wellington MSS., 5 January 1815; *Supp. Desp.*, X. 217.
16 Royal Archives, The Hague, 13 June 1815.
17 Wheeler, pp. 160–1, 29 May 1815.
18 Gore, *Creevey*, pp. 128–9, 24 April 1815; p. 136.
19 De Ros, p. 121.
20 *Desp.*, XII. 462.
21 Stanhope, p. 119.
22 *Supp. Desp.*, X. 61.

21 *HUMBUGGED, BY GOD!*

1 *Birmingham Post*, June 1965; Raymond, *Gronow*, p. 193.
2 *Capel Letters*, p. 102.
3 Jackson, p. 11.
4 Haswell, p. 222.

5 Raglan MSS. No. 24, *Waterloo Memorandum*, [1816?].
6 Müffling, *Passages*, p. 230.
7 Brett-James, *Hundred Days* p. 39, quoting Captain William Verner, 7th Hussars; Richardson, pp. 373-4.
8 Raglan MSS. No. 24, *Waterloo Memorandum*.
9 De Ros, p. 123.
10 Chateaubriand, p. 269.
11 Malmesbury II, 445-6; De Ros, p. 129; Waterloo Letters, p. 2, W. Napier; Oman, Carola, p. 164.
12 Mercer, I. 230.
13 James, Dr John Haddy, p. 13; Hay, Captain William, p. 160.
14 Ellesmere, p. 170.

22 QUATRE BRAS:
THE KNOTTED ROPE

1 Royal Archives, The Hague.
2 Stanhope, p. 108; Maxwell, Sir Herbert, II. 19; Müffling, p. 237.
3 *Croker Papers*, III. 174, 8 January 1845; Maxwell, Sir Herbert, II. 20-3.
4 Fortescue, *British Army*, X. 309.
5 Brett-James, *Hundred Days*, p. 63, quoting Edward Macready, *Ballantyne's History of the 30th Regiment* (1845); Morris, p. 201.
6 Fortescue, *British Army*, X. 309.
7 Houssaye, *1815 Waterloo*, p. 122.
8 Brett-James, *Hundred Days*, p. 63, quoting Edward Macready; Raglan MSS. No. 24, *Waterloo Memorandum*; Brett-James, *Hundred Days*, p. 57, *Battle of Waterloo, Ligny and Quatre Bras, from Eye-Witnesses* (1817).
9 Hay, Captain William, p. 165.
10 *Croker Papers*, 6 May 1826.
11 *With Napoleon at Waterloo*, p. 157, (*The Gordons*, Sergeant D. Robertson).

12 Raglan MSS. No. 24, *Waterloo Memorandum*.
13 *Ibid.*, Allan's diary.
14 Weller, *Wellington at Waterloo*, p. 68.
15 Brett-James, *Hundred Days*, pp. 86-7, quoting Lt. James Hope, *Letters by a British Officer* (1819).
16 Malmesbury, II. 447.
17 Houssaye, *1815 Waterloo*, p. 133.
18 *Ibid.*, Wellington to the King of the Netherlands.
19 Brett-James, *Hundred Days*, p. 86, quoting 'Captain Fritz ———', Kircheisen, *Wider Napoleon!* (Stuttgart, 1911), II. 320-1.
20 Mercer, I. 166.
21 Kurtz, *Ney*, p. 166.
22 Stanhope, p. 121.
23 Frazer, Colonel Sir A., p. 544; James, Dr John Haddy, p. 24.
24 Fortescue, *British Army*, X. 332.
25 Raglan MSS. No. 24, *Waterloo Memorandum*.
26 *Waterloo Letters*, p. 167.
27 Mercer, I. 268-70; Hay, Captain William, p. 171.
28 Anglesey, p. 131; Raglan MSS. No. 24, *Waterloo Memorandum*.
29 Fraser, Sir W., p. 3.
30 Fraser, Sir W., p. 37.
31 Houssaye, *1815 Waterloo*, p. 163.
32 Raglan MSS. No. 24, *Waterloo Memorandum*.
33 Houssaye, *1815 Waterloo*, pp. 155-156 and footnote 70, Book II, Chapter V.
34 *Desp.*, XII. 476-7.

23 WATERLOO: THE FINGER OF
PROVIDENCE

1 *Croker Papers*, I. 74, 27 July 1815.
2 Wheatley, p. 63; Hay, Captain William, p. 164; Leeke, II. 68; Cotton, p. 40.
3 James, Dr John Haddy, p. 33.
4 D'Arblay, VII. 122-6.

5 *Capel Letters*, p. 111.
6 Eaton, (Waldie) p. 60.
7 *With Napoleon at Waterloo*, p. 125, (*The Guards*).
8 Ellesmere, p. 157; Malcolm II. 102.
9 Müffling, *Passages*, p. 243; *With Napoleon at Waterloo*, p. 125, (*The Guards*).
10 Müffling, *ibid.*, p. 244, *Sketch*, p. 112.
11 Leeke, I. 19.
12 Morris, p. 219.
13 Raymond, *Gronow*, p. 68; *With Napoleon at Waterloo*, p. 140, (*The Greys*, Sergeant Dickson); Houssaye, *1815 Waterloo*, p. 175.
14 Gleig, *Life*, p. 268; Raymond, *Gronow*, p. 86.
15 James, Dr John Haddy, p. 33.
16 *Croker Papers*, II. 311.
17 Mercer, I. 287; Wheeler, p. 170.
18 Shakespear and Kennedy MSS.
19 Chandler, p. 1067, quoting A. F. Becke; Chesney, p. 183.
20 Albemarle, pp. 140–1.
21 Houssaye, *1815 Waterloo*, pp. 167–168.
22 Raglan MSS. No. 24, *Waterloo Memorandum*.
23 *With Napoleon at Waterloo*, p. 123, (*The Guards*).
24 Houssaye, *1815 Waterloo*, pp. 191–2.
25 *With Napoleon at Waterloo*, p. 142, (*The Greys*, Sergeant Dickson).
26 Robinson, *Picton*, II. 383.
27 *Waterloo Letters*, p. 89, Colonel Miller; Cotton, p. 60.
28 Shakespear MSS.
29 *With Napoleon at Waterloo*, p. 142, (*The Greys*, Sergeant Dickson).
30 Archives, Museum of the Household Cavalry, Windsor.
31 Brett-James, *Hundred Days*, p. 130, footnote, Wellington to Sir J. Jones.
32 Morris, p. 228.
33 Houssaye, *1815 Waterloo*, p. 203,

General C. Alten to Duke of Cambridge.
34 Lachouque, p. 484.
35 Lawrence, p. 210; Raymond, *Gronow*, pp. 69–72.
36 Ellesmere, p. 179.
37 Creasy, p. 584, quoting Edward Macready.
38 Creasy, p. 586, quoting Edward Macready; Mercer, I. 313.
39 Raglan MSS. No. 24, *Waterloo Memorandum*.
40 Foy, *Vie Militaire*, p. 282; Robert Cecil, *History Today*, 1967, 'General Sir Frederick Adam and the Napier Brothers'; Shaw-Kennedy, p. 23.
41 Wheatley, p. 69.
42 Gleig, *Life*, p. 267 and Haydon, *Journal*, 24 March 1843; Morris, p. 224; Cotton, p. 106; Lennox, William, p. 117.
43 Cotton, p. 134–5; Brett-James, *Hundred Days*, p. 154, quoting Edward Macready; Houssaye, *1815 Waterloo*, p. 217; Kelly, p. 51.
44 Houssaye, *1815 Waterloo*, p. 218.
45 Shaw-Kennedy, p. 128; Cotton, p. 109.
46 Müffling, *Passages*, p. 249.
47 Cotton, p. 106.
48 Creasy, p. 587.
49 *Waterloo Letters*, pp. 246–8, General Lord Saltoun; p. 255, Captain H. Powell.
50 Moore Smith, *Colborne*, p. 255; Kincaid, p. 256; Leeke, I. 55–6 and 58; Cotton, p. 106; *Waterloo Letters*, p. 285, Col. Colborne; pp. 291–4, Lt. Gawler.
51 Müffling, p. 249.
52 *With Napoleon at Waterloo*, p. 163, (*The Gordons*, Sergeant Robertson); Anglesey, p. 148.
53 Lawrence, p. 212; Smith, Sir H., I. 271 and Ellesmere, p. 184; Burghclere, p. 107; *Greville*

Memoirs, 8 November, 1838 and Anglesey, p. 149.

54 Robert Cecil, *History Today*, 1967, 'General Sir Frederick Adam and the Napier Brothers'; Shakespear MSS. *Waterloo Roll-Call*, p. 27; *Waterloo Letters*, p. 116, Major Barton.

55 *Waterloo Letters*, p. 121; Major J. Luard; Gleig, *Life*, p. 270; *Wellingtoniana*, p. 60.

56 Kurtz, *Ney*, p. 180.

57 Stanhope, p. 119.

58 Morris, Thomas, *Recollections of Military Service* (London 1847), p. 227; Marquise D'Assche; *Daily Graphic*, 27 June 1914.

59 Ropes, p. 240.

60 Müffling, *Passages*, p. 248; Smith, Sir H., *Autobiography*, I. 291; Neumann, I. 266, quoting the remarks of General Alava at dinner, 24 December 1831.

61 Royal Archives, The Hague, 19 June 1815, Prince of Orange to King and Queen of the Netherlands.

62 Lennox, William, p. 217–18, and De Lancey, p. 116.

63 *Capel Letters*, p. 122.

64 Montgomery of Alamein, p. 23.

65 Leeke, I. 97.

66 *Desp.*, XII. 484.

67 *Desp.*, XII. 529.

68 *Greville Memoirs*, 10 December 1820.

69 D'Arblay, VII. 134, Mr Saumarez to Fanny.

70 Kincaid, p. 257.

71 Oman, Carola, p. 214.

72 *Supp. Desp.*, X. 531.

73 Brett-James, *Hundred Days*, p. 183 (*Camden Miscellany*, xviii), 19 June 1815, to W. Wellesley-Pole.

74 Shelley, I. 102.

75 Oman, Carola, p. 215.

24 END OF AN OCCUPATION

1 Wellington MSS. 13 April 1829.

2 Richardson, pp. 384–5; *Verner*.

3 *Supp. Desp.*, X. 553, 22 June 1815; *ibid.*, 562.

4 Stanhope, 6 October 1839; Colby, *Waterloo Despatch*.

5 Shelley, I. 87.

6 Moore Smith, Colborne, p. 244.

7 *Desp.*, XII. 590, 8 August 1815.

8 *Gronow*, p. 277.

9 Gleig, *Life*, p. 490.

10 Shelley, I. 108.

11 *Supp. Desp.*, X. 677 Castlereagh to Liverpool, 7 July 1815.

12 Wheeler, p. 179.

13 Broughton, I. 311; Shelley, I. 106; Stanhope, 5 November 1831; 25 October 1838; Houssaye, pp. 238–41.

14 Holland, p. 220.

15 Albemarle, p. 168; Mercer, II. 180; Grattan II. 2nd series, pp. 85–93.

16 *Gronow*, p. 87; Shelley, I. 113.

17 Shelley, I. 99–144; Lennox, p. 166.

18 Broughton, V. 202, 14 June 1839.

19 Wellington MSS., Papal letter, 20 October 1816.

20 Malcolm, II. 35, 19 August 1815.

21 *With Napoleon at Waterloo* (*The Gordons*), p. 166; Moore Smith, *Colborne*, p. 242.

22 Guedalla, p. 299, quoting from the Hamwood Papers.

23 Wellington MSS., 20 July 1816.

24 Cox, pp. 157–8.

25 Cox, 571–3, 11 December 1816.

26 Pange, pp. 25–6, 29 October 1816.

27 Napier, W., I. 197, 26 December 1816.

28 Pange, p. 153, 16 November 1816.

29 *Supp. Desp.*, XI. 592–3, 619.

30 Pange, p. 64.
31 Burghersh, p. 30, Schlegel to Lady Burghersh, 14 August 1817.
32 Raglan MSS. No. 59, 9 July 1817.
33 *Supp. Desp.*, XI. 632, 17 January 1817; Wellington MSS.; *Supp. Desp.* XI. 561.
34 Edgeworth, *Letters from England*, p. 103, M. Edgeworth to Sophy Ruxton describing a talk with Lady Bathurst, 19 September 1818.
35 Wellington MSS., to Mrs Arbuthnot, 7 October 1816; to Wyatt, 25 February 1817.
36 Wellington MSS., Wyatt to Wellington, 27 July 1817.
37 Shelley, I. 378.

25 WESTMINSTER WARRIORS

1 *Supp. Desp.*, XII. 813, 1 November 1818.
2 Redding, II. 75–6; Haydon, *Correspondence*, II. 347.
3 *Supp. Desp..*, XI. 660, Castlereagh to Wellington, 31 March 1817.
4 Warmsley, p. 168.
5 Bamford, I. 166–8.
6 Ziegler, *Addington*, p. 388.
7 Wellington MSS., to Mrs Arbuthnot, 29 July 1820.
8 *Desp.* NS., I. 128, memorandum from Wellington to Lord Liverpool, June 1820; Maxwell, II. 153; Gash, *Peel*, pp. 312–13.
9 *Creevey*, 25 August 1820.
10 Mrs Arbuthnot, I. 52, 10 November 1820, quoting a letter from Charles Arbuthnot.
11 Edgeworth, II. 174–6; Lennox, p. 270.
12 Wellington MSS.
13 Wellington MSS.
14 Wellington MSS.
15 Wellington MSS..

16 Wellington MSS.
17 Stanhope, 1 November 1831; De Ros, p. 175.
18 Holland, p. 295.
19 Byron, *Detached Thoughts*, 110.
20 Mrs Arbuthnot, I. 105.
21 Stanhope, 2 November 1831.
22 Gleig, *Life*, p. 297.
23 Fraser, p. 247.
24 Wellington MSS.
25 Mrs Arbuthnot, I. 168–9.
26 Mrs Arbuthnot, I. 169.
27 Wellington MSS., to Charles Arbuthnot, 18 May 1820.
28 Mrs Arbuthnot, I. 300–1, 11 April 1824.
29 Wellington MSS., [Col. Charles Greville to Lady Charlotte Greville], undated.
30 Shelley, II. 73.
31 Told to the author by Mr Harold Macmillan.
32 Mrs Arbuthnot, I. 185, 29 August 1822.
33 Wellington MSS., to Mrs Arbuthnot, 13 September 1822.
34 Wellington MSS., to Mrs Arbuthnot, 25 March 1823.
35 *Creevey*, 14 November 1822.
36 Byron, *Age of Bronze*, lines 534–5.
37 *Lieven-Metternich*, p. 218, 7 January 1823; p. 227–30, 26 January 1823; p. 243, 28 March 1823.
38 Aspinall, *Arbuthnot*, p. 36, Liverpool to Charles Arbuthnot, 29 December 1822.
32 Stanhope, 19 June 1840.
33 Mrs Arbuthnot, I. 375; Shelley, II. 133.

26 THE CANNING FACTOR

1 *Lieven-Metternich*, p. 209, 20 April 1823; *Wellington and his Friends*, p. 41, 30 October 1823; Mrs Arbuthnot, I. 211, 3 February, 1823.
2 Wellington MSS.

3 Wellington MSS., 13 October 1823; *Creevey*, January 1823.

4 Rolo, p. 134.

5 Mrs Arbuthnot, I. 421, 20 October 1825. The news arrived at Stratfield Saye between 11 and 18 October, while Mrs Arbuthnot was staying.

6 British Museum Add. MSS., 37415, 13 October 1825.

7 Wellington MSS., Keene to Wellington, 19 August 1823; Clancarty to Wellington, 23 April 1823.

8 Wellington MSS., to Mrs Arbuthnot, 13 April 1823.

9 Wellington MSS., 7 June 1823; Mrs Arbuthnot, I. 321, Mrs Arbuthnot's summary of Wellington's letter of 7 June 1823.

10 Wellington MSS., 26 April 1825.

11 Surtees, p. 125, 1 January 1825.

12 *Desp*. NS., III. 56.

13 Peel, *Private Letters*, p. 91, 21 January 1827.

14 Peel, pp. 95–6, 22 January 1827.

15 *Desp*. NS., III. 532–3, Wellington to Peel, 7 January 1827; Peel to Wellington, 8 January 1827; Wellington MSS., 11 January 1827.

16 *Private Correspondence*, pp. 84–94.

17 Bessborough, p. 287.

18 *Greville*, 29 September 1834.

19 Wellington MSS., to Londonderry, 10 April 1827; *Desp*. NS., III. 628.

20 *Desp*. NS., IV. 75, Wellington to Bathurst, 10 August 1827.

21 Morgan, p. 240; *Greville*, 10 August 1827; Wellington MSS., 7 August 1827.

22 Temperley, *Diary of Princess Lieven*, p. 131; *Lieven-Grey*, I. 89.

23 Wellington MSS., description given by Duchess to Rundell the jeweller, 8 September 1828.

24 Inglis, *Hermathena*, LXXXIII, 1954.

25 Stanhope, 21 November 1831; *Desp*. NS., III. 451.

27 PRIME MINISTER

1 *Desp*. NS, IV. 184, 9 January 1828.

2 Wellington MSS., to Mrs Arbuthnot, 10 January 1828.

3 Mrs Arbuthnot, II. 158, 15 January 1828.

4 Wellington MSS., Charles Arbuthnot to Wellington, 23 January 1928; Mrs Arbuthnot, II. 159, 29 January 1828; *Wellington and his Friends*, p. 83, Wellington to Charles Arbuthnot, 26 January 1828.

5 *Croker*, 24 January 1828.

6 Wellington MSS., to Mrs Arbuthnot, 12 December 1828.

7 Colchester, III. 534, 28, 19, 7 and 24 January 1828; Wellington MSS, to Mrs Arbuthnot, 26 January 1828.

8 Ellenborough, I. 3.

9 Wellington MSS., to Mrs Arbuthnot, 7 April 1828.

10 Ellenborough, I. 132, 30 May 1828.

11 *Desp*. NS., IV. 324, 24 March 1828.

12 Anglesey, p. 195, F. Lamb to Anglesey, 24 March 1828.

13 Raglan MSS. No. 48, 7 July 1812.

14 Gash, *Peel*, p. 525, quoting Anglesey Papers, PRO, Northern Ireland, 1068/15f.125.

15 *Lieven in London*, p. 146, 3–15 June 1828.

16 Mrs Arbuthnot, II. 198–200.

17 Ziegler, *William IV*, p. 139.

18 Wellington MSS., to Mrs Arbuthnot, 4 November 1828; 23 November 1828.

19 Wellington MSS., 7 January 1829.

20 Wellington MSS., to Mrs Arbuthnot, 10 and 12 January 1829.

21 Wellington MSS., 13, 15 and 16 January 1829.

22 Wellington MSS., 16 and 17 January 1829.

23 Mrs Arbuthnot, II. 243, 26 January 1829.

24 Colchester, III. 612.

25 *Desp*. NS., V. 518.

26 Mrs Arbuthnot, II. 249, 4 March 1829.

27 Mrs. Arbuthnot, II., 252.

28 *Desp*. NS., V. 538. The story of the duel is taken mainly from *Desp*. NS., V. 527–45, Dr Hume's account to the Duchess; Wellington MSS.; Maxwell, II. 234; Gleig, *Life*, pp. 384–9; Shelley, II. 188; and the memoirs of Greville, Ellenborough and Broughton.

29 Mrs Arbuthnot, II. 264–6, 7 April 1829.

30 Broughton, III. 318, Wellington to Duncannon; Mrs Arbuthnot, II. 260, 28 March 1829.

31 Wellington MSS., Colin Campbell to Duchess, 1 April 1829.

32 Wellington MSS., 17 September 1829; 12 December 1829.

33 *Desp*. NS., VI. 282, 3 November 1829.

34 Mrs Arbuthnot, II. 295, 21 July 1829.

35 Mrs Arbuthnot, II. 312; Peel; *Private Papers*, p. 114.

36 Wellington MSS., to Mrs Arbuthnot, 1 September 1829; 17 September 1829.

37 *Creevey*, 11 April 1829.

38 Wellington MSS., to Mrs Arbuthnot, 29 and 27 October 1829; Moore, p. 20.

39 Wellington MSS., to Rutland, 3 December 1829.

40 Wellington MSS., to Mrs Arbuthnot, 26 November 1829 and 13 December 1829.

41 Wellington MSS., to Charles Arbuthnot, 13 December 1829.

42 Wellington MSS., to Knighton, 15 September 1835.

28 REFORM

1 Eden, p. 198, August 1830.

2 *Desp*. NS., VII. 108, undated.

3 Ridley, pp. 102–3; Airlie, p. 173.

4 *Desp*. NS., VII. 149, 9 August 1830.

5 *Creevey*, 14 November 1829; Ellenborough, II. 370, 28 September 1830.

6 Wellington MSS., to Mrs Arbuthnot, 15 October 1830.

7 Wellington MSS., James Hamilton to Wellington and reply, 14 and 22 October 1830.

8 Wellington MSS., to Sir James Shaw, 18 October 1830.

9 Gordon, p. 104; Seymour MSS.; Gordon, p. 104.

10 Maxwell, II. 252, 12 October 1832.

11 Mrs Arbuthnot, II. 399, 7 November 1830.

12 *Desp*. NS., VII. 223–6, memorandum.

13 Maxwell, II. 194, Salisbury MSS.

14 Neumann, 16 September 1828.

15 *Desp*. NS., V. 184, to Sir Charles Forbes, 29 October 1828; *Greville*, 5 January, 1830; Disraeli, *Bentinck*, p. 215.

16 Broughton, III. 254, 16 March 1828.

17 Stewart MSS., 29 November 1830.

18 Rogers, *Recollections*, p. 218, 21 November 1830.

19 *Lieven in London*, p. 278, 10 November 1830.

20 Mrs Arbuthnot, II. 406, 22 December 1830; II. 404, 29 November 1830.

21 Lady Granville, II. 70,
21 November 1830.
22 *Greville*, 22 November 1830.
23 Martineau, II. 32, quoting from
republican pamphlet.
24 *Lieven-Grey*, II. 296, 2 March
1831; *Greville*, 7 March 1831;
Desp. NS., VII. 410, 14 March
1831.
25 Wellington MSS., to Mrs
Arbuthnot, 9 May 1831;
Brougham, IV. 360;
Buckingham, *William IV and
Queen Victoria*, I. 250, 19 March
1831.
26 *Desp.* NS., VII. 425, 3 April
1831.
27 Albemarle, p. 292.
28 Brougham, III. 118.
29 Wellington MSS., to Mrs
Arbuthnot, 1 April 1831.
30 Edgeworth, *Letters from England*.
pp. 475–7, Miss M. Edgeworth
to Mrs Edgeworth, 22 January
1831; Wellington MSS., to Mrs
Arbuthnot, 8 April 1831, 6 April
1831; Mrs P. S-M. Arbuthnot,
p. 224.
31 Wellington MSS., to Charles
Arbuthnot, 9 May 1831.
32 *Greville*, 22 September 1831;
Wellington MSS., Lord Kenyon
to Wellington, 22 September
1831.
33 Seymour MSS., 4 October 1831.
34 Brownlow, p. 144; *Wellington and
his Friends*, p. 99, to Mrs
Arbuthnot, 12 October 1831.
35 Boulind MSS., 22 October
1831.
36 Wellington MSS., Londonderry,
5 December 1830.
37 *Desp.* NS., VIII. 30,
5 November 1831; Buckingham,
William IV and Queen Victoria, I.
384, 2 January 1832.
38 Salisbury MSS.
39 Aspinall, *Three Diaries* (Le
Marchant), p. 252.

40 *Desp.* NS., VIII. 304, 10 May
1832.
41 *Croker*, 12 May 1832; Aspinall,
Three Diaries (Ellenborough),
p. 250, 12 May 1832.
42 Wellington MSS., to Lady
Burghersh, 14 May 1832;
Seymour MSS.
43 Buckingham, *William IV and
Queen Victoria*, I. 261, 24 March
1831.

29 THE DUKE ON ELBA

1 *Desp.* NS., VIII. 472–3,
4 December 1832.
2 Wellington MSS., Mrs Foster's
memorandum.
3 Copy of letter from the Duchess
of Wellington to General Allan,
thought to be in the possession
of a collector in the USA.
4 Wellington MSS., to Knight of
Kerry, 16 December 1832.
5 Fraser, p. 11.
6 Clark, p. 80; *Desp.* NS., VII.
486.
7 Wellington MSS., Cumberland
to Wellington, 30 December
1832; Wellington to
Londonderry, 7 March 1833.
8 Wellington MSS., 2 and 26
February 1833.
9 Wellington MSS., to Mrs
Arbuthnot, 16 February 1833.
10 Wellington MSS., 13 February
1833.
11 Wellington MSS., Lord
Strangford to Wellington,
14 July 1833.
12 Parker, II. 218.
13 *Lieven-Grey*, II. 453, Lord Grey
to Princess Lieven, 26 June
1833.
14 Morgan, p. 363, 29 July 1833.
15 Wellington MSS., Knighton to
Wellington, 9 March 1832.
16 Albemarle, pp. 376–7.
17 Wellington MSS., to Aberdeen,
21 January 1834.

18 Brownlow, p. 163.

19 Fragment of unpublished autobiography by Miss Yonge printed in Christabel Coleridge's *Charlotte M. Yonge*.

20 Wellington MSS., to Cumberland, 5 October 1834.

21 Fitzgerald, II. 307.

22 Gleig, *Reminiscences*, p. 179.

23 Wellington MSS., to Mrs Arbuthnot, 28 July 1834.

24 Wellington MSS., Halford to Wellington, August 1834.

25 Wellington MSS., Charles Arbuthnot to Wellington, 5 August 1834.

26 Herrick, p. 10.

27 Herrick, p. 19.

28 Herrick, pp. 26–32.

29 Herrick, p. 71.

30 Maxwell, II. 282.

31 Oman, p. 158.

32 Disraeli, *Coningsby*, Bk. II, Chap. 4.

33 *Greville*, 16 and 17 November 1834.

34 *Lieven-Grey*, II. 47, 1 December 1834.

35 Ellesmere, p. 143.

36 Wellington MSS., to Lord Londonderry, 1 December 1834.

37 Oman, p. 156.

38 Wellington MSS., to Egerton, 11 December 1834.

39 Wellington MSS., to Lord Wilton, 19 December 1834; Parker, II. 258.

40 Edgeworth, *Letters from England*, p. 578, Maria Edgeworth to Harriet Butler, 10 January 1841.

41 Lady Granville, p. 195, 7 September 1835.

42 Oman, pp. 158–61, 25 and 29 March 1835.

43 Oman, pp. 163–4, 2 April 1835.

44 *Greville*, 11 May 1836.

45 Wellington MSS., to Peel, 23 March 1837.

30 PILLAR OF STATE

1 Oman, p. 241.

2 Wellington MSS., to Sir H. Taylor, 11 June 1837; Wellington, *Selection*, p. 204, to an unknown correspondent, 26 July 1837.

3 *Greville*, 21 June 1837; Royal Archives, Stockmar Papers, No. 28, Wellington to Lord Liverpool; Oman, pp. 247–8, 9 July 1937.

4 Wellington MSS., to Charles Arbuthnot, 20 July 1837.

5 Wellington MSS., to Charles Arbuthnot, 10 July 1837.

6 Wellington MSS., to Lady Burghersh, 14 September 1837.

7 Wharncliffe, II. 289, Lord Wharncliffe to Lady Wharncliffe, 24 January 1838; Buckingham, *William IV and Queen Victoria*, II. 310–11, 28 January 1838.

8 *Greville*, 15 August 1839.

9 *Greville*, 12 May and 24 June 1839.

10 Stanhope, 17 May 1839.

11 *Wellington and his Friends*, p. 131, to Lady Wilton, 7 February 1840.

12 Stanhope, 14 May 1839; Gordon, p. 115.

13 *Croker*, 21 November 1839; Stanhope, 23 November 1839; *Wellington and his Friends*, 25 November 1839.

14 Wellington MSS., 24 April 1839.

15 Stanhope, 29 October and 4 November 1839.

16 *Croker*, 17 February 1840; Lever, 19 March 1840; Guizot, 6 March 1840.

17 Herrick, pp. 114–18, 13 and 14 March, 3 August 1840.

18 Wellington MSS., 29 December 1839; *Wellington and his Friends*, 31 January 1840.

19 Wellington MSS., p. 157, to Lady Wilton, 15 March 1841.
20 Raikes, 17 July 1841.
21 Gleig, *Life*, p. 386.
22 Wellington MSS., Wellington writing on behalf of Sir James Mountain to Admiral Page, 8 December 1838.
23 Oman, p. 201. See also Wellington MSS., 28 December 1818, when Wellington wrote to Dr Keate that parents could remove their sons if they disliked the headmaster's rules.
24 Wellington MSS., 12 April 1837.
25 Wellington MSS., to Dr Gilbert, 5 November 1837.

31 RIGHT ABOUT FACE!

1 Wellington MSS., to Peel, 17 May 1841.
2 *Wellington and his Friends*, p. 139, to Lady Wilton, 18 August 1840; p. 185, 11 November 1842.
3 *Wellington and his Friends*, p. 198, 2 December 1844, 23 January 1845.
4 Cecil Woodham-Smith, *Florence Nightingale*, p. 41.
5 Parker, II. 509, Peel to Graham, 5 September 1841.
6 Parker, II. 509, Wellington to Peel, 17 February 1842.
7 Martineau, II. 538.
8 Wellington MSS., Peel to Wellington, 15 October 1845; Parker, III. 223–4, Peel to Graham, 13 October 1845 and to Heytesbury, 15 October 1845.
9 *Croker*, 6 April 1846.
10 Parker, III. 283.
11 Parker, III. 296, Peel to Hardinge, 22 December 1845.
12 Wellington MSS., Peel to Wellington, 22 December 1845.
13 *Greville*, 13 January 1846.
14 Wellington MSS., to Redesdale, 21, 28 and 25 December 1845.

15 *Croker*, 28 December 1845 and 3 January 1846; Wellington MSS., to Croker, 6 January 1846.
16 Wellington MSS., to Lord Salisbury, 6 January 1846.
17 *Wellington and his Friends*, p. 203, to Lady Wilton, 27 January 1846.
18 *Wellington and his Friends*, p. 204, to Lady Wilton, 27 January 1846.
19 Wellington MSS., Stanley to Wellington, 18 February 1846.
20 Parker, III. 326.
21 Wellington MSS., to Stanley, 19 February 1846; Gleig, *Life*, pp. 567–72.
22 Blake, *Conservative Party*, pp. 66–7, quoting Derby papers.
23 Maxwell, II. 352.
24 Monypenny, vol. I, bk 2, chap. xii.
25 *Desp.* NS., V. 593, memorandum by Wellington, 22 April 1828.
26 *Wellington Studies*, Foreword by 7th Duke of Wellington.
27 Royal Archives, I. 67. 93, Wellington to Lamartine, 3 March 1848; Russell to Palmerston, 4 March 1848.
28 Chad, p. 22, 29 April 1848.
29 Spicer MSS., Wellington to William Francis Spicer, 22 March 1848.
30 Maxwell, II. 368, 7 April 1848.
31 Lever, Lady Palmerston to Mrs Huskisson, 14 April 1848.
32 Royal Archives, C. 56. 7., Wellington to Prince Albert, 8 April 1848; Wellington MSS., to Lady Wilton, 5 April 1848; Lever, Lady Palmerston, 14 April 1848; Chad, p. 21.
33 Guest, p. 210, 10 April 1848; *Wellington and his Friends*, pp. 210–11.
34 Royal Archives, C. 8. II., Queen

Victoria to Wellington, 12 April 1848.

35 Wellington MSS., to Lord Glengall, 25 March 1848.

36 Wellington MSS., 8 April 1848.

37 Nowlan, p. 107.

38 Wellington MSS., to Edward Booth, Irish Ordnance Office, 29 June 1848.

39 Wellington MSS., to Miss Burdett-Coutts, 30 March 1849.

40 De Ros, p. 147.

41 Wellington MSS., to Miss Burdett-Coutts, 19 October 1848.

42 Wellington MSS., to Miss Burdett-Coutts, 17 October 1847.

43 *Wellington and his Friends*, p. 242, 6, 7 and 8 February 1847.

44 *Greville*, 13 July 1847.

32 THE OTHER SIDE OF THE HILL

1 Guest, p. 270; Burghclere, p. 180, 7 May 1851; Jones, p. 172, 7 October 1851.

2 *Etoniana*, 1965, extracts from Lord Hatherton's Diary.

3 Fraser, p. 52.

4 Maxwell, II. 288.

5 Burghclere, p. 269, 1 May 1852; Guest, p. 297.

6 Fraser, p. 108.

7 Burghclere, 3 and 6 July 1852; *Old Soldier*, p. 87.

8 Elvin, p. 24.

9 *East Kent Mercury*, 26 September 1852.

10 Burghclere, pp. 314, 321.

11 Burghclere, 12 September 1852.

12 This account of the Duke's death comes mainly from (i) a long letter from his valet Kendall written on 21 September 1852 to Kendall's friend Shackle, a footman at Windsor Castle (Royal Archives, Mixed Correspondence III. M.

53. 1848/1853, 189.) (ii) memorandum by Dr Hulke, senior (Wellington MSS.), (iii) a shorter memorandum by Dr John W. Hulke, his son (published in *The Complete Guide to the Funeral of the Duke of Wellington*, C. M. Archer, p. 78, London, 1852).

13 Stanhope, 22 November 1839.

14 Royal Archives, E. 2. 3, Col. Phipps to Prince Albert, 15 September 1852; Bolitho, p. 45.

15 Royal Archives, T. 97. Queen Victoria to King Leopold of the Belgians, 17 September 1852; Royal Archives, E. I. 21, Col. Phipps to Rev. Gerald Wellesley, 17 September 1852.

16 Airlie, 4 and 11 November 1852.

17 De Ros, p. 49; Morgan, p. 522.

18 Royal Archives, C. 61. 117, Prince Albert to 2nd Duke of Wellington, 24 November 1852.

19 Miss E. A. Napier, letter on the funeral of the Duke of Wellington, 18 November 1852, Bodleian Library MS. Eng. Misc. H. 96. f. 333.

20 Moore Smith, *Colborne*, p. 348.

21 Chad, p. 19, 3 July 1836.

22 Royal Archives, Vic. Add. MSS. 119, 20 January 1859.

23 See Lord Holland's *Further Memoirs*, pp. 230–2 and Princess Lieven's *Political Sketches*, p. 111, for critical assessments of Wellington's virtues.

24 Briggs, p. 450; *Wellington Anecdotes*, p. 60.

25 *Wellington and his Friends*, to Lady Wilton, 20 December 1840.

26 Burghclere, p. 153, Wellington to Lady Salisbury, 20 November 1850.

27 Speech in House of Lords, 13 August 1839.

28 Stanhope, 23 December 1840.

29 Gleig, *Life*, p. 428; Rogers,

Recollections, p. 289; Seymour MSS., Col. Grisewood to Sir George Seymour, 14 March 1841.

30 Aspinall, *George IV*, III. Letter 1577, Knighton's diary, 10 February 1830; Stanhope, 21 October 1844; Jeune, pp. 3 and 5.

31 Kelly, p. 386.

32 Edgeworth, *Letters from England*, p. 592, M. Edgeworth to Harriet Butler, 20 April 1841; Ellesmere, pp. 77–8; Fraser, p. 33.

33 Wellington MSS., to Charles Arbuthnot, 17 January 1832.

34 Salisbury MSS., Lady Salisbury's diary, 2 April 1835. (Sir H. Maxwell's transcription contains some small verbal changes.)

35 See a penetrating study of this issue, M. G. Brock, *Wellington Studies*, pp. 75–6.

36 Wellington MSS., 7 July 1846.

37 Michael Glover, 'Wellington and Napoleon,' *History of the English Speaking Peoples*, p. 2748, (London 1971).

38 Stanhope, p. 80, Lord Mahon's rendering of Wellington's views on Marlborough, sent to him for comment on 17 September 1836; Wellington MSS., unpublished reply from Wellington to Mahon, 18 September 1836. Wellington also sent a memorandum comparing himself and Marlborough, which appears in Stanhope, pp. 80–2.

39 Stevens, p. 99.

40 Medwin, p. 9.

41 Gleig, *Life*, p. 428; *The Diaries of Sir Alexander Cadogan* (London, 1971), 22 July 1944.

42 Wellington Memorial Lecture by Field-Marshal Montgomery, *Journal of the Royal United Service Institution*, No. 656, Vol. CXIV, December 1969; Maxwell, II. 112, quoting Salisbury MSS.

43 Wellington MSS., Croker to Wellington, 9 February 1850; Glover, *Wellington as Military Commander*, Preface (1968).

44 Glover, *Legacy of Glory*, p. 165, (New York, 1971).

45 Burghersh, p. 145, 27 March 1843.

46 Wellington MSS., 12 September 1842.

Index

553

VICTORIA R.I.

Elizabeth Longford

Queen Victoria, a woman of diminutive stature and superabundant temperament, gave her name to something more than an age.

Using unrestricted access to material from the Royal Archives, including previously unpublished passages from Queen Victoria's celebrated Journals, Elizabeth Longford's classic account remains the definitive biography of this extraordinary woman. She shows the queen tormented by an unhappy childhood; tantalised by an all-too-brief period of happy marriage; deeply shocked at the Prince Consort's death. She depicts the gradual emergence of the queen's renowned qualities, together with some surprising traits, presenting her in a fresh, affectionate and thoroughly human light.

'It is hard to imagine how Lady Longford's detailed and vivid volume could have been bettered'
Sunday Times

'Gives us more than the general reader has ever had, revealing the queen as a character at once simple and complex, authoritarian and humble'
Daily Telegraph

'Dazzlingly readable, and very enjoyable'
Stella Gibbons

'She has brought Queen Victoria to life again, and has presented to a new generation of readers one of the most truly remarkable personalities of recent history with scrupulous care, fidelity and wit'
Spectator

Abacus
0 349 11255 X

Now you can order superb titles directly from Abacus

☐	Victoria R.I.	Elizabeth Longford	£12.99
☐	The Year of Liberty	Thomas Pakenham	£10.99
☐	The Scramble for Africa	Thomas Pakenham	£14.99
☐	The Age of Revolution 1789–1848	Eric Hobsbawm	£12.99

─────────────── ⬭ ABACUS ⬭ ───────────────

Please allow for postage and packing: **Free UK delivery.**
Europe; add 25% of retail price; Rest of World; 45% of retail price.

To order any of the above or any other Abacus title, please call our
credit card orderline or fill in this coupon and send/fax it to:

Abacus, P.O. Box 121, Kettering, Northants NN14 4ZQ
Tel: 01832 737527   Fax: 01832 733076
Email: aspenhouse@FSBDial.co.uk

☐ I enclose a UK bank cheque made payable to Abacus for £ ....
☐ Please charge £ .... to my Access, Visa, Delta, Switch Card No.

☐☐☐☐☐☐☐☐☐☐☐☐☐☐☐☐☐☐☐

Expiry Date ☐☐☐☐ Switch Issue No. ☐☐

NAME (Block letters please) ....

ADDRESS ....

....

....

Postcode .... Telephone ....

Signature ....

Please allow 28 days for delivery within the UK. Offer subject to price and availability.

Please do not send any further mailings from companies carefully selected by Abacus ☐

THE YEAR OF LIBERTY

Thomas Pakenham

In May 1798, a hundred thousand peasants rose against the British Government in Ireland. By the time the revolt had been put down four months later, thirty thousand dead were literally rotting in heaps in a smoking and desolate countryside. Yet, as Thomas Pakenham's classic account of the rebellion shows, it was not a schoolroom story of the heroic oppressed rising against the brutal oppressor, but the result of a complex, tragic, often absurd and sometimes heroic interplay between different groups of people.

'A notable contribution to the history of Ireland . . . Thomas Pakenham has accomplished brilliantly what he has set out to do'
Observer

'He memorably conveys the utter confusion in which nearly everyone was plunged nearly all the time . . . brilliant narrative, a masterpiece of storytelling'
Irish Times

'A fine, masterly and absorbing book'
Spectator

Abacus
0 349 11252 5